Cambridge studies in medieval life and thought

Edited by WALTER ULLMANN, LITT.D., F.B.A.
*Professor of Medieval Ecclesiastical History
in the University of Cambridge*

Third series vol. 4

THE SPANISH CHURCH AND THE PAPACY
IN THE THIRTEENTH CENTURY

CAMBRIDGE STUDIES IN
MEDIEVAL LIFE AND THOUGHT
THIRD SERIES

TO MY MOTHER AND FATHER

THE SPANISH CHURCH AND THE PAPACY IN THE THIRTEENTH CENTURY

PETER LINEHAN

*Fellow of St John's College
Cambridge*

CAMBRIDGE
AT THE UNIVERSITY PRESS
1971

Published by the Syndics of the Cambridge University Press
Bentley House, 200 Euston Road, London N.W.1
American Branch: 32 East 57th Street, New York, N.Y.10022

© Cambridge University Press 1971

Library of Congress Catalogue Card Number: 75–154505

ISBN: 0 521 08039 8

Printed in Great Britain
by W & J Mackay & Co Ltd, Chatham

CONTENTS

v

Contents

Contents

PREFACE

It is high time that a history of the medieval Spanish Church was written, to replace Lafuente's *Historia eclesiástica*, which is now a century old and has aged badly. But this book is not meant to fill that gap. The materials for a work of synthesis simply do not yet exist. Hence the absence of, for example, any sustained discussion of the monastic Orders which had contributed so much to Spanish life since the eleventh century, or of the rise and fall of the Mendicants – and particularly of the Dominicans in St Dominic's own country. Nor is it a history of the *Reconquista*, although I am not unaware of the part played by churchmen in that operation. Indeed, in view of the consequences for the Spanish Church of that unique movement, some such sub-title as *The Infra-structure of the Reconquest* might well have been appropriate.

For all this, however, it has proved impossible to exclude these topics and others from what was originally conceived as an investigation into the workings of the reform programme, pure and simple, in Spain – the kingdoms of Leon, Castile and Aragon, that is – in the period after the Fourth Lateran Council of 1215. It soon became clear that the subject posed questions of an economic nature regarding the Church's place in society. Nor could such an investigation be limited to Spain, thus defined. The political and ecclesiastical boundaries did not coincide, and so I have not hesitated to wander across the frontier into Portugal, as occasion demanded and as churchmen did then, and to accept the old-fashioned geographical interpretation of *Hispania* which the statutes of the Spanish College at Bologna employed in the late fourteenth century.[1] It is to be hoped that the conclusions reached will now be subjected to criticism based on the documentary resources of particular dioceses. If they merely serve as a set of Aunt Sallies to be shied at, the book will at least have caused students to defend the old assumptions by engaging in the battle of the archives. And that activity had the blessing of Jaime Vicens

---

[1] 'Intelligendo Yspanyam largo sumpto vocabulo prout continet omnia regna illa a montibus Esperie ultra': Berthe M. Marti, *The Spanish College at Bologna in the Fourteenth Century* (Philadelphia, 1966), 132.

Vives – the highest accolade any historian of Spain could desire.[1]

Those students who deem themselves sufficiently intrepid to undertake this task will need also to be prepared to find a cordial welcome awaiting them there. True, they will not always have those invaluable aids to research of which Professor Knowles has written: a railway system and keys that open doors.[2] R.E.N.F.E. was organised without reference to the Division of Wamba, and anyone proposing to visit Mondoñedo, for example, will be obliged either to employ other means or else, as in this case he cannot, to depend from afar upon published catalogues which, when they exist, are very often both maddeningly summary and wildly inaccurate.[3] Yet the trouble and effort will be worth while, for, despite all the depredations of Reds, rats, fires, light fingers and the damp, there is a vast amount of untouched material in the provinces, quite apart from what has been brought by one route or another to Barcelona and Madrid. The *investigador* will soon become rather more *blasé* in his work than the official who warned Heinrich von Sybel in 1851 to respect the dust on the papers of the Committee of Public Safety because it was 'the dust of 1795'.[4] On occasion he will need to employ low cunning and the sort of practical ingenuity which that frustrated bridge-builder, Vicens, possessed.[5] In some places he will discover that Férotin's strictures about the hopelessness of working at Toledo Cathedral are classic and timeless, and that Mr Cobb's excellent stories about his adventures in French provincial archives are, by comparison, quite run-of-the-mill.[6] But, above all, he will learn that that automatic defence-mechanism of *los canónigos archiveros* – the shrugged eyebrows which seem to betoken an absolute veto – is, in fact, more often than not, merely a preliminary gesture which

[1] Cf. *Aproximación a la historia de España*, 8.
[2] M. D. Knowles, 'Denifle and Ehrle', *History*, LIV (1969), 12.
[3] Reference are not given in the footnotes to published catalogues which are mere lists.
[4] Cit. H. Butterfield, 'Some Trends in Scholarship, 1868–1968, in the Field of Modern History', *TRHS*, 5th ser., XIX (1969), 160.
[5] 'Hay en mí una frustrada vocación de constructor de puentes'. Interview of Jan. 1953 published in J. Vicens Vives, *Obra dispersa*, ed. M. Batllori and E. Giralt (Barcelona, 1967), 557.
[6] Cf. M. Férotin, *Le Liber Mozarabicus Sacramentorum et les manuscrits mozarabes* [Monumenta Ecclesiae Liturgica, vol. VI, Paris, 1912], 679; Richard Cobb, *A Second Identity* (London, 1969), esp. 53 ff.

leads before long to most generous assistance and co-operation. I should like to record my gratitude to the many archivists and sacristans who were good enough to allow a total stranger in, and on one memorable occasion eventually to let him out again. At Pamplona, Vich and Urgel, in particular, Don José Goñi Gaztambide, Mossèn Eduard Junyent and Mossèn Lluís Serdà were kindness itself. A list of archives visited will be found at the beginning of the Bibliography.

The other main source of information has been the series of thirteenth-century Papal Registers published by *L'École française de Rome*. Since, however, no less distinguished a scholar than Dom Luciano Serrano was convinced that the editors of that series had denied Spanish correspondence its fair share of column-inches,[1] I have taken care to read all letters to Spain of the period 1216–1303 on microfilm of *Reg. Vat.*, vols 9–50, at Cambridge – though even when material not previously published is alluded to, I have cited the letter in question by reference to the numeration of the *École française* edition. This has been done in order to devote more space to totally inaccessible Spanish material. Despite appearances to the contrary, I have tried hard not to fall victim to what Sánchez-Albornoz has called 'the Spanish craze for inflicting thousands of footnotes upon the reader' (*España: un enigma histórico*, I, 20). For information on the complicated subject of money values, the reader is referred to the work of O. Gil Farrés listed in the Bibliography. Finally I must mention how much I owe to the work of Don Demetrio Mansilla, now bishop of Ciudad Rodrigo. Though I have occasionally disagreed with particular judgements in his *Iglesia castellano-leonesa*, I have certainly learnt more from that book than from any other.

Without the help of friends in England and Spain I could not have written this book. I am particularly conscious of what I owe to Professor C. R. Cheney; El Marqués de Covarrubias and his family; Mr R. A. Fletcher; Professor Antonio García y García; D. Ramón Gonzálvez; Mr Philip Grierson; Professor Edward Miller; Dr D. W. Lomax, who read the work in draft and made a number of helpful suggestions; D. José López de Toro; Dr R. E. Robinson; and many others for much else. My debt to St John's College is incalculable. As a Research Fellow I was able to spend an unforgettable winter and

[1] *Hispania*, I, 8.

a summer in the archives, and then return to genial company in Cambridge. I have also learnt much from the undergraduates here. The map is based on one by Peter Cunningham. No request, for however improbable a publication, was too much trouble for Mr N. Buck and his assistants in the College Library, or for the staff of the University Library. I am most grateful too for the company of innumerable nameless Spaniards in a hundred grubby bars who bore with and let themselves be bored by the enigmatic *inglés* whose attention seemed to be fixed for most of the time on the side-door of the cathedral. I take the greatest pleasure, though, in mentioning three people: Walter Ullmann, an inspiring supervisor and an excellent friend, who has chivvied me along from one hurdle to the next over the past five years; and my parents, who, though they never said so, must have wondered how many more hurdles there were to come, and to whom, at last, this book is fondly dedicated.

P.A.L.

St John's College, Cambridge
15 February 1971

ACKNOWLEDGEMENTS

A version of part of this work was awarded the Thirlwall Prize and the Seeley Medal for 1970–1, and I am grateful to the Managers of that Fund for making a grant towards the costs of publishing the work in its present form. I am grateful also to the Syndics and staff of the Cambridge University Press for their unfailing assistance while the book was in gestation and for personal attention which far exceeded what the professional author had any right to expect.

For what is done, not to be done again
May the judgement not be too heavy upon us

T. S. ELIOT – *Ash Wednesday*

ABBREVIATIONS

I. LIBRARIES AND ARCHIVES

AA	Archivo Arzobispal
AC	Archivo Capitular
ACA	Archivo de la Corona de Aragón, Barcelona (*Cancillería Real*)
AD	Archivo Diocesano
ADB	Arquivo Distrital, Braga
AE	Archivo Episcopal
AGN	Archivo General de Navarra, Pamplona
AHA	Archivo Histórico Archidiocesano, Tarragona
AHN	Archivo Histórico Nacional, Madrid (*Sección de Clero*, unless otherwise indicated)
AM	Archivo Municipal
ASV	Archivio Segreto Vaticano
BAV	Biblioteca Apostolica Vaticana
BC	Biblioteca Capitular
BM	British Museum
BN	Biblioteca Nacional, Madrid
BP	Biblioteca Pública
RAH	Real Academia de la Historia, Madrid

2. PUBLISHED MATERIAL

AA	*Anthologica Annua*
AEM	*Anuario de Estudios Medievales*
AFP	*Archivum Fratrum Praedicatorum*
AHDE	*Anuario de Historia del Derecho Español*
AIA	*Archivo Ibero-Americano*
AIEG	*Anales del Instituto de Estudios Gerundenses*
ALKG	*Archiv für Litteratur- und Kirchen-Geschichte*
AST	*Analecta Sacra Tarraconensia*
BAE	*Biblioteca de Autores Españoles*
BAT	*Boletín Arqueológico, Tarragona*
BCM...	*Boletín de la Comisión de Monumentos de...*

Abbreviations

BEC	*Bibliothèque de l'École des Chartes*
BHS	*Bulletin of Hispanic Studies*
B. Hisp.	*Bulletin Hispanique*
BIFG	*Boletín del Instituto Fernán-González*
BRABL	*Boletín de la Real Academia de Buenas Letras de Barcelona*
BRAH	*Boletín de la Real Academia de la Historia*
BSAL	*Bolletí de la Societat Arqueologica Luliana*
CD...	*Colección Diplomática...*
CHCA	*Congrès d'historia de la Corona d'Aragó*
CHE	*Cuadernos de Historia de España*
CLI	Chronique latine inédite
CODOIN	*Colección de documentos inéditos para la historia de España*
CODOINACA	*Colección de documentos inéditos del Archivo de la Corona de Aragón*
CTEER	*Escuela Española de Arqueología e Historia en Roma: Cuadernos de Trabajos*
DHGE	*Dictionnaire d'Histoire et de Géographie Ecclésiastiques*
EHR	*English Historical Review*
ES	*España Sagrada*
EUC	*Estudis Universitaris Catalans*
HS	*Hispania Sacra*
LDH	Linehan: 'Documentación pontificia de Honorio III'
MDhI	Mansilla: *Documentación pontificia hasta Inocencio III*
MDH	Mansilla: *Documentación pontificia de Honorio III*
MGH	*Monumenta Germaniae Historica*
MHE	*Memorial Histórico Español*
MIöG	*Mitteilungen des Instituts für österreichische Geschichtsforschung*
Part.	Alfonso X: *Las Siete Partidas*
PL	J. P. Migne, *Patrologia Latina*
PMH	*Portugaliae Monumenta Historica*
QFIA	*Quellen und Forschungen aus italienischen Archiven und Bibliotheken*
RABM	*Revista de Archivos, Bibliotecas y Museos*

Abbreviations

RB	*Revue Bénédictine*
REDC	*Revista Española de Derecho Canónico*
RET	*Revista Española de Teología*
RIS	*Rerum Italicarum Scriptores*
RPH	*Revista Portuguesa de História*
RQ	*Römische Quartalschrift*
RTAM	*Recherches de Théologie Ancienne et Médiévale*
SM	*Studia Monastica*
Sched. Baumgarten	: Schedario Baumgarten (see Battelli in Bibliography)
SpGG	*Spanische Forschungen der Görresgesellschaft*
TRHS	*Transactions of the Royal Historical Society*
VL	Villanueva: *Viage literario*
ZSSR	*Zeitschrift der Savigny-Stiftung für Rechtsgeschichte*

3. OTHER

arm.(ario)	cupboard
caj.(a)	
caj.(ón)	box
caixa	
cam.	cameral
d.s.n.	unclassified document
carp.(eta)	folder
estante	shelf
fajo	bundle
gav.(eta): Port.	drawer
inc.	*incipit*
leg.(ajo)	bundle
perg.(amino)	document: parchment
papel	document: paper
vit.(rina)	show-case

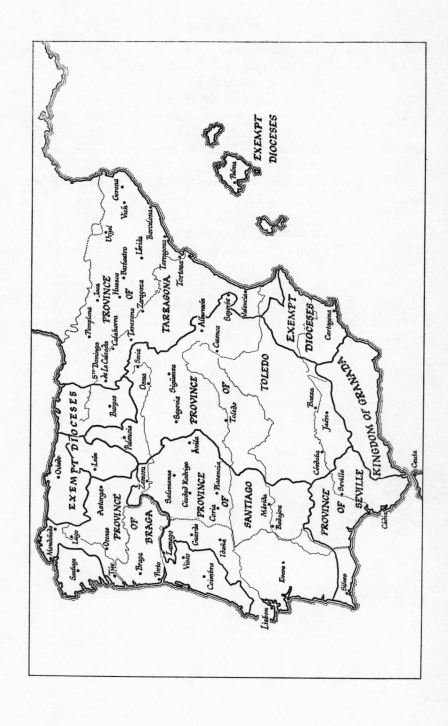

Chapter 1

THE SPANISH CHURCH
AND HONORIUS III

Of necessity historians of medieval Spain subscribe to the Pirenne thesis, for it fits that country's history as it does no other.[1] In the mid-twelfth century the abbot of Cluny, Peter the Venerable, did, fore-shadowing the Belgian scholar by ignoring the Visigoths and arguing that it was not they but the Romans who were overrun by the Moors in 711.[2] And that view still holds. The Visigothic period of Spanish history may be described as no more than 'an appendix' to the Late Empire, and the Middle Ages be defined by the Moorish occupation.[3] Without Muhammad, Spanish historical scholarship down to and including the most recent article by Professor Sánchez-Albornoz would have been inconceivable.

So it is perfectly understandable that the history of medieval Spain should have become the history of the *Reconquista*; that the period of reconquest should be thought of as having left an indelible mark on the Spanish collective personality;[4] and, in particular, that historians should have paid special attention to the points of contact, both military and cultural, between Islam and Christendom.

One consequence of this, though, has been that the presumably less spectacular developments behind the front line have attracted the attention of considerably fewer scholars. The history of the Church,

---

[1] 'Probablemente...a ningún otro país como al nuestro...se puede aplicar la tesis de Pirenne...La idea es especialmente aplicable a España': Maravall, 'La idea de Reconquista', 177–8.

[2] 'Nam statim Romano languescente immo pene deficiente imperio...Arabum vel Sarracenorum hac peste infectorum surrexit principatus, atque vi armata maximas Asiae partes cum tota Africa ac parte Hispaniae paulatim occupans, in subiectos sicut imperium sic et errorem transfudit': *Summa Totius Haeresis Saracenorum*, in J. Kritzeck, *Peter the Venerable and Islam* (Princeton, 1964), 140, n. 111.

[3] Vicens Vives, *Manual de historia económica*, 81; Font y Rius, *Rec. Soc. Jean Bodin*, VI, 264: 'Chez nous le moyen âge commence avec cette invasion et finit avec l'expulsion des maures.'

[4] Vicens Vives, *Aproximación*, 192.

I

for example, has been almost entirely neglected. Though there are hardly fewer ecclesiastical archives than there are tales – and many of them very good tales – about the impossibility of gaining access to them, their contents have still to be sorted and analysed. Since Gams and Lafuente in the middle of the last century, no one has attempted a general survey. Only two names, those of Fita and Mansilla, even deserve mention in a review of the study of the subject since then; and neither the penetrating research of the one nor the patient industry of the other has provided any general perspective of the possibly humdrum history of the thirteenth-century Spanish Church. For while Fita dispersed his energies over a vast field, leaving not what would surely have been an incomparable volume but instead a remarkable series of short papers and articles, Mansilla, intent upon continuing Kehr's *Papsturkunden*, has confined himself almost exclusively to the Vatican archives, which provided the material for his very valuable book published in 1945.[1] The history of that substantial part of the Spanish Church which is not illuminated by the glare of the *Reconquista* has yet to be written.

The subject to be studied, however, does not present anything like the contrast which is suggested by the preoccupation of historians with the frontier area. Wherever they were, all Spanish churchmen were frontiersmen, to some extent. They differed in degree, not in kind. In matters of ecclesiastical discipline they expressed the frontier-spirit by their contempt for distant authority – papal authority included – and their rejection of any reforms which threatened their peculiar institutions, the most ineffectively threatened if not the most peculiar of which was clerical concubinage. The way in which the Spanish clergy as a whole survived and, within a generation, neutralised the fulminations of the Fourth Lateran Council on that topic deserves fuller treatment.[2] Here it is sufficient to observe the working of that frontier-spirit in the diocese of Segovia, and especially at Sepúlveda, in and after 1203 when the combined attempt of Bishop Gonzalo and Archbishop Martín of Toledo to separate the clergy from their women produced not a reformation of clerical morals but

---

[1] *Iglesia castellano–leonesa*, which deals with the period up to 1254. The *Papsturkunden* project has so far only reached the year 1227, and does not incorporate original, unregistered letters, for details of some seventy of which from Honorius III's pontificate, see Linehan, *AA*, xvi, 385 ff.

[2] Below, pp. 51 ff.

widespread clerical revolt.[1] In 1203 Segovia was not, physically, the frontier see that it had been a century before. Yet from the reactions of the clergy there to reforming notions, it is clear that there had been no decay of that sense of aggressive exclusiveness which characterised settlements all along the frontier and had been enshrined in Alfonso VI's confirmation of the celebrated *fuero* of Sepúlveda in 1076.[2]

By then, the year 1203, sanctions against concubinage had a long prehistory, but there is special justification for recalling in particular one earlier occasion on which clerical philandering had been condemned: the national council over which the legate, Cardinal Boso, had presided in February 1117.[3] For the political circumstances of that council illustrate the important point that the truculence of individual clerics or of the clergy in general was far from being the sole obstruction to reform. During the first three and a half centuries of the *Reconquista*, the Christian kings had frequently solved their dynastic difficulties by marriages which took no account whatsoever of the canonical rules of consanguinity. Not until 1023, when Sancho III consulted Bishop Oliva of Vich on the question of the proposed union of his sister, Urraca, and her second cousin, Alfonso V of Leon, is there any sign that they felt themselves bound by the current disciplinary norms; and even then Sancho chose to ignore the inconvenient reply which he received.[4] Now when, in 1117, some thirty years after the death of Gregory VII, the prelates assembled at Burgos, they met beneath the shadow of a similar union of second cousins, Alfonso I of Aragon and Urraca, the daughter and heiress of Alfonso VI of Castile. Canon xiv of the rather laconic review of canonical discipline issued by them, prohibiting marriages within the seventh degree, amounted therefore to a direct challenge to Alfonso VI's political testament. That the attack was led by Archbishop Bernardo

---

[1] In the course of an inquiry into the affair, the abbot of San Tomé, Sepúlveda, stated 'quod ipse scit quod clerici Septempublicenses de villa et de aldeis pro maiori parte tenebant concubinas ante inicium istius cause et multi eorum adhuc tenent': AC Segovia, doc. 16. See also Colmenares, *Historia*, 168–9; González Davila, *Teatro*, III, 538–9. The clergy of Sepúlveda helped to drive the next bishop, Giraldo, into premature retirement over this and other issues: González, *Alfonso VIII*, I, 425–7.

[2] Cf. Sáez, et al., *Fueros de Sepúlveda*, 45–9; González, *Hispania*, III, 243–5; Lacarra, *Moyen Âge*, LXIX, 218.

[3] Fita, *BRAH*, XLVIII, 396.

[4] Pérez de Urbel, *Sancho el Mayor*, 109–14; Abadal, *L'Abat Oliba*, 246–7.

of Toledo, one of the Cluniacs whom Alfonso had invited to Castile to assist him with the *Reconquista*, provided a further element of poignancy. For though Bernardo may have been a reformer (an excellent thing in primates), he happened also to be the champion of the Burgundian candidate to the Castilian throne, the young Alfonso VII.[1] Reform had its political uses and carried with it its political dangers.

This remained true a century after the Burgos Council, at a time when the Spanish Church was in crying need of reform in head and members. Far afield, as far afield as Flanders, tales were told of the incontinence of the Spanish clergy.[2] But the legislation of the Fourth Lateran Council of 1215, 'the most important single body of disciplinary and reform legislation of the medieval church',[3] made no immediate impression upon Castile, Leon or Aragon. For the twenty-three peninsular prelates who, according to the 'official communiqué', were there,[4] the Council's highlight was not so much its solemn decrees as the preliminary slanging match over the primacy issue during which Archbishop Rodrigo of Toledo dismissed the rival claim of Compostela as being founded on an old wives' tale and brought blushes to the cheeks of the archbishop of Braga by recounting in loving detail the unedifying history of Estevão's predecessor, the anti-pope Gregory VIII.[5]

---

[1] Fita, *BRAH*, xLvIII, 398; Defourneaux, *Les Français en Espagne*, 32–7, 201–3; Rivera, *Iglesia de Toledo*, 125 ff.

[2] For the cautionary tale of *quidam presbyter* of 'Hyspania' who had slept with a woman, see *Balduini Ninovensis Chronicon*, 539 (s.a. 1211). Cf. the view of González: 'La moralidad del clero ofrece reducida... documentación, indicio de que no era de nivel bajo': *Alfonso VIII*, I, 419.

[3] Kuttner and García, *Traditio*, xx, 163.

[4] Luchaire, *Journal des Savants*, III, 562, whence Hefele–Leclercq, v, ii, 1730. There are two Toledo MSS., BN, vit. 15–5 (*olim* BC Toledo, MS. 15–22) and BC Toledo, MS. 42–21, which give different lists of Spanish prelates from that of the Zurich MS. used by Luchaire. The former (fo. 22r) notes 'quod XIIII fuerunt episcopi in isto concilio de regno Castelle, Legionis et Portugalie' and mentions the bishop of Oviedo but not those of Astorga, Salamanca or Mondoñedo, while in the other (publ. Rivera, *HS*, IV, 337) the bishop of Astorga's presence is noted, but not that of the others or of the bishop of Segorbe.

[5] BN, vit. 15–5, fos. 22r–3v (Fita, *Razón y Fe*, II, 178 ff.); Foreville, *Mélanges... Crozet*, 1125–7; Kuttner and García, *Traditio*, xx, 136–8; Hefele–Leclercq, v, ii, 1319–20. There is a briefer version of Rodrigo's speech in BC Toledo, MS. 42–21, fo. 1 (Rivera, *HS*, IV, 336–7). For a more balanced account of the career of Mauricio Burdino, the anti-pope, see David, *Études historiques*, 441 ff.

4

The primacy issue was only one of the items which interested them more than reform. There was also, of course, the *Reconquista*. Three years before, the Almohads had been defeated at Las Navas de Tolosa, and the credit for saving 'non solum Yspaniam, set et Romam, immo Europam universam' was due to *Yspania* 'et precipue regno Castelle', as the Castilians were quick to remind the Europeans and some Europeans had the grace to acknowledge.[1] More important, there was the bill for the *Reconquista*. The Castilian victory cost Castilian money, for, though the Moorish account of the 1212 campaign describes the Christians begging pitifully for assistance 'from Portugal to Constantinople', the truth is that that year marked the closing of the period of foreign aid. The few Frenchmen who did come caught dysentery and abandoned Alfonso VIII before the battle. And they had come as mercenaries. Even the king of Aragon was Castile's pensioner and received from Alfonso *stipendia necessaria* for his troops.[2] Regardless of the crusading indulgences which it offered them, foreigners had always made profitability their criterion for assisting in the *Reconquista,* and by 1212 better opportunities for booty were available nearer home. This break with the past was completed in the following year when Pedro II of Aragon died at Muret, with his back to the south, defending his French vassals against the crusading hordes of Simon de Montfort.[3] In 1147 Bishop Pedro of Porto had cajoled the English into abandoning their journey to the Holy Land and joining the siege of Lisbon by promising them booty and quoting the old Spanish proverb that the road is better than the inn.[4] Sixty-five years later these arguments had lost their force; sixty-six years later they were turned against Aragon. The thirteenth-century *Reconquista* would have to be a Spanish enterprise.

The 1212 campaign had cost the Castilian clergy half their year's income.[5] There are no means of knowing quite what this sacrifice meant for them. It was probably not the first such burden that they

---

[1] CLI: *B. Hisp.,* XIV, 357–8; *Sicardi Episcopi Cremonensis Chronica,* 180.

[2] *Anónimo de Madrid y Copenhague,* 122; Defourneaux, 185 ff.; CLI: *B. Hisp.,* XIV, 355.

[3] Defourneaux, 125 ff.; Renouard, *Annales de l'Université de Paris,* XXVIII, 16–17.

[4] 'Non Iherosolimis fuisse sed bene interim invixisse laudabile est': *De Expugnatione Lyxbonensi,* 76. Afonso Henriques' expectation that they might assist him for reasons of religion – *pietas* – and not for loot was soon disappointed: *ibid.* 98, 110.

[5] CLI: *B. Hisp.,* XIV, 355.

had been made to bear. It was certainly not the last. But it can at least be safely assumed that they were not immune to the effects of the nation-wide crisis which dispersed the euphoria of victory and brought the Christian advance to a temporary halt two years later.[1] Economic relief, in the shape of a papal grant of crusading indulgences for warriors on the Spanish front, was requested by the entire Spanish contingent at the 1215 Council *cum quanta potuerunt instantia*. In that, if in nothing else, Rodrigo of Toledo had the support of the archbishop of Compostela.[2] At least two Castilian prelates, García of Cuenca and Giraldo of Segovia, had been reduced to borrowing their fare to Rome;[3] and if, furthermore, they made their stay there last two full years, as did Bishop Martinho of Porto,[4] then the economic consequences of the Council for them may well have been similar to those which forced Bishop Juan Pérez of Calahorra to sell property on his return in order to clear the debts that he had contracted at the Curia.[5]

In these circumstances, it is hardly surprising that the one issue raised at the Council which riveted the attention of Spanish prelates was the fiscal issue: the tax of a twentieth of the income from ecclesiastical benefices to be used for the launching of another crusade.[6] The levying of the tax was given pride of place in the perfunctory passage which Lucas of Túy, writing twenty years later, devoted to the Council;[7] and this emphasis probably reflects pretty faithfully the attitude of the bishops themselves in and after 1215. To them it seemed inequitable that they should be expected to contribute to a foreign War, however Holy it might be, when they were already bearing the heat and burden of the day on their own national front. In this spirit – a spirit which was to endure throughout the century – they devoted their energies not to the business of summoning councils and synods and reforming the Spanish Church, but, instead, to the task of sabotaging the collection of the tax: a task for

---

[1] *Ibid.* 368; *Primera Crónica General,* para. 1023.
[2] Bishop Soeiro of Lisbon and others to Honorius III, autumn 1217, in *Reg. Hon. III,* appendix I, 7 (MDH, 95). [3] Rivera, *HS,* IV, 340–1.
[4] The fact was mentioned in the early 1250s, in the course of a lawsuit between the churches of Braga and Porto: ADB, Gav. dos Arcebispos, 24.
[5] AC Calahorra, doc. 251, 255 : publ. Menéndez Pidal, *Documentos lingüísticos,* I, 126–7.
[6] Hefele–Leclercq, V, ii, 1390–95.
[7] *Chronicon Mundi,* 113. Similarly Gil de Zamora, ed. Fita, *BRAH,* V, 312.

which their spiritual leader, Archbishop Rodrigo, by diverting the funds into his own coffers, proved himself to be admirably equipped. Thus, peculation preceded reform, and because the affair provided the post-Lateran papacy with its first experience of the shortcomings of the Spanish episcopate it is appropriate that some account of it should stand at the beginning of this study.

Throughout Christendom the collection of the triennial twentieth was entrusted by Innocent III to the regional Masters of the Hospital and Temple. In the provinces of Toledo, Braga and Compostela, and the exempt sees of León, Burgos and Oviedo, they were assisted by the cantor and archdeacon of Zamora. Three months after Innocent's deadline for payment, November 1216, nothing had been achieved, and Honorius III sent the Spanish provinces a stiff reprimand. The bishops' ingenuity in interpreting Innocent's mandate had made the collectors' task impossible. Some had alleged that they were not obliged to pay in cash; and others that they were not responsible for summoning diocesan synods for this purpose, although the pope had been quite explicit on this point. In consequence, the collectors had been made to wander the length and breadth of the country, gathering the dues in dribs and drabs of wheat, wine and barley; and at that rate fifty of them, let alone four, Honorius observed, could hardly hope to deal with a province the size of Toledo, which spread over two entire kingdoms. The bishops were reminded that time was short and that the cash was needed immediately. They were to interpret his predecessor's instructions *sano et simplici intellectu* and to centralise and expedite the business of collection.[1] Their Fabian tactics irritated Honorius, as he had already made clear in his reply of December 1216 to a series of questions which the chapter of Compostela had asked concerning the scope of the tax[2]. Yet while the pope fumed, the game continued.

To some Spaniards the capture of the Portuguese stronghold of Alcacer do Sal in the autumn of 1217 seemed to herald the arrival of that moment, the recommencement of military operations, when, in accordance with Innocent III's promise at the Council, crusading indulgences might be granted to the *reconquistadores*. Their argument did budge the pope, but only to the extent of granting favours to the

---

[1] *Reg. Hon. III*, 337 (MDH, 35). Cf. Lunt, *Financial Relations*, 242 ff.
[2] *Reg. Hon. III*, 132 (MDH, 16).

victors of that particular engagement. He was not prepared to release them from the oaths which they had taken to join the Fifth Crusade.[1] Nor would he assign to Spanish purposes the profits of the twentieth; and in February–March 1218 he made a further effort to chivvy the province of Toledo and the rest of the Spanish Church into taking positive action.[2]

When this new approach failed, Honorius tried other methods: the appointment in October 1218 of two papal collectors, Master Cintius, and his chaplain Huguicio, two canons of St Peter's.[3] But, if anything, the cure proved worse than the disease, for Honorius had made no allowance for the villainy of Archbishop Rodrigo. In January 1218 Rodrigo had been invested with legatine authority of a martial character throughout the kingdoms of Leon, Castile and Aragon, in connexion with the fresh Christian offensive;[4] and now, combining his new status with his native wit, he teamed up with Huguicio, to their own shameless advantage and the Church's considerable loss. In February of the year 1219 – a year of disastrous harvests throughout Europe, Spain included[5] – Honorius demonstrated his affection for the archbishop by granting him half of the income of the twentieth in the dioceses of Toledo and Segovia, adding airily (and in the light of later developments, most inadvisably) that there was no need for Rodrigo to tax his conscience overmuch about calculating his share of the takings *ad unguem*.[6] And the recipient was evidently still held in high regard twelve months after, for then the entire uncollected

---

[1] *Ibid.* appendix I, 7; 997 (MDH, 95, 134); Herculano, *História de Portugal*, IV, 80 ff. For the papal attitude, cf. Goñi Gaztambide, *Historia de la Bula de la Cruzada*, 133 ff., except that Goñi refers to a tax of 20% rather than 5% (p. 135).

[2] *Reg. Hon. III*, 1116, 1547 (MDH, 162, 182).

[3] *Ibid.* 1634 (MDH, 187).

[4] AC Toledo, I.4.N.1.20=*Reg. Hon. III*, 1042 (MDH, 148). Cf. Goñi, *Historia*, 141 ff., according to whom Rodrigo had obtained 'el oficio de legado ordinario en España durante diez años' in 1215 (p. 143): an allegation for which the earliest authority dates from the year 1253: BN, vit. 15–5, fos. 22v, 33r. Rodrigo does not figure as legate in the Papal Registers before Jan. 1218: cf. Zimmermann, *Die päpstliche Legation*, 100, 244, The legatine status accorded to Archbishop Estêvão of Braga in Jan. 1219 probably had the same quasi-military quality: ADB, Gav. II das Igrejas, 194; *Rerum Memorabilium I*, 66; Cunha, *História ecclesiástica dos arcebispos de Braga*, II, 96.

[5] 'Per totam Teutoniam, Allemanniam, Frantiam et usque Ispaniam excussa fuerunt grana': *Aegidii Aureaevallensis Gesta Episcoporum Leodiensium*, 119.

[6] *Reg. Hon. III*, 1864 (MDH, 207)=AC Toledo, A.6.H.1.10a; 11b; 11c (three copies).

balance of the tax from the whole area subject to his legatine jurisdiction was made over to him:[1] an act of papal liberality which was
doubtless prompted by favourable reports on the archbishop submitted by Huguicio.

Huguicio had every reason for giving the archbishop a good press.
In March 1218 he had been appointed to the Toledo canonry which
Rodrigo had conferred eight years before upon another Roman clerk;[2]
and between then and July 1220, when the scales at last fell from the
pope's eyes, the *simplex nuntius* passed himself off as a full-blown
legate, committed *multa enormia et abusiva,* and received various
grants from the see of Segovia, of which Rodrigo had recently been
given charge.[3] When, eventually, all this came to light, Honorius acted
purposefully, for once. Rodrigo was administered a stinging rebuke
and informed that his stock at the Curia had fallen sharply.[4] The
archbishop of Tarragona was instructed to investigate and, on the
very same day, 1 July, the pope called Rodrigo's fellow countryman,
Cardinal Pelayo of Albano, to render account of his receipts from the
Hospitallers of Paris. Honorius suspected, perhaps, that the archbishop's chicanery had even wider ramifications.[5] Retribution was
swift. On 4 July Rodrigo was deprived of his income from the twentieth on the grounds that his proposed campaign against the Moors
– which, as the pope now remembered it, had provided the justification for the grant[6] – had never materialised.

In fact, Honorius's memory played him false. The grant of six
months before had been made on account of Rodrigo's past achievements and not in expectation of future action.[7] But inconsistency –
the mark of all of Honorius's dealings with the Spanish Church – was

---

[1] *Ibid.* 2488 (MDH, 269)=AC Toledo, A.6.H.1.10c. On the previous day, 4 Feb.
1220, an identical mandate had been sent to the archbishop: AC Toledo, A.6.H.1.8d;
10 (two copies); and Sparago of Tarragona and other prelates within Rodrigo's
legatine jurisdiction were ordered to render him *auxilium personarum et rerum*: AC
Toledo, A.6.H.1.8b; 9 (MDH, 268); AHA, *Index dels Indices,* fo. 567v. On 5 Feb.
they were directed to pay Rodrigo the balance of the tax: AC Toledo, A.6.H.1.8c.
[2] *Reg. Hon. III,* 1181 (MDH, 167); Potthast, 3921 (MDhI, 420).
[3] *Reg. Hon. III,* 2516, 2716, 414, 2700 (MDH, 300, 326, 43, 323); Colmenares, 185 ff.
[4] *Reg. Hon. III,* 2516 (MDH, 300).
[5] *Ibid.* 2515 (MDH, 299); 2517.
[6] 'Non tamen pro eo quod processeras sed quia procedere intendebas': *ibid.* 2525
(MDH, 301).
[7] *Ibid.* 2488: 'Attendentes expensas et discrimina et labores quos…archiepiscopus…
aggressus est Mauros viriliter impugnando' (MDH, 269).

of less consequence than the fact that the discovery of the scandal dispelled whatever illusions he may still have entertained regarding Rodrigo's integrity. For, though he managed to escape the graver consequences of his actions,[1] Rodrigo would have to wait for Honorius's death for his stock at the Curia to rise again. His legatine status lapsed,[2] and once again Spain was required to contribute to the Fifth Crusade.[3]

Historians have not paid due attention to this archiepiscopal fall from grace.[4] Yet by July 1220 the pope already had other good grounds for despairing of Rodrigo. An earlier incident had shown that the archbishop's zeal for *libertas ecclesiastica*, which Innocent III had entrusted to his care in 1208,[5] was considerably less fervent than his determination not to fall out with the civil power. This incident arose out of Fernando III's refusal to surrender certain property which his grandfather, Alfonso VIII, had bequeathed to the church of Osma. In the autumn of 1217 the bishop of Osma, Melendo, complained in person to the pope and caused Bishop Sancho of Zaragoza and two archdeacons of that church to be commissioned to investigate the affair. The delegates, domiciled in Aragon, found for Melendo, but the very freedom from Castilian pressure which enabled them to reach a decision unfavourable to Fernando prevented its implementation. On-the-spot assistance was needed, and so, in April 1218, they engaged the archbishop of Toledo to act for them. To be required to read his king a lecture was a nightmare for any medieval prelate, and that duty had now devolved upon Rodrigo. He failed the acid test. After some delay he sent the judges a plaintive reply. He had urged the king and queen 'often and diligently' to accept the decision, he said. But he had been unable to bring himself to impose sanctions when the royal couple ignored his admonitions, 'on account of the scandal and not inconsiderable diffi-

---

[1] In Sept. 1220 the allegation of the chapter of Toledo that Rodrigo's grant of the canonry to Huguicio had been made *extra numerum* was referred for a decision to Bishop Domingo of Plasencia, an old friend of the archbishop: AHN, cod. 996B, fo. 44v (MDH, 319); Rodericus Toletanus, *De Rebus Hispaniae*, 202.

[2] The last occasion on which the pope addressed him as legate seems to have been in Nov. 1221. By Sept. 1225, at the latest, he had ceased to use the title: AHN, 3019/1 (MDH, 381); AC Ávila, perg. 12.

[3] AHN, 2129/15; Linehan, *HS*, xx, 180 ff.

[4] Mansilla mentions the papal reprimand, but not its consequences: *Iglesia*, 54.

[5] Potthast, 3680 (MDhI, 398).

culties to which such action might lead'. Let this chalice pass, he pleaded, *quia sicut nobis ita aliis poteritis demandare.*[1]

The lenient judges were obliging, and transferred the burden to the bishops of Burgos and Palencia, Mauricio and Tello. But, alas for justice, they were made of the same stuff as the archbishop, and did nothing. Safe and sound behind a national boundary, Sancho of Zaragoza treated them to a scornful diatribe of quite Innocentian fervour and flavour, calling as his witness *ille qui hominum corda scrutatur et renes.* Had they, perchance, forgotten the text that required them to lay down their lives for their brothers? If they were typical prelates, he concluded, then the prospect was indeed gloomy.[2] Indeed it was, as the same pair of prelates proved in and after 1223 when the pope himself failed to rouse them into assisting the bishops of Cala-horra and Segovia whom the king had exiled and whose churches he was pillaging.[3] It was a serious matter that the three Castilian church-men most frequently commissioned as judges-delegate and executors during Honorius's pontificate[4] seem to have taken Gilbert Foliot as their model rather than Thomas Becket.

Honorius must have known about this spineless display when in October 1219, some months before Rodrigo's unmasking, he sent the archbishop and his suffragans a letter of (for him) quite unusual asperity, the message of which was not at all distorted by its rich assortment of biblical tags. The Castilian Church was in a state of collapse. Heresy was abroad. Monastic discipline had been abandoned. *Modestia clericalis* was neglected. And the fault was theirs. It was the bishops who promoted scoundrels to benefices while themselves dissipating the goods of the churches entrusted to their care. They had ignored completely the message of the Fourth Lateran Council. And they now received a solemn warning: let them hasten to implement the statutes of 1215, 'et illa presertim que salutem respiciunt animar-um'.[5]

---

[1] *Reg. Hon. III,* 743, 776 (=AC Burgo de Osma, perg. 34); 810 (MDH, 84, 89, 93); AC Burgo de Osma, perg. 1, 21 (=AC Toledo, X.2.C.2.1a); Burriel, *Memorias,* 257 ff.; Loperráez, *Descripción,* III, 57 ff.

[2] 'Si enim hoc semper episcopis esset timendum contra reges et principes, semper justitia dormitaret': AC Burgo de Osma, perg. 25; Burriel, 258, 338, 345.

[3] Mansilla, *Iglesia,* 168–71; *Reg. Hon. III,* 4298, 5465, 5922 (MDH, 436, 554, 600).

[4] Registered letters only considered, Mauricio received 19 commissions, Tello 13, and Rodrigo 7.

[5] AC Toledo, I.5.A.1.1. (MDH, 246, from BN, MS. 13116 – not MS. 1311, as

The papal fury was impressive. It might have been Innocent III talking, or Sancho of Zaragoza. The bishops were torpid and negligent, dumb dogs and broken reeds.[1] Still, scalding though it was, Honorius's condemnation of them appears as a cooling draught when set beside the testimony of the Spanish cleric, Diego García. In his devotional treatise of the previous year, *Planeta,* Diego had also called the bishops dumb dogs, and much more besides. They were a positive force of evil triumphant in a dying world.[2] *Tot sunt episcopi quot latrones.* They were the ruin of the Church, the oppressors of the poor, not only unlettered themselves but also enemies of learning, 'non episcopos se putantes esse set dominos'.

His account of their *condicio truculenta* included all the bishops.[3] But there was one in particular for whom Diego reserved his sharpest shafts and his deadliest venom. Hardly surprisingly, the writer did not identify this episcopal sink of iniquity whose stamina in vice placed him beyond the ranks of ordinary mortals.[4] Yet in view of Diego's unqualified devotion to Archbishop Rodrigo, to whom the work is dedicated in the most obsequious terms,[5] it may be presumed that the butt of this savage attack was one of the bishops of the Toledo province with whom in 1218 the archbishop was at odds. Of the various possibilities the most plausible is Bishop García of Cuenca;[6] and because it both provides substance for the pope's gloomy verdict of 1219 and also sheds some light on the murky nature of Rodrigo's dealings with his suffragans, the course of their quarrel is worth following and the issues which divided them are deserving of analysis.

Rodrigo had designs on part of the territory of the see of Cuenca and its rents. When the bishopric of Cuenca had been established in

Mansilla – fos. 10r–11v: Burriel's mid-eighteenth century copy which ascribes the letter to Honorius II).
[1] *Ibid.*: 'dum canes muti proiectum ramulum [*ranunculum* in MDH] in os habent, et sunt quasi baculus arundineus iam confractus'.
[2] *Planeta*, ed. Alonso, 182–97, esp. 184: 'Unde prelati mutis canibus comparati, latratu quodam terribili sepe terrent hospites, nunquam lupos.'
[3] *Ibid.* 185, 405.
[4] *Ibid.* 186–95, esp. 186: 'Cum enim sit quasi cisterna nequicie et sentina odii, templumque tristicie et tronus avaritie, falsitatisque puteus et mare mortuorum viciorum ad instar rufini pessimi.'
[5] *Ibid.* 162 ff.
[6] Diego, obscurely, refers to García, who had been bishop of Cuenca since 1208, as having ruled his church 'per novem annos continuos minus decem': *ibid.* 191.

1182, after the reconquest of the area, it had been given all the rights enjoyed in the Visigothic period by two sees, Valeria and Arcavica, on account of its poverty. Rodrigo now wanted this arrangement annulled because, according to him, Cuenca's income had increased considerably during the intervening period. He was certainly in a position to judge and in possession of information about the economic condition of the diocese, for while he had been at Rome he had arbitrated an involved rents dispute between Bishop García and his diocesan clergy.[1] Yet when he opened his campaign in January 1218 – the year of Diego García's attack – he was careful to disguise his personal ambitions. *Evidens utilitas*, he maintained in his petition to the pope, was what prompted him to raise the matter.[2] It was only at a later stage, at the hearing of the case by Bishop Mauricio of Burgos and his colleagues in March 1220, that what he and his church stood to gain was mentioned: the previous nine years' income of the see of Cuenca. And three months later his proctors put forward a further claim – to the 'villa que dicitur Moia cum terminis suis'.[3]

García, however, was a bonny fighter, and the archbishop's hopes of a quick victory were soon dashed. At the first hearing he attempted unsuccessfully to incriminate the bishop, alleging (of all things) that García had curried favour at court and *falsis persuasionibus* had robbed him of the friendship of the king and queen.[4] The reappointment of the judges-delegate as arbiters proved equally inconclusive,[5] and the case was still unsettled eight years later,[6] by which time García was dead.

Of greater significance, though, than Rodrigo's failure to carry all before him was the unedifying zeal with which he set about discrediting his adversary in 1218. For the suggested identification of Diego García's *cisterna nequicie* is not the only indication of a concerted campaign of vilification directed at the bishop of Cuenca and masterminded by the archbishop of Toledo. García had other

---

[1] On 7 Feb. 1216, together with Cardinal Pelayo of Albano: AC Cuenca, 4–17–243.
[2] *Reg. Hon. III*, 1040 (MDH, 146). Cf. Mansilla, *Iglesia*, 71; Vázquez de Parga, *División de Wamba*, 122.
[3] AC Cuenca, 5–20–276; AHN, cod. 996B, fo. 48ra–vb; Serrano, *Don Mauricio*, 50–1. *Moia*: Moya (prov. Cuenca; part. jud. Cañete).
[4] AC Cuenca, 5–20–276.
[5] AC Cuenca, 4–17–241; AHN, cod. 996B, fo. 48vb.
[6] AC Toledo, I.4.N.1.18: *Significavit nobis* (7 April 1228).

enemies, and one of them was a cleric of his own diocese, the Arch-priest Julián of Huete, who since the very beginning of Honorius's pontificate had been busy at the Curia complaining *oportune et importune* about the bishop's 'intolerable' behaviour.[1] García was charged with simony, mismanagement and incontinence. It was alleged by Julián that, having made a pact with death, he was scurrying thither on all fours; and in December 1217, a month before Rodrigo applied for the division of the diocese of Cuenca, the pope ordered an investigation.[2]

For Rodrigo's purposes the archpriest's accusations were most timely, and appearances suggest that the bishop's two enemies were in league. Their complicitly may be inferred from the fact that papal protection was granted to Julián and his property on the very same day in January 1218 that Rodrigo's case against García was initiated.[3] Moreover, when in the following June the judges appointed at Julián's instigation were reminded of their commission by Honorius, a copy of the rescript was sent to the archbishop, although he had no *prima facie* interest in the matter.[4] They fought together, and they failed together: in January 1221, six months after the unmasking of Rodrigo, Julián's charges were dismissed, and in March 1222 Bishop García was declared by the pope to be held *in odore bone opinionis*.[5]

Rodrigo's tactics against his suffragan do him little credit. The fomenter of sedition within his own province, he was constitutionally incapable of providing the foundation of peace and concord upon which the reform of the Castilian Church might have been based. Instead, he gave an example of truculence and set the tone of ecclesiastical behaviour throughout his province. 'Truculent' was the adjective which Diego García applied to the Castilian bishops, and with a leader of Rodrigo's calibre it is hardly surprising that there should have been 'manifest adversaries' within the episcopate.[6] For

---

1 *Reg. Hon. III,* 924 (MDH, 104). Julián had not been at the 1215 Council: Rivera, *HS,* IV, 337.
2 *Reg. Hon. III,* 924.
3 *Ibid.* 1034, 1040, 1045–6 (MDH, 145–7, 150). No. 1034 is concerned with the recovery of a loan advanced by Julián to enable the bishop of Segovia to attend the Lateran Council. In July 1215 Julián had witnessed a further loan for the same purpose at Segovia: Rivera, *HS,* IV, 340–1.
4 *Reg. Hon. III,* 1460 (MDH, 176).
5 *Reg. Hon. III,* 2954, 3864 (MDH, 356, 396).
6 *Ibid.* 2577 (MDH, 306): García of Cuenca of Melendo of Osma, July 1220.

the Cuenca affair was not an isolated lapse. While it was still at issue, Rodrigo committed further acts of piracy in the diocese of Palencia, demanding excessive procurations while *en route* for an interview with the king and suspending Bishop Tello, regardless of the appeal which had been lodged with the pontiff. 'Deductum est in scandalum et discordias totum regnum', Tello complained to Honorius (whose dossier on the archbishop was already substantial), adding that the primate, who had abandoned Melendo of Osma and had had the effrontery to object to García of Cuenca's connexions at court, had issued his sentence of suspension unceremoniously 'ubi curia regis erat'.[1]

Archbishop Rodrigo was at home *ubi curia regis erat*, and his pre-dilection for the royal court provides part of the explanation for his desultory performance as a reformer. It was a characteristic which was to be shared by Castilian prelates throughout the century, but Rodrigo's biographers have been much exercised by the slur upon their hero contained in the pope's letter of October 1219, and have been at pains to explain it away. The ingenious Estella, having already insisted upon the archbishop's 'indefatigable reforming zeal', was reduced to the argument that his inactivity in this regard was actually yet another endearing attribute, further proof of his essential human-ity. After all, 'manchas tiene el sol y no deja de ser el astro rey, que fecunda e ilumina la tierra'. Moreover – and here the historian of the twentieth century reiterates the justification offered in the thirteenth – *algún discuido* has to be allowed in view of Rodrigo's various contri-butions to the *Reconquista*.[2] Another apologist, Ballesteros Gaibrois, took the other course, and interpreted the thirteenth century in the light of the twentieth. Writing in the late 1930s, he attributed the ills of the Castilian Church, as described by the pope, to Jewish infiltra-tion of the 'clean' Spanish people: an interpretation for which Honorius's bull (which he misdates) provides no support whatso-ever.[3] And when all else fails the archbishop's modern friends are

---

[1] 'In calore animi, nulla monitone premissa, in hora vespertina ubi curia regis erat, non sedens sed stans, statim': *inc. Querelam venerabilis*, 2 March 1221: AC Toledo, X.2.A.2.6 (LDH, 44). The two prelates reached an understanding in the following August: AC Toledo, X.2.A.2.12; AC Palencia, 2/1/35.

[2] Estella, *El fundador*, v, 91–3.

[3] Ballesteros Gaibrois, *Don Rodrigo*, 152. The same author, in 1941, wrote a piece which amounts almost to a caricature of the view of Rodrigo which is questioned

able to cite the Guadalajara Council, which met sometime before
1221, as irrefragable proof of his reforming zeal.[1] They are not discouraged by the fact that, though no record of its statutes has survived,
Rodrigo's intention at Guadalajara seems to have been to abrogate
Bishop Giraldo of Segovia's disciplinary provisions by temporising
with the *clerici concubinarii* of Sepúlveda and Pedraza.[2] He has even
been credited with a whole series of councils, despite the difficulty of
reconciling this claim with the anxiety of Gregory IX and the emphatic
statement of Gregory's legate in 1228 that the provisions of the Fourth
Lateran Council had been almost entirely neglected in Spain.[3]

The fact is that the summoning of councils and synods hardly
figured at all on Rodrigo's list of priorities. He was no saint, no
spartan, no reformer. His own and his church's temporal state were
infinitely more interesting to him; and, as the legate was to observe
in 1229, Archbishop Sparago of Tarragona was hardly less negligent
in the kingdoms of Aragon and Navarre. Apart from a single casual
reference to a Pamplona synod, held probably in 1216,[4] there is no
sign of ecclesiastical assemblies in that region during Honorius III's
pontificate. With that one exception, mention of councils and synods
at this period occurs only in the course of agreements in which the
obligation of a monastic community to be represented at episcopal
synods was mentioned as a token of subjection, without any suggestion that such assemblies were indeed summoned. Such was the case
in the settlements between the bishop of Burgos and the abbey of
Covarrubias in July 1222, and between the bishop of Palencia and the
abbey of San Román de Blaye in May 1224.[5] For the implementation
of reform the twelve years after the Fourth Lateran Council were
twelve years of stagnation in the Spanish kingdoms.

Part of the blame for this must be borne by Honorius himself.
Innocent III's successor lacked the single-mindedness which was most

---

here. The archbishop was represented as 'un hombre de pura e indiscutible *raza
española*, concreto, normal' who at the Lateran Council had defended 'la causa
española': *Príncipe de Viana*, II, 69, 72 (my italics).
1 Ballesteros Gaibrois, 107; Estella, 92.
2 Colmenares, 185 ff.
3 See Ch. 2.
4 García Larragueta, *El Gran Priorado*, II, 168; Goñi Gaztambide, *Príncipe de Viana*,
XVIII, 68.
5 Serrano, *Cartulario de Covarrubias*, 79; AC Palencia, 2/1/37.

urgently needed at this juncture. His fumbling incompetence in dealing with Archbishop Rodrigo was typical. Moreover, in the style of the successors of that other epoch-making pontiff, Gregory VII, he was unduly sensitive to the special pleading of regional groups, and was judicious to a fault in circumstances which called for a measure of recklessness. The policy of stooping to conquer, though at least a century old, had achieved precious little;[1] and in the Spanish situation it was hopelessly inappropriate. That, though, was Honorius's policy, with the result that the earliest post-Lateran stirrings there received from him not encouragement but condemnation. In July 1217 the clergy of the cathedral cities of the southern part of the province of Compostela – those, namely, of Zamora, Ávila, Plasencia, Coria, Ciudad Rodrigo and Salamanca – complained that Archbishop Pedro and their bishops had held a council, 'irrequisitis clericis ipsis', at which a number of constitutions greatly prejudicial to them had been issued, *contra antiquam consuetudinem*. What had aggravated them particularly were the measures taken to restrain abuse of the privilege of clergy in cases involving laymen, and to improve the moral condition of the clergy. The bishops had proposed that facile death-bed repentance should not have the effect of removing all the stigma which a lifetime of vice had merited: rough justice, perhaps, but preferable, on balance, to total episcopal inactivity and the clerical decadence discovered by the legate on his arrival eleven years later. Honorius's cancellation of the conciliar constitutions, without even hearing the bishops' case, was, therefore, as disastrous in practice as it was defensible in point of law.[2] The legate would display no such delicacy; for 'custom' might well be a euphemism for 'corruption', as the province of Braga was reminded by the legate's master in May 1233.[3] And if, furthermore, the pontiff were always to capitulate to objections based on 'difficulty', such as induced him in July 1219 to absolve Archbishop Pedro from the obligation to hold annual councils in the far-flung province of Compostela;[4] then the difficulty which any change for the better necessarily involves would invariably be cited as an objection to reform.

The thirteenth-century successors of Honorius III, Rodrigo of

---

[1] Its advantages were described by Pascal II in March 1106: Southern, *St Anselm*, 178.
[2] *Reg. Hon. III*, 623 (MDH, 63).   [3] *Reg. Greg. IX*, 1324.
[4] *Reg. Hon. III*, 2145 (MDH, 231) = AC Santiago, *Tumbo B*, fos. 224v–5r.

Toledo and Pedro of Compostela would frequently choose the line of least resistance. All the elements of the complex future relationship of the Spanish Church and the papacy were present during this pontificate, and the relative unconcern of Honorious with the issue of reform is the inevitable conclusion of a study of his dealings with Spain, the outbursts of October 1219 notwithstanding. The fiscal question was far more interesting for him, as it would also be for the pontiffs who followed him. Archbishop Rodrigo's misappropriation of funds presented him with the recurrent problem of the means of collection.

In this, however, he was well served by an individual of proven trust, Master Gonzalo García. Between 1215 and 1225 Gonzalo was the key figure – indeed, the only figure – of papal diplomacy in Spain. Innocent III had sent him to collect the Spanish and Portuguese *census*.[1] In 1217–18 he received a number of gifts from the archbishop and chapter of Toledo – though if it was Rodrigo's intention to suborn him, as he later suborned Huguicio, he failed dismally, for it was on the strength of a report from Gonzalo that in November 1221 Honorius revoked the indulgence which he had granted two and a half years before, during the archbishop's salad days and at the request of Fernando III, waiving the conciliar legislation on distinctive dress for Jews.[2] And there is also reason for believing that it was Gonzalo who brought the Huguicio affair to the pope's attention, since in the late autumn of 1219 he had been sent to North Africa on a mission to the sultan and had dealings with the Christian forces there.[3] In 1222, after the archbishop's disgrace, he was again in Spain. At Tarazona on 1 August he received from the prior of Tudela two *aurei*, the previous ten years' *census* of that church,[4] and he was still nearby in the following month.[5] A little later, he seems to have visited Portugal on diplomatic business,[6] and thereafter he becomes less easy to trace. When, at

1 *Reg. Hon. III*, 1635 (MDH, 188). He was in Portugal in 1213: Herculano, IV, 57, 307.
2 *Reg. Hon. III*, 223, 1943 (MDH, 24, 212); Fita, *Actas inéditas*, 235–6; AHN, 3019/1. Cf. Hefele–Leclercq, V, ii, 1386.
3 *Reg. Hon. III*, 2190 (MDH, 243); *Primera Crónica General*, para. 1033.
4 AC Tudela, 5–P–1 (reg. Fuentes, *Catálogo*, 206). The dating clause of the receipt contains an error: August 1222 fell in Honorius's seventh pontifical year, not his eighth.
5 *Reg. Hon. III*, 4113 (MDH, 413).
6 In November 1224 the dean of Lisbon was thanked by the pope for having rendered

Toledo in April 1226, he exchanged some land with the abbot of Valladolid, he was described as *commendator de Castrello de Ferruz*.[1] By March 1231, in which month Gregory IX authorised him to retain the office of sacrist of Osma despite the rules of his Order,[2] it may be assumed that his career as a mobile papal agent had ended.

Gonzalo's role was both diplomatic and fiscal. He collected the *census* and, possibly, the crusading twentieth too after the discovery of the Huguicio-Rodrigo scandal.[3] These matters were uppermost in Honorius's mind in his transactions with the Spanish Church. The bishops remained obdurate,[4] and by October 1225, when another collector was sent to take charge of the balance due from the provinces of Braga and Compostela and the exempt sees of León and Oviedo, the Crusade – which had provided the justification for the tax – was in ruins. This new collector was a Spaniard, Pelayo, bishop-elect of the Palestinian see of Ludd. He had connexions with the church of Orense, and by May 1227 was re-established at Salamanca *in partibus fidelium*.[5] Mindful of the previous fiasco, the pope kept him on a tight rein, for Honorius was very concerned about the repercussions of that affair and about the damage that it had done to the prestige of the Roman Church.[6] The prestige of the Spanish Church, however, which was far more seriously affected by clerical corruption than by archiepiscopal embezzlement, hardly moved him at all. The first, and last, serious attempt to refurbish that reputation had to await his death and the accession in March 1227 of Pope Gregory IX.

---

assistance 'fratri Gonsaldo nuntio nostro in negotiis nostris': *ibid.* 5136 (publ. Sousa Costa, *Mestre Silvestre*, 136, n. 245). Cf. Herculano, IV, 162 ff.

1 AC Valladolid, XXIX-7: publ. Mañueco Villalobos, *Documentos*, II, 110–11, where *Castrello de Ferruz* is identified as Castronuevo de Esgueva.

2 *Reg. Greg. IX*, 564; Delaville le Roulx, *Cartulaire*, II, 416–17. He had been sacrist since at least Aug. 1222: AC Tudela, 5–P–1.

3 This is not certain, but since the pope did turn to the Templars again at this time it is likely. Cf. AC Burgos, vol. 71, fo. 53r (MDH, 387).

4 Sparago of Tarragona was unco-operative, especially while the proceeds were destined for Rodrigo: *Reg. Hon. III*, 3729 (MDH, 390). See also Fabre–Duchesne, *Liber Censuum*, I, 14★: 'Archiepiscopus Compostellanus debet camere pro succursu Terre Sancte DCCC libras.'

5 *Reg. Hon. III*, 4197, 5693, 5888 (MDH, 430, 584, 598); *Reg. Greg. IX*, 101. He had either died or resigned the see by July 1229: AC Salamanca, 3/3/59 (reg. Marcos Rodríguez, *Catálogo*, 181). See also Mansilla, 55.

6 *Reg. Hon. III*, 5693, 2515 (MDH, 594, 299).

Chapter 2

THE LEGATE JOHN OF ABBEVILLE

1228–1229

In 1228 the torpid contentment of the Spanish Church was shattered when Gregory IX sent a legate, the cardinal-bishop of Sabina, John of Abbeville. John was a Frenchman[1] who before his promotion had been archbishop of Besançon, and before that had made a name for himself as a theologian at Paris.[2] Historians from the thirteenth century onwards have stressed the importance of his mission for the prosecution of the *Reconquista*[3] and his concern with the pacification of Portugal during the minority of Sancho II.[4] Until the end of that century, however, it was as a draconian disciplinarian that John was remembered, if he was remembered at all; and when Spaniards referred to him then they recalled – and not infrequently bewailed – the reformer rather than the warrior or the diplomat. In this sense, for ninety years after his departure, he was *the* legate.

Yet this side of his activity has attracted hardly any attention;[5] and what little has been written on the subject is derived from the testimony of Archbishop Rodrigo, to whom the legate's stay, which must have been something of a nightmare for him, seemed to drag on for

---

[1] In the early eighteenth century Thomas ab Incarnatione claimed him as Portuguese, although his true origins had been correctly described almost a hundred years before by Macedo: *Historia ecclesiae Lusitanae*, IV, 275–9; Macedo, *Lusitania Infulata*, 69–71, 78–9.

[2] *Histoire littéraire de la France*, XVIII, 162–77; Feret, *Faculté*, I, 228–31; Glorieux, *Répertoire*, 272–3; Smalley, *TRHS*, 4th ser., XXX, 1 ff.; Stegmüller, *Repertorium*, III, 340–4.

[3] Lucas of Túy, *Chronicon Mundi*, 114; Zimmermann, *Die päpstliche Legation*, 106–8.

[4] Herculano's belief that this was his *motivo principal* stems in part from a misunderstanding about the length of his stay in Portugal: *História de Portugal*, IV, 346. Similarly, Reuter, *Königtum und Episkopat*, 27.

[5] Valls i Taberner has remarked upon his influence on the legislation of the provincial councils of Tarragona, and elsewhere has provided a summary account of the legation: *AST*, XI, 255–6; *San Ramón de Penyafort*, 230 ff. Cf. Gams, *Kirchengeschichte*, III, i, 143–4, 221–4. Almeida has little or nothing to say: *História da Igreja em Portugal*, I, 397–8.

three years,[1] though in fact John was in Spain and Portugal for only half that time. Modern historians have added further complications to the chronology. Having failed to make allowance for the Year of the Incarnation, Herculano concluded that John was at Coimbra both in January 1228 and in January 1229, from which he deduced that Portuguese affairs were uppermost in the legate's mind.[2]

The author of the anonymous Latin chronicle – Bishop Juan of Osma, in all probability – stated quite explicitly that the legate entered 'Spain' in August 1228, at about the feast of the Assumption.[3] But whatever he may have meant by 'Spain', and despite the fact that his is the most circumstantial account that has survived,[4] he was quite clearly wrong on this point, for by then John had been there for at least two months. On 10 June he was at the monastery of San Pedro de Cardeña, Burgos,[5] and he may even have arrived earlier, before 28 March when the chapter of Calahorra provided him with their reply to an enquiry which he had instituted there.[6] Thereafter, between June 1228 and September 1229, it is possible to chart his progress in some detail, and in view of the confusion created by previous writers and the unique importance of his legation there is a strong case for reviewing the evidence.[7]

John spent the year 1228 in the kingdoms of Leon and Castile. The

---

1 *De Rebus Hispaniae*, 202: '...vir bonus, sapiens, litteratus, qui celebratis in singulis regnis conciliis, postquam monita salutis proposuit, ad sedem apostolicam est reversus, tribus annis legationis expletis'.

2 Herculano, 203 ff., 346, following Thomas ab Incarnatione, IV, 277. But the dates of the documents – publ. Santa María, *Chronica*, II, 439–41 – are 'pridie nonis ianuarii' and 'idibus ianuarii *anno domini*' 1228, i.e. 1229. For further examples of this usage in the Peninsula at this time cf. Alamo, *CD Oña*, II, 553–4, 600: on the latter occasion Alamo has noted as an error the identification of *anno domini* 1238 with *era* 1277 'in mense ianuarii', but his misguided acuity has deserted him in dealing with the former. The legate was certainly at Coimbra in January 1229: *PMH*, I, 613, 616.

3 CLI: *B. Hisp.*, XV, 273–4. The attribution of the chronicle to Juan of Osma is suggested by Lomax, *BHS*, XL, 205 ff.

4 *Ibid.* 272–5.   5 Serrano, *Don Mauricio*, 141.

6 Letter dated 'año de Cristo' 1228, publ. González Texada, *Historia de Santo Domingo de la Calzada*, 203–4. He had not left Rome before 22 February, despite Serrano's unsupported allegation that he was in Spain by then: Thorkelin, *Diplomatarium Arna-Magnaeanum*, I, 108 (=Potthast, 8131); Serrano, *Hispania*, III, 572, n. 10. Serrano may have been misled by López Ferreiro.

7 The partial itinerary in Valls i Taberner, *San Ramón*, 231, seems to have been derived from Risco, *ES*, XXXVI, 214–15, *via* Puig y Puig, *Episcopologio*, 217. But Puig's account is confused, owing to his cavalier use of the calendars of the Papal Registers.

arrangements at Burgos Cathedral, apparently his first port of call, were not perfect, but he found much there that was good and laudable, and his only unfavourable comment concerned nothing worse than absence from choir.[1] There were more shocking revelations than that in store for him, and having struck south to visit both Segovia, where he attended the consecration of the new cathedral church, and Ávila, before returning to Burgos, he set off westwards in pursuit of unrighteousness.[2] On 20 August he was at Carrión de los Condes, to the north of Palencia,[3] and it is highly likely, though it cannot be demonstrated, that he visited Palencia itself[4] and Zamora also.[5] This period was, moreover, presumably the occasion of the Valladolid Council, to which we shall return. Sometime, certainly, in the month of September he reached Astorga Cathedral, *in qua nulla erat ordinatio,* and on discovering, not for the last time during his legation, that the distribution of income was quite scandalously unfair, he amended the statutes, as well as reminding the canons of their solemn obligation to attend the services.[6] At the end of that month, on the 29th, he was *apud populum de Gordon* (the modern La Pola de Gordón)[7] to the north of León on the way to Oviedo, where, on arrival, he gave instructions concerning the office of dean and provided a constitution requiring the bishop to distribute vacant prebends among the canons – a constitution which the bishop subsequently sought to evade.[8] By way of the Cistercian house of Villabuena[9] and, probably, Lugo[10], he

[1] Serrano, *Don Mauricio,* 140–1.
[2] Segovia, 16 July: Colmenares, *Historia,* 192; Ávila, 20–1 July: AC Segovia, doc. 144, 311; San Pedro de Cardeña, 8 Aug: Berganza, *Antigüedades,* 143.
[3] Archivo Colegial, Logroño, doc. 18 (reg. Bujanda, *Inventario,* 18).
[4] He granted the Dominicans there his protection: AHN, 1724/15 (Potthast, 8782). Cf. RAH, MS. 9–24–5/4558, fo. 194v. It may be presumed that he visited the schools there.
[5] He excommunicated the rebellious clergy of Toro, and, as Bishop Martín complained in May 1233, demanded benefices at the cathedral for a number of his clerics: *Sua nobis,* 27 March 1230: AC Zamora, 11.i/8; *Reg. Greg. IX,* 1318.
[6] AD Astorga, 2/41: publ. Flórez, *ES,* XVI, 503–5; Rodríguez López, *Episcopologio asturicense,* II, 589–97.
[7] *Bullarium de Calatrava,* fos. 153–6. Cf. Rades de Andrada, *Historia de las tres ordenes,* fo. 27rv.
[8] AC Oviedo, Plomados, 1/6 (reg. García Larragueta, *Catálogo,* 343). Cf. *Reg. Alex. IV,* 1854; BAV, Cod. Lat. 3976. fo. 38v (Schillmann, *Formularsammlung,* 45).
[9] Manrique, *Cisterciensium,* IV, 433; Serrano, *Hispania,* III, 572.
[10] On 3 July 1234 Bishop Miguel of Lugo was empowered to absolve certain clerics excommunicated by John: *Exhibita nobis:* AC Lugo, 21/3/17.

proceeded westward and by 3 November had reached Santiago de Compostela.[1] We then lose sight of him for a couple of months, but since at the very beginning of 1229 he was at the Cortes of Coimbra[2] it is probable that he had spent at least part of the intervening period in Portugal. He definitely visited Guimarães and Porto and provided both churches with sets of statutes,[3] and before arriving at Coimbra he had already penetrated as far south as Tojal, near Lisbon, where the inhabitants had neither church nor priest and wanted both.[4] At the half-way stage of his legation he had covered a very considerable amount of ground.

He was still at Coimbra on 7 January 1229, after which he moved off up the valley of the Mondego by way of Celorico da Beira,[5] and reached Salamanca by 5 February where he presided over a council of the bishops of the kingdom of Leon – a council of which the constitutions have not survived and which has generally been ascribed to the previous year.[6] He was still at Salamanca on the 7th,[7] but by then he had probably concluded his most important business, for on the next day King Alfonso IX departed for Ciudad Rodrigo.[8]

Within five weeks the legate had crossed the Peninsula and was at Zaragoza. What took him there was either a new papal commission directing him to preside over the annulment of the marriage of King Jaime of Aragon and Leonor, daughter of Alfonso VIII of Castile,[9] or alternatively a turn for the worse in the negotiations with the Moorish king of Valencia, which, according to the anonymous Latin chronicler, were the main purpose of John's legation.[10] King Jaime,

---

[1] López Ferreiro, *Historia de Santiago*, v, 135.   [2] *PMH*, i, 613, 616.

[3] Jesus da Costa, *RPH*, iii, 569; publ. *Chartularium Universitatis Portugalensis*, i, 22–3; *Censual do Cabido da Sé do Porto*, 12–13.

[4] Santa María, *Chronica*, ii, 439–40.   [5] *Ibid.* 441.

[6] 'Anno domini .MCCXXVIII. in festo beate Agathe virginis, mense februarii.' Cf. López Ferreiro, v, appendix xv, 46–7; González, *Alfonso IX*, ii, 619–20.

[7] Sousa Costa, *Mestre Silvestre*, 164.   [8] González, *Alfonso IX*, ii, 686–8.

[9] Tejada y Ramiro, *Colección*, iii, 344–8. On 16 March he was attended at Zaragoza by the papal subdeacon 'G. de Almaguera', possibly the *frater Willelmus* from whom the pope had received a progress report on the legation in the previous month. A papal *cursor* of that name had delivered a bull of April 1228 to the church of Huesca, and it is conceivable that it was he who delivered the papal document of Feb. 1229 which approved the royal divorce: *Reg. Greg. IX, 266*; letter *Conquestus est*: note on dorse: AC Huesca, *Extravagantes* (reg. Durán Gudiol, *AA*, vii, No. 59); *Reg. Greg. IX, 267*.

[10] CLI: *B. Hisp.*, xv, 274. Cf. Chabás, *El Archivo*, v, 143 ff.

23

therefore, now redirected the Aragonese war effort towards the Balearics – a project which had the legate's blessing[1] – while discussions over the terms of the annulment dragged on. They were not concluded until the end of April at a council held at Tarazona and attended by contingents of prelates from both Aragon and Castile.[2] But John did not waste these weeks. The Lérida Council occurred at the end of March,[3] and, in addition, the churches of Zaragoza, Huesca and Calatayud,[4] as well probably as those of Tarragona and Calahorra,[5] received visits from him.

Archbishop Rodrigo of Toledo was at the Tarazona Council and, after a brief detour to Tudela,[6] John seems to have accompanied him back into Castile. At Ocaña (some 50 kilometres east of Toledo) on 3 June he published a set of constitutions for Toledo Cathedral which penalised absenteeism and condemned the subdivision of benefices 'contra statuta concilii Turonensis': his two constant preoccupations.[7] Nineteen days later *apud Pariliam* (San Lorenzo de la Parrilla) he issued similar instructions for the church of Cuenca and urged it to model its organisation on that of Toledo 'which you are accustomed to imitate'.[8] Then, moving north, he came to Sigüenza, where on 17

---

1 Desclot, *Chronicle*, I, 88.
2 Tejada, III, 344–8; *Crónica de San Juan de la Peña*, 148. The archive of Tarazona Cathedral was destroyed in the fourteenth century, and no record of this assembly has survived there: Lafuente, *BRAH*, XXIV, 209–15; A. Gutiérrez de Velasco, 'La Conquista de Tarazona en la Guerra de los dos Pedros', *Jerónimo Zurita*, X–XI (1960), 69 ff.
3 Tejada, III, 329 ff.
4 *Reg. Greg. IX,* 386; Durán Gudiol, *HS*, XII, 297–8 (the documents in AC Huesca do not mention the date of John's visit, but it was certainly before the end of May); Chabás, *El Archivo*, V, 147–51 (John was at Calatayud on 20 May); Zurita, *Anales*, I, 125rb.
5 John referred to his visit to Tarragona, for which this would seem the likeliest date, in his letter of 11 Sept. 1229 to the archbishop and chapter. Text: AC Seo de Urgel, cod. 2119, fo. 10r–v; date: RAH, MS. 9-24-5/4558, fo. 192r–v; AHA, *Index dels Indices*, fo. IV. For his motives for visiting Calahorra, if he did, see below. He was never within easier range.
6 On 1–2 May: Tejada, III, 341, 348.
7 AHN, cod. 987B, fos. 29v–30r; BN, MS. 8997, fo. 26r. The reference is to canon i of the Tours Council, 1163: Hefele–Leclercq, V, ii, 971.
8 AC Cuenca, 5-20-275. San Lorenzo de la Parrilla is some 30 kilometres to the south-west of Cuenca. In 1750 Ascensio de Morales mentioned, but did not transcribe, a document of 14 June 1229 in which the legate confirmed a Cuenca constitution of 1190: BN, MS. 13071, fo. 54v. The original could not be found at Cuenca in the summer of 1966.

July, he gave judgement on the age-old boundary dispute between that see and Osma;[1] after which he struck west. He was at León, from where he despatched his constitutions for Guimarães, on 6 August, and at Lerma, to the south of Burgos, on the 17th.[2] That is the last glimpse we catch of him in Castile, and, as far as the anonymous Latin chronicler was concerned, his mission closed at the end of August and he returned to Rome.[3]

But the chronicler was wrong again. For the Catalan Church had still to be dealt with, and the last lap of the legate's marathon took him to Catalonia by way of the area where he had spent the previous spring, through Agreda on 26 August[4] and Zuera on the 31st.[5] When he reached the Mediterranean coast a further papal mandate was awaiting him, containing the pope's reply of the previous March to a number of queries concerning parochial organisation in the province of Tarragona, marriages within the forbidden degree, and the decayed state of the Cluniac Order in those parts. From Martorell, on 10 September, he forwarded his instructions on these points to Archbishop Sparago and his suffragans.[6] On the following day he entered Barcelona and sent the archbishop another letter, ordering him to attend without delay to the particular reforms which he had specified during his earlier visit to Tarragona.[7] He then spent a week in Barcelona, at the end of which he publicly reprimanded Bishop Berenguer on account of his unjust exactions from the property of deceased canons,[8] and issued a set of constitutions for the cathedral which embodied all his objectives as legate.[9] That was on 19 September.

[1] AC Sigüenza, doc. pontificio, 18=*Reg. Greg. IX*, 2298-9: publ. Auvray, *Mél. d'arch. et d'hist.*, XVI, 105-9. Cf. Minguella, *Historia*, I, 30-2; *Reg. Hon. III*, 806, 5652; AC Sigüenza, doc. pontificio, 13 (MDH, 92, 573, 460). The dispute flared up again in 1267: AC Toledo, X.1.F.2.6.

[2] *Chartularium Universitatis Portugalensis*, I, 23; AC Segovia, doc. 226. For the request for absolution made to John by certain laymen of León who had hanged a criminous clerk, see Lea, *Formulary of the Papal Penitentiary*, 22.

[3] CLI: *B. Hisp.*, XV, 275.

[4] 20 kilometres to the west of Tarazona: González Texada, 205.

[5] On the road to Zaragoza: AC Segovia, doc. 184.

[6] *VL*, XVII, 208-9. Texts in Villanueva's papers: RAH, MS. 9-24-5/4558, fos. 193v-5r. Martorell is about 30 kilometres to the west of Barcelona, on the road from Lérida.

[7] AC Seo de Urgel, cod. 2119, fo. 10r-v.

[8] AC Barcelona, *Liber I Antiquitatum*, fo. 238va. Cf. Puig y Puig, 191. The bishop was away, at the siege of Mallorca.

[9] Publ. Martène-Durand, *Thesaurus*, IV, 595-9, whence Mansi, *Conciliorum...Supplementum*, II, 959-64.

The next day found him at Vich;[1] and on the 25th and 26th he was at Gerona.[2] His final port of call seems to have been the Pyrenean see of Urgel where, in the absence of Bishop Pedro de Puigvert, he expanded the size of the chapter.[3] In each of these places his memory was destined to linger on and to haunt the easy-going canons long after his final departure from Spanish territory, for which relief the Spanish Church had cause to be thankful probably at about the beginning of October. His legatine authority was certainly a thing of the past by 29 November, and he had returned, breathless presumably, to the Curia.[4]

In the course of little more than eighteen months the legate had covered the greater part of Christian Spain and Portugal – no mean feat at a time when, 'tum propter alpes et portus et loca periculosa, tum propter fluvios et inundationes aquarum', the comparatively short journey from León to Lugo might take all of five days, even in the summer.[5] The fellow traveller who follows in his footsteps seven centuries after very soon comes to appreciate John of Abbeville's considerable energy. *Experto credite.* And the volume of business with which he dealt as he went was enormous. He intervened in the affairs of the diocese of Calahorra where Fernando III and the local nobility were bent upon frustrating the desire of the canons to move to Santo Domingo de la Calzada where, in a kinder climate and away from the turbulent border area, they might be able – they claimed, among other things – to hold synods.[6] Nor was the bishop of Calahorra, Juan Pérez, the only recently reinstated episcopal exile to receive comfort and assistance from John, and to experience a change for the worse when that support was withdrawn.[7] Bernardo of Segovia, who had

---

1 AC Vich, 37–6–45.
2 AC Vich, 37–6–60; AC Barcelona, *Liber I Antiquitatum,* fo. 238va; AC Gerona, *Causa del Any* 1240.
3 To thirty-three: *Reg. Inn. IV,* 186.
4 On that day Gregory IX referred to him as '*tunc* apostolice sedis legatus': *VL,* xxi, 252.
5 AHN, cod. 267B, fo. 278v. This was in 1247.
6 Mansilla, *Iglesia,* 160–1, 169–70; Pérez Alhama, *REDC,* xv, 396 ff; Lecuona, *Scriptorium Victoriense,* I, 136 ff.; letter *Gravi nobis,* 2 Jan. 1225: AC Calahorra, doc. 240; *Reg. Hon. III,* 5154 (MDH, 526).
7 González Texada, 201–2; *Reg. Greg. IX,* 247. Juan Pérez was at the Curia in Oct. 1224 and semi-permanently thereafter for the rest of Honorius's pontificate; and, despite Gregory IX's instruction of Feb. 1233 that he be represented by a proctor at

shared Juan Pérez's exile, was another,[1] while in Portugal the legate was closely concerned with the promotion of the canonist Vincentius Hispanus to the see of Guarda.[2]

Various disputes, both weighty and trivial, were referred to him. He supervised a settlement between the Master of the Order of Santiago and the Convent of Uclés.[3] In the expectation of his arrival in the north-west, the archbishop of Compostela and the bishop of Astorga delayed their territorial litigation in October 1228 so that either he or, failing him, Cardinal Gil Torres, might give judgement.[4] And while he was in those parts, in the following December, the sacrist of Barcelona and the cantor of Tarragona, far away to the east, chose him as mediator of their own private quarrel.[5] The pressure of purely routine business of this sort was such that he was obliged on occasion to subdelegate his authority both to members of his own entourage and to trustworthy Spaniards. The hearing of a tithe dispute between the church of Albelda and the clergy of Sojo was entrusted to his *dilectus clericus* Master P.;[6] and a couple of cases concerning the monastery of Oña to the bishop of Burgos and canons of that church.[7]

For his main concern was not with these minutiae, but with reform in head and members and, as has been said of the theme of his legislation, with securing 'the rigorous observance of all the rules of the Fourth Lateran Council'.[8] Absolute devotion to those rules inspired everything that John did while he was in Spain. They were reflected in the statutes given to particular churches – to Toledo, Burgos, Cuenca and Astorga in Castile–Leon, to Porto and Guimarães

---

any further hearings there of his case against the king, he was back by Sept. 1234 and died there in Jan. 1237: *Reg. Hon. III*, 5117, 5922, 6190 (MDH, 520, 600, 625); *Reg. Greg. IX*, 1113, 2104, 3470 (=AC Calahorra, doc. 266). In his absence the king pillaged his see, and during his brief return he was forced to sell property to pay his Roman debts: *ibid.* 594 (publ. Sousa Costa, 146–7).

[1] Mansilla, *Iglesia*, 168–9; *Reg. Hon. III*, 6242 (MDH, 639). The legate's indulgences in favour of Bernardo's new cathedral were published by the bishop in July 1232: AC Segovia, doc. 144, 311, 177.

[2] Sousa Costa, 158 ff.

[3] Lomax, *Orden de Santiago*, 61.

[4] López Ferreiro, *Historia* v, 125; Quintana Prieto, *AA*, XI, nos. 49, 52–3.

[5] AC Barcelona, *Diversarum B*, 787.

[6] Archivo Colegial, Logroño, doc. 18.

[7] Alamo, *CD Oña*, II, 559, 567.

[8] Hefele–Leclercq, v, ii, 1502.

in Portugal, and to Barcelona, Gerona and Vich in Aragon. And they were the guiding light of the provincial councils over which he presided.

Unhappily, we are rather ill-informed about John's councils. We may be sure about three, held at Valladolid in the autumn of 1228, at Salamanca in the following February, and at Lérida a month later, for the provinces of Toledo, Compostela and Tarragona respectively, though the anonymous Latin chronicler hints at many more.[1] Yet of these three the constitutions of one only, the Lérida Council, have survived.[2] Nothing is known of the Salamanca Council beyond the fact that it took place,[3] and the proceedings of the Valladolid Council are recorded only in a later (and perhaps incomplete) Spanish translation which Risco discovered in a León manuscript and published in 1787.[4]

Still, this material can be supplemented. There are good grounds for treating the constitutions entitled by Martène *concilium incerti loci* as those of the monastic general chapter of the kingdom of León which was summoned at the legate's behest,[5] and, further, for regarding them as to some extent the equivalent of the lost Latin text of the Valladolid constitutions, to the vernacular version of which they bear as marked an affinity as they do to the Lérida constitutions.[6]

---

[1] No notice has survived of any council in the fourth province, Braga.

[2] Publ. Tejada y Ramiro, III, 329 ff., and Sáinz de Baranda, *ES*, XLVIII, 308ff. The system of numbering canons 15–25 varies in the two versions. Reference hereafter is to the latter, which is cited as *Lér*.

[3] In a synod of 1248 Bishop Aires Vasques of Lisbon referred to a constitution of this council 'in qua cavetur quod pro benedictionibus nubentium et pro annalibus et tricennalibus nichil exigatur': publ. Rosa Pereira, *Lumen* (May 1961), 5. Cf. *Lér*. c. 21.

[4] *ES*, XXXVI, 216 ff.; cited hereafter as *Vall*. They appear to be incomplete, ending abruptly and containing no indication of date.

[5] Martène–Durand, IV, 167 (whence Mansi, XXII, 1090–4: ed. cit. hereafter) 'ex MS. ecclesie Belvacensis'. The internal evidence of its Spanish provenance was noted by Martène (1091), and the note on the dorse of the membrane (1090) points to a connexion with the legate's appointment of the abbots of Samos and Celanova as monastic visitors of the León province: *Reg. Greg. IX, 1756*.

[6] There is almost total identity between these constitutions and *Lér*. c. 12 sqq., except for c. 13 which recalls *Vall*. 225, *De praebendis*. The incomplete state of Martène's MS. would account for the absence of any parallel for *Lér*. c. 1–11. It may be concluded that the original Valladolid constitutions were the model for this chapter; that it met, probably at Villafranca del Vierzo (north-west of Ponferrada) between 1228 and 1233 (cf. Mansi, 1090: 'post annum MCCXV'; Berlière, *RB*, XIX, 374: *c.* 1220); and that, in general, the Valladolid canons were identical with those of Lérida.

The Church and clergy in Spain were in a condition of general decay because, according to the legate's diagnosis, the constitutions of the Fourth Lateran Council had been almost entirely neglected there,[1] and for their recovery they therefore needed a pretty stiff dose of Lateran medicine. Thus, the provisions of the Valladolid and Lérida Councils on a number of issues – annual communion and confession, matrimony, payment of tithes, lay patrons of churches, simony, procedural matters, clerical and episcopal comportment, and triennial monastic chapters – were derived, often *verbatim*, from the 1215 Council.[2] The interest of the legate's programme, however, lies rather in the extent to which it departed from rather than adhered to the Lateran precedent, since these variations highlight the distinctive shortcomings of the Spanish Church. There were no distinctive merits.

One instance may be noted of what appears to have been soft-pedalling in response to secular opposition to an item of reform. The wearing by Jews of special clothes is not mentioned in the Valladolid constitutions. Instead, a prohibition on the use of *cappae clausae* of clerical cut was substituted, in deference perhaps to Fernando III's known view that discrimination had serious political consequences.[3] Otherwise, though, the legate's departures from the Lateran norm were all in the direction of greater stringency. The Spanish clergy, as John of Abbeville found them, were incontinent, largely uneducated and total strangers to the discipline of council and synod. Innocent III had certainly been concerned with clerical morality, yet even that pontiff paled in comparison with John of Abbeville and the vigour with which he terrorised the miscreants. In 1215 *clerici concubinarii* had been threatened with canonical sanctions, but only in general terms. After the Valladolid and Lérida Councils they were left in no doubt about the severity of these sanctions: excommunication, suspension, loss of benefices, and the burial of their consorts – called *barraganas* in

[1] *Vall* 216; *Lér.* c. 1.
[2] IV Lat. c. 21; *Vall*, 221; *Lér.* c. 11 (sacraments); IV Lat. c. 50–1; not in *Vall.*, but *concilium incerti loci* (hereafter *CIL*), c. 4; *Lér.* c. 14 (matrimony); IV Lat. c. 53; *CIL*, c. 5; *Lér.* c. 15 (tithes); III Lat. c. 14; IV Lat. c. 45; *Vall.* 223, 226; *CIL*, c. 15; *Lér.* c. 19, 30 (lay patrons); IV Lat. c. 63–6; *Vall.* 223; *CIL*, c. 7; *Lér.* c. 21 (simony); IV Lat. c. 8; *Vall.* 224–5; *CIL*, c. 11–12; *Lér.* c. 27–8 (procedure); IV Lat. c. 17; *Vall.* 226; *CIL*, c. 16; *Lér.* c. 31 (comportment); IV Lat. c. 12; *Vall.* 223–4; *CIL*, c. 8; *Lér.* c. 23 (monastic chapters).
[3] IV Lat. c. 68; Cf. *Vall.* 222; *Lér.* c. 16; above, p. 18.

Castile – with the beasts.[1] In other respects the Spanish clergy seem to have erred neither more nor less than the clergy elsewhere. They were not remarkable drinkers. Nor, apart from the excessively provocative dress of the Aragonese, which showed rather too much leg for the legate's liking, and the preposterous coiffure of the Castilians which had drawn Diego García's fire ten years before, did their outward appearance merit special criticism.[2] On these issues, therefore, the Lateran legislation was sufficient.[3] But in their fondness for women they were in a class apart, and, even allowing for the fact that virtue brings its own reward but not much publicity, it seems that they always had been and that they always would be. In the eighth century when King Fruela I had attempted to impose celibacy upon them, and both before and since, down to the present century, observers have noted their disregard for ecclesiastical discipline on this point.[4] Indeed, only twenty years after John of Abbeville's councils, the pope himself would feel bound to accept them for what they were.[5]

Diego García had described the Castilian bishops as a bunch of philistines, and to judge by the legate's strictures, their Aragonese brethren and the lower clergy of both nations were just as bad.[6] Of course, if it were allowed to obliterate the achievement of Archbishop Rodrigo and of those many others who, while not shining themselves, at least assisted others who had the capacity to do so, then John of Abbeville's charge would be monstrously unfair; and, indeed, in modern times the legate has been taken to task for his remarks about Spanish culture.[7] Yet John's observations were concerned not with

1 *Vall.* 218–19; *Lér.* c. 8. Cf. IV Lat. c. 14. For the meaning of *barraganas* see *Part.* 4.14.1 (Academy ed. III, 85).

2 *Vall.* 219–20; *Lér.* c. 9; Diego García, *Planeta,* 194. The following century brought scant improvement, if the testimony of Alvarus Pelagius may be relied upon: *De Planctu Ecclesiae,* II, fo. 205ra–b.

3 IV Lat. c. 15, 16, 18. Cf. *Lér.* c. 9: 'Clausa desuper deferant indumenta, nimia brevitate vel longtitudine non notanda [thus far as IV Lat. c. 16] ... vel supertunicis sic apertis ut ostendant latera, sed astrictis ut femoralia non demonstrent ... non utantur.'

4 *Crónica de Alfonso III,* ed. Z. García Villada (Madrid, 1918), 118–19; Thompson, *Goths in Spain,* 304; Gerald Brenan, *The Spanish Labyrinth* (Cambridge, 1962), 49. Cf. Lea, *Sacerdotal Celibacy,* 302 ff.   5 Below, Ch. 3.

6 *Planeta,* 197, 405. *Lér.* c. 5: 'Attendentes quod in partibus Hispaniae, ex defectu studiorum et litteraturae, multa et intolerabilia detrimenta animarum proveniunt.'

7 By Beltrán de Heredia in *RET,* VI, 336, 340–1. On this point cf. Linehan, *Studia Albornotiana,* II.

the gifted élite but with the mass of parish clergy whom in 1225 a Spanish bishop had described as 'pre aliis regionibus inscii litterarum'. The bishop was Tello of Palencia, the very region to which, on account of its nascent university, Beltrán points in rebuttal of John's charge.[1] The rest of Beltrán's case for the defence is hardly less unconvincing,[2] but the point of substance is that it was with the condition of these, the lower clergy, that John was concerned, and for their benefit that at Lérida he went beyond the provision of 1215 for the establishment of schools in such diocesan centres 'quarum sufficere poterunt facultates' and issued instructions for the endowment of *scholae de grammatica* and *magistri* in every archdeaconry, 'ad multiplicem ignorantiam extirpandam'.[3] These schools would at least provide the parish clergy with a smattering of Latin,[4] while, on a rather higher level, the churches of Barcelona, Astorga and Guimarães were reminded of their existing obligation to provide for a master of grammar,[5] and, by having their income guaranteed for a period of three years, student canons were encouraged to take advantage of the opportunity. In order to promote the University of Palencia this period was increased to five years in Castile.[6]

Education costs money, and all the legate's educational reforms were doomed to failure unless the clergy could be established on secure economic foundations. There were too many clergy to provide for. Fewer would perhaps mean better, for the majority simply could not afford not to be pluralists, and with so many of them in quest of a fixed stock of benefices the latter had been devalued by division, thus creating further inflation. Subdivision and pluralism were twin evils: the elimination of the one hinged upon the eradication of the other. The Fourth Lateran Council had railed against

1 *Reg. Hon. III*, 5273 (MDH, 533); Beltrán, 336.
2 For example, he deduces from the fact that John held no councils at Santiago, Salamanca, Zamora or León that 'en este sector del reino de León encontró las necesidades suficientemente atendidas', p. 337. But this is *not* a fact. See the report of the anonymous Latin chronicler: 'Currensque per provinciam convocavit sinodos...': CLI: *B. Hisp.*, xv, 274.
3 IV Lat. c. 11 (cf. III Lat. c. 18); *Lér.* c. 5–6; *Vall.* 217, ordering the establishment of these centres in all conventual churches.
4 *Lér.* c. 7; *Vall.* 217. However, it was recognised that the ignorance of the elderly was invincible.
5 Martène–Durand, IV, 598; Rodríguez López, II, 592; *Chartularium Universitatis Portugalensis*, 22.
6 *Lér.* c. 5; *Vall.* 217–18.

pluralism,[1] but John of Abbeville was determined to deal with its causes.

The ideal was parity between the number of clerics and the number of benefices, and to achieve this the legate invoked Alexander III's constitution which made bishops responsible for providing for clerics whom they ordained *sine titulo*.[2] But remedial as well as preventive action was called for, and as a means of revaluing the benefice John intervened at Toledo and Cuenca, taking as his text canon i of the Tours Council of 1163.[3] One cure of souls, one caretaker: that was the legate's aspiration. However, departure from this rule was common in Spain where, as he lamented, churches were shared by many men, like whores. Both at Valladolid and at Lérida, therefore, he did what he could to make this ecclesiastical polyandry respectable by directing that in each place there should be appointed as chief husband one priest who would take precedence over the rest at the public ministry.[4] Conditions in Castile and Aragon, though, were evidently not identical, for whereas at Valladolid he explicitly forbade subdivision of benefices, at Lérida he was forced to acknowledge that the rents of some parish churches were too meagre for the support of a priest and that, consequently, some degree of pluralism was inevitable.[5] That no such concession had been made at Valladolid in the previous year[6] suggests that the demand for benefices was greater in Aragon and that subdivision had advanced further there than in Castile. To this scramble for income at the parochial level the exclusiveness of the Aragonese cathedral chapters may have contributed, if only marginally. It is striking that whereas in Castile, at Toledo and Cuenca, it was a question of revaluing the canonries and prebends, in Aragon six cathedrals – Tarragona, Barcelona, Gerona, Vich, Urgel and Zaragoza – were either instructed or encouraged to increase the size of their chapters.[7]

[1] IV Lat. c. 29. Cf. III Lat. c. 13.
[2] III Lat. c. 5; *Lér.* c. 13; *Vall.* 221–2; *CIL*, c. 3. Cf. P. Hinschius, *Das Kirchenrecht der Katholiken und Protestanten in Deutschland*, I (Berlin, 1869), 63 ff.
[3] At Porto, likewise, he fixed the numbers of canons and portionaries at fourteen and six respectively: *Censual do Cabido da Sé do Porto*, 12.
[4] *Vall.* 222; *CIL*, c. 6; *Lér.* c. 18.   [5] *Vall.* 225; *CIL*, c. 13; *Lér.* c. 17.
[6] Nor, moreover, in *CIL*.
[7] AC Seo de Urgel, cod. 2119, fo. 10v; Martène–Durand, IV, 595; *VL*, XII, 150; AC Vich, 37–6–60; *Reg. Inn. IV*, 186; *Reg. Greg. IX*, 386 (cf. *Reg. Hon. III*, 1114, 1396; *MDH*, 160, 173).

His policy of streamlining the Spanish Church, not to mention his sense of fair play, also prompted the legate to correct the inequitable distribution of rents in the cathedrals of Astorga and Barcelona where, while some canons and dignitaries were drunk with wealth, others were left to go thirsty.[1] Reforms such as these, though ancillary, were essential to the success of John of Abbeville's master-plan – that of providing the Spanish churches with literate, continent and suitably endowed ministers capable of administering the sacraments and performing the public office. It was in this spirit that he stressed the importance of keeping vestments, fonts and other such paraphernalia clean and decent,[2] and emphasised, wherever he went, that the canons were to attend High Mass and the canonical hours or lose their clothing allowance, the *vestiarium*, and their daily portions of bread, wine, meat and money.[3]

The keystone of John's reforming programme was the institution of provincial councils and diocesan synods, for only by dint of constant pressure from above might the clergy be made to accept this novel régime. And that his constitutions did strike the Spanish clergy as novelties and as the personal lucubrations of an enthusiast – *quedam nova…iuxta sapientiam sibi a Deo datam* – rather than as an expression of the universal law of the Church, we may infer from the account provided by the anonymous Latin chronicler. From the same source we learn also of the unparalleled *sedicio* of both bishops and clergy in response to his instructions about exchanging the pleasures of dalliance for those of learning and the divine office.[4] Knowledge of the extent of resistance to reform was, doubtless, what caused the legate to leave instructions for the more frequent holding of diocesan synods than had been prescribed at the Fourth Lateran Council. A single annual gathering would not suffice. The Castilian dioceses were in need of two a year, and the Aragonese of 'at least one'.

---

[1] Rodríguez López, II, 593; Martène–Durand, IV, 598: 'unde requirit aequitas et hoc ipsum postulat necessitas…'.

[2] *Vall.* 220; *Lér.* c. 10; Cf. IV Lat. c. 20.

[3] Serrano, *Don Mauricio*, 141; AHN, cod. 987B, fo. 30r; *Chartularium Universitatis Portugalensis*, 22 (Burgos, Toledo, Guimarães); AC Cuenca, 5–20–275. At Barcelona the scale of penalties was regulated by the degree of lateness, while at Astorga the Epistle of the Mass and the Gloria of the first psalm at matins and vespers were established as the points of no return: Rodríguez López, II, 591; Martène–Durand, IV, 596–7.

[4] CLI: *B. Hisp.*, XV, 274.

Leaving nothing to chance, John moreover specified the days upon which they were to be held: in both kingdoms on the feast of St Luke in October and, additionally, on the Second Sunday after Pentecost in Castile.[1]

This was indeed the point, and although the Spanish Church during the eleventh and twelfth centuries had not been so totally unaccustomed to councils and synods as has sometimes been supposed,[2] the measure of activity implied by John's prescription, as well as the very content of his reforms, assumed a change of heart among the Spanish clergy for which there was scant evidence when, at the conclusion of his virtuoso performance, the legate returned to the Roman Curia in the late autumn of 1229, reflecting no doubt that the world was a wicked place. The following decade would show the extent to which their capacity for turning a deaf ear to papal and legatine *fiats* had been impaired.

[1] IV Lat. c. 6; *Lér.* c. 3; *Vall.* 216.
[2] Raymundo Guise in the eighteenth century thought that John of Abbeville's Lérida Council was the first council in the Tarragona province since the year 614: BN, MS. 11263, unpaginated. Cf. Valls i Taberner in *AST*, XI, 251 ff.; and, for the kingdoms of Leon and Castile, the various pieces by Fidel Fita in *BRAH* and Mr R. A. Fletcher's forthcoming Oxford D.Phil. dissertation.

Chapter 3

THE REACTION TO
JOHN OF ABBEVILLE'S LEGISLATION

After the legate's departure the onus of reform remained with the archbishops of Spain and their suffragans. The future was in their hands, and depended upon their willingness to take the initiative in summoning provincial councils and diocesan synods and to hammer home the lessons which the cardinal had taught them in 1228–9. Unhappily though they were to prove poor pupils and worse teachers.

While John of Abbeville was still in Spain, Rodrigo of Toledo, who was to survive until 1247, was reminded of his pastoral duty by the pope. Rather less elaborate, but no less explicit, than Honorius III's missive of ten years before, Gregory IX's letter referred to the legate's councils in that province and urged the archbishop and his suffragans most particularly to abide by John's decisions 'super incontinentia clericorum et ordinatione scolarum'.[1] The impressions which he had formed at Valladolid in the previous autumn had evidently induced the legate to call up heavy artillery against the leaders of the Castilian Church. But even this, the ultimate deterrent against disobedience, failed to move them. Though some allowance may be made for the archbishop's illness shortly after the legate had left, this hardly provides adequate excuse for the absence of councils and synods in the province during the rest of his lifetime. The truth was that the bishops of Castile had better things to do and other masters to serve.[2]

This reluctance was shared by the leader of the Aragonese Church, Archbishop Sparago of Tarragona, a royal relation and political churchman whose promotion from the see of Pamplona in the year of the Lateran Council (from which he was absent) had owed nothing

---

[1] AC Toledo, I.6.C.1.21: *Parum est,* 13 Feb. 1229. Note the reference to councils in the plural.
[2] Rodericus Toletanus, *De Rebus Hispaniae,* 202.

to pastoral considerations.[1] But Sparago was more easily overborne than Rodrigo and allowed himself to be dragooned into action by the legate. A month after the Lérida Council John informed him that he had heard reports that there were individuals in his province who were determined to circumvent the recent legislation, and, employing the same text as had prefaced the pope's bull to the province of Toledo in the previous February, he charged the archbishop, on pain of suspension, to deal firmly with them.[2] After the legate's departure, further pressure and threats of suspension were needed to induce the archbishop to fulfil the obligation laid upon him in 1229, that of summoning a provincial council. And the legislation of the gathering of May 1230 – which was attended by only four of his eleven suffragans, three fewer than at Lérida – reflected the grudging spirit in which it had been conceived. Its canons contained a very diluted version of the Lérida programme of the previous year, and, convened under duress, it represented Sparago's solitary contribution to the cause.[3]

It seems, moreover, to have been the only provincial council held in any part of the Peninsula during these years, for the assembly at Compostela in July 1229, while the legate was still in the offing, has the appearance of a diocesan synod, though López Ferreiro thought otherwise.[4] There too, many of John of Abbeville's constitutions were calmly ignored, though it was something that archdeacons were instructed to scour the rural deaneries for clerics deemed *habiles ad studium* but lacking the wherewithal for the Schools.[5] Yet this provision, though perfectly consonant with the legate's ideals, probably owed little or nothing to his having championed the cause of clerical education. For even before 1215 the canons of Compostela had been

---

[1] *VL*, XIX, 176 ff.; Morera, *Tarragona cristiana*, II, 270–1; Goñi Gaztambide, *Príncipe de Viana*, XVIII, 65–7; Fita, *Razón y Fe*, II, 195. Cf. Luchaire, *Journal des Savants*, III, 562.

[2] 'Parum est in civitate ius esse nisi qui illud tueatur existat': *ES*, XLVIII, 325.

[3] Tejada, *Colección*, VI, 28–9; P. de Marca, *Marca Hispanica*, 527; Augustinus, *Opera*, III, 498.

[4] AC Santiago, *Libro I de Constituciones*, fos. 77v–8v; López Ferreiro, *Historia*, V, appendix 16, p. 49. *Libro I* was compiled in 1328: López Ferreiro–Fita, *Monumentos antiguos*, 46. A document in AC Salamanca which seems to record a provincial council of the year 1230 and is described as such by Marcos Rodríguez, *Catálogo*, 185, was misdated by the scribe and does not belong to that year: see below, p. 172.

[5] López Ferreiro, V, 50.

encouraged to study,[1] and the impulse was almost certainly provided by Archbishop Bernardo who, if the content of his library is any guide, was a prelate of traditional but narrow culture with a marked preference for legal learning, as befitted a nephew of the canonist Bernardus Compostellanus Antiquus.[2] And there the common ground of the archbishop and the legate ended. The *acta* of the 1229 assembly bear no resemblance to what was presumably the burden of the latter's Salamanca Council of the previous February. One looks in vain for a condemnation of clerical incontinence. It was only the real property aspect of these dangerous liaisons that attracted Bernardo's attention. There was no objection to clerical offspring being given charge of churches other than those of their fathers. The alternative – that they should be made to beg a living, *in clericale opprobrium* – was inconceivable. Nor was any attempt made to tackle the associated problems of subdivided benefices and pluralism, beyond a perfunctory remark about the need for safeguards;[3] while for the legate's wholesale attack on laymen who abused their patronal rights the archbishop substituted counsels of discretion which would have received the approval of those connoisseurs of the soft option, the episcopal dumb dogs of Castile.[4] Such were the consequences of Honorius III's deference to the 'difficulties' of governing the province of Compostela.

Nevertheless, Archbishop Bernardo's constitutions, far from admirable though they were,[5] are at least a sign of activity of some sort. And in the province of Tarragona for ten years, and in those of Toledo and Compostela for almost thirty years after John of Abbeville's legation, conciliar and synodal activity was extremely rare. Of course, the argument from silence is not infallible. The objection can

---

[1] López, *Estudios crítico-históricos,* 41.
[2] A catalogue of his library, discovered in a Marseille MS., was published by Omont in 1893: *BEC,* LIV, 327–33. But in 1944 Galindo Romeo was credited with its discovery, 'en Mediodía' in 1921, by Portela Pazos who was, understandably perhaps, rather shy about giving references: *Decanologio,* 91, n. 3. Cf. López Ferreiro, V, 121.
[3] *Ibid.* 50–1.
[4] *Loc. cit.:* '...fructibus, censu vel servitiis sibi debitis per pravam consuetudinem sive abusum in Gallecia diu obtentum ipsos patronos de facto non dicimus esse privandos, licet ipsis secundum canones sint privati.'
[5] Cf. González Davila who, with these probably in mind, notes that Bernardo 'hizo constituciones loables para el gobierno de su arcobispado': *Teatro,* I, 54.

always be made that although no record of it has survived or been discovered the seeds sown by John had germinated and produced a flourishing tradition. In view, however, of the quantity of evidence which has survived for the period 1239–50 when in the province of Tarragona ecclesiastical assemblies were frequent occurrences, and the fact that the tentative conciliarism of the provinces of Toledo and Compostela was all too obviously bereft of recent precedent in the late fifties,[1] it is indeed justifiable to regard the argument from silence as tantamount to positive evidence and to dismiss the suspicion that the legate's mission had borne fruit. The obligation to attend the diocesan synod was still acknowledged – by the Cistercians of Monfero, for instance, in 1235[2] – but such promises do not prove that synods were actually summoned, in the diocese of Compostela or elsewhere. Apart from the couple already mentioned, there is evidence – though none of it is first-hand – of only three ecclesiastical assemblies in the decade after 1229. All three were in the province of Tarragona. Bishop Pedro Ramírez of Pamplona reiterated John's legislation on pluralism at a diocesan synod held sometime between 1230 and 1238.[3] At Calahorra Bishop Juan Pérez issued certain constitutions, presumably in a synod, which his successor, Áznar Díaz, confirmed in 1240 but did not specify.[4] And the council held at Lérida in or before 1237, for which the evidence is equally adventitious, appears to have been concerned solely with the repression of heresy – a burden which, significantly, had been shouldered by the secular power in 1233 and not entrusted to the bishops and to ecclesiastical assemblies which hardly ever occurred.[5]

[1] Below, p. 173.   [2] AC Santiago, *Constituciones sinodales y capitulares antiguas,* fo. 17v.
[3] This synod was mentioned in the course of an inquiry into the alleged pluralism of Juan Pérez de Arroniz, which arose out of the Toledo–Tarragona dispute over Valencia: ASV, A.A. arm.I–XVIII.4203. This document has not been incorporated into modern studies of the acrimonious *Ordinatio Valentina,* although others in the Vatican series to which it belongs were published as long ago as 1912 by Martorell in *CTEER,* I, 81 ff. Mansilla's register of this series misdates it '*c.* 1260': *AA,* VI, 322, no. 87. It dates from 1246 and contains the evidence of witnesses concerning the benefices of Juan Pérez, who, until Jan. 1240 had been the Toledo judge in hearings of the *Ordinatio* case. It provides new details about the later stages of the dispute, but eluded the author of the most recent account of the *Ordinatio,* R. I. Burns, despite his 'year of work among the materials pertaining to Spain' at the Vatican: *Crusader Kingdom,* I, 253 ff., 273.
[4] Bujanda, *Berceo,* I, 127.
[5] Devic and Vaissete, *Histoire générale de Languedoc,* VIII, 1011; Tejada, III, 362–6. The

The progress of monastic reform was no less inauspicious. While John was close enough to exert pressure, the holding of triennial chapters under Cistercian auspices, made some headway; and the *acta* of the Benedictine chapter of the Tarragona province in November 1229 betray his distinctive influence.[1] But these hopeful beginnings did not develop. In León the abbots of Samos and Celanova, whom the legate had appointed as visitors of the entire province, devoted themselves to settling old scores of their own until 1234 when it was discovered that the latter was himself excommunicated for keeping a woman.[2] And to judge by the records of the Cluniac visitors of the Spanish houses in 1217–18 and 1228 the abbot's idea of recreation was shared by many of the brethren.[3] The Order's prestige declined steadily throughout the century until, in 1290, its Spanish section had to be written off as *spiritualiter et temporaliter collapsus* even by a set of visitors whose standards were not particularly exalted.[4] John of Abbeville's intervention did nothing to halt this decline. After the fiasco in the León province there do not seem to have been any further triennial chapters. Certainly no record of them has survived, although the *Primera Partida* contains a detailed description of the proper procedure.[5] Such monastic assemblies as occurred were board meetings of business confederations concerned with the economic condition of subject priories. That, rather than the reform of monastic practices,

---

problem of heresy, especially in the diocese of Urgel, engaged the attention of Sparago's 1230 Council: *ibid.* VI, 28; Ventura Subirats, *BRABL*, XXVIII, 88–9.

[1] Tobella, *Catalonia Monastica*, I, 131 ff. For thirteenth-century chapters in the Tarragona province, see the evidence assembled by Tobella, *Analecta Montserratensia*, X, 245 ff. To this may be added the General Chapter referred to in May 1240 as a recent event; and the extraordinary meeting summoned by Pedro de Albalat in the same year: *Reg. Greg. IX*, 5196; below, p. 192.

[2] *Reg. Greg. IX*, 1756, 1908; Escalona, *Historia de Sahagún*, 143. John had also provided for triennial chapters of the Portuguese Augustinians, and had insisted that the visitors appointed thereat be 'aspectu decori, atque honesta canitie venerandi, religione famosi et omni prediti sanctitate': Santa María, *Chronica*, II, 441.

[3] AHN, 1031/11; Fita, *BRAH*, XXVI, 372 ff.; Bishko, *SM*, VII, 352–3; AHN, 1702/11; AC Palencia, 8/15/4.

[4] Robert, *BRAH*, XX, 349. In 1292 the visitors described Valverde as 'spiritualiter in bono statu', although the prior 'diffamatus est de incontinentia et publice tenet meretricem et habet pecuniam ad mensem mercatorum': *ibid.* 352. Cf. Pérez de Urbel, *Los monjes españoles*, II, 527 ff.

[5] Berlière, *RB*, XIX, 374; *Part.* 1.7.19–22: BM, Add. MS. 20787, fos. 57rb–8va: corresponding to laws 17–21 in the Academy ed., I, 307–12. (For a description of the BM MS., see Herriot, *Speculum*, XIII, 278 ff.)

was the purpose of the *generale capitulum* which met annually on 13 November at the abbey of Santa María de Benevivere, Palencia,[1] and of the *universale ac generale capitulum* at San Victorián, Huesca, in 1264-5.[2]

The legate had concluded, correctly, that moral reform depended upon economic reorganisation, and had therefore sought to eliminate pluralism by revaluing the individual benefice and instructing cathedral chapters to adjust their numbers to their resources. In Aragon the closed capitular corporations had hitherto conspired, in the style of certain Oxford and Cambridge colleges in the eighteenth century and after, to ensure that the rate at which the number of shareholding canons increased lagged behind the rate at which capitular income grew, to the great profit of the fortunate few but with consequence for the cure of souls which John of Abbeville could hardly ignore. Consequently, his insistence that they create more canonries touched a neuralgic spot, and the battles which were waged at Tarragona, Vich and Gerona over this issue provide an insight into the strength and determination of those proprietary interests against which the whole of the programme of reform was destined to founder. By seeking to deprive them of part of their income as well as of the pleasures of the flesh he merely succeeded in galvanising them into effective action.

At Tarragona, for example, his inspection of the capitular budget convinced John that there were sufficient resources there for thirty canons and that the sum of 650 *aurei* ought to be earmarked annually for the purpose of providing them with plain and sober garments. In September 1229 he directed the archbishop and chapter to attend to the matter within the month, at the same time obliging those canons who had charge of capitular property to render account of their stewardship twice yearly; and on 1 December Gregory IX confirmed these measures.[3] But the chapter resisted. In September 1232 they appealed on grounds of expense; and by August 1248 they had still not complied, with serious consequences for the cure of souls, as

---

[1] L. Fernández, *Misceldánea Comillas*, XXXVII, 226. The *consuetudines* of Benevivere did, however, provide for an annual chapter of abbots to treat 'de salute animarum': *ibid.* 234.

[2] AHN, 772/17.

[3] AC Seo de Urgel, cod. 2119, fo. 10r-v; AHA, *Index dels Indices*, fo. 567v.

Innocent IV reminded them.[1] Even Archbishop Pedro, the legate's unwavering executor in almost every other respect, was forced to compromise on this issue and, in January 1249, to settle for a figure of twenty-five rather than thirty. For their part the canons surrendered the principle of unanimity which had previously delayed the filling of canonries by election.[2] But their concession cost them little, for thereafter the size of the chapter was steadily reduced, largely on account of their battles with Pedro's disastrous successor, Benito de Rocaberti. Numbers soon fell to twenty-three; to below twenty by September 1264; and to nine by 1272.[3]

It is possible to follow this process in rather more detail in th cathedral church of Vich, to the north, and to substantiate Innocent IV's remark about the spiritual repercussions of such restrictive practices. On visiting Vich in September 1229, John of Abbeville discovered that the number of canons had declined from forty to twenty-three and that three of the canonical portions were enjoyed by laymen who, in view of his lenience in dealing with them, may be assumed to have been individuals of considerable local standing, as traditionally were the canons of the neighbouring see of Gerona. He ordained that their income was to be resumed for the canons, but not until they died, and that the size of the chapter be increased, not to the former level of forty, but to thirty, of whom seven were to be priests and none below the order of subdeacon.[4] The particulars of John's measures for dealing with this declining band have not survived, but some of them may be inferred from the letter sent to Bishop Guillermo on 21 November by Archbishop Sparago, the legate's A.D.C. on this occasion, in response to a number of queries and objections raised by the canons. A month before, on 20 September, the archbishop had demanded full compliance within fifteen days. He had then been present at Vich with the cardinal, which accounts for his uncharacteristic enthusiasm.[5] Four and a half weeks later the memory of

1 *VL*, xix, 231; AHA, *Thesaurus*, fo. 466 (publ. Fita, *BRAH*, xxix, 110).
2 Morera, ii, 286; AHA, *Thesaurus*, fo. 496.
3 Morera, *loc. cit.*; Capdevila, *Seu de Tarragona*, 127; Vincke, *RQ*, xlviii, 205. In Dec. 1255 Alexander IV ordered the chapter, in general terms, to obey the legate's statutes, and in Sept. 1264 Urban IV reiterated the figure of thirty canons: AHA *Cartoral AB*, fo. 36v; *Reg. Urb. IV*, 2112.
4 AC Vich, 37–6–60; Moncada, *Episcopologio*, i, 573; *VL*, vii, 23.
5 AC Vich, 37–6–45.

John was still uncomfortably fresh, and he evidently felt inclined to indulge in the harmless luxury of being a reformer abroad, for the disaffected received short shrift from him. The lay-a-beds and malingerers and those who claimed not to have heard the bell which summoned them to choir were to be penalised for their absence unless they could prove that they actually were stone-deaf; and, in passing, Sparago allowed himself a little moralising which came rather ill from him.[1] Nor was he prepared to adjust their constitutions to the more easy-going practices of Barcelona Cathedral where the canons recited matins of the Virgin in private and in comfort. Moreover, although he was inclined to agree with those who maintained that on a point of canon law John may have overstepped the mark, he was not prepared to expose himself for a principle.[2] And as for the ingenious piece of physiological justification from the fornicating canon who alleged that it had all been an accident, the archbishop was quite unmoved.[3]

While this luckless sinner and his colleagues were being brought to terms with the harshness of modern life, the seven canons whom John of Abbeville had planted in their midst took precautions against the day when the former group, having flexed the muscles of their ingenuity against the archbishop, would set about dealing with them as intruders. In January 1231 they secured papal confirmation of their appointments:[4] a prudent move, for the storm that would threaten them was already gathering.

Bishop Guillermo of Vich was made of sterner stuff than his sluggish chapter. Even before the legate had appeared on the horizon he had taken steps to check some of the abuses in his church. In July 1216, at his own request, Innocent III had empowered the bishop to

---

[1] *Ibid.*: 'Cum...illi qui debiles sunt in spiritualibus frequenter hoc allegarent.'

[2] *Ibid.*: 'Super illo vero articulo utrum canonici sint suspecti vel excommunicati qui ordinationi domini legati obiurant sine causa, licet in hac parte quid iuris sit varient sapientes, ab ore domini legati nos recolimus audivisse quod non erant canonice ferende sentencie set iam late, et ideo super isto articulo contra eius dictum nolumus temere diffinire, licet domini Honorii sit decretalis expressa quod huiusmodi sentencie pocius sunt comminationes quam canonice sentencie promulgate.'

[3] *Ibid.*: '...allegacio quod propter sompnum et quia naturalem rem passus fuit'.

[4] AC Vich, 35–5–17 = *Reg. Greg. IX*, 526. One of the seven was Pedro de Posa who in 1270 bequeathed copies of John of Abbeville's constitutions and sermons, of which he thought highly: 'quamvis ille liber sit scriptus de vili littera tamen multa bona in hoc continetur'. The will is published in *HS*, II, 427–9, but it has escaped the notice of its editor, Mossèn Junyent, that Pedro had special reasons for remembering the legate fondly.

discipline those of the canons who were bent upon preventing the recent Lateran statutes having any effect there, and who, when they deigned to attend capitular meetings at all, were wont to withdraw if what they heard was not to their liking, thereby bringing business to a standstill,[1] Moreover, on 4 June 1229, more than two months before the legate's visitation, Guillermo had implemented one at least of the statutes of the Lérida Council, by granting leave of absence on full stipend to canons who desired to study in Lombardy or in France.[2]

Despite this respectable record though – or, perhaps, because of it, for the capitular backwoodsmen must have regarded the expenditure on education as an absurd extravagance – he fell under suspicion of heresy and, after a wretched journey to the Curia for a hearing of his case before John of Abbeville, resigned his see early in 1233 and became a canon of Vich, having armed himself with a papal exemption from the obligation to be present at High Mass and vespers, upon which, in accord with the legate's provisions, his daily income depended.[3] His successor, Bernardo Calvó was utterly incompetent in his management of the church's affairs (as befitted a saint),[4] and by the time of his death in 1245 the need for capitular economies was urgent. Inevitably there was an outcry against the legatine provisions, and in the late summer of that year the bishop-elect, Bernardo Mur, and the chapter sought Innocent IV's permission to reduce their establishment, irrespective of the fact, which had been known to Gregory IX twelve years before, that the administration of the sacraments had broken down at the parochial level for lack of ministers.[5]

The judges-delegate, two archdeacons and a canon of Lérida, considered the state of the church of Vich and decided that John of Abbeville's estimate had been far too high. In their view, eighteen, not thirty, was the maximum number of canons that the capitular resources could support, especially as funds had been severely stretched by hail, fogs and hospitality to papal legates. Eventually, however, they settled on twenty, and confirmed the legate's requirement

1 AC Vich, 37–6–54: *Cum turpis sit,* 5 July 1216.
2 AC Vich, 37–1: *Privilegis i estatuts,* 13. The provision is misdated by both Moncada and Villanueva: *Episcopologio,* I, 572; *VL,* VII, 24. Cf. Conc. Lérida, c. 7.
3 *Reg. Greg. IX,* 999, 1122; Kehr, *Papsturkunden Katalonien,* 585; Mundó, *VII. CHCA,* III, 77 ff.
4 Junyent, *Diplomatari de Sant Bernat Calvó,* XLVIII–L, 238, 257.
5 AC Vich, 37–5–16: *Dilecti filii,* 2 Aug. 1245; *Reg. Greg. IX,* 1135.

that seven of these should be ordained.[1] Their other arrangements, though, show how little progress had been made in reforming the place since 1229. The three laymen were by now in possession of five benefices there, and although the judges-delegate recommended that they be eased out when opportunity offered, they did not attempt to prevent the recurrence of a similar situation, as had the legate by insisting that all canons be subdeacons. Indeed they acknowledged that *urgens necessitas* and *evidens utilitas* might justify further grants to laymen, as was the practice in their own church of Lérida – a practice which had been ratified only four years after John of Abbeville's council there – *causa reverentie et honoris*.[2] And whereas the legate had stressed the importance of the common life and to that end had ordained that meals be eaten together in the refectory, this practice too was abandoned in favour of money payments during certain periods of the year.[3] The seasonal meat shortage provided a pretext for obliterating the last vestiges of the *vita communis*.

Innocent IV's confirmation of this reassessment[4] removed the name of John of Abbeville from the collective memory of the chapter of Vich. But the saga had not ended yet, for the victory which the bishop and chapter had won by working together proved a hollow victory and a rod for their own backs. By reducing the opportunity of advancement in their church they exposed their alliance to great strain, and the pressure of applicants, upon whose suitability they were obliged to agree, soon drove a wedge between them. And thus it was that the bishop executed a complete about-turn and in June 1256 had the effrontery to represent himself as a partisan of the legate's original assessment, and to allege that the reduction of numbers had been achieved fraudulently (despite his own former advocacy of that cause), and that in consequence the cure of souls had suffered.[5] His true intent, clearly, was to steal a march on his chapter, as he succeeded in doing in the following December when he secured a papal

---

[1] AC Vich, 37–6–44.
[2] *Ibid.*; *ES*, xlviii, 267.
[3] *Ibid.*: 'Verum quia certis anni temporibus carnes recentes et salse nimis inordinate dabantur, statuimus quod loco carnium secundum ordinationem episcopi et capituli denarii tribuantur.'
[4] AC Vich, 37–5–28: *Cum a nobis*, 7 April 1251.
[5] AC Vich, 37–1: *Privilegis i estatuts*, 8 (publ. Valls i Taberner, *AST*, v, 280; Ríus Serra, *San Raimundo: Diplomatário*, 122).

indulgence which entitled him to appoint to two canonries there, the capitular rights of collation and the revised statute *de numero canonicorum* notwithstanding.[1] The partial success of the bishop's campaign in June 1263, therefore, did not in any sense vindicate the legate's judgement.[2] It merely added fuel to the flames of his quarrel with the canons who thereafter followed his example and appealed ever more frequently for papal dispensation from the papal settlement which they had campaigned together to secure between 1245 and 1251.[3]

The receipt by laymen of capitular income was one of the abuses which the legate had attempted to eradicate at Vich, but although they had not been ousted by 1246 the number involved was small. Moreover, the proposals concerning clerical education had received a favourable and immediate hearing there. In the neighbouring diocese of Gerona, however, it was the conjunction of these two issues that provided the forces of reaction with a cause to defend, and the ensuing litigation, of which a partial account has survived in a manuscript volume in the cathedral archive – the so-called *Causa del Any 1240* – provides a clear indication of the nature and strength of resistance to reform. The chapter of Gerona was a closed corporation, entry to which was restricted to a limited caste: the noble, military class. The canons of Gerona, by definition, were deacons only, not priests. In effect, the resources of the church were monopolised by the secular power.[4] The dozen priests who were retained to perform services in the cathedral formed an underprivileged minority group; and battle was joined between them and the canons when, in the light of the constitution of the Lérida Council, they entered a claim for grants such as were available at Vich. But their right to financial assistance hinged upon their right to be regarded as canons, and this

---

[1] *Reg. Alex. IV*, 1569. He attempted to use this indult twice, but was foiled by the chapter: AC Vich, 6–III–22.

[2] *VL*, VII, 39.

[3] A copy of their supplication to Martin IV in May 1282 on behalf of a local worthy, the cleric Pedro de Castello, states that on account of the statute *de numero*, 'de quibusdam certis personis valde necessariis et utilibus nobis et ecclesie nostre providere ad presens commode non possimus': AC Vich, 37–7: *Domus de Angularia et de Cardona*, II, 3.

[4] According to Arberto de Colonico, *miles*, 'a .XC. annis citra [...] clerici qui nobiles genere tantum [...] filii militum et dominorum recipiebantur in canonia Gerundensi, et non alii': AC Gerona, *Causa del Any 1240*, fo. 23va. Many others made the same point: fos. 23ra, 24rb–va. Cf. *VL*, XII, 150–1.

was stoutly denied by their adversaries who, just as the devil can quote scripture, were able to claim that the legate himself – whose increase of numbers from twenty to twenty-four they had, incidentally, ignored – had been aware of but had not objected to this custom.[1] And, in any case, the canons' attitude was that Gerona itself could provide whatever instruction the priests needed.[2] There was no need for them to go gallivanting off to those new-fangled, expensive, foreign places. Nor, perhaps, was there need, given the canons' conception of 'education', and their view that the priests were a species of domestic chaplain whose concern was the humdrum round of church services, not the higher learning of the Schools.

The case was argued at length at Gerona in 1239–40, and documents, rumour and hearsay were quoted by each side until 29 October 1240 when the bishop of Gerona, Guillermo de Cabanellas, and his colleagues, as arbiters, gave judgement against the twelve priests. This, though, was not the end of the affair, as Villanueva believed after inspecting the *Causa* volume during his visit to Gerona.[3] Indeed, on that very day the priests appealed to Gregory IX, and then on Gregory's death to Innocent IV.[4] Eventually, after much further argument, they won their case when in July 1248 Cardinal Gil Torres reversed the sentence of 1240, and in July 1249 their victory was confirmed by Innocent.[5] But it had been a long, uphill struggle for the twelve priests, and the chapter of military men survived the ordeal with their rights pretty much intact.[6]

It had been only by dint of sheer persistence, and the expenditure

---

1 *Ibid.* fos. 25va, 3rb, 11ra–b. Evidence of 'Bernardus clericus presbiter': 'Item audivit dici quod B. de Gusearia (?) dixit coram cardinali … archidiaconum de Albuciano dixisse quod presbiteri non erant canonici.' This was a long shot.

2 *Ibid.* fo. 2ra: 'Item neget ex parte canonicorum quod aliqui de predictis sacerdotibus non debent ire ad scolas cum in ecclesia Gerundensi certos habeant magistros et cantus et grammatici et dialectice facultatis per quos possunt instrui circa intelligendas scripturas et officium ecclesiasticum ad quod sunt specialiter deputati.'

3 *VL*, XII, 125.

4 *Causa*, fo. 26ra; *Reg. Greg. IX*, 5970; *Reg. Inn. IV*, 271. The transcript of evidence ends at Oct. 1240, but the *Causa* was evidently used by the priests' proctor at the Curia in subsequent years. The text is heavily glossed in a hand, presumably his, which is distinct from that of the text itself.

5 AC Gerona, d.s.n.: decree *Ea que iudicio*, 7 July 1249, containing the text of Cardinal Gil's judgement which is dated, according to the *Consuetudo Bononiensis*, 'anno domini 1249 [sic] anno sexto … mense julii die XII intrante'.

6 *VL*, XII, 151.

of 1,200 *aurei alfonsini*,[1] that the student-priests had forced the chapter of Gerona to accept the legate's ordinances of twenty years before; and the canons of Tarragona and Vich proved no less tenacious in defending their property. Vested interests prevailed everywhere. In only two churches in Castile–Leon do the legate's provisions concerning regular attendance at divine office by canons properly dressed and decently shaved, seem to have made any impact during these years. They were incorporated into the constitutions of the church of Burgos in November 1230, while at Zamora Bishop Martín published an elaborate scale of penalties (1217–38).[2] But even there a great gulf still existed between legatine theory and episcopal practice. The order of priorities was quite different. A canon of Zamora's slackness in attending to the vines was regarded as a considerably more serious offence than absence from choir, and the penalties imposed in 1236 were proportionately more severe. Nor can any of the regulations about the divine office have caused the chapter more heart-searching than the concoction of the sections in their constitutions which described the solemn procedure to be followed if their wine were watered or their bread were black.[3]

A great distance separates Zamora from Gerona, but in attempting to understand from admittedly patchy evidence something of the life led by the canons of the cathedrals of Aragon and Castile in the 1230s and 1240s, it will probably do them little injustice to stress both the essentially, if not technically, secular character of the young bloods of Gerona and also the rather fussy concern of the gentlemen-farmers of the other place with the details of their creature comforts, rather in the style of the modern bachelor Fellow. Sacerdotal ordination was sought only by a minority. The legate himself had scarcely pressed the point: at Barcelona in 1229 the dean was the only priest.[4] In October 1232 the canonist-bishop of Orense, Laurentius Hispanus, complained that it was the custom of that church that none but its canons might celebrate at the high altar. Yet *raro aut nunquam* could

---

[1] *Ea que iudicio,* as above.
[2] Serrano, *Don Mauricio,* 145; AC Zamora, *Liber Constitutionum,* fos. 8rb–16vb. The Zamora constitutions are undated. The canons were permitted to miss matins once a week without penalty and, as at Burgos, shaving was *de rigeur* only on feast-days: fo. 8va.
[3] *Ibid.* fos. 6rb, 16rb–va.
[4] Martène–Durand, *Thesaurus,* IV, 597.

the canons of Orense be induced to become priests. And the situation there was unchanged twenty-two years later.[1] Gerona, evidently, was not exceptional. In the year 1280 the proportion of priests to canons was the same both at Huesca in the north-east and at Lugo in the north-west: one to five.[2]

The one inescapable conclusion about John of Abbeville, and the main reason for the failure of his high-minded intervention in Spain, is that he declined to take into account the ineluctable facts of life there. 'The variety of persons and places' which was to provide Innocent IV with a principle in accordance with which he might bow to pressure from the Spanish Church and disown the legate's hard line on clerical incontinence, received no recognition from John himself. His councils supplied a faithful, even a slavish version of the legislation of the Fourth Lateran Council. With rare exceptions he adhered to that model. Making little or no allowance for Spanish idiosyncracies, which were considerable, he deviated neither to right nor to left, but stated and restated the rigid, uniform programme wherever he went. His utter devotion to that programme excluded all consideration of those existing social conditions which, inevitably and easily, survived his assault upon the superstructure: the system of recruiting canons at Gerona, for example, or the customary abuses practised by lay patrons in Galicia which the archbishop of Compostela, wiser in his generation than the children of light, recognised as uncanonical but realised that he must tolerate nevertheless.

John of Abbeville followed Innocent III not wisely, but too well. He was, after all, no politician. He was an academic out of his depth. He had made his reputation as a secular master at Paris, and it was the donnish quality of thoroughness and absolute loyalty to 'authority' that is most apparent during the Spanish legation, his first assignment as cardinal. He was the slave of his sources, which had been most recently codified in 1215, and applied them indiscriminately, invoking the toughest ecclesiastical sanctions in order to ensure respect for his *monita salutis*, as Rodrigo of Toledo called them.[3] *Litteratus*, Rodrigo labelled him, as did another Spanish witness.[4] 'Out of

1 *Reg. Greg. IX,* 916; *Reg. Inn. IV,* 7853.
2 Durán Gudiol, *REDC,* VII, cap. 14–22; AHN, cod. 1042B, fo. 37r.
3 *De Rebus Hispaniae,* 202.
4 *Loc. cit.*; CIL: *B. Hisp.,* XV, 272.

touch' might be a faithful translation. All was cut and dried for John whether he was in the lecture hall at the Schools or confronted with the all too human failings of the rural clergy. He remained as remote and automatic in the second avocation as in the first. His sermons are brittle with this essential dryness. He himself liked to think of them as a popular work for the edification of ordinary people. Yet whenever he came face to face with the texts, training told and the temptation to overload them with a stifling scholarly apparatus proved too much for him.[1] Their apparent success is difficult to understand, and at least one contemporary found them boring, 'sermones valde prolixos', heavy with the weight of their scriptural baggage.[2] The same may be said of his other productions. The so-called treatise on confession proves on closer inspection to be just another piece of quotation-mongering, and his *Expositio super Cantica Canticorum* a mere exercise in sub-Bernardine piety.[3] John lacked the common touch. From the country pulpit he saw pupils not people. Indeed, his work has been described as the swansong of twelfth-century biblical scholarship:[4] a characterisation which is given added point by his almost allegorical encounter in Spain with the Dominican, Raymond of Peñafort, who became his acolyte and went before him preaching and hearing confessions. For Raymond was an ornament of the Order which was destined both to revolutionise biblical studies in general and, in the kingdom of Aragon, to make some part of the legate's reform programme effective during the 1240s and 1250s.[5]

However, the activity of the Dominicans did not get under way in Aragon till 1238, by which time the process of whittling away the legate's various arrangements had got a head-start. Partly this was the work of half-hearted bishops and two-faced abbots. But the papacy

---

1 *Liber Omeliarum* (MS. Trinity Coll. Cambridge, B.15.21), fo. 1ra: 'Hoc opus... non sermonem exactum vel subtilem prurientibus scolarium auribus promittentes sed quasi rudes omelias rudibus rudi proponendas.' What, though, to quote a solitary example, can they have made of his semantic excursus upon Matt. xxi.9: 'Turbe que precedebant et que sequebantur clamabant "Filio David" et est filio dativi casus; "Osanna", id est salva, obsecro: et est compositum ex corrupto osy, scilicet quod est salva et integro; scilicet anna, quod est interiectio deprecantis' (fo. 3rb)?

2 Henry of Ghent, *cit.* Feret, *Faculté de théologie*, I, 231. Lecoy de la Marche calls them the most colourless and unoriginal productions of the age: *La chaire française*, 60. Cf. the opinion of Pedro de Posa.

3 Hauréau, *Notices et extraits*, IV, 148; *Histoire littéraire de la France*, XVIII, 171.

4 Smalley, *Study of the Bible*, 265.   5 *Vita S. Raymundi*, 22; Smalley, 264 ff.

too must take a share of the blame, if blame be appropriate. For considerations of necessity and utility, those elastic concepts that had enmeshed reform at Vich and Lérida, and concern about the very continuation of the ministry in Spain provided strong incentives for compromise. The legate's blanket condemnation of all clergy who failed in any particular to measure up to his exalted standards threatened to bring the administration of the sacraments to a grinding halt, just as the counsels of perfection of extremist reformers had done in the eleventh century.[1] Moreover, papal priorities were being revised at this period. In 1228–9 the legate restated the preoccupation with reform of the Fourth Lateran Council of thirteen years before. But only seventeen years later at the Lyons Council, Innocent IV relegated reform and gave preference to politics in his address on the five wounds of the Church.[2]

The papal reassessment began within three years of John of Abbeville's return from Spain. In the archdiocese of Braga alone the legate's sentences against illegitimate clerics had affected 1,746 holders of benefices; and in July 1232 Gregory IX instructed Archbishop Silvestre Godinho to absolve them all.[3] Two years later, Bishop Miguel of Lugo was empowered to deal with five hundred such unfortunates of his diocese who, strictly speaking, ought to have travelled to the Curia for absolution, and with certain others who had fallen foul of the legate.[4] On the whole, though, Gregory IX was parsimonious with dispensations. He was careful to specify that the Lugo grant did not apply to those whose fathers had been priests or who were themselves guilty of adultery or incest. But Innocent IV, his successor, was much less cautious. At Porto he reversed John's arrangement for the revaluation of canonries and prebends by accepting the argument of Bishop Pedro Salvador that there were insufficient canons for the celebration of services there, and allowing him to subdivide the next two vacant prebends, thereby giving fresh impetus to the spiral of subdivision and pluralism against which the legate had striven.[5] Bishop Pedro Fernández of Astorga was authorised to amend John's statutes for his church, and in particular to

---

[1] Fliche, *La réforme grégorienne*, I, 294 ff.   [2] Hefele–Leclercq, v, ii, 1637–8.
[3] *Reg. Greg. IX*, 829.   [4] *Ibid.* 2068; AC Lugo, 21/3/17.
[5] In July 1245, having two months previously given Archbishop João Egas of Braga leave to convert the next four vacant prebends into twelve: *Censual do Cabido da Sé do Porto*, 17; ADB, Gav. das Dignidades, 15.

modify the penalties against canons who wandered about the place in lay attire during services.[1] It was by his reversal of the sentences of excommunication and suspension against *clerici concubinarii,* however, that Innocent proclaimed the renunciation not only of John of Abbeville's vigorous measures but also of any hope that the Spanish Church might be reformed.

Piecemeal dispensations were issued from the very beginning of his pontificate. In October 1243 'non modica multitudo' of Burgos *concubinarii* was absolved, on payment to the papal funds for the Holy Land of the money that they would otherwise have spent in journeying to Rome for absolution.[2] And in the course of the next three years similar arrangements were made with the clergy of Tarragona and León.[3] Then, in June 1251, only two months after Innocent had confirmed the repudiation of the legate's ordinances at Vich, the statutory sentences of excommunication and suspension imposed at the Valladolid and Lérida Councils were completely withdrawn. Having conferred with his compatriots at the Curia, the Spanish cardinal Gil Torres, to whom the pope had referred the matter, concluded that the legate's efforts *pro animarum procuranda salute* had proved to be counter-productive. For the Spanish clergy, like the Bavarians, did not give a bean for these spiritual fulminations, as the Tarragona Council of 1230 had noted.[4] They carried on regardless and, what was worse, they infected with the contagion of excommunication whomsoever came into contact with them.[5] Thereby they had called the papal bluff, and the pope was obliged to climb down and to abandon the fundamental principles of his predecessor's sometime legate. Shortly after the Lyons Council, Innocent had lamented that in the province of Tarragona ecclesiastical sanctions were ignored and canonical sentences set at naught.[6] Six years later, it was decided to replace John of Abbeville's penalties by a system of fines and to surrender the initiative to individual prelates who had experience of local conditions, lest the Church, like an unskilled doctor, should seem to prescribe the same medicine irrespective of the nature of the

---

[1] In Aug. 1245: Quintana Prieto, *AA,* XI, no. 58.
[2] AC Burgos, vol. 71, fos. 70rb–vb (reg. Mansilla, *AA,* IX, no. 10).
[3] AHA, *Cartoral AB,* fo. 8r (ed. Augustinus, *Opera,* III, 411–12); AC León, doc. 1295: *Ex parte,* 4 Oct. 1245.
[4] Tejada, VI, 28–9; Bayley, *The Formation of the German College of Electors,* 10.
[5] Tejada, VI, 49.   [6] Below, p. 268.

ailment, 'cum per varietatem personarum et etiam regionum poenae sint proinde variandae'.[1]

It was thus accepted that the Spanish clergy could not be expected to conform to the rules of canon law.[2] Innocent IV preferred to cut his losses. He had no alternative. In Castile the legate's plan of reform had been a dead letter all along, and in Aragon even that doughty campaigner Archbishop Pedro de Albalat, who died a month after Cardinal Gil's sentence, did not adhere quite as strictly as he might have done to the line on concubinage.[3] Nor does it seem that the new financial deterrent made much impression. According to the *Primera Partida* the clergy continued with their wenching. It was one of the things that did their reputation most damage.[4] And they did not lack opportunities for their adventures, for, although *barraganas* and *mujeres sospechosas* were warned off, there was no objection to their co-habiting with a wide selection of female relatives. Mothers, grandmothers, sisters and aunts were held to be above suspicion, and in charity ought probably to be accepted as such. But, without undue prurience, one may question the wisdom of including nieces too, and daughters and daughters-in-law by earlier marriages.[5] Small wonder that it was reported of some clerics that in their depravity they managed to commit indiscretions with even these.[6] On the island of Mallorca, where the cause of reform had made rather more progress than in Castile, 'sisters and young cousins' were rejected for what they were: euphemisms for something else.[7]

The year 1251, therefore, witnessed the acceptance of the *fait accompli* of John de Abbeville's failure in Spain. In July 1254 Bishop Juan Díaz of Orense secured a copy of Cardinal Gil's judgement while he was at the Curia,[8] and in the following April the archbishop of

---

1 Tejada, *loc. cit.*
2 *Liber Extra*, III, III. *de clericis coniugatis*, c. 1 (Friedberg, *Corpus*, II, 457). In 1258–9 Cardinal Gil's argument and text were adopted by the archbishop of Uppsala: *Reg. Alex. IV*, 2660, 2837.
3 Below, p. 62.
4 BM Add. MS. 20787, fo. 45rb: *Part.* 1.6.37 (Academy ed. I, 278).
5 *Ibid.* fo. 45va (Academy ed. I, 279).
6 *Ibid.* fo. 45vb (Academy ed. I, 279): *Part.* 1.6.38.
7 'Lurs sors ne lurs cosines joves', whom rectors were forbidden to entertain: Constitution of March 1266, in Nebot, *BSAL*, XIII, 316.
8 *Reg. Inn. IV*, 7885. By Dec. 1255 he had returned to his see: AC Orense, *Escrituras*, XII, 59.

Compostela, Juan Arias, followed suit.[1] It may have been a form of investment: with it, perhaps, prelates were able to recoup some of their Roman expenses by fining their diocesan clergy. Certainly its validity was limited to the lifetime of the recipient, for in February 1290 Juan Arias's successor, Rodrigo, acquired a further copy.[2] So also did six other Hispanic prelates – the archbishop of Braga and the bishops of León, Lérida, Barcelona, Oviedo and Lisbon – in that and the preceding year.[3] But by then the name of John Abbeville had become merely a venerable relic, necessarily mentioned in papal dispensations to pluralists,[4] and roughly synonymous with the defence of *libertas ecclesiastica*. In the year 1282 it was twice invoked in this sense. In April the alliance of the rebel churchmen with the Infante Sancho was denounced by the loyalists as being *contra iura et statuta domini Sabinensis*;[5] and seven months later the abbot of Pombeiro was warned by Archbishop Tello of Braga that his intention of referring a certain property dispute to the royal court had been 'expressly forbidden' by the cardinal-bishop of Sabina, *olim in Hyspania apostolice sedis legatus*.[6] It was scant return for all the energy that John of Abbeville had expended during a Spanish winter and two summers. But in the kingdom of Aragon he had received a better reception and there, at least for a period of ten years, they had taken him seriously.

[1] *Reg. Alex. IV*, 389.

[2] *Reg. Nich. IV*, 2129.

[3] *Ibid.* 757, 519, 2928, 2942, 3018, 3685.

[4] The earliest instance seems to have been in Jan. 1234: *Reg. Greg. IX*, 1737. Between then and 1303 thirty such letters, some of them in favour of more than one clerk, were entered in the Papal Registers. One which was not (for Archbishop Sancho I of Toledo) has the words omitted from the text written in on the fold by the *corrector*, as an afterthought: '[non obstantibus...] et illa quam bone memorie J. Sabinensis episcopus tunc in Ispanie partibus apostolice sedis legatus contra obtinentes plura ecclesiastica beneficia edidisse dicitur'. This was only thirty years after, on 10 April 1259: AC Toledo, A.7.C.2.5: *Pro merente*.

[5] *MHE*, II, 61.

[6] Meireles, *Memórias do mosteiro de Pombeiro*, 129. For similar usage by Archbishop João of Braga in the late 1240s, see *As Gavetas da Torre do Tombo*, III, 235.

Chapter 4

PEDRO DE ALBALAT
AND THE REFORM OF HIS PROVINCE

Circa primam horam noctis on 2 July 1251 the cause of reform suffered its second serious reverse within a month. The death of Pedro de Albalat, archbishop of Tarragona,[1] removed from the Spanish scene a prelate of singular energy and exceptional reforming zeal whose tally of provincial councils, as Argáiz recognised in the seventeenth century, outdid even that of the Visigothic Church.[2] Argáiz credited him with eight councils, but in fact Pedro held ten councils between 1239 and 1250, and the annual cycle was broken only in those two years, 1241 and 1245, when he was called abroad for assemblies of the Universal Church. At the second of these he made a considerable impact.[3] Yet, on account of his pastoral record in Aragon alone, he deserves a wider reputation than he enjoys. Anywhere in thirteenth-century Europe such a record would have been remarkable, and in contrast with the lassitude of the archbishops of Toledo and Compostela of his day it is truly astonishing. With justice he has been described as 'one of the most important figures of the Catalan clergy of his age',[4] but beyond that his achievement has received scant recognition since the sixteenth century when his archiepiscopal successor, Antonio Agustín, published some of the constitutions of his councils.[5] Subsequently, a great deal more material has become available,[6] but the councils and synods of the province of Tarragona, for which he was ultimately responsible, still await serious study. On more than one occasion Villanueva lamented the lack of such a work. 'How

---

[1] *VL*, XIX, 259.
[2] Argáiz, *Soledad laureada*, II, fo. 53vb.
[3] Below, p. 161.
[4] Beer, *Handschriften*, 69.
[5] Cf. *VL*, XX, 32 ff.; Arco, *El arzobispo don Antonio Agustín*.
[6] Tejada, *Colección*, III, 349 ff.; VI, 29 ff., in addition to the works of Marca, Aguirre and Villanuño. Cf. also Fita's perceptive article in *BRAH*, XL, correcting discrepancies in the dating of the councils of 1248–50.

admirably', he wrote, 'might a student employ his talents in elucidating the synodal decrees of the see of Valencia', where Pedro's brother, Andrés, was bishop for more than twenty years. But Villanueva himself was not that student. Having failed to verify the existence of a box of conciliar documents in the capitular archive at Tarragona, he left the job to be done. And it has still to be done.[1] It will never be done if the elimination of the sort of difficulties which deterred Villanueva is to be regarded as prerequisite. Similar obstacles were encountered at the Lérida archive where only the most cursory, and tantalising, inspection was permitted, though it must surely contain material of great value for the present chapter. Nevertheless, it is possible to form from other sources an impression of Archbishop Pedro which the Lérida *fonds* might refine but is hardly likely to invalidate.

Pedro de Albalat was the spiritual heir of John of Abbeville. At his first council, in April 1239, he adopted entire the legate's programme of reform.[2] It was ten years since John's legation, and nineteen months since the legate's death.[3] But the two men had been in contact throughout the previous decade. It is highly likely that they met in 1229, when Pedro was sacrist of Lérida, at the Council which was to provide him at a later date with chapter and verse for the reform of his province, and that his fruitful relationship with Raymond of Peñafort, who was in the legate's entourage, dates from the same time. But it is certain that during the period after his return to the Curia, where he continued to concern himself with the affairs of the Spanish Church,[4] John retained the services of Pedro de Albalat as his agent in the kingdom of Aragon. And the issue which first engaged their joint attention was one in which, as archbishop, Pedro was to show the keenest interest: heresy.

The high incidence of heresy and unorthodoxy in mountainous

---

[1] *VL*, I, 84–5. Cf. *ibid.* x, 195–213; xx, 72–6. Neither Finke's *Konzilienstudien* nor Valls i Taberner's article in *AST*, xi, does more than provide a résumé of Tejada.

[2] Tejada, VI, 30: *De constitutionibus domini Sabinensis servandis.*

[3] Frizon, *Gallia Purpurata*, 213.

[4] He was auditor of the charges against the bishop of Vich in 1232, and of disputes between the archbishop of Toledo and the Order of Santiago, and between the bishop of Barcelona and the monastery of San Cugat del Vallés: above, p. 43; Lomax, *Hispania*, XIX, 334–5; Ríus Serra, *Cartulario de San Cugat*, III, 450.

regions has frequently been noted,[1] and in the kingdom of Aragon throughout the thirteenth century the Albigensian heresy was rampant in the Pyrenean see of Urgel. There had been a serious outbreak shortly before the legate's visit in the autumn of 1229, and at his Council in the following May Archbishop Sparago expressed grave concern.[2] The see of Urgel was at that moment vacant, Pedro de Puigvert (about whose ability to deal with the crisis Honorius III had had his doubts) having resigned in the previous month, possibly in consequence of an unfavourable report submitted by the legate;[3] and Sparago and the bishop of Lérida, Berenguer de Eril, were given joint charge of it until there should be an election.[4] John of Abbeville was extremely interested in the outcome of this election, as is shown by a letter sent by him to Bishop Berenguer in April or May 1230, which has survived in the archive of Urgel Cathedral. The suitability of possible candidates exercised him greatly,[5] and the weight of evidence suggests that the cardinal was being kept informed of developments by Pedro de Albalat. Perhaps it was Pedro who brought this letter from the Curia. Certainly he was an observer – and a highly regarded observer, furthermore – at the riotous process of election at Urgel in May 1230 which resulted in the promotion to the see of Bishop Berenguer's nephew, Ponce de Vilamur, who had been sacrist of Lérida immediately before Pedro himself. Another Urgel document, containing the version of these events submitted to an inquest into the election held soon after by various canons of the church, provides a vivid account of ecclesiastical party politics in thirteenth-century Catalonia. It is a tale of ambushes, bribery, torrid debate and strong-arm tactics. It has a flavour all its own,[6] but the point of interest in the present context is the quite casual reference which it contains to Pedro who, while the beaten side were frogmarching their candidate to the altar, intoned the *Te Deum* which brought the pantomime to an end. Pedro did not escape unscathed. It was assumed that he was an advocate of Ponce, and Ponce's enemies, most

---

[1] Cf. H. R. Trevor-Roper, *Religion, the Reformation and Social Change* (London, 1967), 104–13.
[2] Ventura Subirats, *BRABL*, xxviii, 88.
[3] *VL*, xi, 72; *Reg. Hon. III*, 1958, 2466–7 (MDH, 215, 286–7).
[4] *VL, loc. cit.*
[5] AC Seo de Urgel, d.s.n., publ. Linehan, *AEM*, forthcoming.
[6] AC Seo de Urgel, d.s.n., several extracts published in Linehan, *loc. cit.*

unsportingly, wreaked their vengeance by doing to death one of Pedro's mules and wounding another.[1] And the desperadoes seem to have judged aright, for when Ponce's promotion suffered a further delay Pedro travelled to Rome, presumably for fresh consultation with John of Abbeville. While he was there he secured papal permission to retain the churches of Zaidin, Albalat and Soros together with the income from his office as sacrist.[2]

His visit seems to have disposed of all outstanding objections to Ponce. On 6 February 1231, shortly before he returned to Aragon, John of Abbeville furnished him with a letter addressed to Ponce as bishop, in which the sacrist of Lérida was described as his 'fidelis et sollicitus procurator' and Ponce was urged to prove himself 'acceptus minister Deo' and to nourish the flock which had been entrusted to him 'sacra doctrina pariter et exemplo'.[3] It was not the only commission that he brought with him. Six days later he was appointed, together with the bishop of Lérida and the abbot of Poblet, to protect the chapter of Vich against the archbishop of Tarragona;[4] and the pope's rescript confirming the ex-legate's constitutions for Barcelona, which was issued two days before that, may also have been entrusted to him.[5] The issue of substance, however, is that John's letter referred to Ponce as bishop fully two months before the archbishop of Tarragona received formal notice even of the election.[6] The affair had been stage-managed by John and Pedro, and the latter was an ecclesiastical power in the land eight years before his appointment as leader of the Aragonese Church.

It is curious, and even dramatically appropriate, that Pedro de Albalat's earliest recorded achievement should have been his successful campaign on behalf of Ponce de Vilamur. For the bishop of

---

[1] *Ibid.*: 'Et finito *Te Deum Laudamus* dicta fuit oratio per sacristam Ilerdensem'; 'Gombaldus de Acuta...dixit quod fama publica est in ecclesia Urgellensi quod sacrista [Urgellensis] fecit interfeci unam mulam et alteram vulnerari magistri P. de Albalato.'

[2] AC Lérida, caj. 202, no. 569: *Cum a nobis*, 23 Dec. 1230.

[3] AC Seo de Urgel, d.s.n., publ. Linehan, *AEM, loc. cit.* The letter is dated *Roma in crastina Cinerum.* It is clear from the context that it must belong either to 1231 or 1232; and the morrow of Ash Wednesday (6 Feb.) 1231 may be preferred, since on the corresponding day in 1232 (25 Feb.) the Curia was not at Rome. Cf. Potthast, I, 743, 762 (*ad dies* 29 Jan.–7 Feb. 1231; 21–8 Feb. 1232).

[4] AC Vich, 37–1–17: *Ex parte.*   [5] Potthast, 8659.

[6] *Vida del Illmo Sr D. Felix Amat*, appendix, 162–3.

57

Urgel was to fall far short of John of Abbeville's high standards, and the reformers' white hope of 1230–1 was to be converted into their *bête noire* in the course of the next twenty years, and would dog Archbishop Pedro until his dying day. In the early 1230s, though, this all lay in the future, and Ponce's future career was as inscrutable to Pedro as Pedro's past career is still to us. Where *magister Petrus* had studied, and the truth of the unsubstantiated claim that he was a Cistercian monk,[1] are only two of the questions about him for which no certain answers are available. He was, like so many, *de genere militari*,[2] but all that can be said of his pre-episcopal period is that he was commissioned on at least three occasions to interest himself in the affairs of Aragonese religious communities: to defend the Dominican nuns of Zaragoza; to restrain a clique of Augustinian monks of Santa María de Mur, Urgel, from joining the Premonstratensian Order; and to visit Ripoll.[3] Until October 1236 he remains a shadowy figure.

In that month, however, his many virtues caught the attention of the canons of his own church of Lérida, and they elected him as the successor of Bishop Berenguer de Eril.[4] Pedro was bishop of Lérida for only fourteen months. Yet even in that short period he found time to issue an *ordinatio* which superseded the original *ordinatio* of 1168,[5] displayed his distinctive blend of idealism and realism, and demonstrated his understanding of the practical obstacles which stood in the way of moral regeneration. John of Abbeville had had precious little sense of reality and had acquired none while traipsing round Spain, but Pedro, though no less convinced than the legate that *regimen animarum* was *ars artium*, realised also that it had to be the art of the possible. And so he concentrated upon the logistics of the

---

[1] Though Finistres in the eighteenth century had shown that Pedro was not a member of the Order, Villanueva thought it necessary to disprove what he took to be the contrary view of 'los historiadores de aquella casa'; and in 1967 Burns referred to him as 'a Cistercian monk': *Historia de Poblet*, ii, 242; *VL*, xvi, 135; *Crusader Kingdom of Valencia*, i, 215.

[2] *ES*, xlvii, 22–5.

[3] *Reg. Greg. IX*, 1888 (April 1234); 2838 (Nov. 1235); Beer, *Handschriften*, 68, n. 2. For Pedro as apostolic visitor of exempt monasteries in the early 1230s, see Tobella and Mundó, *Analecta Montserratensia*, x, 427 ff.

[4] *VL*, xvi, 294–6, describing him as 'hominem utique cui aetatis maturitas, morum gravitas et competens quinnimo eminens litterarum scientia suffragatur'.

[5] *Ibid.* 115; J. Lladonosa Pujol, 'Proyección urbana de Lérida durante el reinado de Alfonso el Casto', *VII. CHCA*, ii (1962), 200–2.

problem, upon the economics of reform. The archdeacons of Lérida could not afford to carry out their visitations, 'propter quod grave sequitur dispendium animarum et multa insolencia in subditis enutritur et dissolucio cumulatur': he therefore increased their income.[1] Having himself no *pied-à-terre* within range of the city of Lérida, 'ad quam valeat declinare', he purchased the castle of Bovera from the *communis mensa*;[2] and to ensure a better attendance at cathedral services he created nineteen *dimidiae porciones,* one of which was earmarked for the support of a *magister scolarum* who was given the task of irrigating the intellectual desert thereabouts.[3]

Pedro's *Ordinatio Ecclesie Ilerdensis* was issued on 11 December 1237. By then he was a prominent figure in the Aragonese Church which, since the death of Archbishop Sparago on 3 March 1233,[4] had been leaderless. It was to him, together with Bishop Bernardo Calvó of Vich and Raymond of Peñafort, that Gregory IX referred cases of high ecclesiastical politics during 1237: the revocation of certain actions of the late King Pedro II which had been prejudicial to the rights of the Roman Church; the request of Ponce of Tortosa for permission to resign his see;[5] and appointment to the bishoprics of Majorca and Huesca.[6] Thus, in association with the holiest prelate of the province and the canonist-saint, he had a hand in the religious regeneration of the Aragonese Church even before his elevation to the archbishopric of Tarragona, which occurred in February 1238 after the chapter had resigned its rights of election to Gregory and the pope – almost certainly on the recommendation of St Raymond

---

[1] AC Lérida, caj. 218: *Constitutiones Ecclesie Ilerdensis,* fos. 2v–5r (another copy in AC Seo de Urgel, cod. 2119, fos. 45v–9r), at fos. 3r, 4v. This refers to the 'generalem ordinationem concernentem fundamentum et universum statum Ecclesie Illerdensis tam in capite quam in membris', which Sáinz de Baranda failed to locate (*ES,* XLVII, 24), but which was mentioned by Villanueva (*VL,* XVI, 136).

[2] *Ibid.* fo. 4v.

[3] *Ibid.* fos. 3v–4r: 'Statuimus eciam quod dimidia porcio uni magistro scolarum perpetuo concedatur qui in grammatica regat et doceat et cuius deffectum non modicum imminere nunc usque inventum est studere volentibus detrimentum.'

[4] *VL,* XIX, 180; Junyent, *AST,* XXIII, 150.   [5] *Reg. Greg. IX,* 3708; 3776.

[6] *Ibid.* 3775 (=orig. reg. Pérez Martínez, *AA,* XI, 164, no. 3: publ. *VL,* XXI, 286–7); 3777 (publ. Ríus Serra, *San Raimundo: Diplomatário,* 50–1; Junyent, *Diplomatari de Sant Bernat Calvó,* no. 109). They chose Raimundo de Torrelles (cf. *VL,* XXI, 125 ff.) and the distinguished lawyer, Vidal de Canellas, respectively. Arco assumed that Vidal was elected by the chapters of Huesca and Jaca: *BRABL,* VIII, 465–6. Cf. Durán Gudiol, *HS,* XII, 299–300.

who had declined the position himself four years before[1] – designated
Pedro, the bishop of Lérida of whom he had heard such excellent
reports.[2]

At the time of Pedro's promotion the Christian forces were mass-
ing for the final assault on the city of Valencia, and its capture that
autumn provided the new archbishop with an opportunity of taking
stock of those of his suffragans who were gathered there, in the royal
entourage, in expectation of grants of territory. For five years they
had had no archbishop to give them a lead, and Pedro could ill afford
to lose time in asserting his authority. At 'a council' (as the witness,
Ferrán Pérez de Torolio, remembered it), attended by his bishops
and, significantly, by a number of friars, he stole a march on the archbishop of Toledo and appointed Berenguer de Castelbisbal as bishop
of Valencia.[3] 'A council' held in those conditions, however, amidst
the hurly-burly of military manœuvres,[4] was necessarily an *ad hoc*
affair having little or nothing in common with the formal, full-dress
assemblies of later years. Still, Pedro soon buckled down to his
pastoral responsibilities. In 1239, during which year he was once
described as a legate,[5] a start was made.

---

[1] Raymond's refusal occurred after Gregory IX, in Feb. 1234, had rejected the
chapter's election of Bishop Berenguer of Barcelona, and Cardinal Gil Torres had
declined in the following June: *VL*, xix, 180–1. The account of later developments
in Morera Llauradó, *Tarragona cristiana*, ii, 272–3, requires revision. By Sept. 1234
Guillermo de Mongrí, ex-sacrist of Gerona, was archbishop-elect (*Reg. Greg. IX*,
2103); but he too was uninterested, and preferred to return to Gerona and the
enjoyment of what he had been awarded for leading the assault on Ibiza (*Chronicle
of James of Aragon*, 219–20). This was granted in April 1236 (*Reg. Greg. IX*, 3093),
not April 1238 (as Morera, ii, appendix 21) or Aug. 1237 (as Fita, *BRAH*, xl, 339–
40). However, Guillermo continued as *procurator* of the church until Feb. 1237
when St Raymond was directed to take charge and make arrangements for election
by the chapter (*Reg. Greg. IX,* 3473–4). Two days before, on 5 Feb., Guillermo had
been granted as spoil the property of those who traded illicitly with the Moors,
and it is significant that he arranged for the address of the rescript to be amended to
mark his definitive break with Tarragona: 'Petit quod scribatur sacriste Gerundensi
eodem modo quo hic scribitur procuratori electo Tarraconensi/Supp(licat) sacrista
Gerundensis' (AE Gerona, caixa 6–16=*Reg. Greg. IX*, 3491). Burns assumes that
Guillermo's 'prelacy' continued until 1238:i, 38.
[2] *Reg. Greg. IX*, 4072.   [3] Sanchis Sivera, *La diócesis valentina*, ii, 364.
[4] Fita dates Berenguer's appointment 28 Sept., the very day on which the city was
taken, according to Ibn al-Abbār: *BRAH*, xl, 351; Ghedira, *Al-Andalus*, xxii, 33;
Ubieto Arteta, *Ligarzas*, i, 161 ff.
[5] In an indulgence which he granted to the church of S. Sepulcro, Calatayud:
Sagarra, *AST*, v, 198; Lafuente, *ES*, xlix, 416. Sagarra suggests that the unusual

Pedro de Albalat and reform of his Province

On the day appointed by John of Abbeville, *Jubilate* Sunday, he held his first provincial council at Tarragona. It was attended by seven of his suffragans[1] and lasted until the following Tuesday, three days, in accordance with the procedural instructions of the *Forma de Sacro Concilio Tarracone Celebrando*.[2] The legate's ghost was also there. His legislation was reissued complete, and the point was rammed home by the reiteration of those themes that had been most dear to him: *clerici concubinarii* (predictably); pluralism; marriage within the forbidden degrees; clerical involvement in secular affairs; vagabond monks and canons; and the relaxation of monastic discipline.[3] Yet Pedro had a mind of his own, and two of the items contained in the conciliar constitutions were his own contribution: the declaration of war against heresy, and the encouragement given to his staunchest allies in that war, the friars, whose founders were accorded solemn honours throughout the province.[4] Such was the archbishop's programme. All of the elements of the next twelve reforming years were defined in 1239, and the bishops were left in no doubt about the energy with which he meant to pursue his end. Before he dismissed them, he reminded them once more of the Order of the Day – the constitutions of the Fourth Lateran Council and of John of Abbeville – and warned them that ignorance of those provisions would constitute no defence when he descended upon their churches, as he intended to do, *absque alia praemonitione*.[5]

One of his hearers was able to certify that this was not a meaningless threat, for already, in January 1239, the church of Huesca had

form *dei gratia* (rather than *dei gracia*) may mean that the seal, upon which he is so described, is a forgery. In the summer of 1968 the document, unfortunately, could not be found in the Archivo Histórico Nacional. On no other occasion is Pedro described as legate.

1 Namely, the bishops of Barcelona, Gerona, Vich, Urgel, Lérida, Tortosa and Huesca: a good turn-out, since the sees of Zaragoza and Pamplona were vacant, and the bishop of Valencia was in the throes of organisation. There were only two culpable absentees: the bishops of Tarazona and Calahorra.
2 AC Gerona, *Llibre Vert*, fo. 300r–v; AC Barcelona, *Libro de la Cadena,* fo. 46ra–b.
3 Tejada, VI, 30–1. Tejada also published a set of constitutions 'ex MS. Colbertino' which he took to be John of Abbeville's constitutions as reissued in 1239; III, 367–73. But from internal evidence they must be regarded as a later concoction, as was realised by Finke, who dismissed them as a *Mischmasch: Konzilienstudien*, 68.
4 *Ibid.* cap. 7–8.
5 *Ibid.* VI, 32.

received an archiepiscopal visitation.[1] There was room for improvement at Huesca. The canons had become lax about their vows as regulars, and were rarely to be found in the refectory or dormitory. *Cultus divinus* was not celebrated properly, 'sine barbarismo et soloecismo'. They were reminded of John of Abbeville's statutes (whether those of the Lérida Council or a special set designed for them is not clear) about pawning their goods, wearing flashy clothes and spending the night in town. 'Omnia verbo ad verbum sunt domini Sabinensis', in short.[2] And the same may be said of the archbishop's constitutions for the church of Vich, which he visited in the following August.[3] Yet to this body of doctrine and code of discipline Pedro brought a new spirit of moderation. It is noticeable that on neither occasion did he reiterate the legate's thoroughgoing sanctions against concubinage. Instead, Vidal of Huesca was enjoined to proceed *cum diligentia*, and it was left to Bernardo of Vich to use his discretion in implementing the sentences authorised by John and Sparago.[4] Pedro felt able to trust their judgement, having had a hand in the appointment of the one and having personal experience of the saintliness of the other.

What did concern him, wherever he travelled in his province, was the state of parochial organisation and the removal of obstacles to popular devotion. In some places he was confounded by geography. His own cathedral church when he had been bishop of Lérida, for example, presented its parishioners with a steep climb, 'cum in monte consistat excelso iuxta quem dicta civitas est constructa', as they complained to Urban IV some twenty years later, requesting the provision of facilities for baptism and marriage at a lower altitude.[5] Like-

---

[1] The record of which was published by Arco, *BRABL*, x–xi, 85–7, but with the date – 'II non. januarii anno domini MCCXXXoctavo' – misinterpreted as 1238, before Pedro's promotion. Similarly, *idem, BRABL*, ix, 227; Durán Gudiol, *HS*, xii, 301.

[2] *Ibid.* 86. Cf. *Lér.* c. 24–6 for exact parallels; and above, p. 24, for the legate's visit to Huesca.　　　　　[3] AC Vich, 37–1–19: publ. *VL*, vii, 249–51.

[4] *BRABL*, x–xi, 87; 'ordinationes vero...vestro arbitrio duximus relinquendas, ut in executione ipsarum, secundum quod procedendum videritis, procedatis': *VL*, vii, 250.

[5] AHN, 2249/19: decree *Significarunt*, 29 April 1262. The new cathedral was not established, however, until the eighteenth century when, according to Richard Ford, it was not the laity who pressed for change. 'The steep walk proved too much for the stall-fed canons, whose affections were not set on things above': *Handbook for Travellers in Spain* (London, 1845), ii, 971. Cf. M. Herrera y Gés, *La catedral antigua de Lérida* (Lérida, 1948).

wise, the parochial organisation of the diocese of Zaragoza, which he visited in March 1242, was hopelessly muddled, largely on account of its size – *cum sit latissima et diffusa* – and the inefficiency of its arch-priests upon whom so much depended.[1] But Pedro was less accom-modating than Urban IV, and the citizens of Zaragoza on that same occasion received little sympathy from him in their quarrel over tithes and the sacraments with the cathedral clergy.[2] He was a stickler for the rules. At Huesca he insisted on a strict definition of parish boundaries, which he found *confusas et minime limitatas,* and also on the sovereignty of each resident rector over parochial revenues.[3] In the diocese of Tortosa he emphasised that the parish clergy had to be ordained and resident.[4] And though his main consideration when he visited Valencia Cathedral in June 1242 was that the divine office should be decently administered 'diurnis horis pariter et nocturnis' in the *novella plantatio,*[5] there too he was hardly less concerned about the economic foundations of the recently established frontier parishes.[6] For all this, though, Pedro was a realist and was prepared, as John of Abbeville had not been, to make concessions to human frailty as a means of coaxing the clergy towards a better life. Thus, while both in his own cathedral church and at Valencia he penalised canons for absence from choir, he did allow them one morning each week when they might lie in and miss matins without loss of income.[7]

Tireless though the archbishop seems to have been in visiting the sees of his province, it was upon the bishops that he had to rely if his reforms were to have any permanent significance. The task of admonishing, removing local anomalies and bringing the liturgical practice of each church into line with that of the cathedral of Tarra-gona, 'que ipsius est metropolis et magistra',[8] weighed upon them. So,

---

[1] AA Zaragoza, 5/1/7. [2] Arruego, *Catedra episcopal,* 724–7.

[3] Arco, *BRABL,* x–xi, 87.

[4] AC Tortosa, caj. *Constituciones,* 4 (dated 28 Feb. 1244, addressed to Bishop Ponce, and referring to a recent visitation).

[5] AC Valencia, doc. 2310 (reg. Olmos Canalda, *Pergaminos,* 88).

[6] *Ibid.* He confirmed the bishop and chapter's *ordinatio super divisione patrimonii et creacione dignitatum,* 'hoc excepto: quod primicie omnes parrochialibus ecclesiis relinquntur ut rectores earum inde valeant commode sustentari'.

[7] AHA, *Thesaurus,* fo. 463: constitution *De divino officio observando* (31 Jan. 1249); AC Valencia, doc. 2310. Similar allowance was made at Zamora by Bishop Martín, 'nisi sit festum': AC Zamora, *Liber Constitutionum,* fo. 8rb.

[8] AC Valencia, doc. 2310. Cf. 1242 Council, c. 4, *De celebratione officii:* Tejada, vi, 35.

too, did the duty of attending the annual provincial councils and of passing on the message to their clergy at diocesan synods. By 1242 they seem to have been beginning to wilt under the strain, or perhaps the lack of a council in the previous year had broken the spell. For only three of them appeared at the council that May: a performance which elicited a characteristically firm warning for the future from Pedro. Bishops absent thereafter, 'excusationes frivolas pretendentes', would incur durance vile at Tarragona.[1] This had its effect, and, with the exception of the incorrigible Ponce of Urgel, they all either came or sent representatives to the 1243 Council.[2]

Gradually, as the incumbents died, Pedro was able to safeguard the future by filling the sees with – or, rather, by influencing the electors to appoint – churchmen who shared his outlook. Before investigating this group of prelates, however, it may be as well to consider the situation in the three sees which did not present the archbishop with such an opportunity: those of Tarazona, Tortosa and Urgel, the bishops of which survived from before 1238 until after his death.

Admittedly, none of them remained entirely apart from the mainstream of activity. Even García Frontón of Tarazona (1219–54[3]), was represented at two of the councils, although he attended none of them in person,[4] and it may have been a similar anxiety to that of Pedro for parochial organisation which prompted him in July 1251 to seek papal permission to deal with the disorder of the Calatayud area, and three years later to implement Innocent IV's commission *in pleno capitulo*.[5] But, equally, this may have been an instance of mere acquisitiveness rather than of disinterested pastoral zeal. In the

---

1 *Ibid.* VI, 36.
2 *Ibid.* VI, 37. Bishop Ferrer of Valencia would have been there, had he not been intercepted by Moors while *en route* and murdered: Burns, I, 24.
3 Cf. Lafuente, *ES*, XLIX, 166 ff. He was, however, still alive in November 1254: García Larragueta, *El Gran Priorado*, II, 358.
4 In 1243 and 1249. His proctor on the earlier occasion was the archdeacon of Tarazona, Martín Pérez, who was one of the outsiders whom the chapter of Valencia were prepared to accept as bishop in Oct. 1248. In 1244–5 he was *tercius iudex* in lawsuits concerning the monasteries of Leyre and San Millán de la Cogolla: AC Valencia, doc. 1318 (Olmos, 190); *Reg. Inn. IV*, 444 (=AHN, 1407/9); Férotin, *Recueil des chartes de l'abbaye de Silos*, 189.
5 AHN, 3592/16. The date of Innocent's letter *Cum sicut* – 'Perusii, 2 non. julii anno 9' – may have been miscopied. Cf. Potthast, II, 1185, 1208.

absence of the Tarazona documentation, destroyed long ago, there are no means of knowing. More, however, may safely be claimed for the second of the trio, Ponce of Tortosa, who by 1239 had already been bishop for a quarter of a century, having survived both his chapter's attempt to oust him for simony and perjury in 1218–19, and his own request to be relieved of office in 1237.[1] In spite of his years, he was the most assiduous of Pedro's suffragans, attending all but one of the councils,[2] and possessing a good business brain, as he himself claimed in December 1252 when he instituted an annual *vestiarium* payment of 150 *solidi jaccenses* for each of the canons of Tortosa.[3] In February 1250 the archbishop gained *entrée* to his church when the chapter invited him and the bishop jointly to prepare an *ordinatio congrua* of their rents and rations; and although their deliberations centred largely on the question of cakes and ale, joints of meat and jugs of wine, it was at least possible to oblige the dignitaries of the chapter to publish their accounts twice yearly in imitation of John of Abbeville's Tarragona statute.[4] That, though, seems to have been the extent of Pedro's influence at Tortosa. The wider dissemination of reforming practices and the holding of synods there had to await Ponce's death, and even then progress was not made without an extremely bitter struggle.[5]

If the shortcomings of Ponce of Tortosa consisted in the very soundness of a pedestrian character long set in his ways, those of his namesake the bishop of Urgel, the third of the prelates who preceded and outlived the archbishop and whose election in 1230 had so concerned both John of Abbeville and Pedro himself, were truly spectacular. Since, however, Ponce's final decline occurred at the very end of Pedro's life, and because his destruction formed the crowning achievement of a hard core of episcopal reformers who shared the archbishop's views and owed their advancement to him, some account

---

[1] *VL*, v, 86–90; *Reg. Hon. III*, 1643; 2294; 2480 (MDH, 191; 259; 288).

[2] It was not until 1250 that he spoiled an unbroken record; and the 1250 Council was essentially a political assembly, summoned to excommunicate the king of Navarre: Tejada, VI, 47–8; Fita, *BRAH*, XL, 444.

[3] 'Attendentes quod redditus et proventus camere eiusdem ecclesie sunt per nos adeo augmentati': AC Tortosa, caj. *Común del Cabildo I*, 31. In 1270 the payment was increased to 170 *solidi: ibid.* 25.

[4] AC Tortosa, caj. *Del Camarero*, 12; caj. *Del Sacrista I*, 39 (27 July 1250).

[5] See Ch. 5 below. The earliest record of a Tortosa synod dates from 1274: *VL*, v, 283–4.

of the formation of this party must come before the description of the later career of the hapless bishop of Urgel.

The three sees of Huesca, Calahorra and Pamplona may be considered apart. Though, like the bishops of Tarazona, Tortosa and Urgel, both Vidal de Canellas of Huesca and Áznar Díaz of Calahorra were in charge of their sees in 1238, they fall into a different category. The former owed his promotion partly to Pedro (as bishop of Lérida), and, while he was not flawless, having infringed John of Abbeville's pluralism legislation,[1] the Bologna-trained lawyer who was one of King Jaime's closest advisers nevertheless found time to attend all but two of the archbishop's councils.[2] He remained on good terms with Pedro, who awarded him various churches by way of financial relief;[3] and he held synods, though no first-hand version of his synodal constitutions has survived.[4] More, however, is known about the synod which Bishop Áznar Díaz, a nephew of Rodrigo of Toledo, held at Logroño in April 1240, two years after his election.[5] Virtually every detail of the reform programme of John of Abbeville was included, though Áznar Díaz had missed Pedro's initial council of the previous year;[6] and special attention was accorded to clerical education: their income was guaranteed for three years to clerics who wished to study at the *escuelas generales*, Bologna, Paris, Toulouse or, more modestly, Calahorra itself.[7] On one item, though – concubinage – the bishop soft-pedalled. For though, in general terms, he insisted that his clergy 'vivan castamente e honestamente, segunt que mandan las constituciones de Letrán e las del Legado', he declined to invoke sentences of excommunication or suspension against them. Instead, he antici-

---

[1] AC Huesca, 2–317; publ. Arco, *BRABL*, VIII, 514.
[2] Arco, *BRABL*, VIII, 463 ff; *idem*, *BRABL*, IX, 221 ff.
[3] *Reg. Inn. IV,* 2703; 3240; AC Huesca, 6–189 (reg. Durán Gudiol, *AA*, VII, no. 75).
[4] His successor, Domingo de Sola, incorporated Vidal's constitutions in his own legislation: Ramón de Huesca, *Teatro histórico*, VI, 236. Vidal borrowed and quoted the constitutions of Bishop Vicente of Zaragoza's 1243 synod: AC Jaca, *Libro de la Cadena I*, fo. 1r. Cf. Arco, *BRABL*, IX, 89.
[5] *Reg. Greg. IX,* 3977; Hergueta, *RABM*, XVII, 415–16; Bujanda, *Episcopologio calagurritano*, 16.
[6] Tejada, VI. 30. The legislation is published by Bujanda, *Berceo*, I, 121 ff. It includes provisions concerning clerical dress (c. 12, 18–20, 33); pastoral responsibility; annual penance; knowledge of the *Pater Noster* and *Credo* (c. 4–5, 11, 13–14); pluralism (c. 25); tithes (c. 9, 32, 36, 38–42, 44); clerical involvement in secular affairs (c. 48–9); monastic seizure of parochial income (c. 43); and custody of the Sacrament (c. 51).
[7] *Ibid.* c. 31.

pated by eleven years Cardinal Gil's reassessment, substituting a fine of sixty *sueldos* and concentrating upon securing from priests' sons the undertaking that they would not conspire against his church, just as the archbishop of Compostela had done in 1229.[1] Not that Áznar Díaz was uniquely permissive: Pedro himself had departed from the legate's hard line in the previous year when he had visited Huesca and Vich.

Pedro's first opportunity to intervene in the appointment of a suffragan was provided by the death, in October 1238, of Bishop Pedro Remírez of Pamplona. The archbishop seized the chance and held a diocesan synod *sede vacante* at which the legate's sentences against pluralism were reiterated, and also, presumably, the rest of the reform programme.[2] On the emergence of two candidates for the see (which may have had some connexion with the claim of Rodrigo of Toledo that Pamplona was part of his province) Pedro opposed Guillermo de Oriz who, as a creature of Teobaldo I of Navarre, 'representaba la política de condescendencia, docilidad y servidumbre hacia la corona', and in December 1239 when the pope commissioned him and Rodrigo jointly to nominate a bishop, they chose Pedro Ximénez de Gazolaz, 'el Gregorio VII del episcopado pamplones', as he has been described, with some justice, on account of his sturdy defence of *libertas ecclesiastica*.[3]

Both Pedro Ximénez of Pamplona and Áznar Díaz of Calahorra were enthusiastic patrons of the Cistercians,[4] and their enthusiasm was shared by the archbishop whose affiliations with Poblet have led to

---

[1] *Ibid.* c. 15–16, 52; and c. 2, 6, 8, 17, 29.

[2] In the course of a hearing of the *Ordinatio Valentina* by Cardinal Otto of Porto at Lyons, 17 March 1246, the Tarragona proctor mentioned that 'archiepiscopus Tarraconensis celebravit synodum apud Pampilonam sede vacante de consensu capituli Pampilonensis' at which pluralists had been excommunicated 'iuxta constitutionem domini Sabinensis editam in concilio Ylerdensi': AC Toledo, X.2.K.1.12. It may be inferred from AHN, cod. 987B, fos. 171vb, 174vb, that the synod occurred before the provincial council of April 1239.

[3] *Reg. Greg. IX*, 5020 (the Register entry is written over an erasure); Goñi Gaztambide, *Príncipe de Viana*, XVIII, 95–7. The Toledo claim had been discussed at the Tours Council of 1163, and was certainly revived in 1244: *Chronica Roberti de Torigneio*, 219–20; AHA, *Index dels Indices*, fo. 31v.

[4] For the former's efforts to replace the Black Monks of Leyre with Cistercians, cf. Goñi Gaztambide, *Príncipe de Viana*, XVIII, 116 ff. In 1248 the General Chapter of the Order considered the latter's request 'de uno monacho et tribus conversis secum habendis': Canivez, *Statuta*, II, 329. Cf. also, Hergueta, *RABM*, XVII, 416.

the belief that he was a member of the Order himself. An important role – though a minor one – was played in Pedro's reforming campaign by the White Monks, for whose vitality all over the Peninsula there is evidence throughout the thirteenth century. For this was 'l'âge d'or du Cîteaux portugais',[1] and though, in the *Primera Partida*, Alfonso X dwelt upon their having been corrupted by wealth, he was none the less anxious that they should found a house at Seville.[2] In neither of these kingdoms can Pérez de Urbel's remark about the insignificance of the monastic contribution during this period[3] be applied to them. But it was in Aragon that their Indian summer proved most fruitful. In 1208 King Pedro II praised their 'astonishing virtues' and their attachment to 'true apostolic religion',[4] and twenty years later they struck John of Abbeville as the one hopeful feature of Aragonese monasticism. There was, he informed Gregory IX, no hope of salvation for the Cluniacs there *nisi ad Cisterciensem ordinem convertantur*.[5] Two new foundations were established in the Tarragona province in 1223–4, at Santa Fe and La Baix.[6] Pedro's most reputable episcopal colleague, Bernardo Calvó, was a member of the Order and had been abbot of Santas Creus before his promotion to the see of Vich.[7] And Pedro himself was the Order's special darling. In 1244 the General Chapter directed every monk to commemorate the archbishop of Tarragona during the Mass of the Holy Spirit. For his part, Pedro favoured the Cistercian style – implicitly, as in his instructions that the canons of Huesca and Vich should wear plain, simple garments, and explicitly in his *Summa Septem Sacramentorum* where he insisted that altar linen be kept 'munda et nitida...ad morem Cistercii'.[8] Two of his bishops were

[1] Cocheril, *SM*, I, 82; idem, *AEM*, I, 238–9.
[2] *Part.* 1.7.27 (Academy ed. I, 315): BM Add. MS. 20787, fos. 59rb-va; Canivez, III, 201 (ad an. 1280).
[3] 'La Reconquista avanza pero los monjes no tienen mucho empeño por descender hacia el sur': *Los monjes españoles*, II, 527. Cf. Cocheril, *Études sur le monachisme*, map after p. 440.
[4] Cit. Defourneaux, *Les Français en Espagne*, 52.
[5] RAH, MS. 9–24–5/4558, fo. 193v.
[6] Eydoux, *Cîteaux in de Nederlanden*, V, 175, whose list of foundations corrects that of Janauschek in *Originum Cisterciensium*, 299 ff. See also Cocheril, 372–6; Burns, I, 214 ff.
[7] Junyent, *Diplomatari de Sant Bernat Calvó*, XXXVIII.
[8] Canivez, II, 276; AC Barcelona, *Libro de la Cadena*, fo. 129ra.

Cistercians, and both were zealous pastors. His own successor at Lérida in April 1238, Raimundo de Ciscar, issued synodal legislation which, like the *Summa*, from a version of which it may have been derived, dealt fully with the administration of the sacraments and provided the diocesan clergy with ample information on the subject.[1] Vicente of Zaragoza – whose election was hastily confirmed at the Valencia Council of May 1240 – was equally enthusiastic. By March 1242, when the archbishop visited his diocese, he had held a synod, and before his death in 1244 he summoned at least one more.[2]

Yet although the Cistercians were Pedro's partners in the reforming enterprise, they were unquestionably only the junior partners. Their seniors were the Dominicans. Between 1225 and 1250 the Order of Preachers was the dominant force throughout the Western Church. In Aragon, though – where during the early 1230s heresy was rife[3] – they were warmly welcomed and actively encouraged by the archbishop. So were the Franciscans, and this was rare.

Pedro de Albalat's co-option of the friars stemmed directly from his close association with Raymond of Peñafort. There was a sort of spiritual relationship between them which may have owed something to their common patron, John of Abbeville.[4] During the year 1237, on Raymond's return from Rome to the Barcelona convent, broken in health after his work on the *Liber Extra*, the friar and the bishop of Lérida had been commissioned jointly to settle the succession in the sees of Mallorca, Huesca and Tortosa. But in the following

---

[1] Raimundo died at Lyons in 1247, *en route* for the General Chapter at Cîteaux, according to Finistres, II, 311.

[2] AA Zaragoza, 5/1/7: 'Item constat nobis per episcopum et per alios fidedignos quod clerici in sinodo fuerant amoniti ut in suis ecclesiis residerent'; Argáiz, II, 219r–v. For his election, see *Vida del...D. Felix Amat*, 158 (appendix); for the constitutions of the 1243 synod, Arco, *BRABL*, IX, 89.

[3] See Llorente, *Historia de la Inquisición*, I, 51–3; Lea, *History*, II, 162–6; Maisonneuve, *Études sur les origines*, 275–7. Archbishop Sparago expressed concern in 1230 and received assistance from the Carthusians: Tejada, VI, 28; *VL*, XIX, 310–11. Not even the Cistercians were above suspicion (Canivez, II, 159), and in Feb. 1235 King Jaime issued legislation on the subject: Tejada, III, 362–6 (the date of which cannot have been Feb. 1234, as in Tejada, since Guillermo de Mongrí was present as archbishop-elect: cf. *VL*, XIX, 180). In AA Zaragoza (1/2/2) there is an exemplar of Gregory IX's *capitula* of Feb. 1231 'contra hereticos et fautores heresum'. Cf. *Reg. Greg. IX, 539*; Maisonneuve, 245–6.

[4] Mortier, *Histoire des Maîtres Généraux*, I, 274–5.

year Raymond was elected Master General of his Order and, albeit reluctantly, he accepted the office some three months after Pedro's promotion to Tarragona. In 1240, though, he resigned at the Bologna General Chapter, and returned once more to Aragon. His association with the archbishop – who had already made plain his devotion to the friars – was revived, and almost immediately it bore fruit – appropriately enough, in Raymond's native city of Barcelona.[1]

Bishop Berenguer de Palou died at the end of August 1241, and in the ensuing election the thirty-two canons of Barcelona failed to agree on a successor, nine favouring the prior of the local Dominican convent of Santa Catalina, Berenguer de Castelbisbal, while the majority, twenty-two, opted for their sacrist, Pedro de Centelles. But the choice was not between a friar and a non-friar, for Pedro de Centelles had also fallen under the Dominican spell and had only recently promised to join the Order as soon as he could wind up his secular affairs. The election, therefore, came as something of an embarrassment to him, as he explained to the archbishop who visited Barcelona in mid-October. Pedro de Albalat thought very highly of the sacrist, and on the 15th wrote to the pope praising him to the skies and urging that in spite of his promise he be promoted to the see. But Gregory IX, unbeknown to the archbishop, had died almost eight weeks before, so that the three canons who were despatched to the Curia with letters from Pedro, King Jaime and others, were made to wait until June 1243 for the election of a pontiff to whom they might appeal. Then the Barcelona affair was one of the first items of accumulated business with which Innocent IV dealt. On 4 July the archbishop was instructed to proceed as he thought fit, and in mid-October 1243, in the presence of Raymond of Peñafort, the sacrist was clothed a Dominican by Pedro de Albalat and, with the assembled chapter, *quasi flentes*, chanting 'talem volumus vos habere, talem volumus vos habere', was confirmed as bishop of Barcelona.[2]

Pedro de Centelles was the first Dominican bishop south of the Pyrenees and is, therefore, something of a landmark. The date to

---

[1] *Ibid.* I, 276 ff.

[2] *VL,* XVII, 337–41; *Reg. Inn. IV,* 3; Puig y Puig, *Episcopologio de la sede barcinonense,* 200–2. The date of Bishop Berenguer's death is variously given, as 23 Aug., 24 Aug. and 1 Sept: Puig, 198; *VL,* XVII, 211, 337. The king's approval of Bishop Pedro had been withdrawn by Sept. 1244; ACA, Bulas, leg. VII–3 (reg. Miquel Rosell, *Regesta,* 112).

note, however, is not October 1243. It is October 1241. For Archbishop Pedro had not allowed the papal vacancy to delay the reform
of his province, and through him Dominican influence had been making itself felt at Barcelona during those two years. As at Pamplona in
1239, he seized the opportunity of holding a *sede vacante* synod at
Barcelona during his visit to investigate the election process in the
autumn of 1241. The synod – of 18 October 1241 – witnessed the
publication of two didactic tracts which together comprise Pedro de
Albalat's contribution to the history of the thirteenth-century
Spanish Church, and, individually, reflect the influence upon him of
Raymond of Peñafort.

The first is well enough known. It described the procedure for
dealing with heretics and is regarded as 'le premier document digne
du nom de manuel de procédure inquisitoriale'.[1] It was a business-
like guide, the sort of A.B.C. that Guillermo de Mongrí had asked
for when faced with the problem of apparent repentance on a large
scale six years earlier; and scholars have not hesitated in ascribing
authorship to St Raymond rather than to Pedro, the archbishop who
promulgated it.[2] Its form and content suggest that they are correct. No
such attention, however, has been given to the second tract published
on the same occasion as part of the synodal constitutions, and which
loomed at least as large as *le manuel de l'inquisiteur* in the Tarragona
province during the 1240s and 1250s: Pedro de Albalat's *Summa
Septem Sacramentorum*.

The *Summa*[3] was promulgated by Pedro both at Barcelona and in
his own archdiocese at a synod of uncertain date.[4] In the form in
which it was reissued, almost *verbatim,* by Pedro's brother Bishop
Andrés of Valencia in October 1258, it was published by Aguirre in

---

1 Dondaine, *AFP*, XVI, 96. The synod would seem the likeliest occasion for its
  publication. Douais published the document in *Moyen Âge,* III, 315–25, and dated it
  late 1241–early 1242; Lea, II, 167, and Maisonneuve, 287, favour 1242; and Valls i
  Taberner, *Obras selectas,* I, ii, 305, places it 'en la segunda mitad del año de 1241, o,
  acaso, en 1242'.
2 Douais, 313, and Lea, *loc. cit.,* suggest that it was a joint enterprise; Valls i Taberner,
  loc. cit., makes Raymond the outright author. For Guillermo's difficulties, see *Reg.
  Greg. IX,* 2531; Lea, 164.
3 Ed. Linehan, *HS,* XXII, 9 ff., *q.v.,* for description of the MSS. See also Linehan,
  Studies in Church History, VII, 101–11. References to the *Summa* in the following pages
  are to the copy in AC Barcelona, *Libro de la Cadena,* fos. 127ra–30va.
4 RAH, MS. 9–24–5/4558, fos. 171r–8v.

the eighteenth century.[1] The text used by Andrés was that of the Barcelona synod of October 1241, to which he adhered fairly closely.[2] Yet it cannot be asserted that the Barcelona version was the *editio princeps* of the *Summa*, for Andrés refers also to the 'tract's' having been issued by his brother at a Lérida synod, and it is not clear from the context whether Pedro was bishop of Lérida or archbishop of Tarragona at the time of the said synod. Moreover, the confusion has been further confounded by Aguirre who miscopied his Valencia MS.[3] So this Lérida synod must have occurred either during Pedro's episcopate, October 1236 to February 1238, or *sede vacante* after the death of Pedro's successor there, Raimundo de Ciscar, in 1247 or 1248. Now it is true that Pedro was accustomed to intervening in the affairs of the sees of his province during episcopal vacancies, as at Pamplona and Barcelona, and that he had a direct hand in the appointment of Raimundo de Ciscar's successor at Lérida.[4] Nevertheless, on balance, the later date would seem to be less likely than the other as the occasion of the synod mentioned by Andrés de Albalat – who in September 1248 was himself at Lérida, as a member of the Dominican community.[5] For by 1247–8 the diocese of Lérida had already received, from the late Bishop Raimundo, a sacramental treatise which compares favourably with Pedro's *Summa*.[6]

It compares favourably, and there many points of comparison since both Raimundo's statutes and the *Summa* owe the greater part of their material to that common source of so much of the synodal

---

1 *Collectio Maxima Conciliorum*, v, 197–202.
2 *Ibid*. 202: 'Ista mandavit dominus archiepiscopus Tarraconensis observari in synodo per eum celebrata in sede Barchinonensi, sede vacante, anno domini 1241 in die S. Lucae Evangelistae.' For variations in the Valencia version, see *ed. cit.*, HS, XXII. One of the more interesting is the reduction from three to two of the number of godparents permitted: a restriction designed to promote the growth of the Christian population on the frontier by minimising the bonds of spiritual affinity.
3 'Idem per omnia dicimus et sub eadem poena fieri mandamus de tractatu septem sacramentorum edito per venerabilem archiepisopum *praedecessorem dominum* P...Tarraconensis ecclesiae': BC Valencia, MS. 163 (cf. [Olmos, *Códices*, 122). Aguirre, v, 197, has *praedecessorem domini, viz.* Archbishop Sparago or Guillermo de Mongrí. I am grateful to Don Ramón Robles, canónigo archivero of Valencia, for verifying this point for me.
4 Cf. *VL*, XVI, 141–2, 308–10.
5 *Reg. Inn. IV*, 4172. The date of his profession is not known, but the Lérida convent was founded 'much before' 1230, according to Diago, *Historia de la Provincia de Aragón*, fo. 147v. Publ. *VL*, XVI, 297–308 (undated).

legislation of Western Europe at this period: the statutes attributed to Eudes de Sully, bishop of Paris (1196–1208).[1] Of the two, Raimundo's statutes appear to have followed the Paris statutes rather more closely than does the *Summa*, and to have introduced considerably less that was original.[2] But what is of greater interest here is that there are some grounds for arguing that Raimundo also had access to a version of the *Summa* which had been issued at the Lérida synod to which Andrés de Albalat referred in 1258. For while Raimundo's statutes and the *Summa* have in common a number of phrases which the Paris statutes lack,[3] the former do not contain the distinctive passages on the sacraments and patronage of the friars which appear in the 1241 *Summa*.[4] The Lérida statutes bear no date, but assuming that they were issued before 1241 – an assumption for which there is some support[5] – it may be suggested that they were based on an earlier version of the *Summa* promulgated by Pedro while he was bishop of Lérida – which we may identify as *Summa I* – and, further, that this version had incorporated Eudes de Sully's statutes without adding very much fresh material. Within this hypothesis the final section of the Lérida statutes – for almost all of which no parallel passages may be found either in the Paris statutes or in the *Summa* – would be regarded as comprising Bishop Raimundo's

---

[1] Cf. Cheney, *English Synodalia*, 55–6, 82–4; *idem, EHR*, LXXV, 1 ff.

[2] Of note, among the passages in Raimundo's statutes which figure neither in the Paris statutes nor in the *Summa*, is the chapter *De racionariis* which dealt with a particular local abuse – the lay prebendary: *VL*, XIV, 303. See above, p. 44.

[3] E.g. to the injunction that the sacrament be kept 'sub clave' (Paris, cap. v. 7 [*PL*. 212, 60C]), both add 'si fieri potest' (*Summa*, fo. 128vb; *VL*, XVI, 299); abstention 'ab omni peccato' rather than 'ab omni mortali' as condition of absolution (*Summa*, fo. 128ra; *VL*, XVI, 300. Cf. Paris, cap. VI. 8 [*PL*. 212, 61C]); annual rather than six-monthly synods (*Summa*, fo. 127rb; *VL*, XVI, 297. Cf. Paris, cap. II. 4 [*PL*. 212, 58C]).

[4] *Summa*, fos. 128rb, 130ra. There are many instances of verbal parallels between the Lérida statutes and the Paris statutes which do not occur in the *Summa*, and some instances of parallels between the *Summa* and the Paris statutes which do not occur in the Lérida statutes. E.g. – respectively – the obligation on the clergy to come to the synod 'et si gravi infirmitate detenti, aut alia necessitate *inevitabili*, venire non potuerint' to send their chaplains (Paris, cap. II. 6 [*PL*. 212, 59A]; *VL*, XVI, 297), but 'necessitate *canonica*' in *Summa*, fo. 127rb; the hearing of confession 'in spiritu lenitatis' in Paris, cap. VI. 3 [*PL*. 212, 61A]; *Summa*, fo. 127vb (actually 'in spiritu *levitatis*' in MS.), but 'in spiritu humilitatis' in *VL*, XVI, 300. But we may account for these apparent inconsistencies by assuming that both Raimundo and Pedro, independently, had the Paris statutes before them.

[5] Sáinz de Baranda, in *ES*, XLVII, 175, dates them 1240.

own original contribution.[1] But this *is* only a hypothesis. The terrain is notoriously difficult to negotiate; delusions are legion; a single manuscript as yet undiscovered might easily upset it entirely; and – most substantially – no manuscript of *Summa I* has been produced.

Leaving aside the putative *Summa I* we are on firmer ground with the *Summa* promulgated at Barcelona in October 1241, the earliest known example in the Spanish peninsula of the *liber sinodalis* which contemporaries regarded as the hallmark of an outstandingly zealous prelate.[2] In October 1261 the clergy of the diocese of Valencia were ordered to furnish themselves with copies of the *Summa* by the following Christmas,[3] and though neither the Barcelona nor the Tarragona version contains explicit proof that it had any such didactic purpose in those places, it may nonetheless be assumed that 'las escelentes constituciones sobre sacramentos, vida clerical, etc.' which Villanueva noticed at Barcelona but did not bother to analyse, were promulgated as such by Pedro himself.[4]

The *Summa* is not a strikingly original work. It is far from being a landmark in the literature of pastoral theology. Like the Lérida statutes, it leans heavily on Eudes de Sully, and such texts of the Fourth Lateran Council as are accorded mention are remembered not in the terminology of 1215 but in that of 1229 as they had been transmitted by John of Abbeville at the Lérida Council.[5] Yet though the content of the *Summa* was only very occasionally Pedro's own, positive credit may be given him for the pattern which he imposed on material not his own. It is the arrangement of the *Summa* that distinguishes it from its main source. Whereas the Lérida statutes had followed the Paris statutes indiscriminately and had departed from that model only in their pell-mell rearrangement of the jumble of miscellaneous *communia praecepta*,[6] the *Summa* conflates the old material,

---

[1] *VL*, XVI, 307–8. The injunction that each priest have 'unum manutergium...circa altare ad tergendum os et nares, si fuerit necesse' is, however, based on Eudes de Sully, *Communia praecepta*, 27. Cf. *PL*. 212, 65D.

[2] Artonne, *BEC*, CVIII, 71. See also Cheney, *Synodalia*, 40 ff.

[3] Aguirre, V, 206. [4] *VL*, XVII, 212.

[5] Fo. 128rb: 'Alioquin procedat in pena secundum formam concilii generalis, que talis est: Vivens arcebitur ab introitu ecclesie et moriens carebit *ecclesiastica* sepultura.' Cf. *IV* Lat. can. 21 and Conc. Lérida, can. 11 (*ES*, XLVIII, 314): 'et vivens ab ingressu ecclesiae arceatur, et moriens *christiana* [Lérida: *ecclesiastica*] careat sepultura'.

[6] E.g. the Lérida prohibition on priests who treat the annual synod as an occasion for an illicit holiday among the flesh-pots of the cathedral city appears (*felix culpa*!) in

introduces some that is new, stresses that which Pedro deemed in need of being stressed, and contrives a brief and orderly handbook containing a section on each of the seven sacraments – in a different sequence from that previously adopted – introduced by instructions *De ordinatione sinodi*, which depart hardly at all from Eudes de Sully; and followed by two further sections – *Qualiter Christiani orare debent*, based on nos 10 and 32 of the *communia praecepta*, and *De vita et honestate clericorum*, which also makes use of the *communia praecepta* as well as of additional fresh material. Even when the Paris statutes are most closely followed Pedro adapts them to his own requirements and sub-edits freely. Such is the case in the sections on Baptism, Confirmation and Extreme Unction. In the first, the lapidary sentences are shuffled; further details about godparents are supplied; it is explained that baptism by the child's parents is permitted (which neither the Paris nor the Lérida statutes had mentioned although the practice was tolerated elsewhere at an earlier date);[1] and provision for the baptism of an infant delivered by caesarean section – with which both the other sets of statutes had dealt[2] – is omitted. Further on, the special efficacy of Confirmation is stressed,[3] and the point is made that neither that sacrament nor Baptism was to be repeated, even if the Christian had meanwhile embraced the Jewish or Moorish faith – a problem of immediate concern for the parish clergy of Southern Aragon though not for those of Northern France. Likewise Pedro addresses himself to the sacrament of Extreme Unction since 'nichil in ecclesiis observabatur', and provides for the annual renewal of chrism by the parish priests.[4]

The Paris statutes constantly obtrude, but there are some passages in the *Summa* which, as far as that source is concerned, do seem to be original. The list of penances in the section *De Penitentia* and the quotation from the Fourth Lateran Council *via* John of Abbeville;[5] the description of the sacrament of Matrimony involving Pedro and

the section headed *De multis infortuniis quae eveniunt in celebrando: VL,* XVI, 305. Cf. Paris, *Communia praecepta,* 26 [*PL.* 212, 65C–D]. The Lérida statutes deal with the sacraments in the same order as the Paris statutes; the *Summa* adopts a different order

[1] E.g. Westminster, 1200, c. 3: D. Wilkins, *Concilia Magnae Brittaniae et Hiberniae,* I (London, 1737), 505; Canterbury I, 1213/14, c. 29: Powicke–Cheney, *Councils and Synods,* I, 31.

[2] *PL.* 212, 63D; *VL,* XVI, 303–4.   [3] *Summa,* fo. 127vb.

[4] Fo. 128va.   [5] Fos. 128ra, 128rb.

Berta;[1] certain passages on the Mass;[2] the liturgical instructions appended to the section *De vita et honestate clericorum*;[3] and the instructions regarding ordination:[4] for these Eudes de Sully offers no precedent. Were they, though, of Pedro de Albalat's own invention? Or did he derive them from some other contemporary source? There were many in circulation, and the question which immediately poses itself is whether the most celebrated of them all, Raymond of Peñafort's *Summa de Poenitentia,* is the missing link or one of the missing links. Certainly the same severely practical aim inspires both *Summae,* Raymond's and Pedro's. Both were compiled for the instruction of the clergy in the parish, and particularly in the parish confessional, rather than in the schools.[5] Pedro chose the same tag from St Jerome to preface his piece on Penance as did Raymond.[6] The friars are accorded special honour by Pedro and recommended as confessors.[7] And Raymond is known to have been at hand when Pedro's *Summa* was promulgated at Barcelona in 1241 and to have co-operated with the archbishop on the inquisitorial manual.

For all this, though – and, in truth, it does not amount to very much – it cannot reasonably be maintained that the archbishop's *Summa* must have been inspired by Raymond, except in the sense that Pedro and Raymond breathed the same air and shared the same pastoral concern. Apart from the passages on penance, Raymundian literature offers no obvious source for those few sections of the *Summa* which depart from Pedro's normal authority.[8] It is just possible that

---

[1] *Summa,* Fo. 129rb.

[2] Fos. 128vb–9ra. Here though, certain features of the Paris statutes have been incorporated, and others which had been incorporated in the Lérida statutes have been excluded. Spitting, for example, did not concern Pedro. Cf. *PL.* 212, 65D–6A; *VL,* xvi, 306 (the celebrant to abstain from spitting after his communion; 'sin autem in piscina suaviter spuatur').

[3] Fo. 130ra–b.   [4] Fo. 129va–b.

[5] *Summa de Poenitentia,* prologue *Ad lectorem*: '...ut si quando fratres ordinis nostri, vel alii circa judicium animarum in foro poenitentiali forsitan dubitaverint, per ipsius exercitium, tam in consiliis quam in judicibus, quaestiones multas et casus varios ac difficiles et perplexos valeant enodare'. See also Teetaert, *AST,* IV, 141 ff.; P. Michaud Quantin, 'A propos des premières Summae Confessorum', *RTAM,* xxvi (1959), 264–306; García y García, *REDC,* xviii, 238: 'no es un manual para las aulas universitarias, sino para los confesores'.

[6] *Summa,* fo. 127vb; *Summa de Poenitentia,* 1: 'Quia penitentia est secunda tabula post naufragium.'   [7] Fos. 128rb, 130ra.

[8] *Summa de Poenitentia,* 463–4, deals with the question of interrogation of the penitent

one of the verse *Summulae,* based on Raymond's work and in circulation by about the middle of the century, provided some of the material for the eucharistic section.[1] But it is highly implausible when the man himself was there, and furthermore, it is both pointless to speculate and graceless to imply that the archbishop – *Master* Pedro – was incapable of stringing together a series of fairly commonplace sentences without assistance, simply because he was surrounded by such a wealth of talent. What is both certain and important is that the archbishop was a friend of the canonist of and the Order, and that he sympathised with those developments in pastoral theology which, in the case of confession, considered the merits and personality of the sinner when it came to imposing a penance upon him.[2] For this approach, with its attention to *possibilitas* and associated concepts, was what distinguished Pedro de Albalat from the morality of the market-place enshrined in the old penitentials which Raymond of Peñafort, although fully aware of the difficulties involved, was in favour of abandoning.[3] Not that the Dominicans enjoyed a monopoly of this spirit of emancipation from the letter that killeth.[4] Still it was the Dominicans, rather than the well-scrubbed Cistercians, who were Pedro's main props – as may be seen by passing from the hazardous thickets of amateur textual criticism into the sunlit and more productive pastures of hard fact.

and satisfaction, and urges the priest to teach the penitent the basic Christian prayers. Cf. *Summa,* fos. 127vb–8ra, 129vb. But this material could equally well have been derived from Eudes de Sully: *PL.* 212, 60D–1A.

[1] See, for example, the verse *Summula* (Cologne, 1495, begins: '[S]ummula de Summa Raymundi prodiit ista: non ex subtili sed vili scribimus istam'), xxx(r) ff., on the procedure to be followed if the consecrated host is vomited; which problem also engaged St Raymond and Pedro de Albalat: *Summa de Poenitentia,* 476; *Summa,* fo. 129ra. Raymond's *Summa* was written in 1222–5 and revised in 1234–6 (see Kuttner in *ZSSR, kan. Abt.,* xxxix, 419 ff.), and it is not clear whether metrical versions were current as early as 1241. One of the earliest of these versions was the work of the Cistercian, Arnoul de Louvain, *c.* 1250: *Chronica Villariensis monasterii,* ed. G. Waitz, *MGH, Scriptores* xxv (Hanover, 1880), 208.

[2] *Summa,* fo. 128ra: 'in iniungendis penitentiis caveant sacerdotes quod secundum qualitatem culpe et possibilitatem confitentium eis iniungant...'.

[3] *Summa de Poenitentia,* 472–3, 478: 'et hanc ultimam opiniarem videtur amplecti consuetudo: prima tamen est tutior, licet difficilior.' For the morality of the market-place in contemporary Castile, see below, p. 319.

[4] It was present, for example, in the *Liber Poenitentialis* written soon after 1215 by the Victorine Pierre de Poitiers. See C. R. Cheney, 'La date de composition du "Liber Poenitentialis" attribué à Pierre de Poitiers', *RTAM,* ix (1937), 401–4.

By 1248 the province of Tarragona had five Dominican bishops, four of whom were closely associated with the convent of Santa Catalina at Barcelona, Raymond of Peñafort's base and the powerhouse of the Aragonese Church.[1] The year 1243, in which Pedro de Centelles was installed as bishop of Barcelona, saw also the death of the bishop of Vich, Bernardo Calvó, whose removal from the scene marked the end of an epoch. Though his personal sanctity was not in question, Bishop Bernardo had proved rather too other-worldly for the rough and tumble of a Catalan diocese, remaining so much of a Cistercian that he refused to make a will 'cum simus monachus',[2] and presiding with his high principles intact over the financial shipwreck of his see. In July 1242 the archbishop had gone bail for him when he had been unable to raise a thousand *solidi* in payment of the papal *quinta*.[3] He was succeeded by Bernardo de Mur, archdeacon of Tremp in the church of Urgel, a man who had studied at Bologna and who followed the example of Pedro de Centelles by becoming a Dominican, apparently soon after his election.[4] The neighbouring see of Gerona was the third to receive a Dominican bishop when in December 1245 the chapter chose Berenguer de Castelbisbal, the prior of Santa Catalina, who twice already had come within touching distance of a bishopric – as caretaker of Valencia before the dust had settled there in 1238, and as the beaten candidate at Barcelona in 1241.[5]

---

[1] Diago, *Historia de la Provincia de Aragón*, fo. 103r ff.; Denifle, *ALKG*, II, 202–3, 241–8; Kaeppeli, *AFP*, XXXVII, 47–80.

[2] *VL*, VII, 256–7; Junyent, 250 ff.

[3] Junyent, 238. In Jan. 1234 he was forced to borrow from Pedro Mironis and Raimundo de Cardona of Vich 'tria milia solidorum barcinonensium...ad solvendum pecuniam quam nos pro facto nostri et monasterii Rivipulli (Ripoll) debemus mercatoribus florentinis', which debt was due for repayment at Easter (12 April). By then his resources were slender, to judge by the security offered: 'equum Raymundi de Vallforti de pilo tag [?] et equum Bernardi de Plano de pilo nigro et mulam Peyroni...et nostram capellam et viginti quinque marchas argenti': AC Vich, 6–II–66. Pedro de Albalat had all the goods of the *mensa episcopalis* as security, and the debt to him was still unsettled in Dec. 1250: Junyent, 257; AC Vich, 6–III–5.

VL, VII, 33; Diago, fo. 109v. He had succeeded Ponce de Vilamur as archdeacon of Tremp on the latter's promotion to Urgel in 1230 (AC Vich, 6–II–77; 6–II–84): a reward, doubtless, for having withstood the efforts of the sacrist of Urgel to wean him from Ponce's party at the time of the election, 'cum si hoc faceret magnum commodum esset ipsius B. de Muro et posset semper facere quicquid vellet in ecclesia Urgellensi' – as Berenguer de Mediano remembered having heard the sacrist promise: AC Seo de Urgel, d.s.n. (cit. above, p. 56).   [5] *VL*, XIII, 174.

He was King Jaime's confessor, and in the year after his election he became something of a celebrity when he allowed his tongue to wag too freely and the king caused it to be cut out.[1] It is not known whether the archbishop was active in the promotion of the bishops of Vich and Gerona, but the capitular choice can hardly have displeased him, for when, in 1248, he was twice presented with an opportunity of appointing suffragans, a Dominican received the palm on each occasion. At Lérida, with the assistance of Raymond of Peñafort, he nominated Guillermo de Barberá, prior of Santa Catalina, to succeed his own successor. That was in March.[2] And seven months later when, on the translation of Arnaldo de Peralta to Zaragoza, the chapter of Valencia entrusted the appointment of a successor to him and two of their canons, stipulating that if it were to be an outsider then they must confine their choice to a short-list of nine, at the head of which was the archbishop's brother, Andrés de Albalat, Andrés it was who was selected.[3]

The promotion of Dominicans to these five sees reflected the extraordinary vitality of the Order. They were working wonders on the frontier.[4] It also provided a basis for further expansion. Berenguer of Gerona followed the archbishop's example by founding a convent in his own episcopal city.[5] But it was as pastoral bishops, as spearheads of reform, that the friars contributed most. At Barcelona a diocesan synod was held even before the election of Pedro de Centelles had been confirmed. On the feast of St Luke 1242 – the first anniversary of the archbishop's synod – the archdeacon issued a set of constitutions concerned mainly with annual confession and the detection of heresy.[6] Encouraging though this activity was, however, it was as nothing in comparison with that of Pedro de Centelles who in March 1244, within five months of his induction by the archbishop,

---

[1] *VL*, XIII, 175–7; *Reg. Inn. IV*, 1992. Matthew Paris got wind of the incident: *Chronica Majora*, IV, 578–9.   [2] *VL*, XVI, 141–2, 308–10.

[3] AC Valencia, doc. 1318 (reg. Olmos, *Pergaminos*, 190). The second and third names on the short-list, it may be noted, were both those of Cistercians – the abbots of Veruela and Benifazá.

[4] 'Propter terre novitatem et sacerdotum raritatem' (Bishop Ferrer's words in a charter of Nov. 1242 to the Order of the Sepulchre), there was plenty for them to do there; and plenty was done by very small numbers: AD Barcelona, Pergaminos de S. Ana, d.s.n; Burns, *Crusader Kingdom*, I, 174–5; *idem, Speculum*, XXXV, 346, 350.

[5] *VL*, XIII, 177–8; XIX, 311–12 ('ad instantiam et preces fratris Andreae de Albalato', Nov. 1248).   [6] AC Barcelona, *Libro de la Cadena*, fo. 133ra–b.

held a synod which dealt with the whole gamut of reform, and ordered the parochial clergy to secure copies of the statutes of John of Abbeville and of the archbishop and to have learnt them by the following June. In January 1245 he issued another lengthy set of synodal statutes in the same vein, and published new legislation of his own which dealt with a great variety of issues, amongst which were markets, pimps and prostitutes – particularly those who plied for hire in the streets, who were given eight days to pack their bags and leave.[1] *Clerici concubinarii* received short shrift, as was consistent, and were reminded of the legate's penalties – suspension and excommunication.[2] The same old problem engaged the attention of Bishop Guillermo of Lérida, though in his diocese a system of fines was introduced.[3] At Vich Bernardo de Mur concentrated upon liturgical matters,[4] and at Valencia Bishop Andrés managed to combine his activity in the royal chancery with his pastoral role by summoning various synods at which he waged a relentless if losing battle against clerics who drank more than was good for them, wore outrageous clothes, bequeathed church property to their children and grew their hair so that it covered their ears.[5] If, alone, Berenguer of Gerona failed to distinguish himself in one way or another, allowance must be made for him as a victim of royal persecution which (as he at least appears to have thought) coveted more of him than just his tongue.[6]

[1] Publ. *VL*, XVII, 341–50; but lacking the later part of the second synod, the constitutions of which are in AC Barcelona, *Libro de la Cadena*, fos. 132va–31a, *q.v.* for the prohibition on prostitutes and on the hiring of premises – *operatoria* – to them (fo. 132vb).

[2] *VL*, XVII, 346.

[3] *VL*, XVI, 311. Whether this was done before or after Cardinal Gil's decision of 1251 is not clear.

[4] AC Vich, cod. 147, fo. 1r–v (Feb. 1252). [5] Aguirre, V, 205 ff.

[6] Berenguer had taken refuge at the Curia by Nov. 1246, to judge by the endorsements on papal privileges in his favour which were renewed at that time (AE Gerona, 6/59; 6/60). He was neither present nor represented at the provincial council of April 1247 (Tejada, VI, 44). He died at Naples, still with the Curia, on 6 Feb. 1255, not 1254 – as Eubel, *Hierarchia*, I, 261, following *VL*, XIII, 178 – or 1264 – as Burns, I, 22. Cf. his will, publ. (and misdated) in *ES*, XLIV, 21, 277–9, and the *Libri Anniversariorum* of the Dominican convent of Gerona (which he founded) and of Barcelona: Garganta, *AIEG*, VI, 143; Alcalde, *Homenatge a Antoni Rubió i Lluch*, II, 529. The set of synodal statutes which are attributed to him by Pontich, *Synodales gerundenses*, 145–9; Villanueva, RAH, MS. 62 (9–19–4), sin. pag; and Merino and La Canal, *ES*, XLIV, 18–20, were in fact published by his successor, apparently for the first time, in Oct. 1257: Mansi, XXIII, 927–31.

At the Council of Lérida in 1229 John of Abbeville had ruled that the annual provincial council be held three weeks after Easter, on *Jubilate* Sunday, and the diocesan synod on the feast of St Luke, 18 October.[1] In general this rule was observed. But as regards the synod its inflexibility was a severe disadvantage, for when 18 October fell on a Sunday – as in 1243 and 1248 – it had the effect of depriving the faithful of their mass. Priests could not be in two places at once, in their parish churches and at the bishop's synod. In 1242 the archdeacon of Barcelona obeyed instructions to the letter, with the result that the diocesan clergy were away from their parishes at the weekend:[2] an arrangement which missed the point stressed in the *Summa* – that the people should not lack pastoral care and the sacraments.[3] The synod was planned to last three days, according to the provincial formulary which seems to belong to this period;[4] and since, as the Lérida statutes testify, there was a tendency for clerics to make something of a holiday of it,[5] John of Abbeville's directive was normally modified in order to avoid such a clash.[6]

The pastoral consequences of holding the provincial council on a Sunday were far less serious, and with one exception – the council of January 1244 or 1245[7] – Pedro de Albalat adhered to the legate's

---

[1] *ES*, xlviii, 309.

[2] 18 Oct. 1242 being a Saturday: AC Barcelona, *Libro de la Cadena*, fo. 133ra.

[3] *Summa*, fo. 130ra.

[4] *Forma de sancta sinodo celebranda*: AC Gerona, *Llibre Vert*, fo. 300r; AC Barcelona, *Libro de la Cadena*, fo. 46rb.

[5] '...ne nimis festinent venire Ilerdam occasione synodi, nec magnam faciant moram sic se visitando et reficiendo tam in via quam in civitate': *VL*, xvi, 305. See also *Summa*, fo. 127rb.

[6] At Valencia the synod was held 'tertia feria post festum S. Lucae' in 1255, 1258, 1261 and 1262: Aguirre, v, 197, 205–6. At Gerona 'synodus semper celebretur in IV feria ante festum B. Lucae': Mansi, xxiii, 931. For practice elsewhere, and further literature, see Cheney, *Synodalia*, 15–19.

[7] Valls i Taberner, *AST*, xi, 258, maintains that the council which Tejada, vi, 39–41, dates 12 Jan. 1244, occurred in fact in Jan. 1245. There is evidence both for and against this revision. In Dec. 1251 the abbot and convent of Veruela referred to its constitution *Cum quidem* (against lay aggression on ecclesiastics) as 'constitutionem editam apud Tarrachonam in concilio provinciali ... prid. id. januarii anno domini mccxxxxiiii', i.e. 1245: AHN, 3767/14. However, when, sometime in the period 1309–15, the chapter of Valencia acquired authorised copies ('scriptis et registratis in registro domini Tarraconensis archiepiscopi') of both *Cum quidem* and *Olim excommunicasse* (May 1246: Tejada, vi, 43), the former was said to have been issued 'in quinto concilio Tarraconensi celebrato anno domini millesimo ducentesimo

ruling until the year 1247. The council too was a three-day affair, and in accordance with the provincial formulary the conciliar statutes were issued on either the Monday or the Tuesday after *Jubilate* Sunday[1] down to 1247, when for entirely practical reasons, the customary date was shifted back six weeks. Three weeks after Easter was also the date of the Tarragona fair, and the cathedral city simply lacked sufficient accommodation to cope with both events at the same time. So the council was moved.[2]

During the last four years of his life Pedro's provincial councils seem to have been less concerned with the issue of reform upon which his earlier assemblies had concentrated. At least no such constitution has survived from these years.[3] But this apparent interruption does not imply any cooling of enthusiasm or hardening of the arteries. Quite the contrary, it is an indication of Pedro's achievement. By 1247–8 the inheritance which he had received from John of Abbeville could be passed on with confidence to the new trustees, the bishops of the province, whose own testing time came in July 1251 when the death of their master exposed them to an entirely different climate. That climate and their performance are considered in the following chapter.

quadragesimo tertio, prid. id januarii', i.e. 1244: AC Valencia, doc. 8987 (reg. Olmos, *Pergaminos*, 127, misdated). To whichever year it belonged there must have been some special reason for holding a council in the unaccustomed month of January. The reason may have been royal taxation of the church, and in this regard there is support for the earlier date, 1244, in Innocent IV's letter of May 1244 reprimanding King Jaime for demanding *monetagium* from the Aragonese Church, 'licet idem archiepiscopus (Pedro de Albalat) affectatis sibi quibusdam suffraganeis suis' had urged him not to do so: ACA, Bulas, leg. VII–I (reg. Miquel, 110).

1 Monday 18 April 1239; Tuesday 8 May 1240; Tuesday 13 May 1242; Tuesday 5 May 1243; Tuesday 1 May 1246; Monday 22 April 1247: Tejada, VI, 29 ff.; *Qualiter debeat celebrari concilium Tarraconense*: AC Gerona, *Llibre Vert*, fo. 300v; AC Barcelona, *Libro de la Cadena*, fo. 46rb. A second assembly was held in the year 1240: the hearing of the appeal of the twelve priests of Gerona was postponed from 30 July to 16 Aug. 'propter absentiam domini episcopi qui oportuit in Ylerdam ad concilium sive colloquium ibidem celebrari': AC Gerona, *Causa del Any* 1240, fo. 26ra. But nothing further is known of this meeting.

2 Tejada, VI, 45; Fita, *BRAH*, XL, 445.

3 For the political nature of the post-1247 councils, see Fita, *BRAH*, XL, 446 ff., and below, p. 119.

Chapter 5

TARRAGONA AFTER
PEDRO DE ALBALAT

On the very day of Pedro de Albalat's death, two of his orphaned suffragans, the Dominicans Andrés of Valencia and Guillermo of Lérida had a copy made of Innocent IV's letter *Tua nobis*, of 28 August 1248, which had granted the archbishop permission to establish a number of chaplaincies out of the profits of his successful estate management.[1] It was a wise precaution on their part, for the immediate future was to witness the triumph of forces who had little sympathy with Pedro and his objectives, as Andrés and Guillermo already had cause to know.

Still, Pedro's episcopal friends did not fade away at their master's demise. They were made of sterner stuff than that, and mounted a spirited rearguard action in defence of the cause which he had promoted. For example, and in contrast to the Galician prelates, the Aragonese bishops showed no unseemly haste in taking advantage of the more permissive attitude to concubinage which had received papal blessing only a month before Pedro's death. The archbishop may have regarded the problem as one best left to the discretion of each diocesan bishop, but in his public, conciliar pronouncements he had invariably identified himself with John of Abbeville's hard line,[2] and it was evidently in that light that he was remembered by those suffragans who hesitated to commute the penalties against concubinage which the legate had prescribed. For some twenty years their devotion to his memory proved stronger than the temptation to

---

[1] 'Tam per emptionis titulum quam per industriam tui': AHN, sellos, 65/23. The document was formerly in the archive of Poblet where Pedro was buried on the following day, 3 July 1251.

[2] Conc. Tarragona I (1239), c. 1–2; VI (1246), c. 1: Tejada y Ramiro, *Colección*, VI, 30, 42; *Summa Septem Sacramentorum*, fo. 129vb. The clergy, however, were not dismayed even by these resounding prohibitions. In AC Barcelona, *Constitutiones Synodales et Provinciales*, fo. 183r, this passage of the *Summa* is glossed: 'Nota que mulieres permittuntur habitare cum sacerdotibus.'

adopt the new régime for financial reasons. Guillermo of Lérida's imposition of a fine on the offenders, sometime before 1254, seems to have been an additional, not an alternative, deterrent.[1] Andrés of Valencia continued the campaign until 1268, and even then he did not formally renounce the use of spiritual penalties.[2] The earliest instance of commutation on the basis of Cardinal Gil's ruling appears to have occurred at Barcelona in July 1276 when Arnaldo de Gurb, the successor of Pedro de Centelles, adopted as the normal penalty for beneficed clergy of his diocese the confiscation of one year's income.[3]

It was probably fiscal considerations that drove Bishop Arnaldo to take this step. He had recently built a chapel near his palace, *opere non modicum sumptuoso*, as Bishop Aymo of Vercelli's indulgence to him, granted at Lyons *in concilio generali*, was careful to emphasise;[4] and his provision of cut-price authenticated copies of Gregory X's solemn bull for the Cistercian Order, *In vestitu deaurato*, which both Poblet and Veruela acquired,[5] points to his need for funds at this time. Gradually, other bishops followed his lead, perhaps for similar reasons. The bishop of Tortosa, Arnaldo de Jardino, relented in 1278,[6] and Pedro de Urgel did likewise eight years later – although even after that the bishops of Urgel occasionally revived the legatine penalties.[7] Practice varied from diocese to diocese, since it was left to each bishop either to choose the line of least resistance or to reject it. Thus, while the clergy of Calahorra had been permitted to enjoy themselves, at a price, eleven years before Cardinal Gil's ruling, those

1 *VL*, XVI, 311.
2 Aguirre, *Collectio maxima conciliorum*, V, 208. Six years before, in weary tones, he had excommunicated clergy who bequeathed church property to their children, 'quos debent prorsus a se abiicere, si ordinis honestatem attenderent': *ibid.* 207. Cf. Lea, *Sacerdotal Celibacy*, 309–10.
3 AC Barcelona, *Libro de la Cadena*, fo. 134rb.
4 AC Barcelona, *Diversarum B*, 883 (10 July 1274). On 14 Oct. following, Gregory X contributed a papal indulgence: bull *Solet annuere*: AC Barcelona, *Diversarum B*, 580.
5 AHN, 2283/1, 3769/2: both copies were made at Montpellier on 19 June 1275, only two months after the original issue of the bull. Cf. Potthast, 21020.
6 *VL*, V, 286.
7 *Ibid.* XI, 291–2. Both Pedro and his predecessor Abril had enforced the legate's sentences since 1258. In Nov. 1297 Bishop Guillermo de Moncada, O.P. declared an amnesty and remitted all fines due from *clerici concubinarii* in the deanery of Urgel, but reintroduced suspension as a penalty for future transgressors who were exhorted 'ad frugem melioris vite totaliter se convertant': AC Seo de Urgel, *Registro episcopal fragmentario*, fo. 5.

of Pamplona were made to wait until the late 1270s, when the cost of the French invasion of his cathedral city forced Bishop Miguel's hand,[1] and those of Vich until the first decade of the fourteenth century.[2] Pedro de Albalat cast a long shadow.

Nevertheless, his death was an immediate disaster for the reformers, for it led to the emergence of one of Pedro's old adversaries as a candidate for the succession. Benito de Rocaberti had been chamberlain of Tarragona at the time of Pedro's promotion,[3] but the two men soon fell out, ostensibly on account of Benito's refusal to pay the canons the *vestiarium* in accordance with John of Abbeville's statutes. Deprived of his office by the archbishop, he travelled to the papal Curia, not for the first time, and ingratiated himself with Innocent IV who lent him his support against Pedro and, on 1 October 1248, confirmed him in his office and possession of the *castrum de Reddis* and other property which Guillermo de Mongrí had granted him.[4] On that occasion Pedro had retaliated by declaring him *ipso facto* excommunicate exactly four weeks later;[5] but knowledge of the strength of his support at the Curia must have filled the remnants of Pedro's party with considerable alarm when the chapter and suffragan bishops met at Tarragona to elect a successor in August 1251. According to the incomplete record of that meeting, Andrés of Valencia gave Benito his vote – an improbable departure in any circumstances, and quite impossible to reconcile with the objection to him on two counts, of adultery *et quedam alia objecta*, which Andrés and the bishops of Lérida and Zaragoza, Guillermo and Arnaldo, proceeded to submit to Innocent IV.[6] Innocent, however, either could not or would not find fault with Benito. In January 1252, as prelude to his final decision, he removed the bar on episcopal promotion which

---

[1] AC Pamplona, E 31–2 (reg. Goñi Gaztambide, *Catálogo*, 713), instructing the church's proctor at the Curia to request grants of dispensation from the legate's sentences against both *clerici concubinarii* and pluralists.

[2] AC Vich, cod. 220, fos. 28r–v, 43v–4r (in 1307).

[3] *Reg. Greg. IX*, 3100; Capdevila, *Seu de Tarragona*, 151.

[4] *Reg. Greg. IX*, 5986; *Reg. Inn. IV*, 487, 4140. He had paid an earlier visit to the Curia in Sept. 1232, when Gregory IX had legitimised him: *Reg. Greg. IX*, 869. By July 1248 he was a member of Cardinal Gil's *familia*, and witnessed the settlement of the Gerona dispute at Lyons: AC Gerona, d.s.n.

[5] AHA, *Thesaurus*, fos. 497–8.

[6] *VL*, xix, 259–62; *Reg. Inn. IV*, 5675. Andrés was at the Curia on royal business in Feb. 1252: ACA, Bulas, leg. XII–65 (reg. Miquel Rosell, *Regesta*, 174).

Gregory IX's legitimisation of the chamberlain had contained. A month later he referred the election back to the chapter, and, in April, dismissed the accusations of the three bishops and turned a blind pontifical eye on any flaw which might technically have vitiated the process of election.[1] By the middle of May 1252 Benito de Rocaberti was archbishop of Tarragona.[2]

The succession at Tarragona was symbolic of changes in the Church at large: 'a stormy spring passes straight into winter'.[3] But no contemporary critic engaged in solving the fascinating problem *Utrum ecclesia melius regeretur per bonum iuristam quam per bonum theologum*[4] could have found better material than in the contrast between Pedro and Benito. Moreover, the circumstances of his election and the support that he received from Innocent IV identify Benito as the worldly-wise man of affairs who, according to Marsilio of Padua, had prospered at the expense of the godly and with the assistance of the papacy, and had dragged the Church into a state of spiritual decay.[5] Not that the rebarbative Benito was an invariably 'useful' servant of the papacy. During his sixteen years as archbishop he was locked in constant combat with his chapter, while the papal nuncio who was commissioned to restore peace to Tarragona was led by his experience of Benito to the conclusion that Spaniards were quite impossible to deal with.[6] Much of his sixteen years was spent at the papal Curia in the prosecution of his endless lawsuits. Pedro's mainstay, the Dominicans, found no favour with

---

[1] *Reg. Inn. IV*, 5553–4, 5675.

[2] The election was confirmed on 15 May by the archbishop of Narbonne and his colleagues, in accordance with Innocent's instructions of 12 Feb.: Capdevila, *BAT*, LII, 183; *Reg. Inn. IV*, 5555. Villanueva misdated this letter and, knowing nothing of the last-ditch stand of the three bishops, believed that Benito was archbishop-elect in the previous August. However, on 29 April 1252, Benito was still addressed as *camerario Tarraconensi* by the pope: *VL*, XIX, 186; *Reg. Inn. IV*, 5675.

[3] Beryl Smalley, reviewing Barraclough, *The Medieval Papacy*, in *History*, LIV (1969), 259.

[4] For this *quaestio* of Galfridus de Fontibus, see Glorieux, *Bibliothèque Thomiste*, V, 162.

[5] 'Hos enim tamquam utiles dignificat Romanus pontifex et ecclesie defensores, qui pro temporalibus conservandis vel amplius usurpandis contendere norunt, sacre vero theologie doctoribus tamquam inutilibus reiectis ab eo. "Simplices enim sunt" ut inquit ille cum suorum cardinalium cetu, "et ecclesiam dilapidari sinerent"': *Defensor Pacis*, II, xxiv, 7.

[6] Blanch, *Arxiepiscopologi de Tarragona*, I, 159 ff.; Morera Llauradó, *Tarragona cristiana*, II, 289 ff.

him. They were replaced by the Franciscans,[1] and in common with the rest of the reform party were immediately exposed to the spite of their new father in God.

The significance of the *volte face* of 1252 was very soon brought home to the reform party by Benito's evident sympathy for that persistent villain of the piece, Bishop Ponce of Urgel, the prelate whose election had been witnessed by Pedro de Albalat in 1230 and whose subsequent career had proved such a grave disappointment to the archbishop and his friends. They had had high hopes of him and had greeted his election as marking the revival of his diocese 'tam in temporalibus quam in spiritualibus'. Instead, however, the Counts of Foix had continued to thrive and heresy to flourish,[2] and by 1251, when his chapter sent a deputation to complain about him to the pope, Bishop Ponce had dug his own grave. For the list of charges which they bore with them to the Curia indicated that what he lacked in moral qualities he made up for in stamina. He was, it was claimed, a murderer and *deflorator virginum*, the father of ten children amongst whom church property had been distributed. He had slept both with his sister and his cousin, had forged money, squandered the resources of his diocese, *e moltes altres coses*:[3] stirring stuff, and not unsupported. Ponce's other enemies weighed in too. The Count of Foix provided some pretty damning detail concerning the man of peace by whom he had been persecuted *utroque gladio*.[4] The archdeacon of Aristot recalled that for the last twenty years Ponce had exacted heavy procurations, without ever once visiting his church.[5] The clergy of Lilia complained that, with Ponce's connivance, their provost had stripped the place bare, reduced them to a diet of bread and water which not even the Lenten season had rendered palatable, and had then disappeared 'on crusade'.[6] Most damaging, however, were the letters of Pedro de Albalat – *dels fals Archebisbe que è mort*, as

---

[1] Capdevila, *Franciscalia*, 39 ff.
[2] Menéndez y Pelayo, *Historia de los heterodoxos*, I, 525–8; Miret y Sans, *Investigación histórica sobre el vizcondado de Castellbó*, 207–12. For further details, see Linehan, *AEM*, forthcoming.
[3] *Reg. Inn. IV*, 5592; *VL*, XI, 221–3.
[4] *VL*, XI, 226–7.
[5] AC Seo de Urgel, d.s.n. Ponce had expected the archdeacon to entertain thirty horsemen (12 Aug. 1251).
[6] AC Seo de Urgel, Col·lecció Plandolít.

Ponce's proctor called him – whose councils Ponce had neglected to attend, and who now opined that the church of Urgel was in need of reform both in head and members.[1]

But because by the time that these letters were presented at the Curia Pedro was dead, Ponce's chances of riding out the storm were markedly improved, and it was only by dint of strenuous activity behind the scenes that Andrés de Albalat and his associates (already heavily engaged in their hopeless resistance to Benito's promotion) succeeded in having the case referred to Raymond of Peñafort and the minister of the Aragonese Franciscans.[2] In the light of their findings, the papal auditor, Cardinal Stephen of Palestrina, suspended Ponce and on 15 December 1254 informed the new archbishop of Tarragona of his decision.[3] Benito, however, had a mind of his own, and was not prepared to brook interference in the running of his diocese from his predecessor's associates. So when Raymond called on him to flush Ponce out of Urgel and to superintend the religious settlement there, he refused at first to co-operate, taking refuge beneath several layers of legalistic scruple and alleging a most uncharacteristic concern for the rights of others.

Raymond of Peñafort was now in his eighties, but his was still a name to conjure with. He was quite capable of coping with jumped-

---

[1] *VL*, xi, 221. Ponce had not attended a provincial council since 1242: Tejada, vi, 34.
[2] Ponce's proctor's description of the torrid reception given to the canons of Urgel on their arrival at Perugia in Nov. 1251 is printed in *VL*, xi, 221-2. But Villanueva was wrong to deny that *lo Bispe de Valencia* who assisted them was Andrés de Albalat: 'No sé de qué Valencia seria este obispo, pero es cierto que no era el de la del Cid': *ibid.* 83n. Among other churchmen whom the proctor mentioned as having declared against Ponce were the sacrist of Gerona, Guillermo de Mongrí, who as archbishop-elect of Tarragona had attempted to deal with the heretics of Urgel (AC Seo de Urgel, *Dotium sive dotaliarum ecclesie Urgellensis liber secundus*, fo. 71v); and Ponce's own nephew, the proctor of the bishop of Zaragoza, Arnaldo de Peralta. Arnaldo, a member of the anti-Benito faction, had been translated to Zaragoza from Valencia in 1248. Though not himself a Dominican, he was a great patron both of that Order and of the Poor Clares: Sanchis Sivera, *BRAH*, LXXXII, 40 ff.; Ruiz de Larrinaga, *AIA*, IX, 372.
[3] AHA, *Cartoral AB*, fo. 16r: confirmed by Alexander IV on 7 Jan. 1255: *Reg. Alex. IV*, 93. Villanueva suspected that the commission to Raymond of Peñafort (*Reg. Inn. IV*, 5592) bore no fruit, and has been followed by Valls i Taberner: *VL*, xi, 85; *Obras selectas*, i, ii, 292-3. There is, however, positive proof that Raymond and his colleagues came to Urgel 'prosequentes factum inquisitionis impetrate a sede apostolica contra D. Poncium' in a document recording their expenses on that occasion: AC Seo de Urgel, Col·lecció Plandolít (Nov. 1255).

up archbishops, and Benito was soon brought into line.[1] Still, by his guarded assistance to the unspeakable Ponce, he had proved that the fears of the reformers about the consequences of his promotion were fully justified. And there were other issues. No sooner was his election confirmed than he set off for the Curia to do battle with Andrés de Albalat, claiming jurisdiction over the churches of Jérica and Santa Tecla, Játiva, both of which were already at issue between the sees of Valencia and Segorbe.[2] Nor was it any relief to them that on his return from Italy in April 1253 he summoned a council. For Benito's council was not designed to continue the activity of Pedro de Albalat. Indeed, his view was that there was too much legislation – a view which, in time, would recommend itself to other Spanish prelates[3] – and so, having confirmed in the most perfunctory manner the constitutions of Innocent III, Innocent IV, John of Abbeville and Pedro *en bloc*, he addressed himself to what seems to have been the main object of the exercise, namely the publication and implementation of the cache of papal privileges which he had brought back from the Curia and which empowered him – at a price, no doubt – to absolve pluralists, heretics, *clerici concubinarii*, papal subsidy-dodgers, supporters of Frederick II, traders with the Saracens, and other miscreants, and to dispose of various benefices, collation to which had devolved to the Roman Church.[4]

While at the Curia, Benito had received permission to retain for the next two years the income of the *cameraria* of Tarragona.[5] But

---

[1] The Raymond–Benito correspondence is in *VL*, XI, 231–6. Raymond's remark that Ponce 'nec exemplo praedicavit sufficienter nec verbo' (p. 236) recalls the language of Pedro de Albalat's *Summa*, fo. 128rb. In addition it may be noted that a nephew of Raymond served the chapter of Tarragona as one of their proctors in their struggle against Benito: Blanch, I, 161.

[2] Two letters, both beginning *Venerabilis frater*, 30 Nov. 1251: AHA, *Cartoral AB*, fo. 10v–11r. Cf. Burns, *Crusader Kingdom*, I, 49 ff. The outcome of the dispute is not recorded, but in May 1259 'Bernardus Dominici presbiter de Xerica' was one of the archbishop's household clerks: *Cartoral AB*, fo. 36v.

[3] 'Consideratione habita diligenti quod constitutionum pluralitas non solum confussionem sed etiam animarum periculum plerumque inducit dum ea quae constituuntur non observantur debita reverentia et legitime ut deceret, constitutiones de novo aliquas edere noluimus in presenti': Tejada, VI, 50; below, p. 310.

[4] *Ibid.* 51. Twenty-two acts containing these privileges, all of November–December 1252, were copied into Benito's cartulary: AHA, *Cartoral AB*, fos. 8r, 9v–11v, 33r–v. Some were registered: *Reg. Inn. IV*, 6111–14, 6120–1, 6146.

[5] *Ante promotionem*, 2 Dec. 1252: AHA, *Cartoral AB*, fo. 33r.

this did not satisfy him, and in September 1253 he entered a claim for back-payment from that source in respect of the period during which he had been suspended from the office of chamberlain by Archbishop Pedro. He even had the effrontery to maintain that his predecessor had desired nothing more than that he should receive the full income of the *cameraria*.[1] But Benito was adept at distorting established facts and shifting responsibility on to others. By withholding payment of the *vestiarium* from the canons of Tarragona during the 1240s he had been foremost in obstructing John of Abbeville's reforms there. Yet in December 1255 he insisted that it was the canons who were guilty of the monstrous crime of resisting the legate's 'statuta salubria et honesta'.[2]

His truculent nature poisoned relations with his suffragans also, as a document in the archive of Tortosa Cathedral records. It dates from October 1254 and takes the form of an appeal sent to Innocent IV by the canons of Tortosa who, having, at long last, been relieved of Bishop Ponce,[3] were naturally depressed at the prospect of having one of the archbishop's friends foisted upon them. Their long and detailed account of negotiations during the previous few weeks was not flattering to Benito who, according to them, had employed a mixture of brute force and low cunning in his dealings. In at Ponce's death, he had immediately urged them to elect a successor *de consilio vestro*;[4] and when they resisted, had warned them, *provocatus et commotus*, that there was no escaping him, since however correctly they might proceed they would have to apply to him for confirmation of their choice, and he had no intention of approving any of their own number.[5] They refused to be cowed, though, and chose the archdeacon, Bernardo de Olivella. Thereupon Benito sent a couple of his cronies, canons of Tarragona, down to Tortosa where

---

[1] At a hearing before Cardinal Gil Torres, Perugia, 4 Sept. 1253: AHA, *Cartoral AB*, fo. 12r. Benito's scribe may have miscopied the date. It should perhaps be September 1252, for on that day of 1253 the Curia was at Assisi.

[2] *Petitio venerabilis*, 15 Dec. 1255: AHA, *Cartoral AB*, fo. 36v.

[3] He had died on 29 Aug.: *VL*, v, 89. Neither Villanueva nor Bayerri Bertomeu, *Historia de Tortosa*, VII, 395, mentions the following incident.

[4] AC Tortosa, caj. *Del Arcediano Mayor II*, 29. Their appeal is addressed to Benito.

[5] *Ibid.*: '"Ipsa electio saltem per confirmationem habet per nos transire [they reported him as saying]. Et vix fiet per vos adeo canonica vel justa quod si voluerimus possumus eam cassare." Et dixistis et asseruistis quod nullo modo confirmaretis electionem si eam faceremus de aliqua persona ecclesie nostre.'

they quizzed all and sundry, whether electors or not, in the hope of trapping someone into an indiscretion. Later, when this manoeuvre had failed and Bishop Arnaldo of Barcelona had the temerity to intervene in the cause of fair play – *propter Deum et gratiam ipsius* – Benito proved quite conclusively that he lacked all of the finer feelings. With a look of fury on his face, he clapped spurs to the unfortunate mule upon which he was mounted, let fly a volley of oaths (which the appellants declined to set down, retaining them for the time when to recount them would do him most damage) and declared, more or less, that if Bernardo got Tortosa it would be over his dead body.[1]

In fact, Bernardo did get Tortosa, and without inflicting any physical damage on the archbishop. First, though, he had to negotiate a further obstacle. For Benito cussing from the saddle was only half the picture. When bullying failed and the chapter forwarded its appeal to the pope, Benito had recourse to another means of achieving his end: the law.

Benito's cartulary is a copy-book of documents which served him in his many battles, with the chapter, the king and others, and it contains no dross. So, at first sight, it is strange that it should contain a copy of Bishop Enrico of Bologna's declaration of 1238 excommunicating regular clergy who failed to wear the religious habit while they were at the Schools.[2] Yet this entry is very far from being an exception to that rule of selection which governed the choice of pieces for inclusion, for it provided Benito with an alternative means of excluding Bernardo de Olivella from the see of Tortosa. While he had been studying at Bologna Bernardo had been ignorant of this regulation – or so he claimed when he presented his case to the newly elected Alexander IV. Moreover, he alleged, he had since been absolved by the late bishop of Tortosa's penitentiary. Accordingly, in January 1255, the pope referred the matter for a decision to the prior of the Barcelona Dominicans,[3] and the outcome was evidently

---

[1] *Ibid.*: 'Vos, provocatus et valde commotus, dixistis, asseruistis et affirmastis, stricto repente cum quodam impetu calcaribus mulo quem equitabatis, vultu valde turbato, provocatus et commotus jurastis per Deum et sanctam ecclesiam, votum etiam emittendo et alia verba turpissima dicendo que reservamus suo loco et tempore probare coram judice competenti, quod *a dret ne a tort* dictus electus aliqua ratione non haberet episcopatum predictum quantumcumque homo faceret ibi totum suum posse...'

[2] AHA, *Cartoral AB*, fo. 16v.

[3] *Reg. Alex. IV*, 55: publ. Ripoll, *Bullarium*, I, 269–70.

favourable to Bernardo since, despite the foul means and fair employed by the archbishop, it was he who succeeded to the see of Tortosa later that year, and seventeen years after, following Benito's death and a lengthy vacancy, replaced his old adversary as leader of the Aragonese Church.[1]

It was no coincidence that this, the archbishop's first major reverse, followed hard upon the death of Innocent IV and the election of Alexander IV in December 1254. During Innocent's lifetime nothing had been denied to Benito, but Alexander disapproved of many of the recent developments in Church government and Benito was the very type of Innocentian promotion to whom he took the most particular exception.[2] It was a bad time for Benito to lose friends, for he was adding to his list of enemies all the while. By 1255 he had set King Jaime against him, and in the March of that year the monarch wrote to the pope from Tortosa, complaining bitterly about him and marvelling that the government of thirteen bishoprics should ever have been entrusted to one whose incompetence had been an open secret while he had still been in minor orders.[3] Jaime's letter and the Tortosa affair probably provided Alexander with his earliest impression of the archbishop of Tarragona. It cannot have been favourable, and justifiable foreboding about the sort of reception awaiting him there may well have prompted Benito, who in other circumstances was an enthusiastic habitué of the Curia, not to make his triennial visit *ad limina* in person in 1255.[4] But there was no chance of his escaping papal scrutiny in this way. Self-imposed purdah could not save him while his many adversaries remained vociferous and legates and nuncios travelled back and forth,[5] and in February 1259 Alex-

---

[1] *Reg. Greg. X*, 22. One of his electors on that occasion was the bishop of Barcelona who had spoken up for him in 1254.

[2] According to Matthew Paris, Alexander regarded Innocent as *venditor ecclesiarum*: *Chronica Majora*, v, 492.

[3] AHA, *Cartoral AB*, fo. 79r: 'Non erat regimen XIII episcopatuum seu gubernaculum committendum illi qui in minori officio constitutus domum tenere non novit' (24 March 1255). The king described Benito, aptly, as *de consuetudine litigiosus*, and sent a copy of the letter to the College of Cardinals. In the following August Benito asked Jaime to stop persecuting the Church: AHA, *Corretja*, no. 42. But the quarrel was still raging in Oct. 1258: *ibid.* no. 44: publ. Morera Llauradó, II, appendix 8.

[4] He sent three proctors in his stead, two of them Franciscans: AHA, *Cartoral AB*, fo. 35v: publ. Capdevila, *Franciscalia*, 41.

[5] See Ch. 9.

ander treated him to a lecture which was hardly less withering than Honorius III's denunciation of the Castilian Church forty years before, and lost none of its sting by being in the form of a reprimand which other prelates also received.[1]

It was a negative achievement of no small order to have presided over the spiritual shipwreck of the Aragonese Church and to have reduced it to the state of that of Castile, and all within a decade of the death of Pedro de Albalat. But the collapse was not the responsibility of Benito alone. Alexander's bull was prefaced by an unexceptional cento of biblical *caveats* about the negligent shepherd and his flock, yet it is clear that his particular cause for complaint was the vertiginous decline of clerical morals which had followed the death of Pedro de Albalat; and that was a process which Innocent IV's attitude cannot but have accelerated. For even if most bishops had not yet taken advantage of the relaxation of discipline authorised by Innocent, there were many *concubinarii* who had secured individual letters of dispensation both from Innocent and from Alexander. In February 1259, however, the pope turned the clock back. Just as, four years before, he had repudiated the Innocentian inheritance by dismissing the lengthy queues of benefice-mongers, so now, with a single stroke, he cancelled all general letters of dispensation which failed to specify the circumstances of the beneficiary's case.[2]

The similarity between Benito and Rodrigo of Toledo forty years before extends also to the archbishop of Tarragona's almost total disregard for the papal admonition. Instead of devoting himself to pastoral affairs, he plunged headlong into a further round of litigation. By August 1259 his enemy the sacrist of Tarragona, Jaime Desprats, was at Anagni,[3] and by the following summer Benito had

---

[1] AHA, *Cartoral AB*, fo. 21v: decree *Si vere quod dicimur* (13 Feb. 1259). Cf. *Reg. Alex. IV*, 2853; Potthast, 17480 (for Rouen, Salzburg, Drontheim).

[2] *Ibid.*: 'Si vero huiusmodi concubinarii quorum culpas contigerit canonica districtione feriri, super appellatione aut absolutione vel restitutione sua litteras apostolicas reportarint, illas nisi forsitan in eis appellationis aut excommunicationis seu amotionis seu huiusmodi causam expresserint manifeste, decernimus nullius esse momenti.' Cf. Barraclough, *EHR*, XLIX, 193 ff.

[3] He was with Cardinal Richard Annibaldi on 12 Aug. when the cardinal annulled the Concordat of Estella of 1255 between Teobaldo II of Navarre and the bishop of Pamplona: AM Pamplona, caj. F., d.s.n., XXX, 5 arr. I(=*Reg. Alex. IV*, 2958). Cf. Goñi Gaztambide, *Príncipe de Viana*, XVIII, 112. The sacrist had opposed Benito's election in 1251: *VL*, XIX, 262. Cf. Capdevila, *Seu de Tarragona*, 149.

joined him there for what was to prove an extended stay. The hearings and bickering dragged on for three years, while the church's funds were gradually depleted[1] and Tarragona benefices were granted to the distinguished curialists with whom once more the archbishop was billeted.[2] When, in November 1260, Alexander instructed the provincial churches to hold councils and consider the Tartar menace, Benito was not at his post but at the Curia, 'propter quedam nostra et ecclesie nostre expedienda negotia', frittering away his own energy and his church's wealth; and the bishops of Zaragoza and Vich, Arnaldo de Peralta and Bernardo de Mur, veteran prelates of Pedro de Albalat's following, to whom he delegated his task of summoning the council, hardly disguised their contempt for him in their report to the pope of May 1261. They were not coming themselves to the Curia to inform Alexander of their deliberations, they explained, but were sending proctors, because 'propter angustiam temporis nullus nostrum, scilicet episcoporum, convenienter parare se poterat'.[3] The shepherd had a duty to his flock, they suggested: a very palpable hit.

But Benito did not bruise easily, and preferred to remain at the Curia and to administer his province from there.[4] Nor did he allow himself to be chivvied by Alexander's successor, Urban IV, who reminded him of John of Abbeville's Tarragona statutes and, in particular, of the accountability of capitular officers,[5] for when, at last, he made the supreme effort and summoned a provincial council

---

1 On 9 Aug. 1260 Benito was permitted to borrow 500 marks sterling on the security of his see: *Cum sicut*: AHA, *Cartoral AB*, fo. 39r.
2 On 7 July 1260, 'attendentes bonitatem Petri nepotis dilecti magistri Margariti, Panormitani archidiaconi et rectoris ecclesie de Reddis Tarraconensis diocesis', he appointed Petrus to a canonry in the collegiate church of S. Miguel de Escornalbou, Tarragona, of which he was prior *ex officio*: AHA, *Cartoral AB*, fo. 3v. The church *de Reddis* had previously been attached to the *cameraria* of Tarragona and had been at issue between Benito and Archbishop Pedro in the 1240s: *Reg. Inn. IV*, 4140.
3 Capdevila, *AST*, II, 511, 516. Capdevila was wrong in claiming that 'de la peninsula ibèrica, fins ara, no es coneixia cap assemblea eclesiàstica que s'hagues ocupat d'aquesta qüestió', p. 501. Thirty-three years before, Fita had published, from a Túy MS. of a Commentary on the Psalms, a record of the parallel Braga Council of 1 July 1261: *BRAH*, XXII, 209 ff. (also published, independently, by Feio, *RPH*, I, 141–3). Cf. Hefele–Leclercq, VI, i, 95 ff.; Powicke–Cheney, *Councils and Synods*, I, 600 ff.
4 AHA, *Cartoral AB*, fos. 47v–8r, 58v–66v, 78v. He was still there in Jan. 1263: *ibid.* fo. 48r.
5 AHA, *Index dels Indices*, fos. 571v–2r: two bulls, 5 June and 11 Oct. 1263: formerly Arm. de les butlles apostoliques, 45, 48.

in October 1266, he was concerned not with reform but with ecclesiastical power politics. He had already staked a claim to jurisdiction over the exempt see of Mallorca,[1] and in 1266, as in 1253, he accorded only minimal attention to the constitutions of the legate and of his predecessor, with the laconic injunction that the bishops publish *omnia predicta* at their diocesan synods. It was typical of him that the only conciliar decrees of Pedro de Albalat to receive any extensive treatment were those which dealt with the intrusions of *raptores ecclesiarum* in general[2] and of the archbishop of Toledo in particular.[3] Similarly, his revival of the legate's educational legislation reflected his own legal bias by introducing a provision for the training of canonists, in his image and likeness, as well as of theologians.[4] Meanwhile, he set out to civilise his suffragans by making them eat their meals to the accompaniment of readings from the scriptures: a worthy enough scheme, but one which came ill from Benito of all people and, in the absence of any other sign of anxiety about clerical morality, merely serves to highlight the archbishop's indifference to his pastoral responsibilities.[5]

When Benito died in May 1268, still one jump ahead of justice,[6] the province of Tarragona was hardly recognisable as the scene of Pedro de Albalat's operations. The tradition of annual councils was a

---

[1] *Ibid.* fo. 32v (23 July 1265): formerly Arm. de la dignitat arxiepiscopal, 18.

[2] Tejada, III, 388; VI, 53–4. The constitution was *Olim excommunicasse* (*ibid.* VI, 43), the second of the two constitutions of which the chapter of Valencia secured copies in the early fourteenth century: AC Valencia, doc. 8987 (above, p. 81, n. 7).

[3] Marca, *De primatibus*, 367–9, published two documents from the archiepiscopal archive at Tarragona (identifiable as Arm. de la dignitat arxiepiscopal, 23–4: AHA, *Index dels Indices*, fo. 33r), the second of which reiterated Pedro's constitution *De archiepiscopo Toletano*, issued in May 1240 at the height of the struggle for control of Valencia: Tejada, VI, 33; Burns, I, 274. The documents do not, strictly speaking, belong to the council, being dated 11 and 13 Nov. 1266. They must, however, be mentioned, and not least because in the first of them Benito quoted a canonical tag which he might have pondered more often to his own advantage. He reprimanded the archbishop-elect of Toledo, Sancho of Aragón, for trespassing upon his rights by bearing his cross through the province of Tarragona, 'cum non liceat alicui in alienam messem ponere falcem suam'.

[4] Tejada, VI, 53. Cf. Conc. Lérida, c. 7, which does not mention the study of canon law: *ES*, XLVIII, 311.

[5] Tejada, *loc. cit.*

[6] *VL*, XIX, 187. In the following month Clement IV dismissed various clerks whom he had promoted illegally to reserved benefices: *Reg. Clem. IV*, 1377 (Martène–Durand, *Thesaurus*, II, 607).

distant memory. In sixteen years he had held two, or possibly three,[1] such councils in which the prosecution of his predecessor's policies had been the least of his considerations. None of them, moreover, had met on the day assigned by Pedro.[2] His dealings with his suffragans suggest that his long periods away[3] were less damaging to the government of the Aragonese Church than his rare periods at home. For his behaviour during the Tortosa election was not exceptional. During that very winter he was engaged in a vendetta against the bishop of Pamplona, though the sturdy Pedro Ximénez proved equal to his devious stratagems.[4] Appropriately enough, the two prelates clashed again in the early 1260s over the issue which during Pedro de Albalat's lifetime had provided the Aragonese Church with a focal point of co-operation: the provincial council.[5] It was a sign of the times. Yet, in view of the archbishop's obsessively suspicious nature, as described by the papal nuncio Nicholas of Terracina,[6] it is not surprising that the province should have become an armed camp; and, although a certain measure of joint enterprise did survive Benito's mismanagement, the effect of this disastrous interlude on the progress of clerical reform is not difficult to imagine.

Even in the diocese of Valencia, where Andrés de Albalat and his

---

[1] Tejada, VI, 52, and Valls i Taberner, *AST*, XI, 260, credit him with a third council on 16 May 1256, or 1257. However, its constitutions, as published by Tejada, are exactly the same as those of the 1253 council. Moreover, it is not mentioned among his constitutions in the fourteenth-century MS. BC Tortosa, cod. 187, fos. 24r–6r. Cf. Bayerri Bertomeu, *Códices medievales*, 344–5.

[2] 8 April 1253; 16 May 1266.

[3] According to Morera, II, 295, he was at the Curia permanently from 1257 until 1266.

[4] Goñi Gaztambide, *Príncipe de Viana*, XVIII, 113–14, 224–5.

[5] In 1264 the proctor of the clergy of Murillo claimed that Bishop Pedro's sentences of excommunication were invalid since he himself had been excommunicated for failing to pay his share of the expenses of the agents 'qui mittendi erant ad curiam romanam ratione negotii tartarorum' from the 1261 Council. His share was 155 *maravedís*. The agents had been provided with 1600: AC Pampolona, II Episcopi 23 (reg. Goñi Gaztambide, 655); Capdevila, *AST*, II, 516.

[6] In his letter of Aug. 1257 to Alexander IV, publ. Blanch, 162–6, Benito had objected to Nicholas's dining with the provost and canons: 'et fateor quod verum est, nam et cum ipso archiepiscopo et cum prefatis frequenter et sepe comedi et ipsi mecum, nam nolebam de me dici quod numquam mecum amicus in hospitio receperat caritatem'. His other experiences with Benito led him to speculate about national characteristics: 'nam ex eo quod scio omnes hispanos impatientes esse, ut fama praedicat et facta demonstrant, non solum quod non timeam eisdem hispanis dicere aliquid, imo vereor eos respicere pusillanimus, pavidus et timens, ne ex aspectu provocentur ad iram et reputent se offensos'.

successor Jazpert de Botonach persisted with the holding of synods, the task proved positively sisyphean, and Andrés on occasion seemed close to despair.[1] Indeed, in 1296, despite all their efforts and the promulgation of Pedro's *Summa*, Bishop Ramón Despont O.P. could declare, in the preface to his own *Tractatus de Sacramentis* – a rather more learned and reflective work than Pedro de Albalat's – that the sacraments had as yet received no attention in the synodal constitutions of that church.[2] And elsewhere the situation was at least as bad. When Archbishop Rodrigo Tello visited the diocese of Pamplona in March 1295 he discovered, *inter alia*, the cathedral church seriously understaffed, thirty-three clerics holding benefices in plurality, and four hundred and fifty *clerici concubinarii*.[3]

And yet, for all this, the memory of reform did linger on. Both Rodrigo (1288–1307) and Bernardo de Olivella before him (1272–87) held provincial councils, and even if Rodrigo was rather too ready to accept excuses for absence from his suffragans,[4] at least their legislation harked back to that of the 1240s.[5] The ordinances of John of Abbeville and Pedro de Albalat were Rodrigo's touchstone when he visited Pamplona in 1295,[6] and later that year he learnt that synods were still held in the diocese of Calahorra, although, according to the clergy of Alava, they were summoned in out-of-the-way places, *in*

---

[1] For Jazpert's synods of 1277, 1278 and 1280, see Sanchis y Sivera, *AST*, IX, 143–7.

[2] Publ. Sanchis y Sivera, *AST*, X, 123 ff. Two extracts will suffice to demonstrate the gulf between the *Summa* and the *Tractatus*: cap. 15, *Quod pueri debent confiteri*: 'Reffert enim b. Gregorius in Dialogo quod quidam gravidaverit nutricem in nono anno'; cap. 17, *De penitentiis mulierum*: '...nam sexus mulieris potius debet moneri quam terreri'.

[3] AGN, caj. 4, no. 101 (reg. Castro, *Catálogo*, 581); Goñi Gaztambide, *Príncipe de Viana*, XVIII, 189–90.

[4] In June 1294 he wrote to Bishop Miguel of Pamplona, informing him of the Lérida Council which was planned for August, and adding that 'licet autem ut juris et moris est universos et singulos episcopos suffraganeos nostros ut ad dictum personaliter accedant concilium specialiter convocemus, propter tamen locorum distanciam et viarum discrimina necnon et pericula gravia que possent in itinere inveniri', he would tolerate *paciencer* the sending of proctors instead: AC Pamplona, II Episcopi 38 (reg. Goñi Gaztambide, 821). The contrast with Pedro de Albalat and his contempt for his suffragans' *excusationes frivolas* is most striking.

[5] Tejada, III, 402 ff.; VI, 54 ff.; Valls i Taberner, *AST*, XI, 262–5.

[6] He described pluralism as 'contra constitutionem domini Johannis Sabinensis episcopi et contra ordinationem domini P. predecessoris nostri factam in ecclesia Pampilonensi' (referring to Pedro's *sede vacante* synod there): AGN, caj. 4, no. 101.

locis minus insignibus, instead of at Armentia, the customary place.[1] The mainstream of reform, in spite of Benito's damming operations, had continued to flow, even though it had gone underground. And it sprang up beyond the province, to irrigate the island of Mallorca. In 1266 Bishop Pedro de Morella issued a set of vernacular synodal statutes which borrowed from both Pedro de Albalat's *Summa* and the legatine legislation, and displayed the sort of pristine vigour which was so lamentably absent from Benito's council of the same year, to which futile assembly the archbishop had summoned the insular bishop.[2]

The *Summa Septem Sacramentorum* had a lasting influence. It may have been the model for the set of instructions *De celebratione missarum et sacramento eucharistie et aliis divinis officiis* which the Pamplona synod of March 1301 ordered the diocesan clergy to acquire within the next three months.[3] And in the 1360s and 1370s that section of it which dealt with the sacrament of the Eucharist received a new lease of life when Archbishop Pedro Clasquerin promulgated it at an archi-

---

[1] AC Calahorra, doc. 473 (Estella, 6 Nov. 1295). In 1297 Bishop Almoravid complied with their demand, at Logroño; publ. Bujanda, *Berceo*, I, 132–5. Similarly, the monks of Leyre complained that, though they were exempt from his jurisdiction, Bishop Miguel of Pamplona had summoned them 'ad locum non tutum ad quem propter guerrarum discrimina et viarum pericula que in illis partibus ingruebant, accedere vel destinare ńuntium non valebant': *inc. Sua nobis* (11 Jan. 1303): AHN, 1408/20.

[2] The statutes are published by Nebot, *BSAL*, XIII. Fragments only have survived of the section *De Penitentia* (pp. 195–7), but the connexion with Pedro's *Summa* is suggested by, for example, the instructions *De Matrimoni* beginning: 'per so cor matrimoni es feit corporalment entre totes gents' (p. 253; cf. *Summa*, fo. 129rb). *El cardenal de Sabina* and his constitutions are frequently mentioned (pp. 239–40, 253, 269, 295–7), and the bishop published without modification 'la constitucio del cardenal de Sabina qui fo legat del apostoli en espanya (denunciam) por sospeses tots los preveres, diaches o subdiaches e tots los beneficiats qui tenen o tenran publicament en lurs cases o en altres, drudes e les drudes e altretal dels clergues damunt dits denunciam per vedats, e si es morien en aquest pecat soterrarlos hi han no en cimiteri dons son heretges' (p. 269). *El consyl de Tibur* and a constitution of Gregory IX are also mentioned (pp. 240, 269). The source for the provision of the synod of Oct. 1270 which deterred rectors from visiting Palma and obliged them to attend services in the cathedral when they did (p. 335), may have been the Valencia synod of 1255: Aguirre, V, 197: *Ne clerici in civitatem.* For Pedro de Morella, see *VL*, XXI, 141 ff.

[3] BC Pamplona, *Libro de Constituciones*, fo. XXX(va). Both Sandoval, *Catálogo de los obispos de Pamplona*, fo. 96r, and Moret, *Annales*, III, 274, regarded this as the first Pamplona synod. Cf. Goñi Gaztambide, *Príncipe de Viana*, XVIII, 187.

diocesan synod. On that occasion it was described as *Constitutio sinodalis ecclesie Valentine*.[1] The wheel had come full circle.

What, though, was the significance of 'reform' and 'the tradition of reform'? We run the risk of becoming absorbed in the plumage and forgetting the dying bird whenever we allow ourselves to be convinced by these clichés that anything certain can be known about the state of popular religion. The evidence from the diocese of Valencia alone indicates that frequent synods were no guarantee of effectiveness, and though the survival of synodal and conciliar statutes may provide information about the prelates who issued the legislation, it is no guide to the condition of the people at whom that legislation was directed. The religious life of priests and people in the parishes of thirteenth-century Spain is almost entirely hid from view. Records of episcopal visitations are extremely rare,[2] and it must not be assumed that Archbishop Rodrigo's findings at Pamplona in 1295 were representative of the state of his province either then or earlier. Nor, however, can it be assumed that they were not, though there is reason enough to believe that piety survived at the parochial level and that the translator of Innocent III's *De Contemptu Mundi* was correct in his opinion that there was a market for a vernacular version of the work.[3] Still, the existence of piety at any level of the Aragonese

[1] AC Barcelona, *Libro de la Cadena*, fo. 184r.
[2] The only such thirteenth-century record that has come to light is a single leaf, of the year 1258, contained in the Urgel MS. already mentioned: above, p. 84. Cf. Linehan, *AEM*. The *Index dels Indices* in the AHA, fo. 30r, mentions 'un altre plech que conté diverses visites fetes antigament per los archebisbes y sos visitadors en diverses yglesies catedrals y parroquials de la provincia'; but it is now lost. Visitation records, of great interest, survive from the early years of the next century at Barcelona: Sanabre, *El archivo diocesano*, 14; and at Vich for the years 1330–9: publ. Junyent, *Miscelánea Griera*, I, 369 ff.; while for Huesca a document of the year 1338, which is not a visitation record but is of equal value, is publ. by Durán Gudiol, *Argensola*, VII, 368–9.
[3] Ed. Artigas in *Bol. Bibl. Menéndez y Pelayo*, I–II, from a fourteenth-century MS. Entitled *Libro de la miseria de omne*, the translation may have been made in the mid-thirteenth century (I, 35). The author explains his motives in the prologue (I, 36):

> libro de miseria de omne sepades que es llamado
> conpuso esas rrazones en buen latin esmerado.
> Non lo entiende todo omne sinon el que es letrado
> porque yaze oy muchos postpuesto e olvidado.

A copy of Innocent's original work was in the library of the vicar of S. María de Uncastillo, Sancho Jordan, in 1263: Serrano y Sanz, *Erudición Ibero-Ultramarina*,

Church cannot be deduced from an analysis of its conciliar or synodal legislation.

However, the conciliar tradition of Pedro de Albalat's making did have a significance which was quite independent of the spiritual matters discussed at his councils: a political significance that enabled the Aragonese prelates to defend their temporal interests against the secular power. Benito de Rocaberti himself had reason to be grateful to Pedro for this. But it is an aspect of the ecclesiastical history of thirteenth-century Spain which may most conveniently be considered in the following chapter where the quite different developments within the Castilian Church are discussed.

III, 119, item 49; Escagüés Javierre, *Rev. Bibliografía Nacional*, VI, 203–5. Neither of these MSS. is mentioned by M. Maccarrone in his ed: *Lotharii cardinalis (Innocentii III) 'De Miseria Humanae Conditionis'* (Lucca, 1955).

Chapter 6

THE ECONOMIC PROBLEMS
OF THE CASTILIAN CHURCH, 1

After John of Abbeville's departure, the Spanish Church had to wait ninety years for another legate of similar calibre, by which time it had passed far from its heroic period – according to Lafuente – and deep into the impenetrably gloomy regions of the later Middle Ages.[1] In Lafuente's view, the break came in the mid-thirteenth century with the deaths of, among others, San Fernando, Rodrigo of Toledo and Innocent IV. Yet, if these three were such paragons, it is striking that none of them showed any enthusiasm for continuing the work of John of Abbeville. Whatever else they may have represented, 'las repetidas visitas de los legados' did not, as Villanueva imagined, serve to maintain contact between the Spanish Church and the springs of reform.[2]

The papal legates and nuncios who continued to ply to and fro between the papal Curia and Spain were the servants of Mammon, not of God. They came to collect cash, to raise the wherewithal for the military campaigns and diplomatic operations of the papacy; and they were, of course, bitterly resented everywhere. Spain was no exception. Though, moreover, the kingdoms of Aragon and Castile had no home-grown Matthew Paris to voice their grievances, they did have men with tongues in their heads, a plausible manner and some apparently quite respectable arguments. What right had the pope to expect contributions from them? Was not Christendom already beholden to them for their centuries of exertion breaking Moslem dominance in the Peninsula? Was it equitable, at a time when the Castilian churches had poured their treasure into the coffers of their kings and made possible the astonishingly rapid Christian

---

[1] Lafuente, *Historia eclesiástica*, IV, 280, 330. For the legation of John's successor, Guillaume de Peyre de Godin, also cardinal-bishop of Sabina, see Fournier, *BEC*, LXXXVI, 108–14.
[2] *VL*, V, 91.

advance after the victory at Las Navas in 1212, that they should be called upon to finance harebrained schemes of papal diplomacy in the Eastern Mediterranean? Some such questions seem to have been asked by the Spanish contingent at the Fourth Lateran Council, and they were repeated by the Castilian bishops in the early 1260s. On both occasions they were meant to be questions expecting the answer 'no'. In the interval, however, certain great changes had occurred, changes which affected considerably the confidence of the prelates who asked these questions.

In 1215 the *reconquistadores* were in full cry, especially in Castile. The episcopal chronicler emphasised that all the credit for Las Navas was due to Spain, *et precipue regno Castelle*. The few foreigners who had come had not possessed sufficient *vergüenza* to stay and fight. Even the king of Aragon was a Castilian pensioner. Fifty years later, though, this confidence was evaporating fast. The Reconquest had slowed down to an aimless amble while precious resources had been, and were still being, squandered on their king's chimerical European ambitions. The prelates said that they were poor and they blamed the pope, forgetting that as recently as 1245, when their self-assurance had never been greater, it had been their leaders who had pressed Innocent IV to take even more vigorous measures against Frederick II, promising the pope every assistance 'in personis et rebus iuxta sue beneplacitum voluntatis'.[1]

That they were poor or even claimed to be poor, however, will surprise those historians for whom the wealth of the Spanish Church in every age is axiomatic. According to the doyen of Spanish medievalists, medieval churchmen were enormously wealthy, despite 'los ríos de oro y plata' which flowed towards Rome.[2] The Spanish Church was a hypertrophic growth,[3] and it was never better nourished than during the thirteenth century when, having 'profited enormously from the great conquests', it reached 'the zenith of its social power and prestige'.[4] There is clearly a conflict here between the

---

[1] Below, pp. 160–1. [2] Sánchez-Albornoz, *España: un enigma histórico*, I, 356, 358, 687.
[3] *Idem, España y el Islam*, 39.
[4] 'Probablemente el clero de los estados cristianos alcanzó el cenit de su prestigio y de su potencia social en el siglo XIII, cuando, por una parte, la Iglesia salió enormemente beneficiada de las grandes conquistas, y, por otra, mantenía todavía esencialmente incólume su independencia del poder temporal, alcanzada en los últimos siglos del período anterior gracias al prestigio del Papado': Sobrequés Vidal, *La época del*

medieval bishops and their modern historians, a conflict which has to be resolved before proceeding to any conclusion about the place of the Church in Castilian society and its ability to control not only that society but also its own fortunes.

The tensions which existed between the three points of the eternal medieval triangle – king, pope and bishops – were at least in part economic tensions. But the issue was one of sovereignty, and it was affected by circumstances which were peculiar to each country. The peculiar circumstances of Spain were numerous. One of them was the distance which, it was felt by some pontiffs, separated the Peninsula from Rome. According to Urban IV, for example, Lisbon was at the back of beyond.[1] Naturally enough, therefore, Spanish bishops identified themselves with their king. So, of course, did other bishops elsewhere. In Spain, though, king and bishops had a common Christian mission which drew them even closer together and which in the first half of the thirteenth century was at the forefront of attention: the Reconquest. Yet in this joint enterprise the bishops were quite decidedly the junior partners, for, having given the Church her liberty, the kings of Aragon and Castile felt perfectly free to take liberties with her. And, by implication at least, contemporaries accepted this. It did not surprise Matthew Paris when Innocent IV forgave Jaime of Aragon for having maimed the bishop of Gerona. The king, after all, as he drily observed, 'tam fideliter Deo contra Hispanos Sarracenos militaverat et gloriose triumphaverat'.[2]

Gossipy prelates were not the only casualties, for the Spanish monarchs seem on occasion to have believed that their privileged position placed them altogether above the moral law. Jaime of Aragon was dubbed *the* Conqueror: appropriately enough, for his tally of conquests of Christian ladies was no shorter than that of his assaults on Moorish strongholds, and the adulterous king assumed quite candidly that his undertaking to recapture Murcia would automatically atone for his outstanding violations of the sixth and ninth Commandments.[3] Similarly, the Roman proctor of Sancho IV

---

patriciado urbano, 164. Similarly, J. H. Elliott, *Imperial Spain, 1469–1716* (London, 1963), 20; R. S. Smith in *Cambridge Economic History of Europe*, I, ed. M. M. Postan (2nd ed. Cambridge, 1966), 433.

[1] 'Sita...in remotis mundi finibus': *Reg. Urb. IV*, 305.
[2] *Chronica Majora*, IV, 578–9.
[3] *Chronica...del...Rey En Jacme*, cap. 426, ed. Aguiló, 434–5; trans. Forster, II, 549.

assured the clerk whom he had engaged to forge a bull regularising the king's liaison with María de Molina in 1292, that what he was seeking was for the honour of the Church and, further, that whoever was elected to fill the papal vacancy would certainly ratify the deed. For was not Sancho locked in daily combat with the enemies of the faith?[1] In point of fact, he was not, but it suited him very well to reiterate an argument which had secured so many benefits in the past.

Boundless arrogance was the most striking of the national characteristics which were so jauntily displayed by the Castilian contingent in their almost totally irrelevant contribution to the discussion on the nature of the soul, as related by Virgil of Córdoba.[2] Contemporary fantasy told of the humiliation at the gates of Paris by Fernando I and the Cid of the French king, the German emperor, the patriarch and the pope in response to their demand for tribute from Spain.[3] Their overbearing behaviour gave Spaniards a bad name abroad. That Matthew Paris should not have had a good word to say for them was predictable,[4] but he was not their only critic. The papal nuncio, Nicholas of Terracina, described them as *impatientes*, and did not expect his characterisation to surprise anyone.[5]

Even the canonist Vincentius Hispanus fell victim to this heady propaganda. In his gloss to the *Venerabilem* in the Decretals of Gregory IX he contrasted the admirable Spaniards, who had forged themselves an empire *virtute sua*, with the pathetic Germans whose incompetence had cost them theirs *per busnardiam*. Vincentius ex-

---

[1] Marcos Pous in *CTEER*, VIII, 97.

[2] 'Et quomodocumque omnes homines sint animosi secundum magis et minus super omnes alios sunt Hispani et fortiores omnibus aliis sunt in omnibus factis suis, et hoc habent ipsi a natura sua propria; et robustiores aliis sunt in omnibus et per omnia maxime in proelio', and more in the same vein: 'et semper cupiunt et appetunt mori gladio, et magis homines se interficiunt gladio in Hispania quam per totum mundum': *Virgilii Cordubensis Philosophia*, ed. Heine, I, 226. This was allegedly written *c.* 1290, but cf. Bonilla, *Historia de la filosofía española*, I, 311: 'una superchería'.

[3] *Rodrigo y el Rey Fernando*, ed. Menéndez Pidal in *Reliquias de la poesía épica española*, pp. 257–89, esp. lines 1052 ff. and the king's exclamation (l. 763): 'Quantos en Espana visquieron/nunca se llamaron tributarios.' The poem was probably composed in the 1350s or 1360s, but this incident seems to have derived from a tradition already current in the late thirteenth century. Cf. Deyermond, *Epic Poetry and the Clergy*, 12–14, 22–4.

[4] 'Sunt hominum peripsima, vultu deformes, cultu despicabiles, moribus detestabiles': *Chronica Majora*, V, 450.

[5] Above, p. 96.

pressed these views at a moment when the evidence was very much in his favour, sometime between 1234 and 1248.[1] While Germany was disintegrating, the kingdoms of Castile and Leon, united by Fernando III in 1230, were recovering territory from the Moors at a breathless pace. Within thirty years the peninsular balance of power had been transformed, and even before the reconquest of Córdoba Fernando could quite reasonably stake a claim to imperial dignity.[2] But the climax of Castilian achievement was the taking of Seville in 1248, the year of Vincentius's death, and the eulogy of Spain which the canonist provided in his gloss was a commonplace of nationalistic literature during these years.[3] 'Oh, what blessed times are these', intoned the episcopal chronicler, Lucas of Túy, waxing eloquent over the virtues of a country which was distinguished by the purity of its faith, the active orthodoxy of its kings, the achievements of its arms and the Virgilian contentment of its peasant cultivators.[4] The author of the *Poema de Fernán González* was even more extravagant. With Vincentius he insisted upon Spain's superiority over all other nations of the West. Neither England nor France could boast an apostle to match Santiago. Spain had the best of everything from fresh fish to horses which were sought the world over.[5] (He was right about the horses.)[6] *Pero de toda Spanna Castylla es mejor.*[7] Spain,

---

[1] Publ. Gaines Post, *Studies in Medieval Legal Thought.* 490. Cf. Ochoa Sanz, *Vincentius Hispanus*, 18; Sousa Costa, *Mestre Silvestre*, 473.

[2] 'In Curia Romana talem petitionem proposuit Rex Castellae Fernandus quod nomen imperatoris et benedictionem volebat habere, sicut habuerant quidam antecessores eius': *Chronica Albrici Monachi Trium Fontium*, 936 (s.a. 1234); Chiffletius, *Vindiciae Hispanicae*, 168. On the subject of the *imperium* referred to, see Menéndez Pidal, *El Imperio Hispánico*, 146 ff.; Sánchez Candeira, *El 'Regnum-Imperium' leonés hasta 1037*.

[3] Davis, *Hispanic Review*, III, 150 ff.

[4] 'O quam beata tempora ista, in quibus fides catholica sublimatur, haeretica pravitas trucidatur, et Sarracenorum urbes et castra fidelium gladiis devastantur. Pugnant Hispani reges pro fide et ubique vincunt. Episcopi, abbates et clerus ecclesias et monasteria construunt, et ruricolae absque formidine agros excolunt, animalia nutriunt, et non est qui exterreat eos': *Chronicon Mundi*, 113.

[5] Written *c.* 1250: ed. Marden, verses 145 ff., pp. xxx, xxxv–vi.

[6] *Ibid.* v. 151: 'Nunca tales cavallos en el mundo non viemos.' Giraldus Cambrensis thought highly of Spain's 'equi egregii et generosissimi', and the English court went to great trouble to secure some, the export of which from Spain was normally prohibited: *De Principis Instructione*, 317; *Close Rolls*, *1237–42*, p. 529; *1242–47*, p. 174; *1298–1302*, p. 378. See Renouard in *Homenaje a Jaime Vicens Vives*, I, 571 ff.

[7] *Ibid.* v. 156.

in short, was like paradise,[1] and Spaniards on leave never tired of reminding their hosts of the fact. From the lips of an 'eloquent and elegant' knight, a messenger of Alfonso X, Matthew Paris learnt of the fabulous riches of recently reconquered Seville. Matthew was sceptical, as usual. It all seemed hardly credible to 'us westerners'.[2]

In Spain, however, there was no room for scepticism. Confidence was boundless, and infectious. It was also, in a sense, desperate, even febrile. If there had not been a Seville it would have been necessary to invent one; and if Seville had not been a place of unlimited riches it would have been necessary to treat it as though it were. After their long and hungry haul the Christians needed an oasis, so it is little to be wondered that Alfonso X himself, when singing the praises of the fertile valley of the Guadalquivir, sounded as though he were describing the capture of a granary rather than that of a kingdom. It was a land flowing with milk and honey, rich above all other regions of Spain in the necessities of life, in bread, wine, meat, fish and oil, with a perfect climate to match. But, most important, it was self-sufficient.[3] For ever since 1212 the Castilians had been haunted by the spectre of famine and delayed by its reality. In 1214 the army had been forced to a truce by privation so severe that hardly enough survived to bury the dead and those who did survive were reduced to eating meat during Lent.[4] Limited resources were dangerously extended by the Great Leap Forward. It has been calculated that between the battle of Las Navas and the recapture of Seville the national territory had increased by nearly 50 per cent while population had grown by barely 10 per cent.[5] Men, food and money were at a premium, and to redress the balance spectacular gains were needed in all three – in men especially, since the untaxed frontier acted as a magnet drawing cultivators away from the north and centre. For property owners like the Order of Santiago, with land both in the north and in the south, there was the delicate problem of striking a balance and maintaining

---

[1] *Primera Crónica General*, para. 311.
[2] *Chronica Majora*, v. 233 (s.a. 1251). Elsewhere (v. 311) Matthew again mentions elegance as a Spanish attribute.
[3] 'Et todas las cosas ha de ssuyo complidamente': *Setenario*, 19.
[4] CLI: *B. Hisp.*, XIV, 368. Cf. the account in *Primera Crónica General*, para. 1023, which suggests that the shortage was not quite so widespread.
[5] Vicens Vives, *Manual de historia económica*, 223; Sobrequés, 8, 46. For a brief account of this period, see González in *La Reconquista española y la repoblación del país*, 194 ff.

rents in one sector while populating the other.[1] Many men, however, evidently made their own decision to go south at the time when the supply of manpower from abroad had virtually ceased. In 1268 Pope Clement IV was told by the Portuguese bishops that Extremadura was the most heavily populated area of their country.[2] And the same effect must have been produced in Spain by Fernando III's policy which his son described proudly in the *Setenario*.[3] It was a policy which was to create considerable tension between north and south in the not too distant future.[4] Meanwhile, however, hard-pressed landlords whose tenants were drifting away sought temporary relief in the one cure that was guaranteed to feed the disease: the raising of rents. In 1236 the archbishop of Toledo adopted this ill-advised remedy on his Illescas estates.[5]

Later that year Córdoba was taken. Here, it was confidently assumed, was the panacea. But, instead, settlers flocked there 'as to a king's wedding' in greater numbers than could be accommodated,[6] and for at least the first decade of Christian occupation the area was yet a further drain on resources. On three occasions Fernando III was obliged to provision the place from the depleted regions of the north.[7] Twelve years after, it was the turn of Seville, and, according to a late source, it was in the hope of capturing an excellent standing harvest that Fernando chose to launch his attack when he did.[8]

[1] Lomax, *Orden de Santiago*, 114, 119 ff.

[2] 'In quadam parte regni Portugalie que Extrematura vocatur...maior est populi multitudo a longissimis temporibus quorum memoria non existit': ADB, Gav. das. Notícias Várias, 26.

[3] 'Non poblaua tan ssolamiente lo que ganaua de los moros que fuera ante poblado, mas lo al que nunca ouyera poblança, entendiendo que era logar para ello': *Setenario*, 16.

[4] At the Cortes of 1271 (or 1272) the nobles of the north complained about their loss of rents: González, *Repartimiento de Sevilla*, I, 16. Cf. Ballesteros, *Alfonso X*, 568 ff. González does not mention his authority for this, and it should be noted that if his source is the *Crónica del Rey Don Alfonso X* the meaning of the relevant passage (*BAE*, LXVI, 20-1) is not quite that which he alleges.

[5] The increase was of the order of 7½%. Publ. González Palencia, *Los mozárabes de Toledo*, I, 163 ff.

[6] Rodericus Toletanus, *De Rebus Hispaniae*, 206.

[7] *Primera Crónica General*, para. 1052-5. The third instalment of aid was sent 'a la sazon que el sol escureçio', either 1238, according to *Anales Toledanos II*, or 1239, according to *Chronicón de Cardeña I* and *Anales Toledanos III* (*ES*, XXIII, 408, 373, 422). See also Gómez Bravo, *Catálogo de los obispos de Córdoba*, I, 254.

[8] *Cuarta Crónica General*, 4. Cf. Menéndez Pidal, *Crónicas generales de España*, 141-5.

If the bliss of being alive in that false dawn was somewhat modified by the ineluctable conditions of the frontier, for those broken reeds, the bishops, the consequences of being dragooned into the fight were little short of ruinous. What sustained them through these difficult years was the belief that at the eventual distribution of spoils they would be richly rewarded for all their sacrifices. They were identified absolutely with the struggle against the Moors, naturally as churchmen and necessarily as subjects, in 1212, when the clergy surrendered half their year's income for the Las Navas campaign, and after. Under the leadership of Rodrigo of Toledo, who by his own admission was opposed to any change in the political *status quo*,[1] they were entirely at the royal beck and call.

When Archbishop Rodrigo had given a practical demonstration of what his political philosophy meant, Honorius III had sent him and his suffragans a letter of sharp reproof, but as the Reconquest gathered pace neither of Honorius's successors made any difficulties about royal policy towards the Castilian Church. Both Gregory IX and Innocent IV permitted Fernando III to exercise to the full the right to intervene in episcopal elections – as lord of the land and defender of the Faith – which Fernando's son would enunciate in the *Primera Partida*.[2] Indeed, Gregory was even willing, in December 1237, to revoke his own previous confirmation of the translation of Bishop Juan of Osma to the see of León when it was put to him by the king that Juan, 'tanquam vir magni consilii tibi utilis ac necessarius regno', could not conveniently be spared.[3] The king's concern in the matter was understandable since Juan was his chancellor for both kingdoms – though since the bishop was for that reason almost permanently attached to the court, it is not clear why it should have

---

[1] See above, p. 10, for his plea of justification in the case of Melendo of Osma. The possibility of *scandalum* and *damna non modica* if he should proceed against the king led him to disobey a mandate which had papal authority. See also the remark in his *History* about 'regni prelati, quorum interest regnum et sacerdotium intueri': *De Rebus Hispaniae*, 204.

[2] *Part.* 1.5.18: 'Et la razon por que lo deben facer saber al rey ante que esleyan es esta: porque es defendedor e amparador de la fe, e de las eglesias, e de los que las sierven, e de sus bienes, e otrossi porque es senyor natural de la tierra o son fundadas las eglesias': BM, Add. MS. 20787, fo. 20vb, corresponding to the variant to *ley* 17 in the Academy ed. I, 207. The law printed there as 1.5.18 (p. 208) does not appear in the BM MS.

[3] *Reg. Greg. IX*, 3591, 3967; Mansilla, *Iglesia*, 171–3.

mattered to him which see Juan occupied. What, however, is clear is that Fernando's intervention was decisive and that Gregory complied with his wishes both then, in 1237, and again in March 1240 when, this time with the king's active support, Juan was translated to the see of Burgos.[1]

Nor was Innocent IV any less accommodating than Gregory, despite his reputation for promoting his friends and relations to every vacant bishopric or benefice from Graz to Galloway. Indeed it is probable that his preparedness to co-operate with King Fernando provides the correct explanation of what Bishop Mansilla has recorded as a classic example of papal promotion of a favoured foreigner to a Spanish see: that of the dean of Chartres to Mondoñedo in 1248.[2] For Juan Sebastianes was no Frenchman. His hitherto unnoticed presence at the Paris negotiations of September 1245 between the leaders of the Portuguese Church and the Count of Boulogne indicates that *Johannes Hispanus* – as he was referred to in papal correspondence – was, rather, one of the many ecclesiastical refugees from Castile's westerly neighbour.[3] He was not the only Portuguese *Johannes Hispanus* in circulation at this time, and like his namesake, the bishop of Lisbon, he was supported by revenue from the Castilian Church: by January 1244 he possessed canonries both at Lugo and at Salamanca, possibly as result of a papal grant such as that which had been made to the other *Johannes Hispanus* in May 1238.[4] But a papal grant did not make him a papal pensioner, any more than his French

---

[1] *Reg. Greg. IX*, 5190; Mansilla, *Iglesia*, 176. Serrano, Juan's biographer, admits himself baffled by the king's behaviour in 1237: *Hispania*, I, 15. Part of the reason may have been Juan's promise to the archbishop of Toledo that, in his capacity as chancellor of Castile, he would not accept promotion to any see outside Rodrigo's jurisdiction: *ibid.* 7; AHN, 3019/8. For Juan's chancery career, see Millares Carlo, *AHDE*, III, 282 ff.

[2] *Reg. Inn. IV*, 3681; Mansilla, *Iglesia*, 183: 'Inocencio IV quería sencillamente colocar allí otra persona de su agrado.'

[3] Cunha, *História ecclesiástica dos arcebispos de Braga*, II, 123; Herculano, *História de Portugal*, v, 50–3.

[4] *Reg. Greg. IX*, 4333. In his study of the Mondoñedo election Quintana Prieto fails to allow for this duplicity (or even, perhaps, multiplicity) of *Johannes Hispani*, conflates them, and unwittingly exhumes the bishop of Lisbon (the other John, who had died by May 1244 at the latest: ADB, Gav. das Notícias Várias, 28: publ. Sousa Costa, 427, n. 536) and promotes him to Mondoñedo four years later: *AA*, XIII, 24 ff. For the Mondoñedo John's Spanish benefices, see *Reg. Inn. IV*, 365, 1050. In Aug. 1246 he was alive and well and living at Salamanca, if only temporarily: AC Salamanca, 3/1/40 (reg. Marcos, *Catálogo*, 220).

benefices[1] made him a Frenchman, and the fact that by 1246 he had made a niche for himself at the Castilian court and was regarded as sufficiently eminent to witness the pact between the Order of Santiago and the Latin Emperor, Baldwin de Courtenay,[2] suggests that he was no stranger in those parts and that his promotion to Mondoñedo came as no unpleasant surprise to Fernando III.

Nor was this all. For Innocent also permitted the king to use ecclesiastical benefices and dignities (and the cash that went therewith) as *douceurs* and endowments for his younger sons. At a tender age Sancho and Felipe were given charge, as procurators, of the archbishoprics of Toledo and Seville respectively.[3] Outwardly the brothers had little in common. An Icelandic nobleman who met the pair of them early in 1258 thought the former rather po-faced and eminently suitable for high office in the Church, while Felipe struck him as a thoroughly good fellow but a pretty improbable archbishop.[4] But appearances are deceptive,[5] and at the time of their appointment all that could be said about them for certain was that neither was ordained. Their benefices were simply agglomerations of real estate, and the exchanges which passed between Felipe and his brother, Alfonso X, when the plan for the former to marry Princess Christina of Norway had foundered, express perfectly the view of ecclesiastical offices that was taken by the royal family. In reply to the Infante's complaint that, having resigned an archbishopric and a couple of abbacies, he now lacked both *clerecía* and wife, Alfonso observed that the *tertie decimarum* of the sees of Toledo, Segovia and Ávila were hardly negligible recompense for all that Felipe had suffered.[6]

---

[1] He also possessed the archdeaconry of Tonnerre (Yonne): *Reg. Inn. IV*, 365.

[2] Benito Ruano, *Hispania*, XII, 34. He found himself in the select company of the king's sister, Berenguela; the chancellor, Bishop Juan of Burgos; and Bishop Benito of Ávila. Benito Ruano, p. 22, takes him to be a companion of the Emperor.

[3] Mansilla, *Iglesia*, 186–8. Felipe was appointed in 1249 and Sancho in 1251, before his twentieth birthday: Castejón y Fonseca, *Primacía de la iglesia de Toledo*, 761.

[4] Guzmán y Gallo, *BRAH*, LXXIV, 50. Matthew Paris had been less favourably impressed by Sancho when the Infante had been in London three years before, and described him as an over-dressed adolescent with a failing for blessing crowds. Henry III had been to some trouble to prevent the crowds retaliating: *Chronica Majora*, V, 509; *Close Rolls*, 1254–6, 212. For Felipe, see Hernández Parrales, *Archivo Hispalense*, XXXI, 195 ff.

[5] See Ch. 8.

[6] *Cuarta Crónica General*, 12; *Crónica del Rey Don Alfonso*, 24.

The grant of *tercias* – the third part of the ecclesiastical tithe normally earmarked for the upkeep of the church's fabric[1] – which Alfonso X felt able to use for purely political purposes, had been made to Alfonso's father, Fernando III, by Innocent IV in April 1247 as a contribution towards the cost of the Seville campaign.[2] This was not the first papal grant of *tercias* to the war-chest. Nor was it the earliest indication of secular interest in ecclesiastical revenue. Archbishop Rodrigo had both received such a grant, in March 1219,[3] and earlier restrained Count Álvaro Núñez de Lara, guardian of the young King Enrique I, from helping himself.[4] But it was the first such grant to the *king*, and it was to have many repercussions. After the recapture of Córdoba, Gregory IX had declared that Fernando's military achievement had put the Roman Church in the king's debt.[5] Gregory had repaid the debt, though, by permitting Fernando to dispose of bishoprics to his own convenience. He had not allowed him to make free with the *tercias*, and when the king had attempted to do so in 1228 he had received a sharp reproof.[6] Papal assistance on the occasion of the Córdoba campaign had taken the form of a lump sum, of sixty thousand *maravedís*, from the Castilian and Leonese Churches – a liberal grant indeed at a period of such general hardship, as Burriel observed, though it cost Gregory himself nothing.[7] Yet even if, as he appears to have done, the king contrived to triple the value of that grant,[8] it was still a bargain for the churches, in comparison with the

---

[1] Cf. Giles Constable, *Monastic Tithes from their Origins to the Twelfth Century* (Cambridge, 1964), 47 ff.

[2] *Reg. Inn. IV*, 2538: a grant of half the *tercias* for three years.

[3] *Reg. Hon. III*, 1937 (MDH, 210): half the *tercias* of his province for three years. According to the archbishop, laymen were in possession of the *tercias* anyway, 'pro magna parte'. This was *not* a grant to the king, as Gallardo Fernández, *Origen ...de las rentas*, III, 34, alleged, thus misleading subsequent writers. Cf. Mansilla *Iglesia*, 57.

[4] *De Rebus Hispaniae*, 193. Cf. Fita, *BRAH*, XXXIX, 529.

[5] '...propter quod sic Romanam ecclesiam tibi constituis debitricem': inc. *Si regalis serenitas*, 20 Dec. 1236: publ. García y García, *REDC*, XV, 149–50.

[6] AC Toledo, Z.3.D.1.5=AHN, 3019/5 (publ. Fita, *BRAH*, VIII, 402). Cf. AC Toledo, Z.3.D.1.11 (publ. González, *Alfonso VIII*, III, 717). See Cedillo, *Contribuciones*, 298–9, on the misdeeds of 'un príncipe tan religioso como San Fernando'.

[7] *Reg. Greg. IX*, 3315; Burriel, *Memorias*, 67: 'Fué imposición que en otro tiempo se hiciera insoportable, pero en aquel en que a nuestro Rey todo le parecía poco para dar a la Iglesia, esta nada juzgaba excesivo para aliviar al Rey.'

[8] 'Otrossi say por verdat quel Rey don Fernando gano del papa quellas yglesias del reyno de Leon et del reyno de Castiella le diessen LX mil morabetinos segundo,

concession of 1247. Gregory had done well, better than Innocent, for without the *tercias*, which the kings having secured were never to release, the ecclesiastical community was crippled financially and permanently. Throughout the rest of the thirteenth century and beyond they would treat the *tercias* as a source of regular income, and repeated papal and episcopal *cris de coeur* would fail to recover what had so unheedingly been granted away.[1]

In 1248, therefore, when Seville was taken, the Castilian and Leonese Churches were in a parlous state. Their financial contribution during the previous thirty-five years had been enormous. They had lost control of their future income. They were under the king's heel, and the anxiety which the Spanish bishops had recently expressed for a tougher papal policy towards Frederick II of Germany sprang as much from weakness as from strength, as much from fear lest the German's example of contempt for ecclesiastics and their property should inspire their own monarchs to similar excesses ('cum principes universi exemplum et audaciam in hac parte reciperent ab eodem'), as from their much vaunted confidence in their own powers.[2] They were leaderless: Archbishop Rodrigo had drowned in the Rhône in July 1247 and his successor, Juan de Medina, had followed him to the grave in July 1248, four months before Seville was surrendered.[3] Their fate was in the balance and depended very largely upon the extent to which they were rewarded from the forthcoming

como yo creo, por tres anos', Archdeacon Rodrigo of León recalled in 1267: AC León, doc. 1564. He also mentioned that the executor of the grant, Bishop Juan of Osma, reduced the contribution originally demanded of the church of León – a circumstance which may have some bearing on their desire to have Juan as their bishop at this time.

[1] 'A partir de esta época este nuevo tributo parece haber tomado carta de naturaleza en Castilla': Mansilla, *Iglesia*, 57. In Sept. 1301 Boniface VIII protested to Fernando IV that the *tercias*, which had been allowed to his great-grandfather *ad certum tempus*, were still being exacted by him and his agents 'in tue ac ipsorum animarum periculum, proprie fame dispendium et ecclesiarum ac personarum ecclesiasticarum dampnum, injuriam et jacturam': *Reg. Bon. VIII*, 4407. But such protests were ineffective, and at the end of the fifteenth century the same problem faced Sixtus IV: Azcona, *Elección y reforma*, 288, n. 64.

[2] Huillard–Bréholles, *Historia diplomatica*, v, ii, 1120.

[3] For Rodrigo's epitaph, see Loperráez, *Descripción*, I, 205. Juan de Medina was appointed in Feb. 1248 and died on 28 July: AC Toledo, A.7.A.1.1 (=*Reg. Inn. IV*, 3654); Serrano, *Obispado de Burgos*, III, 385. His will, dated 20 July 1248 (AC Toledo, A.7.A.1.5), mentions a large and varied library. Part of it is published, from BN MS. 13022, fos. 116r–24v, by Alonso Alonso, *Razón y Fe*, CXXIII, 296–7.

distribution of property, the *repartimiento* of Seville. It is generally assumed that they were not disappointed,[1] even though the outlook was far from encouraging. In that very spring the pope had protested that Fernando and his son were dragging their heels on the question of the endowment of re-established cathedral churches.[2] Moreover, the evidence itself simply will not sustain the assumption.

An analysis of the *repartimiento* shows that grants of Seville property to churchmen were restricted, almost exclusively, to a group which had its home in the royal chancery. The recipients represented the Castilian Church only in so far as the Castilian Church had already passed under the direct control of the king. They fell into two main groups: the clique of bishops who were already or who were soon to be most closely associated with the royal administration; and the notaries and chancery clerks who would form the core of the next episcopal generation. Chief among the former group was Bishop Remondo of Segovia, an intimate of the royal house who had charge of the spiritual organisation of Seville from the very beginning and who in 1259, on the retirement from ecclesiastical power politics of the genial Infante Felipe, succeeded to the archbishopric.[3] Four more were bishops of frontier sees who might have been expected to have received sufficient endowments in their own areas. Two of them, Pascal of Jaén and Roberto of Silves, were each sent on diplomatic errands to England in the late fifties,[4] and the former's weight at court was such that in September 1256 the Infante Fadrique chose him as arbiter of a dispute with the archbishop-elect of Toledo, his brother Sancho.[5] Similarly the third of them, Bishop Gutierre who in March 1246 had been appointed to the see of Córdoba at the king's behest 'cum sit genere potens et nobilis, insignis virtutibus et scientia dotatus' – qualities which were to bring about his promotion to Toledo in February 1249 – was awarded the *villa de Bella* for his assistance at the siege.[6] The last of this group was the bishop of

1 Above, p. 102.
2 AC Toledo, I.6.G.I.12 (=*Reg. Inn. IV*, 3770).
3 González, *Repartimiento*, II, 28, 175, 231, 266, 309, 320. For biographical details, see Ballesteros, *Sevilla en el siglo XIII*, ch. 7; *idem, Correo Erudito*, I, 313–18.
4 González, II, 29 (cf. 241, 266); *Close Rolls, 1256–9*, pp. 57, 152, 315; *Close Rolls, 1259–61*, pp. 166–7; Trabut-Cussac, *Mélanges de la Casa de Velázquez*, II, 51–8.
5 AC Toledo, A.7.C.2.11.
6 *Reg. Inn. IV*, 1757, 4341; González, II, 29, 241, 298–9. The grant of Bella was made by the king in March 1249 – that is, seven weeks after Gutierre's promotion – to the

Cartagena, the literary Franciscan Pedro Gallego.[1] Moreover, it was only recently that the churches of Coria and Cuenca, which in the persons of Bishops Pedro[2] and Mateo[3] received grants of land, had ceased to be in the Christian front-line.[4] Indeed, in the early sixties, Mateo's successor but one would maintain that Cuenca was still a frontier see.[5]

In contrast to his relatively generous treatment of these presumably well-heeled prelates, the king's remuneration to churchmen from Leon and Old Castile was paltry. Only five bishops from the region that had borne the financial brunt of the long years of struggle received anything from the *repartimiento*, and for two of them – Pedro of Zamora and Rodrigo of Palencia – the morsels which they were granted did absolutely nothing to alleviate the great weight of debt by which they were encumbered. In fact, on balance the Seville operation left Bishop Pedro out of pocket and contributed marginally to his bankruptcy, as he informed his chapter in January 1255.[6] And Rodrigo's modest receipts had soon to be sold off as his see slid deeper into the mire.[7]

The tentacular archbishop of Santiago, Juan Arias, who to his great chagrin had fallen ill at the siege and had been sent home by the king, nevertheless managed, characteristically, to secure something

---

bishop and chapter of Córdoba jointly 'pro multis et magnis servitiis quae me fecistis in frontaria, et signanter pro servitio quod vos domnus Guterrius...fecistis me in exercitu Sivillae, quando eam acquisivi': publ. Burriel, 507.

[1] González, II, 28–9 (cf. 231), 306 (=*MHE*, I, 9–10). Cf. Torres Fontes, *Hispania*, XIII, 356 ff.; Pelzer, *Miscellanea Ehrle*, I, 407 ff.

[2] González, II, 29 (cf. 241, 266). The episcopal succession at Coria is greatly confused by González Davila, *Teatro*, II, 445, and thence by Eubel, *Hierarchia*, I, 178, and Ballesteros, *BRAH*, CVI, 1234. Sancho was bishop by Oct. 1232 and was still alive in April 1252: Burriel, 404, 536. Vacant: by Feb. 1253, for at least four months: *MHE*, I, 8, 17. Pedro had been elected by 6 Dec. 1253: Ortiz de Zúñiga, *Anales*, 77. He died between Oct. 1259 and Nov. 1260: *MHE*, I, 154, 169.

[3] González, *Repartimiento*, II, 29 (cf. 241, 266), 303.

[4] Mansilla, 122, 132.

[5] Below, p. 178.

[6] González, *Repartimiento*, II, 28 (cf. 241, 266), 40; AC Zamora, 13/7: 'Ex ea (pecunia) enim expensas fecimus: nos ipsos post confirmationem obtentam maiestati regie Burgensi, ut decens erat, personaliter presentando. Item, pro confirmatione nostra Compostellani archiepiscopi presenciam apud eamdem ecclesiam adeundo. Deinde, ad concilium generale Lugdunensem eundo, inibi demorando et abinde redeundo. Postmodum ex vocacione regali nobis facta Yspalim accedendo.'

[7] González, II, 339, 342; see Ch. 7.

for himself.[1] But the only other grants to bishops of older-established sees were to a pair of prelates who had made their name in the royal chancery: Pedro Fernández of Astorga – a see which did achieve economic prosperity during this century, principally on account of the close relationship of each of its bishops with the king;[2] and Benito of Ávila.[3] Benito's see was occupied for much of the thirteenth century by men who spent a great part of their time representing the Castilian monarch at the papal Curia,[4] and he himself was active at this very moment on behalf of one of the king's clerks, Agustín of Osma, whom Benito was determined that the church of San Vicente (Ávila) should provide with a benefice, however much the local clergy might protest.[5] For such was the system: Agustín belonged to that second group which profited from the *repartimiento*, the group which contained at least four future bishops – Fernando of Palencia, Martín Fernández of León, Suero Pérez of Zamora, and Agustín himself, to whom the bishopric of Osma was awarded in 1261.[6]

It was only then, when members of this group became bishops –

---

1 *Primera Crónica General*, para. 1113, 1117; González, II, 23 (cf. 231, 313).
2 González, II, 27 (cf. 241), 298; *ES*, XVI, 235 ff. (for Pedro Fernández) and 225–50 (for the other bishops of Astorga during this century). The almost total destruction of the Astorga archive by the French army in 1810 prevents an analysis of this prosperity, but some information has survived. By March 1224 Bishop Pedro Andrés (d. 1226) had improved the value of the church's property to over nine thousand *aurei* (RAH, MS C2/9.5422, fo. 92r); Pedro Fernández was one of Pedro of Zamora's creditors in 1255 (AC Zamora, 13/7); and Martín González (d. 1301), Sancho IV's boon companion, was able in March 1288 to lend the archbishop of Toledo 20,000 *maravedís monete guerre*, having in the previous May obtained from the impoverished see of Palencia control of the abbey of San Salvador de Cantamuda, in circumstances which are obscure (AC Toledo, A.7.G.2.17; AD Astorga, 4/82). For this bishop, see Hergueta, *RABM*, IX, 328 ff., and Rodríguez López, *Episcopologio*, II, 291 ff. The financial flair of his predecessor, Melendo Pérez (d. 1284) is noted by Flórez, *ES*, XVI, 244.
3 González, II, 29 (cf. 241, 266), 309. Contrary to Mansilla's account, *Iglesia*, 177, Gregory IX's appointment to Ávila of the exiled *magister scolarum* of Lisbon, Estêvão Gomes, in July 1241 (*Reg. Greg. IX*, 6087: publ. Sousa Costa, 243, n. 360) seems to have been ignored. In the following year Benito was bishop, and by 1246 was a member of the king's inner circle: Burriel, 465; above, p. 110, n. 2.
4 For Bishops Domingo Suárez, O.F.M. and Ademar, O.P. at the Curia, see *Reg. Urb. IV*, 233, 2860 (1263); *Reg. Greg. X*, 192 (1272); AC Toledo, A.7.G.1.4/11c (1281); Mondéjar, *Memorias históricas*, 174, 183.
5 *Reg. Inn. IV*, 3943; Loperráez, I, 249 ff.
6 González, II, 31, 231, 320; 20, 139, 264; 70, 243; 69–71 (block grants to the king's *escrivanos* and *clerigos*). On this group, see Procter, *Salter essays*, 115, 120–1.

and even then it was only most tenuously – that the churches of Leon and Old Castile derived any profit from Seville. They had been the victims of an enormous confidence-trick, and though all sections of Castilian society had had to contribute to the cost of military success during the previous three and a half decades, it had been the Church that had been made to sacrifice most. From the *concejos* of Galicia Fernando III had exacted forced loans. But prompt repayment had been promised.[1] There was no prospect, though, of ever recovering the *tercias*. Nor was there any compensation for their loss. The cathedrals of Burgos, Oviedo and León, for example, received nothing from the *repartimiento* of Seville.[2] And the same seems to have been true of the *repartimientos* of Cartagena and Jerez.[3] It was essential to make the Christian presence felt on the frontier, and if northern churchmen were desirous of sharing in the putative pleasures of the south the only course open to them was to uproot themselves and emigrate, thereby further weakening the economy of the north and in some cases creating considerable disharmony in their new surroundings.[4]

---

[1] In June 1248: González, I, 184.

[2] In the case of Burgos this may be more easily appreciated by reference to the extracts from the *Repartimiento* published by Huidobro y Serna, *BIFG*, XXXI, 51 ff., 99 ff. Apart from the royal monastic foundations of S. Isidoro, León (González, II, 43, 243, 305) and Las Huelgas, Burgos (*ibid.* II, 44, 313, 335–6), the only beneficiary in these three places seems to have been the dean of Burgos, Martín González de Contreras. And in Aug. 1258 he met his end, suitably enough after such assiduous attendance at court, when the royal palace of Segovia caved in, with him inside: *ibid.* II, 33, 271.

[3] The cantor of Valladolid who was a royal cleric, and an archdeacon of Toledo, respectively, seem to have been the only representatives of the churches of the north and centre in these two places: Torres Fontes, *Repartimiento de Murcia*, 22, 59, 221, 238; Gutiérrez, *Historia de Xerex*, II, 40. Similarly, at Córdoba the grants of property to Bishop Lope had all been made *before* his election, as the king stressed when he confirmed them in February 1239: Burriel, 443. However, it would be unwise to generalise about the Córdoba *repartimiento* without a careful study of the *Libro de Tablas* in AC Córdoba, which I have not been able to see. The extracts published by Muñoz Vázquez in *Bol. Real Acad. de Córdoba*, XXV, 251 ff., give no clues, while Sr Muñoz Vázquez's study of the subject remains unpublished. The list of landowners owing tithes to the see of Córdoba, admittedly an imperfect guide, mentions only six bishops: Rodrigo of Toledo, Juan of Osma, Nuño of Astorga, Gonzalo of Cuenca, Domingo of Baeza and Sancho of Coria – and three of these had frontier sees: Gómez Bravo, *Catálogo*, I, 264.

[4] For the effects of the Jaén–Soria connexion, see below, Ch. 10. There seems to have been some such affiliation between Córdoba and Burgos: Juan de Medina's MS. of

Moreover, the net profit to the Church of the few grants that were made to churchmen was considerably reduced (if it was not altogether illusory) by the personal circumstances of the recipients. For as civil servants they were almost permanently away from their sees. Their home was the royal court and even their consecration as bishops came second in importance after affairs of state. In October 1255, at Alfonso X's request, the pope postponed for a year that of Suero Pérez of Zamora, the king's notary 'et ei persona plurimum oportuna',[1] while seven years later it was the king himself who instructed the bishops-elect of Osma and Cuenca, Agustín and Pedro Lorenzo, to make arrangements for theirs at Seville, where he and they were occupied for months on end *circa rempublicam,* rather than in their own province of Toledo, 'because we have need of them'.[2] By Raymond of Peñafort's standards, the atmosphere of *curialitas* in which they lived would have prevented such men being ordained, let alone consecrated.[3]

Mention of St Raymond invites comparison with the position of the Church in Aragon and its fate during these years of frantic military activity. There the logistics of Reconquest were rather different, for, having been alloted a much smaller area to resettle by the Treaty of Cazorla in 1179, Aragon had reached its prescribed limits ten years before the fall of Seville.[4] Still, despite the geopolitical advantages which he enjoyed, the decade following the recapture of

the *Compilatio Quinta* passed from Burgos to Córdoba (Fransen, *Rev. d'Hist. Ecclésiastique,* XLVIII, 234; García y García, *REDC,* xv, 147 ff.), possibly *via* Juan's nephew, Fernán Rodríguez, to whom the archbishop's 'decretum et decretales' were bequeathed in July 1248 (AC Toldeo, A.7.A.1.5.). The cantor of Burgos, García de Campo, mentioned in his will that he had Bishop Fernando of Córdoba's copy of Peter Lombard on loan: AC Burgos, vol. 48, fo. 425 (datable to between 1269 and 1274).

[1] *Reg. Alex. IV,* 870. The pope had already issued an indulgence for those attending Suero's forthcoming consecration: *Tue devotionis,* 7 July 1255: AC Zamora, 11.i/5.

[2] '...porque les avemos mester pora nuestro servicio. Ca si por aventura se fuesen consagrar a Toledo o a otro lugar fuera de provincia de Sevilla non nos podriemos tan ayna servir de ellos': Ballesteros, *Sevilla en el siglo XIII,* cxxi. The court was at Seville for most of 1262: *idem. Alfonso X,* 1084. For the phrase *circa rempublicam occupati,* see below, p. 180.

[3] According to Raymond, ordination was to be withheld 'nisi primo sint absoluti a curia': *Summa de Poenitentia,* 287–9.

[4] Valdeavellano, *Historia de España,* I, ii, 567–8; Font y Ríus in *La Reconquista española y la repoblación del país,* 88 ff.

Valencia had presented King Jaime with a multitude of problems. Although the disparity between the area to be colonised and his reserves of manpower was less daunting than in Castile, he too lacked sufficient human resources for definitive resettlement – *la Reconquista lenta*, in Vicens's terminology, as against *la Reconquista militar*.[1] Indeed in 1248 he was especially conscious of this difficulty. The revolt of the Valencian Moors led by al-Azrak had faced him with the difficult choice of either expelling the Moors and rendering the kingdom an economic desert, or retaining them and running the risk of further risings. The dilemma remained with him until his deathbed, when he advised his son and heir to take the former course 'per ço con eren tots traydors', a course which he himself had never been able to take, despite his determination to do so on the morrow of al-Azrak's revolt.[2] Instead he had to content himself with a looser form of control than the Castilian monarch's *repoblación intensiva,* and a practical demonstration of their *dos criterios* was provided in the kingdom of Murcia where both he and Alfonso X had control, in turn, during the 1260s.[3]

Dos criterios are evident also in the treatment which churchmen received from each of these monarchs, and that the thirteenth-century Aragonese Church proved able to defend the endowments of reconquered territory which it had been granted in the past was due in no small measure to its tradition of joint conciliar action.[4] For, in addition to their pastoral function, regular church councils had a political significance which the kings of Castile certainly understood and the kings of Aragon soon learnt to appreciate also.[5] Would-be *raptores ecclesiarum* had to reckon with conciliar constitutions which evidently continued to have some deterrent value sixty or more years after their original promulgation.[6] Moreover, in 1250 the pre-

---

[1] Vicens Vives, *Manual de historia económica,* 143 ff.; Sobrequés, 10–11, 46–7. In maintaining that Castile enjoyed a demographic advantage over Aragon, Vicens, *op. cit.,* 223, seems to ignore the fact that Aragon had a smaller area to colonise.

[2] *Chronica del Rey En Jacme,* cap. 361, 364, 564, ed. Aguiló, 379–80, 382–3, 533; trans. Forster, II, 475–6, 480, 674.

[3] Torres Fontes, *VII.CHCA,* II, 332–3, 336; Font y Ríus, in *La Reconquista española,* 121 ff.

[4] For these endowments, see Lacarra, *RPH,* IV, 272 ff.

[5] Below, Ch. 8. It would be interesting to know what King Jaime's attitude was towards Pedro de Albalat, in 1239 and after.

[6] Above, p. 81, n. 7.

lates of the Tarragona province assembled at Alcañiz solely in order to excommunicate the king of Navarre, in retaliation for the treatment which one of their number, Bishop Pedro Ximénez of Pamplona, had received from him.[1] Teobaldo I of Navarre may have been a pretty negligible quantity. But Jaime I of Aragon was not. Yet he too acknowledged the political weight of the Church, a fact which his spectacular assaults on individual prelates did nothing to obscure. When he received a subvention of tithes in 1248, the grant was made not by the pope and over the heads of the bishops, as in Castile, but by the bishops themselves at a provincial council.[2] Aragonese churchmen were a serious proposition. They were not docile, and the view that 'they are not found at any time at variance with the king as the nobles often were'[3] is profoundly mistaken, as King Jaime, one of Archbishop Benito's victims, had reason to know. Had they been, Jaime would not have recommended his son-in-law in 1269 to endeavour to retain their support together with that of the people and the towns, if it came to a decision, rather than that of the military classes.

The son-in-law who was entrusted with the distilled wisdom of almost half a century of political experience was Alfonso X of Castile,[4]

---

[1] Tejada, *Colección*, VI, 47–8; Goñi Gaztambide, *Príncipe de Viana*, XVIII, 97 ff.

[2] Fita, *BRAH*, XL, 446–7. The provision of *some* form of assistance without delay – 'auxilium...sine difficultate ac tarditate;...opportunum subsidium' – was both authorised by the pope and confirmed by him. But the initiative remained with the bishops; and it was they who granted Jaime the *vicesima* of ecclesiastical income for one year, and in March 1249 extended it for a further year – as the papal confirmation makes clear: 'Cum...tu tuique suffraganei...*unanimi* ad preces et mandatum nostrum conveneritis *voluntate* ut vicesimam...praeberetis...': ACA, Bulas, leg. X–43 (reg. Miquel Rosell, *Regesta*, 153); *Reg. Inn. IV*, 4309 (publ. Baluze, *Miscellanea*, I, 217). Yet Mansilla, when referring to this latter rescript (the text of which he adjusts), implies that the Aragonese grant was identical in form with the *papal* concession of Castilian *tercias*: 'no faltaron tampoco para Aragón privilegiadas concesiones pontificias': 'La Curia Romana y la restauración eclesiástica en el reinado de San Fernando', *RET*, IV (1944), 127–64, at p. 163; *Iglesia*, 57–8. That they were not identical is further indicated by the pope's ability to refer in Jan. 1253 to his explicit concession of *medietatem tertie* six years before as 'illam partem tertie...quam (episcopi) *expedire viderent* (regi)...exhiberi', as though the size of the Castilian grant had been decided by the Castilian prelates too: *Reg. Inn. IV*, 2538, 6316. There could be no such confusion or prevarication in Aragon.

[3] Chaytor, *History of Aragon and Catalonia*, 111.

[4] 'Si a retener nauia negu quen retingues dues partides si tots nols podia retener, ço es la esglesia, els pobles e les ciutats de la terra: car aquels son gent que Deus ama mes

and without being unduly callous he could afford to treat this piece of advice as the fond musings of an old man, for the Castilian Church possessed no such corporate spirit of conciliar activity. The *Primera Partida* – an otherwise exhaustive guide to ecclesiastical discipline and practice, derived largely from Raymond of Peñafort's *Summa* – contains a lengthy description of the procedure at monastic chapters but is silent about councils.[1] Despite the admonitions of Honorius III, John of Abbeville and Gregory IX, Archbishop Rodrigo of Toledo had not been stirred to action. He had been in his element *ubi curia regis erat,* and under his leadership so closely identified were the bishops of Castile and Leon with the king that the royal court rather then the provincial council was their only common forum. To pay the king a visit, *ut decens erat,* was the first thought of Bishop Pedro of Zamora after the confirmation of his election in 1239.[2] Training tells. But at least, Pedro had only one journey to make. His predecessor, Bishop Martín I, had had to cope with two kings and two courts, and the tasks entrusted to him by the pope had come a poor third.[3] Small wonder that the Leonese bishops were such keen supporters of the union of the two kingdoms by Fernando III in 1230.[4]

In gratitude to Bishop Nuño of Astorga for his assistance at that

---

que fa los cauallers, car los cauallers se leuen pus tost contra senyoria quels altres, e si tots los podia retener que bon feria, e si no que aquests .ij. retingues, car ab aquests destruyria los altres': *Chronica del Rey En Jacme,* cap. 498, ed. Aguiló, 486–7; trans. Forster, II, 617. See Valls i Taberner, *B. Hisp.* XXI, 40.

1 Above, p. 39. There is a solitary, casual reference to the provincial council in *Part.* 1.6.54, prescribing penalties against bishops who hunted: BM, Add. MS. 20787, fo. 49ra (cf. Academy ed. I, 285, as *Part.* 1.6.47). For St Raymond's influence on the *Partidas,* see Giménez y Martínez de Carvajal, *AA,* II, 239 ff.; *AA,* III, 201 ff.: the *Primera Partida* is 'integra y exclusivamente canónica', and the *Quarta* 'fundamentalmente canónica' (*AA,* II, 239). Apart from St Raymond ('la principal fuente canónica inmediata de la Primera Partida': *AA,* III, 235) many other sources, from Gratian onwards, are distinguishable – though the title of the Gratian MS. (BC Tortosa, 239), reported by García y García as 'liber decretorum dividitur in tres *partidas',* proves not to have been a *felix culpa* but Prof. García's *culpa: Studia Gratiana,* VIII, no. 33; conversation with the author, Feb. 1967.

2 AC Zamora, 13/7.

3 AC Zamora, 11.ii/8: excusing himself from acting as judge–delegate in a case between the bishop of Burgos and the monastery of Oña 'quia rex Legionis vocat nos ad curiam quam incontinenti est celebraturus apud Legionem, et statim ituri ad colloquium regis Castelle': undated, but from the context an. 1210–11. Cf. Alamo, *CD Oña,* I, 463.

4 Rodericus Toletanus, *De Rebus Hispaniae,* 204.

time Fernando granted him and his church the town of Santa Marina del Rey since, as he explained, kings had a particular duty to reward those who stood by them at times of crisis.[1] Unfortunately, however, for the majority of the bishops, Fernando seems to have altered his opinion by the time of the *repartimiento* of Seville. They then found themselves without the means of defence with which Pedro de Albalat had meanwhile girded the Aragonese Church. As late as 1243, in which year Archbishop Rodrigo concluded his contemporary history on a triumphant note,[2] they probably still shared their leader's optimism. But by 1245 they were evidently uneasy, in 1247 uneasiness must have given way to alarm, and very soon after 1248, when their expectations had been disappointed and the king looked to them ever more frequently for financial assistance, they would have cause to curse the late archbishop for having made so little provision for their welfare.

Their collective change of mind was hastened by a combination of national and international developments. At home, the economic benefits of Seville proved just as nugatory as those which had been expected from Córdoba a dozen years before, and the decade after 1248 was not the blissful dawn predicted by the propagandists but a period of even blacker night. While continuing, with papal approval, to receive the *tercias*, Alfonso X, like his father, failed to honour his undertaking to endow the new sees.[3] It was a bad time for beggars. From the very beginning of Alfonso's reign, in 1252, the economic situation deteriorated. With Seville the Christians inherited all the problems of supply which had induced its defenders to abandon the place,[4] and on his accession the new king's first act was to attempt to reduce demand and to remedy 'las carestias grandes de las cosas que se vendien' by fixing prices, prohibiting exports and publishing

---

[1] 'Sicut ad ultionem malefactorum accingi debet regis auctoritas, sic et ipsius clementia perpetuis tenetur honorare muneribus eos potissime qui tempore discriminis ad eius obsequium fideliter laborarunt', Jan. 1231: Burriel, 376.

[2] *De Rebus Hispaniae*, 207–8.

[3] *Reg. Inn. IV*, 6316, 5216: reproving Fernando III for his failure to provide for the church of Jaén, whose bishops 'propter temporalium rerum carentiam nimium indigentem…inibi pro tempore cogantur in obprobrium pontificalis dignitatis egere', 6 April 1251 (publ. Mansilla, 357). Yet only twenty-four days later he authorised a further grant of *tercias* to the Infante Alfonso from the diocese of Cuenca: BN, MS. 13071, fo. 55r.

[4] *Anónimo de Madrid y Copenhague*, 190; González, *Repartimiento*, I, 207 ff.

sumptuary laws which cast gloom even over wedding-breakfasts:[1] a far cry from the buoyant optimism of four years before. The introduction of a stronger currency which was designed to bring relief produced quite the opposite effect. Having greater intrinsic value, the *dineros prietos* could be struck in only small quantities, and for the same reason they rapidly left the kingdom.[2] Prices soared and an inflationary spiral was established, while the primitive state of communications reduced the limited stabilising influence which such increase of resources as had occurred might otherwise have produced.[3]

In these unpropitious circumstances the king's personal short-comings provided the final, fatal ingredient of disaster. Far from possessing 'a puritan streak', Alfonso was – in the estimation of his Franciscan admirer, Gil de Zamora – the most prodigal of men, and lacked all sense of moderation. It was characteristic of him that, in the very year when his grandees were petitioning John XXI for permission to debase the coinage, he undertook to provision Navarre from his poverty-stricken country which, he claimed, *es tota plantat*.[4] But this was neither his first nor his greatest act of folly, for in the mid-1250s, with Castile still prostrate after its recent exertions, he had embarked on his imperial venture: *una funesta ilusión* Ballesteros pronounces it, echoing Mariana's conclusion that some higher force was bent on deluding him.[5]

---

[1] *Cortes de Castilla*, I, 54 ff.; A. Ballesteros y Berretta, 'Las Cortes de 1252', *Anales de la Junta para la Ampliación de Estudios,* III (1911), 109–43; García Rámila, *Hispania*, V, 205 ff.; Castro, *Rev. Filología Española*, VIII, 6 ff.; Carlé, *CHE*, XXI–II, 303–4.

[2] In May 1277 Pope John XXI was informed of these developments when the Burgos Cortes requested that he permit Alfonso to break his oath to maintain *los dineros prietos* and strike a new coinage *mas comunal*: E(scudero?) de la P(eña?), *RABM*, II, 58–60. Cf. Ballesteros, *Alfonso X*, 836–7; *Crónica del Rey Don Alfonso*, X, 3–4, 6; Gil Farrés, *Historia de la moneda española*, 204.

[3] For 'la espiral inflacionísta', see Carlé, *CHE*, XV, 132 ff., where the great disparity in the cost of horses between Galicia and Castile is noted, p. 137. Spaniards abroad had a down-at-heels appearance: sharp-eyed Matthew Paris noticed that the Infante Sancho's retinue was mounted on mules rather than palfreys: *Chronica Majora*, V, 509. For the currency fluctuation, see Colmeiro, *Historia de la economía política*, 491 ff.; Usher, *Early History of Deposit Banking*, 214 ff.

[4] Guillaume Anelier de Toulouse, *Histoire de la Guerre de Navarre en 1276 et 1277*, p. 126, line 1910. Van Kleffens infers the 'puritan streak' from Alfonso's draconian legislation: *Hispanic Law*, 152, n. 2. Gil de Zamora, ed. Fita, *BRAH*, V, 319. See also Procter, *Alfonso X*, 138; Wolff, *Speculum*, XXIX, 57 ff.

[5] Ballesteros, *RABM*, XXXIV, 219; Mariana, *De Rebus Hispaniae*, I, 555–6. Jofré de

It was to the Church that Alfonso turned for financial backing, both to wind up his old accounts and to underwrite the new. He continued to exact the *tercias*, and his motive in seeking to eliminate irregularities in the collection of tithes during the autumn of 1255 was not, as he piously declared, that the things of God should be rendered unto God, but rather that the things of the Church should be rendered unto him.[1] Apart from suffering from this perpetual haemorrhage the Church was also required to provide further occasional transfusions. In June 1254 when Innocent IV demanded prompt settlement of his father's debts to the Roman Church, the king appealed to the long-suffering bishops of Castile – those of Burgos, Oviedo, León and Palencia – 'como amigos e naturales de mi e de mio lignage'. Even more galling to them than the politely worded demand itself must have been the implication that they were morally if not legally obliged to co-operate, and the reference to Fernando III 'que tanto bien fizo a vos e a vuestras eglesias'. Nevertheless, they obliged,[2] though the money never reached the pope, for in September 1263 the debt was still outstanding and, despite the explanation that it had been intercepted by certain Florentine bankers to whom the king was indebted, a curious coincidence suggests that it may have reached a different destination. On 30 October 1255, as well as writing to thank the bishop and chapter of Burgos for their contribution, Alfonso dispatched the archdeacon of Morocco, García Pérez, to arrange the treaty with the city of Marseilles which formed the basis of his diplomatic campaign to secure the German Crown.[3]

Of the four churches which had responded to the king's request for *servicio*, only Palencia had figured in the *repartimiento* of Seville (and little good that had done Bishop Rodrigo).[4] But by the autumn of

---

Loaisa described the expenses of the imperial venture as 'fere incredibiles': *BEC*, LIX, 337. See also Schramm, *Festschrift Stengel*, 385 ff.

[1] Ballesteros, *BRAH*, CV, 139–40, 149 ff.; Menéndez Pidal, *Documentos lingüísticos*, I, 299–300; AHN, 20/4; *MHE*, I, 70–5; AC Salamanca, 16/3/7, 16/2/11–12 (reg. Marcos, 255, 257, 262). Fernando III had shown a similar interest in the technicalities of tithe collection: AC Salamanca, 16/1/16 (reg. Marcos, 236: text, misdated, in Burriel, 528).

[2] *Reg. Inn. IV*, 8306; AC Burgos, vol. 48, fo. 212 (publ. Ballesteros, *BRAH*, CV, 151–2); AC Oviedo, A/7/14 (reg. García Larragueta, *Catálogo*, 364); AC León, doc. 1092; Fernández del Pulgar, *Historia de Palencia*, II, 340.

[3] *Reg. Urb. IV*, cam. 478; Jordan, *De mercatoribus*, 16; Scheffer-Boichorst, *MIöG*, IX, 242.   [4] Below, Ch. 7.

1255 they were at least aware that the sacred cow, Seville, for which they had sacrificed and been sacrificed during the thirties and forties was, in fact, a white elephant, and, further, that the monster was still hungry and that they were still expected to feed it. For as soon as the Church had been established there under the general management of the Infante Felipe and Alfonso had claimed three years' *tercias* from the new province, it was the provinces of Toledo and Compostela that were made to foot the bill.[1] And again, in July 1257, the Infante successfully petitioned Alexander IV for a grant of three thousand marks from the *tercias* of the northern provinces in order to meet the debts which he had contracted while at the Curia in the previous November.[2] For them Seville was as great a liability after 1248 as it had been before. It was their donations that enabled Alfonso to endow and enhance the church there 'pre aliis ecclesiis Hispanie'.[3]

The glories of Seville Cathedral, then, should not blind the historian to the very real difficulties of the mid-thirteenth-century Castilian Church. For far from providing a physical representation of what most writers have regarded as the medieval Church at its zenith – a misapprehension for which they may have found confirmation in the suggestion that, almost a decade before Alfonso X went a-whoring after strange foreign empires, his father had determined to celebrate Seville's recapture at a secular level by reviving the old Spanish imperial title[4] – those glories ought rather to serve to focus attention

---

[1] *Reg. Inn. IV,* 6214, 6497. The 700 mark subvention was an annual charge, renewed by Alexander IV: *Reg. Alex. IV,* 2078.

[2] *Reg. Alex. IV,* 1921, 2078. He had borrowed £3,000 Tours at the Curia. From his own archdiocese he had been granted the *decimae de oleo* of all churches for life: *ibid.* 99 (January 1255). See also F. C(ollantes) de T(erán), *Archivo Hispalense,* IV, 39–42.

[3] Gil de Zamora, ed. Fita, *BRAH,* v, 321.

[4] This suggestion was made by Schramm in 1950 on the basis of the adaptation to the Spanish context of the imperial coronation *ordo,* the work of a Bishop Ramón, whom Schramm identified with Remondo of Segovia, afterwards archbishop of Seville: Escorial, MS. III & 3, fo. 1–32 (reg. Zarco Cuevas, *Catálogo,* I, 282); *Festschrift Ritter,* 136–8. However, the *ordo* – which previously had been ascribed to the twelfth century and Alfonso VII by Tubino, *Museo Español de Antigüedades,* v, 53–5 – is, in fact, an early fourteenth–century work, done for Alfonso XI by Bishop Remundo of Coimbra, as Sánchez-Albornoz had already demonstrated in *Logos,* II, iii, 75 ff., where the *ordo* is published: a study which became known to Schramm between 1950 and 1952, when he corrected his error: *Festschrift Stengel,* 387, n.1. By then,

on the area to the north where so many dioceses were in difficulties and so many parish churches were falling into decay. It was upon the ruins of these that Seville Cathedral was adorned and Abu Yacub's great mosque converted into a place fit for Christian worship.[1]

Of course, new cathedrals were rising in the first half of the thirteenth century. Lucas of Túy mentions them in the same breath as the town walls, cloisters and bridges as visible proof of Spain's resurgence.[2] Yet, to conclude on the strength either of this enthusiast or of the enduring monuments to his veracity that all the aforementioned signs of crisis may be discounted would certainly be to commit that 'sin which no economic historian should commit' and which Professor Postan has denounced from the pulpit of the *Economic History Review*, taking as his text another age of recession in another country: 'Even if it is proved that the period was rich in acts of private piety, graced by a flourishing religion, embellished by alabaster statues; better educated, more prettily coiffured and gowned, than any other period in the Middle Ages, the basic facts of material development would still be unaffected.'

For 'what do the perpendicular churches prove?'[3] And what can be proved by reference to the laying of the first stone of Toledo Cathedral – a building which was to take as long to complete as the *Reconquista* itself?[4] Certainly not that the kingdom of Castile and the Castilian Church were economically buoyant in the 1220s. The cost of building materials was so high, and Archbishop Rodrigo's income from the *tercias* of his own archdiocese so 'insufficient' that in January 1222 Honorius III was told that the chances of its ever being finished were 'entirely despaired of'. It was the other churches of the province that were made to foot the bill by contributing their *tercias* for the next five years.[5]

though, the error had been popularised by Folz, *L'idée d'empire*, 69. Moreover, when Sánchez-Albornoz republished his *Logos* article, in *Estudios sobre las instituciones medievales españolas*, 739 ff., he made no reference to the Schramm theory.

1 González, *Repartimiento*, I, 525–30.
2 *Chronicon Mundi*, 113.
3 M. M. Postan, 'The Fifteenth Century', *Ec. Hist. Rev.*, IX (1938–9), 160–7, at p. 164.
4 See Lambert, *L'art gothique en Espagne*, 203 ff.
5 *Reg. Hon. III*, 3697 (MDH, 388): '...ad cuius perfectionem, tum pro sui magnitudine, tum pro tenuitate reddituum ipsius fabrice, tum pro lignorum et lapidum raritate, usque adeo insufficientem proponis ecclesiam memoratam, ut de eiusdem consummatione fabrice penitus desperetur, nisi aliud remedium apponatur'. In

The 'magnitude' of that project, which bore thus heavily on contemporaries, has mesmerised later observers in its finished state. Victims of the propaganda of such writers as Lucas of Túy whose enthusiasm could transform even Aristotle into a Spaniard,[1] and heedless both of Postan's *caveat* and of its corollary,[2] historians of the Spanish Church have continued to read prosperity into their subject and have ignored the possibility of the existence of 'economic depression in the midst of artistic plenty'.[3] Yet even if the analogy of the Crown's failure to secure Granada until 1492 cannot shake their faith, it ought surely to weigh with them that only recently the associated doctrine of the extensive Andalucian endowments of the Military Orders has been shown to be ripe for revision,[4] and that documents long in print contain ample proof that in their gifts to the Church the kings were far less liberal than has generally been assumed.[5]

'Liberality' was what Burriel perceived in Gregory IX's dealings with Fernando III (though it was, he opined, as nothing in comparison with Fernando's own liberality to the churches). If, however, Gregory and Innocent IV chose to feel themselves indebted to those 'athletes of Christ', the peninsular monarchs, neither of them was much impoverished thereby. True, Innocent delayed the collection of taxes for the Holy Land in 1248 so that the Aragonese Church might divert its funds to Jaime I.[6] In Castile and Leon, though, it was

---

July 1224 the grant was renewed for a further four years: *ibid.* 5074 (MDH, 512). Rodrigo's stock was evidently rising again at the Curia.

[1] See Rico, *Italia Medioevale e Umanistica*, x, 143 ff.

[2] 'One of the principal tenets of the home-made sociology, which the non-sociological historians commonly assume, is that ages of economic expansion are necessarily ages of intellectual and artistic achievement. As if the generations which make the money also know how to spend it best...': *Ec. Hist. Rev.*, IX, 160–7.

[3] Cf. R. S. Lopez and H. A. Miskimin, 'The Economic Depression of the Renaissance', *Ec. Hist. Rev.*, 2nd ser., XIV (1961–2), 408.

[4] Lomax, 112–13. Cf. Sobrequés, 12 ff., 75.

[5] For example, the 'grant' of Talamanca to Archbishop Rodrigo in Nov. 1214 was in reality compensation for the *apoteca de Talavera*, bequeathed to the archbishop by Alfonso VIII but now resumed by Enrique I's guardians as 'regio fisco necessaria'. Talamanca had been granted to the church of Toledo earlier, but again 'sine beneplacito archiepiscopi Toletani', in compensation for certain property at Alcalá requisitioned by the king; and when Alfonso had restored the Alcalá property in June 1214 he had reclaimed Talamanca: Fita, *BRAH*, VIII, 240, 242.

[6] 'Mandamus quatinus vicesimam ecclesiasticorum proventuum terre sancte deputatam subsidio a prefatis archiepiscopo, episcopis et aliis pro tertio anno usque ad trien-

the local churches, not the Roman Church, that were undermined by the papal grants of *tercias* in 1247 and later years.[1] 'Out of the needs of the Holy Land has arisen modern taxation', it has been written.[2] Taxation of the Spanish Church, however, was occasioned by a Holy War nearer home. 'Bear ye one another's burdens, and so fulfil the law of Christ', Honorius III urged the churches of Rodrigo's province in 1222 when assigning their *tercias* to the Toledo Cathedral building fund[3] – as though they were not already bearing the burden of the war and paying the price of imposing the law of Christ on Islam. As Innocent himself discovered before his death, the effect of his liberal treatment of Fernando was to paralyse the Christian Church in Christian Spain itself. By August 1253 he was aware that the church-lamps were going out all over Sigüenza and the churches falling down, 'pro eo quod partem decimarum...luminaribus, ornamentis ecclesiasticis et fabrice deputatam' had been granted to the king. And the same was true of Palencia.[4]

Moreover there is other evidence – evidence which has not previously been reviewed but which helps to explain the unprecedented activity into which the churches had been galvanised by July 1257 when they were once more required to bear the burdens of the church of Seville. By then the economic problems by which the Castilian Church had been plagued for half a century had produced a crisis in its relationship with the civil power. But before describing that crisis it is necessary to review this other evidence in greater detail.

nium nullatenus exigatis': ACA, Bulas, leg. X-45 (reg. Miquel, 155). For these papal taxes, see below, Ch. 9; for Jaime I as 'fidei specialis adleta': ACA, Bulas, leg. XI-54 (Miquel, 164). See also below, p. 186.

[1] The so-called Formulary of Marinus de Eboli contains a further undated mandate ordering the prelates of *Yspania* to pay their *tercias* to the king 'per biennium': BAV, Cod. Lat. 3976, fo. 291v (Schillmann, *Formularsammlung*, 3001).

[2] By Cartellieri. Cit. R. C. Smail, 'Latin Syria and the West', *TRHS*, 5th ser., XIX (1969), 1–20, at p. 12.

[3] *Reg. Hon. III*, 3697: 'quando etiam lex est Christi ut alter alterius onus portet' – Galatians, vi. 2.

[4] AC Sigüenza, doc. pontificio, 22 (publ. Minguella, *Historia*, I, 571, misdated). For Palencia, see below, Ch. 8.

Chapter 7

THE ECONOMIC PROBLEMS
OF THE CASTILIAN CHURCH, 2

A few weeks after John of Abbeville had left Spain another French-man intervened in the history of the Spanish Church. He was the abbot of St Martin-lès-Aires at Troyes, and on 16 December 1229 he wrote to Bishop Rodrigo of León and his *officialis* ordering them to excommunicate the abbot and convent of San Pedro 'de Alducia'.[1] In comparison with the effect of the recent legation the repercussions of this missive were negligible. But it does not follow that its import-ance was slight, for its despatch had been occasioned by what was for Spanish churchmen throughout the century a much more threaten-ing reality than the spectre of moral reform: an unpaid debt. Having failed to meet the deadline set by their Sienese creditors, Leonardo Jordanis and his three companions, the abbot had then declined to put in an appearance at the hearing of the case against him and his convent at Troyes in the previous March.[2] Moreover, they remained unconcerned even after the bishop had published the sentence against them, so that the Italians petitioned the executors – as the executors, concurring, informed Bishop Rodrigo in March 1230 – 'ut sententiam aggravaremur secundum quod de iure esset aggravanda'.[3]

It is not known what impression this second commination, uttered with candles lit and bells tolling, made upon the abbot of 'Alducia'. But there can be little doubt that already, by 1229,

---

[1] AC León, doc. 507. *Alducia* is not readily identifiable. Possibly *Eslonza* is meant; for which suggestion I am grateful to Dr Derek Lomax. Cf. Calvo, *San Pedro de Eslonza*, where the name appears under various forms: *Aldonza* (p. 314); *Aslucie* (p. 315); *Aldoncia* (p. 326). The abbot of another unidentifiable house, Martín of S. Petrus de Elisontia, was dismissed by John of Abbeville 'propter manifestos excessus': *Reg. Greg. IX*, 1949. The abbot of St Martin was Jean de Boulages: Defer, *Histoire de l'abbaye de St-Martin-ès-Aires*, 45.

[2] On 16 December 'la foire froide' was in progress at Troyes: Bourquelot, *Études sur les foires de Champagne*, I, 83. For the activities of Sienese merchants there at this time, see Sayous, *Annales d'histoire économique et sociale*, III, 199.

[3] AC León, doc. 507.

128

incidents such as this were common, and its various features – loans from Italian bankers, summonses to hearings at the Champagne fairs, and indifference to ecclesiastical penalties – typical. There is certainly ample evidence to show that, in general terms, the entire Peninsula was caught up in Italy's financial web by the end of the thirteenth century,[1] and some to indicate that this situation was by then long established.[2] Yet merely to glance at the work of the most distinguished modern writer on this subject provides sufficient proof that the Spanish manifestations of that most persistent feature of the system – borrowing by individuals and communities – have been studied hardly at all.[3] The subject could not be exhausted in an entire volume, and far less in a single chapter. Since, however, it has a direct bearing on the place of the Church in Spanish – and particularly in Castilian – society, some of the evidence must be considered as prelude to an account of the crisis by which that Church was overtaken at the end of the 1250s.

Although the letter to the bishop of León is silent on the matter, it may be assumed that *Alducia's* debt to the Sienese merchants had its origins in an abbatial visit to the Roman Curia. Throughout the century, Spanish churchmen frequented the papal court, and paid the price. A combination of lengthy lawsuits and a liking for the place involved them in considerable expenditure, and, as did others from elsewhere, they turned for ready cash to the agents of the great Italian banking companies. When, on 19 May 1250, Ramón de Liriis, proctor of the villainous Bishop Ponce of Urgel, borrowed 110 marks sterling from the Roman merchants, Petrus Cinchii de Turre and his two nephews, promising repayment at Michaelmas 'in nostra curia si fuerit citra montes, alioquin...apud Trecas',[4] the

---

[1] Sayous, *EUC*, XVI, 155–98; Rau, *Studi in onore di Armando Sapori*, 717–18.

[2] Verlinden, *Nuova Rivista Storica,* XXXVI, 254–70.

[3] Sapori, *Studi di storia economica medievale*, 654–5. Similarly, there are hardly any references to Spain in the very thorough bibliographical section of his *Le marchand italien*, 43–58. Since then (1952) a single work on one aspect of the subject has been published: Benito Ruano, *La banca toscana*. Neither Espejo and Paz, *Las antiguas ferias*, nor Valdeavellano, *AHDE*, VIII, deal with the international questions.

[4] AC Seo de Urgel, Col·leccio Plandolit, d.s.n. For further details of this case, see *VL*, XI, 82–94; Linehan, *AEM* (forthcoming). The Curia was still at Lyons at the end of September 1250: the Troyes provision, therefore, did not become effective. Petrus Cinchii was one of thirty-six Roman merchants whom Innocent IV had assisted two years earlier in the recovery of money owed them at the Champagne fairs: AGN,

circumstances of the transaction were precisely those in which his and his employer's compatriots acted similarly during the fifty years before and after. All that distinguished it from many other such deals was the location of the Curia at the time, the smallness of the sum involved, and the proctor's choice of creditors.

Being at Lyons, the pope was more than usually accessible to Bishop Ponce and his ilk,[1] while for both him and them 110 marks was very small beer.[2] Where Ramón departed most markedly from the norm, though, was in his choice of *Roman* creditors. For most Spaniards preferred to do business with larger concerns based further north – with the merchants of Piacenza and Pisa, which both had the king of Aragon on their books;[3] of Lucca to whom in the late seventies and early eighties the popes entrusted the transmission from Portugal of the taxes authorised at the Second Lyons Council: a thankless task;[4] and of Siena where in 1298 (when on the brink of ruin, however) the Bonsignori Company could quite justifiably describe itself as 'the most honourable and noteworthy company in the whole world',[5] and whose Spanish clients by then had included the Order of Santiago and the churches of Ávila and Toledo,[6] apart from such smaller fry as the abbot of *Alducia* and those Spanish churchmen with whom their operations as *campsores domini papae* brought them into contact.[7]

caj. 4, no. 17 (reg. Castro, *Catálogo*, 263; publ. Cadier, *Mél. d'arch. et d'hist,* VII, 318–21).   [1] See below, p. 307.

[2] In Oct. 1253 Bishop Ponce borrowed four times as much, £300: *Reg. Inn. IV,* 7044, 7062. His proctor, though, had promised his friend at the Curia, the pope's nephew, payment in kind for services rendered: a pair of fine horses: *VL,* XI, 222. The transportation of livestock was impracticable when the Curia was in central Italy.

[3] ACA, Reg. 6, fos. 28r, 51v, 57r (Piacenza, 1257); Reg. 321, fo. 46v (Pisa, 1296).

[4] *Reg. Nich. III,* 82; ADB, Gav. dos Quindénios, Decimas e Subsídios, 4 (*Reg. Mart. IV,* 242). Archdeacon Giraldo of Couto, the Portuguese collector, informed Nicholas III that the money of that kingdom was *vilis.* Payment, in consequence, was made in a variety of currencies and in precious trinkets, and for these the Italians – the Bactoli and Orlandi Companies of Lucca and the Ammanati of Pistoia – were responsible: Ríus Serra, *Rationes Decimarum Hispaniae,* II, 285; ADB, Gav. dos Quindénios, 6, 7. For their further difficulties, see below, p. 215.

[5] Chiaudano, *Bull. Senese di St. Patria,* n.s., VI, 135.

[6] Benito Ruano, *Banca toscana,* 9–19; *Reg. Clem. IV,* 780; AC Toledo, A.7.C.2.13 (*ante* 1255).

[7] In 1265–6 they were authorised to collect an unpaid debt of 100 marks due to the papal *camera* from the bishop of Palencia, and to take charge of the Spanish estate of the late Bishop Lope of Morocco: *Reg. Clem. IV,* 729, 789.

More widely favoured than any of these, however, were the banking houses of Florence and Pistoia, all of which had at their disposal an impressive international network of control and retrieval. In order to borrow from the Florentines it was not necessary, as Fidel Fita assumed, for Bishop Pedro Pascal of Jaén to visit Florence.[1] Like many other Spaniards before him he was able to avail himself of their services while at the Curia.[2] Almost forty years earlier, during a stay at Anagni which did him little credit, the archbishop-elect of Toledo, Sancho, had turned to Dulcis and Noccius de Burgo when Alexander IV had given him leave to borrow up to 800 marks 'pro expediendis ecclesie Toletane negotiis' and had raised that sum from them and their Florentine associates *de societate Castri Gualfredi*. It is an index of the wide-ranging competence of Sancho's creditors that their principal executor, who was to impose an interdict on the church of Toledo if he failed to meet the deadline for repayment and to cause both him and the *maiores capituli* to be summoned to the Curia if he held out for a further two months, was a Frenchman.[3] Even more impressive, though, is the fact that when these sanctions failed it was the company's own Italian agents who recovered the loan on 21 November 1262, at Burgos.[4] But there was nothing exceptional about this settlement. Four years before, also at Burgos, two other Florentines *de societate Octaviani* had been repaid the sum that had been

[1] *BRAH*, xx, 54.
[2] *Reg. Bon. VIII*, 976–7.
[3] Two letters: *Cum sicut* (11 Jan. 1259); *Significarunt nobis* (1 Feb. 1259): AC Toledo, I.5.C.1.67; I.5.C.1.104. The executors appointed were the prior of St-Hilaire, Paris, and Alexander IV's nephew and chaplain, Blaise, canon of Cambrai. Sancho had previously, on 17 April 1255, undertaken to settle a debt with Florentine and Sienese merchants at the monastery of Ste-Geneviève, Paris, in the following November; and in 1266 the abbot and prior of Ste-Geneviève were made responsible for the collection of a whole host of Spanish debts: AC Toledo, A.7.C.2.13; AHN, 2263/12 (below, p. 132, n. 4). For Castro Valfrido, see Arias, *Studi e documenti*, 81–2.
[4] AC Toledo, A.7.E.1.10. The document transcribes the letters of authority in favour of Senobaldus Fassol and Giambuonus Jacobi, dated Florence 21 April 1261, which charged them with the collection of all debts 'coram domino Alphonso dei gratia Romanorum, Castelle ac Legionis rege illustri et coram omnibus judicibus regie magestatis curie et coram quolibet altero officiali eiusdem curie' and revoked all previous letters of authorisation to their proctors 'in hyspaniarum partibus...et specialiter Tuacium Bernaldi eorum concivem'. Repayment of a further loan from the Florentines, contracted by Sancho while at the Curia, devolved upon his successor, Sancho II: AC Toledo, caj. E.6, d.s.n.

borrowed from them at the Curia by the prior and chapter of Valladolid.[1] The Italians were no strangers at the Spanish fairs. When, in
February 1256, the same Sancho borrowed £4,000 Tours from Petrus
de Ysidolio, a merchant of St Jean d'Angely, it was arranged that his
account should be cleared either at the Alcalá fair during the twenty
days after Easter or else at the Pamplona fair on the feast of the Ascension.[2] Though not on the scale of the fairs of Champagne, these fairs
were evidently coping with rather more than the barter of chickens
and vegetables. In March 1288 Archbishop Gonzalo of Toledo was
able to borrow 20,000 *maravedís* on the security of his receipts from
the three annual fairs at Alcalá, and eleven years later the merchants
of Montpellier thought it worth their while to send Guillelmus Dorna
to represent them there and to act on their behalf.[3]

By then the Florentines had considerable experience of dealing
with Spaniards, and their customers had had occasion to discover
some of the hazards of international finance in a period of dear
money. In 1266 a large group of Florentines of the Castro Valfrido
connection, including Dulcis and Noccius de Burgo, declared themselves unable to meet their considerable debts to Cardinal Richard
Annibaldi, and in lieu of cash made over to the cardinal their Spanish
bonds.[4] Their debtors, both ecclesiastic and lay, whose obligations to
the Florentines comprised quantities of grain, wine and wool as well
as of money, were given two months in which to pay.[5] The executors
appointed by Clement IV were the abbot and prior of Ste-Geneviève
who, in turn, directed the abbots and priors of Poblet and Santas
Creus to oblige the bishop of Lérida, Guillermo de Moncada, either

[1] AC Valladolid, leg. XXIX–61, 11 July 1258. One of the two was Tuacius Bernaldi: publ. Mañueco Villalobos, *Documentos*, I, 331–3. For the dealings of Florentine *campsores* with Alfonso X, see *Reg. Urb. IV*, cam. 478 (above, Ch. 6).
[2] AC Toledo, A.7.C.2.13bis. It is not clear whether Petrus was acting for an Italian company. The Sienese certainly had an agent there by 1293: Paoli and Piccolomini, *Scelta di Curiosità*, CXVI, 64.
[3] AC Toledo, A.7.G.2.17: the fairs were held on the feasts of the Assumption, St John the Baptist and All Saints; A.7.G.1.28, 30 March 1299. Guillelmus was at Alcalá on 5 July.
[4] Two rescripts, both beginning *Cum Castra Gualfredi*, 2 and 8 June 1266: copies in AHN, 2263/12.
[5] *Ibid.*: 'Cum...nonnulli archiepiscopi et episcopi, abbates, priores, capitula, collegia et conventus, communitates, comites, barones, milites, burgenses et quidam alii clerici et laici regni Ispanie in quibusdam pecuniarum summis ac bladi, vini et lane quantitatibus et rebus aliis mercatoribus teneantur eisdem...'

to settle his account with the cardinal or else to come to Paris to explain to them why he had not. The sum involved was only three hundred marks, which hardly justified the copying out of Clement's two lengthy letters, let alone a journey from Lérida to Paris and back.[1] Still, not even experiences of this sort weaned Spanish churchmen away from their dependence on the Florentines. Whether in credit or, which was more usual, in debt, it was to them that Spaniards turned. Before he died, Archbishop João of Braga deposited a tidy little sum, £1,000 Tours, with Dulcis de Burgo and his partners at the Curia,[2] and when, some thirty years later, Archbishop Gonzalo of Toledo authorised his proctors to borrow up to three times that amount he specified two individuals with whom he would prefer to do business (though, prudently, he left them free to raise the loan 'a quocumque mercatori seu alio homine layco vel clerico, seculari sive regulari' since beggars can't be choosers). One was Bocatinus Josepi, merchant of Florence.[3]

The other was Girardinus Donati, a member of the Ammanati Company of Pistoia which, together with the Chiarenti Company, vied with the Florentines for the lion's share of Spanish business at this period.[4] Their agents were in constant contact with the leaders of the Spanish Church, quite apart from acting in the capacity of collectors of papal taxes in the Peninsula. It was with a *campsor* of Pistoia, *Johannes*, that Juan de Parras, canon of Oviedo, who made a will at Viterbo in September 1267, was in credit to the tune of sixty *duplas aureas*.[5] By the same token, probably, Jacobo de Pistoia had secured a Toledo canonry by December 1263.[6] Archiepiscopal or capitular acquiescence in such an appointment is as natural an explanation as papal provision, and it would not be the only case of its kind.[7]

---

[1] *Ibid.* 22 Nov. 1267. The bishop had engaged in litigation at the Curia in 1264: *Reg. Urb. IV*, 1424, 2798. But his debt 'ex causa mutui' may equally well have been contracted at Lérida itself, which was a thriving commercial centre: Benito Ruano, *Hispania*, XXII, 31–3; Altisent, *BRABL*, XXXII, 45 ff.

[2] ADB, *Livro I dos Testamentos*, fo. 10r (21 Oct. 1255).

[3] AC Toledo, A.7.G.1.20 (16 April 1286).

[4] For these two companies, see Herlihy, *Medieval and Renaissance Pistoia*, 165–6. The article by Zaccagnini, mentioned there, was not available to me.

[5] AC Oviedo, B/5/12 (reg. García Larragueta, *Catálogo*, 412).

[6] He was at Orvieto in that month with Cardinal Uberto of S. Eustacius: *Reg. Urb. IV*, 972.

[7] For two other Toledo pensioners, Master Angelus and Master Sinibaldus de Labro, and for a third, Blaise of Anagni, see Ch. 12.

Meanwhile, at the end of the 1270s, we find the treasurer of Toledo, Pedro Roldán, appointing Maestro Chanob de Pistoya as one of his executors and Maestro Chanob doing his duty at Toledo itself.[1]

For elucidation of the circumstances in which these appointments could be made the archive of Toledo Cathedral contains material of considerable interest: the financial papers of Archbishop Gonzalo (1280–98). Similar records have survived from the first half of the century, but not in such profusion, and in order to understand the financial difficulties experienced by the majority of Castilian churchmen in the 1250s it may be useful to tell the story of Gonzalo's dealings with his Italian bankers.

When he was upgraded from the see of Burgos in May 1280[2] Gonzalo inherited not only the primatial see but also the various debts with which that church had been saddled by his ill-starred predecessor – Fernán Rodríguez de Cabañas, whose election Nicholas III had declined to confirm on the grounds that he had bribed the electors.[3] It was therefore in Gonzalo's interest to establish at the outset what was his own personal property, and this he did at Viterbo at the end of that year, just as he had done at the time of his promotion to Cuenca seven years previously, by preparing an inventory of his own goods: an inventory which indicates that since 1273 he had acquired not only several accessions to his already remarkable library but also a taste for dressy garments and exotic nick-nacks.[4]

But this was not all he had acquired. For some of the property which he had brought with him to the Curia belonged not to him but to the church of Burgos, as the new bishop of Burgos, Fernando, lost no time in having recorded, insisting that the accumulated debts for which the church of Burgos was answerable be distinguished from those which were the archbishop's own personal responsibility. The settlement – which, incidentally and valuably, provides information about the current exchange-rate for Spanish currency[5] – was con-

---

[1] González Palencia, *Los mozárabes de Toledo*, II, 261.

[2] AC Toledo, A.7.G.1.2a (*Reg. Nich. III, 649*).

[3] Serrano, *Cartulario de Covarrubias*, LXVII, 119–20.

[4] AC Toledo, A.7.G.1.12 (6 Dec. 1280), mentioning, among much else, a weather-proof of violet samite 'cum aurifrisio de Londoniis', a gold-inlaid razor, Greek tapestries and a quantity of ceramic, some of it Indian. The earlier inventory, of 3 May 1273, is in AC Toledo, A.7.G.1.1. The book-lists contained in each are publ. Alonso, *Razón y Fe*, CXXIII, 303–6, from BN, MS. 13022, fos. 162r–4r, 185r–7v.

[5] AC Toledo, A.7.G.1.4. The abbot of Cardeña was owed 39 marks sterling 'que

cluded at the Curia on 6 November 1281 in the presence of a number of Spaniards, including the Dominican bishop-elect of Ávila, Ademar, and Miguel Pérez, a canon of Burgos who in the following years was to figure as one of the archbishop's principal financial agents.[1] Amongst the items recovered by Bishop Fernando (though not until almost five years had elapsed) were his church's vestments.[2]

In depriving the bishop of Burgos of anything ecclesiastical to stand up in, Gonzalo was following an example set by his own immediate predecessor at Toledo, Fernán Rodríguez, who in his quest for the archbishopric had dilapidated that church by pawning not only the contents of Archbishop Sancho II's chapel in order to pay off that prelate's debts (which had amounted to almost ten thousand *maravedís*), but also various pontifical rings and books, the property of the cathedral church, as a means of reducing his own.[3] The only method of settling old debts was to raise new loans, as the new archbishop soon discovered. In his anxiety to recover the sacred objects surrendered by Fernán Rodríguez, he dragged the church of Toledo far deeper into the financial mire and incurred the sort of difficulties with which by the early 1280s Castilian churchmen had been grappling for several decades.

Already, before his translation, he had been in debt on his own account to the Chiarenti,[4] and it was to them that he again turned in 1281. Other companies also accommodated him: on 30 June 1281 the Ammanati extended the deadline for repayment of two debts, of £2,300 and £1,300 Tours, both of which were due on the following day;[5] and in the autumn the Riccardi Company of Lucca proved no less understanding, granting him a post-dated extension in respect of a

valuerunt tunc M.VI.XXXVIII morabutinos': i.e. one mark sterling = 42 *maravedís*.

[1] Other Spaniards present were Master Álvaro, archdeacon of Ribadeo (Oviedo); Arias Pérez, archdeacon of Compostela; Rodrigo Velázquez, canon of Compostela; and Fernando Pérez, canon of Burgos. Sinibaldus de Labro, archdeacon of Bologna was also there.

[2] AC Toledo, A.7.G.1.5 (1 Nov. 1285).

[3] Fernán had surrendered 'las joyas que fueron de la capiella del arzobispo Don Sancho que Dios perdone' to his creditors' agent on 1 Sept. 1278. The agent was to sell them at Montpellier or Rome 'porque estas cosas...no se podien apreciar ciertamente en esta tierra': AC Toledo, A.7.E.1.4 (publ. *MHE*, 1, 330). The cathedral property is itemised in AC Toledo, A.7.G.2.18; A.7.G.1.32.

[4] For £1,100: AC Toledo, A.7.G.1.4.

[5] AC Toledo, A.7.G.2.16. He had repaid £700 of the smaller.

smaller sum which had been due in mid-July.[1] His main creditors, though, were the Chiarenti, and, in comparison with what he owed them, the sum saved him by the self-effacing curialist, Blaise of Anagni, who at this juncture waived his 100 *maravedís* pension from the archbishop,[2] hardly signified at all. By the end of 1281 they had advanced him £2,900.[3]

His removal to Avignon early in 1282[4] marked no upward turn in his fortunes. *Caelum non animum mutant*... – though he did manage to retrieve the smaller of his debts to the Chiarenti and to repay something over one-third, £858, of what he owed the Ammanati in return for a second period of grace.[5] Meanwhile further debts were mounting up, and by the month of September, when he recovered the Toledo property for a mere £300,[6] he was worth almost £8,000 to the Chiarenti: a sum which he showed no sign of ever being able to raise.[7] Nor, during the winter of 1282–3, did he change his ways. His chaplain, Pedro Diego, and his chamberlain, Juan Martínez, were despatched to raise further loans wherever they could find credit;[8] and it is probably to this same period that we should ascribe the series of blank cheques which, because they were not cashed, still survive

1 £200: AC Toledo, A.7.G.1.11.
2 AC Toledo, A.7.G.1.33 (14 Dec. 1281).
3 Made up of two loans, both advanced at Orvieto: £350 on 30 June, and £2,550 on 24 Sept: AC Toledo, A.7.G.1.27; A.7.G.1.11c.
4 He was there by 16 Feb: AC Toledo, A.7.G.1.26.
5 AC Toledo, A.7.G.1.27 (9 Feb. 1282); A.7.G.1.21 (26 March, six days before the deadline: he was given until 1 Aug. to find the rest of what he owed them – £1,442).
6 AC Toledo, A.7.G.1.32; A.7.G.2.18. He also recovered the container – 'unum pannum de seda veterem cum opere auri in quo erant predicta omnia (*scil.* joye) plicata' – from a representative of the Company's agent, Johannes Galandesch. The same Johannes had supplied the king of Aragon's nuncios at the Curia with funds in 1277–8, and on 17 Sept. 1281 had lent the dean of Ávila, Alfonso Vidal, £270 there: ACA, Reg. 22, fo. 77r; Wieruszowski, *BRAH*, cvii, 591; AC Salamanca, 39/1/19 (reg. Marcos Rodríguez, *Catálogo*, 383). He may therefore have been, like the Florentines Dulcis and Noccius de Burgo, his Company's Spanish specialist.
7 On 31 Aug. the Chiarenti agent at Avignon, Marsupinus Meliorati, granted Gonzalo an extension on two new loans, of £6,100 in all, and a third extension (till 8 March 1283) on the unpaid £1,500 of the previous £2,500 loan. The Company was hardly able to keep up with the archbishop, whose headlong flight into debt was testing even their highly sophisticated system. Marsupinus had not yet received instructions from his colleagues at the Curia about the terms of the most recent loan 'licet utraque pars crederet quod terminus solucionis esset in kalendis septembris vel in aliqua die mensis septembris': AC Toledo, A.7.G.1.11a–b–c.
8 AC Toledo, A.7.G.1.32 (28 Nov. 1282); A.7.G.1.26 (16 Feb. 1283).

with a number of other financial records in the Toledo archive.[1] Not unnaturally, therefore, the Chiarenti – a company which showed quite exceptional patience in its dealings with Spanish churchmen[2] – insisted on the most substantial security to hand: the archbishop himself. Until his debt was cleared Gonzalo undertook to remain at Nîmes, Montpellier, 'seu alia civitate vel terra illis propinqua'; and there he stayed until the spring of 1284 when he was granted permission to depart.[3]

Possibly he was in no hurry to leave anyway. The restriction on his movements may have seemed to him to have come as a godsend, for to have returned to Castile during the civil wars of 1282–4 would necessarily have involved him in choosing between Alfonso X and his rebel son Sancho; and the archbishop, with an eye to the future, may well have preferred to identify himself with neither side at this stage. He certainly resisted the blandishments of Sancho who, anxious for his support, wrote to him twice in 1282 offering to settle his debts for him if he would return.[4]

---

[1] AC Toledo, A.7.G.2.10: a roll of eight documents. The first is clearly a draft: 'Noverint universi quod cum nos G. et c̄ teneamur talibus mercatoribus talis societatis in tanta summa peccunie quam in tali termino tenebamur...' Some are made out in favour of Gonzalo's proctor, Miguel, canon of Burgos. One is a recognition of a debt of £3,100 to Johannes Galandesch and his partners. The whole deserves further study. It is very roughly written.

[2] It was not until 6 Oct. 1301 that the Company received the last instalment, £210.17, of a loan originally advanced to the bishop of Valencia, Andrés de Albalat, at the Curia on 13 Nov. 1276: AC Valencia, doc. 795 (reg. Olmos Canalda, *Inventario*, 928). He had borrowed £1,250.

[3] AC Toledo, A.7.G.1.8; A.7.G.1.20a. (17 March 1284). The Company had demanded the same security from the dean of Ávila two years before: AC Salamanca, 39/1/19 (reg. Marcos, 383). Still, they continued to allow the archbishop credit: on 5 Nov. 1283 he was advanced a further £3,100: AC Toledo, I.5.C.1.20. Miguel of Burgos, though, was fast losing credibility, his permanent task being that of seeking further extensions from the Chiarenti; and on 11 Dec. he was sent reinforcements in the shape of a fresh archiepiscopal proctor, Bertrando de Pradello, *jurisperitus* (as he needed to be): AC Toledo, A.7.G.2.12.

[4] 'Presencia vestra tam nobis quam ipsi ecclesie quam etiam toti regno sit valde necessaria, set prout intelligimus propter obligationem debitorum que pro ipsius ecclesie utilitate contraxisti non est vobis ut expediret ad ipsam liber accessus': AC Toledo, A.7.G.1.6 (Toledo, 22 Feb. 1282); AC Toledo, A.7.G.1.6a (Córdoba, 13 Aug. 1282). Ballesteros, *Alfonso X*, 973, maintains that the archbishop abandoned Alfonso in May 1282, basing his case on a letter of that month (evidently, AHN, 3021/17) in which the Master-General of the Dominicans, at the Vienna General Chapter, thanked Gonzalo for his past kindness to the Order: an inference contain-

In this case, then, the primate of Spain's financial disasters were something of a boon. But such a situation was exceptional, and in normal circumstances the king had no need to bid for the support of the episcopate during the thirteenth century. Alfonso X held all the cards and invented the rules, as did Fernando III and Sancho IV. Moreover, he expressed for the benefit of posterity the view that it was the bishops themselves who, by remaining at the Curia for lengthy periods, were responsible for involving their churches in economic ruin. In the *Primera Partida* Alfonso inveighed against such prelates. At Rome, it was claimed, they ran up enormous debts 'which afterwards their churches cannot pay, so that the churches are reduced' to great poverty from which it takes them much time to recover'. 'E algunas vegadas fican algunas dellas cuemo destroydas'.[1] The destruction of the church of Palencia might be seen as an example of this process, if indeed Alfonso's analysis is reliable.[2] But this, manifestly, it is not.

Debt, of course, is no sure sign of poverty. It may indeed indicate quite the reverse, and the willingness of the Chiarenti Company to continue supplying Archbishop Gonzalo with funds may suggest that they were satisfied with his credit-worthiness and no less confident than modern historians that, of all people, an archbishop of Toledo in the thirteenth century could not in reality fail to be prosperous. However, it is also possible to draw other conclusions from the account of Gonzalo's affairs during the early 1280s, conclusions which are endorsed by such evidence as has already been set against this belief. The Italians, like the historians, may have miscalculated.

Alfonso X, certainly, has misled historians with his account of episcopal mismanagement, by ascribing the temporal and spiritual malaise of the Castilian Church to the irresponsible action of wilful bishops. For the bishops were not bent upon self-slaughter. What dogged them abroad, by and large, were economic disabilities, not

---

ing many curious assumptions, not least the view that the Dominicans were solidly pro-Sancho. Cf. below, p. 223, and, for a sounder estimate of Gonzalo's attitude, Sánchez Belda, *AHDE*, XXI–II, 175, note.

[1] Tit. 5, ley 28: BM, Add. MS. 20787, fos. 22vb–3ra (corresponding to the variant to ley 29, Academy ed. I, 215). The law deplores especially the fact that the faithful are deprived of the sacraments, etc., when penalties of excommunication and interdict are imopsed.   [2] Below, pp. 146 ff.

personal waywardness, and these disabilities stemmed from the same source as those which crippled them at home: their political defence-lessness in a country hard put to finance its own expansion. It was the king who drove them into the hands of the bankers by refusing to allow them to take funds with them out of the country. In 1279 Nicholas III's nuncio, the bishop of Rieti, was instructed to broach the matter as one of the *gravamina* by which the Castilian episcopate was oppressed.[1] It was a restriction similar to, but harsher than that for which Afonso III of Portugal had been taken to task by Clement IV in 1268.[2] As it affected Spanish students at foreign Schools it casts an interesting light on Alfonso's expressions of concern about the spiritual consequences of episcopal indebtedness: educational reform had been one of John of Abbeville's main considerations.[3] But it was against the bishops and higher clergy that the measure was more particularly directed. Conceived in the same spirit as had produced the anti-inflationary legislation of the early fifties, it achieved (or, at least, was capable of achieving) the desirable end of keeping the bishops in leading-strings and at home. Alfonso's Visigothic predecessors had adopted similar policies for fear of clerical sedition operating from a foreign base,[4] and in the early fourteenth century the Castilian bishops themselves were suspected of using like tactics in order to prevent their critics reporting their enormities at the Curia.[5] That, though, does not exonerate Alfonso. Nor did his son's offer to bail out the arch-bishop mark any new departure. It was the exception that proved the rule.

This system of control was no novelty in 1279. Throughout the century bishops fell foul of a succession of kings with monarchical pretensions and were driven by royal persecution to seek sanctuary at the papal Curia. In the twenties and thirties Juan Pérez of Calahorra and Bernardo of Segovia were both victims of Fernando III who,

---

[1] 'Liberum non est prelatis et clericis exeuntibus regnum ex causa studii vel peregrina-tionis aut alia justa causa extrahere pecuniam pro suis necessitatibus extra regnum': *Reg. Nich. III*, 739. For these events, see below, Ch. 9.

[2] Afonso imposed a punitive tax on 'aliqua persona ecclesiastica Parisius commorans vel alibi aut etiam in curia Romana': ADB, Gav. das Notícias Várias, 26: a fuller version of the *articuli* in *Reg. Clem. IV*, 669.

[3] For loans raised by Spanish students at Bologna, see *Chartularium Studii Bononiensis*, vols. V, VII–XI, *passim*; Zaccagnini, *Bull. Storico Pistoiese*, XXXVI, 149–58.

[4] Thompson, *Nottingham Mediaeval Studies*, VII, 26, n. 151.

[5] Góñi Gaztambide, *HS*, VIII, 412.

while the former was incurring debts which he was later to liquidate by selling land, purposefully devastated the diocese and crippled the spiritual administration by conniving at Jewish non-payment of tithes, 'propter quod plures parrochiales ecclesie fere ad nichilum sunt redacte'.[1] And during the seventies there were further casualties. One was Archbishop Gonzalvo of Compostela. Appointed in 1272 by Gregory X – apparently in the hope that he might reform the province – he was hounded out by Alfonso, to whose disappointment at seeing his imperial candidacy fading away had been added the irritation of having his choice for the archbishopric, archdeacon Juan Alfonso of Trastamar, dying on him at the crucial moment.[2] In exile at the Curia the archbishop was maintained by a combination of loans and a notional annual income of £1,500 from his province,[3] though it is not clear how the latter payment can have reached him. Certainly no diocesan funds were available to another refugee of that same decade, Bishop Rodrigo of Segovia, whose offence had been that of defying the king on the issue of the dynastic rights of the Infantes de la Cerda. He remained abroad for eleven years, went the way of all flesh by borrowing beyond his slender means and in February 1281, his creditors' patience exhausted and with the pope who had promoted him in the grave, was excommunicated 'pro eo quod...non solverat quandam quantitatem pecunie Ture et aliis sociis suis civibus et mercatoribus Senensibus in termino iam transacto'.[4] Bitter personal experience underlay his constitution for the province of Tarragona, whither Nicholas IV translated him in October 1288, which forbad ecclesiastics to associate permanently with any secular court.[5]

---

[1] *Reg. Greg. IX*, 594. This abuse continued well into the 1260s: AC Calahorra, docs 310, 337; Cantera, *Sefarad*, XVI, 75–6.

[2] *Reg. Greg. X*, 110, 220; *Reg. Nich. III*, 5, 743; López Ferreiro, *Historia*, V, 239 ff. For the archdeacon of Trastamar, see Mondéjar, *Memorias históricas*, 173–4; below, p. 260.

[3] *Reg. Nich. III*, 530; *Reg. Mart. IV*, 2.

[4] At Viterbo: AC Toledo, X.2.B.2.2. Nicholas III's promotion of Rodrigo to Segovia in Jan. 1279, two years after he had taken the part of the Infantes, should be viewed in the light of the pope's new-found freedom *vis-à-vis* Alfonso: *Reg. Nich. III*, 399; Daumet, *Mémoire*, 48 ff.; The bishop was still at the Curia in 1284: AHN, 1874/4; Colmenares, *Historia*, 229.

[5] *Reg. Nich. IV*, 348; Tejada, *Colección de cánones*, III, 427. Only in July 1288 had Sancho IV given him leave to return to Castile: Daumet, 185.

Such extreme measures, however, were but rarely applied by the Italian bankers, as Master Sinibaldus de Labro and Master Miguel of Burgos, author and witness respectively of the sentence against the bishop of Segovia, were soon to discover in their capacity as agents of the archbishop of Toledo.[1] In that case, as in others, the alleged bogey-men showed surprising patience and moderation, sparing the Spaniards those ecclesiastical sanctions which, as bad payers, they indubitably merited. Nor was it necessarily their motive to encourage their quarry further to ensnare himself by even heavier borrowing before foreclosing, for they were even prepared to waive their profits and settle for the recovery of their original loan. Of the £1,000 lent to Juan Martínez on his promotion to the see of Lugo in March 1279, only £30 had been repaid by the time of the bishop's death, notwithstanding his having disowned all his predecessor's obligations. Yet in October 1282 the bankers of Pistoia were willing to renounce their claims to damages and expenses if only Bishop Alfonso would pay them a further instalment of the principal, of which they had so far received back less than half.[2] And in the same year the Florentines Lapus and Saxutius released the dean of Ávila, Alfonso Vidal, from the responsibility, which he had accepted at the instance of Fernán Rodríguez, elect of Toledo, of guaranteeing repayment of the £220 lent to Juan Ferrández, late treasurer of Salamanca, provided the dean pay them £85 owed on his own account.[3] Like Cardinal Richard Annibaldi fifteen years before,[4] they were prepared to cut

---

[1] AC Toledo, X.2.B.2.2. Tura may have been Tura Bartholomei, an associate of the Bonsignori Company: Chiaudano in *Bull. Senese di St. Patria*, VI, 134.

[2] *Reg. Nich. III*, 450; AC Lugo, letra B, no. 385 (copy in AHN, cod. 267B, fos. 257r–8r). By Oct. 1282 the Ammanati had recovered only £414, and Bishop Alfonso was unable to raise the £225 then demanded. 'Attendentes ad tenuitatem mense nostre, attendentes etiam quod bona ad ipsam spectantia sunt dissipata, destructa et male peracta...et ad solvendum facilius debita ipsius ecclesie Lucensis que multis est debitis obligata', Juan Martínez had renounced his predecessor's debts at Siena on 29 May 1279: AHN, 1331C/7. £250 was repaid at La Rochelle on 3 Dec. 1280. Cf. *ES*, XLI (ed. Risco), 77.

[3] AC Salamanca, 43/3/29;35 (reg. Marcos, 385, 384). Two months later, in April 1282, the dean's sureties for a further loan were Pascal Garcés, treasurer of Toledo, Rodrigo *magister scolarum* of Cádiz and canon of Ciudad Rodrigo, and Juan Pérez, succentor of Ávila. Together with two canons of Plasencia, Juan Pérez and Domingo Ximénez, they were all present at Orvieto: AC Salamanca, 43/3/25 (reg. Marcos, 387).

[4] 'Cum dictus cardinalis...exigi nollet expensas, interesse ac restaurationem dampnorum que dictis mercatoribus...forsitan deberentur': AHN, 2263/12.

their Spanish losses, and even, in the case of one of the dean of Ávila's creditors, solemnly to renounce in advance all recourse to either canon or civil law as a means of recovery.[1]

In the 1240s, similarly, the Master of the Order of Santiago, Pelayo Pérez Correa, had delayed five years in repaying a loan provided at the Lyons Council by the Bonsignori family, and, despite various papal admonitions, nemesis had not followed.[2] The Italian bankers were a symptom, not a cause, of the economic problems of the Castilian Church. Still, for the light that they shed on the economic foundations of that Church during these years, their dealings with Spanish churchmen – and, especially, the constant procrastination of their customers – are essential to an understanding of the Church's position in society there.

The indebtedness of the church of Toledo was part of the legacy of Archbishop Rodrigo. It was from him that the Infante Sancho inherited the debt of 1,450 marks concerning which an *amicabilis compositio* was achieved in April 1255. The loan had been made to Rodrigo at the Curia (possibly on the occasion of his last visit to Lyons in summer of 1247, from which he returned a corpse) and through the good offices of the Spanish cardinal, Gil Torres.[3] The cardinal himself was also a creditor of the church of Toledo, and on his death in 1254 he bequeathed what was owed him to the Cistercians of San Marino del Monte, Viterbo. By the beginning of 1257 pressure was being applied to Sancho for the recovery of this too.[4] Meanwhile he was adding to the burden: he had already borrowed from the Italians before coming to the Curia in the winter of 1258-9,[5] and the expenses of his embassy to England in 1255 – on his return from which, in February 1256, he borrowed £4,000 at St Jean d'Angely[6] – were hardly offset by his brother's six thousand *mara-*

---

1 '...et renuntiavit in hiis omni iuris canonici et civilis auxilio': AC Salamanca, 43/3/64 (reg. Marcos, 388).
2 Benito Ruano, *Banca toscana*, 9–16.
3 AC Toledo, A.7.C.2.13.   4 Potthast, 16706.
5 A papal letter transcribed in ASV, arm. XXXI 72, fo. 222r (Schillmann, *Formularsammlung,* 1787) refers to a loan made by 'B. et R. frater eius et alii socii sui cives et mercatores Senenses' to the proctor of an archbishop-elect of Toledo. It is post-Lyons I and almost certainly concerns Bonifazio and Riccomanno Bonsignori (see Chiaudano, *Bull. Senese di St. Patria*, VI, 132), though the archbishop-elect in question *may* have been Juan de Medina.
6 AC Toledo, A.7.C.2.13bis.

vedís subvention in the following October, however generous Henry III's gifts to him may have been.[1] On his death in November 1261 he left his successor, Domingo Pascal, to settle further accounts with merchants of Condom and Cádiz, which he did at Guadalajara on 27 April 1262.[2] Five days before, Alfonso had written to the archbishop-elect applauding his resolve not to go in person to the Curia to seek papal confirmation but to leave the matter to the king's own proctors there, despite the advice of those canons of Toledo who said that they had been at the Curia and had never known petitions of this nature from the kings of France and Germany to have received a favourable hearing from the pope and cardinals. Well might Alfonso welcome the old man's decision and further discourage him from making the journey at that, 'el mas fuerte tiempo del anno para andar a camino', but to take good care of himself, 'seyendo tan bon ome como vos sodes'.[3] For here was testimony to the effectiveness of the king's economic sanctions. Not even archbishops of Toledo who enjoyed the king's moral and financial support – such as Domingo Pascal's predecessor and successor, Sancho of Castile and Sancho of Aragon, respectively brother and son of reigning monarchs – could stave off financial disaster. Despite Alfonso X's lobbying and Jaime I's subsidies, Sancho of Aragon's chapel passed under the hammer.[4]

An earlier and far more serious casualty of the same process had been the ecclesiastical solidarity campaign which Archbishop Sancho of Castile had betrayed, at a price, in 1259. In the previous two years

1 AC Toledo, A.7.C.2.10 (publ. *MHE*, I, 107–8). Sancho was expected by Henry III in July 1255 and arrived in early September, according to Matthew Paris, whose remarks on the subject are characteristically sour: *Close Rolls, 1254–6*, 114, 116, 212; *Chronica Majora*, v, 509–10, 521 (Sancho's receipt from Henry of 'redditum et thesaurum non modicum').

2 AC Toledo, A.7.C.1.8 (Guirault de Morgat 'mercadero de Sant Pedro de Condom', 700 *maravedís*); A.7.D.1.2 ('Don Pers de Ffriac, mercadero de Cadiz', 1,000 *maravedís*).

3 AC Toledo, A.7.D.1.1. (publ. *MHE*, I, 191–2). In the event the Spanish summer proved too much for him. He died on 2 June: Castejón, *Primacía*, 765–6. Fifty years before he had carried the cross at Las Navas: Rodericus Toletanus, *De Rebus Hispaniae*, 186.

4 For Alfonso's recommendation of Sancho of Aragon and Clement IV's misgivings about him, see *Reg. Clem. IV*, 954, 1036, 1108, 360; for Jaime's financial assistance, Miret y Sans, *Itinerari de Jaime I*, 388; *MHE*, I, 239 (= AC Toledo, A.7.E.1.7); Ballesteros, *Alfonso X*, 445–50.

churchmen had at last been stirred into action by the effects of an economic crisis which had been in preparation for at least a decade before that.[1] During those years quite small debts discovered bishops, who were further removed from the purple than either of the two Sanchos of Toledo, lacking the wherewithal and driven to the unhappy expedient of making inroads into their capital. In order to raise the 400 *maravedís* which his journeys to the royal and papal courts had cost him, Bishop Juan Díaz of Orense had to cancel arrangements which had previously been made for the establishment of an anniversary in honour of St John the Baptist and, in December 1255, recompense his chapter by transferring the charge to property at Sobrado which Innocent IV had permitted his predecessor to annex precisely for the purpose of relieving episcopal poverty.[2] Travelling expenses loomed large also in the financial statement which Bishop Pedro of Zamora presented to his chapter on the first day of 1255.[3] Apart from 200 *maravedís* borrowed from the Jews of Castrotoraf, Pedro owed various sums, none of them crippling, to sixteen individuals, most of them ecclesiastics. Other than Cardinal Gil Torres no one had lent him more than 200 *maravedís*. Yet the sum total was in excess of two thousand, and, of this, unpaid *tercias* accounted for almost one sixth.[4]

However, only one of these sixteen – Arnaldo de Rexac – could be regarded as a foreigner,[5] and Pedro was most scrupulous about sett-

[1] See Ch. 8.
[2] *Reg. Inn. IV*, 1386; AC Orense, *Escrituras*, XII, 59. He had spent 100 *maravedís* in going to the royal court and another 300 at Rome, where he had been in July 1254: *Reg. Inn. IV*, 7875.
[3] AC Zamora, 13/46.
[4] *Ibid.*: 'Debita autem que solvenda remanent sunt hec: debent solvi domino Egidio cardinali CCC minus X mor. quos de mandato suo debuimus distribuere inter quosdam pauperes consanguineos eius. Item eidem XC mor. de redditu hereditatis de La Franca; episcopo Astoricensi C mor; episcopo Salamanticensi CC mor; capitulo Zamorensi C et LII mor; abbati de Morerola C mor; magistro E. cantori Zamorensi C et XLVII mor; terciariis P. Petri quondam cantoris CC mor; terciariis P. Johannis quondam thesaurarii Legionensis C mor; Fernando Ramiri C mor; Petro Johannis clerico abbatis Fusellensis C mor; domino Andree portario XC mor; Arnaldo de Rexac C mor; Garsie Munionis domini regis iudici L mor; domino Garino L mor; Stephano de Gaiat XXXV mor...' Again in Nov. 1267 Pedro Pérez, by then dean of Zamora, was appointed to collect royal taxes in the kingdom of Leon: Ballesteros, *BRAH*, CIX, 452.
[5] If it was he who, as sacrist of S. Pedro de Cereto (Elne), was provided to a Cartagena canonry at the instance of Bishop Andrés of Valencia in Dec. 1274, then it is hardly

ling his accounts with the Florentines, Jacopo Bonacontri and partners, from whom (perhaps at I Lyons) he had borrowed 160 marks. Indeed his servant, R. Gonzálvez, presented himself at Provins on the very first day of the St-Ayoul fair – 14 September 1247 – six days before the Italians were ready to do business.[1] Other Spanish prelates, though, were rather more casual and considerably less solvent. Bishop Nuño of León was one. In the spring of 1247, when Fernando III was granted the *tercias*, both León and Oviedo were in debt. But whereas Innocent IV left Bishop Rodrigo Díaz of Oviedo to work out his own salvation he summoned Nuño to the Curia to give an account of his stewardship.[2] The outcome was disastrous. Possibly because he was short of ready money the bishop granted León benefices to curialists. One of the prebends which he had previously been permitted to establish *extra numerum* in order to accommodate unbeneficed local clergy was awarded to a Roman, Nicholas, 'clericus de Urbe'. A nephew of Cardinal Richard Annibaldi, 'Stephanus dictus Surdus', received various *prestimonia* of the late dean, Pedro Arias.[3] Thus the rents of a Spanish cardinal's relative were transferred to a total stranger;[4] and the process of erosion continued during the two-and-a-half-year vacancy which followed Nuño's death in April 1252, while a group of León canons campaigned, unsuccessfully, to exclude the royal candidate for the see, the royal notary, Martín Fernández. Consequently the church's financial position continued to deteriorate, despite the favours showered upon the new bishop by the king and, at the king's behest, by the pope.[5] Martín Fernández's proctors at the Curia, the archdeacon Pedro Núñez and the treasurer Fernando Abril, were driven to borrow from the Bonsignori, not

credible that he was the same Arnaldo 'de Rassaco' who died as archbishop of Monreale in 1324: AC Valencia, perg. 478, 'Lugduni, id. decembris, anno tertio' (reg. Olmos, 489, misdated 1273). Cf. Burns, *Crusader Kingdom*, II, 387, n. 111.
[1] AC Zamora, 13/48. Cf. Bourquelot, I, 82.
[2] *Reg. Inn. IV*, 2499, 2655.
[3] *Ibid.* 1735 (Oct. 1245), 4573 (April 1249), 5113 (Feb. 1251).
[4] For Pedro Arias's uncle, Cardinal Pelayo, see below, Ch. 12.
[5] *ES*, xxxv, 313 ff.; *Reg. Inn. IV*, 7919. On 20 Oct. 1255, at the king's request, Alexander IV cancelled the debts which Martín had inherited 'nisi probatum fuerit legitime debita ipsa in utilitatem ipsius ecclesie fore versa', as Innocent IV had done fourteen months before: AC León, doc. 1299, *inc. Tuis et karissimi*; *Reg. Inn. IV*, 7923. This was repeated in Oct. 1256, and in the period 1255–9 Alfonso granted the bishop and church of León some twenty privileges: *Reg. Alex. IV*, 1637; García Villada, *Catálogo*, 142–4.

only for their own maintenance but also in order to pay the arrears of income awarded by the pope to William of Parma, vicechancellor of the Roman Church, and William's nephew, Hugolin. Repayment was due after only four months, at the beginning of 1255. So the church of León was in no condition to rally to the financial assistance of the king in the October of that year.[1]

León's easterly ecclesiastical neighbour was even less well equipped to bail out its 'amigo natural'. The history of the church of Palencia in the first half of the century – and particularly in the decade after the capture of Seville – provides, and was regarded by contemporaries as providing, a succinct account in miniature of the misfortunes of the Castilian Church; while its university, at which the youthful St Dominic had studied in the 1180s, serves in its decline as a barometer recording the pressures to which not only it but also the national Church at large was subject. Of these, episcopal extravagance during Roman holidays was one. But, the *Primera Partida* notwithstanding, it was very far from being the greatest.

Amid the already encircling gloom, the saint had been so affected by the extent of poverty there that he had sold his books in order that the poor might eat bread, having no wish to be nourished by dead skins while human beings suffered. 'Povres gens moroient de fain/Por defaute d'avoir don pain'.[2] But fondness of this order was rare at Palencia. Normally the weakest and poorest-represented went to the wall, and in 1225 the diocesan clergy were required both to contribute to the upkeep of the university with a quarter of their *tercias* for a further quinquennium,[3] and, from the same source, to provide Bishop Tello with a 'moderate subsidy' towards the expenses that he had incurred in the Reconquest.[4] Even if they had been in receipt of their entire tithe revenue their situation would have been difficult; but they were not. In that same year the pope acted on the bishop's complaint that the nobles of the diocese were withholding payment.[5] The reprimand was evidently ignored, however, for

---

[1] *Reg. Inn. IV*, 7861, 7909, 7980; above, Ch. 6. They owed 527 marks.

[2] *The Life of St Dominic in Old French Verse*, ed. Manning, lines 1007–12. The *Life* is not contemporary, but it is supported by earlier evidence: Manning in *Mediaeval Studies in Honor of J. D. M. Ford*, 139 ff.; Jordan of Saxony, *Libellus de principiis*, 30–1.

[3] *Reg. Hon. III*, 5273 (MDH, 533). Cf. *ibid.* 2742 (MDH, 331) '...cum in hoc modicum graventur ecclesie'.

[4] *Ibid.* 5694 (MDH, 586).   [5] AC Palencia, 3/8/7 = *Reg. Hon. III*, 5681 (MDH, 578).

in 1229 Gregory IX had to issue letters against both the predatory vassals of King Alfonso IX and their attacks on the church's property, 'Palentino episcopo intimante',[1] and also the Jews of those parts who, while refusing to pay tithes on property acquired from Christians (contrary to canon 67 of the Fourth Lateran Council), were able to build themselves ever more lavish synagogues and to emphasise their economic prosperity by establishing their cemeteries adjacent to those of the Christians, thus creating considerable scandal and disturbance.[2]

Gregory's informant, clearly, was John of Abbeville who, while at Palencia in the previous autumn, had experienced another pastoral manifestation of the church's economic infirmity: the rooted opposition of the bishop and chapter to the Dominican Order. Tello's much publicised enthusiasm for the cause of clerical education did not extend to patronage of the friars who were best able to raise standards, even at the founding father's *alma mater*. For in the estimation of the hard-pressed chapter the friars represented above all a further threat to their resources. In August 1231 the pope censured them for having refused to allow the newcomers to celebrate publicly and bury the dead, contrary to the legate's ordinance.[3] Thus, in Castile as elsewhere, unlike Aragon during Pedro de Albalat's pontificate, the group which even hidebound John of Abbeville had recognised as constituting the white hope for church reform was hampered at every turn, and the outbreak of the Albigensian heresy which affected those parts in the late 1230s could not easily be contained because the means of doing so had been rejected in advance.[4] In that sense, then, there was truth in the analysis of the *Primera Partida* concerning the spiritual consequences of economic regression, whatever its causes. Contemporaries noted the connexion, reversing cause

---

[1] AC Palencia, 2/1/46, *Desideramus cum te,* 8 June 1229.

[2] '...et iuxta christianorum cimiteria sua faciunt ita vicina et cum quandoque christianum et judeum eadem terra sepelire contingat per clamores judeorum impediuntur exequiae christiani, et vitari non potest quin aqua benedicta qua ibidem christiani asperguntur de more perveniat ad judeos', *RAH*, MS. 9–24–5/4558, fo. 194v–5r (19 March 1229). Cf. Hefele–Leclercq, v, ii, 1385.

[3] AHN, 1724/15 (Potthast, 8782).

[4] *Reg. Greg. IX*, 3271; AC Palencia, 2/1/47, letter *Antiquorum memorie*, addressed to Fernando III, 21 March 1236, specifying that natives of Palencia were contaminated. Cf. Fernández del Pulgar, *Historia de Palencia*, II, 304, blaming interlopers from León since the local people were 'ocupados en obras de piedad y religión'.

and effect. In the neighbouring diocese of León drought and famine were held to be a consequence of the toleration extended there to a clutch of heretics.[1]

A further charge levied on the church of Palencia – and on the Castilian Church in general[2] – during the thirties was that of supporting exiled Portuguese ecclesiastics. Bishop Martinho of Porto died there, sometime before April 1235,[3] and in the previous year the bishop-elect of Coimbra, Master Tiburcio, ex-sacrist of Palencia, was permitted to continue drawing income from that source.[4] But it was during the next decade, after the death of Bishop Tello in 1246 and in the shadow of the capture of Seville, that the affairs of the church entered their darkest phase. For the election was disputed by the cantor, Rodrigo Gonzálvez, and the archdeacon of Cerrato; the two candidates resigned their claims into the hands of the pope; and on 4 April 1247 Innocent IV rejected both and appointed the papal chaplain, Master Rodrigo.[5]

Probably Rodrigo was one of the Spanish clerks whose home at the Curia was the household of Cardinal Gil Torres. Possibly, like the cardinal, he had some connexion with Burgos.[6] And, although it is not certain that he was a royal nominee, it may be assumed that in 1247, of all years, any Castilian bishop appointed by the pope would have enjoyed at least the king's blessing. But, whatever his pedigree, Bishop Rodrigo was loth to leave the Curia. The letter which he sent to Archbishop Rodrigo of Toledo soon after his appointment – a

---

1 Lucas of Túy, *De altera vita*, ed. Mariana, 170–1. The drought lasted ten months 'et arescebant omnia siccitate'. It ended (miraculously) on the expulsion of the heretics. See also Risco, *Historia de Léon*, I, 73–81.

2 *Reg. Greg. IX*, 4333, 6083; above, Ch. 6.

3 ADB, Gav. dos Arcebispos, 24, art, cxvii. Cf. Sousa Costa, *Mestre Silvestre*, 208.

4 *Reg. Greg. IX*, 2075. On 10 June 1229 Tiburcio had been at Perugia in the company of Cardinal Gil Torres and a group of ranking Portuguese churchmen: *ibid.* 307. Possibly he was Portuguese himself.

5 AC Palencia, 3/8/9 (publ. Fernández de Madrid, *Silva Palentina*, I, 244–5). On the following day the cantor, who in Sept. 1246 had been styling himself 'elect of Palencia', was consoled with a papal grant permitting him to retain his benefices in plurality: Serrano, *Hispania*, I, 30; *Reg. Inn. IV*, 2497.

6 For Cardinal Gil and his circle, see below, Ch. 12. The dorse of AC Palencia, 3/8/9 is marked 'Sanctorum Cosme et Damiani', which points to the cardinal's intervention. Since Rodrigo named the property granted him at Seville *Palençiola*, he may have been the archdeacon of Palenzuela of that name who was at Burgos in Sept. 1240. In that case he must have resigned the archdeaconry by Dec. 1246: González, *Repartimiento*, II, 28; AHN, 3020/3; *Reg. Inn. IV*, 2317.

letter which reveals a shaky mastery of Latin[1] – implies that he regarded it as his proper habitat. It was there, at Lyons, that he swore allegiance as a suffragan of Toledo on 6 June 1247.[2] During the next two years he was entrusted several times with the task of assigning rents in Castilian churches to foreign clerks designated by Innocent, and of executing provisions in their favour.[3] But if these commissions took him to Castile he had returned to the Curia by May 1253 when he acted as auditor at Assisi of an appeal lodged by the church of Limoges,[4] was still absent from his diocese four months later,[5] and seems to have died there in September 1254 or shortly before.[6]

Innocent was evidently well disposed towards Bishop Rodrigo. But he was unable to provide him with any financial relief. In June 1247 Rodrigo was granted a half of the *tercias* of his diocese for a period of one year to alleviate his church's 'great burden of debt'.[7] However the bishop was made to take his place in the queue behind the king who had pre-empted him by two months, and in March 1253 he was still waiting[8] while Alfonso X tightened his hold on the church's revenue. It was this situation, superimposed upon Palencia's other earlier woes – and not simply Rodrigo's taste for life at the Curia – which drove him to the next stage of the episcopal rake's progress: failure to repay the loan advanced him by Folcarinus

---

[1] AC Toledo, X.2.A.1.1, undated but evidently written April–May 1247. It may have been this letter, which warned the archbishop of certain archdeacons of Braga 'litteras ecclesie vestre derogantes potentie et nichilominus maiestatis vestri dignitati detrahentes', that provided Rodrigo with a motive for his final visit to the Curia.

[2] AC Toledo, X.2.1.1.1d. On 17 June he was absolved from his promise to make a triennial visit *ad limina*: *Reg. Inn. IV*, 2809.

[3] *Ibid.* 3938 (May 1248) for John of Parma, *scriptor pape*, 'in aliqua ecclesiarum cathedralium Yspanie' – despite his assurances of the previous year to the archbishop ('Me siquidem a vestra utilitate et servicio nulla animadvertet occasio. Sed utpote ecclesie vestre humillissimum [sic] suffraganeum et servicio vestro per omnia appositum me proculdubio habere non ambigatis', AC Toledo, X.2.A.1.1) he lit upon Toledo: *ibid.* 7863. But this was equitable since John acted as Toledo proctor in the period Aug. 1252–Aug. 1254 (AC Toledo, A.7.C.1.3; 3a; 5; I.7.I.1.2c); *ibid.* 4167 (Sept. 1248) for Theobald, brother of Petrus Johannis de Lavania, senator; *ibid.* 6629 (Dec. 1248) for Petrus Gaietanus at Toledo (below, Ch. 12); *ibid.* 4573 (April 1249) for Nicholas 'clericus de Urbe' at León (above, Ch. 6).

[4] *Ibid.* 6960.

[5] AC Palencia, 8/15/7.

[6] On 29 Sept. the pope entrusted the late bishop's *familia*, 'clerici, laici et medici', to Cardinal Gil's care: *Reg. Inn. IV*, 8079.

[7] AC Palencia, 2/1/53 (= *Reg. Inn. IV*, 2775, publ. Mansilla, *Iglesia*, 339).

[8] *Reg. Inn. IV*, 6439.

Jacobi, Jacobus Scambii and their Florentine partners at the time agreed, the St-Ayoul fair at Provins in September 1248. Five months later he was issued with the inevitable solemn warning.[1] Yet even if the pope's attempt to set him on a sounder financial footing had borne fruit it would have been achieved only at the expense of the other churches of his diocese.[2] The papal practice of robbing Peter to pay Paul may have had scriptural authority but it was no solution, since Peter was on the bread-line too, as Innocent knew perfectly well.[3] Still, that practice – of seeking to relieve ecclesiastical poverty by battening on other equally hard-pressed sectors, provincial, diocesan or capitular – was characteristic of the thirteenth-century Castilian Church and, at once, both cause and effect of its weakness and divisions. So when Bishop Rodrigo was prevented from enjoying diocesan revenue which the king had appropriated, he naturally set about despoiling his own chapter.[4] And while the Church devoured herself it was the king and the nobles who scavenged to greatest effect. On the death of Archbishop João Egas of Braga in November 1255 Alfonso X seized property of his which had been deposited both at Palencia, 'dum esset in lecto egritudinis consitutus', and elsewhere throughout the kingdom.[5]

By then though there were signs that the Castilian Church might be capable of some measure of common purpose. A spirit of resistance was abroad and, significantly, it chose to defy the pope by way of rehearsal for the more serious confrontation which lay ahead, with the king. In the following month, December 1255, Alexander IV's attention was drawn to 'quidam ecclesiarum prelati Yspanie ac aliunde' who had refused to pay the pensions assigned by his predecessor to the vice-chancellor of the Roman Church, William of Parma, and William's nephew Hugolin. Alexander retaliated by threatening them with the ultimate deterrent: exclusion from the

---

1 *Reg. Inn. IV.* 4642. See Arias, *Studi e documenti,* 82, n. 2.
2 'Ita tamen quod ecclesiis civitatis et diocesis predictarum pro earum reparatione, libris et aliis ornamentis, quas his noveris indigere de medietate reliqua provideas competenter': AC Palencia, 2/1/53.
3 Similar grants were made to the bishops of Coria (Feb. 1241), León (Aug. 1254) and Osma (Jan. 1257): *Reg. Greg. IX,* 5408; *Reg. Inn. IV,* 7960; *Reg. Alex. IV,* 1899.
4 Below, Ch. 8.
5 ADB, Gav. das Propriedades e Rendas da Mitra, 32: letter *Sicut venerabilis,* 24 May 1256. João had died at Valladolid on 16 Nov.: Ferreira, *Fastos episcopaes,* II, 46.

Curia and all its benefits.[1] The sums of money at issue were trifling. None was greater than twenty marks,[2] and the wherewithal for payment of two years' arrears formed only a small proportion of the loan raised at the Curia by the bishop of León's proctors in August 1254.[3] There was as yet no such resistance to the much larger demand made by the king that autumn. That, however, was to be the next step. For the autumn of 1255 was the first of the seven lean years to which the Castilian bishops would look back in the winter of 1262–3. And by then they had learnt the truth about Seville. A hundred years before, Bishop Pedro of Porto had inveigled the Jerusalem-bound English crusaders into joining the assault on Lisbon instead, by arguing that the road was better than the inn.[4] Even so it had proved necessary to allow them to sack the place. Now, though, the Castilian bishops, having glimpsed the promised land of official propaganda, had to conclude that what they had hankered after and beggared themselves for was not an oasis but a mirage.

[1] *Reg. Alex. IV*, 1014.
[2] They affected the churches of Astorga, Compostela, Oviedo, Burgos, Cuenca, Segovia, León and Ávila: *Reg. Inn. IV*, 6615, 6623 (Feb. 1252).
[3] 84/527 marks: *ibid.* 7861, 7980.
[4] Above, p. 5.

Chapter 8

THE ECONOMIC CRISIS
OF THE CASTILIAN CHURCH

The years 1257–8 constitute an important but hitherto unacknow-
ledged political and geopolitical landmark in the history of the
Spanish Peninsula, for in the course of a few months the kingdoms of
Aragon and Castile both embarked upon extra-peninsular adventures
which, by divergent paths, were to decide the fate of each throughout
the later Middle Ages. Aragon, having completed the reconquering
stint which it had been assigned at Cazorla, turned to the Mediterranean. Of course, what Dufourcq has called *l'orientation thalas-
socratique* of the Catalans was no new phenomenon. It was almost
co-eval with the *Reconquista* itself, having its origin in the recovery of
Barcelona in 801 and developing imperceptibly out of the struggle
against the Saracen.[1] The attack on the Balearic Islands which John of
Abbeville had blessed for that reason in 1229 thus provided Jaime I
with a base from which his son would confound papal diplomacy by
driving the French out of Sicily in 1282,[2] the supreme irony of that
reverse being the purposefulness with which Martin IV's predecessors
had encouraged the king to interest himself in the politics of that area.
As early as 1238, even before the recapture of Valencia, Gregory IX
had attempted to cajole him into taking command of the Lombard
opposition to Frederick II,[3] and when Jaime announced his intention
of intervening in the affairs of the Latin Empire eight years later he
received every encouragement from Innocent IV.[4] Yet Martin IV,
together with the rest of Europe, was amazed by Pedro III's coup.
On the eve of the Sicilian Vespers Aragon hardly seemed a serious
proposition. The pope had only scorn for 'little Aragon' and its

[1] Dufourcq, *L'Espagne catalane et le Maghrib*, 28 ff. Cf. Tramontana, *Nuova Rivista
Storica*, i, esp. 546–66.
[2] Desclot, *Chronicle*, i, 88.   [3] Zurita, *Anales*, i, 152vb–3rb.
[4] ACA, Bulas, leg. VIII–20 (reg. Miquel Rosell, *Regesta*, 131). This was in March
1246, at which very time the Order of Santiago was being encouraged by the pope to
send relief to the Latin Empire. Cf. Benito Ruano, *Hispania*, XII, 14 ff.

'feeble' king, according to Desclot.[1] Five years later, though, Jordan of Osnabrück voiced the opinion that recent events marked a revolution in European power politics. The humiliation, *contra opinionem*, of the French 'que se maiorem reputat omni gente' by the insignificant Aragonese was in his view a sign of the times, the secular prefiguration of the imminent destruction of the *ordo clericorum* by the friars.[2] And he was right. There had been a revolution. But it had not been unheralded. The coming storm had been rumbling for at least twenty years.

During the 1260s Jaime's sights were set on Sardinia as part of the Hohenstaufen inheritance to which Pedro had a claim after his marriage to Frederick II's grand-daughter, Constanza, in June 1262.[3] But the betrothal of the pair, and the beginnings of Aragon's new foreign policy, dated from 28 July 1260.[4] Two years before that, on 11 May 1258, Jaime had accepted the consequences of his own father's defeat at Muret in 1213 and by the Treaty of Corbeil had resigned virtually all his suzerain rights in the Midi, Louis IX in return surrendering his notional authority over the County of Barcelona which dated from the reign of Charlemagne.[5] Thus the king of France released those Aragonese energies which, having attached themselves almost immediately to the Hohenstaufen cause, succeeded twenty-four years later in ousting his younger brother from Sicily. That same year, 1258, witnessed also Jaime's ratification of ordinances for the port of Barcelona which would enable the commercial community to exploit that victory to the full and establish its firm hold over Mediterranean trade during the next century.[6]

Aragon, then, does not conform to the all-purpose concept of the Closing Frontier which has been conjured by Professor Lewis from

1 *Chronicle*, II, 48.
2 'Sicut igitur in tempore iam precedente gens Gallicorum...per gentem Aragonum parvam, nudam corporis et rerum prodigam et ad omne genus laboris pronam et succinctam, contra opinionem humiliata est': *Noticia Seculi*, ed. Wilhelm, *MIöG*, XIX, 669.
3 V. Salavert y Roca, *Cerdeña y la expansión mediterránea de la Corona de Aragón* (2 vols., Madrid, 1956), I, 128–9, 202–3.
4 Girona Llagostera, I. *CHCA*, 241; Soldevila, *Pere el Gran*, I, 91 ff.
5 Publ. *CODOINACA*, VI, 129–38. Cf. Lognon, *La formation de l'unité française*, 138–41; Abadal, *Revue historique*, CCXXV, 319 ff, and *Annales du Midi*, LXXVI, 315 ff. For the effect of Muret, see Renouard in *Annales de l'Université de Paris*, XXVIII, 16–17.
6 Publ. Capmany, *Memorias históricas*, II, 23–30. Cf. R. S. Smith, *The Spanish Guild Merchant*, 9 ff.

the evidence of recession in Europe during the century after 1250; and Professor Lewis admits it.[1] What he did not appreciate in 1957, however, when he read his paper to a conference of historians was that that very year was no less significant a centenary for *Spanish* history than the year 1893 when his mentor, F. J. Turner, had read his. For 1257–8 marked an epoch in Castilian fortunes too. Rather less stealthily than the king of Aragon, Alfonso X also struck out in a new direction – straight up the imperial cul-de-sac. On 1 April 1257 he was elected to the shadow of the Hohenstaufen inheritance, the kingship of the Romans, leaving the substance, Sicily, for the family of his father-in-law King Jaime.[2] Thus, astonishingly, only five years after being the first monarch to succeed to the joint kingdoms of Castile–Leon, Alfonso chose to concentrate such resources as his exhausted realms could muster on winning control of Germany, the one European state to have retained the elective principles that had so dogged his remote ancestors during the first centuries of the *Reconquista*. Grasping enthusiastically the old Germanic nettle which earlier Spanish rulers had spent such effort in eradicating,[3] he squandered that reputation for pragmatism as a national virtue with which Vincentius Hispanus had only recently contrasted the folly and incompetence of the Germans. It was not for want of alternatives. Apart from the completion of the *Reconquista*, other imperial possibilities presented themselves. Early in 1259, at the Toledo Cortes which he had summoned for a discussion of the finances of the German venture, his vassal, Ibn el-Ahmer – the Nasrid king of Granada – attempted to divert his attention to the 'much greater and better empire than that' which was his for the taking in North Africa,[4] and in the September of that year he seems even to have been toying with the idea of reviving the old *imperium Hispaniae*.[5] His pursuit of that chimera indicates the extent of his political wisdom, the lack of which experience did nothing to repair. When in Nov-

---

[1] *Speculum*, XXXIII, 477–8.
[2] Bayley, *EHR*, LXII, 473 ff.
[3] See esp. Sánchez-Albornoz, *Bol. de la Acad. Argentina de Letras*, XIV, 35 ff.
[4] According to Alfonso himself in a letter of June 1264, publ. Minguella, *Historia de Sigüenza*, I, 599. Cf. Ballesteros, *Alfonso X*, 226, 362. For Alfonso's relations with North Africa, see Dufourcq, *Rev. d'hist. et de civ. du Maghreb*, I, esp. 37–8.
[5] Hüffer in *SpGG*, Reihe I, III, 384, for Jaime I's suspicions on this point. Cf. Maravall, *Concepto*, 461–2. Castilian ambitions of this sort had been abandoned implicitly in 1179, at the Treaty of Cazorla. See Valdeavellano, *Historia*, I, ii, 567–8.

ember 1282 he drafted his will he did so in the conviction that the French were in the ascendant in Europe and that God would be best served 'si firmiter amor Françie et Ispanie omni tempore uniatur'.[1] Seven months before, the French had been humiliated in Sicily.

As the grandson of Philip of Swabia, though, he was perfectly entitled to bid for the debris of Frederick II's empire. He regarded it as his exclusive preserve. Pedro of Aragon's betrothal to Constanza was, he informed King Jaime, a personal affront to him such as no man had been made to suffer before.[2] By then, 1260, his attitude was well set. Since 1239, at the latest, the Castilians had been actively concerned about the interests of Beatrice of Swabia, Fernando III's queen,[3] and during the forties they, like the Aragonese, had been encouraged by the papacy to press their claim against Frederick. On 3 May 1246, at a time when the Castilian *Reconquista* was in full cry, Innocent IV had written to the Infante Alfonso in that sense, promising whatever assistance the Roman Church might lend *cum Deo et honestate*.[4] It was papal policy to multiply Frederick's difficulties, and Innocent evidently felt that this might be done without detriment to that other crusade which was being waged in Spain. Only nine days before, he had granted the usual indulgences to those fighting the Saracen there.[5] By 1257, however, the number of those who were confident of the king of Castile's ability to carry on a struggle on two fronts had been reduced to Alfonso himself, his immediate circle and such foreign admirers as Gutetus de Mixigia, the Milanese notary whose verses on the theme that 'rex regum comiti preferri debet aperte' expressed their own delusions in the heady language which had been employed by the Castilians themselves in the previous decade.[6] For though the pope praised Alfonso in similar terms, declaring him worthy of special consideration *inter alios principes terre* on account of his signal services to the Church,[7] it was vacillation on the

---

1 Publ. Daumet, *BEC*, LXVII, 84. He characterised the French as 'divites et pacifici' and his countrymen, predictably, as 'fortes et rigorosi et intenti circa arma et etiam pleni guerre'.

2 *CODOINACA*, VI, 153–4 (20 Sept. 1260).

3 *Reg. Greg. IX*, 5164. See Giunta in *Studies pres. E. M. Jamison*, 137 ff.; A. de la Torre in *Atti...Federiciani*, 161 ff.

4 *Reg. Inn. IV*, 1816. Cf. Bayley, *EHR*, LXII, 474.

5 *Reg. Inn. IV*, 1832.   6 Ed. Hahn, *Collectio monumentorum*, I, 394–6.

7 For example, probably *c.* 1259, Alfonso received a papal letter beginning 'Dum fidei puritatem, virtutis constantiam, strenuorum magnificentiam operum et

part of Alexander IV rather than any favourable expectation about the likely outcome that resulted in the king's entering the imperial lists against the count, Richard of Cornwall. Moreover, the papal panegyrics began to sound a note of alarm about Alfonso's failure to press the assumed advantage of the capture of Seville. A papal letter preserved in the collection of Richard of Pophis opened cheerfully enough, but then came to the point. What had possessed Fernando III to make a pact with the king of Granada after the success of 1248, and Alfonso to renew it on his accession?[1] Although, as it happened, Ibn el-Ahmer's views on Castilian foreign policy concurred with Alexander's, it was nevertheless, in the pope's view, a scandal that the king of Granada should have been the king of Castile's vassal at all in 1259.

In view of their recent experiences it may be assumed that the Castilian bishops were even less enthusiastic about the German business than the Moor. For them in 1257 Seville was not the Golden City but the bottomless pit into which they were currently being required to empty their income. They can have been in little doubt about their attitude – and even, perhaps, about their *collective* attitude – to fresh expensive foreign ventures, and such doubts as did exist must soon have been resolved when the pope sent his nuncio, Angelo patriarch of Grado, for discussions with the king on the subject in the autumn of 1258. On 21 October Alfonso wrote from Segovia, where the Patriarch was established five days before, to inform his allies in Siena of his arrival.[2] But the seriousness of his

ingentia merita quibus progenitores tui semper inter alios principes catholicos quodam presigni titulo specialiter claruerunt, intra nosmetipsos memori cogitatione recolimus' and reassuring him – 'te tanquam filium benedictionis et gratie inter alios reges terre sincerioris dilectionis brachiis complectentes': ASV, arm. XXXI. 72, fo. 288r, no. 2476 (Schillmann, *Die Formularsammlung des Marinus von Eboli*, 2491). For the context, see below, p. 157, n. 3.

[1] BM, MS Lansdowne 397, fo. 108r: 'Inter ceteros principes orbis terre catholicos tu, sicut clara et manifesta tue celsitudinis opera manifestant, inpendisti hactenus et incessanter inpendis sollicitos ac indefessos circa cultum fidei christiane labores illamque divina fultus potencia laudabiliter ampliasti, propter quod humane preconio laudis attolleris et apud Deum grandia premia promereris...Sane audivimus et mirati sumus quod olim tempore acquisitionis...civitatis...et...pater tuus cum...rege Granate sarraceno quedam iniens...conventiones et pacta iuramento prestito observare...' (Batzer, *Z. Kenntnis*, 379). Alfonso was ordered to terminate the treaty.

[2] AHN, 1977/5; Winkelmann, *Acta imperii inedita*, I, 464.

mission failed to restrain the nuncio, who since his resignation as archbishop of Crete had been keeping body and soul together with whatever morsels he could procure at the Curia,[1] from attempting to repair his fortunes at the expense of the Spanish Church. When news of his exactions reached the pope, Archbishop Benito of Tarragona was set to investigate, presumably on the assumption that it takes a thief to catch a thief.[2] Possibly this was also the occasion of the letter to the king in the Marinus Formulary in which the pope assured Alfonso that news of the misconduct of various papal nuncios had come as a great shock to him and the cardinals.[3] Yet despite Alexander's evident disapproval of what had occurred, the patriarch's 'unheard-of exactions' were still fresh in the bishops' minds in the winter of 1262–3 when they wrote to Urban IV on the subject, and the pope who had sent him rather than the king for whose sole benefit he had been sent was made the butt of their collective criticism.[4]

And the charge stuck. The conclusion of their disingenuous analysis – that the Roman Church was responsible for 'prelatorum ac ecclesiarum destructio'[5] – has long since been established as the authorised version. Modern historians such as Sánchez-Albornoz repeat it, apparently unconscious of its incompatibility with their no

---

1 *Reg. Alex. IV*, 1412–13, 1802.

2 AHA, *Cartoral AB*, fo. 23v: 'Quia patriarcham Gradensem credebamus utpote approbate religionis veram fidem et modestiam in suis processibus servaturum, ipsum olim in Ispaniam ad karissimum in Christo filium nostrum regem Castelle illustrem duximus destinandum. Sed ipse, quod dolentes referimus, eundo morando et redeundo, ut alia in quibus insolenter excessisse dignoscitur taceamus, immoderatas exactiones procurationum et necessarium suorum pretextu ab ecclesiis et locis ecclesiasticis faciendo, postquam etiam id eidem per nostras curavimus litteras sub pena quam ipso facto incurreret districtius inhibere, ac alias recipiendo donaria inhoneste, Romanam ecclesiam que in suis nuntiis mensuram gerit et exigit, infamavit...' (22 Sept. 1259).

3 'Porro super eo quod idem nuntius nobis et eisdem fratribus [*scil.* cardinalibus] retulit te olim a quibusdam predecessoris nostri nuntiis gravatum fuisse indebite et offensum non levi fuimus dolore turbati, scientes id de voluntate dictorum predecessoris et fratrum nullatenus processisse, cum potius firma semper ipsorum intentio fuerit, et nos nunc impari proposito intendamus, tuis et tuorum progenitorum exigentibus meritis, tuam inter ceteros principes efficere personam honorificentia potiori et te apostolico munientes presidio tuos et tuorum profectus multipliciter procurare' (Schillmann, 2491: above, p. 155, n. 7). The only other possible context for this letter is the year 1263, and the tone of Urban IV's broadside to the bishops on that occasion was quite different.

4 Publ. Benito Ruano, *HS*, XI, 12–17, esp. 17.

5 Linehan, *EHR*, LXXXV, 730 ff.

less perennial belief in the fabulous riches of Spanish ecclesiastics, and would regard the Patriarch of Grado incident as confirmation of their view that throughout the Middle Ages 'rivers of gold and silver' flowed to Rome from meek, uncomplaining Spain.[1] This, naturally, was the view of regalist writers in the mid-eighteenth century – of Nicolás de Azara who calculated that when Spain had been a Roman province its tribute had not amounted to half as much as the popes had exacted since its so-called independence,[2] and of Ascensio de Morales who discovered a copy of the bishops' letter of 1262–3 together with Pope Urban's uncompromising reply in the archive of Cuenca Cathedral and regarded it as a perfect example of 'la antigua tiranía con que hemos sido tratados de la Corte Romana y sus ministros' who 'han mirado siempre a un fin, que es el de sacar hasta la última gota de sangre a nuestros naturales'.[3] It is much more telling, though, that Benedict XIII should have believed it too at the beginning of the fifteenth century and should have reflected the prejudices of his Aragonese origins by arguing that his own demands on Castile had been negligible in comparison with the 'magnas pecunias' and 'pingua beneficia' exacted by his predecessors.

The occasion of these remarks was the irritation of the queen of Castile, Catherine of Lancaster, at being refused permission to enjoy the *tercias* unless she devoted them to the war effort against the Moors.[4] By 1415 such restriction must have seemed intolerable. It was 168 years since Innocent IV had first granted this form of ecclesiastical revenue to the Castilian monarch – an event which the bishops glossed over in their letter to Urban IV. And their eloquent silence, a tribute in itself to the effectiveness of royal discipline, was all the more remarkable in view of the economic crisis through which they were indeed passing and which had only very recently been prevented from bearing political fruit in the form of those assemblies which John of Abbeville had prescribed for quite different reasons: pro-

---

[1] Sánchez-Albornoz, *España: un enigma histórico*, I, 356, where the author laments the lack of any Castilian equivalent to the resistance of Henry IV, Frederick II and Philip the Fair to Gregory VII, Innocent III [sic] and Boniface VIII respectively.

[2] Cit. Sarrailh, *L'Espagne éclairée de la seconde moitié du XVIIIe siècle*, 624–5.

[3] Morales to Carvajal, 10 Feb. 1751: BN, MS 13072, fo. 2v. Morales's attitude to the papacy is further illustrated by his suggestion to Fernando VI that 'la desgracia' of the loss of Constantinople which occasioned Urban IV's appeal for funds was 'quizá causada por culpa de los Romanos': *ibid.* fo. 62r.

[4] Suárez Fernández, *Castilla, el Cisma y la crisis conciliar*, 73–4, 298–9.

vincial councils. The conciliar movement of 1257–8 was inspired neither by enthusiasm for papal reform nor by resistance to papal taxation, but by the economic consequences of *royal* control.

Even before the capture of Seville the normally docile Spanish bishops were beginning to show signs of strain. Though, for example, their intervention at the Lyons Council of 1245 was no more overtly suggestive of their disaffection with the king than was their letter to Pope Urban, nevertheless it will clearly bear this interpretation. To Urban they were to complain about the burden of taxation imposed upon them by Innocent IV.[1] Yet what had distinguished them in 1245 had been their keen advocacy of vigorous action against Frederick II, and their willingness to underwrite the costs of such action. Their enthusiasm may have been partly an extension of that over-weening national confidence in their own powers which drew strength from the collapse of the Moors at home. But ecclesiastical self-interest was at least as strong a motive. From a cultural point of view Menéndez Pidal has observed a 'marked similarity' in the careers of Frederick II and Alfonso X, and has remarked upon their 'parallel lives'.[2] In view of their recent experiences may not the same coincidence have struck the peninsular prelates in 1245, including those who were subject to the king of Castile, 'nuestro divino rey San Fernando' as Burriel called him?[3] Some such irreverent reflection may well have occurred to the canons of Calahorra and made them all the more willing to contribute to the pope's fund for the defence of *ecclesiastica libertas* when Innocent IV sent his chaplain Master Raymond to collect cash for that purpose in January 1244.[4] Less than twenty years later they would remember Master Raymond as one among many agents of the insatiable papacy,[5] but on the eve of the

---

1 'Item dominus Innocentius quartus imposuit subsidium pro facto istius imperii Constantinopolitani, ratione cuius ipse imperator [*scil.* Baldwin II] habuit a prelatis Hispanie quadraginta millia aureorum et plus; sed quod ipse imperator operatus est cum ipsa pecunia omnes sciunt': Benito Ruano, *HS*, XI, 16. Benito regards this as 'una nueva aportación hispánica a la defensa del Imperio Latino hasta ahora totalmente desconocida' (16, n. 32). The reference, however, is clearly to the universal tax prescribed by canon 14 of the Council. Cf. Hefele–Leclercq, v, ii, 1651–2.

2 *Boll. Centro di studi filologici e linguistici Siciliani,* III, 8, 14.

3 Burriel to Castro, 30 Dec. 1754, ed. Valladares de Sotomayor, *Semanario Erudito,* II, 44.

4 *Illam de vestre,* 11 Jan. 1244: AC Calahorra, doc. 278.

5 Benito Ruano, *HS,* XI, 16.

Lyons Council Innocent's appeal could strike a chord at Calahorra and elsewhere, for in the emperor who showed such scant respect for churchmen, Spanish churchmen could see their own rulers writ large. Some Spaniards had had personal experience of Frederick's severity, having seen the inside of his prison after their capture by the Pisan fleet while *en route* for Gregory IX's abortive Roman Council in May 1241. One who had was Master Juan who was on a mission to the Curia on behalf of Bishop Martín Rodríguez of León. He acquitted himself fairly well – as he remembered it all when dean of León in 1267 – having the presence of mind to throw his letters of credit into the Mediterranean on arrest.[1] Others though were less reourceful, and their miserable fate was still remembered by the appellant bishops in 1262–3.[2] According to the pope's man in Germany, Albert Beham, those who survived the experience emerged as but shadows of their former selves.[3] But the effect of the incident on the boatload of peninsular prelates who escaped unharmed seems to have been hardly less traumatic, and in their joint letter to the pope, Archbishop Pedro de Albalat and the bishops of Astorga, Orense, Salamanca, Plasencia and Porto volunteered their all in the struggle against Frederick and made no pretence of their fear that, if he were not thoroughly chastised, other princes would soon follow his 'exemplum et audaciam'.[4] If their prose was somewhat disjointed that was because they were looking over their shoulders as they wrote; and, within the decade, the fate of the bishop of Gerona, mutilated on royal orders, would show that their alarm was fully justified.

Between then and July 1245, when the emperor was condemned at Lyons, their ardour did not cool. In that aviary presided over by the papal peacock – as an anonymous Ghibelline versifier described the assembly[5] – the Spanish bishops were the hawks. Constituting the

1 AC León, doc. 1564. '…he quando elos otros furon pressos enna mar del emperador echo aquellas letras del empresado enno mar'. By the time of his escape and return to León Nuño Álvarez was bishop. He was therefore detained till at least Jan. 1244. Cf. *Reg. Inn. IV*, 412.
2 '…qui prelati in manus inimicorum ecclesie incidentes, captivitatem cedent, miserabilem inediam, ammissionem familie, jacturam rerum passi sunt': Benito Ruano, *HS*, XI, 15.
3 *Albert's von Beham Conceptbuch*, ed. Höfler, 77.
4 Publ. Huillard-Bréholles, *Historia diplomatica*, V, ii, 1120.
5 *Pavo de figura seculi*, ed. Karajan, esp. lines 63–74. Composed in the 1280s. Cf. Hirsch, *MIöG*, XL, 317 ff.

largest national group, according to the *Relatio*, they reiterated not only their faith in the hard line but also their willingness to meet the cost;[1] and Frederick's condemnation of the archbishops of Tarragona and Compostela for interfering in matters which they did not understand[2] missed the essential point that, although possibly Pedro de Albalat and Juan Arias were ignorant of many of the details of his struggle with Innocent, nevertheless they were both fully experienced in the business of dealing with the likes of him in their own setting – though there they would not have dared to speak out so recklessly. Each in 1245 had his equivalent to Frederick II. In the province of Tarragona Teobaldo I of Navarre was hardly less of a menace, as the bishop of Pamplona informed the pope in September 1245,[3] and by his firm refusal to allow his secular rights to be judged by any ecclesiastical authority, even the highest, he invited comparison with the emperor and three years later brought down upon himself a sentence of excommunication.[4] The province of Compostela provided an even closer parallel in Sancho II of Portugal whose outrages against the Portuguese bishops subject to the jurisdiction of Juan Arias incurred him in a papal sentence tantamount to that loosed against the emperor and issued one week later.[5] Nicholas of Curbio, Pope Innocent's biographer, was not the only observer to be struck by this coincidence.[6] Frederick himself drew Fernando III's attention to the case of Sancho in a letter the burden of which was to remind the king of Castile of the pope's temerity in interfering in his affairs

1 'Postmodum surrexit archiepiscopus de Yspania, qui multum dominum papam animavit ad procedendum contra imperatorem, referendo plurima que contra ecclesiam fecerat, et quomodo tota sua fuerat intentio ut deprimeret ecclesiam iuxta posse, promittens quod ipse ac alii prelati Yspanie, qui multum magnifice ac generaliter melius quam alia natio ad concilium venerant, domino pape assisterent in personis et rebus iuxta sue beneplacitum voluntatis': *Relatio de Concilio Lugdunensi*, ed. Weiland, 515.

2 Matthew Paris, *Chronica Majora*, IV, 540.

3 AM Pamplona, J, d.s.n. 6–1: *inc. Venerabilis frater*, 6 Sept. 1245: reg. Goñi Gaztambide, *AA*, x, No. 107.

4 Details in Goñi Gaztambide, *Príncipe de Viana*, XVIII, 97 ff. At the hearing of the case at Lyons in May 1247 the king asserted through his proctor, Jacobus de Maringiaco, 'quod nullo modo super temporalibus in Romana curia responderet. Predictus vero rex per litteras apostolicas postmodum evocatus nec per se nec per procuratorem super predictis temporalibus voluit respondere': AC Pamplona, IV Episcopi 27 (reg. Goñi Gaztambide, *Catálogo*, 555).

5 Peters, *Studia Gratiana*, XIV, 255 ff.

6 *Vita Innocenti IV*, 96.

'in quibus non minus vestrum quam nostrum vertitur interesse'.[1]

The Spanish bishops' sense of foreboding was justifiable and would be justified, although when translated into action it at first mistook its adversary. Within ten years of the Lyons Council they had raised the rebel flag against the pope.[2] But the pope was not their real problem, and by 1257 they were at last frank enough to acknowledge it. In that year the formal announcement of Alfonso's imperial candidacy was added to the accumulation of their existing woes. But it was, perhaps, a quite different phenomenon that drove them to the edge and, for a short time, kept them there: the weather. This is not to suggest that politics – and ecclesiastical politics least of all – go by the weather. Still, their obsession with that *gravissima afflictio* of seven years' duration when they wrote to Urban IV in the winter of 1262–3[3] suggests that the meteorological history of Castile in the 1250s has at least something to do with the bishops' short-lived political activity during that period.

Such fragments of information as have survived on this most important aspect of Spanish history[4] indicate, hardly surprisingly, that the thirteenth century there was a dry century. If an age may be judged by its intercessions, then *siccitas* and *ariditas* rather than Moors and heretics were its real bugbears. The miracle most frequently requested of San Isidro, the patron of Madrid, was that of rain-making. In 1252 he came up to expectations, just as he had done twenty years before while at León Lucas of Túy had been bribing the people to disavow the local Albigensians by promising them showers from above.[5] In 1258 the *madrileños* were again beholden to the Saint.[6] But unhappily either his compassion or his competence

1 *Petri de Vineis Epp.*, 120; 122: 'Vos tamen, quorum in hoc non minus vestra causa quam nostra nunc agitur'; 123: 'Et ut non longe petatur a nobis exemplum, qualiter in regno Portugalie honoris sibi usurpaverit dignitatem, curas vestras et animos excitetis'. In the early 1290s Jaime II of Aragon was anxious to secure a copy of the 'dictamina magistri Petri de Vinis et processus domini Frederici imperatoris, dive memorie, abavi nostri' for Sancho IV of Castile: Rubió y Lluch, *Documents...de la Cultura catalana mig-eval*, II, 3–4.
2 Above, Ch. 7.
3 Benito Ruano, *HS*, XI, 14.
4 For some general observations, see Olagüe, *La decadencia española*, IV, 249 ff.
5 *Leyenda de San Isidro por Juan Diácono*, ed. Fita, *BRAH*, IX, 114–16, 119; above, Ch. 7.
6 *Leyenda*, 117.

was limited, for in that year there were bad harvests at Burgos and 'great hunger' at Sigüenza,[1] while, apart from drought, severe frosts also took their toll, and the price of wine soared.[2] 1258 was a bad year everywhere. Albertus Miliolus recorded it as one of *caristia*,[3] and in England the chroniclers were at one in lamenting the hardness of the times. Matthew Paris wrote of fifteen thousand Londoners dying in the course of the summer (a fate which overtook the French capital in the following year); men were reduced to seeking nourishment from nettles, tree-bark, horsemeat 'et quod deterius est'.[4] So great was the demand for the services of gravediggers that they were obliged to consign the corpses to the ground *glomeratim*.[5]

In Castile where, as Alfonso X was to acknowledge, food-supply was essential for keeping the fight going,[6] the effects of *caristia* were certainly no less substantial than in England on the eve of the Barons' War; and the Church there had little left to lose, having become almost totally identified with the king. During the winter of 1257–8, while the recluse of St Alban's was dreaming that the church-tower was in danger of collapsing, the royal palace at Segovia actually did collapse, taking the dean of Burgos (the only member of that church to have benefited from the *repartimiento* of Seville) with it, and damaging several bishops, but leaving the king intact.[7] If, as they dusted themselves down, the walking wounded compared their position with that of their episcopal brethren in Aragon, they must have been aware of certain striking differences. Climatically, of course, that kingdom can hardly have been much better off – though the rising of the Ebro which did so much damage at Zaragoza in 1261 suggests

---

1 *Chronicón de Cardeña*, ed. Flórez, *ES*, XXIII, 374; Minguella, I, 208–9. The passage in *Chron. Cardeña* contains no mention of plague, though it is the only authority for the assertion of Verlinden (who cites it at second hand) that 1258 was a plague year in Western Spain: *Rev. Belge de philol. et d'hist.*, XVII, I, 105, n. 2. 'Fue el año malo de pan' is all that it says.

2 *Chron. Cardeña*, 374. Late frosts were the cause of the bad harvest of 1234 also: *Anales Toledanos II*, ed. Flórez, *ES*, XXIII, 407–8.

3 *Liber de temporibus et aetatibus*, ed. Holder-Egger, 525.

4 *Chronica Majora*, V, 690, 693–4, 701–2, 746–7; *Bartholomei de Cotton...Historia Anglicana*, ed. Luard, 137; *Chron. Lanercost*, ed. Stevenson, 65. Also *Ann. Monastici*, ed. Luard, II, 166, 351; III, 462; IV, 120.

5 *Gesta abbatum monasterii S. Albani*, ed. Riley, I, 389.

6 *Part.* 2.20.8 (Academy ed. II, 196).

7 *Gesta abbatum*, I, 388; *Chron. Cardeña*, 374; Gil de Zamora, 'Biografías', ed. Fita, *BRAH*, V, 322–3.

that drought was not a universal complaint.[1] Yet Bernat Vidal de Besalú thought it at least worthwhile to remind the king of Castile, when Alfonso and Jaime met at Soria in 1257, that he would be ill advised to fight a war over Navarre, observing 'that in the army of the king of Aragon there were such stores of bread and wine and meat and corn that they counted these almost as naught, by reason of their abundance, but that in the army of the king of Castile there was so great dearth of all things that soldiers and horses were dying of hunger'.[2] This may have been a debating point, but it is hardly credible that the chronicler would have made such an assertion if the evidence was against him. Certainly the Aragonese economy was subject to the effects of natural disasters too. In August 1248 Innocent IV had come to the assistance of Pedro de Albalat 'cum...propter sterilitatem terre ac alias necessitates urgentes debitorum onere sis gravatus'.[3] But Pedro, the zealous persecutor of Frederick II, had done more for his church and province than merely secure piecemeal papal relief. He had provided them with a tradition of provincial councils which, quite apart from making a direct contribution to the reduction of popular poverty by revising the number of feast-days,[4] and resisting royal tyranny by excommunicating the king of Navarre for pestering the bishop of Pamplona, provided the Aragonese Church by virtue of their very existence with that which the Castilian Church lacked: a political bargaining position. Whether or not the real advantages which the Aragonese Church had derived from the Reconquest during the twelfth century had been continued into the thirteenth,[5] and irrespective of the bitter struggles between the king and Pedro's archiepiscopal successor at this very time and of Jaime I's spectacular assaults on the persons of individual prelates, that was an achievement of considerable significance. 'Llama la atención', wrote Cedillo of the twelfth century, 'la diferencia que existe entre el número de los concilios reunidos en Cataluña y en

---

[1] According to the sixteenth-century writer Diego de Espés. Cit. Arco, *BRAH*, LXXII, 517.

[2] Desclot, *Chronicle*, I, 147. For the date of this, cf. Valls i Taberner, *B. Hisp.*, XXI, 25. Desclot's remarks indicate the change that had occurred in the peninsular balance since 1212 when the king of Aragon had been Castile's pensioner at Las Navas.

[3] *Cum sicut nobis*, 30 Aug. 1248: AHA, *Cartoral AB*, fo. 8v.

[4] '...cum in illis eo quod non laborant pauperes aggravantur': Tejada, *Colección de cánones*, VI, 35.

[5] Lacarra, *RPH*, IV, 272 ff.

otras partes de España y la gran escasez por lo que respecta a Castilla y León'.[1] And the disparity can have been hardly less evident to Castilian churchmen in April 1257 when King Jaime granted their Aragonese colleagues a large measure of exemption from the terms of the rigorous export restrictions then in force.[2] Indeed it is certain that it was not. For by April 1257 the Castilian Church was actively engaged in looking to its own defences.

The stirrings of resistance occurred at all levels of the Castilian Church. Of varying degrees of intensity it identified the enemy sometimes as the local chapter and sometimes as the pope and the king. At the lowest level it was formalised in the literally parochial pacts whereby the local clergy of Ávila in 1258[3] and of Salamanca in April 1259,[4] recalling the *collaciones* which dated from the establishment of the Christian frontier in those places,[5] undertook to defend their interests against the encroachment of bishop and chapter. But other co-operative ventures involving clerical groups were rather more ambitious. Activating the *cabildos de curas* – those associations of clergy normally devoted to purely pious purposes such as had existed at Guadalajara since 1081[6] – the clergy of Toledo made common cause with those of Talavera in February 1258 by a *carta de hermandad* which pledged their bodies and all their possessions in mutual defence against the archbishop-elect and other prelates. Their motives, they insisted, were strictly defensive and in keeping with the traditional nature of such *cartas* which normally contained nothing more seditious than undertakings to reciprocate prayer and hospitality.[7] For

---

1 *Contribuciones é impuestos*, 259–60.
2 Publ. Tejada, III, 386; contemporary copies in AC Vich, 37-3-55; AGN, caj. 3, no. 7 (reg. Castro, *Catálogo*, 317).
3 Ariz, *Historia de las grandezas de la ciudad de Ávila*, I, 36r–v. Noted by Lafuente, *Historia*, IV, 276, as marking the transition in 1258 from the Spanish Church's *período heroico* to its *período crepuscular*. As a further indication of transition Lafuente referred to Alexander IV's promotion in that year of Bishop Abril of Urgel, on which see Linehan, *AEM*. Lafuente's observation is repeated, without acknowledgement, by Sobrequés, *La época*, 166.
4 AC Salamanca, 13/4 (reg. Marcos Rodríguez, *Catálogo*, 276); Dorado, *Compendio histórico de la ciudad de Salamanca*, 217; González, *Hispania*, III, 427–30.
5 Lacarra, *Moyen Âge*, LXIX, 211, 218.
6 Núñez de Castro, *Historia eclesiástica y seglar de Guadalaxara*, 50.
7 AC Toledo, Z.3.D.2.10: 'E nos esta hermandat non la fazemos a desden de nuestros prelados nin por les fazer perder dignidat, mas fazemosla a defendimiento e a amparamiento de nuestras ordenes e de nuestros beneficios e de nuestras eglesias e de

all their protestations though, their action had a more positive significance. Quite apart from the extreme measures which it envisaged,[1] it was by virtue of its very timing a technical act of sedition. In that very month, at the Valladolid Cortes, all associations except such as professed strictly charitable ends were prohibited by the king.[2] And one month later the Toledo clergy dispensed with equivocation and, in their *carta de hermandad* with the clergy of Rodiellas, added the pope and the king to the list of potential aggressors.[3]

The lower clergy were not acting in a political void, but took their cue from the very churchman about whom they were currently expressing such serious reservations, the Infante Sancho, archbishop-elect of Toledo. His antecedents hardly marked him out as the Castilian Pedro de Albalat or the champion of ecclesiastical independence.[4] Nor indeed was he. For, as was soon discovered, he was playing a political game, taking advantage of his brother the king's temporary weakness which had enabled the *hermandades* to declare themselves,[5] and making ecclesiastical discontent serve his own ends. Faithless opportunist though he was, however, there is no denying that he showed remarkable energy and single-mindedness in canalising dissent and inducing the warring ecclesiastical factions to sink their differences and devote their dissipated energies to the common cause. His recorded activities throughout 1257 and for the greater part of 1258 provide clear testimony; and his first step was to provide the Castilian Church with that potentially political weapon – the habit of provincial councils. On 15 January 1257 at Alcalá de Henares, together with five of his suffragans – Fernando of Palencia, Gil of

---

nuestros patrimonios por que la clerezia e la santa eglesia e la fe catolica non sea abaxada nin aviltada.' Cf. Ruiz Jusué, *AHDE*, xv, 422 ff; Suárez Fernández, *CHE*, xvi, 5 ff.

[1] '...si por aventura nuestro sennor el electo don Sancho o qual quier prelado o su vicario o su procurador por auctoridat dellos o por su propria voluntad algun agravamiento quisiere fazer al cabildo de la clerezia de Talavera...nos el cabildo avandicho de la clerezia de Toledo somos tenudos delos ayudar con cuerpos e con averes e con beneficios e con todo nuestro poder.'

[2] *Cortes de Castilla*, i, 61 (cap. 36).

[3] Publ. Sierra Corella, *RABM*, xlix, 113–14. The two pacts are otherwise virtually identical.

[4] Above, p. 110.

[5] 'La causa inmediata que produjo el nacimiento de la Hermandad parece bien clara: es la debilidad, más temporal que permanente, de la monarquía': Suárez Fernandez, *CHE*, xvi, 7.

Osma, Remondo of Segovia, Pedro of Sigüenza and Mateo of
Cuenca – he ordained that thenceforth the bishops of the province
should observe a biennial cycle of councils, meeting on St Martin's
Day (11 November) and fifteen days after Easter, at Alcalá, Buitrago
(twice) and Brihuega respectively, beginning that November 'ac sic
deinceps in succedentibus annis singulis'. If necessary, Sancho might
amend these arrangements – necessity being left to his judgement of
the 'great danger' that the Church might suffer by their delaying so
long. Absentees with unconvincing *alibis* would be fined two
hundred *maravedís*. The agreement concluded with a statement of the
signatories' devotion to Alfonso X.[1] He at the time was far away in
the south-east, attending to the affairs of the kingdom of Murcia;
and there he remained for the greater part of 1257.[2]

Till almost the end of the year there is no record of communication between the brothers; and, in view of Alfonso's situation, such
absence of information may well faithfully reflect a deliberate lack of
contact on the king's part. For – always assuming that he knew of the
Alcalá meeting – Alfonso must have viewed with some alarm the
emergence of political consciousness among the prelates, including
the hitherto utterly reliable Remondo of Segovia, at the very moment
of his accepting the imperial invitation. The most plausible assumption, then, from such negative evidence is that the king was hopeful
that, given time, the Church would divide itself and that he might
then rule it again; which was a very reasonable expectation in view
of its inherent lack of solidarity. When Bishop Gil of Osma subscribed
to the Alcalá declaration, for example, he was within eight days of
having his request for half of the *tercias* of his diocese granted by
Alexander IV;[3] while by mid-April the economic problems of the
church of León had led the chapter to charge Bishop Martín Fernández with having mismanaged their financial affairs.[4] Such were the
tensions within ecclesiastical society that it could not long afford the
luxury of an independent, co-operative stand. Still, if the mere grant
of rights of justice at Santander, which he made to Sancho on 5

---

[1] 'Salvo iure et dominio regis quod nos in omnibus et per omnia conservare semper
intendimus fideliter': AC Toledo, I.5.A.I.8: publ. Fita, *BRAH*, x, 152-4, from
Burriel's transcript (BN, MS. 13069, fos. 91r–2r).
[2] Ballesteros, *Alfonso X*, 175 ff.
[3] *Reg. Alex. IV*, 1899.
[4] Risco, *ES*, xxxv, 315.

November (six days before the date proposed for the first council), was intended to buy off the opposition, then the king had under-estimated the opposition.[1] Sancho too could wait, and raise his price. In 1258 he did. Early in January Alfonso gave the Norwegian delegation no reason to believe that Sancho was anything other than capital archiepiscopal material;[2] which within a few weeks Sancho confirmed – though after his own fashion rather than his brother's – by persuading the parish clergy of Toledo to withdraw their opposi-tion to a contributory educational fund of his devising:[3] no mean feat in the very month of the publication of their general defiance. The legislation dealing with clerical dress, issued by the Valladolid Cortes in the third week of January, may possibly have irked him,[4] the matter coming more appropriately within the competence of his new-fangled council. But in mid-March he replied in kind, using the hospitality of the king's court to restore 'pax et caritativa concordia' to Bishop Pedro Garcés of Segorbe and his chapter.[5] On 5 July the king scored a point by granting the debt-ridden Bishop Martín Fernández his receipts from the *tercias* of the diocese of León, as he was in a position to do.[6] Eight days later they were both at Palencia, giving a helping hand to the recently elected Fernando and his chapter. But while Alfonso, having mediated between the bishop and the local nobility, hastened on to Arévalo,[7] Sancho remained and undertook an enquiry into the respective responsibility of Fernando and the chapter for the various debts bequeathed to the church by Bishop Rodrigo. He issued his compromise settlement at Brihuega on the 21st. It was based on the notion that *ecclesiastica utilitas* was well served when ecclesiastics refrained from poaching on one another's preserves:[8] Sancho's *leitmotiv* for the time being, the wisdom of

[1] Cit. Ballesteros, *Alfonso X,* 1077.
[2] 'Gravem virum et ad gerendum archiepiscopatum Toletanum idoneum': Guzmán y Gallo, *BRAH*, LXXIV, 50.
[3] AC Toledo, A.7.C.1.6: 'veyendo e entendiendo que el ayuda que nos demandava nuestro sennor don Sancho por ayr a escuelas que era a nuestra pro e a ondra de la clerecia e que era demandada con derecho queriendo nos facer guisado'.
[4] *Cortes de Castilla,* I, 55 (cap. 5).
[5] *VL*, III, 237–9.
[6] '...en ayuda para quitar debdas de su iglesia': publ. Risco, *ES*, XXXVI, p. clvi.
[7] AC Palencia, 3/2/24. Cf. Ballesteros, *BRAH*, CVI, 126–7.
[8] AC Palencia, 3/2/23: 'Cupientes insuper inter se pacem et quietem indissolubili caritatis fibula observari; intelligentes etiam quod nichil deperit ecclesiasticis

which was amply demonstrated by the united front with which his settlement enabled the church of Palencia to confront the acquisitive local *concejo*.[1] And though it seems that he failed in carrying the principle to the point of reconciling the bishop and chapter with the Dominicans there,[2] two days after the Brihuega compromise he did himself provide an example of the spirit of self-abnegation which he had been preaching by renouncing the traditional archiepiscopal right to a share of the property of deceased canons of Toledo.[3]

But his debts were pressing him hard, and it was only a matter of time before he would be forced or tempted to abandon a policy which required considerable resources for its maintenance. Already in June 1257 he was wavering: Alexander IV's cancellation, at his request, in that month of past grants of his church's lands and tithes which earlier archbishops had authorised (including grants which had received papal confirmation[4]) was totally at variance with the concept of *ecclesiastica utilitas* currently being canvassed by him. Then, towards the end of 1258, he turned his coat and showed its lining to be made of the traditional, royal stuff. Possibly he was still in Castile at the end of October and met the Patriarch of Grado at Segovia. But soon after he must have left. He was not, as Ballesteros believed, the life and soul of the Toledo Cortes which discussed the imperial affair at the end of the year and at the beginning of 1259.[5] For he was nowhere near Toledo. He was at Anagni.

He had arrived there by 11 January, on which day the pope empowered him to borrow up to 800 marks on behalf of the church of Toledo.[6] But that was small beer. Sancho had his eyes on a greater prize: the income of his province. And by the end of the month he had secured it. On the 26th, in reply to his petition 'quod Toletana ecclesia magno premitur debitorum onere a tuis predecessoribus contractorum', Alexander IV granted him two-thirds of all the *tercias* of his province for the next five years;[7] to which was added the entire

utilitatibus si quae sunt aliena reddantur.' Cf. Fernández del Pulgar, *Historia de Palencia*, II, 334.
[1] Caamaño, *AHDE*, XI, 519–20.
[2] Ripoll, *Bullarium*, I, 392; Fernández del Pulgar, II, 325.
[3] Publ. *MHE*, I, 138–9.
[4] AC Toledo, A.7.C.2.4, *Sicut dilecti*, 13 June 1257.
[5] *Alfonso X*, 225.
[6] AC Toledo, I.5.C.1.67.
[7] AC Toledo, Z.3.D.1.15, *Affectu benevolentie* (publ. Linehan, *EHR*, LXXXV, 750).

takings of one *decimarius* in every parish for the same period,[1] and presentation to a canonry in the cathedral churches of each of his suffragans.[2] The last of these rescripts was issued on the 28th: in two days the Infante Sancho had completely reversed his ecclesiastical policy of the previous two years. *Ecclesiastica utilitas* was sacrificed to *Toletana necessitas*. Not that his profitable stay at Anagni had yet ended. He remained there till at least the middle of April, and was consecrated there on or before 2 April.[3] On that day his departure was evidently imminent, for the pope wrote to Archbishop Juan Arias of Compostela and to both his and Sancho's suffragans instructing them to observe what Sancho would tell them from him concerning certain unspecified matters.[4] The cautious tone of that communication suggests that the pope may have been referring to their recent activities: a suspicion which is strengthened by a further letter, addressed to the king on 9 April, which recommended the new archbishop to his brother and described him as 'negotiorum tuorum promotor precipuus'.[5] How much longer Sancho stayed at the Curia we do not know. But he was back at Toledo by 31 August,[6] having sought before leaving Anagni to extend his ecclesiastical piracy beyond his province by securing papal confirmation of the rights of the church of Toledo in terms which Benito de Rocaberti, who had recently arrived at the Curia himself, adjudged to be prejudicial to Tarragona's authority in the diocese of Segorbe.[7]

By the time of his return the incipient ecclesiastical opposition was shattered. It had been his own doing. Mud from a muddy spring, the Infante had reverted to type, abandoned the party of his own making, and striven to secure his own comfort at his recent

---

1 See below.
2 AC Toledo, A.7.C.2.2, *Tuam volentes honorare*.
3 But not before 7 March when he was still 'electus': AC Toledo, A.7.C.2.3a; caj. I.12, d.s.n. Cf. Castejón's assertion that he was consecrated at Toledo: *Primacía*, 761.
4 AC Toledo, A.7.C.2.3, *Inter alias sollicitudines*.
5 AC Toledo, A.7.C.2.6 (publ. *MHE*, I, 147–8, wrongly ascribed to Sancho of Aragon). The next day he received permission to retain the abbacies of Santander and Santillana which he had possessed before his consecration: AC Toledo, A.7.C.2.5, *Pro merente*.
6 AC Toledo, A.7.C.2.9.
7 AC Toledo, A.7.C.2.1 (Potthast, 17606); Marca, *De primatibus*, 369–72 (Potthast, 17646; 29 July 1259). Benito had arrived at the Curia by 17 May, having been ordered to report there by the Patriarch of Grado: AHA, *Cartoral AB*, fo. 36v.

colleagues' expense. Not that he had long to enjoy his ill-gotten goods. Yet neither his death in October 1261[1] nor his suffragans' success in inducing the pope to reduce the grant of revenue sometime before September 1260[2] could put the clock back to January 1257. Prelates such as Fernando of Palencia – who sent him a pathetic appeal on 1 November 1259 asking to be allowed to retain his revenues for that year 'pora quitar los grandes debdos que delexaron los nuestros antecessores la eglesia de Palencia obligada, assi como vos sabedes'[3] – would not be duped a second time into risking royal displeasure. 'The intolerable burden' placed upon them, which Bishop Pedro Lorenzo referred to in January 1263 as having caused their 'manifest destruction',[4] had other than financial implications. It meant not only the *coup de grâce* for the already faltering University of Palencia, deemed 'dissolved' by Urban IV in May 1263,[5] but also the fragmentation of such ecclesiastical solidarity as had been achieved.

That development was in process even before Sancho's apostasy of January 1259. When the Leonese bishops congregated on 2 December 1258 they did so at Madrid, where the king was. And although theirs apparently was a more politically motivated assembly than the Alcalá meeting, containing Spanish prelates from the Braga province but no Portuguese from that of Compostela, their only recorded act was to issue a collective indulgence in favour of León Cathedral.[6] It might of course be argued, on the grounds that on occasion no evidence is more significant than any evidence, that they would naturally have ensured that this *was* their only recorded act. Equally cogent though is the view that they had been infiltrated and tamed by Alfonso who was in the vicinity; and the royal favours granted on

---

[1] Castejón, 764.
[2] AC Toledo, Z.3.D.1.15bis, *inc. Inter alia munera*, 6 Sept. 1260, referring to the grant of the receipts of the single *decimarius* in every parish of the province – which had already been curtailed 'ex certa causa'; and confirming the grant of the entire income from the *tercias* for five years – which was more than the bull *Affectu benevolentie* had specified in Jan. 1259. Publ. Linehan, *EHR*, LXXXV, 750–1.
[3] AC Toledo, X.2.A.2.4.
[4] AC Cuenca, 8/34/678.
[5] 'Non sine multo eiusdem provintiae dispendio': *Reg. Urb. IV*, 240. See J. San Martín, *La antigua Universidad de Palencia* (Madrid, 1942); Ajo y Sáinz de Zúñiga, *Historia de las universidades hispánicas*, I, 195 ff.
[6] AC León, doc. 1533 (publ. *ES*, xxxv, 268–9).

the 5th and 9th to the church of Coria and the clergy of the Zamora diocese respectively suggest how this may have been done.[1] Archbishop Juan Arias of Compostela knew his place and his suffragans knew their price. There is fragmentary and confusing evidence of episcopal consultation in that province at about this time, none of which says much for their spirit of independence. On 11 September either in 1259 or 1260 the suffragan bishops of Compostela, 'vocati apud civitatem compostellanam ad sinodum', debated solemnly the question of who should have precedence over whom at their meeting (in itself a fair indication of their inexperience in these matters).[2] It was perhaps that assembly – though a date three or four years later might be preferred – that roared like a mouse and objected to royal intervention in episcopal elections, always provided that their objection were not made public.[3] Characteristically, they were considerably less reticent about taking the pope to task for having deprived the archbishop of his right to confirm episcopal elections and consecrate his suffragans, after Juan Arias had interfered in the affairs of the see of Ávila *lite pendente*: an abuse upon which their local genius, Bernardus Compostellanus, had occasion to comment.[4]

[1] Ballesteros, *BRAH*, CVI, 134. The latter guaranteed clerical freedom from arrest. On the same day Mondoñedo Cathedral was similarly favoured.

[2] AC Salamanca, 14/2/20. The names of the bishops who were present indicate that the 'synod' occurred between 1253 and 1260, though the scribe entered the date as 'era 1268', i.e. 1230. Marcos Rodríguez, *Catálogo*, no. 185, fails to notice this discrepancy and adds a further confusion of his own by reading as 'III id. *aprilis*' what is, unmistakably, 'III id. *septembris*'; and González, *Correo Erudito*, III, 194, ascribes the document to the year 1240. 1260 is possible, on the assumption that the scribe meant to write 'era MCCLX^V VIII' but wrote MCCLXVIII by mistake; but 1259 may be preferred since the Lisbon representative is described as 'vicarius *ecclesie* Ulixbonensis'. Bishop Aires Vasques had died in Oct. 1258 and the election of his successor, Mateus, was confirmed between Jan. and March 1260: Cunha, *História ecclesiástica da igreja de Lisboa*, I, 166v, 171r; *Reg. Alex. IV*, 3183–4.

[3] 'Item statuimus quod solempnis electio tantum principi presentetur, nulla prius ab eo licentia postulata. Volumus tamen quod ad presens non publicetur': López Ferreiro, *Historia de Santiago*, v, app. 29, cap. 18.

[4] Such would appear to be the context of cap. 12: 'Cum ecclesia Compostellana fuerit in ista quasi possessione a tempore quo non extat memoria ut providere possit de pastore iure metropolitico ecclesie sue suffraganie viduate, non solum in casu negligentie set (etiam) in quocumque alio, (cum) sive propter formam sive propter vicium persone cassetur electio per canonicos eiusdem ecclesie celebrata, et Romana ecclesia, ut publice asseritur, eamdem hoc iure privare intendat...' The ban on Juan Arias was imposed between Sept. 1261 and Feb. 1263: Ballesteros, *Sevilla en el siglo XIII*, cx–cxi; *MHE*, I, 204; *Reg. Urb. IV*, 331, 2826. The copies of the *acta* of the

In view of their collective timidity, Fidel Fita's interpretation of the Alcalá meeting of January 1257 is clearly very wide of the mark. 'That important document' recording the bishops' intentions shed a 'profound light' on the ecclesiastical history of Spain. No longer, he wrote in 1887, could the total absence of councils in the Toledo province be contrasted with the 'multitude' of such assemblies which the thirteenth century witnessed at Tarragona. The Alcalá declaration, despite its consciously inaugural character, suggested to him that there existed a tradition of regular councils and synods which had not been broken since John of Abbeville's legation:[1] a theory which in turn served Gorosterratzu as firm ground upon which to base his belief that even before 1228 councils and synods were common occurrences.[2] All that was needed in order to establish the nature of their influence was evidence: 'resta averiguar cuáles fueron'.[3] Fita badly miscalculated. There is no record of any such councils, not even of the first four planned for November 1257– April 1259. The detailed progress-report compiled by Burriel in December 1752, after more than two years of work in the Toledo Cathedral archive, contained no mention of conciliar or synodal material for this period.[4] For some historians such lack of evidence is proof positive that councils were summoned with great frequency, indeed that they 'were then so commonplace that they occasioned no more mention...than does a faculty meeting in local newspapers today'.[5] That conclusion, however, cannot be applied to thirteenth-century Castile. The reason why neither Burriel nor any writer since has unearthed such records is that there was nothing then to record.[6] The Alcalá meeting stands in a void. What it produced was not proof of past achievements, but a blueprint for the future which was soon

---

council in AC Santiago – *Tumbillo de Tablas,* fos. 79v–80v; *Libro I de Constituciones,* fos. 9v–11v – mention no date. López Ferreiro, v, 186, suggests 'post-1245'. For the observations of Bernardus Compostellanus, see Johannes Andreae, *Glossa ordinaria,* C. 18 in VI⁰ 1, 6 gl. ad v. *Devolvetur* (publ. Barraclough, *Cath. Hist. Rev.* XIX, 291–2).

[1] *BRAH,* x, 154.   [2] *Don Rodrigo Jiménez de Rada,* 220–2.
[3] *BRAH,* x, 159.
[4] Burriel to Rábago, 22 Dec. 1752, ed. Valladares, *Semanario Erudito,* II, 5 ff.
[5] Kay, *Cath. Hist. Rev.,* LII, 162–3.
[6] No trace of evidence was found in the cathedral archives of Toledo, Palencia, Cuenca, Sigüenza, Segovia or Burgo de Osma. For an account of such material as exists in the cathedral archives of Galicia, see Ochoa Martínez de Soria, *Scriptorium Victoriense,* VII, 345 ff.

rejected. At Peñafiel in April 1302 the bishops tried again, having before the council began to settle the order of precedence of the suffragans at its sessions.[1] Some forty years earlier, the prelates of the Compostela province had been faced with the same problem. Neither group had any tradition upon which to draw. By leaving his colleagues in the lurch and being at Anagni in April 1259, instead of in Castile preparing for the Brihuega council which he had arranged more than two years before for the 28th of that month, Sancho of Toledo had thwarted the establishment of such a tradition.

He had also betrayed a revolution, for in Castile, where the summoning of one council implied revolt, the prospect of a conciliar programme was tantamount to revolution. As the prelates informed Nicholas III in 1279, the king did not tolerate assemblies at which they might discuss their grievances;[2] and in employing such stark terms as these it is not necessary either to embrace the almost cosmic concept of Lewis's Closing Medieval Frontier or to ignore Elliott's strictures against the historian's too ready assumption that 'political disagreement' has significance for him only when 'social revolt' can be postulated.[3] In the context of the medieval Castilian Church, and of the historiography of the subject, the emergence of mere 'political disagreement' is no small matter.

But the king had not eliminated dissension by dispersing it. True, he could continue to appease the prelates by allowing them some part of the revenue which by right was theirs already, just as he had done in dealing with the bishop of León in July 1258 or in conniving at the pope's grant to his brother in January 1259. By these means he bound Bishop Fernando of Córdoba and his chapter to the royal cause in June 1260, promising them 'las dos partes de los diezmos de las fabricas que nos avemos en las iglesias del obispado' as from the year 1266 (having three days previously dealt with tithe evasion in that diocese, on the grounds that the church was greatly defrauded thereby);[4] and ten years later a similar grant was made to the bishop-

---

[1] BC Toledo, MS 23–16, fo. 24v. The Peñafiel constitutions are publ. in Tejada, III, 433–46.

[2] 'Item prelatis vel capitulis terre sue non est liberum simul convenire et tractare de gravaminibus et injuriis que inferuntur, aut ipsa apostolice sedi referre': *Reg. Nich. III*, 743. See below, Ch. 9.

[3] *Speculum*, XXXIII, 475 ff.; *Past and Present*, XLII, 44–5.

[4] *MHE*, I, 162–3. Cf. above, p. 123.

elect of Cartagena, García Martínez.[1] But this form of palliative, the thief's concession to his victim, hardly indemnified the prelates. Elliott's observations cease to be appropriate when he associates himself with 'Tocqueville's perception that revolution tends to come with an improvement rather than with a deterioration of economic conditions'.[2]

The mutterings of dissent continued. Many churchmen, clearly, might have read as a description of their own situation the reference at the beginning of the eighteenth chapter of Isaiah to 'a nation meted out and trodden down'; and, had they consulted the scriptures (which appearances suggest they did not often do), some might even have endorsed the interpretation of the passage offered by the Joachimite, Gerard of Borgo San Donnino, to whom it suggested that Alfonso X was Antichrist.[3] And Alfonso himself, by depriving the bishops of the means of giving their complaints a public airing, drove them underground and left them no alternative but sedition. It was to be expected that when Clement IV authorised him in June 1265 to exact ten per cent of their income for the next five years, ecclesiastical bodies such as the chapter of Zamora should have appealed to the pope for remission, informing him that they had already been beggared for the king.[4] What was politically unforeseeable though – and for Alfonso politically ominous – was that less than four months later the newly appointed archbishop of Toledo of his choosing, Sancho of Aragon, should have been in secret session with his suffragans at Brihuega. The meeting was markedly better attended than the Alcalá gathering of January 1257, was graced by prelates of such impeccably curialist pedigree as Pedro Lorenzo of Cuenca and Agustín of Osma, who made no secret of their concern for the security of church property during episcopal vacancies, and censured the king for his preference for Jewish advisers – a subject about which they

---

[1] Publ. Torres Fontes, *Col. documentos del reino de Murcia*, I, 57–8.
[2] *Loc. cit.*, 39.
[3] Salimbene, *Cronica*, ed. Holder-Egger, 456 (s.a. 1253).
[4] AC Zamora, 1/3: 'cum ab eodem rege ecclesia nostra multipliciter sit gravata... proventus nostri sunt adeo diminuti quod vix ex eis possumus sustentari' (28 Nov. 1266). The papal grant was occasioned by the war against Granada. The dean of Zamora, Pedro Pérez, who appealed with the chapter, was, incidentally, engaged in collecting the tax for the king in the kingdom of Leon: a nice example of the dual personality of such churchmen: AM León, 1/7 (Ballesteros, *BRAH*, CIX, 452).

were to inform the pope more fully twelve years later.[1] In the privacy of his own chapter, too, Archbishop Sancho deplored the extent of lay interference in ecclesiastical affairs,[2] but having no provincial council at which they might openly have protested against the levy they were helpless and, whispering they would ne'er consent, they consented.[3] Before much longer, though, they were presented with an opportunity of breaking clean away from the stifling intimacy of Alfonso's court. When the Infante Sancho – who, like their frustrated desires, had been born in 1258[4] – raised the rebel flag in 1282 he was immediately joined by precisely those bishops who had been most closely associated with his father and had made their careers in his chancery. The reaction of such men to the restrictions of Alfonso's régime is strikingly reminiscent of the behaviour of those eleventh-century German bishops who, having risen to eminence in Henry III's chapel, abandoned his system and his son most readily in 1076.[5]

In 1259 though, there was not even that panacea in the offing, and the bishops' immediate concern was simply to survive the current crisis of Castilian society in common with other churchmen through-

---

[1] AC Palencia, 4/1/3: 'nephas est ut blasfemantibus [?] Christi iudeis maior habeatur fides quam christifidelibus christianis'. Cf. *Reg. Nich. III*, 743: 'Item judaeos christianis preponit multipliciter, unde multa mala proveniunt.' The Palencia document is the only record that has survived of this meeting. It is barely legible. Apart from Sancho, the bishops of Cuenca, Osma, Palencia, Segovia, Sigüenza and Segorbe were present, as well as the proctors of the bishops of Jaén and Córdoba, and representatives of the cathedral chapters. Dated 7 March 1267, it sheds new light on the attitude of the archbishop to the king. Cf. Ballesteros, *Alfonso X*, 445 ff.

[2] 'Eapropter dampnamus et reprobamus illam non consuetudinem sed potius corruptelam qua in aliqua ecclesia amore vel forte timore potentium inolevit, videlicet quod fiebat promissio vel receptio a prelato sine capitulo, vel a capitulo sine prelato, de canonia vel portione vel beneficio proximo vacaturo': *De constitutionibus et consuetudinibus ecclesie Toletane*, BN, MS 13041, fo. 14r (undated). *Consuetudo* and *corruptela* had been similarly contrasted by Gregory IX in the early thirties: above, Ch. 1.

[3] A document of Aug. 1267 contains a casual reference to an episcopal assembly at Ponferrada at some earlier date: 'Item quando el arzobispo de Santiago fizo xamar todos los bispos sos sufraganeos he elos otros bispos e los procuradores de los cabildos a Ponferrada...': AC León, doc. 1564. Was this perhaps the council which muzzled its resentment of royal interference in episcopal elections?

[4] Mondéjar, *Memorias históricas*, 211.

[5] Cf. Fleckenstein in *Adel und Kirche (Festschrift Tellenbach)*, 233–4. Gonzalo of Toledo, who avoided the embarrassment of having to declare his allegiance at this time had his equivalent in 1080 in Benno of Osnabrück, who, rather than commit himself at the Synod of Brixen, spent the day hidden under the altar.

out the Peninsula who looked to the pope in these years for protection against secular aggression.[1] The church of Palencia had a rougher passage than most. The effect of Archbishop Sancho's *volte-face* was to reopen the controversy between bishop and chapter over their common property and the debts bequeathed by Bishop Tello, which had been settled amicably in the previous summer. Indecision characterised the actions of both parties. In May 1259 the dean and chapter failed to prosecute an appeal which they had entered against a papal provision there, and were fined.[2] While he was at the Curia in March 1262 Bishop Fernando sold for a song property which he had possessed, Quinqueyuga, since before his promotion.[3] He had already been obliged to part with his modest receipts from Seville, but all to no avail, for by June 1263 his only income was the *sustentatio tenuis* allowed him by his Florentine creditors who had assumed full control of his financial affairs. Amongst those creditors was Dulcis de Burgo, one of the many Florentines whose Spanish clients were referred to the tender mercies of Cardinal Richard Annibaldi in 1266. If Fernando's successor Alfonso was still on their books then – and Fernando's failure over the previous three years to settle a 100 mark debt with the papal *camera* suggests that he probably was – then the events of the year 1266, the second year of the royal levy on ecclesiastical revenues authorised by Clement IV, must have marked the absolute nadir of the fortunes of the church of Palencia.[4]

That impression is confirmed by the various letters which the prelates sent to Urban IV during the winter of 1262–3,[5] in which they protested against the pope's demand for assistance towards the expenses involved in reversing the recent disasters in the Latin Empire, arguing that they were neither liable, on account of their many services *Deo et domino regi* during the *Reconquista*, nor able to provide funds for that purpose. A more or less historical account of what had happened since Las Navas, together with a number of rather arch

---

[1] For example, Alexander IV and Urban IV received appeals for help from churches as far apart as Urgel and Mondoñedo: *inc. Conquesti sunt*, 5 Dec. 1259; *Loca divino*, 28 April 1263: AC Seo de Urgel, d.s.n.; AC Mondoñedo, d.s.n.

[2] *Reg. Alex. IV*, 2911.

[3] AC Sigüenza, doc. pont. 26: publ. Minguella, I, 589–91.

[4] González, *Repartimiento de Sevilla*, II, 339, 342; *Reg. Urban IV*, cam. 156; *Reg. Clem. IV*, 729, 781; AHN, 2263/12.

[5] For full discussion and texts, see Linehan, *EHR*, LXXXV, 730 ff.

asides, served to substantiate their first point. With regard to the second, they cited the case of Palencia where, so they claimed, eleven thousand had died in a single year *mediante fame*, as Alexander IV and the cardinals had been informed already. And other areas had registered disasters of almost equal magnitude over the past seven years. The *gravissima afflictio* of continuous famine had obliged every man to shift for himself: fathers had had to abandon their sons, and sons their fathers; 'qui divites erant facti sunt pauperes, et qui pauperes mortui sunt'. Churchmen were reduced to begging their living, since 'redditus suos pro maiori parte habent in decimis' and their income from that source had plummeted as those settlers whom the current scourge had spared migrated to the frontier 'quia ibi habent possessiones pro nihilo, et quia ibi tributa non solvunt'.

Thus the Castilian Church suffered from the drift of population southwards. By 1245 the rents of the church of Segovia had diminished for that reason,[1] but less than twenty years later a far more ominous development was occurring, to which Bishop Pedro Lorenzo of Cuenca adverted in his letter to Urban IV in January 1263: depopulation even of the area immediately behind the Christian front-line.[2] The ease with which the rebel king of Granada was able to penetrate far into Christian territory in the following year proved that the bishop was no scaremonger.[3] Alfonso's reaction was to place an embargo on property transactions at Murcia for a period of five years, in the hope of stabilising the situation,[4] while Clement IV took fright and wrote drawing Jaime of Aragon's attention to a problem of which he was perfectly well aware: the indigenous Moorish population within his realms. They were a serpent within his breast, said the pope. Arguments of *utilitas* must not seduce him

---

[1] AC Segovia, doc. 241: 'Ceterum quia propter sterilitatem possessionum et raritatem inhabitancium, occasione quorum redditus ecclesie vestre diminuti dicantur, certitudinem non habemus an vacancia prestimonia ad complementum dicte provisionis in presenti sufficiant' (Cardinal Gil's *ordinatio*, Oct. 1245: see below, p. 271).

[2] AC Cuenca, 8/34/678: '... et cum ecclesia nostra, in confinibus paganorum sita, non sit in firmo statu, et habitatores discurrunt undique depopulando nostram diocesim et cotidie transeundo ad inhabitandum Ispalensem et alias frontarias – quocirca loca singula plures de nostra diocesi, immo maior pars, inhabitat'. Cuenca had been reconquered in 1177, but it was still a frontier see. Cf. Mansilla, *Iglesia castellano–leonesa*, 132–3.

[3] Ballesteros, *Alfonso X*, 362.

[4] Publ. Torres Fontes, *Col. documentos del reino de Murcia*, I, 22 (May 1266).

into tolerating this fifth column. They must be expelled.[1] The various inter-related difficulties raised by demographic resources and internal migration had been starkly posed two hundred years before at the recapture of Toledo,[2] and had remained a constant threat to security ever since. Events of the early 1260s indicated the gravity of the situation, which the conviction expressed shortly afterwards by Archbishop Sancho II of Toledo did nothing to relieve. He felt able to revoke the rule of his church, which forbad canons to retain their income from Toledo when appointed to a benefice elsewhere, on the grounds that there had been a complete change in the situation that had originally made such a rule necessary. Toledo was prosperous and in no danger from the Moors, he argued.[3] Yet in October 1275 Sancho himself met his end confronting a Moorish army of invasion at Martos in the diocese of Jaén. And the experiences of Archbishop Gonzalo only seven years after that certainly do not give an impression of prosperity.[4]

The letters sent to Pope Urban were rich in detail concerning the woes of the Castilian Church. Debts were heavy and income negligible; buildings were falling down for lack of funds; Alexander IV's grant to Archbishop Sancho had been an 'intolerable burden', costing the churches almost a quarter of their total assets, 'ex quo sequitur ecclesiarum destructio manifesta'; and a succession of papal nuncios, a list of whom was supplied in the bishops' joint letter,[5] had contributed further to their misery. Indeed, the entire emphasis of their

---

[1] 'Considera igitur, fili, considera: cum te tam experientia cogat advertere, quam familiaria etiam exempla ignorare non sinant, quam gravibus sit res plena periculis, Sarracenorum in terra tua retentio; qui licet ad tempus occultent iniquitatis sue, necessitate cogente, propositum, illud tam avide quam ardenter, immo etiam quam inique, captata occasione, revelant': Ripoll, I, 478–80 (Potthast, 19911).

[2] Ibn Bassam records Count Sisnando's advice to Alfonso VI, not to interfere in the internal affairs of the kingdom of Toledo after its reconquest, because 'you will not find other people to maintain its prosperity or another governor as obedient as Ibn Di-l-Nun': advice which the king ignored, thus providing fertile ground for the Almoravids: García Gómez in *Al-Andalus*, XII, 32; Menéndez Pidal, *Imperio hispánico*, 116. Cf. Olagüe, I, 253, who regards the late fifteenth century as providing the earliest instance of these processes.

[3] BN, MS 13041, fo. 17r–v: 'Nos considerantes quod causam illi dederit edicto novelle ecclesie paupertas reddituum et nimia sarracenorum incivitas metuenda, propter quod canonici ab ecclesie residentia inviti forte plusquam voluntarii divertebant, consuetudinem illam vel statutum duximus revocandum cum iam facultates ecclesie supercreverint Toletane et sarraceni agant iam, deo gratias, in remotis et tuta sit via circumquaque que ducit ad ecclesiam Toletanam' (undated).

[4] Ballesteros, *Alfonso X*, 755 ff.   [5] Benito Ruano, *HS*, XI, 15–17.

letter was that it was those nuncios, and ultimately the pope, who were responsible for their fate. The king's role, about which they had been actively concerned only three years before, was not mentioned. In 1204 Alfonso VIII had admitted to having filched settlers from the estates of the church of Toledo in order to man his *populationes* on the frontier, and to having caused *multa dampna* thereby.[1] More recently, in 1253, Innocent IV had acknowledged that the church of Sigüenza was falling into disrepair on account of the grant of *tercias* to the king 'and to certain of his sons'.[2] Yet the appellants of 1262–3 referred to neither of these facts in the course of their diatribes, not even the chapter of Toledo, which stressed particularly the state of collapse of churches throughout the province.[3]

Evidently they had been purged of their recent evil thoughts against Alfonso. Pedro Lorenzo made no attempt to disguise where his first loyalties lay. In March 1262 he had agreed to be consecrated where it best suited the king, at Seville; and it was from the royal court there that he forwarded his appeal in the following January, explaining in passing that he was fully engaged in that aspect of the king's service which was synonymous with God's work.[4] Eight months later he was still there when he appealed again, this time against a charge imposed upon his church by the executor of a papal mandate in favour of Paolo di Sulmona and family, refugees of the Italian wars. He had not been at Cuenca, he explained somewhat artlessly in support of his objection that the executor had failed to instruct him sufficiently in the matter. He had been occupied *circa rempublicam* in the royal chancery: an alibi which illustrated the weakness of the Castilian prelates no less perfectly than his protests against the executor's allocation of the total charge amongst the provincial churches reflected their lack of any corporate sense.[5] The contrast with Aragon

---

1 Fita, *BRAH*, VIII, 232–3.
2 AC Sigüenza, doc. pont. 22: publ. Minguella, I, 571 (misdated).
3 AC Cuenca, 8/34/678: 'nobis pro paupertate nimia fabricis ecclesiarum subvenire non valentibus, constructe corruunt et iniciate consummari non possunt'.
4 *Ibid.*: 'cum...nos simus totaliter occupati circa Dei et regis servicia, contra sarracenos tam Ispanie quam Affrice in guerra continua laborantes, eciam circa populacionem terre de novo reddite cultui christiano, circa quam necessarie intendentes cum exinde formidetur perniciosum periculum Ispanie et sancte Dei ecclesie provenire'. Previously archdeacon of Cádiz (Seville), Pedro Lorenzo had been elected on 6 Dec. 1261: AC Toledo, X.1.E.2.4.
5 AC Cuenca, 8/34/679: 'cum essemus in regno et non latitandi vel subterfugiendi

is immediately apparent: there in 1250 such negotiations had been a subject for the provincial council.[1] Moreover, at Lérida in April 1263, the Aragonese Church was led by King Jaime in its refusal to subscribe to any fund for the Eastern Empire.[2] Their reasons seem to have resembled those of the Castilian prelates, but the latter had had to shift for themselves. With no archbishop to lead them, they had received no moral support from Alfonso, who had very good reasons for not complying with the arrangements envisaged in the pope's instructions to Raymond of Paphos, the nuncio whose arrival had produced the outcry: namely, the summoning of an assembly of bishops at which the question of aid for Constantinople might be discussed.[3]

It is clear that, by omitting the king from their catalogue of scourges, the Castilian bishops completely misrepresented the situation. The fact was that they were in the position of the English bishops as described by Matthew Paris: the victims of a confederation between pope and king, who succumbed because they were divided, bent the knee unto Baal with hardly an exception, and allowed themselves to be mulcted for the Sicilian business.[4] The pope may have been an unwilling party to the scheme, his acquiescence in Alfonso's seizure of ecclesiastical revenue being the price of placating the Reconqueror-turned-imperial candidate. But the parallel is otherwise extremely close. For at this very moment Alfonso and his brothers were taking a serious interest in Mediterranean power-politics. Sometime between June 1258 and May 1261 the king helped the Emperor Baldwin's wife, Marie de Brienne, to recover her son from the Venetians to whom he had been pawned;[5] and in the first half of 1263 the impecunious emperor himself was scrounging his way round the Peninsula, not for the first time.[6] Moreover, the turbulent Infante

---

causa, immo circa rempublicam occupati populando de mandato domini regis terram a sarracenis de novo acquisitam et in cancellarie officio constituti'. Pedro de Peñafiel, archdeacon of Lara (Burgos), the executor, had charged Toledo and Palencia 400 *maravedís* each, Segovia, Cuenca, Sigüenza and Osma 250 each, Jaén 150, and Córdoba 100. The bishop calculated that Toledo was at least four times as wealthy, and Sigüenza twice as wealthy, as Cuenca.

1 Tejada, VI, 48.
2 AHA, *Index dels Indices*, fo. 2r–v. Details in Linehan, *EHR*, LXXXV, 735.
3 ADB, Gav. dos Quindénios, decimas e subsídios, 9: Linehan, *loc. cit.*
4 *Chronica Majora*, v, 584–5 (ad an. 1256).   5 Wolff, *Speculum*, XXIX, 64.
6 *Ibid.* 71–2; AHA, *Index dels Indices*, fo. 2r–v. Cf. Benito Ruano, *Hispania*, XII, 3 ff.

Enrique was not the only one of Alfonso's brothers with a stake in that area.[1] In August 1264 the ex-procurator of Seville, Felipe, was planning to lead an expedition to Romania to 'expunge the heretical Greeks'. That, indeed, was the purpose for which the nuncio Sinitius was directed to seek 'an appropriate subsidy' from the Castilian Church in that month.[2]

Naturally, though, the prelates disregarded all this in their account. It was much more convenient for men in Bishop Pedro Lorenzo's circumstances – men who were doing the state some service, *circa rempublicam occupati* – to externalise their misfortunes and blame a combination of natural disasters of biblical duration and papal avarice. In the early fourteenth century the author of the Chronicle of Fernando IV displayed the same prejudice by describing in consecutive sentences the great expense involved in securing papal legitimisation of Sancho IV's offspring, and the extensive famine throughout Castile which claimed as much as a quarter of the population, the juxtaposition implying cause and effect.[3] And modern writers have accepted this version: Sánchez-Albornoz is outraged at the indignity of María de Molina's having to apply to the pope in order to legitimise a king of Castile. It prompts him to reflect on the 'rivers of gold and silver' which flowed from Spain to Rome, and the meek and mild bishops who never resisted such impositions.[4]

The question of gold and silver deserves a chapter to itself,[5] but some comment is appropriate at this point on Sánchez-Albornoz's characterisation of the prelates, which is rebutted by such a wealth of evidence. The bishops did not kowtow to the pope. By and large they ignored him. There is great truth in George Borrow's remark that 'love of Rome had ever slight influence over her – that is, Spain's – policy'.[6] In the first millennium B.C. it was to Tarshish in Andalucia that Jonah repaired in his anxiety to escape the presence of the Lord;[7] and in the second millennium A.D. Spanish prelates adopted

---

[1] Giudice, *Don Arrigo Infante di Castiglia*, esp. 117–20.
[2] AC Toledo, E.7.C (xiii).7.1. Details in Linehan, *EHR*, lxxxv, 743. Cf. Geanakoplos, *The Emperor Michael Palaeologus and the West*, 175–80, 252–4.
[3] *BAE*, lxvi, 119. This is a near-contemporary account: Puyol, *BRAH*, lxxvii, 507 ff.
[4] *España: un enigma*, i, 356.
[5] Ch. 9.
[6] *The Bible in Spain* (Everyman's Library ed.), 3.
[7] Jonah i, 3. Cf. Schulten, *Tartessos*, 8 ff.

the same tactic, with more success. In this they were assisted by the popes themselves, who in general shared Urban IV's opinion that Lisbon, for example, was at the ends of the earth,[1] the corollary of which was that at Lisbon and elsewhere throughout the Peninsula papal mandates were commonly either quietly ignored or flagrantly defied. Thirteenth-century Spanish churchmen had inherited something of that spirit of independence which the bishops of Santiago had shown three centuries earlier when they described themselves as 'totius orbis antistites'.[2] The clerk who adapted the imperial coronation *ordo* for Spanish usage did not hesitate to retain the title *apostolicus* for the archbishop of Toledo.[3]

Papal provisions were worthless without local approval. Innocent IV's petty grants to the vice-chancellor of the Roman Church and his nephew encountered widespread resistance. In September 1260 the canons of Compostela vowed to reject all future provisions, and a provincial council there openly challenged the pope's right to discipline the contumacious archbishop.[4] For at least two and a half years Bishop Suero Pérez turned a deaf ear on Alexander IV, and in December 1268 his chapter imposed a stiff penalty on local clerks who attempted to secure papal provision to any church in the diocese on the strength of capitular authorisation.[5] Real foreigners ventured there at their peril. One night, probably in the 1260s, the proctor of the pope's own treasurer was set about by 'certain sons of perdition'. He survived, but the treasurer's goods were stolen, his sister who was ill in bed was treated *feraliter,* and her small son was killed, as later was one of their accomplices.[6] There is a Portuguese quality about the

---

[1] Above, p. 103; Vincentius Hispanus, similarly, 'hoc... *de mundi fine* remittit opus'. See Fransen's observations on Ochoa's paper at the *Congrès de Droit Canonique Medieval*, in July 1958: *Bibl. de la Rev. d'hist eccl.*, XXXIII, 175.

[2] Valdeavellano, *Historia de España*, I, ii, 217.

[3] BC Toledo, cod. 39–12, fos. 163r–70v. Noted by Elze, *Die Ordines für die Weihe und Krönung des Kaisers und der Kaiserin*, 55, rubric no. 22.

[4] López Ferreiro, V, 158.

[5] *Reg. Alex. IV*, 306, 1668 ('tu preces et mandatum nostrum pertransietis, aure surda id efficere non curastis'), 2309; AC Zamora, *Liber Constitutionum*, fos. 1vb–2ra. See also Ch. 12.

[6] 'Preterea quendam yspanum qui patrati maleficii conscius fuerat et particeps, ne per ipsum tantum crimen revelari contingeret, dicuntur miserabiliter occidisse.' *Inc. Horrendum facinus*, BM, MS Lansdowne 397, fo. 113v (Richard of Pophis Formulary: Batzer, 396). The earliest known reference to a papal treasurer is of the year 1262: Gottlob, *Aus der Camera Apostolica*, 95.

atrocity. It compares well with the treatment received by some of Afonso III's long-suffering bishops.[1] In this case, though, the criminals were not laymen, but clerics themselves who as a preliminary punishment were deprived of all their benefices in their city and diocese. Similarly, when the *familiares* of Laurentius de Urbe, Cardinal Peter Colonna's chamberlain, arrived at Burgos in the early nineties to take possession of a canonry there, they were attacked by the canons, with the dean to the fore and the king's blessing, and all but drowned. Two months later Laurentius gave up the unequal struggle and cut his losses, exchanging his Spanish rents for the English and Italian benefices of an archdeacon of Braga who, being Portuguese, presumably felt either that he would not receive or that he could take that sort of treatment.[2] Not that brute force was their only weapon at Burgos. They were quite capable of simply ignoring papal reservations;[3] and in 1307 they succeeded in proving that, irrespective of Clement IV's constitution *Licet ecclesiarum*, the practice there was – and had been for at least sixty years – that benefices remained at the disposal of the dean and chapter even if the last holder had died at the Roman Curia.[4]

The 'foreigner' in question on that occasion was an archdeacon of Oviedo. Clerical carpetbaggers were usually Spaniards from a neighbouring diocese rather than Italians; yet they were utterly foreign – *alieni* – and bitterly resented.[5] One such pluralist whose patron did him proud was the dean of Tarazona, Ramón de Peralta, who came from Aragon to Castile with Archbishop Sancho II of Toledo and profited greatly from his master's revocation of the capitular statute against absenteeism.[6] The chief patron, though, was the king. Many

[1] Cf. *Reg. Clem. IV*, 669. The prelates were incarcerated and threatened 'expressis eorum nominibus quod ultra presentem diem nec tu Bracarensis eris archiepiscopus nec tu Colimbriensis eris episcopus': ADB, Gav. das Notícias Várias, 26, cap. xxii.
[2] *Reg. Nich. IV*, 6214; *Reg. Bon. VIII*, 537, 692.
[3] Although the next vacant benefice was reserved for Landulf, son of the nobleman Frederick de Prefectis, the chapter awarded it to Master Simon de Carrión (later bishop of Sigüenza) in June 1296; and the curialist was still without satisfaction in Feb. 1299: AC Toledo, d.s.n. in caj. 0.9. and I.12; *Reg. Bon. VIII*, 3648.
[4] AC Burgos, vol. 62, ii, fos. 85–113 – 'quamdiu vacaverint et quomodocumque vacaverint et ubicumque vacaverint', fo. 112. See Linehan, *EHR*, lxxxv, 745.
[5] See below, Ch. 11.
  Treasurer of Toledo by Oct. 1272. By the time of his death in 1276 he had accumulated a Toledo archdeaconry, and rural deaneries at Illescas, Benquerencia, Caravaca, Perales, Tielmes and Embid, as well as Aragonese benefices at Tarazona, Zaragoza, Calatayud and Teruel: *Reg. Greg. X*, 73; *Reg. Nich. IV*, 3837.

papal provisions were made at his behest in favour of his immediate circle of clerical servants. Thus, in August 1262, while the Castilian Church was preparing its case against the demands of the nuncio, Master Gonzalo – the future archbishop of Toledo – was appointed to the deanery of that church, though he was not yet in sacred orders.[1] It was on Alfonso's recommendation also that, in December 1263, Urban IV granted that recent proponent of ecclesiastical solidarity, Bishop Pedro Lorenzo of Cuenca, permission to set aside the rights of the ordinary collators, his chapter, and appoint two of his clerics to canonries in that church.[2] At least eleven provision-rescripts for royal clerks and chaplains were secured by Alfonso's proctor at the Curia in July–August.[3] In Castile, as elsewhere, it was the king rather than the pope who derived the profit from their *confederatio*, at the expense of the divided Church.[4]

It is necessary to labour this point since historians have made much of such incidents as the presentation to Alfonso XI at the Madrid Cortes in 1329 of the protest about the harm done to the national Church by papal provision to benefices of 'perssonas estrannas que non sson mios naturales nin del mio sennorio', but have given less than due weight to papal complaints about the indignities to which its agents were being subjected by Spanish churchmen at that very period.[5] John XXII's collectors were ambushed, but passive resistance produced hardly less striking results, as Clement V had learnt in the previous decade. When the cost of collection exceeded the revenue raised he might well have echoed Clement IV's view, expressed in August 1265, that Spain was a liability to the Roman Church.[6]

In a letter to Cardinal Ottobono Fieschi, two years later, Clement IV described the state of the Spanish churches as *multum collapsum*.[7]

---

[1] AC Toledo, I.9.B.1.7; 12, two letters, both *Etsi ad provisionem*, 19 Aug. 1262.

[2] *Reg. Urban IV*, 2346.

[3] Details in Linehan, *EHR*, LXXXV, 740–1.

[4] Cf. Deeley, *EHR*, XLIII, 497 ff.; Barraclough, *Papal Provisions*, esp. Ch. IV.

[5] *Cortes de Castilla*, I, 432–3. Cf. Goñi Gaztambide, *AA*, XIV, 77–8.

[6] *Ibid.* 81. For the effectiveness of passive resistance, see the report of the collector, Juan Fernández archdeacon of Castro, discussed below, pp. 247–9. Cf. *Reg. Clem. IV*, 923: 'Thesaurus apud nos nullus latet...Anglia adversatur, Alamania vix obedit, Francia gemit et queritur, Yspania sibi non sufficit, Italia non subvenit sed emungit' (Martène–Durand, *Thesaurus*, II, 174).

[7] *Ibid.* 1278 (Martène–Durand, II, 542).

Ten years after the collapse of the independence movement, and twenty years after the exuberance generated by the Seville campaign, they were indeed in ruins; and over those ruins presided that true sovereign, Alfonso X. He could ignore his father-in-law's advice about taking the Church seriously because in political terms it was negligible. It was also, for the same reasons, in moral terms degenerate. For the sort of information which the legislation of the Aragonese councils provides on that topic, we have to turn to Alfonso's *Primera Partida*. Neither is this an accident, nor is it all. Alfonso's influence was not merely restrictive and negative. Clerical concubinage received his blessing. The bequeathing of ecclesiastical property to priests' children – already a problem at Palencia in the 1220s – was said to have been made mandatory by that 'athlete of the Christian faith', Fernando III, for the diocese of Calahorra in 1231.[1] That may have been malicious rumour, but there can be no question about Fernando's son's interference in a sphere which in Aragon was indisputably the prerogative of the ecclesiastical councils: at least twice he authorised groups of clergy thus to provide for their offspring.[2] The royal author of the filthy poem about the astonishing sexual prowess of the dean of Cádiz[3] bore no small responsibility for the circumstances in which such exploits could be performed and recorded. 'If we meet a subdeacon, deacon, priest or bishop with a lady on his arm', it has been written of the English Church after 1123, 'we guess that she is probably not his wife'.[4] If, however, the lady and her escort are Spanish, we may assume that they are not unduly perturbed by our speculations, since, for practical purposes, the distinction hardly matters. In the year after his gloomy pronouncement about the state of the Spanish churches, Clement IV's penitentiary absolved a chaplain of the church of Pedagaes in the Braga diocese from the sentences which he had incurred by keeping a woman. He claimed ignorance of the law,[5] and there must have been many like him in that part of the Braga province which lay in the kingdom of Castile–Leon. Unlike

---

[1] AC Palencia, 2/1/42 (MDH, 536, 538); *Reg. Greg. IX*, 594. For this description of Fernando, see ASV, arm. XXXI. 72, fo. 288r (Schillmann, 2491).

[2] The clergy of Salamanca, June 1262, and of the rural deanery of Roa (Osma), June 1270: *MHE*, I, 193; Loperráez, *Descripción de Osma*, III, 204–5.

[3] *Cancioneiro da Biblioteca Nacional*, ed. Machado, II, 372–4.

[4] C. N. L. Brooke in *Cambridge Historical Journal*, XII, 5.

[5] ADB, Gav. das Notícias Várias, 13 (24 July 1268).

João Fernandes, though, they were probably more interested in the king's law than the pope's.

The king's bishops certainly were, and through his control of them the king ruled the Church. However the word *curia* were derived – from blood or trouble, *cruor* or *cura* – they were curialists, even by that strict definition which would restrict the term to 'those who, possessing no particular qualification, became bishops as a result of court influence'.[1] To them the nuances of the word's etymology mattered little: either of the gloomy alternatives is fair comment on their situation. They were ensnared, and the Church was the preserve of the upper crust. Such was the implication of the off-guard observation of Fernando III's taxgatherer, that sanctity was an exclusively seigneurial attribute. In that case retribution was swift, because San Isidro, who was working-class, overheard his remarks and took them personally.[2] But San Isidro was in Heaven and the pope was in Italy. *Nulla est comparatio.* The king of Castile was out of reach, and such was his predominance over the bishops that not even a political revolution could alleviate their lot. As prologue to a description of their experiences at the hands of Sancho IV, though, it is necessary to consider the Spanish Churches from his, the pope's, point-of-view, and to review – as the Castilian prelates in 1262–3 reviewed – the activities of the papal legates and nuncios by whom they had been visited in recent years.

[1] 'To call them "curialist bishops", as is sometimes done, is surely misleading. The term "curialist" has come to have a pejorative meaning. The implication is that, if they served the Crown, or owed their promotion to the Crown, they must automatically as bishops have belonged to a Court Party': Highfield, *TRHS*, 5th ser., VI, 115–16.

[2] The tale is told in the *Leyenda* of the Saint written in 1275. What the taxgatherer said was 'Ego bene crederem quod qui esset filius principis vel alicuius magnatis bene posset fieri vere sanctus, set virum laboricii seu ruricolam non credo ullatenus fore sanctum.' Ed. Fita, *BRAH*, IX, 118.

Chapter 9

THE PAPACY AND SPAIN

'In terra summus Rex est hoc tempore nummus', wrote Adán Fernández, the versifying archdeacon of Compostela in the early 1230s;[1] and by that token the various papal legates and nuncios by whom Spain was visited in the thirteenth century can have seemed little better to his countrymen than a succession of regicides. That, certainly, is the impression given by the bishops' letter thirty years later. Yet no serious effort has ever been made to assess the impact on the Peninsula of papal fiscal policies or even to provide a list of the agents involved. The editor of the bishops' letter was unable to put flesh on the bare bones of the catalogue supplied in 1262-3.[2] In this chapter, therefore, an attempt will be made to fill this gap, and because papal emissaries who had no brief to collect cash occasionally overstepped the mark and followed in the footsteps of that peculant pair, Huguicio and the Patriarch of Grado, the survey will include diplomats as well as collectors. It will not, however, make too rigid a distinction between those whose destination was Castile and those whose destination was Aragon, for the popes themselves seem to have thought in terms of the entire Peninsula rather than of its constituent kingdoms, instruments concerning all three being stored in a single box in the papal treasury, according to the inventory made in 1339.[3]

The bishops' collective memory reached back to Gregory IX's pontificate, but papal legates had been visiting the Spanish kingdoms for many years before that,[4] and Spanish churchmen were accustomed

---

[1] Publ. Amador de los Ríos, *Historia crítica de la literatura española*, II, 355-6. Cf. López Ferreiro, *Historia de Santiago*, V, 354, 366; *Cancioneiro de Ajuda*, ed. Michaëlis de Vasconcellos, II, 818.

[2] Benito Ruano, *HS*, XI, 16-17. Cf. the section *De Apostolicae Sedis legatis in Lusitaniam* in Thomas ab Incarnatione, *Historia ecclesiae Lusitanae*, IV, 301-5; Lafuente, *Historia eclesiástica*, IV, 581-2.

[3] Ehrle, *ALKG*, I, 330.

[4] Benito Ruano, *loc. cit.* 15. For a list of legates from 1065 to 1197, derived from Kehr and published sources, see Säbekow, *Die päpstlichen Legationen*, 76-9.

to dealing with them, degrading though the payment of tribute may have seemed to the popular imagination.[1] In the kingdom of Aragon responsibility for paying their procurations was discussed during the negotiations of April 1227 between Bishop Sancho of Zaragoza and his chapter, while at Vich the cost of accommodating them was mentioned in June 1246 as being equally damaging to the capitular economy as the effects of hail and fog.[2] 'Accommodation' meant more than mere hospitality. In 1214, during the legation of Cardinal Peter of S. Maria in Aquiro, for example, Bishop Raimundo of Gerona had been persuaded to grant an annual pension of £15 *barchinonenses* to the papal scribe Petrus Tusci.[3] Even that pillar of rectitude, John of Abbeville, is known to have interfered in the collation of benefices at Zamora and León.[4] Legates and nuncios were no strangers in Castile either. At Burgos a fund had long been established by 1250 out of which the expenses of their visitations were met, and when Fernando III attempted to bulldoze his own nominee into the abbacy of Sahagún, the injured party, Abbot Guillermo, asked that one be sent to hear his case.[5]

Yet up to that point, the mid-1230s, the number of missions was not excessive. Although Honorius III sent three cardinals to the kingdom of Aragon, a papal fief which required close supervision during the minority of Jaime I,[6] he was otherwise chary of risking a

---

1 *Reliquias de la poesía épica española*, ed. Menéndez Pidal, 279.

2 AA Zaragoza, *Cartulario Pequeño*, fo. 6v; AC Vich, 37–6–44.

3 *Reg. Hon. III*, 644 (MDH, 67). The cardinal came in the aftermath of the Albigensian Crusade to assist the infant king of Aragon, Jaime I. He reconciled a number of heretics in the diocese of Urgel: Zimmermann, *Die päpstliche Legation*, 44–5; AC Seo de Urgel, *Dotium sive dotaliarum liber secundus*, fo. 72v; Diago, *Historia de la Provincia de Aragón*, fo. 8r; Miret y Sans, *Itinerari de Jaime I*, 268. Zimmermann's statement (p. 85) that he returned to Aragon as legate in Dec. 1217 is not supported by the evidence. Cf. *Reg. Hon. III*, 943 (MDH, 107); Lafuente, IV, 581.

4 For Zamora, see below, p. 293. The provision, of 'el prestamo de Religos per mandado del bispo de Sabina que fuera legado de Roma en Espanna' to Master Rodrigo canon of León and later dean of Plasencia, was remembered in 1267: AC León, doc. 1564.

5 Mansilla, *Iglesia castellano–leonesa*, 361–2; Escalona, *Historia de Sahagún*, 143 (1233 X 1236). No legate was sent; instead Guillermo went to the Curia, and eventually became a cardinal. Moreover, the tables were turned on the king's man, the abbot of Celanova: above, p. 39; *Reg. Greg. IX*, 1281; Escalona, 587.

6 Bertrandus of Ss. John and Paul (*ante* June 1217–*post* July 1219): *Reg. Hon. III*, 612, 842, 1664, 2162 (MDH, 61, 94, 194, 234); Conrad of Porto (*ante* June 1222–*ante* Jan. 1224): *ibid.* 4061 (MDH, 409; cf. 487); Romanus of S. Angelo (*ante* Sept. 1225–*post*

repeat of the Huguicio fiasco and preferred to use as his agents the Hospitaller, Master Gonzalo García, and the bishop-elect of Ludd, Pelayo, Spaniards both. Gregory IX followed the same policy. During his first seven years there is no sign of any papal agent in the Peninsula other than John of Abbeville. The legations of Cardinal Rainerius Capocci and Bishop Navarrus of Coserans are spurious.[1] Gradually though, as the struggle between Empire and Papacy developed and the *Reconquista* forged ahead, the frequency of visits increased. In 1234 Fernando III received two emissaries – possibly in connexion with his current imperial pretensions:[2] Thomas, *cubicularius pape*, in the January,[3] and the papal *scriptor*, Bartholomew of Anagni, at the end of the year.[4] Within four years the pope was thinking of the king of Aragon as a possible leader of resistance to Frederick II, and by September 1239 Cardinal James of Palestrina, sent in the previous year as legate to the territory of Raymond VII of Toulouse, was devoting his energies to assuring that good relations were maintained between Jaime and the pope's Genoese allies.[5] Until his capture by the enemy in the spring of 1241 the cardinal continued to keep Aragon under surveillance. At the end of October 1239 he wrote from Nice to Archbishop Pedro de Albalat and the Aragonese Church, enclosing papal letters of the previous month which enumerated Frederick's various crimes against humanity, and reminding them that they must prevent his being given any assistance.[6] High

---

March 1226): *Reg. Hon. III*, 5633, 5848 (MDH, 572, 597). See also Zimmermann, 87, for Cardinal Centius of Porto. According to Lafuente, IV, 581, he came *c.* 1226: seven years after his death.

[1] The alleged visit of the first to Cardeña in 1228 is based upon an evident misreading of his source by Pérez de Urbel, *Los monjes españoles*, II, 568. Cf. Berganza, *Antigüedades*, II, 143. An undated document (no. 92) in AC Jaca mentions Navarrus 'apostolice sedis legatus': publ. Sangorrin, *El libro de la Cadena*, 325–8, who dates it 1229 for the most curious of reasons. Arco attributes it to the early 1230s, *BRAH*, LXV, 65. But Navarrus was bishop of Coserans from 1208–11. Cf. Gams, *Series episcoporum*, 541.

[2] Above, p. 105.

[3] *Reg. Greg. IX*, 1758. For details, see Lomax, *Hispania*, XVIII, 30.

[4] AC Toledo, A.6.H.1.30: *inc. Gratum gerimus*, 8 Dec. 1234, recommending Bartholomew to Archbishop Rodrigo. On 14 May 1235 the nuncio was at Arcos de Nájera: González Texada, *Historia de Santo Domingo de la Calzada*, 209.

[5] ACA, Bulas, leg. VI–24, 25 (reg. Miquel Rosell, *Regesta*, 106–7); *Reg. Greg. IX*, 4934.

[6] Publ. Junyent, *Diplomatari de Sant Bernat Calvó*, no. 196, where the letter is dated

politics was not his sole concern, though. He received the protest of the chapter of Urgel against the pluralist archdeacon of Aristot, Ricardo;[1] and found time to arrange for Master Guillaume, brother of the archdeacon of Beauvais, to be appointed to a benefice in the Pamplona diocese.[2] In Castile, meanwhile, frater Carsilius, formerly the pope's head cook, was collecting money during 1238 and 1239.[3]

The bishops in 1262 did not mention Carsilius. Their grievances against Gregory IX were confined to events of the years 1240–1 – to the miseries to which those Spanish churchmen who responded to his summons to the Roman Council were subjected, and to the subsidy imposed by him which the collectors insisted be rendered in pure gold 'sicut audivimus a maioribus nostris'.[4] It is not clear how genuine the first complaint was, or whether the canon of León's imprisonment was cheered by the company of any of his compatriots. We may be sure that Bishop Pedro of Zamora would have mentioned the experience, had it befallen him. Yet even if most of them escaped this fate, the cost of the round trip – which in the case of Bishop Pedro Salvador of Porto lasted eight months – cannot have been negligible.[5] More, however, is known about the subsidy which they mentioned, the *quinta*. In May 1241, while the bishops were compiling their blow-by-blow account of the sea-battle, the nuncio Master Philip de Ceccano and his underlings were already at work in Castile and Aragon. The pope's letter of April 1240, introducing

Oct. 1240. For his capture, see *Reg. Greg. IX*, 6007; Huillard-Bréholles, *Historia diplomatica*, v, ii, 1118 ff.

[1] AC Seo de Urgel, d.s.n. (May 1243), apparently referring to a date before March 1241. Cf. *Reg. Greg. IX*, 5391.

[2] In the teeth of capitular resistance Guillaume eventually secured the church of Arcos. He may have been the 'Guillelmus dictus Specta' with whom Bishop Pedro Ximénez was at odds in March 1246: *Reg. Inn. IV*, 274, 1783.

[3] At Palencia on 1 July 1239 he collected three gold marks and thirty *maravedís* from the Order of Santiago as dues for the previous three years: Arch. Uclés, 88/24 (I owe this information to Dr D. W. Lomax). Gregory had recommended him to Archbishop Rodrigo on 28 Aug. 1238: *inc. Devotionem tuam*, AC Toledo, A.6.H.1.14. For Carsilius *supercocus*, see Fabre–Duchesne, *Liber Censuum*, I, 448 (May 1233).

[4] Benito Ruano, *HS*, XI, 15.

[5] ADB, Gav. dos Arcebispos, 24, art. cxvii, *ad fin*. Cf. AC Zamora, 13/7. See above, for the prelates who avoided capture, p. 160. It is not clear why Bishop Adán Pérez of Plasencia was with them, since only six weeks before, in late March 1241, he was already at the Curia together with his neighbour, Bishop Fernando of Coria: *Reg. Greg. IX*, 5408, 5954, 5964, 5967.

Philip to Archbishop Rodrigo of Toledo, had not mentioned any statutory tax: it was left to him to make a voluntary contribution. The gift of five hundred marks which he had sent, 'ut devotus filius', in the previous year was remembered, and it was asked that his present subscription should be such as would shame the other archbishops into generosity.[1] The time for petty charity had clearly passed: the Black Monks of the four provinces were called upon to supply sufficient funds for a new military operation in Lombardy;[2] and in Aragon at least, collection of the *quinta* had begun by the following year, the voluntary method having evidently failed to produce results. Whereas in England only the benefices of foreign clerks were liable, the native clergy also were taxed, and the record of receipts prepared by the subcollectors at Urgel states that it was levied on both capitular and individual incomes.[3]

Churchmen high and low were short of ready cash and in order to pay were forced to pawn their most prized possessions: at Urgel the cleric Zacharias parted with his sword for 5s. 5d.; for £50 the bishop of Vich, Bernardo Calvó, offered everything he had.[4] And although Gregory's death in August 1241 and the twenty-two month papal vacancy which followed (broken only by a fortnight of Celestine IV) afforded them a breathing-space, the election of Innocent IV in June 1243 heralded a period of even greater stringency. Within weeks the new pope had sent another nuncio, his chaplain Master Raymond, to the Spanish kingdoms. All that the kings of Aragon and Navarre were told was that Raymond had come 'pro quibusdam ecclesie Romane negotiis'.[5] In addressing the churches of Calahorra

---

1 'Quod alii archiepiscopi exemplo tue liberalitatis illecti ad subveniendum ecclesie facilius inducantur': *Firmiter credit*, 5 April 1240: AC Toledo, A.6.H.1.27.

2 AHA, *Index dels Indices*. fo. 568v (5 April 1240). Pedro de Albalat summoned the abbots of his province for the following September: BP Tarragona, MS 176 (*Resumen ... de algunos documentos ... de S. Pedro de Ager*: an eighteenth-century summary; unpaginated), no. 199: cit. Morera, *Tarragona cristiana*, II, 280.

3 AC Seo de Urgel, d.s.n: a list of 58 payments by the canons and clergy of Urgel 'tam de communi quam de proprio', to the abbot of Ripoll and A. de Yuarcio monk of Poblet, collectors 'pro magistro Philippo in diocesi Urgellensi', totalling 2,348 *solidi* and 2 *denarii*, 8 June 1241. Cf. Lunt, *Financial Relations*, 197.

4 *Ibid.*; above, p. 78.

5 *Inc. Cum te tamquam*, 3 and 11 Sept. 1243: ACA, Bulas, leg. III–1; AGN, 4/15 (reg. Miquel, 109; Castro, *Catálogo*, I, 238). Miquel assumes the nuncio to have been Raymond of Peñafort; but the bishops in 1262 mentioned that he was subsequently

and Segorbe, though, Innocent was less mealy-mouthed: Raymond was there because, notwithstanding all Gregory IX's efforts, the Roman Church was in debt; cash was needed 'pro catholice fidei, ecclesiastice libertatis et patrimonii sui defensione...ac terre sancte negotiis'.[1]

This reads like the *agenda* of the Lyons Council of 1245 at which, as has already been observed, the Spanish contingent volunteered their all in the struggle against the deposed emperor. The Spaniards were there in large numbers, and their spokesman was one of their archbishops, if the author of the *Relatio* may be trusted.[2] For quite how many of them he spoke we cannot be sure, however. The archbishops of Tarragona and Compostela, Pedro de Albalat and Juan Arias, were there by 13 July;[3] Pedro of Barcelona within a week of that;[4] and Pedro Ximénez of Pamplona by 6 September.[5] So, to his cost, was Pedro of Zamora.[6] The list might be extended by assuming that the various prelates who received indulgences granting financial relief between late July and late October were also all personally present. These were Lorenzo of Orense,[7] Rodrigo Díaz of Oviedo,[8] Martín of Salamanca,[9] Nuño Álvarez of León,[10] Pedro Ferrández of

bishop of Béziers: *viz.*, either Raymond de Salles or Raymond de Valhauquès (successive bishops of Béziers, June 1245–July 1247 and Sept. 1247–June 1261 respectively): Benito Ruano, *HS*, XI, 16; M. H. Fisquet, *La France pontificale: metropole d'Avignon: Montpellier*, II (Paris, 1868), 93–4.

[1] *Inc. Illam de vestre*, 11 Jan. 1244: AC Calahorra, doc. 278. Villanueva's papers mention another apparently identical letter of 13 Jan. in AC Segorbe. But it is not there now. RAH, MS 9–24–5/4560, unpaginated. Cf. C. Tomás Laguía, *Catálogo de la sección de pergaminos del Archivo de la S. I. Catedral de Albarracín*.

[2] Above, p. 161.

[3] ASV, A.A. arm. I–XVIII. 98 (publ. Sousa Costa, *Mestre Silvestre*, 434–5).

[4] ACA, Bulas, VIII–13 (reg. Miquel, 124).

[5] Above, p. 161. Nicholas of Curbio, *Vita Innocentii IV*, 96, states that the pope sent a nuncio, Master Bernardus Neapolitanus, to Navarre at this juncture to make peace between the bishop and the king. But this seems to be an error: the case was to be heard at the Curia, and Bernard's mission occurred in the autumn of 1251 when he was dean of Patras: AC Pamplona, IV Episcopi 1, dorse – 'littere...misse decano Patracensi' (reg. Goñi Gaztambide, *Catálogo*, 585).

[6] AC Zamora, 13/7.

[7] *Reg. Inn. IV*, 1386. Lorenzo (the canonist Laurentius Hispanus) made a great impression at the Council, according to the eighteenth-century historian of the church, Muñoz de la Cueba, *Noticias históricas*, 253.

[8] *Reg. Inn. IV*, 1387, 1431.

[9] *Ibid.* 1439.

[10] *Ibid.* 1735.

Astorga,[1] Adán Pérez of Plasencia,[2] and Vidal de Canellas of Huesca.[3] Such evidence, though, hardly suggests that they were in any state to honour the archbishop's promises, and the *Yspani* of the *Relatio* almost certainly included the Portuguese episcopal exiles at the Curia.[4] But however many there were of them there, they were all bound by the fiscal provisions announced at the Council's final session: for the relief of the Latin Empire a three-year tax of half their revenues on clergy who were absent from their benefices for six months of the year or more, and of a third on those others with a total income in excess of one hundred silver marks; for the Holy Land the *vicesima* of the Fourth Lateran Council was revived.[5] It was these provisions, rather than the proposals designed to strengthen them and their churches financially, that the bishops remembered with displeasure in 1262–3.

By their reckoning the Emperor Baldwin received forty thousand *aurei* from them; 'sed quod ipse imperator operatus est cum ipsa pecunia omnes sciunt'.[6] The collection of the subsidies for Constantinople and Jerusalem dragged on throughout the rest of Innocent's pontificate, and year by year it became clearer that these causes inspired considerably less enthusiasm in them than did the persecution of the Emperor Frederick. Though no articulate Gallican objections were immediately forthcoming,[7] it was hardly to be expected that the Castilian Church, which was already paying so heavily for the privilege of the *Reconquista*, would rejoice at this new burden. Such, however, was Innocent's regard for the *Reconquista* that he appointed as collector of the tax for the Latin Empire, Bishop Juan of Burgos, chancellor of the kingdom.[8] Ten years before, Juan had been busying himself in the task of conveying ecclesiastical revenue

---

[1] *Reg. Inn. IV*, 1519; Quintana Prieto, *AA*, XI, 211, no. 58.

[2] *Etsi clericorum*, 12 Sept. 1245: copy in RAH, MS C/7–9/5427, fo. 134r–v.

[3] AC Huesca, 2–317 (reg. Durán Gudiol, *AA*, VII, 363, no. 71).

[4] Herculano, *História de Portugal*, V, 13 ff. *Rex Yspanie* sent a representative, according to Nicholas de Curbio, *Vita*, 93: this was probably Jaime of Aragon's nuncio, 'nobilis vir Ensiminus Petri': ACA, Bulas, VIII–12 (reg. Miquel, 123).

[5] Hefele–Leclercq, v, ii, 1651–2, 1657–61.

[6] Benito Ruano, *HS*, XI, 16.

[7] Cf. Matthew Paris, *Chronica Majora*, VI, 100; Lunt, 250 ff.

[8] In a letter of 9 March 1247 to the chapter of Calahorra, the cardinal-bishop of Albano, Petrus de Collemedio, referred to this appointment: AC Calahorra, doc. 291.

into the royal treasury.[1] Now he was called upon to perform an about-turn and, with Seville still unwon, to supervise a massive transfer of funds out of the kingdom. His only honourable course was to die, which he promptly did.[2]

In Aragon, meanwhile, Pedro de Albalat had appointed bishops Vidal of Huesca and Pedro Ximénez as collectors of the subsidies, in accordance with the pope's permission to him to subdelegate the thankless task;[3] and by February 1247 at least one protest about them had reached Lyons, from the abbey of Montearagón.[4] In Portugal, similarly, João Martins, *custos* of the Lisbon Franciscans, encountered various difficulties, the clergy of the Braga archdiocese assuring him that, conditions being what they were, there could be no question of their being able to contribute to the cause.[5] Such delays were intolerable. As the pope had insisted at the Council, the subsidy had to be collected quickly if it was to serve any useful purpose at all.[6] In January 1247, therefore, he appointed one man to co-ordinate collection throughout the Peninsula: the Franciscan, frater Desiderius.[7]

Desiderius had only recently returned to the Curia from Aragon where from August till October 1246 he had been attending to the absolution of King Jaime from the sentences which he had incurred on account of his attack on the bishop of Gerona.[8] His new mission had more than one purpose. Both the border warfare between Castile and Portugal,[9] and the eternal conflict over the property of the Tarragona *cameraria*[10] engaged his attention. His main concern,

---

[1] Above, Ch. 6.   [2] On 1 Oct. 1246: Serrano, *Obispado de Burgos*, III, 389.

[3] *Inc. Ad liberacionem imperii*, 31 Oct. 1245: contemporary copy in AC Seo de Urgel, d.s.n.

[4] AHN, 642/14 (=*Reg. Inn. IV*, 2388); Ramón de Huesca, *Teatro histórico*, VII, 327.

[5] 'Cum autem pro rerum inopia et gravi statu regni Portugallie, sicut dicunt, facultatem solutionis hujusmodi non habentes': *Reg. Inn. IV*, 3561: publ. Wadding, *Annales Minorum*, III, 191. The clergy of Coimbra told the same tale. Cf. Potthast, 12822; Esperança, *História seráfica*, I, 490.

[6] 'Sane ut festina fiat et utilis imperio prefato subventio': Hefele–Leclercq, V, ii, 1652.

[7] For whom, see López, *La provincia franciscana de España*, 380–8. He was at the Curia on 21 Jan: ACA, Bulas, IX–27; 28 (reg. Miquel, 138–9).

[8] ACA, Bulas, IX–24 (reg. Miquel, 135: publ. *ES*, XLIV, 282–4); *VL*, XIII, 319. At the final settlement at Lérida on 18 Oct. he was accompanied by Bishop Philip of Camerino. The historian of that church loses track of Philip in the previous March: Cappelletti, *Le chiese d'Italia*, IV, 254–63.

[9] *Reg. Inn. IV*, 3027, 3565.

[10] He found against Benito de Rocaberti who had the sentence reversed by Cardinal Gil Torres in 1252–3: AHA, *Cartoral AB*, fo. 12r.

however, seems to have been the subsidies, collection of which he entrusted to a number of native members of his Order. Thus, at Zaragoza, on 2 March 1247, he appointed the guardian of the Gerona convent, frater Aimerico, as his lieutenant in the kingdom of Aragon.[1] Aimerico was assisted by frater Pedro de Tarragona.[2] Frater Martín was made responsible for the archbishopric of Toledo,[3] and frater João Martins again – it would seem – for the kingdom of Portugal.[4]

But the friars were denied immediate results. When frater Aimerico first arrived at Seo de Urgel he failed to secure the necessary information, as he had hoped he might, and had to appoint as a further deputy the local archdeacon.[5] Frater Martín seems to have had a similar experience when he met the dean and chapter of Toledo at Illescas. All he was able to do was to treat them to a rather sententious lecture. With Christ and the scriptures as his authorities, he assured them that resistance was futile. 'Mas val obedecer que sacrificar; e esto nos demostro el fijo de dios que fue obedient al padre fata la muerte.' Not that he was thinking in terms of capital punishment. Being a Franciscan he preferred the way of 'mayor omildad con menor sentencia'. Still, if they had not paid by the following Easter they would be excommunicated and denied Christian burial. Leaving them with the text of a statement explaining the conciliar constitutions, to be read in every rural deanery throughout the

---

1 AC Seo de Urgel, d.s.n: 'Cum collectio vicesime a summo pontifice mihi per totam Hispaniam sit commissa, nec per me negocium ipsum propter alia que mihi iniuncta sunt a prefato domino congrue valeam expedire...' On 22 May Pedro de Albalat ordered that all payments be forwarded to Tarragona by the feast of John the Baptist, 24 June. By then Aimerico was *custos* of the Valencia convent (*ibid.*).

2 On 2 Feb. 1248 fr. Pedro acknowledged receipt of '13 morabotines menos 15 sueldos barcelonenses por razón del nuevo subsidio' from the abbot of Ager: BP Tarragona, MS 176, no. 204.

3 AC Toledo, caj. E.6, d.s.n, undated.

4 Thomas ab Incarnatione, IV, 304–5. João Martins was bishop of Cádiz from May 1267, and in Dec. 1278 was translated to Guarda where he seems to have survived till March 1301: *Reg. Clem. IV*, 457; Mansilla, *HS*, x, 245 ff.; *Reg. Nich. III*, 214; Pereyra da Sylva Leal, *Catálogo dos bispos da Idanha e Guarda*, unpaginated, sec. V.

5 AC Seo de Urgel, d.s.n: 'Notum sit omnibus quod ego frater Eimericus, custos Valencie, ad Sedem Urgellensem personaliter accedens pro vicesima, media et tercia plenam, ut optabam, recipere rationem, de consensu domini episcopi Urgellensis dilecto nostro R. de Todiniano, archidiacono eiusdem, vices meas et locum committo.'

province, and a solemn warning not to allow any revenue to absentees who had yet to pay, he made his departure, asking them first for their prayers.[1]

Their prayers they may have granted, but evidently not their money, for in March 1248 the pope was obliged to send another collector to *Hispania*: his *scriptor*, Master James de Mirbello.[2] And he, in turn, was succeeded by another: Master Manfred de' Roberti. The bishops in 1262 remembered Manfred,[3] and there are signs that by the time that he had reached Castile, in May 1249,[4] the sense of grievance which was to inspire their protest was already taking possession of churchmen there. For when he attempted to recover certain property of the Roman Church, possibly receipts of subsidy, which Bishop Vicente of Guarda (the canonist Vincentius Hispanus, who had died in September 1248) had deposited with the Master of Alcántara, the brothers of Alcántara drew their swords and drove him off.[5] Yet not until 1255 were his attackers brought to justice and made to pay.[6] We do not know whether resistance, either active or passive, was the reason for the general interdict which he imposed on the diocese of Calahorra.[7]

No papal collector could reasonably have expected a cordial reception so soon after the fall of Seville. Still, Innocent did not relent, but fed the flames with a stream of nuncios. Apart from frater Miguel de Tudela O.F.M. who dealt with the *census* while Desiderius was at

1 '....E rogamos vos que roguedes a dios por nos': AC Toledo, caj. E.6., d.s.n.
2 *Inc. Cum olim*, 29 Feb. 1248: AHA, *Index dels Indices*, fo. 573r; 1 March 1248: BN, MS 13094, fo. 122r (eighteenth-century copy from archive of S. Clemente, Toledo). His commission mentions only the *vicesima*.
3 Benito Ruano, *HS*, XI, 16. For Manfred's subsequent career as a papal agent in Italy, see Waley, *Papal State*, 164.
4 *Reg. Inn. IV*, 4568, instructing him to communicate a message to Fernando III. In June 1250, as cantor of Antioch and 'nuncius in Yspania', he attended the Portuguese Cortes at Guimarães: *PMH* I, 185–9. In the same year he was at Seville: Zurita, *Anales*, I, fo. 163va.
5 *Inc. Licet tibi*, 1 Sept. 1255; *Turbamur plurimum*, 3 Sept. 1255: AHN, Ordenes Militares, Calatrava, eclesiásticos, 1/48 (reg. Uhagón, *BRAH*, xxxv, 73, no. 48), 1/49. By then Manfred was rector of the Campagna-Marittima. His tenure of the office is not mentioned by Waley, 319.
6 *Inc. Dudum dilecto*, 11 March 1256, confirming the settlement whereby the Master – by then Master of Calatrava – promised to pay 'quandam morabutinorum summam' to Manfred by the feast of the Ascension: AHN, Ordenes Militares, Calatrava, eclesiásticos, 1/50.
7 Lifted by Cardinal Gil Torres, July 1252: AC Calahorra, doc. 312.

work,[1] they were all concerned with the conciliar subsidies. One of these was the nuncio, Master Petrus de Viccovario, who was at Barcelona in July 1249,[2] by which time it was clear that whichever of the two archbishops it was who had offered the resources of the Spanish Church four years before, he had spoken out of turn. Pedro de Albalat himself was in difficulties, and died in July 1251 owing the Roman Church 1,500 *aurei* 'de vicesimo et subsidio' – a debt which was not settled until 1259.[3] When the *collector vicesime*, Petrus de Piperno, arrived in the autumn of 1252, Pedro's successor, Benito de Rocaberti, was allowed a further period of grace,[4] as were Remondo of Segovia and Pedro Ximénez of Pamplona.[5] In the diocese of Zamora many clerics had been excommunicated for non-payment, and in October 1253 the pope felt obliged to engage the services of their own bishop, Pedro.[6] And thus matters stood in December 1254 when Innocent's death automatically annulled the powers granted to

---

1 Miguel was sent to the king of Aragon in Nov. 1246 to inform him of the attempt made on Innocent IV's life 'per malefactores illos qui Acinini vocantur'. He belonged to the Pamplona convent: ACA, Bulas, IX–25 (reg. Miquel, 136: publ. López, *La provincia franciscana*, 345). On his behalf, fr. Pedro de Tarragona (the assistant of Desiderius) received 'X uncias boni auri' – ten years' *census* – from the prior of Urgel (Lérida, 3 Sept. 1247): AC Seo de Urgel, *Dotium sive dotaliarum liber secundus*, fo. 18r. The Castilian bishops in 1262 remembered him too as 'frater Michael Navarrus...qui non minus alias ecclesias pergravavit': Benito Ruano, *HS*, XI, 16.

2 AD Barcelona, pergaminos de Santa Ana, d.s.n. (publ. Felíu, *AST*, VIII, 102). No evidence has been discovered, however, for the alleged papal tenth in Aragon during Innocent IV's pontificate which Ríus Serra infers from the entry in the collectors' accounts for that kingdom in 1279–80: 'Ascendit decima totius dominationis regni Aragonie secundum levationem quam fecit de tempore domini Innocentii pape IV [1243–54] dominus Fulco Pererius, pro tunc collector regni Aragonie.' Thus Ríus, *Rationes decimarum*, I, x, from ASV, *Collectorie* 25. In *AST*, I, 397, though, Ríus refers to *Collectorie 35* and Fulco, *Penerrii*. Possibly the pope referred to was Innocent V. Alternatively, the *levatio* may have dated from Innocent IV's pontificate, but have been connected with the *vicesima* and used to double-check the *decima* accounts thirty years later.

3 *Reg. Inn. IV*, 6537.

4 *Ibid*. From 24 June to 29 Sept. 1253. A further extension, to Michaelmas 1254, was granted in May 1254: *ibid*. 7474.

5 *Ibid*. 5982, 6083. For this collector, see Lunt, 616.

6 He was authorised to absolve those excommunicated for not paying the *vicesima* and to collect from those whose obligation was less than 20 *solidi turonenses*: 'quantitatem autem eorum quam propter hoc reciperitis nobis per vestras litteras quantocius intimare curetis': *inc. Petitio tua*, 21 Oct. 1253. In Jan. 1255 he had 80 *maravedís* of this money in hand: AC Zamora, 11.i/4; 13/46.

his last nuncio, frater Velascus O.F.M., who had set out from the Curia in the previous May bearing confidential messages for the kings of Portugal and Aragon, unsettled accounts for the king of Castile, and a commission to collect what was still owed.[1]

In 1262 the bishops mentioned the names of three of the nuncios sent by the pontiff who now succeeded, Alexander IV;[2] but their list was not exhaustive. They made no mention of his first representative, Master Gregorius, dean of Messina, sent in the spring of 1255 to collect the *census* in Spain and Provence. On 11 May Sancho of Toledo was asked to assist the nuncio in his dealings with Alfonso X.[3] During the next six months, however, he left no trace, although by 29 November when he confirmed various papal privileges belonging to the Cistercians of Osera in the diocese of Orense – who owed an annual *census* of one *maravedí* – it may be assumed that he had reached the north-west of the Peninsula.[4] Three months later he was in the north-east, at Alagón near Zaragoza, where representatives of the collegiate church of Tudela paid him their *census* for the previous twenty-seven years;[5] and a fortnight after that, on 12 March 1256, he wrote from Tarragona to the prior and chapter of Urgel demanding payment within twelve days of the *census* for that year and for five years of Innocent's pontificate.[6] At Cubellas, a short distance north, he was with Archbishop Benito on the 15th, and received from him an undertaking to settle his various debts to the Roman Church. These included not only the balance of Pedro de Albalat's account – namely, 1,068 *alfonsini* and five *oboli auri duplices* – but also a further 2,720 *alfonsini* which, on the instructions of Petrus de Piperno, had been deposited with him by Sancho of Toledo, and which Benito,

[1] *Reg. Inn. IV*, 7787, 8306, 8307–8. For Velascus, appointed bishop of Guarda in Sept. 1267, see López, *Biblos*, XVIII, 249 ff.

[2] The Patriarch of Grado, fr. Gabriel O.F.M., and Andreas de Ferentino 'qui bis accessit ad partes Hispanie': Benito Ruano, *HS*, XI, 17.

[3] *Fidei sincere integritas*: AC Toledo, A.7.C.2.7.

[4] AHN, 1526/18. Cf. *Liber Censuum*, I, 223. The fragment of an *inspeximus* in AHN – 1646/21: among the *documentos sin procedencia* of the Oviedo province, and described in the Summary Catalogue as 'sig. XIII: trozo de bulla' – seems also to have been issued by him.

[5] 53 *solidi sancxetorum*: AC Tudela, 5–Q–2 (reg. Fuentes, *Catálogo*, 358), 27 Feb. 1256. Cf. *Liber Censuum*, I, 216: 'II solidos illius monete, videlicet sancettorum.'

[6] AC Seo de Urgel, d.s.n: '...Set et quinque uncias auri ad pondus Burgense quas pro eodem censu quinque annorum preteritorum, videlicet quinti, sexti, septimi, octavi et noni pontificatus felicis memorie domini Innocentii pape IIII debetis.'

characteristically, had then refused to release.[1] The archbishop failed to keep his promise, though, and with the pope's patience exhausted he was excommunicated by the nuncio Nicholas of Terracina in the following year, and so remained until March 1259 when, on payment of what he owed to frater Velascus – the papal penitentiary and nuncio of 1254 – Alexander IV absolved him.[2]

Nicholas of Terracina deserves our gratitude for having supplied us with an account of his impressions of his stay at Tarragona, for statements of the thirteenth-century nuncio's case are as rare as contemporary criticism of them is commonplace. In March 1255 King Jaime denounced Benito to the pope and requested that an inquiry into his misdeeds be undertaken 'per aliquem legatum vel aliquam providam personam'.[3] Nicholas was appointed in August 1256, and met with the king's approval,[4] but not with the archbishop's, as the report which he sent to the pope from Barcelona in August 1257 emphasised. His task had been to bring peace to the church of Tarragona – 'miserabilem immo potius miserandam ecclesiam' – and there he had been for almost a year, except for the brief visit to the Castilian court which he had made on Alexander's instructions.[5] From the beginning the archbishop had created difficulties. He had objected to the nuncio's being accommodated in the cloister as the provost's guest, although, as Nicholas observed, 'certe honestius erat vestro nuncio morari infra ambitum ecclesiae quam per vias discurrere eundo per alia hospitia civitatis'. Nicholas admitted to having invited the canons to eat with him. He had also invited Benito. After all, he did not wish to be thought mean: 'nolebam de me dici quod numquam mecum amicus in hospitio receperat caritatem'. Certainly he had struck up various friendships in Tarragona. He would rather

---

[1] AHA, *Cartoral AB*, fo. 35v. Cf. Capdevila, *Franciscalia*, 43.

[2] *Ibid.* fo. 36r: *inc. Cum dilectus filius*, 11 March 1259. Where and when Velascus had received the money is not recorded, though it may be mentioned that only two months before he had been sent to England and may have met the archbishop *en route*. See Treharne, *EHR*, XL, 403 ff.

[3] *Ibid.* fo. 79r.

[4] *VL*, XIX, 313; AHA, *Cartoral AB*, fo. 80r–v: '...de cuius vita et conversatione laudabile testimonium ferimus, qui ad partes Catalonie pro factis eiusdem ecclesie destinastis' (Jaime to Alexander IV, 17 Oct. 1256).

[5] Blanch, *Arxiepiscopologi*, 166. For his intervention in the case of the Order of Santiago and their Florentine creditors, probably at this time, see Benito Ruano, *Banca toscana*, 114–15.

be criticised, as the archbishop had criticised him, for that than for the opposite: 'malo enim de familiaritate humili quam de electione et superbia reprehendi'. How, he asked, was a papal nuncio expected to behave? In the year before the memorable visitation of the Patriarch of Grado, whose 'unheard-of exactions' the Castilian bishops remembered so vividly in 1262, the question strikes a balance which naturally was lacking in Spanish accounts of the activities of such men. Nicholas may be forgiven for concluding that Spaniards were tetchy creatures.[1]

Their attitude to legates and nuncios combined familiarity with contempt. Thus, when invited by Alexander IV to suggest means of countering the Tartar peril in 1261, the Aragonese prelates conceded that if a subvention were demanded they would respond 'sicut cetere provincie', despite their state of poverty which had been caused by papal provisions, the demands of the papal Curia and the expenses of papal nuncios; yet suggested that the most efficacious method of raising Christian morale would be to send out cardinal-legates who would induce the Christian princes to collaborate against the enemy without.[2] Cardinal-legates were no rarity in Aragon: in June 1256 the nuns of Santa Clara, Barcelona, were exempted from payment of procurations to papal agents 'nisi fuerint cardinales'.[3] Nor were they in Castile. But those who came after 1257 must be carefully distinguished from those who had come before, for it was Alfonso X's imperial ambitions that brought them there. The king, if anyone, rather than the pope was ultimately responsible for the abuses perpetrated by the Patriarch of Grado. So also was he for the missions of Goddefredus de Alatro and Andreas de Ferentino, whom Alexander IV sent to set the royal mind at rest,[4] and for those of a whole host of nuncios whose names might be prised from documents in any European archive.[5] They can hardly be regarded in the same light as the collectors of the taxes authorised at the Lyons Council. Innocent's

---

[1] Nicholas's version, contained in his letter of 5 Aug. 1257 to the pope, is publ. by Blanch, 162–6.
[2] Publ. Capdevila, *AST*, II, 514–15.
[3] Fita, *BRAH*, XXVII, no. 42.
[4] Fanta, *MIöG*, VI, 103. Andreas was at Burgos on 11 July 1258: Mañueco Villalobos, *Documentos de Valladolid*, I, 331–3.
[5] For example, the papal courier, Johannes Sardus, sent to Spain on 15 March 1264: Herlihy, *Pisa in the Early Renaissance*, 12.

nuncios had come from the Curia to Castile; Alexander's came to Castile from the Curia. The former had been sent because the pope wanted Castilian money; the latter because the Castilian king needed papal assurances.

Further, the kingdom of Castile could boast two semi-permanent legates during these years, the Franciscans Lope Fernández de Aín and Lorenzo de Portugal, bishops *in partibus* of Morocco and Ceuta respectively.[1] Technically, of course, both were papal agents with special responsibility for the Crusade in North Africa, towards which the pontiffs had been attempting to divert the attention of the king of Castile since at least 1246.[2] That, though, was neither Lope's sole nor his prime concern. Alexander IV used him as a roving peninsular consul. In Castile he was commissioned to supervise the delimitation of dioceses and to appoint bishops in recently reconquered territory;[3] in Navarre to investigate the case of Sancho VII's natural daughter, Blanca, who wished to continue as abbess of the Cistercian nuns at Matellas;[4] while from Aragon he supported the application for papal dispensation of the noble couple Pedro and Berenguela de Pulcrovisu, who had married within the forbidden degree,[5] and informed the pope of the forthcoming dedication of the convent church of Sijena in the Lérida diocese.[6] In January 1257 he was at the Curia – although, only thirteen months before, the pope had released him from his obligation to pay a quinquennial visit, ostensibly on account of his work for the Church in Africa.[7] Not that it was the affairs of that region that brought him to Rome, for he had already been authorised to employ deputies for the exercise of his legatine functions rather

[1] Biographical details of Lope, in López, *Memoria histórica*, 12, 21 ff.; Ballesteros, *Al-Andalus*, VIII, 102–3; Matute y Gaviria, *Archivo Hispalense*, I, 121–8; Mansilla, *Iglesia castellano-leonesa*, 60 ff.; Dufourcq, *Hespéris*, XLII, 78–9; of Lorenzo, in Golubovich, *Biblioteca bio-bibliografica*, II, 319–24; Wadding, *Annales*, II, 116–18.

[2] Lope's mission was launched in Oct. 1246: Potthast, 12307. See also Ballesteros, *Al-Andalus*, VIII, 105–6; Abate, *Miscellanea Francescana*, LV, 351–2, nos 175, 187. For Lope as legate, see *Reg. Alex. IV*, 274–5, 483, 862.

[3] *Ibid.* 873, 902 (Oct.–Nov. 1255); Mansilla, 85–7.

[4] *Ibid.* 553 (May 1255). He was one of a number of prelates, both Spanish and foreign and including the bishop of Hereford, who granted an indulgence in favour of the new church of the Augustinian nuns of S. Pedro de Rivas, Pamplona, sometime before Aug. 1258: AHN, 1422/7.

[5] AHN, 2233/16: *Exhibita nobis*, 21 July 1256.

[6] In Dec. 1257: Pano, *BRAH*, XXIX, 422–3.

[7] *Reg. Alex. IV*, 907; Esperança, I, 483.

than visit North Africa in person.[1] It was in the king's interest that he was there, in connexion with Bishop Juan Díaz of Orense's refusal to admit Alfonso's notary, the dean of Braga, as rector of S. María de Crastello.[2] The royal court was his real centre, and royal diplomacy in general his main concern;[3] and the same may be said of the bishop of Ceuta after Lope's demise.[4] Indeed, it is only because Lorenzo assisted at the negotiations regarding the Empire at Marseilles, Soria and Segovia during 1256 that we know of him as 'predicator crucis in tota Yspania' and 'legatus domini pape in Yspania'.[5] Ten years later he was no nearer gaining possession of his see beyond the Straits.[6] He had survived the period of episcopal discontent, and, though both he and Lope were papal legates and the latter was a permanent charge on the province of Toledo,[7] Lorenzo can never have been in danger of being mistaken for one of the Roman agents of odious memory whom the Castilian bishops reviled in 1262. For his sympathies were so far removed from the interests of the Curia that he felt able to subscribe the bishop of Cuenca's protest against the award of income to Paolo di Sulmona in August 1263.[8]

As Franciscans, Lope and Lorenzo shared many of the attributes of the man about court, Gil de Zamora O.F.M., tutor to the future

[1] In April 1255: *Reg. Alex. IV*, 298.   [2] *Ibid.* 2202.

[3] In the summer and autumn of 1254 he was the Castilian negotiator at the Treaty of Bordeaux with England, and then went to the Curia to pursue that business: Rymer, *Foedera*, I, i, 297, 305; *Close Rolls, 1254–6*, 390; *Reg. Alex. IV*, 298. For his receipts from the *repartimiento* of Seville, see González, *Repartimiento de Sevilla*, II, 29, 43, 134, 242.

[4] He was *bone memorie* by 8 April 1260 (AC Segovia, doc. 187). According to Golubovich, I, 234–5, he had retired in 1257 and gone on pilgrimage to the Holy Land. Of his successor, Blanco, who was also a legate, and was appointed before May 1261 (*Reg. Nich. IV*, 2121), López, *Memoria histórica*, 29–31, could find no trace. He did, however, confirm a copy of a bull of Innocent III (Potthast, 2816) at Barcelona on an unspecified date: AHA, *Cartoral AB*, fo. 24v; and another in the archive of S. Francisco de Guimarães: Esperança, I, 500. The beginning of Lorenzo's episcopate is placed by Dufourcq 'en 1260 au plus tard' (*Hespéris*, XLII, 77), and by Golubovich, II, 324, 'verso il 1266'. But 'L. Ceptensis (episcopus)' was at Valladolid on 18 March 1258 (Benito Ruano, *Banca toscana*, 113), though Benito, confusing the sees of Morocco and Ceuta, interprets *L* as *Lupus* instead of *Laurentius*. In May 1260 he was at the royal court: Ballesteros, *BRAH*, CVII, 30.

[5] Scheffer-Boichorst, *MIöG*, IX, 246; Bayley, *EHR*, LXII, 477.

[6] On 5 July 1266 he was 'in his palace' at Seville: Ríu y Cabañas, *BRAH*, XVI, 53.

[7] *Reg. Inn. IV*, 5171; *Reg. Alex. IV*, 1114. In a sense Lope earned his keep as *procurator in spiritualibus* to the Infante Sancho: *Reg. Inn. IV*, 5182.

[8] AC Cuenca, 8/34/679.

Sancho IV and author of a set of *sermones curiales pro curiis magnatorum*.[1] Many mendicants identified themselves with the secular powers that be, to the alarm of their superiors.[2] They may properly be considered in the same category as those royal clerics and diplomats, such as the archdeacon of Trastamar, whose substantial income was supplied by the Castilian Church either on the king's sole authority or else with the connivance of a compliant pope.[3] The late 1250s, when Alfonso X mounted his elaborate diplomatic campaign in order to buy his way into Europe, provide various examples of such careers. For elaborate diplomatic campaigns require elaborate diplomats; and they, in turn, require funds. One of these was the king's chief permanent negotiator during these years, García Pérez, archdeacon of Morocco – a church which could not support its bishop, let alone its archdeacon, being, like Ceuta, 'un évêché fantôme in partibus'.[4] García Pérez relied for his income on the Castilian Church. Nest-feathering was a frequent topic of conversation among the members of his circle. When Archbishop Sancho of Toledo was at the Curia in the spring of 1259 as *promotor precipuus* of the king's business, and the pope granted his cleric Gonzalo (subsequently archbishop himself) the income of a Toledo canonry for five years while he studied civil law, Sancho wrote post-haste to Paris to give the archdeacon of Morocco the good news.[5] Of course it did not cause Sancho any anguish that it was his own chapter that bore the brunt of this. Neither capitular nor episcopal resistance was tolerated. When the bishop of Orense attempted to exclude the king's man, Fernando Johannis de Portucarrario, dean of Braga, from the church of Crastello, he was unceremoniously slapped down. The dean had

---

1 López, *AIA*, xxxi, 26; *Liber de preconiis Hispaniae*, ed. Castro y Castro, lxxvii–cv.
2 Below, p. 239.
3 Above, p. 185. For his benefices, see below, p. 260.
4 Dufourcq, *Hespéris*, xlii, 79. For García Pérez in 1256–7, see Ruffi, *Histoire de la ville de Marseille*, 135–6; Scheffer-Boichorst, 241 ff.; Bayley's note in *EHR*, lxii, 483; Procter, *Alfonso X*, 126.
5 The pope's rescript, *Sicut dilectus filius* was issued on 2 March (AC Toledo, caj. A.12/I.7). On the 7th Sancho wrote to García Pérez who acknowledged receipt on 17 April, and to the beneficiary (AC Toledo, caj. I.12, d.s.n; caj. A.12/I.7a). With García Pérez at Paris were Tello, archdeacon of Palencia, and 'Didacus Garsie filius ...Garsie Martini domini regis Castelle protonotarius', whose father had been a member of the Castilian legation to Paris in 1255. Nothing, however, is known of the 1259 mission. Cf. Daumet, *Mémoire sur les relations*, 5–6.

influential friends himself at the Curia, but appropriately it was Bishop Lope of Morocco who administered the rebuke just eight days after the bishops had tentatively inaugurated their resistance movement at Alcalá de Henares.[1]

By October 1263, six and a half years later, when Alfonso sent the dean on a tour of duty in Portugal, Leon and Galicia,[2] that movement had been betrayed, and the bishops had identified the pope as the root of all evil and issued their summary of legatine extortions. But the evidence hardly bears them out, either in their allegation that they had had considerable numbers of Italian refugees foisted upon them,[3] or in their observations about the unending stream of curial harpies. The truth was that they had been made to finance the foreign policy of an empire-builder *manqué* who was not destined to be presented with a Sicilian Vespers. The papacy had derived little or nothing from Castile or from Spain at large since the death of Innocent IV, apart from the *census*. The mission of Raymond of Paphos was a new papal departure occasioned by a new papal reverse – the loss of Constantinople; and both the speech prepared for him by Urban IV in July 1262, which was designed to remind the Castilian bishops about its dire consequences for the Holy Land, and the nature of the taxes which he was authorised to levy – *media, tercia* and *vicesima* – recalled the discussions and decisions of the 1245 Lyons Council. The bishops' outburst against him, appealing before he had had time to state his carefully prepared case, was literally pre-emptive, and, as such, it fully merited the papal rebuke which his successor, Master Garinus, dean of Châlons, brought with him in October 1263.[4] Yet

---

[1] *Reg. Alex. IV*, 2202. The church of Crastello had been a bone of contention between bishop and king since at least 1198, and in Oct. 1256 the dean and another royal cleric, Juan, had been excommunicated by the archdeacon of Túy for harassing the rector appointed by the bishop, Juan Suárez: AC Orense, Obispo, 47; ADB, Gav. I das Igrejas, 202. The dean owned property at Seville, and may have been the *Ferrán Ibáñez* mentioned in the *repartimiento* among the king's *oficiales diversos* and *criazones*: Ballesteros, *Sevilla en el siglo XIII*, clxviii; González, *Repartimiento*, II, 71, 244. In the 1230s he had toadied to the king of Portugal and incited the citizens of Porto against their bishop: Sousa Costa, *Mestre Silvestre*, 422. In Aug. 1257 he was at the Curia with Cardinal Octavian Ubaldini, whose chaplain he had been for at least twelve years: *Reg. Inn. IV*, 1302; *Reg. Alex. IV*, 2296. See, further, below, p. 259.

[2] ADB, Gav. das Notícias Várias, 11.

[3] Details in Linehan, *EHR*, lxxxv, 738. Cf. Benito Ruano, *HS*, xi, 17.

[4] Linehan, *loc. cit.*; *Reg. Urb. IV*, 740 ('Vos autem, *presentientes* ipsum pro predicto

the dean's instructions, too, hark back to the constant theme of recent years: he had already been directed to summon the king to the Curia for a further round of discussions on the imperial affair, and to investigate the whereabouts of the money which Alfonso had allegedly forwarded in settlement of his father's debt to the Roman Church.[1] Moreover, a further imminent disaster – in Castile itself – was to render this papal initiative extremely short-lived.

During October 1263 subsidies for the Holy Land were demanded from both the Aragonese and the Portuguese Churches, the task of collection being entrusted to Bishop Domingo of Huesca and Archbishop Martinho of Braga respectively.[2] No such mandate is known to have been sent to any Castilian prelate. Nor was the king of Castile informed, as were those of Portugal and Aragon, when Urban sent an old cameral hand, Master Sinitius, to the Peninsula in March 1264 to collect the *census* and other outstanding debts of the Roman Church.[3] Three months later, though, there seem to have been no exceptions when the pope sent the bishops of the three kingdoms a long letter describing the damage done to the Church by Saracens, heretics and Manfred of Hohenstaufen, and asking them to deliver 'some decent sum of money' to the collector 'with liberal promptitude'. It was an impressive letter and Benito de Rocaberti had it copied into his cartulary, though the vagueness of its demands cannot have given that pastmaster of evasion many sleepless nights.[4] In

negotio...pervenisse...antequam vobis apostolicas super hoc litteras presentaret, in appellationis vocem ad sedem apostolicam prorumpentes, nuntios vestros ad nostram presentiam transmisistis').   [1] *Reg. Urb. IV*, 351; cam. 478.

[2] AC Huesca, 2–261 (reg. Durán Gudiol, *AA*, VII, no. 85); ADB, Gav. dos Arcebispos, 31, 1 Oct. 1263, allowing the prelates retinues of 12 horsemen and 18 *persone* in the first case, 16 and 25 in the other. Cf. Potthast, 18663–4. On 23 Oct. the pope reissued Innocent III's crusading indulgences of Dec. 1215 (Potthast, 5012): ADB, Gav. dos Quindénios, 2. In Aragon the tax was a quinquennial hundredth: AC Huesca, *Extravagantes* (reg. Durán, no. 84). Archbishop Martinho had already received a papal appeal, in July 1262: Battelli, *Schedario Baumgarten*, 3087–8.

[3] *Reg. Urb. IV*, cam. 455–6–9 (publ. García Larragueta, *El Gran Priorado*, II, 413). Fabre described Sinitius as 'particulièrement distingué dans l'exercice de ses fonctions', *Mél. d'arch. et d'hist.* X, 371. He had recently been in England and France: Lunt, 616–17.

[4] *Ibid.* cam. 463–4; AHA, *Cartoral AB*, fos. 55r–6r. The only omissions from the list of addressees in the Register were the archbishops of Toledo and Compostela and the bishop of Badajoz. In the version sent to the province of Tarragona the thoroughgoing condemnation of Manfred, whose daughter had married the Infante Pedro in June 1262, was toned down. Cf. Girona Llagostera, I, *CHCA*, 254.

normal circumstances the Castilian prelates might well have wished
that they had not already shot their bolt against Raymond of Paphos,
for Sinitius was a far more serious proposition, being allowed considerable procurations for his retinue and supplied with churchmen
of the calibre of Raymond of Peñafort and Guillermo de Mongrí as
his liaison officers.[1] But circumstances were not normal: at the end of
May 1264 – a fortnight or so before Urban issued his appeal – the
king of Granada, Ibn el-Ahmer, had risen in revolt against Alfonso X.[2]

The rebel's immediate successes bore out the bishop of Cuenca's
recent remarks about the fragility of Castile's frontier; and even in
Tudela, far to the north, there was a keen sense of 'stress and danger'.[3]
In Rome, which had never approved Alfonso's tolerance of the
Moor, Clement IV panicked. 'Ignoramus quid agere debeamus', he
confessed to Cardinal Richard Annibaldi in May 1265, three months
after his election.[4] But what he *had* already done was to abandon his
predecessor's policy of making the Peninsula contribute to the
defence of the Holy Land, instructing the archbishop of Seville in
Castile, and the archbishop of Tarragona and bishop of Valencia to
preach the Crusade against the immediate foe in Aragon, on the
grounds that to assume responsibility for one's neighbour house
when one's own was threatened by fire was 'satis absonum et
contrarium rationi'.[5] He had also, in March, made an award of
Castilian and Leonese ecclesiastical income to Alfonso – a quinquennial hundredth, such as the bishop of Huesca had recently been
collecting for the Holy Land from the Aragonese Church.[6] Three
months later, this was improved to a triennial tenth, though not without considerable misgivings on the pope's part. He was loth to
revive the unfortunate precedent of 1247, and made the grant condi-
tional upon Alfonso's renouncing his unauthorised possession of the
tercias – 'illam rapinam vilissimam tam dampnabilem quam dam-
nosam', about which he claimed to have remonstrated with the
king even before his promotion – 'cum sit indecens quod spoliatori
subsidium conferant spoliati':[7] a conclusion with which the despoiled

---

[1] *Ibid.* cam. 460, 473.   [2] Ballesteros, *Alfonso X*, 370.
[3] See the lament of Shem Tob Falaquera in Baer, *History of the Jews in Christian
Spain*, I, 203.
[4] *Reg. Clem. IV*, 895.   [5] *Ibid.* 15, 19, 128.
[6] *Ibid.* 16, Cf. Goñi Gaztambide, *Historia de la Bula de la Cruzada*, 197–8.
[7] *Ibid.* 890, 896 (publ. Martène–Durand, *Thesaurus*, II, 137–8, 144–5).

canons of Zamora were in full agreement.[1] But Clement's instructions to the archbishop of Seville (who was, in any event, hardly the best man to hold the king to a bargain) were less than resolute regarding the seriousness of this condition; and irresolution cut no ice with Alfonso X.[2] Neither was Jaime of Aragon, to whom a like grant was made in July, obliged to feel unduly concerned when the pontiff censured him for subjecting the Aragonese Church 'exactionibus indebitis', for allowing the church of Valencia to languish in poverty, and for failing to dispose of the serpent in his breast by expelling his Moorish subjects from the kingdom.[3] The grant of ecclesiastical revenue ought not, strictly speaking, to have been made at all while these abuses continued, Clement reminded him in the autumn.[4] But the grant *had* been made, because Clement believed Christendom to be in peril on its Spanish flank – in such great peril, indeed, that he was prepared to revoke the appeal for funds from Spain for the Holy Land, thus rejecting implicitly the traditional view and sole justification for such a grant: that Spain and the Holy Land were two fronts in one Holy War. His use of the fire metaphor was, in this respect, particularly significant. The giving of aid to a blazing neighbour had not struck his predecessors as irrational. They had taken the opposite

[1] Above, p. 175.
[2] At one stage Clement opined that, if the king refused to surrender the *tercias*, it would be 'better' to suppress the decree authorising the *decima*, and on another he instructed the archbishop to proceed with the collection of a different tax 'sicut in alia littera quam tibi mittimus plenius continetur'. But this *alia littera* has not survived, and in June 1267 he wrote again to the archbishop after the king had complained of his not having proceeded with the collection: 'causa tamen quare cessaveris ignoramus' (which hardly accords with the Zamora appeal of Nov. 1266), and implying that Alfonso had undertaken to renounce the *tercias* only for the duration of the *decima* grant: *Reg. Clem. IV*, 890, 896, 1205.
[3] *Ibid.* 134, 848 (text completed from Diago, *Anales del reyno de Valencia*, I, 374v–5r). The bishop of Valencia, Andrés de Albalat, co-executor of the grant with Benito de Rocaberti, delegated his powers to Bishop Arnaldo of Zaragoza in a letter of 13 Aug. 1265 from Perugia, reserving only the collection in his own diocese: AC Seo de Urgel, d.s.n. For his strife with the king over diocesan tithes, see Burns, *Crusader Kingdom*, I, 144 ff.
[4] *Reg. Clem. IV*, 928: 'Porro debet illud advertere tua sublimitas, quod si per juris tramites ordinate vellemus incedere, nullum tibi fuisset impendendum subsidium ab ecclesiis terrae tuae donec gravamina revocasses earum' (13 Aug. 1265). Jaime had recently earned the pope's gratitude, however, by securing the release from the clutches of Manfred of the bishop-elect of Verona, Manfred de' Roberti (the nuncio of 1249–50): Martène–Durand, II, 98–100, 192; Waley, 172.

view and had quoted Horace in support.[1] In 1265, though, Clement IV felt that he was in no position to bargain, and the kings of Castile and Aragon knew it.

'Yspania sibi non sufficit', he calculated in the August of that year; and at the beginning of 1268 assured Louis IX of France that it was not financially worthwhile to send a legate to Aragon.[2] He might have been surprised, therefore, had he known that, on the security of the grant of subsidy, 'Christ's prize-fighter' the king of Aragon was able to borrow 100,000 *solidi* at Valencia at the end of October 1265 and supplies worth a further 60,000 at Alicante soon after.[3] On 9 October Jaime's chapel clerk, Pedro de Pinu, had been sent to Urgel for the first year's instalment from that diocese, which was to be paid within six weeks.[4] Of course, the Aragonese Church, like the Castilian, had been mulcted before. But the 1265 grant of revenue differed markedly from its most recent precedent, that of 1248-9. Then – at least formally – the bishops had retained the initiative. Sixteen years later – during which they had lost Pedro de Albalat and gained (if *gain* be the word) Benito de Rocaberti as their leader – they were not consulted. They were hardly better placed than their colleagues in Castile, who protested but succumbed.[5]

Clement IV was no match for either monarch. He fondly assumed that Alfonso would not dare go to war with the sin of the *tercias* on his soul. Alfonso, however, shared Jaime's view that God's champion, however occasional, had an automatic right to absolution.[6] If a papal grant of church revenue were not forthcoming, then he took what he wanted, grant or no grant. In 1279 he was charged by Nicholas III

---

[1] Honorius III to the province of Compostela, Jan. 1224, urging it to assist the bishop of Lisbon against the king of Portugal 'eo quod vestra res agitur paries cum proximus ardet': *Reg. Hon. III*, 4864 (MDH, 490). Similarly, *ibid.* 2906 (MDH, 341), 2917. Cf. Horace, *Epistles*, I, xviii, 84; R. W. Hunt, in *Classical Influences on European Culture, A.D. 500–1500*, ed. R. R. Bolgar (Cambridge, 1971), 54.

[2] *Reg. Clem. IV*, 923, 1288.

[3] *Ibid.* 134 ('strenuus Christi pugil et magnificus, ac victoriosus Christiane fidei propugnator'); ACA, reg. 13, fo. 283r (reg. Martínez Ferrando, *Catálogo*, I, no. 619); AC Seo de Urgel, d.s.n. Jaime was at Alicante between 9 March and 2 April 1266: Miret y Sans, *Itinerari*, 384–5.

[4] AC Seo de Urgel, d.s.n.

[5] Benito did offer some *personal* resistance: Vincke, *Staat und Kirche*, 111 ff.

[6] 'Quis enim sapiens bellico se committit discrimini cui conscientia bellum intestinum indicit?': *Reg. Clem. IV*, 890.

with having made use of expired papal privileges for this purpose;[1] and there is evidence to support the charge. In June 1264 – at the time of the Granada uprising but before Clement had authorised either the hundredth or the tenth – he demanded aid from the bishops on the strength of a couple of bulls issued in April 1246 and July 1259.[2] And Jaime was cast in the same mould: contemptuously arrogant by nature, he proved difficult when at the Second Lyons Council Gregory X suggested that he might pay the arrears of tribute due from his kingdom to the Roman Church. The *census* of 250 *oboli auri*, promised as an annual payment by his father Pedro II in 1204, was more than £550 in arrears. But the king's attitude, as recorded in his Chronicle, was that 'it was not becoming in him to ask for anything, but rather to give to me', for 'I had done such service to God and to the Church of Rome that those trifles should not intervene between me and them'.[3] His son and grandson were of that opinion too: in 1282, when Martin IV refused to follow custom and allow Pedro III crusading revenue for his much-publicised African expedition, since 'the treasure which cometh from tithes is not gathered together to be spent in Barbary nor in any other place save only in the Holy Land beyond the sea', Pedro deemed this sufficient pretext for turning his attention to Sicily;[4] and seven years after that momentous intervention, in May 1289, Alfonso III had the effrontery to challenge Philip the Fair's request for 'la decima a .X. ans sens tota condició',[5] although the king of France was the current papal champion and, as leader of a crusade against him, had as good a claim to such privileges

---

1 'Item privilegiis sibi ab apostolica sede concessis ad tempus abutitur, immo magis abutitur transacto tempore, nec eorum etiam originalia ostendit': *Reg. Nich. III*, 743.
2 AC Cuenca, 1/4/36 (20 June 1264): as publ. by Minguella, *Historia de Sigüenza*, I, 599–601. Cf. *Reg. Inn. IV*, 1832.
3 *Chronica del Rey En Jacme*, cap. 537, ed. Aguiló, 514–15; trans. Forster, II, 651–2. *Liber Censuum*, I, 216.
4 Desclot, *Chronicle*, II, 48, 54. Cf. Dufourcq, *L'Espagne catalane*, 251–2.
5 ACA, Cartas Reales Diplomáticas, Alfonso II, caj. 4, no. 14: report from the royal proctor, Galcerán de Timor, almost entirely illegible, dated 'en la ciutad de Roma dimecres despres Santa Creu de Maig'; *viz.*, 4 May 1289, in view of the reference to the pope's promotion to Zaragoza of 'el pabord de Massellia' (Hugo de Mataplana: cf. *Reg. Nich. IV*, 873). Neither Finke nor Vincke refers to it, nor is it mentioned in modern accounts of the diplomatic manoeuvres of the period: Klüpfel, *Die äussere Politik Alfonsos III von Aragonien*, 53–4; Digard, *Philippe le Bel et le Saint-Siège de 1285 à 1304*, I, 67–71.

as his own forbears had had until, by precipitating the break with Rome, they had been reduced to pillaging the Aragonese Church without the blessing of the hitherto compliant papacy.[1]

Papal receipts from Spain during the decade 1264–74 seem to have been extremely slender. There is record of one collector only, Master Adegarius of Parma, who was sent to collect the *census* in 1273–4.[2] Nothing further is heard of contributions for the Holy Land or the Latin Empire. Moreover, it is clear that the events of 1264 had prevented the then nuncio, Master Sinitius, from securing 'some decent sum of money' from each of the bishops for those needs. Even the *census* had been denied him, for in 1273–4 Adegarius received arrears of the previous eighteen years – for the interval, that is, which had elapsed since the visit of the dean of Messina. Such was the case at Brioca on 15 September 1273, in respect of Roncesvalles and the three Burgos monasteries of Oña, Silos and San Pedro de Cardeña;[3] at Tudela on 26 May 1274;[4] and at Perpignan where the canons of Urgel rendered payment on 4 September.[5] Elsewhere, at Huesca and Valladolid, the interval was even greater – twenty and twenty-five years respectively; and at both places the nuncio encountered stout denial. The canons of Huesca dug in and refused to pay, declaring that they were perfectly prepared to argue the case at the Curia. All that saved them from themselves was the nuncio's chance meeting with their bishop, Jaime Sarroca, at Barcelona. Having just returned from the Curia himself, Jaime could appreciate the canons' folly, and Adegarius was promised his gold.[6] Not that he absolutely insisted on

---

[1] Vincke, 129 ff.

[2] Adegarius must not be confused with his contemporary, Albertus, who was also a canon of Parma and papal *scriptor* and had been sent to Spain by Urban IV in Oct. 1261: *Reg. Urb. IV*, cam. 2. See Affo, *Memorie degli scrittori e letterati Parmigiani*, I, 170; Mercati, *Saggi di storia e letteratura*, I, 115–20.

[3] AC Toledo, A.7.E.I.8: the money was in two denominations: 112½ *duplas marrochinas aureas, decem et octo untias auri ponderantes* from Oña, and 126 *morabutinos alfonsinos de auro in bona pecunia numerata* (90 from Silos, and 18 each from Cardeña and Roncesvalles). Cf. *Liber Censuum*, I, 217–19. It was entrusted to Archbishop Sancho for delivery at the papal *camera* 'infra tempus ordinati generalis concilii' (Lyons, 1274).

[4] AC Tudela, 5–Q–2: 'XXXVI turonenses grossos et VI parvos pro XXXVIII solidos sancxetorum usualium'.

[5] AC Seo de Urgel, d.s.n. Both here and at Tudela Adegarius was shown receipts issued by the dean of Messina.

[6] AC Huesca, 2–262, 13 Aug. 1274 (reg. Durán Gudiol, *AA*, VII, 373, no. 101).

pure gold – which the Castilian bishops had remembered as Gregory IX's offence: he was quite prepared to receive Urgel's due in what local experts assured him was the equivalent in current coin 'cum aurum in hac terra non inveniatur nunc ad vendendum'.[1] He was also prepared to wait: at Valladolid the canons were less mulish than at Huesca, but more hopelessly muddled. They had looked high and low for their records, could not trace them, and were short of ready money. So they were allowed a breathing-space in which to organise their affairs and raise the wind.[2] No feature of that episode – neither the canons' uncertainty nor the nuncio's patience – accords well with the accepted version of exigent curialists making constant demands. Moreover, they were then given ample opportunity to forget afresh: another eighteen years passed before another nuncio was sent to collect the Spanish *census*.[3]

But during those eighteen years they had the king to contend with, for Alfonso's imperial pretensions had still to be liquidated; and no sooner had the ticking of that unexploded bomb, the kingdom of Granada, become temporarily inaudible than he returned to the fray. In June 1266 his fleet would not sail for lack of funds; yet in October 1271 he was assuring his friends at Pavia that his plans for the relief of Lombardy were far advanced, and as late as October 1274 financial aid was being demanded from his subjects 'pora fecho del imperio'.[4] By then, though, it must have been clear even to him that his imperial future was not bright: at the Lyons Council earlier in that year a score of Spanish prelates had witnessed Gregory X's acclamation of Rudolf of Habsburg as King of the Romans.[5] The following

---

1 AC Seo de Urgel, d.s.n: 'LVIII turonensibus per priorem Predicatorum et plures campsores fidedignos de Perpiniano diligenter pro qualibet auri untia computatis.'
2 AC Valladolid, XXXII–1.A, at León, undated. The canons were required to pay their due at the Dominican convent at Toledo by the following January 'in bono auro seu argento monetato tantum...ad computum vigintiquinque morabutinorum bone et veteris monete Burgalensis pro quolibet anno, videlicet de vigintiquinque annis preteritis': publ. Mañueco Villalobos, II, 328–31.
3 Raimundus Bulgarelli, canon of Messina, collector in 1290–1. See Mercati, *Bull. Ist. Ital. e Arch. Muratoriano*, XLVI, 121 ff. In March 1291 he was at Zamora: Benito Ruano, *Banca toscana*, 118.
4 Dufourcq in *Rev. d'hist. et de civ. du Maghreb*, I, 45; Zanelli in *Archivo Storico Italiano*, 5th ser., X, 122–6; Torres Fontes, *Col. documentos del reino de Murcia*, I, 88.
5 On 13 July 1274 at least twenty peninsular prelates were at Lyons; namely, Compostela, Plasencia, Segovia, Osma, Ciudad Rodrigo, Lisbon, Zaragoza, Valencia, Lugo, Toledo, Palencia, Segorbe, Coria, León, Guarda, Tarragona, Barcelona,

year brought the final break, for while Alfonso and Gregory were in conference together at Beaucaire, the bomb exploded, with shattering effect. The Merinid invasion from North Africa and the conjunction of those forces with the Moors of Granada distracted the king's attention at the crucial moment, while providing the pope not only with manifest proof that Alfonso's destiny was to serve Christendom by fighting the enemies of the Faith at home, but also with a pretext for offering him some *douceur* to accompany the bitter pill of disappointed ambition: namely, the sexennial tenth which the Council had authorised for the relief of the Holy Land.[1] And it *was* a bitter pill for the king to swallow: he devoted one of his most scornful *cantigas* to the subject of papal perfidy: 'Se me graça ffazesse este papa de Roma'.[2] Still, he had the papal grant, and its palliative character was further enhanced by the appointment as its collector in Castile of Master Fredulus, prior of Lunello (Maguelonne) and his promotion to the vacant see of Oviedo in November 1275.[3] The promotion ought to have been doubly advantageous, for Fredulus knew Alfonso of old, having been involved in the imperial negotiations for at least eight years, while from his new vantage-point he might ensure that the king observed his part of the bargain by not reverting to the use of titles which he had renounced at Beaucaire.[4]

Tortosa, Mallorca and Porto; the first nine of whom were still there on 23 July, as were the bishops of Coimbra, Jaén, and Silves: ASV, A.A. arm.I–XVIII.2991 (reg. Mansilla, *AA*, vi, 324, no. 91); AC León, doc. 1514. Archbishop Sancho of Toledo had changed his mind since 1 Feb. when he had arranged not to attend: AC Toledo, I.5.A.3.1; BN, MS 1529 (Pérez, *Archiepiscoporum Toletanorum Vitae*), fo. 60r.

[1] Ballesteros, *Alfonso X*, 728 ff.; *Reg. Greg. X*, 649 (Oct. 1275); Ríus Serra, *Rationes decimarum*, ii, 309–12.

[2] *Cancioneiro da Biblioteca Nacional*, ii, 308–9.

[3] *Reg. Greg. X*, 639. The capitular choice, Master Ferrán Martínez, had died before his election was confirmed. A royal notary and one of the king's men at the Curia, he had returned to Castile in June 1274, bringing Fredulus with him: *ES*, xxxviii, 197–8; Ballesteros, *Alfonso X*, 712–13. Then another bishop-elect, Master Álvaro, made a brief appearance: to the evidence for his existence adduced by Risco (*ES*, xxxviii, 203–4) may be added Nicholas III's reference in Jan. 1278 to the time 'quo idem magister Alvarus eidem ecclesie presidebat': *Reg. Nich. III*, 218.

[4] *Reg. Greg. X*, 650. In Sept. 1267, while a scholar at Bologna, Fredulus had been appointed to examine the claims of the imperial candidates at Frankfurt. In June 1274, and again six months later, Gregory X had sent him to Castile for discussions with the king: *Reg. Clem. IV*, 589; *Chartularium Studii Bononiensis*, v, 148; vii, 29, 65, 71; Kaltenbrunner, *Mittheilungen aus dem Vat. Archive*, i, nos. 48–50, 63, 67–8; Müller, *RQ*, xxxvii, 102. At the latter date he was not yet bishop-elect of Oviedo, as Mondéjar alleged: *Memorias históricas*, 191.

In March and April 1276 Innocent V confirmed Gregory's arrangements and reiterated the venerable papal belief that vigorous action in Spain would lend assistance to the Holy Land;[1] and during that autumn Fredulus nominated sub-collectors of the *decima* for the dioceses of Toledo, Burgos and Calahorra[2] as well, presumably, as for the rest of the Castilian Church – that tired old mare which stood to derive no advantage from the horse-trading between king and pope.

For Bishop Fredulus was a pronounced trimmer. He soon endeared himself to Alfonso and was sent on diplomatic missions to both the French and papal courts. He had chosen a bad moment, though, thus to expose himself, since while he was abroad the rebellion of the Infante Sancho occurred, and by the disaffected the bishop of Oviedo was regarded with the deepest loathing. Sancho threatened to have his head; rather than risk which, Martin IV translated him to the less perilous see of Le Puy in June 1284, a month after the death of Alfonso and the accession of the sanguinary Infante.[3] The strength of feeling against him was not due simply to his foreign origins. He had made himself especially hateful by exceeding his brief as collector, ignoring Alfonso's remission of the first year's payment of the *decima* which the churches had declared themselves incapable of raising 'absque gravi incommodo', and taxing incomes of less than £7

---

[1] *Inc. Attendens sollicite*: '...pensans meditatione sollicita quod Sarracenorum impugnatio predictorum in grandem favorem magnumque cedit auxilium dicte Terre', 23 March 1276: ASV, Instrumenta Miscellanea, 56 (reg. Milian Boix, *AA*, xv, 521, no. 15); bull *Sarracenis de partibus* (partially ed. Raynaldi, *Annales*, III, 399; reg. Laurent, *Innocent V*, 490, no. 194, *sine nota chronologica*), 11 April 1276 (date in AC Toledo, I.5.C.1.35).

[2] Gonsalvo García and Master Juan, sacrist and cantor of Burgos, for Burgos (Burgos, 11 July); Ramón Bernardo, archdeacon of Calatrava, and Pedro Pérez Bonet, canon of Toledo, for Toledo (Brihuega, 3 Sept.); Master Juan, archdeacon of Alava, and Pedro de Arne, *socius* of Calahorra, for Calahorra, who at Albelda on 11 Feb. 1278 received the *decima* of the bishop's diocesan income for the year 1276: 1,898 *mor.* 6 *sol.* and 3 *den.* 'illius monete albe que facta fuerat tempore guerre de Granada': AC Toledo, I.5.C.1.35; I.7.G.1.12; AC Calahorra, doc. 383.

[3] *ES*, XXXVIII, 207; Mondéjar, 384–5; *Reg. Mart. IV*, 505. Fredulus seems to have taken the hint and stayed at the Curia during the civil war. He was there on 13 Dec. 1283 and 23 March 1284; and on the latter date was already describing himself as 'Aniciensis seu Podiensis episcopus', some eleven weeks before the issue of the pope's bull of appointment: AC Calahorra, doc. 404; AHN, 1874/4. Later that year Sancho IV relented to the extent of allowing his nephew, Jofré archdeacon of Ribadeo (Astorga), to remove his property: Gaibrois de Ballesteros, *Sancho IV*, I, clxxvi.

turonenses contrary to the conciliar constitution. This he had done not for the pope, but for the king who stood to gain; and in April 1278 Nicholas III responded to the appeals forwarded by the clergy of a number of sees by ordering the over-zealous Fredulus to desist and to undo those things which he ought not to have done.[1]

But at least Alfonso X had been granted the *decima*. His royal neighbours helped themselves. Afonso III permitted the collector, Archdeacon Giraldo of Couto, to gather what was due from the Portuguese Church, and then locked it all up, pocketed the key, and coolly announced that he could not tolerate its removal from the kingdom.[2] Pedro III of Aragon also took the law into his own hands. Having received an evasive reply from John XXI to his application for a grant, he proceeded, in the manner of Alfonso X, to revive a papal concession previously made to his father, and – two months later, at the siege of Montesa in August 1277 – simply to demand then and there £15,000 from the collector.[3] He later argued that, had he not acted thus, his army would have melted away, and asked Nicholas III to treat what had been a forced loan as a retrospective grant. When Nicholas proved less accommodating than his predecessors, and even sceptical about the king's version of what had happened, Pedro retorted that the facts of the case were well enough known *in Ispania* and that there ought to be no question of argument, particularly since other kings had received such grants who had done precious little to deserve them.[4]

He obviously had Alfonso in mind, but his argument failed to convince the pope who saw Pedro's contemptuous treatment of papal mandates as an extremely dangerous precedent and was determined to check the contagion before it spread further.[5] And his

---

[1] *Reg. Nich. III*, 27–41 (for Túy and twelve other dioceses).

[2] Ríus Serra, *Rationes Decimarum Hispaniae*, II, 285, publishes Giraldo's report of the incident to Nicholas III.

[3] *Reg. John XXI*, 143 (April 1277); Ríus Serra, II, 315 (June 1277); Soldevila, *Pere el Gran*, II, i, 100: 'ex speciali gratia et urgente eciam necessitate qua propter guerram sarracenorum dictam peccuniam quamplurimum necessariam habebamus'.

[4] *Reg. Nich. III*, 199 (Dec. 1278); Vincke, 124; Ríus Serra, II, 319: '...cum quibusdam aliis regibus super dicta decima concedenda gratiam fecerit dominus Papa, qui pro tuitione fidei christiane contra sarracenos ad alium actum hactenus minime processerunt nec adhuc compleverunt' (July 1279).

[5] Pedro's request was refused 'ne...predicte presumptionis in exempli perniciem *refrenanda temeritas* si rex exegerit impunita remaneat': *Reg. Nich. III*, 199.

collector of the *decima* in Aragon and Navarre, Master Benenatus de Lavania,[1] took the same view, and emphasised the point when he informed Nicholas that the French troops who had sacked Pamplona Cathedral in September 1276 had carried off not only various relics and chalices – 'quod est valde orribile' – but also all the fruits of his labours, the sum total of the Navarre *decima* which had been deposited in the treasury there.[2] But both pope and collector were powerless, and if the king of Aragon's method of pirating papal funds was rather less spectacular than that of the king of France, it was certainly no less effective. For when Nicholas remained adamant and demanded repayment in full, Pedro took to playing hide-and-seek with the collectors, causing the archbishops of Arles and Narbonne to wonder whether the cost of chasing him all over the kingdom might not be in excess of the sum at issue.[3] So the game continued until, with the start of the War of the Vespers, the fifteen thousand purloined pounds passed into oblivion, the king having displayed in his successful coup of 1277 and his conduct of the ensuing war of attrition those qualities of patience and scorn which were to serve him in the greater cause after 1282.[4] And the further cost to the pope of replacing the collectors' mounts as they expired in pursuit of Pedro underlined the futility of his attempt to bring the king to justice.[5]

---

1 A member of the family which produced two thirteenth-century popes – Innocent IV and Adrian V – and, as canon of Narbonne, himself one of the electors in Oct. 1259 of the future Clement IV as archbishop: Ríus Serra, II, 299; Baluze, *Concilia Galliae: Narbonensis* (Paris, 1668), app. p. 161. He was at Tudela by Sept. 1275 and as late as March 1281 was at Agreda: López Polo, *Catálogo del archivo del Capitulo General Eclesiástico*, 29, no. 19; *MHE*, II, 37.

2 'Et nisi istud factum tam orribile bene puniatur timeo quod alia pecunia decime, que est in aliis locis deposita, per principes et alios male et peius tractetur, si peius etiam dici posset': Ríus Serra, II, 290, 294, 303. For the sacking of Pamplona, see Goñi Gaztambide, *Príncipe de Viana*, XVIII, 146 ff.

3 Ríus Serra, II, 288. Though the pope's decision had been final, Pedro continued to insist that the central issue was the gravity of his *necessitas* at Montesa, but prevented the archbishops from interviewing witnesses of that incident: *ibid.* II, 319; *Reg. Nich. III*, 199.

4 £1,000 *turonenses* of the Aragonese *decima* was still at Barcelona in June 1296: *Reg. Bon. VIII*, 1166.

5 Ríus Serra, II, 307. Benenatus himself all but died in harness in the summer of 1279, and the Portuguese collector Giraldo of Couto was so wearied by his dealings with Afonso III and Dinis that in May 1284, 'senex, debilis et valetudinarius', he was evidently ready to hand over to his successor, Monaldus de S. Anatholia (or, de

But Nicholas III also tackled Alfonso X and, though he failed again there, it is noteworthy that it was he rather than any of his predecessors who did so. As cardinal deacon of S. Nicholas in Carcere Tulliano, John Gaetan Orsini had always shown special interest in the affairs of the peninsular Church. Dante condemned him to painful contortions in the Eighth Circle of Hell on account of his notorious simony,[1] but the two Spanish cardinals, Pelayo Gaitán[2] and Gil Torres,[3] evidently had a higher opinion of him, since they both chose him as executor of their wills. In April 1246 he had been appointed to investigate the circumstances of the Evora election, and in November 1254 to unravel the extremely complicated border dispute of the dioceses of Coimbra and Guarda.[4] When Clement IV felt that he was being railroaded by Alfonso X into appointing Sancho of Aragon to the see of Toledo, it was to Cardinal John that he turned for guidance.[5] The cardinal's household contained a number of Spaniards, and at the Lyons Council he and Cardinal Richard Annibaldi were the two prelates whom Gregory X consulted before ruling on the question of the Aragonese *census*.[6]

Nicholas III was therefore something of a Spanish expert. But, more important, he was also the first pontiff for twenty years who in his dealings with Alfonso, king of Castile, did not have to make allowances for Alfonso, king of the Romans. Clement IV, at his firmest, had felt obliged to assure the king that he would always respect his wishes concerning episcopal elections by acting 'iuxta morem a tua domo regia prescriptum', which was tantamount to

Mathelica, Camerino), O.F.M.: *ibid.* II, 287, 312; ADB, Gav. dos Quindénios, 7; *Reg. Mart. IV*, 242 (ADB, Gav. dos Quindénios, 4).

[1] *Inferno*, XIX, 70.
[2] AC León, doc. 1603; Risco, *Historia de León*, I, 72; Cañizares, *BCM Lugo*, II, 152; Fernández Catón, *Archivos Leoneses*, VII, 108.
[3] *Collectionis Bullarum Sacrosanctae Basilicae Vaticanae*, I, 137. The will of Rodrigo Pérez, archdeacon of León, instructed his executors 'ut...solvantur CCC morabutinos Petro Benedicti magistroscolarum Zamorensi, quos recolo me a domino Egidio bone memorie Sanctorum Cosme et Damiani diacono cardinali mutuo recepisse, ita tamen si habet specialem mandatum recipiendi predictam pecuniam a domino Johanne Gagitano vel a domino Egidio bone memorie' (19 Nov. 1268): AC León, doc. 1569.
[4] *Reg. Inn. IV*, 1864; *Reg. Alex. IV*, 947; Sousa Costa, *Mestre Silvestre*, 327 ff.
[5] *Reg. Clem. IV*, 1108 (5 Aug. 1266).
[6] Below, Ch. 12; *Chronica del Rey En Jacme*, cap. 538, ed. Aguiló, 515; trans. Forster, II, 652.

agreeing never to liberate the Castilian Church from its bondage.[1] But the ghost which had haunted Clement had been laid at Beaucaire in 1275, and Alfonso was now on a par with other crowned mortals. Nicholas could afford to face him squarely: one of his first acts as pope was to reprimand the king for his persecution of Archbishop Gonsalvo of Compostela. That was in February 1278. Two months later he intervened to check the abuse of the *decima* grant;[2] and within a year he had decided to attack Alfonso on a broad front.

In view of the disturbed state of Castile, he informed Alfonso in March 1279, he would have held his peace, had not conscience impelled him to protest (which, being interpreted, is, had not the changed diplomatic circumstances permitted him to protest). On an occasion of this kind it becomes more than a moral duty to speak one's mind. It becomes a pleasure. Out of regard for the king, though, he would spare him the indignity of letters patent which would bruit the news abroad. Instead he was sending a special nuncio, Bishop Pietro of Rieti, with a *memoriale secretum* cataloguing Alfonso's offences against the Church.[3]

The *memoriale secretum* defined and denounced every detail of the system which had kept the Castilian Church in a state of subjection during living memory. It was an explosive document and, if any good was to come of it, the bishop of Rieti would need to tread carefully. His instructions, therefore, like those of Raymond of Paphos in 1262, were unusually comprehensive. On arriving at the Castilian court he was to present an amiable appearance, breathe not a word about the purpose of his mission, keep his eyes open for likely allies, and, when a suitable opportunity offered, casually to explain in very general terms why he was there. Act One having thus been safely negotiated, he might then withdraw. The co-operation of the king in this, for him unrehearsed, charade was taken for granted. At a later date the bishop was to descend to particulars and to deal, in order, with the various grievances of the Castilian Church. There

---

[1] *Reg. Clem. IV,* 954 (6 Sept. 1265); a sop to the king, when refusing his request for Sancho of Aragon's promotion to Toledo. Within the year, though, Clement had capitulated on that point also: *ibid.* 360.

[2] *Reg. Nich. III,* 5.

[3] *Ibid.* 739. For Pietro, see Ughelli, *Italia Sacra,* I, 1205; Cappelletti, *Le chiese d'Italia,* v, 324.

were seven articles, of which two are of only incidental significance.[1]

The first two issues (upon which the bishop was instructed to concentrate his fire) were the *tercias*, predictably, which Alfonso had continued to treat, irrationally and unjustly, as a permanent source of revenue; and royal depredations of church property during vacancies, which Nicholas deemed 'similiter inexcusabilis...quia novus'.[2] His vendetta against the churches of Compostela and León constituted items three and four. Item five covered a multitude of sins, being a rag-bag of episcopal complaints which the nuncio might not be able fully to substantiate without further information. So he was urged to avoid confrontation with the king on these points, at least until he had had the opportunity of briefing himself in private discussions with the bishops and others.

Nevertheless, this fifth item is by far the most interesting. For the *gravamina prelatorum* described with a remorseless thoroughness the royal method of controlling ecclesiastical persons and things. It is an impressive document which would have heartened Ascensio de Morales and his friends, a regalist's *vademecum*. It mentioned, point by point, the 'preces, minaces et impressiones' used in order to ensure the election of suitable bishops; extortion of money and attacks on church treasuries; the breaking of promises and spoliation of ecclesiastical property 'licet ecclesia sit munita legitima prescriptione'; disregard for *libertas ecclesiastica* and the operations of secular justice of a rough and ready sort; the abuse 'transacto tempore' of papal indulgences granted 'ad tempus'; prohibition of the publication of spiritual penalties and papal letters in the interest of others; the practice of forcing bishops to append their seals to 'cedulas vacuas'; the exaltation of Jews over Christians, about which the episcopal caucus had complained in 1267, 'unde multa mala proveniunt'; and the denial of the means of redress by banning episcopal assemblies and appeals to Rome, and by withholding funds for foreign travel. The bishop's *memoriale* enumerated these abuses, and details of 'alia multa gravamina' were contained in the

---

[1] *Ibid.* 743. The sixth concerned Portugal; the seventh 'est ultimo et secreto tangendus, videlicet de oppressionibus et gravaminibus multis illicitis et injustitia subditorum'.

[2] 'Videtur quod primo fiat descensus ad articulum *tertiarum* [thus ASV, Reg. Vat. 40, fo. 56v: not *terrarum*, as ed. Gay, *Registres de Nicolas III*, 343]...In quarum perceptione nec concessionem nec consuetudinem nec prescriptionem allegare potest. Peccat ergo graviter in percipiendo, peccat etiam in modo percipiendi...'

dossier of written evidence with which he had been furnished. Twenty years before, the bishops had whispered in corners against the king, while in public blaming the pope for their misfortunes. In 1279, though, with Alfonso preoccupied by mounting political troubles, they revised their opinion, abandoned timidity and prevarication, and, taking their cue from the Portuguese churchmen who had presented their *gravamina* to Clement IV in 1268,[1] looked instead to the pope as their saviour and liberator. For nothing less than that – their liberation under guarantee from the excesses of royal supervision – was the purpose of the mission of 1279. The bishop of Rieti was not to be fobbed off with vague promises and excuses. Action was demanded.[2] But it was not forthcoming. There is no evidence either that the bishop was permitted to present the ultimatum or that the two nuncios who did come in 1280 – the Templar, Pontius de Broet, and Petrus Teobaldiscus de Urbe, *sergens noster*[3] – succeeded in wringing from the king any of the concessions demanded by the dissident prelates. The pope and his agents were powerless to free the Castilian Church from its bondage, and all that was left to the prelates was to seek a solution through direct political action. They were soon provided with an opportunity.

When the Infante Sancho raised the rebel's flag at Valladolid in May 1282 he was immediately joined by droves of abbots and half a dozen bishops, at least two of whom had risen to eminence in the royal chancery and owed their position almost entirely to the man whom they were now rejecting, Alfonso X.[4] Sancho's success in

---

[1] For the Portuguese *gravamina,* see Herculano, *História,* v, 208 ff. A doctored version of them was entered in *Reg. Clem. IV,* 669; the full text is in ADB, Gav. das Notícias Várias, 26. The prohibition of councils and seizure of *tercias* were only two of the items repeated in the 1279 *memoriale.* Moreover, the archbishop of Compostela, who may well have stage-managed the Castilian appeal, must certainly have known about the earlier appeal from his Portuguese suffragans. See also the terms of the Portuguese concordat of 1289–90, and King Dinis's concession of Aug. 1292 regarding clerical export of money: *Reg. Nich. IV,* 716; Monte Pereira (ed.), *Documentos históricos da ciudade de Évora,* i, 35. Cf. above, p. 139.

[2] *Reg. Nich. III,* 743: 'Notandum quod intentio est domini nostri: non perfunctorie, non verbaliter, non generalibus verbis, non quesitis coloribus, non excusationibus frivolis, sed factis et congruentibus cautelis rex satisfaciat votis eius.'

[3] *Ibid.* 676 (Feb. 1280); AC Toledo, I.7.I.1.3.: *Cum dilectum,* 10 April 1280.

[4] *MHE,* II, 67–70. For Melendo of Astorga and Suero Pérez of Zamora, see, respectively, *ES,* XVI, 243–4; below, Chs 10, 12. The other four were the bishops of Mondoñedo, Túy, Badajoz and Coria.

attracting such men was a judgement on his father's refusal to allow them a life of their own. For all their conservative instincts – their resentment of the mendicants, for example, 'cosa especialmente curiosa' in the view of one recent writer, and their anxiety about recent administrative innovations[1] – the rebel churchmen cannot be cast as ecclesiastical backwoodsmen, as distinguished from political prelates who remained loyal. No 'court–country' polarity will account for the taking of sides for and against Alfonso X. Political rebellion was the result of ecclesiastical repression: there had been faint rumblings fifteen years before. But it was not the golden gate to *libertas ecclesiastica*, because rebels and loyalists were all playing the same, political game. Their more or less well-attuned antennae picked up different signals, but the main preoccupation of both groups was the preservation of their association, in however servile a capacity, with the civil power. Hence, neither the rebels, who made plans to hold regular councils,[2] nor the loyalists, who identified themselves with John of Abbeville and the defence of *libertas ecclesiastica*,[3] can be described as 'reformers'. Moreover, since 1279 the episcopal programme and the papacy had parted company: in August 1283 Martin IV declared for Alfonso and against Sancho and his conciliar bishops.[4]

It remains to be seen how far the new king would depart from his father's methods in order to accommodate the demands of his episcopal friends.

[1] *Ibid.* ii, 95–6: 'Quod adhibeatur remedium super molestationibus predicatorum et minorum quas cotidie inferunt ecclesiis et clero et monasteriis, iura eorum contra suum ordinem indebite usurpantes' (cf. Suárez Fernández, *CHE*, xvi, 16); 'Quod dominus Sancius ordinet chancellariam suam prout consuevit a suis avis et proavis ordinari.' (I have emended the *MHE* text).

[2] At Valladolid they arranged for biennial councils, the first of which was to be at Benavente on *Jubilate* Sunday (9 May) 1283. On that occasion they revised their plans: councils were to be annual and were to occur on 26 April 'in loco ubi germanitas regnorum Legionis et Galleciae fuerit celebranda': *MHE*, ii, 70, 97.

[3] *Ibid.* ii, 61 (above, p. 53). In Jan. 1283 Martin IV refused a request from Alfonso, of all people, that a papal legate be sent: *Reg. Mart. IV*, 300.

[4] *Ibid.* 479.

Chapter 10

THE CASTILIAN CHURCH
AT THE END
OF THE THIRTEENTH CENTURY

The rebel bishops of 1282–3 imagined that they were witnessing the dawn of a brave new world in which they would be permitted to consult freely together while the king restrained the mendicants whose 'molestations' they so energetically deplored. But it was a false dawn. The Infante Sancho was using them just as his uncle and namesake had used them in 1257–8. Very soon they discovered, like Falstaff, the difference between the reckless youth and the reverend signior. The former had led them to believe that the clock might be turned back. All that the latter turned, though, was his own coat, which he did with all the dexterity of the late archbishop of Toledo.

For the bishops not the least galling feature of Sancho IV's treatment of them was his positive enthusiasm for the mendicants: by the close of 1284 the king had lent a helping hand to four Dominican houses,[1] and in the following February he gave solemn warning to the bishops and clergy of the awful consequences of harassing the Franciscan Order in his realm.[2] Thus their expectation that Sancho would curb the friars was disappointed. There had been nothing 'curious' about their attitude. It was an episcopal commonplace throughout Europe and shared by all who felt their interests threatened by those comparative newcomers. The mendicants represented as great a threat to the 'old order' in the Church as did emergent Aragon in the sphere of international politics at that very time.[3] But poverty made the Spanish Churches especially sensitive to the success of these interlopers in securing a share of the limited supply of ecclesiastical alms and patronage. All over the Peninsula the friars

---

[1] Toledo, Salamanca, Burgos, the nuns of Madrid: Gaibrois de Ballesteros, *Sancho IV*, III, v, xi–xii, xviii–xxiii (nos 7, 16–18, 31, 33–4, 37).
[2] Publ. Carrión, *AIA*, v, 127–30.   [3] Cf. Jordan of Osnabrück, above, p. 153.

clashed with bishops, cathedral chapters and the older Orders.[1] At court, though – and especially at the Castilian court – they won a firm foothold early on and, as confessors, soon established squatters' rights on the king's conscience.[2] In 1264 Alfonso X openly expressed his devotion to them, and episcopal resentment was hardly less notorious: it was hinted at in the 1279 submission to Nicholas III, given a public airing four years later, and reported to Honorius IV in 1285 when the Order of Preachers sought papal protection against 'nonnulli qui nomen domini recipere in vacuum non formidant'.[3]

By then, though, the mendicants were as firmly bound to Sancho as they had been to his father, even during the civil war (*pace* Ballesteros).[4] Their unique capacity for changing masters stemmed from their intrinsic value to the king. Possessing, as they did, such a monopoly of talent and ability, they were essential to Sancho. So were they to the Castilian Church at large, as was proved during the civil war itself, in the very year of the bishops' complaint about them, when the illiterate clique within the chapter of Jaén had to engage the assistance of certain Franciscans because they were not able to cope with the Latin language themselves.[5] But their alliance with the new king did not necessarily presuppose the advancement of the principles of education, religion or learning. The expertise of the friars was not infrequently misapplied. It was, for example, a Dominican who forged the papal dispensation in favour of the illicit liaison of Sancho and María de Molina.[6] Moreover, it boded ill for the cause of reform – which the Dominicans had done so much to advance in Aragon forty years before – that the individual of that Order most signally

---

[1] See below, Ch. 12.

[2] For royal patronage of the friars in the 1230s, see Lucas of Túy, *Chronicon Mundi*, 113. Alfonso X's nephew, Juan Manuel, advised his son always to have a Dominican confessor: *Libro Infinido*, ed. Gayangos, *BAE*, LI, 266. For Franciscan confessors, see López, *AIA*, XXXI, 5 ff.

[3] Finke, *Ungedruckte Dominikanerbriefe*, 55; *Reg. Nich. III*, 743: 'Item occasione nove religionis institute ab eo ecclesie multipliciter aggravantur'; *MHE*, II, 96; *inc. Habundans malitia*, 13 Sept. 1285: AHN, 3022/8.

[4] See above, p. 137. In April 1282, the prior provincial of the Dominicans (Munio of Zamora), together with other leading friars and the Franciscan bishop of Burgos, Fernando, remained loyal to Alfonso in the face of immediate danger: *MHE*, II, 59–63. Cf. Ballesteros, *BRAH*, CXIX, 175.

[5] Ximena, *Catálogo de los obispos de Jaén*, 228.

[6] Marcos Pous, *CTEER*, VIII, 97.

favoured by the king, and promoted at his instance to the see of Palencia in 1294, was very far indeed from being a paragon of virtue. The prelate in question was Munio of Zamora who, three years before, had been removed from the post of Master-General of the Order by Nicholas IV on account of certain serious but unspecified offences. It is necessary, however, that we pry a little into the circumstances of his case – circumstances over which the pope deemed it prudent to draw a discreet veil. The incident cannot be dismissed as 'a Castilian interlude hardly worth the solving'.[1] For it illustrates both the frustration experienced by those bishops who had put their trust in the rebel Infante in 1282, and the attitude of the rebel, after he had become king, to the associated questions of royal control and episcopal prestige.

The papal vendetta against Munio of Zamora has been ascribed to a variety of causes. It has been suggested both that Nicholas IV was by nature an hispanophobe and that Boniface VIII, who forced him to resign the see of Palencia in July 1296, suspected him of being implicated in the fabrication of Sancho's marriage bull.[2] Not until 1925, though, was a plausible explanation offered when, in her study of Munio, Gaibrois de Ballesteros drew attention to a letter of July 1281, which had then only recently been published, in which the prioress of S. María de Zamora informed Cardinal Ordonho of Tusculum of the havoc that had been caused in her house by a group of nuns within the community who had denied the bishop of Zamora's authority and his rights of visitation, associating themselves instead with the local Dominican friars. And by association the prioress, María Martínez, meant precisely that. The friars had frequently spent the night there, had accompanied the young nuns to private rooms, had dallied with them 'muy desulutamientre', had exchanged habits with them, and had wandered about the place in their birthday-suits 'comol dia que nascian'. Their leader, she added, was *ffre Monio*.[3]

Was this the Munio of Zamora who, at Florence seven weeks before, had been appointed Spanish provincial by the General Chap-

---

[1] Boase, *Boniface VIII*, 198. For a detailed account of Munio's career, see Mortier, *Histoire des Maîtres Généraux*, II, 251–93.

[2] Hernando de Castillo (1584), *Historia general de Sancto Domingo*, I, fo. 491v; Boase (1933), *loc. cit.*

[3] Publ. Castro, *B. Hisp.*, XXV, 196–7: orig. in AC Zamora, 13/60 (together with a Latin version of the same).

ter of the Order? Mercedes Gaibrois insisted that it was: here was 'la respuesta categórica' to the hitherto unanswered questions about his dismissal.[1] And there is further evidence which suggests that she was right. It does not appear that there was more than one Munio of Zamora, and that the deposed Master-General was punished for the sins of a namesake. Had there been, then the archdeacon of Zamora, Pedro Anays, would have taken the trouble to specify which of them it was who owed him 573 *maravedís*, when he made his will in August 1294.[2] Moreover, when Bishop Suero Pérez visited the convent in July 1279 in order to reinstate María Martínez as prioress, he was told that *frater Munio* had taken a leading part in the disturbances which had marred the régime of the anti-episcopal prioress, Jimena, threatening with perpetual imprisonment any lady who remained loyal to the bishop's jurisdiction.[3] Two of the most energetic of the rebels, Elvira Pérez and Sancha Garcés, were referred to as 'consobrines fratris Munionis' in the following March by the prior of Valladolid, executor of the papal mandate against them issued by Nicholas III after the bishop had informed the pope of his findings there.[4]

Bishop Suero Pérez was a fiery character and adept at making enemies for himself. But he was not a doctrinaire opponent either of these nuns in particular or of the Dominicans in general. In March 1264 he consecrated the nuns' new church after they had been flooded out of their former establishment,[5] and in the following February he

---

[1] Mortier, II, 171–2; Gaibrois de Ballesteros in *Finke Festschrift*, 140.

[2] AC Zamora, 18/20: 'ffrey Monio y la priora allende rrio'.

[3] AC Zamora, 13/61: 'frater Munio comminatus est istis qui fovebant partem ecclesie Zamorensis quod caperet eas et poneret eas perpetuo in catenis'.

[4] AC Zamora, 13/62, containing the text of the letter (*Sua nobis*, 1 Dec. 1279), together with that of the prior's summons of 31 March 1280. Some thirty nuns were summoned to a hearing at Valladolid on 29 April. Not having appeared – 'maguer las atendi diez dias despues del termino' – they were excommunicated on 8 May.

[5] Gaibrois de Ballesteros, *loc. cit.*, 140, n. 58, There is some doubt about the date of their move (1238?), since the nuns' miraculous relic which saved them from a watery grave in the Duero allowed their records to perish: J. López, *Tercera parte*, 237; Álvarez Martínez, *Historia de Zamora*, 190. However, on 23 Jan. 1259, Alexander IV associated the community with the Augustinian convent at Madrid, at the instance of the noblewoman, Jimena Rodríguez: *inc. Cum sicut*, AC Zamora, 1/3. 'Augustinian', of course, meant 'secundum instituta ordinis fratrum predicatorum': thus began the trouble. The ladies were decently scrupulous about trifles – for example, the possibility of simony in their purchase of a church from the bishop, about which the papal *familiaris*, fr. Petrus de Regio, set their minds at rest on 2 May 1273 (AC Zamora, 1/5). For the bishop's other problems, see below, Ch 12.

granted the friars of Salamanca an indulgence to assist them with the construction of their new premises in the wake of a similar disaster there.[1] By the autumn of 1272, however, he and the prioress had fallen out, and Gregory X was requested to make his sentence of interdict against her effective. Not that the papal mandate had any immediate effect: it was only in October 1279 that its León executors referred it to the cantor of Ávila for immediate attention.[2] And by then the bishop had gained *entrée* to the embattled nunnery and had emerged with new and astonishing revelations.

The record of his visitation of July 1279 contains the evidence submitted by some thirty nuns who said that they had resisted the advances of the friars and had contented themselves with the thought of episcopal jurisdiction. The others had gone. Led by Dona Catherina of Zamora and her paramour, they were touring the surrounding villages selling things. Those who were left behind were possibly vindictive and almost certainly disappointed women, and allowance should be made for this when considering their version of events. Yet, even with this proviso, their account of what had happened since the previous episcopal visitation would have been worthy of Coulton's attention – or, alternatively, of that of Havelock Ellis whose account of Spanish nuns as bandits and bullfighters is well known.[3]

> Nuns fret not at their convent's narrow room,
> And hermits are contented with their cells.

Not so, however, the nuns and hermits of Zamora during the 1270s.

When last there, Suero Pérez had dismissed Dona Jimena and established María Martínez as prioress in her stead. He had also forbidden the Dominicans to enter the place. But that deprivation proved insupportable to those ladies who looked to the friars for the consolations of religion and what may, charitably, be described as companionship. Almost immediately their promises to the bishop were forgotten. It was not only the rule of silence that was broken, as everyone admitted. So were the gates. The party without maintained

---

1 AHN, 1894/16. They had moved in 1256, after the Tormes had overflowed a second time: AHN, 1893/16 (Potthast, 10417); Cuervo, *Historiadores del convento de San Esteban de Salamanca*, I, 10; III, 628.

2 AC Zamora, 13 / 63, containing the text of Gregory's letter of 31 Oct. 1272, *Sua nobis*.

3 *The Soul of Spain* (London, 1937), 100.

contact with a fifth column within, where Dona Stefanía led the resistance. Missives were brought in by womenfolk 'scriptas in digitis'. When the friars lobbed a letter into choir from outside it was greeted by a *Te Deum* intoned by Stefanía, 'quia dicebant quod moniales incorpore erant ordini fratrum predicatorum'. For that reason María Martínez was given a miserable time, being told by the dissidents that 'she was not their prioress but St Augustine's'. They called her a heretic and abused the memory of her mother and grand-mother. They insulted her 'cum digitis ad oculos'. They made up dirty songs about her, one of which had the refrain: 'Marina, bacallar, caraça, asnal.' To all this she responded cheerfully by putting the troublemakers in the stocks. But they were immediately released, and stones were thrown. Dona Catherina's lover warned her that if she did not go away she would be locked up and killed. Meanwhile they put her between two doors and squeezed. This was not good for her. And they threatened to treat the bishop likewise, marching about and brandishing sticks the while.

While some of them were out walking in the town one poor nun had her bottom pinched by a friar on the bridge. But, bad as that was, it pales in comparison with the scenes that were enacted when they opened the main gate and let the friars in. '"Aqui casamiento de bon lugar", exclaimed brother Juan. So did brother Nicolás, and immediately made love to Inés Domínguez.' They were not alone. Each of the brothers had his sister, and some had several. Inés, in fact, made three hearts beat as one; and Juan Daviáncos (who was old enough both to have known better and to have attempted less) sat with her in the infirmary and disparaged his rival, saying 'mia mengengelina, non diligatis puerum sed diligatis me senem, quia magis valet bonus senex quam malus puer'. It was hardly the time to use the second person plural. Still if 'old me' was out of practice he made the most of his chances. While he was supposed to be preaching he wandered around the choir muttering 'mia mongelina'. Munio, meanwhile, was saying that he would remove Orobona's habit – and apparently not merely as a symbolic gesture. Pedro Gutiérrez was in full cry, running hither and thither. Eventually he cornered a clutch of girls in the kitchen. They did not reciprocate his feelings, were forced to seek the seclusion that an oven grants, and all but suffocated. Not every night was like that, but there was a regular arrangement whereby the nuns took in the friars' washing, received smart presents in return and retained certain rather intimate garments as souvenirs. Much of the time they seem to have spent stark naked, though doubtless they dressed up when they all went off together for an evening's drinking, leaving the battered prioress to recite compline by herself.[1]

The bishop had a good case, then, and, even with his record, could expect to be vindicated by the commission of enquiry which Nicholas III entrusted to the prior of Valladolid at the end of 1279.[2] And two years later his chances of success looked even brighter. For the Infante Sancho was friendly also, and took his part against the civil authorities of Zamora when they chose him as arbiter of their differences.[3] It is hardly surprising that the dean, Pedro Yáñez, stipulated in his will of April 1281 that his 50 *maravedís* bequest to the local mendicants should be executed only 'if it please my lord bishop'.[4] Nor need we look any further for explanation of the *molestationes predicatorum et minorum* to which Suero Pérez, together with the other rebel bishops, alluded in May 1283. There was nothing 'especially curious' about that grievance.[5]

Yet, in the event, the civil war robbed Suero Pérez of satisfaction. When the case next attracted papal attention, six years after his visitation, it was the friars' version, not his, that was contained in Honorius IV's bull of September 1285. It reads like a classic case of episcopal highhandedness. Unprovoked – so their version ran – he had forbidden them to preach and administer the sacraments either to the people or to the nuns. When the prioress – Dona Jimena, evidently – had objected, he had come to the convent 'as an enemy', dismissed her 'without reasonable cause' and intruded his own appointee in her place, incarcerating some of the sisters and excommunicating others. Some forty of them he had expelled, so that for many years they had been forced to wander about dragging out a miserable existence 'in

[1] AC Zamora, 13/61.
[2] AC Zamora, 13/62. On 5 Dec. 1279 the pope instructed the dean of Salamanca, Pedro Pérez, to investigate the wholesale alienation of conventual property which had occurred. The hearing was held in the following November. The nuns had had permission to acquire property, but not to sell it, since 2 July 1265: AC Zamora, 1/6 (text of *Ad audientiam nostram*); 13/65; 13/64 (*Devotionis vestre*).
[3] AC Zamora, 11.ii/10, containing the text of Martin IV's letter, *Sua nobis*, confirming the Infante's findings, 7 May 1281.
[4] AC Zamora, 18/9.
[5] Cf. above, p. 221.

animarum suarum periculum'. For this Archbishop Gonzalo (who four days before had been commissioned to protect the Order from episcopal excesses throughout the kingdom) was charged to summon him to the Curia within four months.[1] His death in the following spring meant that Honorius remained unenlightened,[2] and in April 1287 his successor, Bishop Pedro, was persuaded by Sancho IV to make a settlement which was wholly favourable to the friars and conceded unreservedly to them jurisdiction over the convent of nuns.[3] True, justice of a sort eventually caught up with Munio, and not even the king's friendship and funds could protect him from the papal campaign when at last it was launched.[4] But the faults that make us men – which were adduced in his favour at the General Chapter of 1290[5] – evidently did endear him to Sancho, and suggest that an old reprobate would make a capital bishop of Palencia.[6]

It was not only his episcopal adherents that the ex-rebel betrayed by advancing a churchman with a record such as Munio's. He also betrayed his better self, as expressed in his *Castigos* – a treatise which was in the course of preparation in the very year of Munio's promotion.[7] 'El buen perlado', as envisaged by Sancho, would have met with the approval of John of Abbeville himself. He was to be learned and chaste, concerned not for his own well-being or with that of his *linaje* but solely for that of God's Church. If the Almighty granted him prosperity, let his motive for rejoicing be that he was thereby enabled to be even more generous in almsgiving.[8]

---

[1] AHN, 3022/8; *Reg. Hon. IV*, 147.
[2] Suero Pérez died between May and mid-June: Gaibrois de Ballesteros, *Sancho IV*, I, 128. Álvarez Martínez, 200, prints the text of his epitaph.
[3] J. López, *Tercera parte*, 240–1.
[4] Gaibrois de Ballesteros, *Finke Festschrift*, 141–2. The king's gift of money to Cardinal Ordonho in July 1285, to which she refers (citing the royal accounts: AHN, Códices, 1009bis, fo. 12v) *may* have been designed to purchase the silence of one who had been informed about Munio four years before by María Martínez. But that is not the *only* possible explanation: Sancho had other business pending at the Curia.
[5] 'Nunquam in capitulis generalibus, exceptis dumtaxat quibusdam levioribus culpis, sine quibus hec vita non ducitur, quas constitucio inter leves culpas connumerat, culpabilis est inventus': *Litterae encyclicae*, ed. Reichert, 154.
[6] Mortier, II, 573 ff. In 1291 the Dominican General Chapter met at Palencia, at Sancho's express wish: *Acta Capitulorum Generalium*, ed. Reichert, I, 270.
[7] Ed. A. Rey from MSS. which are free of the later interpolations that have devalued the work as a reliable source. Cf. Rey's discussion, 9 ff.
[8] *Ibid.* 104 ff.

But the episcopate, it had to be admitted, fell far short of this ideal. Indeed, what it enshrined – to Sancho's official despair – were the seven deadly sins.[1] And, reverting to reality, we may ascribe much of the blame for that to the moralising monarch himself. During the civil war itself he had provided a grim example of what, in practice, he meant by 'el buen perlado'. When Bishop Juan Alfonso of Palencia remained loyal to Alfonso X in April 1282,[2] Sancho attempted to oust him from his see and replace him with the dean of Seville, Ferrán Pérez, an archetypal curial cleric with a distinctly unimpressive *curriculum vitae*.[3] It was no difficult task for the old king to paint a sombre picture of a servant whose record and antecedents had not struck him as objectionable while he had observed the political proprieties, and the dean's dossier was duly published by Alfonso's proctor, Master Benedict of Pontecorvo, at Martin IV's court at Orvieto on 24 April 1284, by which time – unbeknown apparently to those present – the king was dead.[4] Significantly, Master Benedict's main point was not that the dean had sinned against nature, as was well known, but that he had infringed the king's patronal rights, his 'possessio vel quasi' of control of elections in the cathedral churches of Castile and Leon. In the apparently erroneous belief that Bishop Juan Alfonso had died,[5] therefore, the proctor protested most vigorously against the dean's intrusion without reference to the king, as was customary.[6] Details of the man's personal record seem to have

[1] *Ibid.* 109–10: 'Ca oy dia sy pararemos mientes, todos los siete pecados mortales en los servidores della los fallaras.'
[2] *MHE*, II, 59 ff.
[3] Alfonso X had employed him in negotiations with the rebel Infante Felipe, through whose good offices he had secured the deanery of Seville in Jan. 1255: *Crónica del Rey Don Alfonso* (*BAE*, LXVI), 16; *Reg. Alex. IV*, 131. Muñoz Torrado, *Iglesia de Sevilla*, 142–3, confuses him with another royal agent, Ferrán Pérez de Foçes. Cf. Zurita, *Anales* I, fo. 232ra–b; *MHE*, II, 15. In 1280 Nicholas III suspected him of having received bribes from the would-be archbishop of Toledo, Ferrán Rodríguez: Serrano, *Cartulario de Covarrubias*, 119–20.
[4] Cf. Ballesteros, *Alfonso X*, 1056.
[5] Unless he had a successor of the same name, Juan Alfonso lived until Nov. 1293: Fernández del Pulgar, *Historia de Palencia*, II, 346 ff. Indeed, in Jan. 1287 Sancho IV assured the *concejo* of Palencia that he meant no harm to them by the privileges which he had accorded to Juan Alfonso 'quando eramos Inffante, nin despues que ffuemos Rey': Gaibrois de Ballesteros, *Sancho IV*, III, lxxxix (no. 144).
[6] AC Toledo, X.2.A.2.5: '...cum de consuetudine et de iure sit quod mors prelati in ecclesiis cathedralibus regnorum Castelle et Legionis notificari debeat et consueverit

been regarded by the proctor as rather less damning than that. Damning they were, though. His sodomy was public knowledge, and but for *reverentia ordinis clericalis* the secular courts would have consigned him to the flames long since. He possessed the deanery of Palencia as well as that of Seville and prebends at Toledo, Burgos, Cuenca and Husillos – all without papal dispensation. Moreover, he was not ordained and was rarely seen in choir, preferring to spend his time hunting and engaged in secular pursuits. He was excommunicated as a partisan of the rebel Infante and *conspirator publicus*. Indeed, he was alleged to have encouraged Sancho to break with his father; which was not surprising since he was a descendant of that arch-traitor, Vellido Adolfo.[1] The recital certainly justified the rather lame conclusion, that Ferrán Pérez was not episcopal material.[2] Yet he continued to enjoy Sancho IV's favour, and efforts were made to secure for him the sees of Sigüenza and Seville.[3]

Sancho's support of the unsavoury dean provides further proof of the bishops' naivety in assuming that the events of 1282–3 might be turned to their and the Castilian Church's advantage. They had merely exchanged one slave-driver for another. Personal promotion remained the prime consideration, and continued to be most surely secured in the royal service. Arias of Lugo, for example, was elected by the chapter in 1294 at the direction of the king whose interests he was guarding at the papal Curia. And on his return a grateful monarch rewarded both him and his see.[4] But the grapes of wrath were as sour as the fruits of victory were sweet. On Sancho's accession the archdeacon of Oviedo, Ferrán Alfonso, paid the penalty for having

---

notificari regi eidem, et morte notificata huiusmodi et iam electione celebrata eidem regi per sollempnes nuntios presentari, ut benignum sicut moris est prebetur assensum; et in ista possessione, vel quasi, dictus dominus Alfonsus tempore suo et predecessorum suorum suis temporibus fuerit pacifice et quiete tam in ecclesia Palentina, cuius est ipse patronus, quam in aliis ecclesiis regnorum suorum, et nunc ecclesia Palentina per mortem domini Johannis Alfonsi vacante...'

1 *Ibid.*: '...cum...fueritque et sit proditor et de genere proditorum descendens, scilicet de genere Bellid Adolfe qui dominum suum dominum Sancium quondam regem Legionis prodiit et interfecit'. Vellido Adolfo murdered Sancho II of Leon and Castile in Oct. 1072. See Valdeavellano, *Historia de España*, i, ii, 319.
2 *Ibid.*: 'et est minus sufficientis scientie ad dignitatem episcopalem obtinendum'.
3 *Reg. Hon. IV*, 670; *Reg. Nich. IV*, 493. It cannot have been much to his advantage that Honorius IV referred the Sigüenza affair to the bishop of Palencia in Nov. 1286. For his political services to Sancho, see Sánchez Belda, *AHDE*, XXI–II, 177.
4 *ES*, XII, 86–90; *Colección de documentos históricos*, i, 88–9.

remained loyal to Alfonso X in 1282[1] by being deprived of his benefices and driven out of the country on the flimsiest of pretexts. That was bad enough in itself, as Cardinal Jordan of S. Eustacius – whose chaplain the archdeacon was – reminded the king in August 1287, and not the sort of thing that Fernando III, his exemplary grandfather, would have done, the cardinal fondly imagined.[2] The worst aspect of the affair, though, was, in his opinion, the part played by Bishop Martín of Astorga who, with not a thought for *libertas ecclesiastica*, had actually led the attack on the archdeacon.[3]

Clearly the cardinal was quite hopelessly out of touch with Castilian reality. Bishop Martín was the king's man first and the Church's second, if at all. He had his family to consider, and but for being the king's man he would not have been a bishop anyway. It was only because he and his predecessors had allowed themselves to forget where their first loyalties ought perhaps to have lain that the bishops of Astorga presided over a relatively prosperous see.[4] Moreover, Spanish churchmen, then as previously, were peculiarly susceptible to the whispering-campaign and backstairs-politics which had been the undoing of the cardinal's protégé: he was not the only one to feel the draught of royal disfavour during Sancho's reign. Gómez García, who died as bishop-elect of Mondoñedo in July 1286, was another victim of the same witch-hunt as had brought about the archdeacon's discomfiture and which was automatically incurred by whomsoever the king suspected of not sharing his own conviction about the im-

---

[1] *MHE*, II, 59.

[2] AC Toledo, E.7.D.2.3: '...quia fuerat vobis suggestum quod negotia per vos commissa vestris procuratoribus in Romana curia expedienda idem archidiaconus impediverat expediri...Rex Ferrandus avus vester...consimiles litteras contra ecclesiasticas personas in dignitatibus constitutas ad suggestionem simplicem alicuius forte malevoli non mandasset...Credendum est potius suggestionibus callidis emulorum per subreptionis astutiam quam ex deliberatione vestri consilii manavisse.' This was to take the charitable view of both grandfather and grandson. Cf. above, pp. 139–40.

[3] *Ibid.*: 'Utinam dominus Astoricensis, in regno Legionis vester prothonotarius, ut cum reverentia ipsius loquamur, curam sibi commissi officii et debitum regiminis pastoralis ac statum ecclesiastice libertatis ante subscriptionem predictam provida deliberatione pensasset.' There was a special reason for the cardinal's sense of disappointment in Bishop Martín: only nine months before he had been one of the three cardinals who had authorised his translation from Calahorra to Astorga: *Reg. Hon. IV*, 717.

[4] *ES*, XVI, 246; Hergueta, *RABM*, IX, 330 ff.

portance of securing papal approval of his illicit liaison with María de Molina – a cause for which he was himself prepared to lie and cheat.[1] But whereas, ironically, Sancho's spite brought Ferrán Alfonso a bishopric,[2] the malevolent gossip about Gómez García had the desired result of costing him his, so that his epitaph in Toledo Cathedral, with its phrases about the ephemerality of worldly achievement and its refrain of 'here today, gone tomorrow', may be regarded as rather more than just another exercise in formal rhetoric.[3] It may quite properly serve to commemorate many more of his colleagues, bishops and others, who, having set out to fish for rich prizes at court, soon discovered that their main preoccupation there was to stay alive and afloat.

In December 1283, while the rebel bishops were planning the constitution of the *post-bellum* Church, some of the consequences of this continuing royal tutelage were considered in the course of a letter written by the local clergy, *los naturales*, of the church of Jaén. The letter, which was sent to Archbishop Gonzalo of Toledo, was a potted history of their diocese, and it had a moral.[4] It recalled that

---

[1] Jaffé–Finke, *AHDE*, III, 298 ff.

[2] After a further clash with the king and a spell of imprisonment he took refuge at the Curia. By then he was dean of Oviedo, and in 1295 he was awarded that see by Boniface VIII on the death there of the capitular candidate: *ES*, xxxviii, 218, 220; *Reg. Bon. VIII*, 580; AC Oviedo, A/11/1; AHN, 1602/16 (reg. García Larragueta, *Catálogo*, 512, 510). But for Sancho's vendetta against him it is unlikely that he would have been at hand. He was not at the Curia by choice, and in his will referred to Sancho's reign as 'primo tempore quo eram in curia Romana': AC Oviedo, B/6/12 (reg. García Larragueta, 565).

[3]   ...Quam sit vita brevis, quam sit brevis...
    In me cognosce qui mea metra legis.
    Qui quondam potui, qui quondam magnus habebar,
    Jam meo nil possum pulvis et ossa manens.
    Nil mihi divicie, mihi nil genus adque juventus
    Profuit. Hec vita nichil est aliut nisi ventus.
    Ergo tibi caveas, ne te deceptio mundi
    Fallat. Nam poteris cras, sicut ego, mori:
publ. Fita, *BRAH*, xx, 458. For the circumstances of his fall from grace, see Gaibrois de Ballesteros, I, 88 ff. It was very sudden. In the previous year the king had recommended him as enjoying 'locum excellentiorem' among his clerics, and he was still in favour as late as May 1286: Robert, *BRAH*, xx, 345; *As Gavetas da Torre do Tombo*, I, no. 217.

[4] AC Toledo, X.1.D.2.1. Parts of this letter were published by Ximena in the seventeenth century – but parts only, 'por no ofender la modestia y piedad cristiana de los que la leyeren', in view of the 'incredible calumnies' about the bishops which it contained: *Catálogo de Jaén*, 211, 225–6, 228, 235.

ever since the re-establishment of the Christian religion at Jaén in 1246 the cathedral chapter had consisted of two groups: themselves (*los naturales*) and *los de Soria*. Soria, some four hundred kilometres to the north, was prolific of royal clerks – for which reason Alfonso X had urged its elevation to cathedral status in 1267: a nice illustration, incidentally, of the royal scale of values;[1] and, according to *los naturales*, *los de Soria* had been using Jaén as an ecclesiastical convenience, monopolising the best benefices in the cathedral church. To date, they complained – ignoring the unhappy history of the Dominican bishop of Baeza, Domingo, in the pre-1246 period[2] – all three of their bishops had been Sorians. The first, Pedro Martínez the royal chancellor, had arrived there as a corpse, having died on his way back from Rocamadour. So they could hardly complain about him. They remembered his successor, Pascal, though. In general an admirable person, he had had only one serious fault: his tendency to bend over backwards in his anxiety to award benefices to *los de Soria* rather than to *los naturales*.[3] And Martín, the third bishop, had bent even further.[4]

1 *Reg. Clem. IV*, 406 (publ. Loperráez, *Descripción de Osma*, III, 200–2): 'Famosum inter alia loca illarum partium et fecundum in populis, tales producit alumnos tam clericos quam laicos per quos non solum regalis curia verum etiam tam propinque quam remote partes Yspanie honorantur.' The results of a census which was done only three years later do not, however, support the claim that the place was well populated: 777 inhabitants in Soria itself and a further 2,385 scattered among 238 villages, with an average population of 1.18 per square kilometre is hardly *fecundus*. See Jimeno, *BRAH*, CXLII, 216–17. Had Jaén attracted the cultivators as well as the clerics, as the frontier area had done elsewhere? Or was its royal nursery, in reality, Soria's only recommendation? For Soria clerics in Fernando III's chancery, see Millares Carlo, *AHDE*, III, 289–90.

2 Paralysis forced Domingo into early retirement: in Jan. 1246 Innocent IV reminded him of the 'exemplum beati Job': *Reg. Inn. IV*, 1664. He subsequently made a thorough nuisance of himself, making off with books and ornaments belonging to the church of Jaén and leading 'vitam detestabilem et in conspectu Dei ac hominum displicentem'; and, with the reputation of the Dominican Order in mind, the pope ordered him to be placed under house arrest in a distant convent: ASV, arm. XXXI. 72, fo. 107r (Schillmann, *Formularsammlung*, 461).

3 For Pascal, see above, Ch. 6; for his connexion with Soria, *Reg. Inn. IV*, 4901. In April 1251 the pope scolded Fernando III for having failed to endow the church of Jaén: *ibid.* 5216. Alfonso X proposed Pascal for Toledo in March 1266. He died abroad in Dec. 1275: *Reg. Clem. IV*, 1036; AC Toledo, X.1.D.1.1.

4 AC Toledo, X.1.D.2.1: 'En ninguna cosa non remedo al bispo don Pasqual qual si non en levar los suyos adelant e posponer los naturales de aca mucho mas que non fizo don Pasqual.' In July 1264 he had been cantor of the church and one of the king's clerics: *Reg. Urb. IV*, 1680.

Martín, however, had just died, and *los naturales* were determined to hold out for home rule and have a local man as bishop for a change. Civil war was being waged, and the king's attention was otherwise engaged: they would never have a better chance. But they managed to muff it, thanks to some particularly maladroit electoral tactics, and yet another Sorian, Juan Ibáñez the *magister scolarum*, was elected. This left them with only one card to play: an appeal to the archbishop. It was their method of playing this card that brought blushes to the cheeks of their historian almost four hundred years later.

Despite the nature of his office at Jaén, Juan Ibáñez was not one of their great minds. In fact he was illiterate, and, what was worse, even the choir-boys knew it. Amongst those always severe critics he was a laughing-stock; which must have pained him, for – as *los naturales* slyly remarked – he had children of his own. He also had a plausible way with him and talked them into signing his election decree. They did this (they explained later) lest they should appear bad sports. That settled, the bishop-elect set off with his friends for the court of the rebel Infante, having first arranged for some Franciscans from afar to deal with the archbishop, thus saving himself an interview which, because he had no Latin, Juan Ibáñez did not relish.[1] It was at this point that *los naturales* wrote their letter, and, having had the worst of it for almost forty years, concluded with the lapidary generalisation that 'la falta de los perlados letrados e complidos de mucho bien a traido la tierra a este estado'.

Their appeal was a failure. Juan Ibáñez joined the ranks of Sancho IV's bishops where he was not the only father of a family,[2] and Jaén continued to serve as a rest-home for civil servants. But that final lamentation did not refer merely to the capitular in-fighting of a frontier see. It was a judgement on Alfonso X's choice of bishops and his dealings with the Church in general. It is true that both Alfonso

[1] *Ibid.*: 'E el cabildo pronon semeiar cosa de moços non quiso nenguno contradeçir e firmaron luego el decreto...E tomaron los de Soria el fecho sobre si e la mensageria por yr a don Sancho con el, e son ydos, porque han de razonar en romance. Ca si ante Vos oviessen a yr non querrien a ello meter porque avrien a proponer en latin. E han puesto mas de enviar freyres menores a Vos por la conffirmacion.'

[2] Ximena, 229. Almost four years passed though before, still *ordinandus*, he took his suffragan's oath to the archbishop: AC Toledo, X.1.D.1.1e. Martín of Astorga was also married, and Sancho's secretary and chaplain, Gonzalo Pérez (archdeacon of Úbeda, abbot of Santander; bishop of Jaén, 1301) had two sons: *ES*, XVI, 246; Ximena, 236, 321.

and Sancho are on record as favouring prelates who were *letrados*,[1] and the former's court was certainly a haven of learning where Juan Ibáñez would have been an embarrassment both to himself and to others. But the intellectual disciplines most assiduously cultivated there had no particular relevance to the episcopal calling. The bishops of Astorga and Segorbe were notable or notorious for translations of Arabic texts[2] and medical diagnosis[3] respectively. No theologian, though, of comparable calibre was promoted to a Castilian see during these years. The traditional theology was not a feature of the court's cultural activity, the *Primera Partida* notwithstanding. There is indeed a suggestion in one of Salimbene's anecdotes that by at least some Spaniards the subject was regarded as unworthy of their attention and best left to foreigners.[4] Of course, the shortage of theological bishops was a general European phenomenon, and not confined to Castile. In Castile, however, the combination of this cultural climate and the political status of the prelate did induce a marked reluctance towards episcopal promotion in many of the abler candidates. Adán Pérez took refuge with the Dominicans at the very thought of Plasencia, and Hermannus Alemannus begged Clement IV *humiliter ac instanter* not to appoint him to one of the country's richest sees and claimed to be a bastard so that he might remain a scholar as well.[5]

[1] *Part.* 1.16.2 (Academy ed. 1, 411); *Castigos*, 106.
[2] Hermannus Alemannus, bishop of Astorga, 1266–72. See *ES*, XVI, 241–3. Luquet's article, *Rev. de l'hist. des religions*, XLIV, 407 ff., discusses his translations of Averroes but says nothing of his presumably German origins. At Paris he had studied with the future Clement IV and shared lodgings with him; in Castile he was patronised by Bishop Juan of Burgos: *Reg. Clem. IV*, 1157; Millás Vallicrosa, *Las traducciones orientales*, 56. See also Haskins, *Studies in the History of Medieval Science*, 16.
[3] Aparicio, bishop of Segorbe, 1284–1300 (for these dates, AC Toledo, X.1.G.1.1i–j. Cf. Eubel, *Hierarchia*, 1, 443). His unostentatious bearing and pastoral zeal (which extended to collecting samples of urine) attracted much criticism; and not until the seventeenth century were his eccentric habits appreciated: *VL*, III, 62–3; Villagrasa, *Antigüedad de la iglesia catedral de Segorbe*, 107; Zunzunegui, *AA*, XVI, 15–16. The medical pope, the Portuguese John XXI, was thought equally unprepossessing by Ptolemy of Lucca who criticised him for making himself too approachable. 'Et quamvis magnus fuerit in scientia, modicus tamen fuit in distinctione': *Historia Ecclesiastica*, lib. 23, cap. xxi, *RIS*, XI, 1176.
[4] On failing to qualify as a magician at Toledo, the clerk Philip (archbishop of Ravenna in 1251) was told by his tutor there: 'Vos Lombardi non estis pro arte ista, et ideo dimittatis eam nobis Hyspanis qui homines feroces et similes demonibus sumus. Tu vero, fili, vade Parisius et stude in scriptura divina, quia in ecclesia Dei adhuc futurus es magnus': *Cronica*, ed. Holder-Egger, 393–4.
[5] *Reg. Greg. IX*, 5964 (below, Ch. 12); *Reg. Clem. IV*, 1157.

Amongst the lower clergy for whom the bishops were responsible illiteracy was widespread, John of Abbeville's strictures having apparently produced little practical improvement.[1] And the problem was a practical one. It was hardly surprising that sentences of excommunication were so blandly ignored at Salamanca, as the canons of that church complained to the king in August 1289. Less than thirty years before, a Compostela provincial council had explained why. It was impossible to apply the intricate rules for formal excommunication which IV Lateran and I Lyons had established 'propter imperitiam clericorum qui sententiam excommunicationis non scribere nec formare sciunt'.[2] And the higher clergy were very often no better. From the strictly pastoral point of view the learning of men such as Master Martín, the canon of Orense whose copy of Avicenna was deposited for general use in the cathedral pulpit in 1281, was hardly less barren than the total illiteracy of eight canons of Palencia – almost 20 per cent of the chapter, including the dean and the *magister scolarum* – thirteen years later.[3] By the mid-fourteenth century, at the latest, the papacy had come to accept the situation, and was prepared to admit to benefices 'in tota Ispania et Vasconia' clerks whose minimal intellectual achievements were deemed inadequate elsewhere.[4]

The fault lay with the bishops and, beyond them, with the king whose creatures they were. When John XXII deplored the decay of the Castilian Church in 1318 they were all too clearly the lineal descendants of those who had received such a bad press from Diego García exactly a hundred years before. They kept concubines quite openly, endowed their offspring with church property, forcibly prevented their victims and critics from appealing to the Holy See, and

---

[1] In so far as they concerned the parish clergy, that is.
[2] Gaibrois de Ballesteros, *Sancho IV*, III, clviii (no. 262); López Ferreiro, *Historia de Santiago*, V, appendix 29, cap. 10.
[3] Duro Peña, *HS*, XIV, 187; AC Toledo, X.2.A.1.1 (publ. Mortier, II, 573 ff.). Of 31 canons of Pamplona in Nov. 1254, one only was a graduate and four were illiterate; while at the Cuenca election of March 1280 neither the *capellanus maior* nor the archdeacon of Alarcón knew how to write: Goñi Gaztambide, *Príncipe de Viana*, xviii, 132; AC Toledo, X.1.E.1.1g.
[4] 'Juramentum examinancium in Romana Curia deputatorum', publ. Tangl, *Die päpstlichen Kanzleiordnungen*, 48. Cf. Tihon, *Bull. Inst. hist. belge de Rome*, V, 77. For remarks about Spanish culture in the Statutes of the Spanish College at Bologna (1375–7), see references in Linehan, *Studia Albornotiana*, II.

regarded the diocesan visitation merely as a means of fund-raising.[1] Some idea of the seriousness with which the *visitatio* was treated may be gathered from a treatise devoted to the subject – the *Liber Septenarius* – which was composed not long after 1318 by Rodrigo de Palencia, the archpriest of Carrión, and dedicated to his bishop, Juan de Saavedra.[2] Rather optimistically the author expressed the hope that the work might enliven the bishop's dull moments. But if he derived any pleasure from the *Liber*, then Bishop Juan must have been a very dull fellow indeed. Conceived in terms of the essential sevenness of things, it is extremely heavy going, and for its own sake would not be worth rescuing from oblivion.[3] All that makes it worthy of mention here is the contrast between the theory and the practice of diocesan visitation which, quite incidentally, it highlights. While the text insists that annual visitation is merely the *minimum* obligation, the prologue acknowledges that in fact the bishop's various other preoccupations have a prior claim on his attention.[4]

'For the greater part of the year' the bishop of Palencia was at the royal court or otherwise engaged. The pastoral activity of such prelates was necessarily limited. One such was Bishop Alfonso of Coria, chancellor of the rebel Infante Sancho and subsequently of his widow. During a thirty-year pontificate he hardly ever visited his see, and

---

[1] Goñi Gaztambide, *HS*, VIII, 413.

[2] BC Burgo de Osma, cód. 17, fo. 1ra: 'Reverendo patri domino speciali ac refugio meo singulari, domino Johanni divina clemencia episcopo Palentino ac nobilissimi Infantis domini Petri maiori cancellario, Rodericus vestra plantula et factura vester archipresbiter ac servus inutilis cum debita reverentia ac humilitate servili terram coram vestris pedibus osculatur.' The MS is summarily described by Rojo Orcajo, *BRAH*, XCIV, 728. Cf. García y García, 'La canonística', 432. Bishop Juan was *canciller mayor* to the Infante Pedro by Feb. 1325, and had retired from the position by Jan. 1343: Fernández del Pulgar, III, 14–15.

[3] Fo. 1rb: 'Idcirco in hoc opusculo consideravi si possem... aliquantulum vestrum tedium sublevare.' In addition to sections on the seven sacraments, seven vices, etc., the Clementines are treated as the seventh *liber decretalium,* and under the heading 'Septem sit species falsitatis litterarum apostolicarum' Innocent III's decretal on that subject is reproduced (fos. 27ra, 35rb). Cf. Poole, *Lectures on the History of the Papal Chancery*, 156–7.

[4] Fo. 4vb: 'Non solum semel in anno debemus visitare sed et bis vel ter, si opus fuerit et subditos tales se reddiderint.' Cf. fo. 1va: 'Quia fere pro maiori parte anni estis cum domino rege vel regina seu infante ab ipsis vocatus, et pluribus ibi suis et vestris ac subditorum vestrorum negociis et circa plurima occupatus, ita quod non potestis, ut desideratis, insistere circa subditorum vestrorum salutem studio et labore...'

when Archbishop Rodrigo of Compostela came there in 1315 he found it in a state of almost total collapse 'propter negligentiam et excessus notorios'.[1] The royal court exerted a fatal fascination over the entire peninsular Church. Bishop Soeiro of Lisbon complained to Honorius III about the clergy of his diocese who had abandoned their flocks and were dancing attendance on the king.[2] As early as 1241 it was necessary to remind the Dominicans that, if they went there at all, they ought to concern themselves with creating a peaceful climate and not with prosecuting contentious lawsuits.[3] The openings there for the educated cleric, as royal counsellor or preacher, were stressed even by Ramon Llull when he was attempting to persuade indolent monks to devote themselves to learning;[4] and the clergy of Talavera, who, in the Archpriest of Hita's tale, were ordered to renounce their mistresses, clearly regarded the royal court rather than the papal Curia as the spiritual tribunal of final appeal.[5]

From the vantage-point of a Portuguese see, Alvarus Pelagius opined that Spain's bishops were the world's worst. Not one in a hundred was undefiled by simony. They were a public scandal, luxurious, bearded and effeminate, going about with bare arms, not wearing shirts 'ex lascivia' and sporting *risqué* outfits.[6] He reminded them that they were forbidden to fight, even against Saracens;[7] and though, as Alvarus described them, they would seem to have been

1 BN MS 13076 (Calderón de la Barca, *Memorias...de Coria*, 1752), fos. 21v, 131v. Cf. *MHE*, II, 109. In 1288 Nicholas IV had declined to authorise his translation from Coria to Sigüenza since Sigüenza required 'sponsus legitimus et ydoneus', which Alfonso was not: ASV, arm. XXXI.72, fo. 351r (Schillmann, *Formularsammlung*, 3138). Cf. *Reg. Nich. IV*, 341.

2 *Reg. Hon. III*, 4665: 'qui vel sectando regalem curiam vel se aliis negotiis mancipando in ecclesiis suis residere non curant' (Jan. 1224).

3 Douais, *Acta Capitulorum Provincialium O.F.P.*, 607 (AC Burgos, 1241, cap. ix); similarly, *ibid.* 610 (Palencia, 1249, cap. ii).

4 *Libro de Evast y Blanquerna*, in *Ramon Llull: Obras literarias*, ed. M. Batllori and M. Caldentey (Madrid, 1948), 313–14.

5 *Libro de Buen Amor*, 'Cantica de los clerigos de Talavera', copla 1696: 'Ado estavan juntados todos en la capilla, / levantose el dean a mostrar su manzilla, / diz': Amigos, yo querria que toda esta quadrilla / apellasemos del papa ant'el rey de Castilla', ed. J. Corominas (Madrid, 1967), 625–31.

6 *De Planctu Ecclesiae*, II, fos. 54ra, 55rb, 205ra–b, on the 'vainglorious Spaniards' 'in suis pessimis moribus et vitiis gloriantes'.

7 *Ibid.* II, fo. 55rb: 'Tamen non possunt pugnare manu propria, etiam contra saracenos...Contra quod prelati in Hispania et Alemannia faciunt tota die, de hoc conscientiam non habentes.'

ill-equipped for it, martial activity was certainly a characteristic feature of the peninsular prelates. They were fighting men. Benito de Rocaberti's speech was well-stocked with parade-ground ribaldry. Sitting booted and spurred astride his mule he uttered 'very dirty words'.[1] On one occasion Innocent III had to remind Bishop Rodrigo of Sigüenza of the text of St Paul's Epistle to Titus after that sturdy man of God had carried the battle into his own cathedral church, lashed out with his pastoral staff and inflicted fatal wounds on a member of the congregation.[2] Even when the Holy War had become a distant battle these attitudes persisted, and for all his pious protestations Alvarus Pelagius himself was as deeply imbued with the military spirit as were the brethren whom he upbraided. In his eyes Alfonso XI of Castile was a monarch among kings since, while the others praised God with their voices, Alfonso risked his neck for Him.[3] And, rather shamefacedly, he was forced to admit that even he was accustomed to kiss the king's hand, as the 'vile Spanish prelates' did – but 'more out of fear than humility', he added brightly, remembering an escape clause from the *Liber Extra*.[4]

Being a good lawyer and knowing all about inward reservations, Alvarus survived with his conscience intact. The choice for him, as for the rest, was between hypocrisy and sedition. Churchmen in Castile were regarded as having chosen the latter course when they attempted to hold councils, and it was only at moments of serious political unrest – in 1257, 1279 or 1282 – that they tabled their plans. On this last occasion they were duped by Sancho IV, and the continuing contrast between the Castilian Church, with its lack of experience of concerted action, and the Aragonese Church in which – despite Benito de Rocaberti and the interdict occasioned by the War of the Vespers – something of the practices inculcated by Pedro de Albalat still survived, was graphically illustrated some seven years after

---

[1] Above, p. 91.

[2] Potthast, 3850 (MDhI, 412): 'Oportet enim episcopum...esse...non percussorem' (*Ep. ad Titum*, i. 7).

[3] '*Quomodo regnum Castelle praecellit alia:*...Alii reges vocibus laudant Deum: tu pro eo corpus exponis': *Speculum Regum*, ed. Pinto de Meneses, I, 22. Cf. Castro, *Structure of Spanish History*, 124: 'A few Renaissance thinkers *wrote* Utopias, but the Spaniards *have shed their blood* for such dreams on more than one occasion.'

[4] *De Planctu Ecclesiae*, ii, fo. 52ra: '...Sed qui ex timore facit iam non facit, extra de reg. iii *qui ex timore*.' Cf. Friedberg, *Corpus Iuris Canonici*, II, 928.

Sancho's accession, when Nicholas IV ordered councils to be held in every province of the Western Church to consider ways and means of dealing with recent disasters in the Holy Land. The loss of Acre called for prompt action, and in his two bulls of 18 August and 25 September 1291 the pope stipulated that proctors from the councils should reach the Curia by the following February, or, when that time-schedule had been disrupted by delay in delivering the mandates, as soon after as possible. Accordingly, the provinces of Milan, Tours and Canterbury made haste.[1] So also did the province of Tarragona: Archbishop Rodrigo received the papal letters on 2 January 1292 and on the very next day summoned his suffragans 'primo, secundo, tercio et peremptorie' for 1 March. At the same time he forwarded to the bishop of Calahorra a copy of the bull *Illuminet* in which the indulgences available to crusaders were specified.[2] Before the end of April the conciliar proctors were on their way to Rome, while the archbishop took advantage of the assembly and reissued and revised provincial legislation relating to clerical morals and discipline.[3]

In the province of Toledo, meanwhile, nothing happened. Although the pope's letters were delivered to him on 12 December 1291, it was not until 6 January – twenty-five days later – that Archbishop Gonzalo sent word to his suffragans to assemble at Valladolid on 20 April – if, indeed, the summonses *were* sent.[4] No record of the Valladolid meeting has survived. Instead, the archbishop proceeded to

---

[1] *Dire amaritudinis; Inter cetera* (Potthast, 23783, 23828); Hefele–Leclercq, VI, i, 327; Powicke–Cheney, *Councils and Synods*, II, 1097 ff.

[2] AC Seo de Urgel, d.s.n; AC Calahorra, doc. 456 (Potthast, 23756).

[3] AGN, 3/43 (reg. Castro, *Catálogo*, 421, misdated: Goñi's correction in *Príncipe de Viana*, XVIII, 189, is confirmed by the reference in the document to one of the proctors as Bishop B(ernardo Peregri) of Barcelona); Tejada, *Colección de cánones*, III, 409 ff. The council belongs to the year 1292, not 1291 as Tejada believed: and its *acta*, as Tejada published them, contain at least one subsequent addition. Cf. Valls i Taberner, *AST*, XI, 264; Hefele–Leclercq, VI, i, 329.

[4] AC Toledo, I.5.A.1.2 (*Inter cetera*), dorse: 'Nuncii pape venerunt xij die decembris.' The summonses are still in AC Toledo, addressed to the bishops, etc. of Cartagena, Burgos, Oviedo, Palencia, León (3 copies) and Cuenca: I.5.A.1.2a–b–c–d–g–h–h: bis–k. One of the León copies is publ. by Tejada, VI, 58–9. In the mid-eighteenth century Burriel made copies of some of these, and suggested that the León summonses were not used because the archiepiscopal scribe had erred in addressing the bishop of León as *Fernando*: BN, MS 13116, fo. 23v. But even if this explanation were correct (which it is not) it would not account for the preservation of the other summonses at Toledo. Furthermore, none of the cathedral archives of the province contains any mention of the council.

use the papal mandates as a means of establishing authority over the exempt see of Cartagena, thus turning the tribulations of the Universal Church to the advantage of the church of Toledo.[1] And the chapter of Braga *sede vacante* did likewise, having the effrontery to subpoena the bishop of Oviedo, another exempt see.[2]

The archbishop of Tarragona had not let a second sun go down upon his mandate, but almost a month passed before the archbishop of Toledo took action. Possibly he did not feel able to obey the pope until he had consulted the king. Certainly Sancho IV kept the Compostela Council under surveillance. From Zamora on 21 April 1292 he wrote to the assembled prelates asking them to offer prayers for the success of the siege of Algeciras.[3] Since both the assemblies in his kingdom were planned for the same day there was no chance that one would give the other a lead – a coincidence that was perhaps too much to the king's advantage to have been entirely fortuitous. And, finally, there is the symbolic aspect of his request for prayers. With the fall of Acre, 'the Crusading movement began to slip out of the sphere of practical politics',[4] leaving prayer as virtually the only weapon left to the beleaguered Christians. And Sancho IV claimed even that for himself.

He and his father had already denuded the Church of its more substantial endowments. The abuses listed in the bishop of Rieti's *memoriale* all continued unchecked: expired papal grants were resur-

---

[1] Cf. Fita, *Actas inéditas*, 189–92; Torres Fontes, *Hispania*, XIII, 524–5. Toledo had had no such opportunity since Innocent IV had declared Cartagena an exempt see in 1250: Potthast, 14032; Fita, *BRAH*, III, 273. No mention has survived of any Toledo council in 1261 to discuss the Tartars.

[2] ADB, Gav. dos concílios, 1: the chapter's letter (21 April) informing bishop Miguel that the terms of *Dire amaritudinis* applied 'provincie prelatis tam regularibus quam secularibus tam *exemptis*' and summoning him to a council on Whitsunday (25 May), 'cum sitis licet exempti de provincia Bracarensi'. The bishop stalled, promising 'que el daria aquella respuesta que deviesse' if they could justify their claim (3 May). Cf. Ferreira, *Fastos episcopaes*, II, 93. The archbishop of Toledo also had designs on Oviedo which, *licet exempta*, the papal penitentiary in 1280 had believed to be part of the province of Compostela: AC Toledo, I.5.A.1.2.c; Eubel, *Arch. kath. Kirchenrecht*, LXIV, 33. For the origins of this confusion, see David, *Études historiques sur la Galice et le Portugal*, 119 ff.; Mansilla, *HS*, XIV, 9–11; Gaiffier, *Anal. Bollandiana*, LXXXVI, 77; Rivera, *Iglesia de Toledo*. 252–5.

[3] The letter was seen by Morales in the archive of Badajoz Cathedral in 1753–4: Rodríguez Amaya, *Rev. Est. Extremeños*, VIII, 408.

[4] Runciman, *History of the Crusades*, III, 427.

rected[1] and the *tercias* exacted. Meanwhile, far from receiving 'rivers of gold and silver' from Spain, Nicholas IV, like Clement IV before him, had occasion to complain that Spain contributed nothing to papal funds.[2] If there were any churchmen who took heart from the council or councils of the spring of 1292, then they received a rude shock before the year was out and they were required to come to the aid of the king, the country and Christendom with financial assistance towards the expenses of the siege of Tarifa.[3] Sancho IV was not a man to be trifled with, as Archbishop Rodrigo of Compostela discovered two years later when he failed to obey immediately a demand for eighty thousand *maravedís* for the war against Aben-Jacob, and the king thereupon ordered his property throughout the kingdom to be seized.[4] And worse followed after Sancho's death during the minority of Fernando IV. In August 1295 at the Valladolid Cortes the bishops were denied access to their only public forum, the royal court. With the sole exception of the royal chaplains, churchmen were ordered to abandon the young king's entourage and return to their own quarters, 'los arçobispos e obispos e los abbades...asus arçobispados e obispados e asus abbadias, et los clerigos asus logares'. The royal household was to be staffed with 'omes bonos delas villas'

---

1 At the Haro Cortes of Aug. 1288 Sancho freed his subjects from 'la demanda dela deçima que el Papa dio a nuestro padre por seyes annos pora ayuda dela guerra': hardly a generous concession, since the six-year grant had been made thirteen years before: *Cortes de Castilla*, I, 103; above, p. 213. And later still – between 1289 and 1294 – Innocent V's bull of 28 March 1276, *Exurgat Deus* (Potthast, 21135, undated) which had committed the preaching of the peninsular Crusade to the then archbishop of Seville, was being used by Miguel, abbot of S. Millán de Lara, 'vicario e procurador general de don Garcia arçobispo de Sevilla, executor del negocio de la Cruz': AC Lugo, 21 / 3 /22.

2 *Reg. Nich. IV*, 6857: 'De terris vero Castelle subiectis nichil umquam percepit ecclesia, cum felicis recordationis Gregorius papa...clare memorie Alfonso regi Castelle ipsam decimam ex certis causis duxerit concedendam' (to Edward I of England, Feb. 1292).

3 On 18 Dec. Sancho received 35,400 *maravedís* from the sees of Palencia, Burgos and Calahorra 'pora la hueste de Tariffa'. His total receipts from the Church exceeded 800,000 *maravedís*, and in March 1294 he informed Bishop Gil of Badajoz that, because of the heavy costs of the campaign 'que sera grant onrra et grant pro de nos et de toda la Christiandat, et sennaladamente de toda la nuestra tierra...avemos menester gran aver, el cual non podemos escusar, como quier que no sea mui grave': AC Burgos, vol. 48, fo. 213; Gaibrois de Ballesteros, *BRAH*, LXXVI, 75, 431, 432 ff.

4 Gaibrois de Ballesteros, *Sancho IV*, III, ccclxvii, ccclxxxi–ii (nos 534, 562): 'e tomad todo quanto ffallarades en los sus çillos e peyndrat a los sus vasallos otrossi quanto les ffallaredes'.

as in the reign of Fernando III, which the anti-clericals regarded as a Golden Age, just as Sancho's episcopal partisans had regarded it, by their very different standards, a dozen years before; and the seals were to be entrusted to two lay notaries.[1] The effect of these measures would be to exclude ecclesiastics from the councils of the kingdom, thus cutting their one political lifeline. On 16 August Archbishop Gonzalo of Toledo entered a strong protest, having reminded the Cortes four days before of the 'muchos agrauiamientos' which churchmen were accustomed to receiving from kings and nobles. He mentioned, in particular, the excesses committed by laymen during episcopal vacancies. So serious were the depredations that very frequently it proved impossible to give the deceased prelate a decent funeral. Nor were the churches allowed to elect a successor *liberamiente*, being forced to choose 'contra sus voluntades'. And the same applied to other benefices. Even Bishop Martín of Astorga was willing to join the resistance movement, for the situation was critical.[2] Yet when they proceeded to lay claim once more to what they had always been denied – the right of free assembly – they were again charged with sedition. And the charge stuck.[3]

The Castilian Church continued to be at the king's mercy. The lord king gave, and the lord king took away: the charters which he granted it were commonly either neglected or revoked by him, as the bishops complained in 1279.[4] Appropriately, it was an exclamation from the Book of Job that sprang to the lips of Archbishop Gonzalo of Toledo when he wrote to his chapter from the papal Curia during Sancho's reign.[5] The church of León was currently being reminded of the value of royal concessions. Having waived its debts to him in

---

[1] *Cortes de Castilla*, I, 131. Cf. above, p. 221.

[2] AC Toledo, I.5.A.1.6; *Cortes de Castilla*, I, 133–5.

[3] In the nineteenth century the regalist criticism of those prelates who had attended the 1302 Peñafiel Council was voiced by Lafuente: 'No era noble, en verdad, hacer alarde de rigor contra una mujer virtuosísima y un niño de catorce anos, los que tanto habían callado ante el temible y astuto Sancho el Bravo': *Historia eclesiástica*, IV, 407. Fita, very properly, called this 'regalismo farisaico', since the Peñafiel legislation was altogether defensive and restrained: *Actas inéditas*, 181. Cf. Tejada, III, 433 ff.

[4] *Reg. Nich. III*, 743.

[5] AHN, papel, Toledo, 7216/2, d.s.n.: 'Conceptum sermonen tenere quis poterit?': hanc quidem Job exclamationem proponimus, quia reticere non possumus quod sentimus' (Job, iv, 2); in response to a whole stream of complaints about their plight (c. 1288).

April 1288, so that 'en nuestro tiempo sea mas rica e non pierda lo que ha', the king forgot all his promises and assurances when he needed funds for the siege of Tarifa four years later.[1] No church was exempt from that levy. Palencia, for example, was mulcted to the tune of sixty thousand *maravedís*;[2] and if Palencia had recovered from the catastrophe of thirty years before when allegedly eleven thousand had died there, fresh disasters were already in store for it. Of all the cities of Castile Palencia suffered most during the civil wars of the late 1290s 'et iacturam maximam est perpessa', according to a contemporary witness, Jofré de Loaisa.[3] And meanwhile the richest local benefices were assigned to men such as Alfonso Pérez, the king's scribe and the queen mother's chaplain, who in June 1288 was granted property at Monzón 'por jure de heredat'.[4]

To the papacy, however, the Castilian Church continued to be a dead loss. 'Hispania...suis gravatur oneribus', as Clement IV had observed and Nicholas IV confirmed.[5] By way of illustration, both of this and of other matters discussed in the foregoing chapters, we may conclude with some account of the Spanish Crusade when the Christian kings took the initiative once more in the early fourteenth century.

In April 1309 Clement V gave his blessing to the campaign which Fernando IV of Castile and Jaime II of Aragon proposed to mount against the kingdom of Granada. Jaime's man at Avignon, Bernat dez Fonollar, advanced the traditional argument: since it was in the Almighty's interest that Granada should be recaptured, the pope and the cardinals were morally obliged to provide every assistance. They, not the kings, would be responsible if the enterprise failed. And, though there were those at the Curia who hinted that the king of Castile's intention was not to rid the Peninsula of what Clement called that 'fetidam nationem', but rather to give them a fright and

---

1 Gaibrois de Ballesteros, *Sancho IV*, III, cxv–vi; *idem*, *BRAH*, LXXVI, 437 ff. Bishop Martín's will of Dec. 1288 lists debts of more than 30,000 *maravedís*: *ES*, XXXVI, clix.
2 Gaibrois de Ballesteros, *BRAH*, LXXVI, 432.
3 Ed. Morel-Fatio, *BEC*, LIX, 363. Palencia's reduced population in the early fourteenth century is noted by Carande, *RBAM*, IX, 255–6. See also Deyermond, *AEM*, I, 613 ff.
4 BM, MS Egerton 442, fo. 34r. By May 1308 he was prior of Husillos, and canon of Palencia and Murcia: *ibid*. fo. 34v.
5 *Reg. Clem. IV*, 1117; above, pp. 185, 243.

enrich himself, the pope accepted the argument and granted Fernando a tenth of the ecclesiastical revenue of his kingdom for three years.[1]

By the end of 1309, however, the progress of the campaign was lending some credence to the reservations of the sceptics. In October the king's uncle, the Infante Juan, and Juan Manuel broke faith and abandoned the siege of Algeciras,[2] and if the pope was uncertain about how he should respond to Archbishop Fernando of Seville's appeal for more funds for the king in February 1310,[3] the events of the following months did nothing to reassure him. Eventually, in July, he declined to authorise a fresh grant and instead directed the three archbishops subject to Castilian jurisdiction to hold provincial councils and report to him on both the general state of the kingdom – 'ac precipue ecclesiarum, prelatorum et ecclesiasticarum personarum dicti regni' – and the military campaign.[4] That the initiative for consultation, even at this late stage, should have come from the pope rather than from the Castilian prelates themselves is not surprising. When, after a four-year absence, Archbishop Rodrigo of Compostela returned to his church after the Vienne General Council and was informed of the impending Cortes, he had to badger the archbishop of Toledo into taking any precautions at all 'concerning those things which concern yourself, ourselves and our churches'. Clearly neither was accustomed to such a procedure: Rodrigo suggested not a council but a gathering.[5] In Aragon, by contrast, Jaime II had already acted before Clement contacted the leaders of the Castilian Church, having requested Archbishop Guillermo of Tarragona in the previous October to summon a provincial council for discussion of the ecclesiastical contribution to the fighting fund, 'conspicientes atta-men, quod hec absque celebracione generalis concilii nequeunt utiliter explicari'; and, in view of what was said on that occasion, had even interceded for them and requested Clement to relieve the Aragonese Church of its 'onera importabilia' by suspending the collection of the

---

[1] *Reg. Clem. V*, 4046; Finke, *Acta Aragonensia*, III, 200–2; Gallardo Fernández *Origen...de las rentas de la Corona de España*, III, 70 ff. For details of these negotiations, see Goñi Gaztambide, *Historia de la Bula de la Cruzada*, 265 ff.

[2] Giménez Soler, *Don Juan Manuel*, 367 ff.

[3] ASV, *Instrumenta Miscellanea*, 490 (reg. Milian Boix, *AA*, XV, 531, no. 43).

[4] *Reg. Clem. V*, 5484, 5494.

[5] The word he used was *ayuntamiento*: AHN, papel, Toledo, 7216/2, d.s.n. (1 Dec. [1312]).

decima.[1] Admittedly, allowance must be made for the political machinations of a king whose fondness for his national Church had not prevented him from asking the pope in 1309 for enormous grants of ecclesiastical revenue such as not even the wars against Frederick II and the ransoming of St Louis had warranted.[2] Still, if only in that Jaime took the trouble to manipulate the Church, there is a marked contrast between his approach and Fernando's; and at least some weight may be attached to his assertion, that he felt bound to plead on behalf of the Aragonese Church which had so readily assisted him in the past.[3]

Moreover, the aftermath of Clement V's intervention provides even more telling evidence concerning the ineffectiveness of papal collectors in the kingdom of Castile. For after the pope had suspended the *decima* grant in June 1311, for reasons which he did not care to specify but which very probably were connected with Fernando's extortion of the *tercias*,[4] he then relented and in July 1312 instructed the bishops of Córdoba and Ciudad Rodrigo to secure all unpaid contributions, forward what was owed to the king's naval allies, and provide him with a full account of their dealings.[5] This account has survived, and it records in vivid detail some of the difficulties facing papal collectors in Castile, even when their receipts were ultimately destined for the king himself. It was prepared not by the appointed bishops, but by two clerics – Juan Fernández, archdeacon of Castro and later dean of Córdoba, and Juan Gonzálvez – and their assistants, to whom the prelates had the wisdom to refer the whole tedious business.[6]

And it was, indeed, a tedious, dangerous and cold haul that lay before them when they began their task in November 1313. For

---

[1] Vincke, *Documenta selecta*, nos. 151, 153.

[2] Finke, *Acta Aragonensia*, III, 207–11.

[3] Vincke, no. 153: '...attento quod prelati et clerus dicte provincie semper prompti existunt beneplacitis nostris obtemperare et subvenire pro posse, pro eis intercedere et pro ipsorum relevacione preces effundere reputamus nos forcius obligatos' (March 1311).

[4] *Reg. Clem. V*, 6939: 'iustis tamen et rationalibus causis que impresentiarum animum nostrum movent inducti'. See above, p. 207, for Clement IV's misgivings about granting church revenue to the royal *spoliator*.

[5] *Ibid.* 8591.

[6] ASV, *Reg. Avinionensia*, 91, fos. 225r–41r. Cf. Loye, *Les archives de la Chambre Apostolique au XIVe siècle*, 209.

Fernando IV had died thirteen months before and the country was in the throes of a civil war of peculiar complexity,[1] so that when they summoned the abbots of the surrounding monasteries to meet them at Osma in April 1314 none came. They were not prepared to venture out into the war zone on such a trifling errand.[2] For the same reason the collectors drew a blank at Calahorra, and failed to pin down the bishop of Palencia who dared not show his face in his own episcopal city.[3] At Toledo 'terra erat destructa' and nothing could be collected because the local population were at war with their archbishop and Juan Manuel.[4] The word *carestia* occurs frequently in their account, and their living expenses were considerable 'quoniam terra Castelle erat tunc cara'.[5] It was bitter weather through that winter: 'cum pessimo tempore quo tunc erat' their shoes wore out almost as soon as they were replaced – which was frequently, and not inexpensive.[6] The men themselves succumbed to the weather: having been sent on an errand to Villarreal and Alcaraz, Fernando Garcés was brought back an invalid to Toledo on the back of an ass, the snow having affected his legs. The cost of carriage, medication and a new pair of shoes amounted to fifty-six *maravedís*, all for no return.[7] And their horses succumbed too. The first to go was a mount belonging to Diego Garcés, a nephew of the archdeacon, which had cost its owner four hundred *maravedís* (sixty *maravedís* less than was successfully claimed in compensation after its demise at Sigüenza).[8] Such modest profit, though, was as nothing compared with what the archdeacon himself made when his steed was taken ill (witness Don Oliverio) as they left Tudela del Duero. Carting the creature to Valladolid on a litter and having it personally attended to for four months cost three hundred *maravedís*. When it then gave up the struggle a further three thousand was claimed.[9] The vast quantities of wax and parchment which they purchased as they went were, in comparison, cheap, though the services of notaries (when they were

1 See Giménez Soler, 51 ff.
2 'Non audebant exire de locis suis propter guerram quam habebat, et timebant si exirent incurrere mortem, quam nolebant recipere propter nos': *Reg. Avin.*, 91, fo. 234v.
3 *Ibid.* fos. 237v, 239r.   4 *Ibid.* fo. 226r.   5 *Ibid. passim*; fo. 229r.
6 *Ibid.* fos. 231r, 232r: 'Et omnes ipsos sotulares dabamus hominibus propter magnas nives que tunc erant, et rumperunt statim sotulares propter hoc.'
7 *Ibid.* fo. 229v.   8 *Ibid.* fo. 233r.   9 *Ibid.* fo. 240r.

able to find them)[1] were not. At Magaz, for example, where there was no competition, Alfonso Rodríguez could demand fifty *maravedís*, and then a further thirty in settlement of his scruples about preparing the document which excommunicated his lord, the bishop of Palencia,[2] while at Sigüenza extra had to be offered so that their hired hand might pen his compositions in a suitably minatory style.[3] Papal mandates alone convinced no one. Gonzalvo Rodríguez, canon of Palencia, carried far more weight than Clement V, bishop of Rome, and if anything was to be achieved it was necessary to purchase his assistance; and similar arrangements had to be made with the bishop of Sigüenza's vicar-general 'ut nobis esset bonus et non impediret nos'.[4] Indeed their expenditure was so considerable that by September 1314, when they reached Burgos, they were not covering their costs.[5] And thus it remained until, at the final tally, they found that, having allowed for their various equine misadventures, several changes of clothes and expenses at the rate of thirty-five *maravedís* daily, their seventeen-and-a-half-month peregrination had cost almost thirty-two thousand *maravedís* while their receipts had produced rather less than thirty thousand.[6]

Any assessment of the economic relationship of the Roman Church, the Spanish Churches and the Spanish monarchs must give due weight to figures such as these. They are not to be disregarded merely because the collectors were natives and their claims for expenses were so questionable. After all, in Aragon thirty-five years before, foreign collectors had expressed similar fears as they trudged around in pursuit of Pedro III; and, in spite of everything, Juan Fernández rose to be dean of Córdoba. Meanwhile, moreover, Fernando IV was able to assure Clement V that it was 'customary' for him and his predecessors to receive two-thirds of the *tercias*,[7] and

---

1 *Ibid.* fo. 234v: 'De Gormaçio non deportavit Petrus Ferrandi testimonium quia non invenit notarium publicum.'
2 *Ibid.* fo. 239r.
3 *Ibid.* fo. 231r: 'ut littere haberent maiorem roboris firmitatem et plus timerentur'.
4 *Ibid.* fo. 239v: 'ut esset nobis bonus et favorabilis quum sine ipso nihil poterat fieri in illa terra'; fo. 231r.
5 *Ibid.* fo. 239v: 'Nos feceramus magnos sumptus multo plus quam inde habueramus.'
6 *Ibid.* fo. 240v: 'videntes quod primo comederemus in duplo ante quam collegissemus'; fo. 241r.
7 On 1 Jan. 1308 the pope granted the king two-thirds of the *tercias* for three years after Fernando had submitted 'quod...de tertia vero parte hujusmodi decimarum

Clement could observe, when granting four years' procurations to the archbishop of Toledo, that only with papal assistance might that church be relieved of its debts.[1] Yet, then as now, Spaniards naturally assumed that all their woes were attributable to papal collectors, that papal collectors were all as disreputable as the Patriarch of Grado, and that – the experiences of Adegarius of Parma notwithstanding – no papal collector would settle for anything less than pure gold. Also at the beginning of the fourteenth century Bishop Fernando of Córdoba wrote to the archbishop of Toledo, warning him in advance of the imminent arrival of certain papal emissaries and advising him to grease their palms well in view of the harm that they might do him. He had been at the Curia, had met their type before, and knew what he was talking about, he said.[2]

Gossip of this sort, though, does not prove that the criticisms of 1262–3 had any foundation. All that it proves is that some bishops have suspicious minds. For, though it may be possible to produce evidence in support of the bishop of Córdoba's pessimistic view of human nature, the fact remains that it was the king and not the pope who controlled the destiny of the Spanish Church. Asked about the pope's temporal power, an illustrious contemporary admitted that it was considerable, but added that he was certain of one thing only: the pope had less power in Castile than anywhere else. More than that he did not know. Nor could more have been said. The author of the dialogue, Juan Manuel, was a nephew of Alfonso X, and he too, like the bishop of Córdoba, was in a position to know what he was talking about.[3]

quae dicitur fabricae, tu et progenitores tui consuevistis ab olim percipere duas partes'. For his no less traditional abuse of this grant the king was later excommunicated and his kingdom interdicted: AC Toledo, Z.3.D.1.7 (publ. Gallardo Fernández, III, 67–70); *Reg. Clem. V,* 9727.

[1] AC Toledo, A.7.H.1.3c: 'a quibus non potest absque nostre provisionis auxilio relevari' (= *Reg. Clem. V,* 2032).

[2] 'E ha mester, Sennor, que les mandedes fazer honra e los fagedes merced, ca tales omes son que pueden enpeçer por el oficio que traen que aprovechar. E comoquier, Sennor, que lo vos bien sabedes, enpero mejor lo sabemos nos ca los conosciemos alla en la Corte a estos e a otros e sabemos qual es su oficio': AC Toledo, X.1.C.2.4.

[3] 'Otrossi ha muy grant poder en lo temporal; mas cuál o cuánto es este poder, porque yo sé de Castiella, et los reys de Castiella et sus reinos son mas sin ninguna subjeccion que otra tierra del mundo, por ende non sé yo mucho desto': *Libro de los Estados,* ed, Gayangos, *BAE,* LI, 357.

Chapter 11

SPANIARDS AT THE CURIA, 1

The bishop of Córdoba's attitude to curialists had a lengthy pedigree. Since the late eleventh century, at the latest, when a canon of Toledo had described in loving detail the deep potations in which the distended cardinals engaged while his archbishop angled for a grant of legatine powers,[1] Spaniards – no less than Frenchmen and Englishmen – had visualised the Curia as an unwholesome place inhabited by mercenary knaves. In September 1301 Jaime II of Aragon was informed by his proctor, Giraldo de Albalat, that on account of the bribes which they were offering Boniface VIII, the agents of Castile and Portugal would almost certainly secure the marriage dispensation which they sought, 'quia tamen papa in adquirendo pecuniam nimis avidum se ostendit';[2] but, right though he may have been about Boniface, there was nothing especially *fin de siècle* about his suspicions. Throughout the century that had just closed they had been very frequently expressed. Skulduggery and the Curia were synonymous. If in the early 1260s Rome's long grasping fingers could reach as far as Compostela and deprive the archbishop of his inalienable rights, was it not natural that when the bishop of Salamanca set off for the Curia at about the same time without so much as a word of explanation to his chapter, a jittery dean should fear the worst and send a frantic letter to his friend, the bishop of Urgel, beseeching him to use whatever influence he had at Rome to prevent the disaster which they all feared?[3] For the clergy of Barcelona Rome was the Forbidden City; and 'Rome' meant 'wherever the pope was', according to the *Partidas*.[4] Castilian churchmen in Castile

---

[1] *Tractatus Garsiae Tholetani canonici de Albino et Rufino*, ed. Sackur, MGH, *Libelli de lite*, II, 423–35. Archbishop Bernardo's journey to Rome in 1088 provides a possible context for this incident. See Rivera, *Iglesia de Toledo*, 136 ff.
[2] Finke, *Acta Aragonensia*, I, 102.
[3] *VL*, XI, 238. See Linehan, *AEM*, forthcoming.
[4] *Reg. Inn. IV*, 3757; *Part.* 1.9.4. (Academy ed., I, 330).

could hardly believe that Castilian churchmen at Rome had honourable motives for being there: Fernando Alfonso's bequest of 1294 in favour of student canons of Salamanca stipulated that 'a los que estodieren enna corte de Roma...les non den ende nada'.[1] And, contrariwise, Castilian churchmen at Rome were wont to protest – indeed, to protest too much – to their friends at home that they were by no means savouring their stay and that their only thought was of their return. Rome was an expensive place, as Archbishop Gonzalo of Toledo (with good reason) assured his chapter in 1288: he timed his exile by the increasing lightness of his pocket.[2] Their suspicion that he was inventing 'excusationes frivolas' in order to spin it out rather irritated him, therefore; and the account which they had sent him of their own misfortunes left him cold, wrestling manfully as he was against hopeless odds and pitiless creditors.[3] The tone of his letter was precisely that of the undergraduate reassuring his increasingly sceptical parents that he will be coming down soon. Their shrewd suspicion that, not only was he rather enjoying himself, but was probably more often tipsy than not, was difficult to allay. So Gonzalo had a tricky letter to write when they decided to make him a Fellow, and the new cardinal-bishop of Albano had to break the news that he would not be coming home at all. He made a poor job of it. There he had been, spending a virtuous evening with his teetotal friends, he told them – inserting, as an afterthought, that he had been waiting for his final *exeat* – when what should happen but that Pope Boniface should promote him. Imagine his surprise![4] All of which was made no more plausible by his forgetting the Latin for Cuenca and Olmedo.[5]

---

[1] AC Salamanca, 20/2/25–2 (reg. Marcos Rodríguez, *Catálogo*, 432).

[2] AHN, papel, Toledo, 7216/2, d.s.n: 'nos qui in isto exilio vivimus satis in bursa nostra sentimus'.

[3] *Ibid.*: 'ut de fame et nuditate qua vos perire dicitis et affligi decentius taceamus;... nos qui tantorum honere debitorum quasi sub importabili fasce deprimimur, quos usurarum vorago consumit, quos expense gravant multiplices...'

[4] AHN, papel, Toledo, 7216/2, d.s.n: 'Sane pridem dum sederemus in foribus domus domini cum humilibus servis suis in civitate Reatina cum aliis curialibus permanentes (et ad reditus nostri licentiam laborantes: inserted), placuit memorato patri suorumque cardinalium sacro collegio de vestra ad Albanensem ecclesiam nos transferre et ad preeminentem cardinalatus erigere dignitatem. Ex quo tam subita mutabilitate status et insufficientie nostre conditione pensatis... stupor mentis et varia cogitationum fluctuatio nos invasit': a rough copy, with corrections, on paper.

[5] *Idem*: informing his nephew, Gonzalo Palomeque, of his translation 'de Cursensi

Gonzalo strove hard to give the impression of feeling out of place at Rome: a view of themselves which Spaniards have tended to foster in modern times. In 1584 the historian of the Dominican Order blamed the downfall of Munio of Zamora on a curial conspiracy of Frenchmen and Italians, by whom 'la nación Española siempre ha sido aborrecida'; and, as recently as 1956, the same attitude was expressed by Mansilla in his discussion of the part played by the Spanish cardinal, Petrus Hispanus, in the election of Pope Clement V. The Spaniard, it is suggested, was clay in the hands of the unscrupulous Napoleon Orsini and changed sides simply because 'como buen castellano no entendía ni de dobleces ni de intrigas'.[1]

It is an attractive theory, perfectly consistent with the celebrated 'Spanish inferiority complex' and wholly creditable to those on whose behalf it is advanced; but, in reality, there is nothing to be said for it. Neither Munio nor Petrus was a political tyro. Munio was as much sinning as sinned against, and his sins were sins of the flesh. Petrus, a boon companion of Boniface VIII, was no stranger to curial intrigue, as the chapter of Toledo acknowledged by engaging him to intercede for them with the pope.[2] Indeed, the rather elaborate precautions which he took on the occasion to which Mansilla refers – arranging to meet Cardinal Napoleon 'ad latrinam, quia alibi loqui non poterant ita secreto' – suggest that he may even have derived a morbid pleasure from some of its finer points.[3]

And what was true of Petrus Hispanus was true also of Spaniards throughout the previous century. They were in their element at the

---

[sic] ad Toletanam ecclesiam. At the end has been added: 'Sane vos volumus... qualiter provisum est Cusensi ecclesie de archidiacono Treverensi.' Cf. *Reg. Bon. VIII*, 2832, 2908 (Jan.–Feb. 1299).

1 Hernando de Castillo, *Historia general de Sancto Domingo*, I, fo. 491v; Mansilla, *HS*, IX, 271.

2 AHN, papel, Toledo, 7216/2, d.s.n. To Cardinal Gonzalo of Albano, asking him to expedite the return of his nephew, their new archbishop: 'Ca sabed por cierto, Sennor, que mucho es mester que el electo venga a su Eglesia pora razon de muchas guerras e mucha tribulacion que ha en la su tierra e en la su provincia...Et bien sabedes...pedir merçed a nuestro sennor el papa e rogar al Refferendario, nuestro companero e nuestro amigo que guisasse con nuestro sennor el papa que nos cubiasse a nuestra eglesia' (1299–1300). Cf. Boase, *Boniface VIII*, 284, 346–8; Mansilla, *loc. cit.*

3 Finke, *Aus den Tagen*, lxiv. Another report, sent to the king of Aragon, mentioned, rather more delicately, that the two cardinals had conferred 'ubi deponebant superflua': Finke, *Acta Aragonensia*, I, 193.

Curia and hastened there with relish, as flies to the jampot. Like Tawney's early seventeenth-century businessmen at the royal court, many of them, doubtless, went the way of moths around the candle-flame instead.[1] But the fate of these did nothing to stem the flow of new arrivals. 'Whosoever went to Rome a fool returned a fool', according to a contemporary Aragonese aphorism.[2] Neither that *caveat* though – even if 'poverty' were substituted for 'folly' – nor such misgivings about the Roman climate as Alfonso X mentioned to his archbishop-elect of Toledo in 1262, provided an effective deterrent. Raymond of Peñafort seems to have been exceptional in withdrawing from the Curia for that particular reason.[3] During the pontificate of Urban IV another Petrus Hispanus made himself so comfortable there that it proved necessary to obtain from him a promise to leave 'statim quam assecutus fuerit pacificam provisionem in ecclesia Mindoniensi'.[4]

Seven months later, though possessed of his Mondoñedo canonry, he was still there.[5] What was keeping him was that which had induced him to make the long journey in the first place: his determination to jump the queue for benefices in his crowded church, and the equal determination of the bishop and chapter of Mondoñedo to bar his way, provision mandate or no provision mandate – just as only recently they had successfully resisted the pope's reservation of the archdeaconry of Montenigro for Pedro, *magister scolarum* of Lugo.[6] Looking about him, *Aprilis* – the ingenuous cleric in the verse dialogue about life at the Curia, written in the early 1260s – saw that others with nothing like his qualifications had received fat prebends from the pope. So he decided to go to Rome himself, secure in the belief that the pope would be only too pleased to help him too.

---

[1] Cf. the review of Tawney's *Business and Politics under James I* (Cambridge, 1958) by K. G. Davies, *Ec. Hist. Rev.*, 2nd ser., XI (1958–9), 517.

[2] 'Qui foll sen va a Roma, foll sen torna': *Chronica del Rey En Jacme*, cap. 542, ed. Aguiló, 517; trans. Forster, II, 655.

[3] Above, p. 143; *Vita S. Raymundi*, ed. Balme–Paban, 24–5.

[4] *Reg. Urb. IV*, 353 (Aug. 1263).

[5] *Ibid.* 1023. He was in the company of Cardinal Stephen of Palestrina.

[6] ADB, Gav. das Dignidades, 24: *inc. Viros litterarum*, 23 Feb. 1262. Bishop Nuño Pérez ignored this mandate and awarded the archdeaconry to Fernando Yáñez. At Orvieto in July 1263 Bishop Matheus of Lisbon, as auditor, adjudged the *next* Mondoñedo vacancy to Pedro of Lugo who, until then, was to receive an annual pension of £40 *leoneses* from Fernando: *ES*, XVIII, 158; *Reg. Urb. IV*, 1118.

Abril was a Spaniard – 'Hyspana gente profectus' – and while there is little reason for treating him as a representation of the bishop of Urgel of that name, his motives for going to Rome were indeed precisely those which would induce the canons of Salamanca – where Bishop Abril was an archdeacon before his promotion – to disqualify themselves from receiving grants from the bequest of Fernando Alfonso.[1] Nor, but for papal support, would Pascal Pérez, a native of Zamora with only a pleasant voice to recommend him, ever have reached the head of the queue for prebends in that church, to which Urban IV promoted him in May 1264 after an examination of no great difficulty at the Curia.[2]

Petrus Hispanus, and Pascal Pérez with his pass degree, were thus provided with at least a notional advantage over their friends at home, where, in common with the other churches of Castile, León and – though, perhaps, to a lesser extent – Aragon, Zamora and Mondoñedo were in the throes of an economic crisis to which bishops and chapters were reacting by adopting ever more niggardly measures in order to preserve what they still had. Thus each of them was doing, at a lower level, precisely what the leader of the Castilian Church had done in 1259 – seeking his own well-being at the expense of his colleagues. The urgent need for solidarity between bishops and their chapters – to which Alfonso X himself drew their attention – was commonly ignored; and the result, in the judgement of an early seventeenth-century bishop, was that the autonomy and authority of the Spanish Church was lost to king and pope.[3] The king's capacity for dividing and ruling has already been considered. It remains to be seen how far the pope also profited from their struggles.

Everywhere in the thirteenth century episcopal elections were a nightmare, for they provided any single individual with the opportunity of indulging his own ambition to the detriment of the rest of the chapter: *haec pestis*, as Bishop Bruno of Olmutz called it in his report

---

[1] *Carmen Apologeticum*, ed. Grauert, *Magister Heinrich der Poet* (cit. hereafter as *Carmen*), lines 51, 59 ff. For a critique of the identification of Bishop Abril of Urgel, as subject (cf. *Marca Hispanica,* 534), and as author (cf. Lambert in *DHGE,* III, 1070), see Linehan, *AEM*, forthcoming.

[2] *Reg. Urb. IV,* 1715. But that was not the end of it: see below, pp. 301–3.

[3] *Part,* 1.14.9 (Academy ed., I, 397); Sandoval, *Catálogo de los obispos de Pamplona,* fo. 97v.

to Gregory X on the state of Europe in 1273, which put self first and produced double elections both in the Church and in the Empire.[1] Ideally, the only sure way of preventing such an outcome was for the cathedral chapter to vest all its powers of election in one man, as happened at Ciudad Rodrigo in 1264 when Domingo Martínez, thus empowered, repaid his colleagues' confidence in him by choosing himself.[2] The usual practice, though, was to proceed *per compromissionem*, entrusting selection to two or three canons, and, in the later part of the century, to require them to reach their decision in the time that it took a candle to burn right down. Yet even with this mesmeric aid to concentration *compromissarii* sometimes failed to agree.[3]

Just how serious the consequences of a divided election might be may be judged from the course of events at Burgos after the death of Bishop Juan de Villahoz in August 1269. For though he had only three votes – as against the forty-three cast for the dean, D. Martín – Pedro Sarracín, archdeacon of Valpuesta, nevertheless took the case to Rome, and, on account of the long papal vacancy prior to the election of Gregory X, it was not until September 1275 that the affair was settled by the translation to Burgos of Bishop Gonzalo of Cuenca (the future archbishop of Toledo and cardinal). Meanwhile vacancies occurring in the cathedral chapter had remained unfilled, until in October 1272 Gregory had intervened – not, however, to impose a bevy of venal Italians on Burgos, but instead to invite a committee of the canons then at the Curia to forward nominations.[4] He was prompted to act not by the prospect of rents but by the cure of souls which, while the local Dominicans were taking advantage of the

---

[1] 'Homines se ipsos amantes praeponunt commodo reipublicae rem privatam': ed. Höfler, *Analecten z. Geschichte Deutschlands u. Italians,* 19–20.

[2] BN, MS. 7112 (Sánchez Cavañas, *Historia Civitatense*), unpaginated, cap. 6; Nogales–Delicado, *Historia de Ciudad Rodrigo,* 64.

[3] Ballesteros, *Historia de España,* III, 418, notes this practice (which seems to have originated in Castile), but his references are faulty. The earliest recorded instance was at Oviedo in 1275, where it failed in its objective, as it also did at Cuenca in 1280, *Reg. Greg. X,* 639; AC Toledo, X.1.E.1.1g. But it was successful there in March 1290, at Jaén in March 1300, and, at about the same time, at Segovia and Ciudad Rodrigo. Soon after, the chapter of Guarda introduced it into Portugal: AC Cuenca, 4/18/252; AC Toledo, X.1.D.1.1i; *Reg. Bon. VIII,* 4043, 4207, 4470.

[4] *Reg. Greg. X,* 632; Mansilla, *HS,* IV, 329; AC Toledo, A.7.G.1.1: *inc. Illarum ecclesiarum,* 12 Oct. 1272.

sede vacante situation to expand their temporal possessions at the chapter's expense, was being dangerously neglected.[1]

Although the see of Burgos was directly subject to Rome, Gregory refrained from pressing his advantage: a point which deserves to be stressed, particularly since his theoretical right to intervene in such situations was no more challenged by the secular power in Castile than it was by those other critics elsewhere who took exception to the occasional glaring abuse of power but not to the power itself.[2] Spanish churchmen, however, were themselves frequently as hazy about the precise nature of papal powers of collation as they were utterly convinced of the rigour with which they were, or would be, applied. The constitution *Licet Ecclesiarum* was a dead letter both at Burgos and, at the end of the century, at Tudela where the dean, Master Gil Álvarez, imagined that what prevented him from disposing of the benefice of a canon who had recently died at the Curia was not the universal law of the Church which had been in force since at least 1265, but rather a recently enacted regulation of Boniface VIII.[3] Yet, at the same time, the dean and chapter of nearby Calahorra were plagued by visions of an unsleeping papal monster forever on the *qui vive* for a false move, whom three years later they forestalled by filling a vacant benefice worth all of five *maravedís*, lest 'per negligentiam episcopi ad quem potestas conferendi jure ordinario termino pertinebat' collation should devolve to the Roman Church.[4]

There is evidence to suggest that the pontiffs did not deserve this evil reputation. On occasion they were even generous in their dealings with the Spanish churches. During the first half of the century both Compostela and Túy owed a debt of gratitude to Gregory IX and Innocent IV respectively for tolerating a combination of capitular

---

[1] AC Toledo, A.7.G.1.1.: 'Accepimus quod ecclesia Burgensis...ex eo quod plures dignitates, canonie et tam maiores quam minores portiones iamdudum vacarant ibidem, cum sede Burgensi vacante non sit preter Romanum pontificem qui conferre possit easdem, legitimis erat servitoribus et defensoribus destituta'; AHN, 184/9 (below, Ch. 12).

[2] *Part.* 1.16.11 (Academy ed., I, 418); Juan Manuel, *Libro de los Estados,* ed. Gayangos, *BAE,* LI, 360; Barraclough, *Papal Provisions,* 148, 166 ff.

[3] Above, p. 184; AC Tudela, 41–12–9: 'Intelleximus a personis gravibus et fidedignis sanctissimum dominum Bonifacium octavum collaciones beneficiorum in curia romana vacancium reservasse simpliciter sue collacioni' (reg. Fuentes, *Catálogo,* 442), 29 Jan. 1299.

[4] AC Calahorra, doc. 492, 18 March 1302.

division and electoral sharp practice;[1] and in the 1290s the church of Córdoba twice laid itself open to papal intervention and was twice reprieved. First, when the *magister scolarum* of León, Juan Fernández, resigned his rights as bishop-elect at Perugia during the papal vacancy in February 1294 – possibly on account of his illegitimacy[2] – the chapter held another election and secured the assent of their choice, the archdeacon of Ribadeo (Astorga), within a week of Celestine V's appointment; and their action was permitted to pass unchallenged.[3] Then, on the death of Gil Domínguez and the division of the chapter nine to seven, Boniface VIII admitted the holder of the bare majority, Fernando Gutiérrez, allowed him to borrow his living expenses when he came to Rome, and absolved him from the obligation to make the visit *ad limina* in person thereafter. Yet on his return to Castile Bishop Fernando showed the extent of his gratitude by telling the old tale that all curialists were scoundrels.[4]

Boniface may have been acting in the knowledge that certain of Spain's more distinguished churchmen – men, that is, who had the ear of the king – had reached the conclusion that the episcopal dignity involved more trouble than it was worth. It was certainly an expensive business: Bishop Vicente of Porto, who died in April 1296, reckoned that he had spent at least £7,000 of his own money 'in servitia et deffensione nostrae ecclesiae cathedralis'.[5] Then there was the disagreeable prospect of being brought face to face with two masters at one remove. Rodrigo of Toledo had suffered some nasty moments in the early part of the century when his two worlds clashed; and similar considerations may well have been in the mind of

---

[1] *Reg. Inn. IV,* 7425. For Compostela, see below, p. 265.

[2] He was dispensed in July 1295; *Reg. Bon. VIII,* 333.

[3] AC Toledo, X.1.C.2.7; X.1.C.1.1h: 'Quia predictus Egidius Dominici absens electus fuit et inscius, nec nobis ad plenum constabat ubi esset, licet ab aliquibus diceretur quod Bononiensi studio insistebat', they sent out a search-party on 15 May. He was found near Pamplona on 30 June and after the customary show of resistance ('utinam essem dignus ad tantam ecclesiam regendum') he accepted the offer.

[4] AC Toledo, X.1.C.2.8 (= *Reg. Bon. VIII,* 3634); Gómez Bravo, *Catálogo de los obispos de Córdoba,* I, 285; *Reg. Bon. VIII,* 3632bis, 3846; above, Ch. 10. Boniface also provided Córdoba Cathedral with certain constitutions, mentioned in a papal bull of 1556; but no record of them has survived. Cf. R. Fawtier, *Hand-list of Charters, Deeds, and similar Documents in the possession of the John Rylands Library,* I (Manchester, 1925), 71.

[5] *Censual do Cabido da Sé do Porto,* 419–20.

João Martins de Soalhães when he rejected the primatial see of Portugal in May 1292, though the reason he gave the canons of Braga was that the burden of episcopal office was not something that ought to be assumed *perfunctorie*.[1] For when this royal counsellor and diplomat was offered the see of Lisbon twenty months later he accepted it with alacrity and with none of the soul-searching of the previous occasion.[2] Lisbon was less problematical. It straddled the politico-ecclesiastical borders. As a suffragan of Compostela it provided its occupant with more room for manoeuvre.

In the 1230s and 1240s the two *Johannes Hispani* had led a similar double life.[3] So had Fernando Johannis de Portucarrario, dean of Braga and notary to Alfonso X, in the fifties, sixties and seventies, as a servant of the Castilian Crown with property in Galicia on both sides of the political frontier[4] but little or no sense of gratitude to those amongst whom he had prospered, to judge by the absence of Castilians from the list of beneficiaries in his will.[5] It is remarkable,

---

1 ADB, Gav. dos Arcebispos, 16: 'Cum negotium de quo agitur sit arduum et tantum onus subire et suis humeris subportare sit quamplurimum difficile, grave et quodammodo importabile secundum fastigium tante dignitatis, considerando etiam quod nichil est adeo terribile quam officium episcopale si perfunctorie agatur'; ADB, Gav. dos Privilégios do Cabido, 5; *Reg. Bon. VIII*, 344; Ferreira, *Fastos episcopaes*, II, 94.

2 ADB, Gav. dos Arcebispos, 17, 19. On 4 Oct. 1297 Boniface VIII forgave him certain offences at the request of King Dinis. In 1301 he was one of the king's proctors at the Curia: ADB, Gav. das Notícias Várias, 21 (*inc. Celsitudinis tue*); *ibid.* 20; Finke, *Acta Aragonensia*, I, 102; *Reg. Bon. VIII*, 4121.

3 Above, Ch. 6.

4 Above, p. 204. He was prior of Guimarães as well as dean of Braga; and in León, apart from Crastello, he held property of the abbey of Celanova at Ecclesiola and Sande (Túy). The document confirming his rights there was witnessed at Seville in July 1263 by Bishop Juan of Orense, the injured party in the Crastello episode: ADB, Gav. dos Arcebispos, 33; Gav. das Religioens, 10.

5 He prepared his will at Burgos in Nov. 1272. It provided for wine to revive the canons of Braga after vespers; a standing offer of one *maravedí* for any canon who managed to attend matins every day for a month; and £50 for the Franciscans and Dominicans of Guimarães with the request 'quod si in aliquo eis erravi parcant mihi': ADB, *Livro I dos Testamentos*, fos. 13r–14r. Not that these provisions were necessarily executed, for, on 31 March 1276, Innocent V informed Pedro Hispano, cardinal bishop of Tusculum (the future John XXI) that, after the dean had died 'curiam nostram sequentem apud Sanctum Saturninum [Saturnia, 60 kilometres north-west of Viterbo?]', his property had been seized by his nephew, Martinho Peres de Portucarrario, and by João Martins de Soalhães, 'non sine camere nostre ad quam taliter decedentium bona de antiqua et observata consuetudine spectare noscuntur preiudicio'. The cardinal was charged with its recovery, and on 16 May

though, that a man of such standing never became one of Alfonso's bishops, for his training had certainly fitted him to act *perfunctorie* in that office. Perhaps he shared the view of the natural son of Alfonso IX of León, Fernando Alfonso, who declined the see of Salamanca in 1246, preferring to continue as archdeacon of that church; which he did for another forty years, combining that office with the deanery of Compstela and receipt of a pension from Ávila, and by his longevity delaying the more equitable distribution of rents in favour of the other three Salamanca archdeaconries which Cardinal Gil Torres had authorised the year before his rejection of the mitre.[1]

It was not, then, only saintly men and retiring types, like Hermannus Alemannus, who resisted episcopal promotion. For – though there were, of course, always some whose one ambition was to wield a pastoral staff[2] – it must have been clear to many that the pastoral staff reversed was a rod for their own backs. Moreover, by exposing themselves to papal scrutiny as contenders for sees, well-heeled archdeacons ran something of a risk, as the cautionary tale of the archdeacon of Trastamar shows. By 1267 Archdeacon Juan Alfonso had, with the king's help, accumulated a fine collection of benefices, but in that year his campaign to secure the archbishopric of Compostela had the result of causing his adversaries in the chapter to draw attention to the fact that Innocent IV's original indulgence to him, upon which the whole soaring superstructure of pluralism was based, had been obtained under false pretences. Whereupon the entire edifice collapsed, and Clement IV reserved all his benefices.[3] There

---

he wrote from Rome to Archbishop Ordonho of Braga, instructing him, in accordance with the mandate *Dilectum filium*, to have the dean's goods entrusted to Giraldo, archdeacon of Couto: ADB, Colecçao Cronológica, d.s.n. Conceivably, the dean had been in Italy on Alfonso X's business.

[1] *Reg. Inn. IV*, 2317. For his relationship to Alfonso IX, *ibid.* 1275. The fifteenth-century *Memoria de los aniversarios* in AC Salamanca (fo. 17v) described him as 'el fijo del rey Don Fernando que gano a Cordoba y a Sevilla'; and Mondéjar, *Memorias*, 490, as a son of Alfonso X. For Cardinal Gil's Salamanca constitutions, Mansilla, *Iglesia castallano–leonesa*, 325. See also Portela Pazos, *Decanologio de Santiago*, 99–102; Julio González, *Alfonso IX*, I, 314; *idem, Correo Erudito*, III, 194 ff.

[2] One such was Martín, the dean of Burgos who almost won that see in 1269, and eventually secured Sigüenza in May 1275; *Reg. Greg. X*, 608. In 1263 he had made a bid for Ávila, and in 1264 for Toledo. On that occasion Urban IV had warned him that if his claim proved flimsy he would be punished by being deprived of his benefices: *Reg. Urb. IV*, 331, 664, 2826.

[3] *Reg. Clem. IV*, 545. In Aug. 1264, when Alfonso X had written on his behalf to

was much to be said for the private enterprise of Alfonso IX's bastard, and others followed his example, recognising the nettle for what it was, and choosing not to grasp it.

Understandably, therefore, the popes wooed the reluctant and rewarded the acquiescent with grants and favours. When Mateo Riñal, archdeacon of Palenzuela (Burgos), was promoted to the see of Salamanca in December 1245, and then, eight months later, was translated to Cuenca before he had been consecrated, he received a bonus from Innocent IV on each occasion. His Burgos canonry and prebend were allotted to his brother, Juan; and the debts which he had amassed during his stay at the Curia were referred for settlement to the church of Salamanca which had never seen him.[1] Similarly, Bishop Pascal of Jaén's Osma benefices were awarded to his brother, Bartolomé; Bishop Juan of Mondoñedo was permitted to draw the income of his Spanish benefices for two years after his consecration; and Archbishop Sancho of Toledo distributed his among his *familiares*.[2] Felipe of Seville and Suero Pérez of Zamora received the same treatment from Alexander IV;[3] and at the end of the century the practice was continued by Boniface VIII, who allowed Fernando of Oviedo to retain his Palencia benefices for three years, in view of the heavy debts of his new church; Martinho of Braga to assign his to six of his *clerici familiares*; and Pascal of Cuenca to continue to receive the income of the archdeaconry of Olmedo (Ávila).[4]

The effect of grants and favours such as these was to assist the poor at the expense of others who were no better off. This was an old Spanish practice, but Burgos still needed some persuading when,

Urban IV that 'nullum (es) adhuc in regnis ejus per sedem apostolicam vel aliquem prelatorum dictorum regnorum ad precum ejusdem regis instantiam, beneficium assecutus', he possessed – apart from the archdeaconry of Trastamar – the archdeaconry of Carballedo (Astorga), the deanery of Lugo, the secular abbacy of Árbas (Oviedo), rents at Orense and a León canonry – all of which the pope was prepared to believe were worth less than forty marks *per annum*: so he was provided to a León dignity: *Reg. Urb. IV*, 2080, 2093. See above, p. 140.

1 *Reg. Inn. IV*, 2317, 3142; AC Burgos, vol. 71, fo. 77v (reg. Mansilla, *AA*, IX, no. 12); *Reg. Inn. IV*, 3191.
2 *Reg. Inn. IV*, 4901 (Oct. 1250); 4162 (Oct. 1248); 7334 (March 1254): the last of these made an exception in favour of poverty-stricken Palencia. In the event Sancho retained his Burgos benefices: above, p. 170.
3 *Reg. Alex. IV*, 98 (Jan. 1255); 871 (Oct. 1255).
4 *Reg. Bon. VIII*, 1301 (= AC Oviedo, A/11/8: reg. García Larragueta, *Catálogo*, 529, misdescribed); ADB, Colecçao Cronológica, III/4/24; *Reg. Bon. VIII*, 3240.

together with Salamanca, it was required to subsidise Mateo Riñal.[1] Palencia in the 1290s had no charity to spare for Oviedo or for anyone else, as Bishop Álvaro made clear in the following year by disobeying a provision mandate, only to be reminded by Boniface that, having himself been translated through no merits of his own ('absentem et ignorantem') from that backwater, Mondoñedo, he had a moral – not to mention a legal – duty to conform.[2] It was a bitter pill to swallow; and so was the grant to Pascal of Cuenca, since when Gregory X had originally assigned him the archdeaconry of Olmedo, the chapter of Ávila had retaliated, though in vain, by stripping the dignity of the rents which the constitutions of 1250 had attached to it, and transferring them to the episcopal *mensa*.[3]

The rights of the churches to which the bishops were promoted were also plundered, to provide funds to cope with the burden of inherited debt and the demands made by needy relatives.[4] Frequently, papal largesse to bishops took the form of grants of collation to benefices which was normally shared with the chapter[5] or – as in the case of Alexander IV's aforementioned concession to Sancho of Toledo – which belonged to other churches within the province.[6] When applying for such a grant in October 1247 Mateo Riñal masqueraded as a reformer, stating that it was his intention to introduce literate clerics into the Cuenca chapter;[7] but if that was ever the actual effect of this form of papal intervention, it was never its self-confessed purpose.

In fairness to the pontiffs who made so free with the rights of others, though, it must be said that they were no less lavish with what was

---

[1] *Reg. Inn. IV*, 3283 (Oct. 1247).

[2] *Reg. Bon. VIII*, 1807, 2879, 2640.

[3] AC Toledo, caj. I.12, d.s.n (*inc. Ad audientiam nostram*, 1 April 1286); X.2.D.1.5. For the Ávila constitutions, see Mansilla, 346.

[4] Sancha Páez wrote from Galicia to her brother, Bishop Abril of Urgel, asking him to take one of her sons into his household and to send her some of the money reserved for the poor of his diocese: AC Seo de Urgel, d.s.n: publ. Linehan, *AEM*, forthcoming.

[5] For Oviedo, March 1257, renewing a grant of Innocent IV: *Reg. Alex. IV*, 1919; Vich, Dec. 1256: above, p. 44; Palencia, pre-June 1263: *Reg. Urb. IV*, 281; Cuenca, Dec. 1263: above, p. 185; Seville, May 1264: *ibid.* 1625; León, July 1264: *ibid.* 1946; Barcelona, Sept. 1265: *Reg. Clem. IV*, 147; Compostela, March 1273: *Reg. Greg. X*, 135.

[6] Renewed for Sancho of Aragon in Oct. 1272: *Reg. Greg. X*, 125.

[7] *Reg. Inn. IV*, 3284.

theirs, by granting collation of benefices which had devolved to the Roman Church[1], providing protection against the sentences of judges delegate,[2] and remitting the bishops' obligation to make costly visits *ad limina*.[3] The second of these privileges could be, however, and frequently was nullified; and while the popes were evidently far from anxious to have the Curia cluttered up with Spaniards, the Spaniards themselves were at least as determined to come as Innocent IV and others were determined to keep them away. For the visit *ad limina* provided a useful opportunity for combining business, and even pleasure, with duty. Rodrigo of Palencia was not the only prelate who preferred to ignore a papal indulgence of this nature.[4]

[1] Oviedo, July 1245: *Reg. Inn. IV*, 1387; Oct. 1290: AC Oviedo, A/10/12 (reg. García Larragueta, 496); Sept. 1296: *Reg. Bon. VIII*, 1367; Pamplona, June 1247: AC Pamplona, V Episcopi, 20 (reg. Goñi Gaztambide, *Catálogo*, 557); Tarragona, Dec. 1252: *Reg. Inn. IV*, 6114; León – together with grants of annates and *tercias*, Aug. 1254: *ibid.* 7959–61; Dec. 1256: *Reg. Alex. IV*, 1641; Sept. 1290: *Reg. Nich. IV*, 3403; Compostela, July 1264: *Reg. Urb. IV*, 1872; Feb. 1290: *Reg. Nich. IV*, 2128; Seville, Sept. 1289: *ibid.* 1460; Huesca, March 1291: AC Huesca, 2–82 (reg. Durán Gudiol, *AA*, VII, no. 127); Ciudad Rodrigo, July 1298: *Reg. Bon. VIII*, 2619; Toledo, Jan. 1300: *ibid.* 3510 (=AC Toledo, A.7.H.1.5).

[2] During Innocent IV's pontificate alone: Calahorra, *Etsi libenter*, 21 March (year missing): AC Calahorra, doc. 276; Oviedo, 17–8–1245: *Reg. Inn. IV*, 1432; Valencia, *Vestris devotis*, 22–10–1245: AC Valencia, perg. 2382 (reg. Olmos Canalda, *Pergaminos*, 175: misdated); Toledo, *Dignus es*, 25–10–1245: AC Toledo, A.6.H.1.2; A.6.H.2.4a; Gerona, *Tue pacis*, 27–2–1246 (renewed, 24–11–1246, with superscription 'Petit eciam episcopus Gerundensis sub nova data renovari de gratia speciali'): AE Gerona, 6/57; 6/59; Astorga, *Personam tuam*, 26–9–1246: AD Astorga, 3/53 (reg. Quintana Prieto, *AA*, XI, no. 60); Palencia, 4–6–1247: *Reg. Inn. IV*, 2743; Tortosa, *Sincere devotionis*, 23–10–1248: AC Tortosa, caj. del Illmo Sr Obispo II, 33; Mondoñedo, *Meritis tue*, 7–3–1251: AC Mondoñedo, diplomas sig. XIII, d.s.n; Toledo, *Exigentibus tue*, 12–8–1252: AC Toledo, A.7.C.1.3a; Tarragona, *Affectu benevolentie*, 2–12–1252: AHA, *Cartoral AB*, fo. 33r.

[3] Porto, 'de biennio ad triennium', Oct. 1235: *Reg. Greg. IX*, 2812; Palencia, June 1247: *Reg. Inn. IV*, 2809; Lisbon, reduced from biennial to triennial, July 1263; abolished completely, June 1267: *Reg. Urb. IV*, 305; *Reg. Clem. IV*, 476. During the pontificates of Honorius IV, Nicholas IV and Boniface VIII, the bishops of Lamego, Astorga, Salamanca, Sigüenza, Cartagena, Tarazona, Seville, Ávila, Huesca, Lérida, Valencia, Barcelona, Tarragona, Oviedo, Gerona, Osma, Pamplona and Calahorra all received either partial or total remission: *Reg. Hon. IV*, 615, 730; *Reg. Nich. IV*, 20, 903, 1433, 1470, 1499, 2735, 2830, 2931, 4162, 7119; *Reg. Bon. VIII*, 520, 2228, 2071, 3822, 3846. It may be noted that the archbishop of Tarragona's obligation, reduced from biennial to triennial on 30 Jan. 1292, had previously been triennial: AHA, *Index dels Indices*, fo. 37r; *Reg. Alex. IV*, 908 (Nov. 1255).

[4] Above, p. 149. On 3 Jan. 1298 – only four months after his obligation had been remitted – Bishop Bernardo of Gerona sent proctors to the Curia 'ad limina

The pope could suspend the rule concerning devolved benefices in particular cases – as when the bishop of Segovia, in whose diocese there were many vacancies, dithered at the Curia;[1] and he could grant indulgences which would or might attract alms to their churches.[2] When it went beyond this, though, *favor apostolicus* infringed the rights of others. For example, one type of grant – permission to employ substitutes for the diocesan or provincial visitation[3] – was tantamount to a grant of income tax, since there were few prelates as scrupulous as Gonzalo Palomeque of Toledo who, on hearing that his agents had taken 3,500 *maravedís* from Jaén and 4,500 from Córdoba, issued a stern rebuke and ordered them to make restitution.[4] And grants of diocesan annates – normally good for three years,[5] but on at least two occasions for five[6] – had the same effect of pandering to the acquisitive instincts of prelates who were hardly in need of any encouragement. The zeal with which the cuckoo-archbishop of Toledo, Sancho of Aragon, proceeded to raise huge loans on the security of his church's revenues as soon as he was promoted and irrespective of the undertakings which he had given to Clement IV,[7] was shared by others whose pastoral reputation stands higher. His two successors at Toledo, Gonzalo Gudiel and Gonzalo Palomeque, uncle and nephew, both picked their churches clean before moving on to their next posts. The activities of the former –

apostolorum...visitandum, ad impetrandum etc. et exponendum domino pape vel aliis loco sui miserum nostrum et ecclesie Gerundensis statum et oppressiones quibus una cum ipsa ecclesia affligimur': *Reg. Bon. VIII*, 2228; AE Gerona, *Liber Notularum* (1294–1300), G.1.1, loose doc. between fos. 77 and 78.

1 *Reg. Nich. IV*, 482 (Feb. 1289).
2 Salamanca, Feb. 1289: AC Salamanca, 16/1, fos. 8v–9v (reg. Marcos, 415, 414); Oviedo, July 1290; July 1291: *Reg. Nich. IV*, 3019; AC Oviedo, *Plomados*, 3/15 (reg. García Larragueta, 500); Valencia, June 1291: *Reg. Nich. IV*, 5370.
3 Oviedo, July 1290; Zaragoza, July 1291: *Reg. Nich. IV*, 2994, 5716.
4 'Lo erraran muy gravamente...non debieran rrecibir dinero si non la visitacion fecha': AC Toledo, X.1.C.2.3 (Dec. 1301). The pope had issued the grant, which was good for two years, on 21 Jan. 1299. One of the executors – Bartholomew of Capua – ordered the province to pay within six days. It had been renewed in 1300: AC Toledo, A.7.H.2.1 (*inc. Venerabilis frater noster*); A.7.H.2.2b; *Reg. Bon. VIII*, 3310.
5 Sigüenza, May 1289; Zaragoza, June 1289 (renewed July 1291); Tarragona and Seville, Sept. 1289; Tarazona, Oct. 1289: *Reg. Nich. IV*, 904, 1020, 5726, 1385, 1604, 1602.
6 *Ibid.* 2040 (= AC Salamanca, 23/75: reg. Marcos, 420), 4491.
7 *Reg. Clem. IV*, 1156 (Nov. 1266).

whom an admirer described as being concerned for the welfare of all the faithful – have already been mentioned.[1] His nephew was no better. On his translation fron Cuenca to Toledo in 1299 he took with him most of that church's goods and distributed the rest among his lay friends. Three years passed before his successor at Cuenca, Bishop Pascal, received compensation, during which time he, in turn, was dependent on his Ávila income.[2] Spanish churchmen, like the fleas in the verse, lived off others all along the line.

One of Juan Manuel's tales described the career of a dean of Santiago who rose to be pope, thanks to the magical powers of his tutor Don Illan de Toledo, but was then spirited back to Toledo for having assigned his benefices to his own relatives rather than to the magician's son, as he had promised.[3] (It was easier to make and un-make a pope than to secure a canonry!) That the perfidious dean should have been associated with Compostela was particularly appropriate, since, apart from being the home of those archetypal pluralists – the historical dean, Fernando Alfonso, and the archdeacon of Trastamar, Juan Alfonso – Compostela was also the anchorage of one of the great ecclesiastical pirates of thirteenth-century Spain, Archbishop Juan Arias.

Juan Arias (1238–67) owed his promotion to Gregory IX's admission of a minority appeal from the chapter of Compostela against the postulation of the canonist-bishop of Orense, Laurentius Hispanus, 'eo quod multi in eadem ecclesia reperiebantur idonei'.[4] In his dealings with others, though, the archbishop showed no such tender feelings for local rights and home rule. Like his predecessor, Bernardo, he stopped at nothing in his determination to extend the

---

1 See Alonso Alonso, *Comentario al 'De Substantia Orbis' de Averroes por Álvaro de Toledo*, 275–6; above, pp. 134–5.
2 Pascal's grievance was referred to judges delegate in Feb. 1299, but it was Bishop Simón of Sigüenza, as arbiter, who awarded him damages of 20,000 *maravedís* in March 1302: *Reg. Bon. VIII*, 2832; 3338; AC Toledo, X.1.E.2.2. The state of Cuenca after Gonzalo's ravages may explain why the archdeacon of Talavera, Sancho Martínez, declined the see in Feb. 1299: *Reg. Bon. VIII*, 2908.
3 *El libro de los Enxiemplos del Conde Lucanor et de Patronio*, ed. Knust, 45–51.
4 *Reg. Greg. IX*, 4177, 4588; Mansilla, *Iglesia castellano-leonesa*, 174–5; García y García, *Laurentius Hispanus*, 16–17. López Ferreiro, *Historia de Santiago*, v, 151, bases his account of the election of Juan Arias on the passage in the *Tumbillo de Tablas*, AC Santiago de Compostela, fo. 83v, which states simply that he was elected 'per viam Spiritus Sancti'.

hegemony of Santiago.[1] Though absent from the capture of Seville, he received property in the *repartimiento*, had his cross carried before him through that province, and pressed for the payment of *vota Sancti Jacobi* both there and at Badajoz.[2] Adept at finding benefices in other churches for his own dependents, he secured provision at Orense for his relative Pedro Yáñez, and at León for his Roman proctor Martín Yáñez – at a time when León could hardly afford to support its own man, Pedro Pérez.[3] He took advantage of divisions within the church of Salamanca – where Alexander IV had reserved the next election after certain enemies of Bishop Pedro Pérez had reported that he was at death's door, and the dignitaries were at odds with the canons over burial rights in the cathedral – and rode rough-shod over the local clergy and a papal mandate by intruding his own creatures into benefices from which he had ejected Gonzalo Peláez and other denizens, in contempt of Alexander's explicit instructions that they were to remain unmolested while waiting for full canonries to become vacant.[4] Again, by misinterpreting a papal mandate he interfered in the rights of collation of churches in his own arch-diocese.[5] Meanwhile he proved as good a gamekeeper as he was a poacher, and kept his own preserve shut to outsiders. When the representative of Master Abril – the future bishop of Urgel who had

---

[1] For Bernardo's prevention of the restoration of the see of Mérida – a skeleton in Compostela's cupboard since 1120 – see Mansilla, 78–81; Lomax, *Orden de Santiago*, 24; *Reg. Greg. IX*, 3226; Valdeavellano, *Historia de España*, I, ii, 418. He trespassed within the dioceses of Astorga and Oviedo, and demanded *vota Sancti Jacobi* from the *concejos* of the archdiocese of Toledo: Quintana Prieto, *AA*, XI, nos 49, 52–3; AC Santiago, *Tumbillo de Tablas*, fos. 100v–103v; AC Oviedo, B/4/15–16 (reg. García Larragueta, 266, 281); AC Toledo, Z.3.D.1.20, *inc. De Toleto*, 13 Aug. 1228.

[2] Above, Ch. 6; Ballesteros, *Sevilla en el siglo XIII*, cx–cxi; *inc. Venerabilis frater noster*, 28 Feb. 1259: AC Santiago, *Tumbillo de Tablas*, fo. 84r; ADB, Gav. dos Votos, 9, fo. 1r–v.

[3] *Reg. Alex. IV*, 864, 1647; *Reg. Inn. IV*, 6317; *Reg. Urb. IV*, 906, 2826. After Arch-bishop Juan's fall from grace, the León proctor was made a charge on Compostela: *ibid.* 2025.

[4] AC Salamanca, 23/33; 28/1/53; 23/31; 23/66: 'asserens portiones ipsas eo pretextu quod dicti portionarii in predicta ecclesia in canonicos sunt recepti tanto tempore vacavisse quod ad eum erat ipsarum collatio devoluta' (reg. Marcos, 295, 283, 292, 294); Beltrán de Heredia, *Cartulario...de Salamanca*, 67.

[5] AC Santiago, *Tumbillo de Tablas*, fos. 85v–6r: 'Credens per hoc datam tibi per litteras ipsas potestatem ad providendum de alienis beneficiis prorogari in ecclesia ipsa et aliis ad eorundem prioris et capituli collationem spectantium': *inc. Dilecti filii prior*, 7 Aug. 1257.

an expectancy there – requested that the Compostela prebend made vacant by the death of the archdeacon of Palencia be assigned to him, Juan Arias flatly refused, observing that only if the pope intervened in person would Abril receive satisfaction.[1] And by September 1260, when he and his chapter vowed to disregard all future papal provisions, his attitude had hardened even further. Bernardus Compostellanus may well have had him in mind when he explained that the pope had been moved to reserve episcopal elections 'quia prompti essent archiepiscopi in cassandis electionibus, ut provisionum potestas rediret ad eos.' Contempt for the rights of others, which Juan Arias attributed to the pope, was indeed his own besetting sin.[2]

The squabbling canons of Salamanca laid themselves open to Juan Arias, and – as at Burgos in the early 1270s – the luxury of discord proved expensive in material terms. Spiritually too the repercussions were grave, since the type of deadlock reached at Burgos meant that, while unbeneficed clergy were clamouring for livings, cathedral chapters dwindled almost to vanishing point and pastoral administration was brought to a standstill – the same situation as obtained at Tarragona, Zaragoza, Huesca and Sigüenza because there it was proving increasingly difficult to recruit properly qualified canons who were prepared to abide by a regular rule.[3] To the Church leaders the spiritual issue may have appeared the less important of the two. Many treated the parish as an economic unit rather than as a social or religious entity. Archbishop Martinho of Braga, for example, wrote to his chapter from Montpellier in April 1302 to assure them that the forty days' residence qualification for new members applied only to their canonries, not to their parochial income. 'Esto non foy nossa entençao', he insisted.[4] But popular attitudes, which were conditioned

---

1 AC Seo de Urgel, Col.lecció Plandolít: publ. Linehan, *AEM*, forthcoming.
2 Barraclough, *Cath. Hist. Rev.*, XIX, 291–2; López Ferreiro, v, 158.
3 In the late 1240s Pedro de Albalat sought to regularise the chapter of Zaragoza on account of the lack of 'persone litterate et ydonee' in those parts: ASV, arm. XXXI.72, fo. 101v (Schillmann, *Formularsammlung*, 401). Cf. *Reg. Inn. IV*, 4567 By June 1265 the Augustinian chapter of Sigüenza was reduced from twenty canons to six, for the same reason, 'sicque dicta ecclesia defectum in divinis officiis et in suis juribus non modicam patitur lesionem...cum non sit qui pro ea se tunc murum defensionis opponat ac jura tueatur ejusdem quampluribus diripientibus bona ejus': *Reg. Clem. IV*, 129. Change, though, was delayed for almost forty years: see below, Ch. 12, and for Huesca; for Tarragona and Burgos, above, pp. 41, 256.
4 ADB, Gav. dos Privilégios do Cabido, 7.

by the selfish antics of the higher clergy, *were* relevant for the Church at a time when spiritual sanctions were proving increasingly ineffective. It was not only in Germany that there was disregard for the thunderings and fulminations issuing from Rome in the 1240s. The malaise was general, and Spain too had its crisis of confidence in the clergy, for which crisis the clergy themselves were responsible. Lucas of Túy noted that the in-fighting among the canons of León over a successor to Bishop Rodrigo in the early thirties played straight into the hands of the Albigensians of those parts 'qui semper sitiunt discordiam cleri' and accounted for the enthusiasm with which the heretics were received there.[1] At Salamanca, as the constitutions of 1245 observed, popular criticism concentrated on the monopoly of benefices by the few and the exclusion from preferment of worthy local candidates; and simoniacal practices added fuel to the flames.[2] Soon after the Lyons Council, Innocent IV admitted that the spiritual sword was losing its edge in the province of Tarragona – an impression which cold steel and the bishop of Gerona's injuries served merely to confirm for Matthew Paris.[3] The private lives of the clergy were beyond redemption, and the pontiff was soon to have to admit defeat on that score too. But while Pedro de Albalat and his assistants in Aragon continued to defend this last ditch, even after the High Command had given the order for retreat, the battle in Castile was shifted to lower ground and an attempt was made to eliminate the causes of clerical discord by providing constitutions which would regulate the internal economy of the cathedral churches.

This task, like the question of clerical concubinage, was referred to Cardinal Gil Torres. It seems, indeed, to have been in the light of his investigations into the financial affairs of the Castilian churches that the cardinal became convinced of the futility of John of Abbeville's thoroughgoing measures, his reversal of which has all the appearances of a decision of secondary importance, reached during the discussions

---

[1] *De altera vita*, III, ix, ed. Mariana, 169.

[2] 'Unde non levis instantia et contemptus gravis tam adversus episcopum quam clerum in populo consurgebant': publ. Mansilla, 323; *Reg. Hon. III*, 2272 (MDH, 252). See also *Fueros leoneses*, ed. Castro and Onís, 167, 192–3, for the penalties prescribed in the *fuero* of Salamanca for abusing bishop or clergy.

[3] 'Hispania usque ad ascisionem linguarum episcopalium desaevit': *Chronica Majora*, IV, 579; above, p. 79; '*Non absque dolore* cordis et plurima turbacione didicimus quod ita in plerisque partibus ecclesiastica censura dissolvitur et canonice sententie enervuntur...': AHN, 161/2, 2 Oct. 1245.

about the level of incomes – the really important issue – on the advice of Spaniards whose primary purpose in coming to the Curia had been concern for personal property, not alarm about the decline of clerical morality.[1]

Neither the concept of written constitutions nor the intervention of a cardinal represented any new departure for the Castilian Church. In the 1170s the legate Hyacinth had fixed the number of canons and prebendaries at Lugo; John of Abbeville had adjusted the incomes of dignitaries at Astorga and Barcelona; and Pelayo Gaitán had provided a set of constitutions for León – where, possibly, he had once been bishop-elect[2] – as well as attending to the internal affairs of Cuenca and Mondoñedo.[3] Characteristically, Juan Arias had not looked for any lead from Rome but had already in 1240 worked out Compostela's salvation, dividing capitular property among the canons, issuing a statute *de numero canonicorum* which received papal approval six years later, and subsequently urging his suffragans to deal likewise with the parishes for which they were responsible.[4]

Innocent IV's approval of the Compostela constitutions reflected the anxiety which had been expressed at the Lyons Council about the material prosperity of cathedral and collegiate churches.[5] It was pressure from below that brought Cardinal Gil into action in 1245.[6] Gil's constitutions, though, differed markedly from earlier examples of the genre. Based on detailed *inquisitiones* – surveys of capitular endowments of great topographical interest[7] – they were far more extensive than Cardinal Pelayo's for León and, having as their object the partition of the *mensa communis* between bishop and chapter, were distinct

---

1 'Nos cum prelatis et aliis viris discretis Hispaniae apud Sedem Apostolicam constituti': *VL*, v, 285–6.
2 Mansilla, 194; above, Ch. 2. For the León constitutions, see *Reg. Hon. III*, 5017 (MDH, 504); Mansilla, *AA*, I, 53 ff.; for Pelayo, below, Ch. 12.
3 AC Cuenca, 4/17/243; *Reg. Hon. III*, 5629 (MDH, 571).
4 López Ferreiro, v, 156–7, 186–9; appendix 22.
5 Can. 13, *Cura nos pastoralis*: Hefele–Leclercq, v, ii, 1649–51.
6 AC Segovia, doc. 241: 'Hinc est quod clamoribus vestris quod tenuitate proventuum intolerabili, ut asseritis, pressi, subveniri vobis de prestimoniis vestre ecclesie supplicastis, dominus papa...sub dissimulatione non potuit preterire...' (Lyons, 3 Oct. 1245).
7 The Burgos *inquisitio* was publ. by Flórez, *ES*, XXVI, 482–9; and the Calahorra *inquisitio* by Hergueta (from BN, MS 704: a late sixteenth-century copy), *RABM*, XVII, 423–32. Those for Ávila and Segovia – AC Ávila, doc. 15; AC Segovia, doc. 17 – seem never to have been published. There is no *inquisitio* in AC Salamanca.

in conception from those of John of Abbeville who had set such store by the corporate existence of the cathedral canons. Since Mansilla has written of them and has published the text of those that were transcribed into the papal registers, there is no need to cover the same ground again. That author, though, underestimates Gil's achievement by confining himself to Vatican sources. He deals at length with only four sets of constitutions – those for Salamanca, Ávila, Burgos and Calahorra. Details of two more – for Plasencia and Segovia – which he merely mentions in passing, are preserved in Spanish archives; and in addition, Córdoba, Cuenca and, possibly, Ciudad Rodrigo were also beholden to the cardinal.[1]

Gil's constitutions were based on two principles which many other Spanish churches adopted piecemeal during the course of the century. One was the partition of endowments between bishop and chapter which Gregory IX described as 'iuxta generalem consuetudinem aliarum ecclesiarum Ispanie' when he sanctioned it at Guarda in June 1234.[2] The other – the 'one year rule' whereby the *prestimonia* of deceased canons were paid to their executors for that, or sometimes a shorter period after their death – had been in operation at Palencia as early as 1155.[3] Cardinal Gil thoroughly approved of it, describing it in his Plasencia constitutions as 'consuetudinem laudabilem que in

---

[1] Mansilla, 193 ff., 321 ff., 344 ff., 359 ff., 371 ff. For Segovia, see following pages; for Córdoba, Gómez Bravo, I, 263–4; Muñoz Vázquez, *Bol. R. Acad. de Córdoba*, XXVI, 71. The text of the Plasencia constitutions (mentioned by Fernández, *Historia de Plasencia*, 36) is in RAH, MS C/7–9/5427, fos. 134v–43r. The only record of his intervention at Cuenca is in Morales' reference to a document, seen at AC Cuenca *c*. 1750, concerning Gil's reduction of the number of *racioneros* and *medio-racioneros* to ten and twelve respectively (April 1251): BN, MS 13071, fo. 55. The date of the Ciudad Rodrigo constitutions – Jan. 1252 – suggests that Gil may have had a hand in their preparation: BN, MS 7112, cap. 4.

[2] *Reg. Greg. IX*, 2087. In March 1224 Bishop Pedro of Astorga and his chapter had prepared a *distinctio* of the property of the see, in order to avoid any *occasio discordie*: conf. by Honorius III, *Cum venerabilis*, 7 June 1225 (LDH, 66).

[3] Lomax in *Homenaje Vicens Vives*, I, 286. Adopted at Compostela, Feb. 1223: AC Santiago de Compostela, *Tumbillo de Tablas*, fo. 109r; León, Jan. 1241: *ES*, xxxv, 428–9 (conf. Jan. 1256, not 1227 as García Villada, *Catálogo*: AC León, doc. 1528); Vich, Feb. 1246: AC Vich, 37–1–11 (conf. July 1251; Aug. 1293: AC Vich, cód. 220, fos. 47v–8r; 37–16–10); Córdoba, March 1255: Gómez Bravo, I, 270; Oviedo, May 1255: AC Oviedo, B/5/1 (reg. García Larragueta, 359); Gerona, Sept. 1255: AC Gerona, *Cartulario Carlomagno*, fo. 75r; Zamora, July 1256: AC Zamora, 13/49; Valencia, Aug. 1277: AC Valencia, perg. 1289 (reg. Olmos, 527); Cartagena, June 1281: publ. Torres Fontes, *Documentos del sig. XIII*, 67–8. A 'six month rule' was

plerisque ecclesiarum Hispanie laudabiliter observatur'.[1] Laudable though it may have been, however, it was primarily a protective measure and was associated with the rule that a canon or prebendary was to receive no income during his first year of tenure.[2] It was designed to prevent absenteeism and, at Cuenca for example, was very strictly applied.[3]

Once the cardinal's partition had received papal confirmation, members of the chapter and their successors in perpetuity were bound by its terms. If, as happened at Calahorra, it proved to be to their disadvantage, the disinherited had no redress but were wholly dependent for relief on episcopal charity.[4] The chapters were, therefore, all the more anxious to secure the best possible terms, and it was probably their concern that accounts for the long delay which occurred in the process of issuing all but one of Gil's constitutions.[5] At Segovia, for example, the battle lasted almost two years. In October 1245 Gil expressed some doubt about the feasibility of his provisional allocation of rents to each member of the chapter and, in view of the state of the economy, made its adoption contingent upon the findings of the dean and the archdeacons of Segovia and Sepúlveda whom he

adopted at Mondoñedo, April 1251: AC Mondoñedo, diplomas sig. XIII, d.s.n; and at Urgel, March 1258: AC Seo de Urgel, *Dotium sive dotaliarum liber secundus*, fos. 20v–2r. Generally, the rule was effective only when death occurred at a particular period of the year: e.g. after 24 Dec. at Burgos, Jan. 1264, and Cuenca, 1265: ES, XXVI, 329; AC Cuenca, 3/L/11/149; after matins on Christmas Day, at Calahorra, conf. Sept. 1270: AC Calahorra, doc. 356; between vespers on Holy Saturday and the end of that *era*, at Toledo, conf. May 1291: BN, MS 13041, fo. 20r; after 15 Aug. at Salamanca, Dec. 1299: AC Salamanca, 43/2/82 (reg. Marcos, 463); before 1 Sept. at Jaca, Feb. 1298: Arco, *BRAH*, LXV, 70.

1 RAH, MS C/7–9/5427, fo. 138v.

2 Huesca: Durán Gudiol, *REDC*, VII, cap. 114–16; Lugo, March 1285: AHN, cod. 1042B, fo. 21v; Palencia, Aug. 1288: AC Palencia, 4/1/5.

3 '...quod omnes illi qui decetero recepti fuerint sive in canoniis sive in portionibus teneantur facere residentiam in ecclesia Conchensi per unum annum integrum ita quod si una dies defuerit iterum teneantur annum incipere, et tempus quo antea servierint minime computatur. Alioquin non detur eis portio seu canonia in studio seu extra': AC Cuenca, 5/20/277 (an. 1250).

4 Bishop Rodrigo, in Nov. 1281, and Bishop Fernando, in May 1303, assisted the canons with grants of revenue, the latter referring to the 'magnam lesionem' which Gil's constitutions had inflicted upon them: AC Calahorra, doc. 396, 506.

5 The exception was Salamanca – where Bishop Martín was on the point of retiring, and had, perhaps, no stomach for a fight. Only a fortnight elapsed between the cardinal's decision and registration: *Reg. Inn. IV*, 1262 (= AC Salamanca, 15/2/51: reg. Marcos, 215, 217); 1439.

made responsible for the preparation of the *inquisitio* as a basis for the chapter's negotiations with Bishop Bernardo.[1] His reservations were justified. Even with the assistance of the abbot of Sotosalvos, a disinterested outsider, the parties were unable to provide Gil with their final settlement before 30 April 1247, and its revised terms indicate that the canons had had the worst of the recent tug-of-war. Moreover, though Gil approved their agreement later that year, on 14 September,[2] he was still involved with certain details of it in the autumn of 1250.[3]

Evidently the bishop of Segovia had fought a hard fight. Whether it had been an entirely clean fight is less clear though, for Cardinal Gil was amenable to pressure and there is reason to believe that he had a special weakness for bishops. Having confirmed the Ávila constitutions on 30 March 1250, he immediately adjusted them in favour of Bishop Benito, explaining that, although he was bound by the rules of fair play, he nevertheless felt obliged to express in tangible form his affection for the prelate. So he offered him, for life, either the 230 marks' pension which the dean of Compostela, Fernando Alfonso, received annually from that church, or, alternatively, the rents of Piedrahita del Barco, Foncalada and Ancados, which the constitutions had assigned to the chapter; and, choosing to alienate his cathedral chapter and not the royal bastard, Benito chose the latter.[4] Similarly, the newly elected bishop of Salamanca, Pedro Pérez, was left to settle the details of the demarcation of the archdeaconries of that see, and, while the Calahorra constitutions were still *sub judice*, Bishop

[1] AC Segovia, doc. 241. See above, p. 178.

[2] AC Segovia, doc. 17 (the *inquisitio*, dated 1 June 1247); doc. 36. Each member of the chapter had the 1245 proposed allocation reduced by 30 *maravedís*: thus the canons, whose share was cut from 80 *maravedís* to 50, were much harder hit than the dean (400–370). The episcopal *mensa* was endowed with rents worth five thousand *maravedís*. Colmenares, *Historia de Segovia*, 201, mentions only this final settlement.

[3] On 10 Aug. 1250 he wrote from Lyons, approving their agreement about the size of the chapter, and ordering measures to be taken against dignitaries of the church who had failed to provide, at the time of their admission, 'una decentem capam de xamito vel de alio pretioso panno serico...prout in ordinatione nostra plenius continetur': AC Segovia, 224, 265.

[4] AC Ávila, doc. 14 (copy in AHN, cod. 1443B, fo. 11va–b). The bishop had been with Gil in the previous month: *Reg. Inn. IV*, 4751. In Oct. 1256 the Ávila constitutions were supplemented also: López-Arévalo, *Un cabildo catedral de la Vieja Castilla*, 297–302. By then the rents in question had been restored to the chapter; the canons had the bishop's letter of renunciation (of July 1255) confirmed by the pope: *Reg. Alex. IV*, 920.

Aznar was allowed to reorganise the affairs of the collegiate church of Armentia.[1] Three years elapsed between the completion of the Calahorra constitutions and their eventual registration.[2] That in the case of Plasencia the interval was of only five weeks was probably due to the determination of the dean, Martín Pérez, who had a long-standing grievance against Bishop Adán Pérez. Anyway, there was not much for them to squabble about at Plasencia.[3]

The fundamental cause of tension between the bishops and their chapters was the question of promotion to benefices. Both at Segovia and at Salamanca that was the root of almost all the trouble,[4] as it was, indeed, throughout the century and throughout Europe. Whatever their personal merits, and whether they came in under the bishop's cloak or with a papal mandate, outsiders were *alieni* and were bitterly resented by the local-born *oriundi*. They were not welcome and that was that. The chapter of Mondoñedo expressed the classic home-rule view when, in 1297, they told Boniface VIII that any of their number would be 'more useful' as bishop than an outsider. And the same consideration applied to canonries. There was little sympathy for the attitude of Archbishop Gonzalo of Toledo who had put it to his chapter nine years earlier that, provided he appointed suitable men, it mattered not whence they came.[5] For 'suitability' was defined by a

---

1 *Reg. Inn. IV*, 2419 (Feb. 1247); AC Calahorra, doc. 302bis (July 1249).
2 *Reg. Inn. IV*, 6379 (publ. Mansilla, 371–7, misdated). In the registered version of Nov. 1252 the cardinal's judgement was dated Oct. 1249; but the constitutions were prepared by March 1249, in which month the proctor of the twelve priests of Gerona copied them onto a spare leaf of his *libellum*: AC Gerona, *Causa del Any 1240*, fo. 32ra–vb. AC Calahorra contains two pieces of correspondence between Aznar and Gil – doc. 296, 300 – but neither is legible. The date of the final *ordinatio* is May 1257: AC Calahorra, doc. 229. Hergueta assumed this to be an error in the BN copy (*RABM*, xvii, 414); but it is perfectly consistent with the extended negotiations that occurred.
3 22 April–29 May 1254: RAH, MS C/7–9/5427, fo. 143r. Cf. *Reg. Greg. IX*, 5964, for Martín Pérez's opposition to the bishop in 1241; Fernández, *Plasencia*, 36.
4 AC Segovia, doc. 36: 'Intelleximus quod prefati scandali radix et seminarium, origo ac fomes ex eo potissime pullularat...Unde de facili sequebatur adversum patremfamilias non levis occasio murmurandi et mortalis infirmitas cui molestum est per inopiam affici et indigentiam perpeti difficulter scrupuloso corde commota videbatur sibi iustam habere materiam conquerendi'; Mansilla, 322–3.
5 'Pensantes aliquem de ipsius Mindoniensis ecclesie gremio utilius quam extraneum ad ipsius fore regimen assumendum': *Reg. Bon. VIII*, 2227; 'cum etiam si omnes posuissemus extraneos, dum tamen ydoneos, jure nostro utentes, nulli crederemus iniuriam intulisse': AHN, papel, Toledo, 7216/2, d.s.n.

man's origin, and, moreover, there were *oriundi* who, though also *ydonei*, could not be accommodated in their native place.[1] Bishops and chapters were not invariably divided on this issue. Together, at Salamanca in the early 1220s, they invoked, with success, their statute *de numero canonicorum* against one *D. presbiter*: an incident which became memorable, since Honorius III's decretal entered Canon Law – though perhaps the most remarkable passage of the pope's letter, which recorded *D*'s having voluntarily withdrawn from the contest on encountering resistance, was not included in the *Liber Extra*.[2] Benefice-mongers were normally rather more brazen than the self-effacing *D*. At Salamanca and Zamora in the thirties and forties, *alieni* were so persistent that the local clergy despaired of preferment and reverted to secular life,[3] while at Toledo the local residents took the law into their own hands. By October 1236, according to the capitular proctor, Archbishop Rodrigo had brought in so many outsiders that hardly one in four of the chapter was of local stock.[4] But by January 1245 the chapter had been expelled and sent packing to Alcalá, 'paucis exceptis qui de illis partibus oriundi sunt'.[5] So it was predictable that Cardinal Gil's constitutions should have included regulations in favour of the *oriundi*.[6] Such protective legislation was widely

[1] Two such cases, both from Burgos: Pedro Alejándrez, canon of Étampes, 'qui, sicut asserit, de civitate Burgensi traxit originem et diu disciplinis scolasticis insudavit' at the court of Blanche of Castile, widow of Louis VIII of France: *Reg. Urb. IV*, 1623. Master *J*. could secure only a half portion there, although 'ipse longo tempore Parisius in artibus, medicina et demum in iure civili adeo studuit laudabiliter et profecit quod in medicina et artibus ipsis licenciam habuit et rexit ibidem': ASV, arm. XXXI.72, fo. 205r (Schillmann, 1457).

[2] 'Asserens quod super receptione sua potius volebat implorare gratiam episcopi et capituli quam contra eos invitos per sententiam obtinere': *Reg. Hon. III*, 5237 (MDH, 530). Cf. *Decretal. Greg. IX*, II, xxviii, de appell, c. 63 (Friedberg, *Corpus Iuris Canonici*, II, 439).   [3] Mansilla, 323; below, Ch. 12.

[4] AC Toledo, A.6.H.1.24 (publ. Gorosterratzu, *Don Rodrigo*, 303–5). Estella, of course, makes a case for Rodrigo: *El fundador*, 173–5. The creation of twenty *capellanías* for the new cathedral had been authorised in the previous January: AC Toledo, E.1.A.1.2(= *Reg. Greg. IX*, 2904). Cf. Lambert, *L'art gothique en Espagne*, 296.

[5] *Reg. Inn. IV*, 908. Estella notes the move, but fails to account for it.

[6] Mansilla, 323 (Salamanca), 347 (Ávila); RAH, MS C/7–9/5427, fo. 136v (Plasencia). Neither at Calahorra nor at Burgos were *alieni* explicitly excluded: instead the principle of promotion by seniority within the chapter was stressed, 'nisi litterarum scientia vel generis nobilitas et morum honestas vel alia causa rationabilis ipsum exigant'. The same qualifications were admitted for Salamanca archdeaconries – with the exception of *generis nobilitas* (they already had the dean of Compostela on their hands): Mansilla, 364, 372, 324.

sought after. In the diocese of Salamanca the collegiate churches obtained access to the cardinal's seal after his death and forged letters for themselves which accorded them the same protection against intruders as Gil's constitutions had accorded to the cathedral church. At least, that was what Alexander IV was told in August 1255 by Bishop Pedro Pérez, who, now that he was prevented from filling the cathedral chapter with his nominees, was all the more anxious to retain his other sources of unearned income. And the enquiry held at Zamora in the following March bore out the bishop's story. The defendants, who included the *concejo* of Salamanca, offered no evidence and were condemned, the sentence being confirmed by Pope Alexander in November 1257.[1]

The spirit of autonomy which the fabrication of these pseudo-constitutions indicates was typical of Castile in the mid-1250s. By November 1254, though, when Cardinal Gil died, it was painfully clear that the cause of autonomy had been ill served at Salamanca even by the authentic version. Hitherto we have allowed the Spanish cardinal to remain a two-dimensional figure, obtruding occasionally into the narrative but remaining for the most part offstage, blandly issuing constitutions from afar. But, in fact, he was at the centre of the stage, at the Curia, throughout;[2] and he had friends, not all of whom were bishops. Well before December 1253 he had been asserting himself at Salamanca, reserving, with papal approval, the next three vacancies there for his protégés.[3] The chapter of Ávila, too, had discovered that their bishop's notional loss of influence was not entirely their gain. On the very day on which the constitutions were issued for the benefit of *indigeni civitatis et diocesis* the cardinal had ordered them to provide for a final dozen Castilian clerics before the shutters went up.[4] Cardinal Gil's constitutions provided the Castilian churches with only as much protection from interference as the cardinal himself was prepared to allow them. Just how much that was is the subject of the following chapter.

---

[1] *Reg. Alex. IV*, 747 (Aug. 1255). The rest of the story is derived from Alexander's bull *Hiis qui* (9 Nov. 1257) which Bishop Pedro of Salamanca had registered in Dec. 1291: *Reg. Nich. IV*, 6365. Cf. Beltrán, *Cartulario*, 65–6.

[2] *Contra*, Beltrán, 61, 71, 73.   [3] *Reg. Inn. IV*, 7302.

[4] Mansilla, 347; AHN, cod. 1443B, fos. 11vb–12ra: the list included two of the dean's nephews, a nephew of the cantor (who was at the Curia at this time), Adán of Burgos, and Domingo Domínguez and Domingo Martínez, both of Soria.

Chapter 12

SPANIARDS AT THE CURIA, 2

Towards the end of May 1239, at a time when the critical situation of the Roman Church was keeping them fully occupied, two cardinals – James Pecoraria and Richard Annibaldi – were set to work as research assistants by Archbishop Rodrigo of Toledo. If the Roman Church was about to be drowned in the Tiber by the Emperor Frederick then Rodrigo's duty was perfectly plain to him: he must keep his powder dry. After all, popes and emperors came and went, but the primacy issue in the Peninsula remained. So – fortunately for Toledo, as it happened – the archbishop acquired copies of various twelfth-century privileges of his church and engaged those two busy men to scour the Register of Innocent III, 'ne regestis ipsis perditis casu fortuito aut vetustate consumptis, ius ecclesiae contingat cum pereuntibus deperire'. And, obligingly, they did as they were asked.[1] Coming from Rodrigo, such a request was not remarkable. All that was remarkable about it was that it was addressed to that particular pair of cardinals rather than to the Spanish cardinal deacon of Ss Cosmas and Damian, Gil Torres, for very little happened in the Spanish Church or to Spanish churchmen at Rome with which Cardinal Gil was not acquainted. From 1217, when Honorius III brought him from Burgos to Rome, until his death on 11 November 1254, Gil Torres was, literally, Spain's man at the Curia.[2] In May 1234 the canons of Tarragona had tried, unsuccessfully, to bring him back as their archbishop; and so, in 1247, did the canons of Toledo. But Innocent IV would not part with that tower of strength – 'columpna firmissima' – and the cardinal stayed at the Curia.[3]

---

[1] Reg. Greg. IX, 5025-40 (= AC Toledo, X.7. [Primacía] 3.7a–d). Cf. Auvray, Les registres de Grégoire IX, II, 1241 ff., and, for the destruction of the papal archive in 1244, Poole, Lectures on the History of the Papal Chancery, 203–4.

[2] Eubel, Hierarchia, 5; Serrano, Obispado de Burgos, III, 391.

[3] VL, XIX, 180; Reg. Inn. IV, 3654. Cf. Bayerri, Historia de Tortosa, VII, 417, n. 2, and Blanco Díez, BRAH, CXXX, 275, who offer no evidence for their allegation that Gil visited Spain after his elevation.

And that, virtually, is the sum total of certain knowledge about him. 'La figura de este Cardenal español no es aún hoy plenamente conocida', wrote Mansilla in 1945, since when no advance has been made.[1] There are misconceptions, though, in abundance: that he was a canonist of note,[2] of Portuguese origin[3] or, rather more plausibly, 'natural de Burgos',[4] and that his family came from the Rioja area;[5] all of which must be dispersed in favour of what may be verified, just as he himself insisted that the smell of charcoal should be dispersed from Ávila Cathedral so that the odour of the incense might be appreciated there.[6] Other than that his *humilis clericus* João de Deo dedicated the *Notabilia cum Summis super Titulis Decretalium* to him, there is no reason for connecting him either with canon law or with Portugal[7] – except in so far as *every* thirteenth-century cardinal had, perforce, to be something of a canonist – unless Zamora be considered part of the kingdom of Portugal. For, while Gil Torres had contacts in every Castilian and Leonese cathedral church, it was with the church of Zamora that his links seem to have been strongest. He established an anniversary there for his parents and his sister;[8] he persecuted the bishop and chapter with his favours;[9] and, according to his near-contemporary, the Franciscan polymath, Juan Gil de Zamora, he was an authority on the etymology of the place-name.[10] Possibly,

---

[1] Mansilla, *Iglesia castellano–leonesa*, 179, n. 148.

[2] 'Prestigiosa canonista': Castell Maiques, *AA*, XIV, 28.

[3] Thus various Portuguese writers down to the 1967 re-edition of Almeida, *História da Igreja* (ed. Peres), I, 256.

[4] Serrano, *Don Mauricio*, 70–3 (the fullest account to date: Serrano claimed to have much more material on Gil 'en nuestras papeletas', 73, n. 4; but he never published it); Mansilla, 225. The two papal bulls – *Reg. Inn. IV*, 4436, 5723 – state merely that he was promoted from that church to the cardinalate, not that he was born there.

[5] Hergueta, *RABM*, XVII, 413: solely on the strength of his constitutions for Burgos and Calahorra.

[6] 'Thus in altari et choro cotidie ministretur copiose ut fumus thuris redoleat, non carbonum offendat': Mansilla, 350.

[7] Sousa Costa, *Itinerarium*, I, 299–300.

[8] AC Zamora, 12/1: on the cardinal's behalf, Gil, canon of Zamora, spent $114\frac{1}{2}$ *maravedís* on the purchase of property 'in suburbio Zamorensis' for this purpose. The cardinal stipulated that twelve *maravedís* a year for life was to be paid to the poor cleric Juan, his *alumpnus* ('Actum Zamorensi in claustro ecclesie cathedralis, III kal. novembris'; no year).

[9] See below, pp. 292–4.

[10] *De Preconiis Hispanie*, ed. Castro y Castro, 245. Also 152: 'qui tanquam animal oculatum, fuit discretione preditus, et tanquam animal pennatum, sublevatus titulis

therefore, that was where he hailed from – but only possibly, for contemporary estimates of Cardinal Gil are not necessarily to be trusted. Matthew Paris, for example, gave him a favourable obituary notice, praising him for having remained aloof from curial skulduggery during his lifetime.[1] What had earned him the rare distinction of kind words from that improbable source, though, was clearly less a European reputation for probity than the fact that quite recently he had spoken up for Robert Grosseteste and had had the grace to acknowledge that there was much truth in the bishop of Lincoln's criticisms.[2] That Gil was no paragon, however, Grosseteste himself was aware. While he had still been archdeacon of Leicester he had been asked to provide the cardinal's nephew with a benefice, and, as bishop, he had responded to another such request from the Spaniard with one of his famous terrifying letters.[3] Perhaps it was remorse that caused Gil to spurn the system towards the very end of his life when, in 1254, he declined to act as executor for the archdeacon of León, Rodrigo Pérez, though there are other explanations for his behaviour on that occasion,[4] and he had certainly shown no such tender feelings before.

In 1229, for example, Cardinal Otto of Montefaltro, legate in the Low Countries, forced the church of Verdun to provide Gil's nephew, Master Esteban, with a benefice. Esteban of Husillos was a great collector of benefices.[5] The salient detail, though, is that with his uncle's help he was accumulating his fortune in this way while John of Abbeville was busy trying to eliminate such practices in Spain itself.

honestatis'; at which passage Castro's MS *E* (fifteenth-century) refers to Egidius *Zamorensis*.

[1] *Chronica Majora*, v, 529: 'qui, aetate ferme centenarius, singularis pare carens extitit columpna in Curia Romana veritatis et justitiae, et munerum aspernator, quae rigorem aequitatis flectere consueverunt'.   [2] *Ibid.* v., 393.

[3] *Roberti Grosseteste episcopi quondam Lincolniensis Epistolae*, ed. H. R. Luard (Rolls Ser., London, 1861), 125–8, 138–40; also 137–8, 196 (thanking Gil for his kindness). The English Franciscans were also in touch with Gil: *Monumenta Franciscana*, ed. J. S. Brewer (Rolls Ser., London, 1858), 377.

[4] *Reg. Inn. IV*, 8303: 'Sane quod idem cardinalis [Egidius] facultatem hujusmodi recipere noluit, nos in te [Cardinal Octavian Ubaldini] transferentes eandem...' The archdeacon owed Gil money; Cardinal Octavian got him accommodated at Oviedo: above, p. 217; *Reg. Alex. IV*, 745.

[5] *Reg. Greg. IX*, 2695 (July 1235), referring to the appointment as having been made during Otto's legation, for the date of which see *Annalium Laubiensium Continuatio*, ed. Pertz, 26.

For the Spanish cardinal had very little in common with that idealistic Frenchman. Though he was well aware of the evil consequences of clerical concubinage and mentioned them in his constitutions for Salamanca, Ávila and Plasencia, he spared his countrymen the tedious diatribes on the subject for which John is remembered, and in 1251 was responsible for the suspension of the legate's energetic measures against the abuse.[1]

Gil justified that decision in medical imagery; and he was, in Innocent IV's estimation, very highly skilled at that level.[2] On his promotion in 1217 he had at first acted as the junior partner of his fellow-countryman, Pelayo Gaitán, cardinal-bishop of Albano, who until then had been the chief refuge of Spaniards at the Curia.[3] The pair of them worked together as auditors of cases concerning the peninsular churches until Pelayo's death in January 1230, by which time Gil had acquired sufficient experience to take over the practice himself.[4] He completely outshone the other Spanish cardinal, Guillermo the ex-abbot of Sahagún, whom Innocent IV appointed to the title of the Twelve Apostles in 1244. Guillermo was very infrequently mentioned.[5] Gil was the great luminary to whom

---

[1] Mansilla, 328–9, 355; RAH, MS C/7–9/5427, fo. 143r; above, Ch. 3.

[2] 'Poenae sint proinde variandae, ne ad instar imperiti medici omnium curare occulus uno colyrio videremur': *VL*, v, 286. Cf. the pope's appointment of Gil as auditor, pre-Feb. 1244, 'cum ignotam causam curare medicus nullus possit': *Reg. Inn. IV*, 448.

[3] For Pelayo, see Mansilla, *AA*, I, 11 ff. He came from León, and at Rome was an authority on the affairs of the peninsular churches: during the Toledo–Braga primacy debate at the Fourth Lateran Council, it was alleged on behalf of Braga that Pedro Mendes, the archbishop-elect (d. Nov. 1212) had never received the pallium which had been sent to him, 'sed episcopus Legionensis habet illud, secundum quod bene novit dominus Albanensis' (ADB, Gav. dos Arcebispos, 20a). But had Pelayo also been bishop-elect of León – a possibility which has not been considered? The anonymous Latin chronicle refers to him quite explicitly as 'quondam electus Legionensis', and this is confirmed by one of the letters of Cardinal Thomas of Capua (CLI, ed. Cirot, *B. Hisp.*, xv, 278; Hahn, *Collectio monumentorum*, I, 383). Risco too refers to a León document of Feb. 1208 which mentions a bishop-elect of this name. The difficulty is that by Feb. 1208 Pelayo Gaitán had been a cardinal for almost two years, and that Pedro Muñoz was bishop of León till 1207: *ES*, xxxv, 281–2; Mansilla, *loc. cit.*, 13.

[4] *Reg. Greg. IX*, 2490. For their joint action, see *Reg. Hon. III*, 5011 (publ. Sousa Costa, *Mestre Silvestre*, 174–5), 5614 (MDH, 570). Gil was with Pelayo at Perugia a few days before he died: AC León, doc. 3807; Fernández Catón, *Archivos Leoneses*, VII, 108.

[5] For Guillermo (d. 1250) and the circumstances of his appointment, see Escalona, *Historia de Sahagún*, 141–4; *Reg. Greg. IX*, 5163; above, p. 189; as joint auditor with

Spaniards had recourse when they came to the Curia, and by whom, as early as April 1218, Afonso II of Portugal was persuaded to grant tithes to the prelates and dioceses of his kingdom.[1] Even before Pelayo's death visiting bishops and clergy gathered around Gil: at Perugia in June 1229 he had a houseful of them.[2] He was auditor of their lawsuits;[3] he lent them money[4] and arranged loans for them;[5] he supported their petitions, by, for example, writing to the Cistercian General Chapter;[6] and when they died there he acted as executor of their wills.[7]

Apart from casual visitors, there were also the permanent fixtures – the proctors of the Spanish churches whose names and initials are found on the back of papal rescripts. Not every church, of course, retained a permanent proctor.[8] Some Cistercian houses, for example,

---

Gil in June 1247: *Reg. Inn.* IV, 2811. The will of Bishop Juan of Burgos (Sept. 1246) named him and Gil as *superexecutores*; and in his (July 1248), the archbishop-elect of Toledo, Juan de Medina, made two bequests to members of Guillermo's circle: 220 *maravedís* to the cardinal's nephew, *Stephanus armiger*, and 100 to 'Bartolomeus olim serviens': AC Burgos, vol. 46, fo. 430 (Serrano, *Hispania*, I, 40); AC Toledo, A.7.A.1.5a.

[1] Sandoval, *Antigüedad de Túy*, fo. 147v; Sousa Costa, 67–71, 396. It may also be mentioned that the sixteenth-century Mexía copy of the *repartimiento* of Seville records grants to 'don Gil de Torres' and to 'don Xil, sobrino del arcidiano (and 'del deán') de Roma': Julio González, *Repartimiento de Sevilla*, II, 224, 232, 265.

[2] Seven of them witnessed his judgement of an Italian dispute: Master Tiburcio, archdeacon of Palencia, and Master *Johannes Burgensis* were two of them: *Reg. Greg.* IX, 307.

[3] Bishop of Pamplona – king of Navarre (Jan.–March 1246): Goñi Gaztambide, *Príncipe de Viana*, XVIII, 98; Irurita, *Municipio de Pamplona*, 124 ff.; the 12 priests of Gerona (July 1249): above, Ch. 3; bishop of Astorga – S. Martín de Castañeda (Feb. 1250): AD Astorga, 3/59 (= *Reg. Inn.* IV, 4751), 3/63; Lisbon rents of Bernardus Compostellanus (Oct. 1250): *Reg. Inn.* IV, 5268; *cameraria* of Tarragona (Sept. 1252): above, p. 90.

[4] For his loans to Archbishop Rodrigo of Toledo, Bishop Pedro of Zamora and Rodrigo Pérez, archdeacon of León, see above, pp. 142, 144, 217). In Sept. 1246 Bishop Juan of Burgos owed Gil 300 *meajes dobles*, and Gil's chamberlain 20 marks; and the will of the cantor of Burgos, García de Campo (late 1260s) acknowledged a 200 *maravedí* debt 'por el cardenal Gil', which words have been crossed out and 'por un bon ombre' put in: Serrano, *Hispania*, I, 40; AC Burgos, vol. 48, fo. 425.

[5] For Archbishop Rodrigo in 1247; above, p. 142; for the church of Sigüenza (pre-April 1239): Minguella, *Historia de Sigüenza*, I, 563.

[6] In 1246, on behalf of Alfonso López de Haro, and probably at the behest of Bishop Áznar of Calahorra: Canivez, *Statuta*, II, 312–13.

[7] As sole executor of Archbishop Silvestre of Braga (d. July 1244): Sousa Costa, 15–17.

[8] On the permanent proctors, see Heckel, *Studi e Testi*, XXXVIII, esp. 317 ff., and Herde,

acquired their copies of common privileges through neighbouring abbots or members of the Order who had particular reasons for visiting the Curia. When the abbot of Ríoseco (Burgos), Pedro Garcés, was at Perugia in June 1235 he obtained privileges not only for his own house but also for Gumiel;[1] and in 1250 Fernando Rodríguez did the same for the nuns of Villamayor (Burgos) and the monks of Palazuelo (Palencia).[2] Alternatively, the services of Italian professionals could be hired. The Spanish Cistercians were served by a number of these – including the tireless Pietro de Assisi, the proctor general of the Order who was 'perhaps a succession of men acting under one name';[3] *Jorinus O. Cist.*, whose sign was the head of a man wearing something rather like a trilby hat;[4] *P. B. Cist.*, whose mark was a coxcomb;[5] Cardinal John 'of Toledo', the Englishman;[6] and many others.[7] Master Leonardo of San Germano protected the interests of the Augustinians of Roncesvalles, and in 1247–8 made himself heard at least three times, challenging the issue of bulls confirming the property rights of the Cistercians of Fitero and Poblet and of the church of Toledo.[8] He, evidently, was an Italian. But it is not always clear whether a proctor who is known only by

Beiträge, esp. 80 ff. In the following account the *incipits* of bulls cited have not been given.

1 AHN, 353/10 (19 June 1235); 353/11; 231/11 (22 June 1235): 'Petrus Garsie abbas de rivo sicco impetravit hoc privilegium' on each one.

2 For Villamayor, 21 May and 11 June; for Palazuelo, 13 June: Serrano, *BRAH*, CIV, 190–2; AHN, 3430/12.

3 Brentano, *Two Churches*, 32 ff., *q.v.* for literature on Pietro. The *Archivo Histórico Nacional* contains at least forty bulls for thirteen Cistercian houses, delivered to him and his associates between 1250 and 1301.

4 For Poblet, 31 May 1235: AHN, 2175/2; sellos, 5/21; for Piedra (Tarazona), 2 June 1235: AHN, 3667/10; 3667/12.

5 For Rueda (Zaragoza), 31 July 1258: AHN, 3755/2. See Battelli's comments on signs of this type, in *Schedario Baumgarten*, I, xxxii.

6 As *Cardinalis Cisterciensis* or *Albus*, for Sobrado (Coruña), 27 June 1248: AHN, 541/13–17; for Oliva (Navarre), 13 Sept. 1249: AHN, 1421/7; for Poblet, 13 Nov. 1258, 13 Nov. 1259: AHN, 2240/3; sellos, 90/13.

7 No attempt has been made to exhaust the theme in this context, where further elaboration would be out of place. A full account will be published elsewhere. The nature of the evidence for this type of study makes it one which will prosper only through co-operation between scholars throughout Europe. Meanwhile, see the excellent list of names, endorsements, etc. in Herde, *Beiträge*, 89 ff.; and Anton Largiadèr, *Die Papsturkunden der Schweiz von Innozenz III. bis Martin V. ohne Zürich*, I (Zürich, 1968).

8 AHN, 1398/15 (14 May 1247); 2211/3 (5 Oct. 1247); AC Toledo, I.5.C.1.1 (29 March 1248).

his initials or his Latin name was a Spaniard or not. Such is the problem with Petrus Berengarii who, on behalf of Bishop Andrés of Valencia, appeared before the *auditor contradictarum*, John of Camecano in December 1251,[1] and between 1257 and 1277 acted for various Spanish clients – Poblet, the king of Aragon, the archbishop of Toledo and the bishops of Pamplona and Zaragoza.[2]

Many churches, however, kept their own man at the Curia; and, as the century advanced and bishops grew ever more anxious to pre-empt papal provisions by prompt action,[3] the number of these increased. In the 1220s Bartolomé de Arguedis was there on behalf of Toledo, and acted for Ávila and Palencia also. He received papal permission to draw the income of his benefices *in absentia*,[4] and after his retirement and return to Toledo was, perhaps, called upon by the archbishop on occasions when his curial contacts and experience might prove useful.[5] His successor was Fortunius who took charge of virtually every Toledo rescript issued between May 1234 and March 1247,[6] and represented the collegiate church of Tudela also.[7] This was hack work, and only very rarely is Cardinal Gil's name found on

---

[1] AHA, *Cartoral AB*, fos. 10v-11r. Archbishop Benito's claim to the churches of Jérica and S. Tecla, Játiva was at issue.

[2] AHN, 2235/19; 2241/6; 2241/8; 2241/13; sellos, 49/14; ACA, Bulas, leg. XIV-2 (reg. Miquel Rosell, *Regesta*, 181); AC Huesca, 2–136 (reg. Durán Gudiol, *AA*, VII, no. 107); AC Toledo, A.7.E.1.1–1a–1b–7a; AM Pamplona, E, d.s.n. (publ. Irurita, 143–4); AA Zaragoza, 2/16; 2/4/41.

[3] Cf. Durandus, *Speculum Iudiciale* (Lyons, 1556), c.3 in VI°.3.4, gl. ad v. *per seipsos*: 'Ante constitutionem Clementis [IV: *viz. Licet Ecclesiarum*] prelati habebant suos procuratores in curia, qui quamcito contingebant vacare aliquod beneficium ad eorum collationem spectans, illud conferebant, et sepe dominum papam in conferendo preveniebant, et sibi illudebant...': publ. Göller, *RQ*, XX, 84–5. Also Barraclough, *Public Notaries*, 27 ff.

[4] *Reg. Greg. IX*, 329: 'Cum...apud sedem apostolicam pro libertate ecclesie Toletane ac aliarum regni Castelle ecclesiarum necnon et iure ipsarum sollicite ac fideliter laboraris' (Aug. 1229); AC Ávila, doc. 9 (Nov. 1223); AC Palencia, 2/1/43 (= MDH, 580, Oct. 1225). In April 1223 he had been with the two Spanish cardinals at the Curia: *Reg. Hon. III*, 5614 (MDH, 570).

[5] If Bartolomé was the archdeacon of Calatrava, *B*, he was sent to the Curia in Dec. 1234 and – for hearings of the *Ordinatio Valentina* – in Dec. 1240 and March 1246: AC Toledo, A.6.H.1.30; AHN, cod. 987B, fo. 171rb; AC Toledo, X.2.K.1.12. In March 1243 he was at Toledo: Serrano, *BRAH*, CIV, 189–90.

[6] AC Toledo, X.2.P.1.2c; X.2.C.1.7.

[7] AC Tudela, 30–C–4; AE Tudela, fajo AB–6; AC Tudela, 29–P–2; 30–C–5; I–C–4 [Jan. 1237–April 1239]: reg. Fuentes, *Catálogo*, 242, 1132, 244, 246, 256: all of these are concerned with the Tudela–Zaragoza property dispute. In view of the Toledo-

papal rescripts.[1] But it was minions like Fortunius who became his chaplains, received his protection and owed their advancement to his patronage.

Some idea of the composition of his *familia* may be gained by comparing the lists of Spaniards who witnessed his judgements of July 1248 and February 1250, in favour of the twelve priests of Gerona and the bishop of Astorga respectively.[2] On the first occasion there were ten of them, apart from the three interested proctors: Master Soeiro dean of Lisbon; two Burgos dignitaries, the archdeacon Master Juan Mateo, and Domingo Pérez, abbot of Castrojériz; the cardinal's chamberlain, Pedro Yáñez, archdeacon of León; Master Bernardo, canon of Compostela, and Master Martín Gómez, both papal chaplains; the chamberlain – and future archbishop – of Tarragona, Benito de Rocaberti; Master Pascal Cornelio; Master Lope, canon of Toledo and chaplain of Cardinal John 'of Toledo'; and Master Raimundo 'rector de Reddis'. Eighteen months later some of these had gone,[3] and others had taken their place. The bishop and cantor of Ávila, Martín Pérez, and the Cuenca archdeacons,

Tarragona struggle for the church of Segorbe it is of interest that his name appears also on the dorse of a bull of Jan. 1237 which urged the king of Aragon to restore reconquered territory to that church: ACA, Bulas, leg. VI–16 (reg. Miquel, 99).

[1] For Palencia: letter *Cum sicut*, protecting the church against further provisions until it was capable of paying the customary rents to those already there, 4 June 1246: AC Palencia, 3/8/10. For Burgos: his constitutions and the letter appointing conservators thereof, May 1252: AC Burgos, vol. 62.i, fo. 108 (= *Reg. Inn. IV*, 5723); vol. 62.i, fo. 109 (two further copies: vol. 7.i, fo. 371; vol. 10, fo. 400): reg. Mansilla, *AA*, IX, nos 18, 20.

[2] AC Gerona, d.s.n. (above, Ch. 3); AD Astorga, 3/62 (= *Reg. Inn. IV*, 4751). Serrano, *Don Mauricio*, 71–2, mentions some of Gil's *familiares*. With Gil in April 1223 and again in Sept. 1245 was Johannes Suerii, canon of – and, subsequently, archdeacon of Alava – Calahorra: *Reg. Hon. III*, 5614 (MDH, 570); *Documentos para a história da Cidade de Lisboa*, 179. Cf. Bujanda, *Berceo*, I, 122; Cunha, *História da igreja de Lisboa*, I, 161. In the early 1250s he was in Portugal; he may have been the archdeacon of Calahorra, Johannes Severini (or Severii) whom the canonist Domingos Domingues acknowledged as his master: *PMH*, I, 185–9, 644, 664; Merêa, *Bol. da Fac. de Direito (Univ. de Coimbra)*, XLIII, 166. Cf. *Reg. Inn. IV*, 1118.

[3] Master Soeiro, an exile at the Curia, whose deanery had passed to Bernardus Compostellanus, the canonist and co-witness of the Gerona judgement by Oct. 1250 (*Reg. Inn. IV*, 938–9, 5268); the archdeacon of Burgos and Master Martín Gómez (abbot of Cervatos, Burgos, in 1246: AC Burgos, vol. 46, fo. 430); Benito de Rocaberti; Master Lope – who returned as treasurer of Toledo in 1259, had his bar sinister removed, and was rendered *episcopabile* (*Reg. Alex. IV*, 2826, 2869–70); and Raimundo de Reddis, Benito de Rocaberti's proctor in Dec. 1252 (AHA, *Cartoral AB*, fo. 10v).

Martín Gonzálvez and Domingo Pérez, were there presumably in connexion with the preparation of the cardinal's constitutions for their churches. The bishop of León and Fernando Abril, canon of that church, also had their reasons for being present.[1] The *magister scolarum* of Astorga, Nuño Velázquez, however, and two who remained from July 1248 – Gil's chamberlain, Pedro Yáñez, and the abbot of Castrojériz – were members of the permanent staff.

Nuño Velázquez was the León proctor, and by following his career – which can be done in some detail – it is possible to offer some conclusions about the effect on the Spanish Church of others of his ilk. He is already known to readers of historical footnotes as the victim of a student prank at Vercelli who, the morning after the night before, was reminded that while in his cups he had promised to join the Dominicans and was required to hand over his property to them.[2] He was already *magister scolarum* of Astorga[3] at the time of this uncharacteristically intemperate escapade which, ironically, marked the beginning of his rise in the world since, on coming to Rome in order to clear his name, he became one of Cardinal Gil's *clerici*. By November 1246 he was pressing his claim to an Oviedo canonry and the prebend of San Millán 'quod quondam Agnes amita eius obtinuit'.[4] It was not his first visit to the Curia. The chapter of León had sent him there in November 1238 to secure confirmation of the election of Bishop Martín;[5] and, despite his Oviedo canonry and another at Palencia to which he was provided in February 1253, it was for that church – León – that he acted as proctor,[6] and from

---

1 Above, Ch. 7. The cantor of Ávila secured a benefice for his nephew and by Oct. 1250 was one of the cardinal's chaplains: AHN, cod. 1443B, fo. 11vb. *Reg. Inn. IV*, 5268.
2 H. Rashdall (ed. Powicke–Emden), *The Universities of Europe in the Middle Ages*, II (Oxford, 1936), 27, n. 5; *Reg. Inn. IV*, 529, 1348–9.
3 Not of Asti. Cf. R. W. Southern, *Western Society and the Church in the Middle Ages* (Harmondsworth, 1970), 293.
4 *Ibid.* 2913. He had become *magister scolarum* since Nov. 1235: AD Astorga, 2/35.
5 AC León, doc. 1294 (= *Reg. Greg. IX*, 4594).
6 *Reg. Inn. IV*, 6711; AC Lugo, 21/3/19: letter *Sua nobis* (concerning the León–Lugo struggle for Triacastela), dorse: 'Munio Velasci magisterscolarum Astoricensis, canonicus et procurator episcopi et capituli ecclesie Legionensis [petivit]; Rodericus Petri portionarius et procurator episcopi et capituli Lucensis ecclesie contra[dixit]. Fiant littere de conveniencia quod dicti judices debeant avenire apud Villamfrancam de Vallecarceris', 5 Oct. 1247. Cf. Cañizares, *BCM Lugo*, II, 151. In May 1254 the Lugo proctor, Rodrigo Pérez, also received permission to hold benefices in plurality: *Reg. Inn. IV*, 7555.

León that he received a further benefice in November 1252 – through the intervention of the cardinal's nephew, Esteban de Husillos.[1] Yet another benefice was awarded him in the following January, on which occasion he took the precaution of insuring his León rents by resigning them to the papal notary John of Capua and receiving them back again.[2] By March 1259, when he made a will, he had added the León archdeaconry of Çea to his hoard and acquired extensive property elsewhere.[3]

Nuño's successful career owed a very great deal to Cardinal Gil's assistance in securing benefices not only at León but also at Oviedo and Palencia where the *magister scolarum* of Astorga was one of those *alieni* whom the cardinal's constitutions elsewhere declared unacceptable. Another who profited in the same way, though rather more modestly, was Gil's chaplain, Master Pascal Cornelio, who by July 1250 was possessed of canonries both at Toledo and Burgos.[4] Meanwhile Pedro Yáñez, the cardinal's chamberlain, had fared (arguably) better. Gil possibly inherited Pedro, together with the Castilian brief, from Cardinal Pelayo.[5] By February 1250, though, he was rid of him, for Pedro had become bishop of Córdoba.[6]

---

[1] *Ibid.* 6701.

[2] *Ibid.* 6232: 'Retulisti humiliter coram nobis quod cum...M(artinus) Legionensis episcopus quedam prestimonia tunc vacantia, prout spectabat ad ipsum, tibi liberaliter contulisset, ac postmodum ad tuum pervenisset auditum quod idem episcopus tempore collationis huius astrictus excommunicationis vinculo tenebatur, tu volens in hac parte conscientiam habere pacificam et quietam...'; 6233.

[3] AC León, doc. 1538. He bequeathed five hundred *maravedís* 'pora las oras' with which property at Villamor was purchased: AC León, doc. 1603. The will of Bishop Suero Pérez of Zamora in May 1285 mentioned 'domos meas que fuerunt M. Velasci in Tauro': AC Zamora, 12/14.

[4] *Reg. Inn. IV*, 4163, 4751.

[5] As archdeacon of León he owed Pelayo money, and was at the cardinal's deathbed in Jan. 1230: AC León, doc. 617, 3807 (cit. Fernández Catón, *Archivos Leoneses*, VII, 108–9). When Innocent IV awarded the Infante Sancho a Toledo archdeaconry on 29 Oct. 1247 he instructed Gil Torres to invest Pedro with it 'nomine suo': *inc. Apostolice sedis*: AC Toledo, A.7.C.1.1.

[6] Mansilla, 181. He remained bishop of Córdoba till at least Nov. 1254: Rymer, *Foedera*, I, 310 (but cf. Torres Fontes, *Col. de documentos...de Murcia*, I, 3, for Bishop Lope Pérez of Córdoba in June 1253). Yet in July 1258 the chapter of Palencia claimed that their bishop owed them 100 *maravedís* 'pro Petro Johannis camerario domini Egidii cardinalis nunc episcopo *Ovetensi*' (AC Palencia, 3/2/23). Since Bishop Pedro of *Oviedo* had been in possession of that see since May 1251 at the latest (*ES*, xxxVIII, 38), and by July 1258 both Bishop Pedro of *Córdoba*, and Lope Pérez his successor, were dead (AC Toledo, X.1.C.1.1g), the likeliest explanation of

By then the church of Segovia also had been made aware of the pernicious consequences of the ability of certain Spaniards whose merits attracted the attention of pope or cardinal, for their proctor, the archdeacon of Cuéllar and papal chaplain, Master Nicolás, was receiving from them an annual pension of five hundred *maravedís* which had been declared sacrosanct during the reorganisation of the church's finances in 1245–7.[1] He therefore had ten times what a canon of Segovia was allowed, quite apart from the revenue of his archdeaconry.[2] And, what was worse, he came from Burgos.[3] Master Nicolás was no less *alienus* – and he was considerably more expensive – than the Italian, Petrus Gaietanus, to whom in June 1246 the dean and chapter had assigned an annual pension of eight marks.[4] Moreover, since Petrus Gaietanus was a chaplain of the cardinal-bishop of Albano who at this time had a hand in the collection in Castile of the taxes levied by the Lyons Council,[5] the eight marks may have been very well invested. The archbishop-elect of Toledo, Juan de Medina, certainly regarded the annuity which he settled on Petrus Gaietanus before leaving the Curia as an investment. He said so.[6]

this difficulty may be simply that the canons of Palencia were muddled. Possibly, though, Cardinal Gil had two chamberlains of the same name. To add to the confusion, Gil's nephew, Esteban de Husillos, had a cleric called *Petrus Johannis* in Jan. 1255: AC Zamora, 13/46.

1 AC Segovia, doc. 241: ' Salva provisione sive gratia quingentorum morabutinorum quam dominus papa magistro N. subdiacono suo archidiacono Collarensi in prestimoniis predecessoris sui vel equivalentibus ecclesie vestre sibi voluit et mandavit' (Oct. 1245). This predecessor was Gutiérre – conceivably the bishop of Córdoba consecrated by the pope in March 1246. In Jan. 1235 Cardinal Gil had had another archdeacon of Segovia – Giraldo – with him at Perugia. It was Nicolás who brought the chapter's request for confirmation of their statute *de numero canonicorum* to Lyons in Aug. 1250: *Reg. Inn. IV*, 1757, 2863; *Reg. Greg. IX*, 2491; AC Segovia, doc. 224.

2 In the Segovia *inquisitio* the 'prestimonia provisionis magistri Nicolai' are listed separately from the rents of his archdeaconry: AC Segovia, doc. 17.

3 Serrano, *Hispania*, I, 40; *idem*, *Obispado de Burgos*, III, 379 (commemorating his death, as dean of Segovia, in March 1258).

4 At Lyons (20 June 1246); witnessed by Cardinal Gil and Bishop Bernardo of Segovia: copy in *Reg. Inn. IV*, 6629. The Segovia *inquisitio* valued the *prestimonia* of 'P. Gaetanus concanonicus' at 66 *maravedís*, 17 *solidi* and 9 *denarii*, which was above the limit set for each canon.

5 Above, p. 194, n.8.

6 'Noveritis quod nos ob reverentiam patris venerabilis domini episcopi Albanensis et tam propter probitatem vestram quam propter obsequium quod ex persona vestra ecclesie nostre proventurum spectamus', he granted him a pension of two

Had he lived, he would have been disappointed, though, as his church and the church of Segovia were, and have discovered the snag about such arrangements. For when Petrus Gaietanus was promoted to the see of Todi in 1252 his benefices (but not necessarily his loyalties) were transferred to the vicechancellor of the Roman Church, William of Parma.[1] Still, the same risk was attached to the benefices of Spaniards at the Curia. When the abbot of Castrojériz, Domingo Pérez – the Burgos proctor and familiar of Cardinal Gil[2] – died there, his abbacy (which normally was in the bishop's gift) together with the four hundred *maravedís* income which Gil's Burgos constitutions had annexed to it, were assigned by the pope to a protégé of the king of Castile, Fernando Velázquez, to finance him for five years at the Schools.[3]

Fernando Velázquez came from Segovia and was to become its bishop in 1265; so the transaction contained an element of rough justice, considering what Burgos, in the person of Master Nicolás, had received from Segovia.[4] But it is unlikely to have appeared thus to the parties concerned. Indeed, experiences of this sort seem to have led the Castilian churches to reconsider their policy of allowing their proctors at the Curia, whether nationals or foreigners, to retain vulnerable benefices. In the past churches had sought assurances that their control of such benefices would not be prejudiced by the death at Rome of their curial occupants.[5] By mid-century, though, they

hundred *maravedís per annum* in expectation of a Toledo benefice 'quod vel que liberalitatem dantis deceat et recipientem', Lyons, 31 March 1248: copy in *Reg. Inn. IV*, 6629. Petrus took some interest in Spanish affairs at the Curia: he was a witness of the Astorga–Castañeda plea in Sept. 1245, and in 1267, as bishop of Todi, he secured a common privilege for the Cistercians of Armentera (Coruña): *Reg. Inn. IV*, 1519; AHN, 1762/2.

1 *Reg. Inn. IV*, 6617, 6629. See also Herde, 4–5, and above, Ch. 7.
2 His association with Gil dated from July 1244 when he was at Città Castellana: Sousa Costa, 17, n. 50. As abbot of Castrojériz he was at the Curia in July 1248 and Feb. 1250. His name appears on the dorse of papal rescripts for Burgos in March 1249 and Aug. 1255: AC Burgos, vol. 7.ii, fos. 5–6, 8–10 (reg. Mansilla, *AA*, IX, nos 14, 31; *Reg. Inn. IV*, 4436; *Reg. Alex. IV*, 700).
3 Mansilla, 360, 364; *Reg. Inn. IV*, 6727; *Reg. Alex. IV*, 588, 3022, 3142.
4 *Reg. Urb. IV*, 1915; Colmenares, *Historia de Segovia*, 224.
5 For anxieties at Jaca and Monteáragon in the 1220s about the fate of the archdeaconry of Sodoruel and the church of Larraga, then in the possession of Jacinthus canon of St Peter's, see AC Huesca, 9–279; *Reg. Hon. III*, 4130 (MDH, 271, 418). These grants to Jacinthus – who also had an annuity from Urgel which in March 1236 the bishop and canons were scolded for having failed to pay – probably dated from the winter

were adopting different tactics and imitating the action of the beaver. It is noticeable that the church of Toledo did not appoint a successor in the style of Fortunius, but preferred to employ Italians and to pay them from time to time in cash – cash which the Italians were prepared to wait for and even understandingly to forego altogether.[1] This was a prudent policy to adopt, even before *Licet Ecclesiarum* defined the risks involved in 1265; and its wisdom was demonstrated in 1263 when Vivián the bishop-elect of Calahorra arrived at the Curia as spokesman of the Castilian Church and, though he was no innocent there, was relieved of the archdeaconry of Guadalajara which he had occupied at the time of his promotion.[2]

Unless one were an Archbishop Juan Arias with a genius for getting someone else to support one's proctor, the only other possible solution was that of Archbishop João of Braga who kept Johannes de Pinello waiting for payment until his will was proved.[3] This method of retrospective settlement was also favoured by Bishop Pedro of Zamora at the end of the century,[4] but while it may have worked

of 1219–20 when the bishops of Huesca and Urgel were both at the Curia: AC Huesca, *Extravagantes* (reg. Durán Gudiol, *AA*, VII, 62–3); *Reg. Hon. III*, 2298, 2466, 2480 (MDH, 260, 286, 288). Despite Honorius III's assurances, Larraga was awarded by Innocent IV to a nominee of the king of Aragon in March 1245: *Reg. Inn. IV*, 1144.

1 At Lyons on 26 May 1274 Master Angelus, canon of Cambrai and Châlons 'in romana curia advocatus' received £280 Tours in payment of the 100 *maravedí* annuity settled on him by Sancho of Castile 'quamdiu viverem'; and on 26 Nov. 1291 Master Sinibaldus de Labro, archdeacon of Bologna, was paid £100 Tours 'pro penssione quinque annorum mihi assignata ab...archiepiscopo [Gonzalo Gudiel]': AC Toledo, I.5.C.1.42; A.7.G.1.25. For John of Parma and Blaise of Anagni – two other Toledo retainers – see above, Ch. 7.

2 The recipient was a nephew of Cardinal Uberto Coconato. When that nephew died the archdeaconry was transferred to another nephew, together with Vivián's other Toledo income, 'ne dictus cardinalis hujus gratie frustretur effectu': *Reg. Urb. IV*, 1787. Cf. Linehan, *EHR*, LXXXV, 737; and, for Vivián's earlier visits to the Curia, in Jan. 1234 for Fernando III and in Jan. 1245 for Archbishop Rodrigo, *Reg. Greg. IX*, 1758; *Reg. Inn. IV*, 929, 950.

3 ADB, *Livro I dos Testamentos*, fo. 10r: 'Item mando Johanni de Pinello procuratori meo in curia, cui nondum providi in beneficio aliquo, C. morabutinos et unam equitaturam mediocrem de mille libris turonensibus quas dimisi in curia penes Dulcem mercatorem Florentinum et socios suos' (21 Oct. 1255). Johannes de Pinello was the archbishop's proctor by 28 July 1253, and in Aug. 1254 also acted for the bishops of Salamanca and Burgos: ADB, Gav. dos Concílios, 4 (*inc. Sua nobis*); AC Salamanca, 23/28 (reg. Marcos Rodríguez, *Catálogo*, 259); AC Burgos, vol. 46, fo. 423 (reg. Mansilla, *AA*, IX, no. 25): *Nostris est nuper*: dorse of each.

4 AC Zamora, 12/15: 100 *maravedís* bequest to *Lope* 'por que ffu a corte de Roma por nos' (an. 1302).

well, given a clear understanding between the parties, with substantial proctors who had a large clientele, lesser men were greatly inconvenienced by being treated by their employers as long-term creditors. There is at Tudela a particularly interesting letter sent sometime during the 1290s[1] to the dean and chapter of that church by their proctor Berenguer de Açanis, the agent between 1281 and 1300 of various Castilian and Aragonese interests.[2] It is the proctor's lament. Ever since his master, the bishop of Tarazona, had recommended them to him – he chided his clients – he had worked unsparingly for them. He had been a model servant, working away from them like nobody's business; but all for absolutely no return.[3] He had done battle with three 'great lions' (by which he meant his fellow proctors, one of whom was Aragonese[4]) who had been baying for the salaries

---

[1] AC Tudela, 41–26–19, dated Orvieto 'die mercurii proxima post festum S. Johannis Baptiste' (reg. Fuentes, 1114, as 'copia simple del sig. XIII', though it appears to be the original version). The reference to 'magister S(ancius) abbas monasterii S. Saturnini Tholosani [St Sernin, Toulouse] qui erat tunc archidiaconus' suggests a date in the 1290s. Cf. *Reg. Bon. VIII*, 1151, 4278; Devic and Vaissete, *Histoire générale de Languedoc*, IV, 526.

[2] For Bishop Suero Pérez of Zamora, 7 May 1281: AC Zamora, 11.i/10; for Guillelmus de Villa 'perpetuus capellanus in ecclesia Barchinonensi', 15 July 1281: AC Barcelona, d.s.n; for Alfonso Sánchez 'perpetuus portionarius ecclesie S. Jacobi de Medrit', 15 Oct. 1290: AC Toledo, Z.3.D.2.14; for the dean and chapter of Tudela, 20 Aug. and 9 Sept. 1291: AC Tudela, 5–C–8; 5–C–9 (reg. Fuentes, 430–1); for Bishop Pedro of Tarazona, 11 May 1298: AHN, sellos 72/7; for Poblet, 7 and 10 March 1300: AHN, sellos 5/36; sellos 90/21:23:25–26; 2355/19:20; 3224/14; for the nuns of Santa Clara, Barcelona, 31 March 1300: Fita, *BRAH*, XXVII, 475. Since Tarazona has no archive he is difficult to identify; but he may possibly have been the *Berengarius dictus de Insula* who was a canon of that church in Oct. 1292 and its cantor in Jan. 1299: AC Tudela, 5–C–10; 41–26–9 (reg. Fuentes, 433, 442).

[3] 'Recepi litteras vestras cum magnis promissionibus et modica utilitate, de qua non modicum sum turbatus…Debetis scire, domini, quod ego fui valde liberalis vobis quando dominus Tyrasonensis, dominus meus, rogavit me pro vobis et recommendavit mihi negocium vestrum sicut suum proprium. Feci sicut fidelis procurator laborando et ordinando sicut aliquis de mundo potuisset bene ordinare ut possent littere impetrari…'

[4] The three were Andreas de Setia, Johannes de Trebis and Egidius Petri de Pertusa. Though Pertusa is in the Lérida diocese (cf. *Reg. Greg. X*, 370), Gil Pérez's connexions were with the church of Huesca, which sent him to Bologna as a scholar (June 1268: *Chartularium Studii Bononiensis*, VII, 290; VIII, 213). He may have been related to Juan López de Pertusa, *consiliarius familiaris* of Alfonso IV and canon of Zaragoza (cf. Vincke, *AEM*, I, 348). By 1277 he was proctor of the bishop of Zaragoza (Herde, *Archiv. f. Diplomatik*, XIII, 274). He also acted for Bishop Miguel of Pamplona, 11 July 1281; and for the abbey of Montearagón (Huesca), 7 May 1288: AC Pamplona, II Episcopi 14 (reg. Goñi Gaztambide, *Catálogo*, 739); AHN, 653/18.

due to them from Tudela, and when one of them had lost patience and taken the matter to court he had told an effective sob-story on his clients' behalf and got the better of the plaintiff – whom he had then paid out of his own pocket.[1] Ditto the other two; on which account he was worse off to the tune of thirty-four gold florins. And what had the dean and chapter sent him in return? Airy nothings; no cash. This really would not do. He couldn't offer his creditors air as payment, such as they seemed to think they could offer him. It had been going on now for five years.[2] Even their instructions to him were hopelessly vague. Had they no idea? They weren't much help. What he had to put up with![3]

They were hard of heart, he concluded, like Pharoah.[4] So, not unreasonably, he and others in his position took their cue from the Israelites and shifted for themselves as best they might, attaching themselves to any ranking curialist who might be of assistance, and preferably to a cardinal. Others too, who were not proctors but were anxious to jump the queue for benefices, sought patrons, and though the associations thus formed brought them into contact with a wide range of non-Spanish dignitaries, the two most sought-after cardinals down to 1254 were, not unnaturally, Pelayo Gaitán and Gil Torres. With the help of one or other of these, scores of petitioners secured provision to cathedral and collegiate churches throughout the Peninsula, John of Abbeville's anti-pluralism legislation notwithstanding.[5] For the favoured individuals the system was a blessing. But

[1] 'Deinde reddimus ad iudicium et allegavi ego quod ecclesia erat in malo statu propter guerram et quia est in frontaria. Duravit diu set per sententiam auditoris habuit.VIII. florinas de auro tantum, quas ego solvi ei de bursa mea. De qua predictus abbas [of St Sernin, the arbiter] et plures alii fuerunt valde gavisi, quia ipse E(gidius) noluerat acceptare compromissum.' Gil Pérez had claimed £20 Tours; the 'compromise' figure had been £4.

[2] 'Quid plura? Ut breviter transeam: bene scitis etiam quod salarium mihi debitum non misistis... Ex tunc non vidi litteras vestras nec modo cum similibus promissionibus. Hoc non sufficit mihi quia non possum solvere creditoribus meis de vento, sicut vos actenus solvistis mihi. Non creditis paccare in quinque annis cum sustinui.'

[3] 'Nimis scribitis breviter in omnibus. Quare non misistis copiam affirmationis? – et ad quid posuistis exceptionem in procuratorio, set generalem mittere – et etiam de iudicibus. Quid est magna brevitas non est bona, quia quandoque pars adversa proponit aliquem exceptionem legitimam contra loca et iudices producta in iudicio, et propter hoc sunt plura loca necessaria. Etiam quanta ego sustinui pro vobis utinam vos scretis...'

[4] 'Potestis dicere sicut alibi dicitur: induratum est cor farahonis (Exodus, vii. 12).'

[5] Only one case of (prudent) remorse on that score has been noted, that of Gil's nephew,

for the corporations to which these individuals belonged it was deplorable – deplorable, that is, when other individuals turned it to their advantage. Thus deprived of their rights of collation, bishops and chapters protested; and none protested more vigorously than the bishops and chapters of the two churches with which Pelayo and Gil were most intimately connected, the churches of León and Zamora respectively.

When Honorius III conferred the León *prestimonium* of San Martín del Valle on the *magister scolarum* of León, Pelayo's nephew Juan Galvani, in February 1220, he urged Bishop Rodrigo to bear in mind the tremendous advantages which that church derived from having a cardinal at the Curia, and so to admit Juan Galvani with good grace.[1] Evidently the bishop was in some need of persuasion. He was not impressed by the allegedly charismatic cardinal, who was at the time not at the Curia but in Egypt leading the Fifth Crusade to disaster, and had been giving the cardinal's friends and relations an uneasy time.[2] And, sure enough, in July 1223, when the bishop had attempted to elude the pope's reservation of an archdeaconry there and to curry favour with Pelayo by assigning it to Juan Galvani,[3] the benefits of the cardinal's friendship proved entirely nugatory. Rodrigo was made to accept a set of constitutions of Pelayo's concoction, was suspended for two years from the collation of benefices in his church, and was convicted of being 'negligent, tepid and remiss'.[4]

Pelayo had high hopes for his nephews, both in Church and State. In November 1216 Honorius III had suggested to Alfonso IX of Leon that Juan Galvani be made chancellor of the kingdom in recognition of his uncle's services to the king;[5] and while Pelayo was

Pedro *magister scolarum* of Zamora, who made a clean breast of his pluralism in Sept. 1238 'quia ipsum conscientia remordebat ex eo quod...Sabinensis episcopus... contra plura beneficia obtinentes quandam constitutionem edidisse dicitur et eam excommunicationis sententiam roborasse': *Reg. Greg. IX, 4525.*

[1] *Reg. Hon. III,* 2331 (MDH, 272): 'Quidem si diligenter adverteris quem, qualem et quantum ad Legionensem ecclesiam et personam tuam dictus Albanensis gerat sinceritatis affectum, quid debeas patruo in nepote monstrabis.'

[2] *Ibid.*: 'Si diligenter adverteris quantum hispanis cedat ad titulum talis et tanti virtus hispani, non sic illius abicies post terga memoriam quod eum [not *sum,* as Mansilla] in suis habere credaris absentem.' Cf. Linehan, *HS,* xx, 178 ff.

[3] 'Intendens, ut creditur, ut favor iamdicti Albanensis episcopi per apostolice auctoritatis assensum, collationi huiusmodi robur daret': *ibid.* 4414 (MDH, 449).

[4] *Ibid.* 5017, 5023, 5534 (MDH, 504–5, 563).

[5] *Ibid.* 100 (MDH, 10).

away on Crusade, Cardinal Thomas of Capua had written in similar terms, 'rogans quatinus quem ad patruum geritis, in nepote monstretis affectum', the *nepos* on this occasion being one *P.* – possibly *P. Aurie* whom the pope legitimised in September 1217.[1] By October 1232 *P. Aurie* was dean of Salamanca; Juan Galvani was dean of Compostela; Pedro Arias, another nephew, was dean of León; and their uncle was dead. His death, indeed, had produced a determined campaign against them which Gregory IX condemned as 'hateful ingratitude', particularly since its leaders were themselves protégés of Pelayo Gaitán and – 'veluti manuum suarum factura' – ought to have had greater respect for his memory.[2] The pope assured the deans' persecutors that Pelayo Gaitán was still a name to conjure with: at Rome his memory lingered on.[3] So, for that matter, did it linger on at León. But it was not a particularly happy memory. For Juan Galvani was still *magister scolarum*, as well as being dean of Compostela;[4] and when Pedro Arias died his *prestimonia* were to pass to another cardinal's nephew who was not even a Spaniard.[5]

The León *prestimonium* awarded to Juan Galvani in February 1220 was vacant on account of the election of the archdeacon of León, Martín Rodríguez, to the see of Zamora three years before.[6] Zamora in 1217 was in a state of both spiritual and temporal collapse after twenty-three years of misrule by Bishop Martín Arias.[7] But the new bishop was not allowed to reorganise his chapter's affairs, for Zamora was blessed with the curse of Cardinal Gil and through him the provision of benefices to his relatives and dependents was immediately short-circuited.[8] Collectively the bishop and chapter offered resistance, which elicited from Honorius III letters of reprimand akin to those sent to León. Surely – he observed on three separate occasions – they ought to welcome the opportunity of showing their gratitude

---

[1] Publ. Hahn, *Collectio monumentorum*, I, 383–4. Cf. *Reg. Hon. III*, 782 (MDH, 90).

[2] *Reg. Greg. IX*, 918; Fernández Catón, *Archivos Leoneses*, VII, 108; AC Salamanca, 3/1/40–2 (reg. Marcos, 188).

[3] '...cuius apud nos vivit memoria, et cum eo decedente non decidat...nepotes suos habeamus in visceribus Jesu Christi': *Reg. Greg. IX*, 918.

[4] *Ibid.* 604.

[5] *Reg. Inn. IV*, 5113 (above, p. 145).

[6] *Reg. Hon. III*, 984 (MDH, 125). His archdeaconry passed to Master *L*, a chaplain of Pelayo Gaitán.

[7] *Ibid.* 629–30 (MDH, 64–5).

[8] See the list of recipients in Mansilla, 234–42.

to the cardinal whose chief anxiety was to enhance their state. They should meet with his wishes cheerfully – *ylariter* – instead of defying apostolic mandates.[1] Instead, however – again collectively – they framed a set of constitutions which sought to prevent such intervention in their affairs. In certain respects their legislation foreshadowed the cardinal's own constitutions of the late 1240s, though they hesitated to adopt his central principle of separate endowments for bishop and chapter.[2] Not until 1266 did they take that step, in the form of a *divisio* of their resources arbitrated by the dean of Compostela, Fernando Alfonso, and a solemn undertaking that neither party would admit anyone to membership of the church without the agreement of the other, under any circumstances.[3] Prior to that agreement their attitude to the entire system of papal provision – and to Cardinal Gil as a feature of that system – was ambivalent and typical of the thirteenth century: as a body they deplored it while as individual members of that body they made thorough use of it.[4] Thus Bishop Martín Rodríguez protested to Gregory IX that the last thirteen benefices in his church had been disposed of by John of Abbeville and the two Spanish cardinals; that in thirteen years as bishop he himself had not been permitted to appoint to a single full prebend; and that the local clergy, whose ancestors had endowed the church, were passed over in favour of *extranei* and *peregrini*. But in each case the outcome was that he was authorised to fill vacancies himself, the chapter's shared rights of collation were set aside, and such clergy as did not enjoy his favour once more sought the assistance of Cardinal Gil.[5] For their part, the dean and chapter sent letters to the pope claiming that their bishop was bent on destroying the church of Zamora, and offered them 'non beneficia sed maleficia, non gratiam sed iniuriam'.[6] While each side looked to Rome and the

1 *Reg. Hon. III,* 1277, 2405, 4878 (MDH, 169, 277, 498).
2 AC Zamora, *Liber Constitutionum,* fos. 8rb–16vb, Xrb. There were to be twenty-four canons and twelve portionaries only; only portionaries could be admitted to canonries; no one beneficed elsewhere could possess a benefice at Zamora.
3 *Ibid.* fo. 3vb: 'Item diffinio quod nec episcopus per se vel capitulum per se aliquem recipiant in socium vel in fratrem, sive proprio motu sive per litteras apostolicas'; AC Zamora, 6/1-1a-1c.
4 Cf. Barraclough, *Papal Provisions,* 145.
5 *Reg. Greg. IX,* 1318 (May 1233); 2009 (July 1234); 3258 (Aug. 1236).
6 '...ut earum verbis utamur': ASV, arm. XXXI. 72, fos. 189v–90r (Schillmann, 1310). The letter refers to the tender age at which the bishop in question had been appoin-

cardinal for some advantage over the other, all that they were able to agree upon at home was their failure to agree upon anything, which they enshrined in a statute requiring total unanimity in the conferring of benefices. This was tantamount to the postponement *sine die* of the exercise of their rights of collation, but even after its condemnation by Innocent IV as uncanonical they continued to attempt to operate it.[1]

In circumstances such as these Cardinal Gil was able to insinuate his *nepotes* into Zamora with the greatest of ease. Indeed, Bishop Pedro – who succeeded on the translation of Martín Rodríguez to León in 1238 – may have been one of them.[2] For both bishop and chapter implicitly accepted the cardinal's mediation as constituting the normal method of collation in their church. It was not a growth industry: there are very few cases of Zamora clerics securing benefices, through his agency, elsewhere.[3] At the Curia, meanwhile the cardinal's *nepos dilectus*, Esteban the abbot of Husillos, was going from strength to strength. Between 1229 and 1252 he had accumulated benefices at Compostela, Zamora, Toledo, Palencia, Oviedo, Salamanca, Ávila and Calahorra. Further afield, the churches of Chartres, Châlons, Douai and Prague, as well as Verdun, owed him a living; all of which may cause the reader to look askance at Mansilla's assurance that this type of early fourteenth-century excess 'no tiene aún aplicación para la primera mitad del siglo XIII'.[4] The precise nature of Esteban's activities at the Curia is not clear, though during his uncle's declining years he did emerge as something of an entrepreneur in benefices.[5] It seems that on Gil's death he may have been

ted, and Schillmann takes this to mean Bishop Martín Rodríguez, on the strength of a mistaken interpretation of *Reg. Greg. IX*, 2009 (which he cites as no. 1009). It may apply equally to Bishop Pedro or – more plausibly – Suero Pérez.

[1] AC Zamora, 11.i/11 (= *Reg. Inn. IV*, 2003: publ. Mansilla, 218), 10 July 1246. Cf. *Reg. Urb. IV*, 1615.

[2] Pedro Benítez, the Zamora proctor in 1251–2, was a nephew of both the bishop and Esteban of Husillos, the cardinal's nephew: *Reg. Inn. IV*, 5564, 5805.

[3] Gil Yáñez 'in provincia Compostellana', Jan. 1252 (*Reg. Inn. IV*, 5565); Elías (episcopal proctor in Oct. 1253: AC Zamora, 11.i/4, dorse), Salamanca canonry, July 1253 (*ibid.* 7675); Gil Guillérmez, 'propter...merita et consideratione bone memorie Egidii...cardinalis cuius nepos esse diceris', Palencia benefice, pre-Oct. 1257: (*Reg. Alex. IV*, 2298).

[4] *Reg. Inn. IV*, 6044. Cf. Mansilla, 242.

[5] He secured a dignity at Zamora and another elsewhere in Castile–Leon for his *familiaris*, Carasco, May–Aug. 1252: *Reg. Inn. IV*, 5827, 5907; a Zamora canonry

exposed to the sort of reprisals suffered by the nephews of Cardinal Pelayo.[1] Soon, though, he found himself a new master, Cardinal Stephen of Palestrina,[2] and so was able to continue the family business of benefice-broking into the pontificate of Gregory X when, with his sights on the bishopric of Salamanca, he died.[3] The churches which had been made to invest in him paid the customary penalty, the abbacy of Husillos passing to the Portuguese curialist and future cardinal-bishop of Tusculum, Ordonho Álvares, at a moment when, in common with the other collegiate churches of the Palencia diocese, it was fast approaching a state of utter collapse.[4] Yet even that was not the end of the Torres dynasty: although somewhat etiolated, the family's reputation for pluralism survived in the person of Pedro Benítez, Esteban's nephew and the cardinal's executor, who was still thriving as cantor of Zamora and *magister scolarum* of Salamanca in December 1285.[5] And some credit too may perhaps be claimed for Bernardo of Zamora, the curial scribe who penned such elegant letters during the years 1276–8.[6]

for Bernardo, portionary of that church, June 1252 (*ibid.* 5851); a benefice 'in provincia Compostellana' and at Zamora for Pedro Benítez, Nov. 1251–Jan. 1252 (*ibid.* 5564, 5805); a Ciudad Rodrigo benefice for his cleric, Jaime archdeacon of Coria, March 1252 (*ibid.* 5806); an Astorga benefice for Juan Rodríguez, a relation of the cardinal, Nov. 1252 (*ibid.* 6696).

1 On 18 May 1255 Gil, cantor of Zamora, wrote from Husillos absenting himself from a hearing of the Braga–Porto dispute 'propter urgentissima negotia ecclesie Fussellensis que coram domino rege Castelle vertuntur': ADB, Gav. dos Arcebispos, 29.

2 There is in AC Toledo (E.7.D.2.4) a barely legible letter from Cardinal Stephen to Alfonso X on behalf of Esteban, whose benefices appear to have been in jeopardy (dated Viterbo, 18 Oct; no year). In March 1259 Esteban's benefices were re-confirmed, as they had been in Oct. 1252: *Reg. Alex. IV*, 2897.

3 *Reg. Greg. X*, 245 (May 1273). In Sept. 1267, when Juan de Parras, canon of Oviedo, made his will at the Curia he directed that his loose change be entrusted to Esteban: AC Oviedo, B/5/12 (reg. García Larragueta, 412).

4 *Reg. Greg. X*, 275. In March 1271 the church and cloister of Lebanza (Palencia) 'esta mal parado e ha mester todo de refazer', according to Archbishop Sancho II of Toledo. Yet in 1279 the bishop and chapter understandably refused to assign any further funds to these collegiate churches: AE Palencia, doc. de Lebanza, 4; AC Palencia, 4/1/5. In Aug. 1252 Esteban had secured exemption for himself, his *familia* and for the laity of Husillos from payment of papal subsidies: *Reg. Inn. IV*, 5924.

5 AC León, doc. 1569; *Reg. Urb. IV*, 1205, 1831, 2046; *Reg. Hon. IV*, 261.

6 For B. Çamoren as papal scribe, see Battelli, *Sched. Baumgarten*, 3841–2, 3874, 3884, 3897, 3921–2, 3924, 3938 (as *Bern. Zamor.*). Baumgarten listed two bulls of Innocent V, 3841–2, both 'prächtige Schrift': these rescripts are in AHN, 3756/1–2, which contains two more examples of Bernardo's handiwork: sellos 49/15 (2 April 1276);

There was nothing unique about the beneficial activity of Gil Torres at Zamora. But it must be stressed that, as Mr Barraclough has demonstrated, pressure came from below. Gil was in much the same position with regard to Zamora as his colleague Cardinal Thomas of Capua, who was at pains to explain to his old friends at Capua that, much as he loved both them and the church that had nourished him, he was simply unable to meet all their requests *statim*.[1] Nor was Zamora's disorganisation exceptional. The register of *litterae beneficiales* of Urban IV's third year records applications for provision mandates in favour of individuals submitted by the prelates and chapters of other peninsular churches which had not been supplied with formal constitutions by Gil: Compostela, Toledo and Palencia as well as Zamora.[2] The kings of Castile and Aragon too made requests for their clerics, irrespective of residence rules and statutes *de numero canonicorum*, thus sapping as petitioners the defences which they erected as patrons.[3] That aspect of John of Abbeville's reform programme had not long survived the legate, but closer contacts with the Curia made the abrogation of tiresome regulations a more easily accomplished task. When the chapter of Guarda supplicated Innocent IV for relaxation of their statute *de numero* in favour of a local worthy, Vicente Rodrigues, they were careful to mention his relationship to Master Martinho, the prior of Guimarães who was no mean personage at the pope's court.[4]

For the same reason, that papal grants were so frequently reversed,

425/19 (3 April 1276). On 15 Oct. 1276 Bernardo served Bishop Pedro de Urgel as proctor: AC Seo de Urgel, d.s.n: letter *Sua nobis,* dorse. Was he the Bernardo who had been awarded a Zamora canonry in June 1252 (*Reg. Inn. IV,* 5851)? Cf. Herde, *Beiträge,* 210, n. 265.

[1] Publ. Heller, *Archiv f. Urkundenforschung,* XIII, 283.

[2] *Reg. Urb. IV,*1783, 1829, 2606; 1936; 2040; 2499.

[3] *Reg. Inn. IV,* 913–7 (including a request for leave of absence from Zamora with full stipend for Master Pelayo, canon and physician to the Infante Alfonso), Oct. 1243. In July 1245 Jaime I of Aragon was granted a canonry for his clerks in each of the cathedral churches of his kingdom, 'certo ecclesiarum ipsarum canonicorum numero vallato...vel quod iidem clerici alias beneficiati existunt nequaquam obstantibus': ACA, Bulas, leg. VIII–8 (reg. Miquel, 119). Cf. Sancho IV's prohibition in 1287 of the reception to canonries at Covarrubias 'sinon quando vacasse': Serrano, *Cartulario de Covarrubias,* 133.

[4] '...et quia magistro Martino priori Vimariensi capellano vestro attinet linea parentole', Aug. 1253: ADB, Gav. das Dignidades, 17. By May 1256 Master Martinho had been appointed archbishop of Braga: *Reg. Alex. IV,* 1365. Cf. Ferreira, *Fastos episcopaes,* II, 49 ff.; Cerchiari, *Capellani papae,* II, 11–12.

the rescripts exempting churches from further provision – such as the bishop of Zamora had received at the time of his second protest to Gregory IX and which were acquired by all but a few during the 1240s and early 1250s[1] – were basically worthless, and after Innocent IV's death demand for them waned. They could do nothing to combat the real sources of grievance which Innocent mentioned in a letter of May 1250 to the abbey of Eslonza.[2] Nor could *Execrabilis* – Alexander IV's constitution of April 1255 which wrote off all but four of the provisions to *prebendae vacaturae* in any church – though various parties chose to regard it as a more general panacea than it really was. The chapter of León thought that it provided them with the means of disposing of providees to portions as well as to canonries;[3] and, although it applied only to those *iam admissos* in 1255, it

---

[1] *Reg. Greg. IX*, 2009. During Innocent IV's pontificate various forms of protection were granted: the ordinary as sole executor in his diocese: *Et tua supplex*, 13–11–1250 (AE Gerona, 6/9) and 21–1–53 (AD Astorga, 3/66: reg. Quintana, *AA*, XI, no. 82); *Intendentes ecclesiam*, 2–11–52 (AHA, *Cartoral AB*, fo. 33v); exemption of the episcopal *mensa* [Osma], 13–11–48 (*Reg. Inn. IV*, 4208); resumption of prebends held by *alieni*, 3–11–53 (AC Palencia, 2/1/59; AC Santiago de Compostela, *Tumbillo de privilegios*, fo. 112r–13v: Potthast, 15162); exemption from payment of daily rations to absentees [14–11–50: *Paci et tranquillitati*], and from general letters of provision addressed to the province [4–4–51: *Fraternitatis tue*] (AE Gerona, 6/20; 6/11). But the most common form was the guarantee against provision: Compostela, 28–7–45 (AC Santiago, *Tumbo B*, fo. 224v); Astorga, 10–8–45 (reg. Quintana, no. 59); Oviedo, 17–8–45 (*Reg. Inn. IV*, 1431); Plasencia, 12–9–45 (AC Plasencia, d.s.n.); Gerona, 29–1–46 (AE Gerona, 6/13); Huesca, 15–3–46 (AC Huesca, 2–723: reg. Durán Gudiol, *AA*, VII, no. 74); Cuenca, 26–7–48 (BN, MS 13071, fo. 55r); Oviedo, 31–1–50 (AC Oviedo, Plomados 1/7: reg. García Larragueta, 350); Astorga, 29–7–50 (AD Astorga, 3/65: reg. Quintana, no. 78); Cartagena, 5–8–50 (Fita, *BRAH*, III, 274); Gerona, 29–8–50 (AC Gerona, *Llibre Vert*, fo. 204r); Valencia, 13–12–51 (AC Valencia, perg. 269: reg. Olmos, *Pergaminos*, 214); Braga, 23–10–52 (ADB, Gav. das Dignidades, 18.ii); Palencia, 3–12–52 (*Reg. Inn. IV*, 6128); Compostela, 23–12–52 (AC Santiago, *Tumbo B*, fo. 247v); Braga, 21–5–53 (ADB, Gav. dos Privilégios do Cabido, 2; Gav. das Dignidades, 18.i), 19–12–53 (ADB, Gav. das Dignidades, 19); Salamanca, 27–1–54 (AC Salamanca, 23/69: reg. Marcos, 248, misdated); Braga, 26–2–54 (ADB, Gav. das Dignidades, 18.iii); Orense, 9–8–54 (*Reg. Inn. IV*, 7915); León, 11/20–8–54 (*ibid.* 7922, 7958); Zamora, 23–8–54 (AC Zamora, 1/1: attrib. to Innocent III by Matilla Tascón, *Guía-inventario*, 114); Lisbon, 12–9–54 (*Reg. Inn. IV*, 8013); Burgos, 19–11–54 (AC Burgos, vol. 10, fo. 413: reg. Mansilla, *AA*, IX, No. 26).

[2] 'Super provisione plurium de iudeismo ad fidem catholicam conversorum et subsidio carissimi...regis Castelle et Legionis contra hostes christiane fidei dominantis...non modicum aggravatur', 22 May 1250: AHN, 968/3.

[3] *Reg. Alex. IV*, 1290, 1339. Cf. Barraclough, *EHR*, XLIX, 207.

was cited three years later by the chapter of Valencia against Miguel de Spigol, canon of Vich, as well as by the chapter of Vich, including Miguel de Spigol, against Guillermo de Planis.[1] Indeed, the Spanish evidence provides little support for those historians who regard Alexander IV's pontificate as a watershed in the history of provisions.[2] Pressure from below was maintained. By April 1258 the pope was being petitioned for relief by the church of Oviedo, where to Innocent IV's ten outstanding provisions 'many' of his own were said to have been added. He reduced the waiting list, and in February 1261 did the same for Calahorra[3] – as did his successor Urban IV, for León, Toledo and Seville.[4]

While *Execrabilis* was welcomed by the ordinary collators, many canonists criticised it severely – and none more so than Bernardus Compostellanus.[5] This was understandable, since his own career had owed a great deal to the abuses which *Execrabilis* hoped to check and, as one well established at the Curia by 1255, he was loth to have his

---

[1] AC Valencia, perg. 8161: 'Cum sint in ecclesia Valentina quatuor recepti canonici ad vacaturas prebendas et adhuc spectent, et super hoc edita sit constitutio quod ecclesie ubi quatuor sunt spectantes vacaturas prebendas seu episcopi et capitula earundem per litteras apostolicas providere aliquibus minime teneantur', March 1258 (reg. Olmos, 250); AC Vich, 37–6–43; 6–III–21; 6–III–26, Sept. 1258. Cf. Barraclough, *loc. cit.*, 198.

[2] Barraclough, *loc. cit.*, 212, opines that the 'conscious object and real merit' of Alexander's pontificate 'was to renew the normal and accepted organization which Innocent had thrown out of working order'; and Vincke, *RQ*, XLVIII, 200, observes a sharp drop in provisions to Spanish churches. This tendency to exaggerate the 'improvement' under Alexander stems partly from Baier's list of provisions (*Päpstliche Provisionen*, 234) which, because it was compiled before the completion of the calendars of the Registers of the pontificate, is disproportionately brief.

[3] *Reg. Alex. IV*, 2531 (Yet within the month he was enforcing one of Innocent IV's provision mandates there: *ibid.* 2564); AC Calahorra, doc. 330: four clerics had been received into canonries 'ad mandatum nostrum' and 'nonnulli alii super receptione ac provisione sua in eadem ecclesia a nobis litteras impetrarint': *inc. Decet et expedit*, 18 Feb. 1261.

[4] At León, Alexander had provided 'many' and Urban a dozen by Dec. 1263. Ten provisions had been authorised during the archiepiscopal vacancy at Toledo. At Seville the sense of *Execrabilis* was reiterated *hac vice*: *Reg. Urb. IV*, 1206, 1296 (July 1264), 2020 (Feb. 1264).

[5] 'Dicam dictam constitutionem esse odiosam et contra iuris rationem': cit. Barraclough, *EHR*, XLIX, 210. Benito de Rocaberti had the text of *Discrimen preteriti* (*Reg. Alex. IV*, 998) entered in his cartulary: AHA, *Cartoral AB*, fo. 15r; and the archbishop of Braga obtained copies of *Execrabilis*, *Nuper super* and *Contingit* (*Reg. Alex. IV*, 1004–5): ADB, Gav. das Dignidades, 3, 22, 21,

powers of patronage curtailed.[1] His fears, though, proved groundless. Men in his position, curialists and cardinals, continued to exert the old influence. As the benefice-market became more difficult, their value was enhanced. In July 1263 three cardinals – Bishop Rudolf of Albano, Ottobono Fieschi and Matthew Rosso Orsini – managed to persuade Bishop Matheus of Lisbon, whose church had just had all but four expectancies cancelled by Urban IV, to provide Velasco Fernandes and Domingos Peres, *magister scolarum* of Braga, with canonries, 'revocatione non obstante predicta';[2] while, though only one of the five whose rights were safeguarded later that year when the number of León expectancies was reduced to six seems to have been a non-Spaniard,[3] two were the chaplains of cardinals,[4] a third was a nephew of Bernardus Compostellanus,[5] and the other was the bishop's proctor, Pedro Pérez.[6]

After the death of Cardinal Gil, Spaniards at the Curia found themselves new patrons. Some followed the abbot of Husillos into the household of the Hungarian cardinal, Stephen of Palestrina.[7] Others took refuge with Innocent IV's nephew, Cardinal Ottobono Fieschi, a man whose influence was able to secure rents of £500 *portugalensis monete* and a Lisbon canonry for Gil Martins, a poor cleric of that place who came to the Curia in November 1262 with

---

1 For Bernardo's own Spanish benefices, see Barraclough, *EHR*, xlix, 490–1; for his activities as patron, *Reg. Inn. IV*, 6317, 8089; *Reg. Alex. IV*, 383. He died between June and Dec. 1266: AC Burgos, vol. 40.i, fo. 333 (cf. Barraclough, 491).

2 ADB, Gav. das Dignidades, 23.

3 *Reg. Urb. IV*, 1206 (1 Dec. 1263): Rainerius, nephew of Cardinal Uberto Coconato.

4 *Ibid.*: Master Dominicus *physicus*, chaplain of Cardinal John Gaetan Orsini; and Pedro Domínguez, archdeacon of León and chaplain of Cardinal James Savelli. The former cardinal's household contained two canons of Orense in Nov. 1254 – Pedro Rodríguez and Pedro Codarii; and in 1256 his chaplain, Master Gonsalvo canon of Astorga, received a further benefice: *Reg. Alex. IV*, 947, 1683. Cardinal James was host to a whole colony of Spaniards in 1263–4. Pedro Domínguez, his 'domesticus et commensalis capellanus', was archdeacon of Triacastela: *Reg. Urb. IV*, 233, 1027, 1680, 2360.

5 *Ibid.*: Rodrigo Sánchez, archdeacon of León.

6 *Ibid.*

7 For Cardinal Stephen's Spanish friends, see Linehan, *AEM*. One of them, Bishop Abril of Urgel, who seems to have owed his see to the cardinal's intervention, showed his gratitude by challenging the award of the archdeaconry of Tremp to Stephen's chaplain, Timothy (canon of Pécs; later bishop of Zagreb) in 1259–60: Linehan, *loc. cit.*; ASV, *Collect.*, 397, fos. 52r–3r. In July 1260 Stephen was entrusted with the task of sorting out the multitude of claims to benefices at Burgos: *Reg. Alex. IV*, 3142.

only four marks to his name.[1] The Lugo proctor, Martín, owed his dignity in that church to the good offices of John Pirunti, nephew of Cardinal Jordan Pirunti;[2] and the Astorga proctor, Abril Rodríguez, was beholden for his further benefices to Cardinal Octavian Ubaldini.[3] Octavian – who for Dante was *the* Cardinal – assisted other peninsular churchmen also.[4] He corresponded with the king of Castile and the archbishop of Compostela,[5] and wrote twice to the archbishop of Braga urging him to assign a prebend to Master Pedro Garini who was a canon of that church and his own chaplain. Master Pedro's quest for income had involved him in 'tot et tantis laboribus et expensis' that he had vowed not to leave the Curia until he was promised satisfaction.[6] Hordes of clerics had provision mandates. What gave any individual the advantage was a letter of this sort from a cardinal who had it in his power to promote or obstruct the bishop's affairs at the Curia. Two cardinals, of course, were better than one; and, in view of the historians' assurances about their diametrically opposed views on the subject of local ecclesiastical

---

[1] *Reg. Urb. IV*, 179; AHN, 1331B/23. Ottobonos was host to Pedro Pérez, canon of Zamora, in Aug. 1254 (*Reg. Inn. IV*, 8300); to Gil, *abbas Burgensis* in Oct. 1257 (*Reg. Alex. IV*, 2625: publ. J. Ptaśnik, *Monumenta Poloniae Vaticana*, III (Cracow, 1914), no. 87); and to Martín dean of Burgos, and Melendo archdeacon of Astorga in June 1264 (*Reg. Urb. IV*, 1113). He was auditor of the disputed elections to the sees of León in 1254, Lérida in Sept, 1256, and Ávila in July 1263; of the Braga–Porto jurisdiction case in June 1254; and of the troubles at Tarragona during the career of Benito de Rocaberti. In 1267 he toyed with the idea of visiting Spain: *Reg. Inn. IV*, 7919; AHA, *Cartoral AB*, fo. 17r; *Reg. Urb. IV*, 331; ADB, Gav. dos Arcebispos, 86; AHA, *Thesaurus*, fo. 51–2; *Reg. Clem. IV*, 1278.

[2] *Reg. Urb. IV*, 1704 (June 1264). He had been proctor for two years or more. During the pontificate of Boniface VIII *Martinus Lucensis* served as proctor for the church of Oviedo, certain Galician monasteries, and the archbishop of Toledo: AC Oviedo, Plomados 4/20 (reg. García Larragueta, 570 = *Reg. Bon. VIII*, 4751); AHN, 545/14; 1488/14–15; 1917/5; AC Toledo, X.2.B.2.5 (= *Reg. Bon. VIII*, 4043): dorse of each.

[3] *Reg. Alex. IV*, 2372 (Dec. 1257). Cf. AD Astorga, 3/62–3: dorse (July 1250).

[4] Amongst whom were his chaplains, the dean of Braga in Feb. 1245; Pelayo Rodríguez canon of Zamora in Nov. 1257; and Pedro Martínez, canon of Palencia, his 'capellanus commensalis' in Dec. 1263: above, p. 205; *Reg. Alex. IV*, 2374; *Reg. Urb. IV*, 2413. Cf. *Inferno*, x, 120.

[5] *Registri dei cardinali Ugolino d'Ostia e Ottaviano degli Ubaldini*, pubblicati a cura di Guido Levi (Istituto Storico Italiano: fonti per la storia d'Italia, viii (Rome, 1890)), 174–5.

[6] ADB, Gav. das Dignidades, 84 (undated). Pedro Garini was at the Curia with Archbishop João in Jan. 1254: ADB, *Livro I dos Testamentos*, fo. 7r–v.

autonomy, it is instructive to find the future pontiffs Innocent IV and Alexander IV appealing jointly, while they were still cardinals, on behalf of Master Lope Rodríguez to Archbishop Rodrigo of Toledo.[1]

The outcome of the contest for the deanery of Zamora, which was enacted at Orvieto during the winter of 1263–4, proved the value of such contacts.[2] In the decade after Cardinal Gil's death, the advent of the combative Bishop Suero Pérez and the nation-wide upheavals of the late 1250s had further intensified the battle for benefices at Zamora. The bishop's practice of turning a deaf ear to papal provision rescripts – a practice which was to lead eventually to his excommunication[3] – produced an inevitable clash when the dean, Juan Yáñez, died and Juan's nephew, Martín Vicéntez, claimed the office on the strength of an expectancy granted him by Urban IV. In October 1263 the case was heard by Hostiensis himself, and there was no lack of Zamora clerics present at the Curia to offer evidence. The plaintiff was Martín Vicéntez, the bishop's dean – García Núñez – having been inducted in the previous January;[4] but there had been a third candidate also, canon Pedro Pérez. Martín Peláez, the bishop's proctor, submitted that there had been no vacancy; and that even if there had been it could not have been filled by Martín Vicéntez, since 'non esset idoneus, immo prorsus indignus ad decanatum'. Confirmation of this was supplied in the name of the chapter by Alfonso Mini, a man with a personal grudge against the plaintiff.[5] For his part, Martín Vicéntez claimed that the bishop had deprived him improperly of the office while an appeal to the pope was pending,

---

[1] AC Toledo, I.4.0.1.20: 'ut eundem magistrum Lupum in vestram, domine archiepiscope, tamquam filium in parentis gratiam quantum decet et convenit reducatis', 17 April 1243. Cardinal John 'of Toledo' was a third signatory of the letter. Cardinal Raynald dei Conti (Alexander IV) was indistinguishable from his colleagues in this respect: in March 1252 he demanded a benefice in the province of Toledo for his chaplain, Johannes: *Reg. Inn. IV, 5821*.

[2] The following account has been constructed from the transcript of the submissions of the various parties at the hearing of the case by Cardinal Henry of Ostia (AC Zamora, 11.ii/5); a letter (seemingly of Clement IV) in the Marinus Formulary (ASV, Arm. XXXI.72, fo. 205r: Schillmann, 1455); and the Register of Urban IV.

[3] In May 1269 (not 1231, as Matilla Tascón, 141): AC Zamora, 11.ii/6. See above, Ch. 8.   [4] AC Zamora, *Liber Constitutionum*, fo. 5ra.

[5] Martín and two others – one of whom was Pedro Pérez – were bent on preventing Alfonso's admission to a benefice at Zamora, though the bishop and the *maior pars* of the chapter approved of him. This was reported in the following Feb: *Reg. Urb. IV, 1615*.

and demanded £200 Tours expenses and one thousand marks in lieu of lost income. Then his proctor, Pascal Pérez, produced further information: the bishop ought to have assigned to Martín Vicéntez the *prestimonium de Fontis Peradis* which had become vacant on the promotion of Don Andrés to the see of Sigüenza. Instead, in defiance of the pope's mandate he had awarded it to one of Alfonso X's clerics, Juan de Santiago.[1]

The final item of information contained in the transcript of the various *libelli* is that on 3 October 1263 the various appeals of the would-be dean were referred for decision to Cardinal Stephen of Palestrina. This was done at the instance of Cardinal Jordan of Ss Cosmas and Damian, the successor to the title of Gil Torres, with whom Martín Vicéntez, his chaplain, was staying during this period.[2] If, however, Martín and his patron were counting on a favourable issue of the deanery case emerging from this transfer, then they were to be disappointed, for that office was occupied successively by Martín's two rivals – García Núñez and Pedro Pérez,[3] and the highest post that Martín ever secured at Zamora was that of treasurer.[4] It may have afforded him some consolation that in June 1264 Cardinal Stephen, as arbiter rather than as judge, awarded half the *prestimonium de Fontis Peradis* to him rather than to the bishop's nominee, Esteban Domínguez.[5] Yet on balance the bishop had got the better of the contest, and Martín's allies shared his discomfiture. Pascal Pérez, for example, paid the penalty for having served as Martín's proctor. In May 1264 Urban IV granted him the next Zamora vacancy,[6] but by 2 October, when Urban died, Pascal had achieved nothing, and Bishop Suero Pérez had no difficulty in

---

1 This had occurred while Andrés was still bishop-elect, sometime since 1261. Cf. Minguella, *Historia de Sigüenza*, I, 214.

2 *Reg. Urb. IV*, 992, 1000, 2364 (Nov. 1263–Feb. 1264).

3 García Núñez was dean till Nov. 1266 at least (AC Zamora, 4/2, 4/3); Pedro Pérez by Dec. 1267 (Ballesteros, *BRAH*, CIX, 452). He was succeeded by Pedro Yáñez, June 1278 to Jan. 1281 (AC Zamora, 13/53, 12/16) who had previously, until Sept. 1275 at least, been cantor (AC Zamora, 16.i/10; AD Barcelona, documentos de S. Ana, d.s.n); as had his successor as dean, Alfonso Pérez, June 1282 to 1286 (AC Zamora, 12/16, 24/6bis, *Liber Constitutionum*, fo. 2ra).

4 By 1279 till, at least, Jan. 1281: AC Zamora, 13/61, 12/16.

5 *Reg. Urb. IV*, 1047, where the previous occupant is named as Bernardo. Esteban was promised the next Zamora vacancy, until which time Martín was to pay him half the income of the *prestimonium* and of the prebend to which it was attached.

6 *Ibid.* 1715.

holding off his egregious executor – Amador, canon of Salamanca, who was also at Orvieto on his own behalf in December 1263 – and preventing any grant being made by the *distributor proventuum* at Zamora until October 1266 when Clement IV referred the whole affair to new judges.[1]

Neither that letter nor an earlier mandate which Clement had allegedly sent for Pascal Pérez was registered, and this at least emerges clearly from the foregoing account of Zamora's kaleidoscopic condition in the early 1260s: that the plethoric flow of contradictory papal mandates made curial aid a *sine qua non* for provision. For any individual applicant, either at Zamora or anywhere else, to enjoy the unanimous support of bishop and chapter was very rare. Rather surprisingly, Martín Vicéntez managed somehow to secure it eventually, in the form of letters to the pope sealed by the bishop, the dean and the chapter.[2] But this method was open to abuse, and in December 1268 – by which time Suero Pérez and the canons had drifted apart again on the question of their respective jurisdiction over the clergy of Toro – the dean and chapter forbad it.[3] Appearances suggest that the bishop had broken faith and was not abiding by the arbitrated settlement of 1266.[4] All that is certain, though, is that there was, as usual, trouble in the camp there, and that all of those who had derived any benefit at all during the transactions of 1263–4 had been clerics with a friend at the Roman Curia.[5] 'A final judgement on the provisions system' is indeed 'to be sought

---

1 *Sua nobis,* 4 Oct. 1266: executor's copy: AC Zamora, 11.ii/7. Cf. *Reg. Urb. IV,* 1065.

2 '...prout in litteris inde confectis sigillatis sigillis episcopi, decani et capituli': ASV, arm. XXXI. 72, fo. 205r.

3 AC Zamora, 6/1; *Liber Constitutionum,* fo. 1vb–2ra: 'Statutum et ordinatum est a decano et capitulo Zamorensi quod nunquam apponatur sigillum capituli in litteris alicuius destinandis ad curiam romanam pro beneficiis impetendis in ecclesia nostra vel in aliqua alia ecclesia civitatis vel diocesis Zamorensis.'

4 On 8 May 1286, when the bishop had died, the dean and chapter confirmed the dean of Compostela's statutes and stipulated that no future bishop 'possit se excusare ab observacione...predictorum dicendo quod tempore quo hec constitucio seu ordinacio fuit edicta vel ordinata non erat ipse episcopus Zamorensis': *Liber Constitutionum,* fos. 2rb–4ra, 8ra.

5 Pedro Pérez had been with Cardinal Ottobono Fieschi in July 1254 (*Reg. Inn. IV,* 8300); Esteban Domínguez had been known there since March 1253 (*ibid.* 6728; *Reg. Urb. IV,* 2383); Martín Vicéntez had the support of Cardinal Jordan and when he was at last beneficed his admission was prompted at least as much 'consideratione dicti cardinalis' as by the letter from Zamora: ASV, arm. XXXI.72, fo. 205r.

not in Rome but in the provinces'.[1] Yet it was to Rome that the provincials looked for the expedient solution.

When Rome took the initiative, however, then the cry went up amongst them that their rights were being tampered with and that they would be reduced to penury. In the course of a single sentence a man of the stamp of Archbishop Juan Arias could conjure *ius* out of *quasi possessio* and cast the pope as the villain of the piece. Not much credit was given to the popes for the trouble they took to allay such suspicions, reassuring the chapter of Tarragona when it appeared necessary to delay somewhat an archiepiscopal election, and stipulating that a provision mandate was to be executed only if it were found that none other had been sent to the church in question – Tarazona – during that pontificate.[2] Spaniards assumed the worst and were ever on the alert for indications of papal duplicity in the letters they received. Boniface VIII was obliged to rephrase letters of safe-conduct for Jaime II of Aragon when that monarch espied a loophole through which he suspected the pope might squeeze.[3] And as textual critics churchmen, too, were thoroughly alert, with a keen eye for defective *non obstante* clauses in provision mandates[4] – alert to a fault on occasion, as in the case of the archdeacon of Lérida who misspelt his formal objection to the form and appearance of one of John XXII's.[5] The papal pensioner, Paolo di Sulmona, was kept on the bread-line for several months because a papal scribe had not been able to cope with the Latin for Guadalajara.[6] Yet, since there was no rule, indulgence, constitution or custom, licit or – as in the case of the 'unanimity rule' practised at Zamora and elsewhere[7] – otherwise,

---

[1] Barraclough, *Papal Provisions,* 38.

[2] 'Sane non ista scribimus ut ex tunc vestram velimus eripere libertatem sed quoniam indecens arbitramur ut illis eiusdem ecclesie canonicis absentia sua noceat', May 1268: *Reg. Clem. IV,* 1375; July 1264: *Reg. Urb. IV,* 1921.

[3] 'Te ac illos quos tecum duxeris in personis et bonis sub b. Petri et nostra custodia' was emended to 'te cum regnis et terris tuis, comitatu Barchinonie ac aliis bonis immobilibus atque mobilibus que impresentiarum tenes et possides', Sept. 1296: ACA, Bulas, leg. XX–10, 15 (reg. Miquel, 265, 270).

[4] E.g. the chapter of Barcelona in Jan. 1298: *Reg. Bon. VIII,* 2416.

[5] '...sunt in eis manifesti et notorii deffectus...tam in falsa grammatica, in constructione et intellectu congruo quam etiam in orthogrophia [*sic*] ut cuicumque intelligenti potest liquide apparere', Feb. 1317: AC Lérida, *Regestre de presentasions de prebendes* (arm. AB, no. 53), fo. 2v.

[6] AC Cuenca, 8/34/679, Jan. 1263: publ. Linehan, *EHR,* lxxxv, 752–3.

[7] At Tarragona till 1249, and at Oviedo in Jan. 1248: above, p. 41; *Reg. Inn. IV,* 3585.

that was proof against the appropriate *non obstante* clause, objections such as these merely delayed the evil hour; and all that was left to the protesters was stout denial or plain disobedience, in the style of Bishop Suero Pérez. Between 1255 and 1264 ten peninsular churches were reprimanded on this score,[1] but eventually they capitulated and came no nearer an open breach than the canons of Huesca whose constitutions hinted at rebellion in one sentence and made an affirmation of fidelity in the next,[2] consoling themselves by taking direct action against the alien providees if they had the temerity to put in an appearance either at Huesca or elsewhere.[3]

The reason why they invariably capitulated was that they themselves could not survive that sanction which was available to the pope – and which Alexander IV employed to curb the 'ingratitude' of the Spanish prelates in 1255: denial of access to the Curia and its services.[4] Spaniards needed Rome, and whether in search of benefices or of legal aid they came there in droves. They were certainly not strangers to the place. As a Castilian, Cardinal Petrus Hispanus could draw on a wealth of experience accumulated over the previous century. If he played his political cards badly it was not on account of any national genetic defect. The papal court and the system of law which it operated have struck one recent student as hopelessly confusing and confused, 'irresistibly' reminiscent of 'the dizzying, incomprehensible administration of Kafka's *Das Schloss*'.[5] But Spaniards knew their way about the endless passages. They had friends in high places.

---

[1] Compostela (*Reg. Alex. IV,* 410); León and Oviedo (*ibid.* 809, 2980–1; *Reg. Urb. IV,* 2216, 2360); Lisbon (*Reg. Alex. IV,* 1861, 2764); Braga (*ibid.* 819); Calahorra (*ibid.* 2291); Salamanca (*ibid.* 2641); Corias, O.S.B. (*ibid.* 2920); Palencia (*Reg. Urb. IV,* 1831); Burgos (*ibid.* 2061).

[2] '*De inhabilibus*: Nullus defectum in natalibus patiens de utero non assumatur in canonicum Oscensis ecclesie quamvis cum eis fuerit per ordinarios vel per Sedem Apostolicam super defectu huiusmodi dispensatus, salva in omnibus auctoritate Sedis Apostolice', 1301: publ. Durán Gudiol, *REDC*, VII, no. 33.

[3] The canons of Huesca set about the representative of Bishop Ademar when he was translated from Ávila in 1290, 'per capillos trahentes ipsum per terram et ignominiose tractantes': *Reg. Nich. IV,* 2458, 3598; Aynsa, *Fundación de Huesca,* 405–6. See above, Ch. 8.

[4] 'Eorum suadente ingratitudine...tales vel procuratores seu nuncii ipsorum vel alii pro eis ad impetrandum vel contradicendum in curia nostra pro ipsis vel eorum ecclesiis aliquatenus admittantur...duximus decernendum': *Reg. Alex. IV,* 1014.

[5] R. J. Brentano, *York Metropolitan Jurisdiction and Papal Judges Delegate, 1279–96* Berkeley, 1959), 164.

When Fernán Rodríguez was denied the see of Toledo in 1280 he was advised and consoled by four cardinals who spoke to him 'como amigo a amigo'.[1] And twenty-two years later, Archbishop Gonzalo Palomeque heard from the archdeacon of Guadalajara's proctor, Nicasius, how two others – Peter of Piperno and Francis Cajetan – had asked how he was, listened with evident pleasure to an anecdote about his recent escapades, and declared him a thoroughly good fellow.[2] That some, with Petrus Hispanus, were unseated is no proof that they had never ridden.[3]

The consequences of the Roman Habit were profound and expensive. It is difficult to calculate the cost of a journey from 'the ends of the earth', but if Castilians took as long in travelling to the Curia as did papal bulls in the opposite direction, then it may be assumed that the six-and-a-half-months' allowance granted to canons of Zamora who took that road cannot have lasted them till their return.[4] It was, of course, quicker to and from Aragon: in July 1233 executors at Tarragona were implementing a papal mandate which had been issued at the Lateran only twenty days before.[5] But while churchmen were more determined to come to the Curia than the popes were to restrain them, it is hardly surprising that so many were forced to borrow from the Italian banking companies on arrival. In 1298 Bishop Álvaro set off from Palencia simply in order to challenge a papal provision,[6] and in the following year a mere archdeacon in far-flung Túy thought nothing of sending two local clerics to Rome as

---

[1] Serrano, *Cartulario de Covarrubias*, 119–20.

[2] 'Petierunt a me...quomodo habeatis vos; et ego tamquam vester non fui mutus nec tardus quin ego exultarem tandem vestram [...] corde et ore in quantum potui. Item narravi eis de sententia quam tulistis contra rusticum de lochis [?] et qualiter non permisistis vos corrumpi pro suis vaccis et qualiter divisistis eas. Et ipsi habuerunt multum pro bono. Et tunc dixit D. Petrus...quod habebatis bonam faciem bene faciendi, et multa alia bona dixit de vobis': AC Toledo, A.8.H.2.10 (undated, but apparently early 1302).

[3] One who fell was Velasco Pérez whose association with the Colonna cost him the see of Ciudad Rodrigo, Aug. 1297: *Reg. Bon. VIII*, 2031.

[4] AC Zamora, *Liber Constitutionum*, fo. 5rb (an. 1219). News of Alfonso X's death in April 1284 took at least three weeks to reach Orvieto, and in the autumn of 1291 the bull *Inter cetera* (Potthast, 23828) took eleven and a half weeks to reach Toledo: above, pp. 230, 241.

[5] AC Seo de Urgel, d.s.n.

[6] On reaching Perugia, however, either his purse or his nerve failed him: *Reg. Bon. VIII*, 2640.

his proctors at hearings of a property dispute.[1] Boniface VIII's Register records twenty-two loans raised at the Curia by or for the bishops of eighteen Spanish and Portuguese sees.[2] The proximity of the papal court while Innocent IV was at Lyons during the 1240s obviously reduced both the distance and the expense involved – as it did in the following century.[3] But the effect of that period may well have been to create habits which were not broken when the means of indulging them were subsequently withdrawn again to Italy.

As the century advanced so the cost of the drug rose. In 1261 the Tarragona Council allowed its agents sixteen hundred *maravedís* for their curial expenses; for the same purpose in 1292 fifteen hundred *turonenses argenti* were demanded from *each* suffragan.[4] The price of papal mandates and privileges rose too.[5] But the addicts were far from being discouraged. Indeed, their determination increased also: they pillaged their churches and sold their lands to raise the necessary funds.[6] For, though not all curialists were the peculant rogues who

1 ASV, *Instrumenta Miscellanea*, 288 (reg. Milian Boix, *AA*, xv, nos. 23–4). On 8 March 1261 the archdeacon of Astorga, Melendo Pérez, appointed three proctors – two Spaniards (Fernando Garcés, canon of Zamora, and Master Domingo Gonzálvez, *clericus chori* of León) and one foreigner (Antonius Narniensis) – to press his claim to the archdeaconry of Valdemora against the bishop of León; and on 9 March Master Domingo set off from Astorga for the Curia: ASV, *Collect.*, 397, fos. 113v, 115v.

2 *Reg. Bon. VIII*, 303, 603, 976, 1326, 1730, 2190, 2392, 2630, 2631, 2892–3, 3309, 3632bis, 4121 (joint loan), 4126, 4177, 4256, 4681, 4735, 4743. Some of these loans – those to Fernando of Calahorra and Fernando of Segovia, for example – were raised in order to pay the *servitia communia* and *servitia minuta* which were due from prelates appointed at the Curia: *ibid.* 3632bis, 4177; AC Calahorra, doc. 489, 491; Baethgen, *QFIA*, xx, 212. By 1303 *servitia* had been paid by over half the sees of Castile and Portugal, but by only three in Aragon – Calahorra, Urgel and Zaragoza. In 1320 the archbishop of Zaragoza was reminded that 'singuli moderni predecessores' had paid the tax: Haller, *QFIA*, I, 287; Hoberg, *Studi e Testi*, CXLIV, 26, 35, 127 and *passim*; Kirsch, *Die Finanzverwaltung*, 87.

3 From Avignon, *cursores* were allowed eight days for a journey to Pamplona, ten to Valencia, and fifteen to Toledo. In 1321 the costs of a party of twenty-three, eight of them mounted, from Tortosa to Avignon and back, were reckoned to be £62.8 *sol*: Renouard, *Revue Historique*, CLXXX, 29; Schäfer, *Die Ausgaben*, 492; Göller, *Die Einnahmen*, 298.

4 Capdevila, *AST*, II, 516; AGN, caj. 3, no. 43 (reg. Castro, *Catálogo*, 421).

5 As the notes on a couple of Poblet bulls, of roughly similar length, record: 'solvit pro ista P[etrus] B[eren]g[arii] VI solidos et VI denarios in grosso [.?.] et bulla'; 'P[etrus] de Ass[isio]...XX turonenses': AHN, 2241/3 (June 1259); 2298/5 (June 1282).

6 Bishop Julião of Porto helped himself to the treasure of his church in 1230; and in his will of Aug. 1294 Pedro Anays, archdeacon of Zamora, recalled having pawned

plagued the imagination of the clerk Abril, 'hispana gente profectus', it was nevertheless a serious matter to be out of pocket at Rome – as the agents of the church of Huesca reminded the chapter in April 1273 when the bishop-elect died there and the appointment of a successor rested with Gregory X.[1] Money talked, despite the crushing reply that Abril received when he suggested that any ship was worth a ha'porth of tar.[2] Clearly not all of the six thousand *solidi*, which in 1267 Bishop Pedro of Gerona received from the king of Aragon 'ratione viatici', can have been meant for his living expenses in the strictest sense of the word.[3] Less portable gifts – such as the pair of fine horses which Bishop Ponce of Urgel's proctor promised the pope's nephew in the early 1250s – might be sent from the Pyrenees to Lyons, and they were, perhaps, not quite so pointed as hard cash. There would, though, have been little sense in transporting a mule from western Spain to central Italy, and in a codicil to his will of January 1267 Bishop Domingo of Salamanca bequeathed instead 150 *maravedís* to Uberto Coconato, the cardinal who had taken that church under his wing a few months before.[4] The Aragonese monarchs – who had contacts at the Curia well before the end of the century when the Chancery Registers provide the mass of detail about them which Finke published in *Acta Aragonensia*[5] – preferred such arrangements as the £50 annual pension granted to Imbertus de

his land before going to Rome, and losing on the deal: *Censual do Cabido da Sé do Porto*, 397–8; AC Zamora, 18/20.

1 AC Huesca, *Extravagantes*: 'Scribatis nobis qualiter nos agere debeamus, taliter facientes quod propter defectum expensarum honor Oscensis ecclesie circa prosecutionem predictam non valeat impediri' (reg. Durán Gudiol, *AA*, VII, no. 91).

2 'Ille modus non est, Aprilis, in Urbe...': *Carmen*, lines 367 ff.

3 ACA, Reg. 8, fo. 78r. In Feb. 1286 P. de Olivaria received only 1,302 *solidi* for 129 days' service at the Curia: Reg. 321, fo. 32v.

4 'Al cardenal don Uberto de Cucu nato CL morabutinos pora .i. mulo que le enviamos prometer por nostra carta': AC Salamanca, 20/1/33 (reg. Marcos, 315). The cardinal's letter of Sept. 1265, taking the church 'sub protectione et favore nostro libenter...honores et profectus vestros promovere quantum cum Deo et honore nostro possumus favorabiliter intendentes', begins with the papal formula *Grandis affectus* and has all the appearances of a papal bull: AC Salamanca, 40/43–1 (Marcos, 311). Cf. above, p. 130, n. 2.

5 The papal notary and future cardinal, Jordan Pirunti, assured Jaime I 'quod quando vixero attentus et sollicitus ero ut nichil fieri possit in curia quod excellencie vestre debeat displicere', undated, but apparently *temp.* Alexander IV: Finke, *SpGG*, IV, 361–2. For the king's appeal to the College of Cardinals on the subject of Benito de Rocaberti at this time, see above, Ch. 5.

Bociacis, the pope's *domicellus*, in the same month as the bishop of Salamanca's bequest.[1] So did the archbishops of Toledo,[2] for too much was at stake to depend on, for example, the tardy needle-women who failed to finish on time the altar-cloths promised by Bishop Thomas of Hereford in 1279.[3]

The kings of Aragon, as of Castile, could afford not to stint their envoys, for they made the Church – and on one occasion the pope himself – pay their bills. In April 1287 Alfonso III wrote to Daroca for assistance with the cost of the Roman mission since 'in ipsa tam utili ac tam grandi negotio expense habundant', and his demand for fifteen thousand *solidi* 'in subsidium nunciorum quos...ad romanam curiam destinastis' figured in the list of *gravamina et oppressiones* presented by the archbishop and chapter of Tarragona two years later.[4] In 1294 Jaime II exacted one hundred thousand *solidi* for the same purpose.[5] Churchmen were less fortunate, though the popes lent a hand when they could with grants of vacant benefices and annates, and by remitting part of the debts which bishops inherited with their sees.[6] It was very rare, however, for a Spaniard at the Curia to find a compatriot willing and able to advance him a loan.[7] So when he returned he brought with him – apart from the occasional sack of relics: volatile currency![8] – a collection of debts to Italian bankers. Some bishops, such as those of Barcelona and Calahorra,

---

1 'Attendentes grata servicia quod vos...in curia...nobis fecistis et facitis et facere cotidie non cessatis': González Hurtebise, II.*CHCA*, 1237.
2 Above, pp. 136, 288.
3 *Registrum Thome de Cantilupe*, ed. R. G. Griffiths and W. W. Capes (Canterbury and York Soc. 1907), 223–4.
4 ACA, Cartas Reales Diplomáticas, Alfonso II, caj. IV, extra series, 113; AHA, *Corretja*, no. 59.
5 Vincke, *Documenta selecta*, no. 66. For Boniface VIII's loan of £10,000 to defray the costs of Jaime's own visit to Rome in 1296, see ACA, Bulas, leg. XX–13 (reg. Miquel, 268: publ. Finke, *Acta Aragonensia*, III, 59, misdated).
6 Above, Ch. 11. Grants of vacant benefices to Tarragona, Jan. 1244; León, Aug. 1254; Barcelona, Feb. 1258: *Reg. Inn. IV*, 382, 7923; *Reg. Alex. IV*, 2514; and of remission of debt to Calahorra, May 1247; León, Aug. 1254 and Oct. 1256; Toledo, Feb. 1275: *Reg. Inn. IV*, 2710; above, p. 145; *Reg. Alex. IV*, 1637; *Reg. Greg. X*, 456.
7 The only known instance is Gonzalo of Toledo's loan of 500 *torneses* to Pascal of Cuenca in 1299: AC Toledo, X.1.E.2.2.
8 For the job-lot which the abbot of S. Cugat brought back with him in May 1238 ('...alias famosissimas mixtas'), see Ríus Serra, *San Cugat*, III, 459 ff. A collection of relics *de Romania*, complete with guarantee from an unknown archbishop of Athens, Crecencius, found its way to Segovia: AC Segovia, doc. 181.

could demand a diocesan subsidy at this stage,[1] and others had cost-sharing schemes with their chapters. The issue of responsibility was debated at great length at León in 1267,[2] while at Silves capitular liability was defined in April 1273 by Bishop Bartolomé, the successor of Alfonso X's ambassador to Rome, Bishop García.[3] To repay the Italians by borrowing at home, as Archbishop Tello of Braga did in January 1292,[4] was merely to delay the evil hour. Bishop Pedro Yáñez of Orense was granted a reprieve in September 1293 when Pedro Ordóñez, the dean, bequeathed him the thousand *maravedís* quos sibi mutuavi quando venit de curia romana'.[5] But such windfalls were exceptional. God knew where the abbot of Besalú was to find the wherewithal.[6] But there was one other solution.

Debt touched and paralysed the Church's spiritual functions at every level: only when his executors had repaid the four hundred marks which Master Pedro Guilherme, *doctor decretorum*, owed the chapter of Braga, might a start be made on the ten thousand masses that were to be said for the repose of his soul.[7] However, the ingenuity of desperate bishops produced a redemptive variation on this theme. Though the synod as a source of reform – John of Abbeville's synod – was in decline, since Benito de Rocaberti's dictum, that there was no need for further legislation as there was too much already, had been adopted by others,[8] might not the synod have other uses? Benito had thought that it might, and at Mondoñedo and Braga in the early fourteenth century the synod was resurrected by debt-

1 Martène–Durand, *Thesaurus*, IV, 603; AC Calahorra, doc. 473.
2 AC León, doc. 1564.
3 Silva Lopes, *Memórias do bispado do Algarve*, 563; *Reg. Urb. IV*, 233, 712, 2860. In Oct. 1266 García had been discovered, penniless at Montpellier, by Archbishop Sancho II of Toledo: AC Toledo, A.7.E.1.3; 6.
4 At Braganca he borrowed 4,900 *maravedís de León* 'pora vestir nostra companna' and a further 66,000 and £500 *de portugal* 'pora pagar deudes que nos devaamos en corte de Roma alos mercadores en pro e en serviço de la nostra eglesia de Bragaa': ADB, *Coleçcao Cronológica*, III/4/5.
5 AC Orense, *Escrituras*, II, 33.
6 'Pro obtinenda confirmatione electionis' he had to pay fifteen thousand *sous*, 'quos unde solvamus, nisi dominus nobis ab alto provideat, ignoramus': cit. Vincke, *AST*, VII, 342.
7 ADB, Gav. dos Legados, 15 (July 1309).
8 Above, p. 89. Lisbon, 1271; Tortosa, 1324; Cuenca, 1344: Rosa Pereira, *Lumen*, xxv (May 1961), 6–7; *VL*, v, 299; BN, MS 13071, fo. 218r–v. No record has survived of the various constitutions which, according to Bishop Bernardo of Cuenca, had been published 'in diversis sinodis...diversis temporibus celebratis'.

ridden prelates as a fund-raising occasion.[1] The diocesan clergy of Mondoñedo were encouraged to co-operate by the bait of an extra year's income which their executors might claim after their death – a doubly generous version of the right enjoyed by the cathedral chapter since 1251.[2] And thus, literally, was the future mortgaged to pay for the past.[3]

Developments in the church of Valencia, far away to the south-east, indicate the extent to which this general judgement may be applied to the fate of other aspects of reform. For at mid-century Valencia was one of the richest sees in the Peninsula, in both spiritual and material terms. In 1251 its territorial wealth greatly exceeded that of the County of Barcelona, and its bishop, Andrés de Albalat, was a pastor of outstanding zeal.[4] But, in a sense, the bishop's very distinction was a liability to the church of Valencia, since both pope and king claimed his services – the one as visitor of exempt monasteries,[5] and the other as Chancellor, in which capacity he had frequently to travel to the papal court.[6] There he died in December 1276 and,

---

1 In Aug. 1324 the diocesan clergy of Mondoñedo granted Bishop Gonsalvo twenty thousand *maravedís* 'pora pagardes a deveda que devedes aos mercadores na Corte de Roma': AC Mondoñedo, *Kalendario Antiguo I*, fo. 151v. Cf. Sanjurjo y Pardo, *Los obispos de Mondoñedo*, 50. In Nov. 1330 at a synod 'enas sas casas de Bragaa' Archbishop Gonçalo was granted three years' diocesan annates to meet the great costs which he had incurred 'per muitas ydas a casa del Rey e a outros logares': ADB, Gav. I das Igrejas, 5.

2 AC Mondoñedo, *Kalendario Antiguo I*, fo. 152r; above, p. 270, n. 3.

3 The bishops of Mondoñedo were much at Rome on behalf of the kings of Castile at the turn of the century and were invariably behind with their payments of *servitia*: BN, MS 5928 (Villaamil, *Noticias...de Mondoñedo*), fo. 65v; AC Toledo, I.5.C.1.69; *Reg. Bon. VIII*, 2437, 2637; Göller, 239, 259, 266.

4 *Reg. Inn. IV*, 5315; above Ch. 4.

5 In Sept. 1248, before his election, he was sent to visit Ager, O.S.A. (Urgel) and reform the place. The task was committed to him again in March 1257, and his prohibition on this occasion of 'camisas castellanas' and 'vestidos cortos o largos' recalls the legislation of his brother: *Reg. Inn. IV*, 4172; *Reg. Alex. IV*, 1835; BP Tarragona, MS 176, no. 220. In the same month – March 1258, not March 1257, as Ramón de Huesca, *Teatro*, vii, 390; Arco in *Universidad*, vii, 28 – he was similarly engaged at Montearagón: AC Barcelona, *Diversarum A*, 2015.

6 He was there in Feb. 1252, April 1257 and Aug. 1265: ACA, Bulas, leg. XII–65; XIV–2 (reg. Miquel, 174, 181); above, p. 208. Then, having accompanied King Jaime to the Lyons Council in 1274, he remained with Gregory X who sent him on diplomatic missions to Castile: *Chronica del Rey En Jacme*, cap. 526, ed. Aguiló, 505; Quétif–Echard, *Scriptores*, I, 360; ACA, Reg. 37, fos. 66r, 78r (reg. Martínez Ferrando, *Catálogo*, I, 1752); Müller, *RQ*, xxxvii, 108–10.

though John XXI's reservation of the see was reversed within the month,[1] by then Valencia had entered a difficult period. In February 1257 Andrés had been driven to seek papal relief from his debts. The 1260s witnessed some improvement, but on his death he bequeathed to the church a debt to the Chiarenti Company which was not finally cleared until 1301.[2]

Well before 1301, though, the consequences of Andrés's costly service to the king had been brought home to Valencia. His successor, Jazpert de Botonach – who was engaged in the same expensive capacity[3] – was obliged to adopt a policy of retrenchment, and since, as he recognised in his will, reform costs money,[4] it was there that the axe fell. In January 1280 his economies touched the very life-principle of reform as understood by John of Abbeville and his followers: clerical education. Andrés's constitution in favour of student canons was 'modified' by the introduction of a residence qualification.[5] This was not in itself a mortal blow, nor was Jazpert a philistine.[6] But the ripples which had now reached Valencia were part of a flood that had been advancing across the Peninsula throughout the century and had already engulfed Castile by the mid-1240s when Cardinal Gil's constitutions had all included restrictions on student canons.[7] Some individuals, having cast their bread upon the waters and seen it sink, secured themselves a place in the dry with the help of an upwards heave from a curial hand. But the waters had moved on, and by the end of the century the churches of Galicia

---

[1] *Reg. John XXI*, 46, 54.

[2] *Reg. Alex. IV*, 1749; *Reg. Urb. IV*, 2130; above, p. 137. A fortnight before he raised this loan he had received papal permission to assign £1,500 in his will from episcopal funds for his *familiares* and creditors: *Reg. John XXI*, 55.

[3] When he was sent on embassy to France in Feb. 1284 he had to borrow money to supplement the expenses allowed him: Martínez Ferrando, *Catálogo*, II, 1861–2.

[4] 'Cum spiritualia sine temporalibus diu esse non possint...': AC Valencia, perg. 5565 (reg. Olmos, *Pergaminos*, 665).

[5] Of six months 'post receptionem': Miedes, *Constitutiones sive Ordinationes... Ecclesiae Valentinae*, fo. 13r.

[6] He is regarded as the patron of Arnau de Vilanova: R. Verrier, *Études sur Arnaud de Villeneuve* (Leiden, 1947), 20–2; J. Carreras Artau and M. Batllori, 'La patria y la familia de Arnau de Vilanova', *AST*, XX, (1947), 5–75, at 12 ff. It should be noted, however, that Arnau's dedication of the *De Improbatione Maleficiorum*, is to 'Jo. presuli Valentino': ed. Paul Diepgen, *Archiv f. Kulturgeschichte*, IX (1911–12), 385–403, at 388. This would suggest not Jazpert but Bishop Jean of Valence (1283–97). Cf. Eubel, *Hierarchia*, I, 513.

[7] Mansilla, 327, 353, 376; RAH, MS C/7–9/5427, fo. 141v.

were submerged. 'Volentes consuetudines aliarum ecclesiarum pro viribus imitari', the chapter of Lugo lowered its sights in 1290, from the upper limits – fixed since 1173 – of thirty canons and twenty portionaries to ten and twenty respectively, 'cum tot sint ponendi in ecclesia quibus possint suppetere facultates'. Times were hard at Lugo: in the early nineties a portion was granted on condition that the recipient never be away for more than eight days at a time, and in May 1293 the same restriction was imposed on the *magister scolarum*.[1] Nearby at Orense, where in 1256 the *magister scolarum* had been a student at Modena, the autumn of the year 1302 found the chapter denying the dean, Gonçalvo Núñes, his income 'en quanto el fosse en studio' on the grounds that they paid nothing to an earlier dean, Pedro Rodríguez, during the five years which he had spent at Rome 'en serviço da iglesia':[2] an admission of the type of niggardliness which explains why so many Spaniards threw themselves into the arms of curial patrons.

It was a tide which washed away the unsteady bastions of reform, and by the end of the century the Dominicans, who once had faced the flood, were sailing with it. Familiarity with secular courts was one of the developments within the Order that its early provincial legislation had viewed with alarm and, though Andrés de Albalat had shown that a man of affairs could still retain many of the virtues of the founding fathers, justification for that alarm was soon supplied in the person and pre-history of Andrés's successor but one as bishop of Valencia, Ramón Despont. By January 1291, when Nicholas IV appointed him to the see after a divided election, the task of reform had to be started afresh there; and though Bishop Ramón, as a Dominican, gave his mind to it,[3] his was a mind of very different stamp from that of Bishop Andrés. Ramón was an administrator who became a friar late in life; with Andrés it had been the other way about. In his early years he had been attracted to law rather than to theology: not a good sign.[4] His pre-episcopal period had been spent

---

1 *ES*, XLI, 378–9; AHN, cod. 1042B, fos. 24r, 31v.
2 AC Orense, *Escrituras*, I, 23; XVII, 39bis. Pedro Rodríguez was dean between 1253 and 1257. Cf. Duro Peña, *AEM*, I, 297.
3 *Reg. Nich. IV*, 3950; above, Ch. 5.
4 Diago, *Historia de la Provincia de Aragón*, fo. 15r. He had Hostiensis at his fingertips: *VL*, I, 188. Cf. the *admonitiones* of the 1299 Provincial Chapter, cap. viii, xiv, xvi, in *Acta*, ed. Douais, 647 ff.

at the papal court in the service of his king. In March 1286 Alfonso III had written to him there, thanking him for all that he had done on behalf of his father and himself.[1] At that time he was carving out a career for himself in the papal service too: by June 1288 he was *sacri palatii auditor* and dean of Compostela *in absentia*,[2] and even after his appointment to Valencia he remained in Italy, as rector of the March of Ancona, while his royal and papal masters were public enemies.[3] He was a natural choice as Celestine V's envoy to the Isola peace-talks with Jaime II in October 1294.[4] In April 1303 Boniface VIII would speak of him as an old and trusted friend when appointing him his legate in Sicily, a man with broad shoulders; and in the following January Jaime would recommend that he be made a cardinal.[5] At the see of Valencia, though, he was a superannuated diplomat who was predisposed to return to the active list – in short, a *fin-de-siècle* friar.

In the same year as Ramón Despont was appointed to Valencia, Munio of Zamora was removed from the Master-Generalship of the Order. The tremors of that affair activated the 1290s: the Provincial Chapter of 1299 cannot but have had that in mind when it forbad friars to pay visits to nunneries, since 'scandala sequantur plurima atque nota'.[6] Munio, though, was merely a symbol of the Order's loss of innocence. Simple philandering, of which he seems to have been guilty, was far from being the lowest depth to which the friars had descended. Darker things were hinted at in 1299.[7] Anyway, the rot had set in at least half a century earlier. St Dominic – as a saint can afford to do – had admitted to a liking for the conversation of young women. The death of the lyric spirit and the emergence of

---

1 ACA, Reg. 63, fo. 94v.
2 ACA, Reg. 77, fo. 1r. He was still *auditor* in April 1289: Mansilla, *AA*, VI, 326, no. 95. As dean he seems to have been the immediate successor of Fernando Alfonso, who had died at León in Jan. 1286. Cf. Portela Pazos, *Decanologio*, 102–4, who finds no trace of him before Sept. 1290 and is ignorant both of his identity and of his successor as dean on his promotion to Valencia – Guillelmus Baravi, archdeacon of Agde (*Reg. Nich. IV*, 4021).
3 Waley, *Papal State*, 316.
4 'Natione et familiaritate probabiliter tibi gratum': ACA, Bulas, leg. XVIII–1 (reg. Miquel, 208; Potthast, 23992).
5 ACA, Bulas, leg. XXIII–2 (reg. Miquel, 311 [= *Reg. Bon. VIII*, 5202]). Cf. Finke, *Acta Aragonensia*, I, xli–ii; Olmos, *Los prelados*, 76 ff.; Vincke, *Documenta Selecta*, no. 100.   6 Douais, 648.
7 *Ibid.* 647: 'crimen nefandissimum quod absurdissimum est etiam nominare'.

what may be termed *dominicainisme politique* had occurred, it might be argued, when the General Chapter had had this detail struck from the record in 1242. Thereafter, the dangers of *familiaritas* had been constantly discussed,[1] while in Castile the story was told of the friar who, having preached his sermon, produced a stream of blue jokes, and of the priest who fondled young women, claiming to be a different person from the man who had said mass that morning.[2] Moreover, sins of the flesh were not their only sins. As early as 1240 the cantor of Salamanca, Master Pedro, had bequeathed his civil law books to the local friars.[3] Law and medicine – particularly medicine – were displacing theology in the Dominican curriculum, and not only in Spain – although there the availability of Moorish and Jewish science provided the friars with splendid material to which they might apply that mastery of the semitic languages which they had originally acquired for purposes of biblical exegesis. St Francis had loved all creation; but members of his Order and of Dominic's in the next generation wanted to know how it worked. Their books were the running brooks; their sermons in stones; and, indeed, in a sense, the curiosity of such as Ferrarius Catalaunus O.P., who wondered whether original sin was transmitted in the semen, was theological.[4] Certainly it had pastoral connotations – to the alarm of the 1249 Provincial Chapter which sought to restrain the *fratres phisici* from taking in patients, scrutinising urine and prescribing medicine.[5] Their work – they were reminded in 1281 – was supposed to be *utilis* rather than *curiosa*.[6] By 'useful' theological was meant, and in 1299 unlicensed study of law and medicine was forbidden and the friars were recalled from the pleasures of the chase to the discipline of theology.[7]

It was not until this late stage that the Dominican ethic, for what it

---

1 *Acta Capitulorum Generalium*, ed. Reichert, I, 24; *Litterae encyclicae*, ed. Frühwirth, 59, 118, 121, 128. Cf. R. F. Bennett, *The Early Dominicans* (Cambridge, 1937), 151.
2 'Non so yo aquel que dize la missa, ca el que dize la missa es sacerdote e yo so un mançebo que agora juego': ed. Foulché-Delbosc, *Rev. Hispanique*, VIII, 508.
3 'Digestum vetus, digestum novum, codicem inforciatum et Summam Azonis et libellum Institutionis': AC Salamanca, 20/1/20 (reg. Marcos, 198).
4 Glorieux in *Bibliothèque Thomiste*, V, 109–10 (*c.* 1276). For Ferrarius, see Quétif Echard, I, 349.
5 Douais, 610.
6 *Ibid.* 631. Cf. Reichert, I, 208–9.
7 *Ibid.* 647 ff.

was then worth, began to have any appreciable effect on the high command of the Castilian Church. John of Abbeville had been accompanied during his legation by Raymond of Peñafort, but Castile under the spiritual leadership of Rodrigo of Toledo failed to benefit from the first flush of the Order as Aragon did, through those friars whom Pedro de Albalat drafted into the episcopate. Only in frontier sees, beyond the reach of the metropolitans, were members of either mendicant Order established by the middle of the century, and, though by the mere act of summoning a diocesan synod Pedro Pérez O.F.M., bishop of Badajoz, provided a glimpse of the resources which might still have been tapped, the Golden age of the Mendicants had passed by then.[1] The Dominican bishop of Silves, Roberto, was a fallen idol who served Alfonso X on foreign embassies, as did the two bishops of Ávila, Domingo Suárez O.F.M. and Ademar O.P.[2] Twice only in the entire century did cathedral chapters elect members of either Order.[3] It was the pope who appointed the Franciscan, Fernando, to Burgos in 1280 and, six years later, Pedro Fechor O.F.M. to Salamanca and Rodrigo Gonsálvez, Prior Provincial of the Dominicans, to Compostela.[4]

There is little need to stress how greatly the friars were needed by the 'established Church', at a time when the canons of Jaén were incapable of expressing themselves in the Church's language without their assistance; but the opposition that Rodrigo Gonsálvez encountered from the chapter of Compostela both indicates the extent of

---

[1] March 1255: Solano de Figuerora, *Historia de Badajoz*: I, III, 13–20. For two other frontier prelates of the Franciscan Order, Pedro Gallego of Cartagena and Juan Martínez of Cádiz, see Pelzer in *Miscellanea F. Ehrle*, I, 407 ff.; Sancho de Sopranis, *Hispania*, IX, 370–73; Mansilla, *HS*, X, 243–53. Bishop Lope of Morocco had a hand in the appointment of all three: Mansilla, *Iglesia*, 86–7.

[2] Above, Ch. 6; Eubel, *RQ*, IV, 218. It may be noted that the Jaén successors of Bishop Domingo of Baeza were not, like him, friars.

[3] Martin O.P. 'qui fuit quondam archidiaconus Valentinus', Segovia, May 1259: AC Toledo, X.2.B.2.1a (Eubel, *Hierarchia*, I, 442, makes him a Franciscan); Fernando Álvarez, O.F.M., who died before consecration, Oviedo, 1293: *ES*, XXXVIII, 216. Archbishop Remondo of Seville was not a Dominican, *pace* Eubel, I, 277. Cf. Ballesteros, *Correo Erudito*, I, 315–16. Nor was Pedro Pérez of Salamanca (1248–64), though Eubel, I, 428, and all previous authorities since González Davila, *Historia de Salamanca*, III, 240 – with the exception of Dorado, *Compendio*, 215–18 – have so described him. There is no document in AC Salamanca to support them, and when the bishop is mentioned in royal charters he is not accorded the prefix *frey*.

[4] *Reg. Nich. III*, 651; *Reg. Hon. IV*, 320, 536.

resentment against them – which only recently had been given public utterance – and helps to explain why the kings of Castile, whose influence in episcopal elections was as great as their devotion to the mendicants, failed to introduce more of them into Castilian sees.[1] Throughout Europe the friars clashed with the ordinaries and the older Orders, but Castile's economic crisis made the contest all the more bitter there. Spain alone was excluded from the terms of the truce with the Franciscans which was announced at the Cistercian General Chapter of 1276.[2] At Burgos the struggle between the Benedictines of Silos and the Friars Minor engendered such violent passions that it was still recounted by locals in the late nineteenth century in a modernised version which had the two parties exchanging shots in true First Spanish Republic style.[3] Meanwhile the cathedral chapter was fairly permanently embroiled with the Dominicans from 1262 until the beginning of the fourteenth century. The canons sent a hooded man to steal the friars' privileges, preached sermons inciting the people 'similitudinibus et comminationibus' to take their convent by storm, and tormented them with body-snatching and brick-hiding expeditions.[4] The date 1262 points to the reason why the canons of Burgos conducted their campaign with such ferocity: they had just survived the seven lean years and were in no mood for allowing such revenues as they received by preaching, administering the sacraments and burying the dead to pass to the friars. The same period saw similar clashes concerning these same issues at Calatayud and, predictably, at Palencia.[5] As the chapter of Braga insisted, when denying the mendicants a foothold there in March 1279, ecclesiastical resources simply could not accommodate new foundations.[6] Yet, with the kings' support, they were accommodated.[7]

---

[1] *Reg. Nich. IV*, 677, 1511, 1817.   [2] Canivez, III, 152.

[3] Férotin, *Recueil des chartes de Silos*, 312 ff.

[4] Documents in AHN, carpetas 183–5. They have not been used by Mansilla, who refers to the affair in *HS*, IX, 253, or by Hoyos, *BIFG*, XLIII, 182 ff.

[5] Ripoll, *Bullarium*, I, 363, 392 (Potthast, 17245, 17846).

[6] 'Specialiter pensantes quantum posset dampnificari ecclesia et civitas Bracarensis si religiosi aliqui, et maxime fratres predicatores et minores construerent seu edificarent monasteria seu domos ad habitandum in civitate vel cauto Bracarensi...cum vix pauperes verecundi propter tenues helemosinas possent sustentari': ADB, Gav. das Religioẽs, 16.

[7] When the Burgos Dominicans came to terms with the chapter in 1301 they were made to promise 'quod...non procurent per se nec per alium cum domino rege nec

There were times, even in Aragon, when the Dominicans felt ill at ease. In the late 1240s some of their benefactors interpreted the king's *attentat* on the bishop of Gerona as a sign that the Order was to be ostracised, and withdrew their support accordingly.[1] Also, as the century advanced, there was a number of burial disputes: at Huesca in the 1260s with the Cistercians of Veruela for the body of the Infante Alfonso,[2] and on Mallorca in the 1290s with the cathedral chapter. There they came to blows over a very small matter.[3] But such incidents were rare in Aragon and they soon passed,[4] whereas in Castile they were frequent and long-drawn-out. For the regular clergy they were, moreover, counter-productive, since, judging the mendicants by the enemies they kept as much as by the virtues they displayed, the already discontented laity tended to patronise the friars. The losses suffered in this way at Salamanca were mentioned in the constitutions of 1245 – and relations with the mendicants were rather better at Salamanca than elsewhere in Castile–Leon.[5] Thus the gulf widened and bitterness increased. Anyway, there was no denying that the friars were a force to be reckoned with. They were worth having as allies both in this world and the next. In 1262 the chapter of Toledo had their appeal to Urban IV published in the convents of both Orders,[6] and career churchmen who had spent their entire lives

cum regina nec cum proceribus nec cum concilio Burgensi nec cum aliquo istorum aliquid in preiudicium nec in gravamen aliquid Burgensi ecclesie vel capitulo eiusdem'. This recital, however, struck the bishop, Cardinal Petrus Hispanus, as insufficient, and before he had the settlement confirmed by the pope and registered he amended the clause: 'nos addimus *nec cum aliquo alio*': a fair illustration of the suspicion with which the friars were regarded: *Reg. Bon. VIII*, 4676 (ASV, Reg. Vat. 50, fo. 194v); AHN, 185/12.

[1] *ES*, XLIV, 280.
[2] Diago, *Historia de la Provincia de Aragón*, fos. 268r–9r; Sagarra, *BRABL*, IX, 295–8; AHN, 593/19–20.
[3] 'Corpusculum cuiusdam pueri defuncti': AHN, 92/2–3 (Potthast, 24751, 24802). Some fifteen years earlier the Cistericians of La Real had promised the chapter that they would not inter 'masculos minores XIIII annis nec mulieres minores XII annis': Nebot, *BSAL*, XIII, 109.
[4] In 1268 Bishop Domingo of Huesca elected to be buried with the Dominicans; and ten years after the Mallorca dispute the Order was granted burial rights on the island: AHN, 594/10; 93/6 (cf. Potthast, 21555).
[5] 'Celebris sepultura maiorum, de quarum ultimis voluntatibus Salamantina ecclesia consueverat in temporalibus grata suscipere incrementa, penitus abdicaretur ab ea': Mansilla, 323. Cf. Cuervo, *Historiadores...de San Esteban de Salamanca*, III, 627–9.
[6] AC Cuenca, 8/34/678.

doing battle with the mendicants frequently remembered them in their wills.[1]

For all this, though, the mendicants had the effect of impoverishing the Castilian Church rather than enhancing it, even while they were at their best. For the sort of man who might have become the *buen obispo* of whom Berceo wrote – leading his flock 'non como solda-dero, mas como pastor'[2] – was tempted to join them, whereupon he automatically debarred himself from episcopal promotion.[3] Indeed, when Adán Pérez of Cuenca was elected to the see of Plasencia he sought refuge from that dreadful fate with the Dominicans of Bologna, where he was a student.[4] His break for freedom failed, but at Burgos it was such a conversion late in life – that of the archdeacon of Valpuesta, Juan Tomé, who took the Dominican habit and chose to be buried in their church – that was mainly responsible for the trouble there.[5] Only in the see of León were the mendicants given the opportunity of practising their pastoral skills: both Bishop Martín Fernández, their patron, and his synodal legislation, with its recommendation of the friars, were unique.[6] And by then, the 1260s, the friars were not what they had been. The original spirit, which Pedro de Albalat had captured, was gone, and, in contrast to Aragon, where the penitential legislation of councils and synods broadcast the so-called doctrine of circumstances, Castile was represented by the contemporary tract for the confessor which had the priest telling the penitent that when fixing the size of the penance they were 'in a market' – a seller's market, evidently, where mortal sins cost seven years.[7] While Pedro de Albalat's *Summa*, in accord with the teaching

---

1 The archdeacon Pedro Pascal, one of their chief persecutors at Burgos, bequeathed them twenty *maravedís* in March 1277: AC Burgos, vol. 48, fo. 316; AHN, 183/5, 184/7; and others there did the same. See also the terms of the dean of Braga's bequest in Nov. 1272: above, p. 259.

2 *Veintetres milagros*, ed. Marden, 52.

3 One who did so was the dean of Palencia and nephew of Bishop Tello, St Pedro González: *ES*, xxiii, 131 ff. The sole exception to the rule was the bishop of Segovia, Martín, who had renounced an archdeaconry previously and joined the Dominicans.

4 *Reg. Greg. IX*, 5964.

5 AHN, 183/4: *inc. Significarunt nobis*, 5 July 1262. A raiding-party of canons had stolen his body from the friars' church.

6 *ES*, xxxvi, 229–55 (esp. cap. 46–7); Risco, *Historia de León*, ii, 173.

7 ' "Amigo, cada pecado mortal mereçe siete annos mas; que yo e tu estamos como en mercado, por exo íe he yo a dar aquela penitencia que tu sofrir puedas" ': ed. Morel-Fatio, *Romania*, xvi, 381. Cf. above, Ch. 4.

of Raymond of Peñafort, had been striving against these antiquated attitudes, the only employment for the Dominicans that had occurred to Rodrigo of Toledo had been, appropriately enough, that of urging the faithful in sermons and the confessional to pay the tithes which they owed the church of Toledo.[1]

In March 1288 – with much moralising about the weakness of womankind and the need for rigid enclosure, which must have galled those who had followed his career closely – Munio of Zamora gave the nuns of Caleruega, Dominic's birthplace, permission to have extra mattresses to keep them warm in bed.[2] The mendicants were past their best. They were feeling the cold more, and in seeking their own greater comfort they had assumed the acquisitive characteristics of their persecutors. Diago Rois, a Franciscan of Palencia, for example, succeeded in gaining possession of the library of Bishop Lope of Sigüenza and refused to deliver the books to Lope's executors on the pretext that they belonged to the queen of Portugal – a pretext which caused Alfonso X's wife, Violante, to remark in a letter to him that he ought to have known better than to suppose that queens read books like those.[3] Acquisitiveness was the order of the century. Acts of disinterestedness – such as the founding of an anniversary at Zamora by Rodrigo Pérez after the chapter had spurned him[4] – were rare indeed. The law of the jungle drove many to the Curia while perpetuating at Astorga the enormous variations in salary – *scandalum et animarum non modica turbatio* – which John of Abbeville had deplored in 1228.[5] It hastened the complete breakdown of capitular life by secularisation of the cathedral chapters and distribution, in the style of Cardinal Gil's constitutions, of property previously held in common, since before such change was made at Sigüenza in 1302 the cathedral fabric was nobody's business because it was everybody's business, and priests coming to say mass there had to bring their own candles with

---

[1] *Ex parte*, 22 Sept. 1245: AC Toledo, I.7.G.1.2.
[2] Martínez, *Colección diplomática...de S. Domingo de Caleruega*, 350–2.
[3] AC Toledo, A.7.E.1.2: '...et fray Diago, bien sabedes que tales libros como aquellos non serian dela reyna' (publ. Minguella, I, 221).
[4] 'Ob reverenciam domini mei Martini secundi [Martín Rodríguez] quondam episcopi Zamorensis qui me nutrivit ac beneficiis exaltavit', Aug. 1243: AC Zamora, 12/8; *Reg. Greg. IX*, 4594.
[5] Rodríguez López, *Episcopologio asturicense*, II, 593. Cf. *Reg. Urb. IV*, 2676 (July 1264).

them.[1] By excluding the Dominicans it had also prevented the reform of the Castilian Church, since by the time they were admitted to the episcopal heights at the end of the century the Dominicans were hardly distinguishable from the rest. Indeed, like the pigs and the men at the end of *Animal Farm,* already it was impossible to say which was which.

[1] AC Sigüenza, doc. particular, 79. Miguel Martínez, archpriest of Molina, quoted the example of 'otras eglesias que solian seer reglares que son agora meior servidas porque son seglares'. For some of these other churches, see above, p. 267. The Sigüenza statutes of 1302 are publ. Minguella, II, 359–71, misdated. Cf. *Reg. Bon. VIII*, 4134. Secularisation had been authorised thirty-seven years earlier but had been constantly delayed. In the same year Boniface VIII took similar action at Huesca where the issue had been debated for just as long: Ramón de Huesca, *Teatro,* VI, 239 ff.

CONCLUSION AND EPILOGUE

'You would be surprised in Paris to learn that in Madrid of all your major political acts it is your Civil Constitution of the Clergy that has had the most success. You did not know that we southern people, adorers of Madonnas and burners of unbelievers, are not at all courtesans of the pope': *Gazette nationale ou le Moniteur universel*, 30 May 1791, in Richard Herr, *The Eighteenth-Century Revolution in Spain* (Princeton, 1958), 406.

'When Ferdinand III captured Seville and died, being a saint he escaped purgatory, and Santiago presented him to the Virgin, who forthwith desired him to ask any favours for beloved Spain. The monarch petitioned for oil, wine and corn – conceded; for sunny skies, brave men, and pretty women – allowed; for cigars, relics, garlic, and bulls – by all means; for a *good government* – "Nay, nay", said the Virgin, "that never can be granted; for were it bestowed, not an angel would remain a day longer in heaven".': Richard Ford, *Gatherings from Spain*, 1846 (Everyman's Library ed.), 46–7.

'If the Minister of Agriculture goes on quoting Papal Encyclicals to defend his drafts, you can be sure that we shall end up by becoming Greek schismatics': José María Lamamié de Clairac, Traditionalist deputy, in 1934. Quoted by Richard Robinson, *The Origins of Franco's Spain* (Newton Abbot, 1970), 201–2.

In 1892, as Spain approached the inglorious end of its imperial phase, Menéndez y Pelayo spoke at Seville on the subject of *El siglo XIII y San Fernando*. In that of all Spanish cities he was, of course, preaching to the converted when he spoke of the king as a happy blend of sanctity and strength, and of his century as second only in *grandeza* to the age of Carlos V and Felipe II, for which it had been 'memorable ensayo y providencial preparación'[1]. And the sermon had been preached before – often. His litany of illustrious men and their achievements harks back to the triumphal panegyric of Bishop Lucas

---

[1] *Estudios y discursos de crítica histórica y literaria*, VII, 47 ff., esp. p. 60.

of Túy. The reference to the battle of Las Navas as *Christendom's* greatest victory since the time of Charles Martel recalls the speech of another bishop – Alfonso García de Santa María, bishop of Burgos – who at the Council of Basle in September 1434 had based his countrymen's claim to precedence over the English contingent there primarily on Spain's 'estension de los terminos de la yglesia e enssalçamiento e enssanchamiento de la fee catholica'.[1] His lecture was, in short, a classic exposition of the Spanish superiority complex. If God was not actually a Spaniard then he was at least an ally. Could one fail to discern the intervention of the Almighty, the action of the divine hand in all this?[2]

The foregoing pages have been devoted to the experiences of a group who would surely have answered such a question in the negative: Fernando's own ecclesiastical contemporaries to whom so much of the cost of *Christendom's* successes was charged. In so far as the Roman Church spoke for Christendom, Christendom's debt to Fernando and his house was freely acknowledged; and it was paid by allowing the king to reimburse himself from the national church. To the pope it seemed perfectly equitable that the monarch who was responsible for smoking out 'the filthy pagans' from the south of Spain should be given a fairly free hand in the frontier church and also further north.[3] The monarch's failure to honour his side of the bargain by attending to the endowment of the new ecclesiastical foundations did not affect the issue.[4] He remained in control. As elsewhere, 'useful' bishops were appointed – useful to the king, that is, not, as Marsilio of Padua imagined, to the pope. Clement IV assured Alfonso X that he accepted the principle of royal domination that was enshrined in the *Partidas* (of which the victims of this papal–royal collusion

[1] Above Ch. 6. Santa María's discourse is publ. *Ciudad de Dios*, XXXV, 524. Cf. Suárez Fernández, *Castilla, el Cisma y la crisis conciliar*, 116; Tate in *Studies... González Llubera*, 387 ff.
[2] Menéndez y Pelayo, VII, 57–8.
[3] ASV, arm. XXXI.72, fo. 319v: 'Quod impugnator paganorum habeat ius presentandi in ecclesiis quas acquiret:... Cum itaque tu, fili benedictionis et gratie, ad hoc sis omni virtute sollicitus ut de frontaria regni Castelle... paganorum eliminata spurcitia ibi plantetur et vigeat religio christiana', the pope granted the Infante Alfonso right of presentation *una vice* to churches 'in cunctis villis aut castris dicte frontarie' (Schillmann, *Formularsammlung*, 2885). Cf. Mansilla, *Iglesia castellano-leonesa*, 89–90.
[4] Above, p. 121.

were reduced to tampering with the text).[1] Papal 'prestige' and papal 'theocracy' made far less impression on contemporaries than they do on such writers as Sobrequés and Ferrer Flórez.[2] By the pope's yardstick Spain was much further away from the Curia than the Curia was to the many Spaniards who managed to evade royal controls and swell the swarms of petitioners, proctors and officials of whom the author of the *Carmen* wrote.[3] Despite the eloquent assurances of the eighteenth-century regalists and of Sánchez-Albornoz, papal nuncios did not succeed in bleeding Spain white. Instead they encountered in both king and clergy the attitude that the Roman Church was a Welfare State to be sponged on but not contributed to. And, although on one occasion a pope retaliated by withholding the benefits, this attitude persisted.[4] Rome could exert little enough influence over its feudal dependents in the Peninsula, the kingdoms of Aragon and Portugal. Far-fetched though they may be, there is a substantial element of truth in the contemporary legends of the Black Bishop of Coimbra and of the papal legate threatened with mutilation by Afonso Henriques, Portugal's first king, who owed his royal title to Rome.[5] Castile, moreover, was not even notionally dependent – a fact which provided the bishop of Burgos with a debating point against England in 1434,[6] and underlay that sense of *ecclesiastical* auto-

---

[1] Above, pp. 86, 108, 217. Cf. Jaime II's letter of Jan. 1301 to Boniface VIII, complaining about the activities of the late Bishop Diego of Cartagena ('non pastorali sed hostili more...quodque eo solo quod castellanus origine et a nostrarum gencium nacionibus alienus, procuravit nobis semper incomoda et iacturas') and informing the pope that he had ordered the canons to elect 'talem...episcopum... qui Deo, vobis nobisque complaceat' as prelate of that exempt see: Vincke, *Acta Aragonensia*, I, 95–6. For 'useful' bishops in England, see C. R. Cheney, *From Becket to Langton* (Manchester, 1956), 21. For the whittling away of royal rights in later MSS. of the *Primera Partida*, see Herriot, *Romance Philology*, V, 170–1.

[2] Sobrequés, *La época del patriciado urbano*, 164. Ferrer Flórez on Gregory IX's exemption of the see of Mallorca from metropolitan jurisdiction as an example of 'la idea teocrática' in action: *AST*, XXIII, 19–20.

[3] *Carmen*, lines 139 ff., 213 ff.: his metaphor was drawn from bees.

[4] Above, p. 150.

[5] Livermore, *History of Portugal*, 66–7. Cf. *Chronica Rogeri de Hoveden*, II, ed. W. Stubbs (Rolls Ser., 1869), 333 (*sub anno* 1187). Afonso Henriques had put his mother in chains – 'parum imitatus Coriolanum Romanum', as Rodrigo Sánchez de Arévalo learnedly observed in the fifteenth century. According to this version the king answered the legate's criticism by showing him his scars. Publ. Gonzaga de Azevedo, *História de Portugal*, IV, 292–3.

[6] 'Ca esta ssingularidat tienen los reyes de espana que nunca fueron ssubjectos al ymperio romano nin a otro alguno; mas ganaron e alçaron los regnos de los dientes

nomy that was implied by Alfonso XI's attempt to have the Indulgence made available to Castilians visiting Santiago rather than Rome on the occasion of the 1350 Jubilee celebrations.[1]

But this sense of ecclesiastical autonomy was *royal*, and was one aspect of the total *lack* of autonomy and independence of the Spanish Church *vis-à-vis* the civil power. When John of Paris noted that, Christian though they were, the kings of Spain had no need of priestly unction, he was stating an observable social fact as much as a highfalutin' generalisation about the limits of spiritual authority.[2] The priests lacked standing, and, if Ptolemy of Lucca can be believed, they may have been subject to outbursts of anti-clericalism, which was, he said, something of a Spanish characteristic.[3] Well might the pope quote them altruistic passages from the New Testament, and their own leaders ruminate upon that most appropriate Book of the Old.[4] But the burdens which they bore were financial burdens, and without funds reform was doomed, as the bishop of Valencia understood. They could not resist the quick returns which they might secure by abandoning the high moral line. Thus fines from *concubinarii* helped the bishop of Barcelona pay for his new chapel, and the subjects of the two poems of Adán Fernández which have survived are women and money.[5] The scramble for a place in the sun – or, rather, in the shade – undermined John of Abbeville's attack on pluralism and its attendant evils.[6] While the warriors on the frontier were being

de los enemigos ssegunt dise la glosa in c. adria in lxiiii dist. x. vo. iiij. E juan andres por prosupuesto pone que los reyes de castilla e de leon non reconosçe superior. *In c. et ssenecte (sic) de dona. inter vi. et ux.* De la cassa real de ynglaterra non sse lee esta perrogativa.' The first king of England, 'llamado thoel', had received the kingdom from the Romans on payment of tribute; and more recently England had become a feudal dependent of the Roman Church when Innocent III had sent a legate ('galacio vercelense') to King John: *Ciudad de Dios*, xxxv, 214–15.

[1] López de Meneses, *Est. Edad Media de la Corona de Aragón*, VI, 377–8. Pedro IV of Aragon supported the idea in principle, but not Alfonso's proposed embargo on pilgrims out of Spain.

[2] *De Potestate Regia et Papali*, cap. xviii, ed. J. Leclercq, *Jean de Paris et l'ecclésiologie du XIIIe siècle* (Paris, 1942), 229. Cf. E. H. Kantorowicz, *The King's Two Bodies* (Princeton, 1957), 326.

[3] *Breves Annales, sub anno* 1277, describing Pope John XXI as 'magnus in Philosophia, sed in actionibus spiritu Hispanico plenus, quia exosos habuit religiosos', for which God punished him by making the ceiling collapse: *RIS*, XI, 1291.

[4] Above, pp. 127, 244.

[5] Above, Ch. 5; Ríos, *Historia crítica*, II, 355–7.

[6] Contemporaries did not share the enthusiasm of a later age for either Mallorca or

reminded that they were at war with the Moors not for booty but for Christ,[1] in the hinterland the spirit was getting the worst of it. The economic obstacles to reform even hindered the adoption in the province of Tarragona of the uniform clerical dress which Archbishop Rodrigo in 1291 described as an expression of *con*formity through *uni*formity. Twenty-three years before, Bishop Andrés de Albalat had had to postpone the introduction of a measure to this effect, 'volentes parcere sumptibus et expensis propter aliquorum indigentias'.[2] More seriously, a little over a century after the Fourth Lateran Council, a Tarragona Council had to command priests and rectors to celebrate at least three times a year;[3] and at Basle in 1435, within weeks of the bishop of Burgos's stirring address on Spain's outstanding virtues, the king of Castile's delegates attempted to amend the council's decree against concubinage so that it should not prejudice royal laws and customs on the subject.[4] Such were the long-term consequences of having given due weight in the past to such corrosive concepts as custom, which was a synonym for corruption; necessity and utility, which permitted laymen to occupy prebends; and difficulty, which induced the pope to release the archbishop of Compostela from the obligation to summon a provincial council as often as once a year.[5]

Popes of the past had soft-pedalled on this last point too, and it is both interesting and opportune to note that at the Toledo Council of 589 one of the first acts of the Catholic bishops after the adoption

the Algarve. Bishop Pedro could not tolerate the climate of his island see, and in Aug. 1268 was given permission to stay elsewhere; while at Silves five years later it was reported that the cathedral church was destitute of *servitores* between June and October 'cum aer, ut dicitur, eo tempore distemperantior apud Silvium sit': *Reg. Clem. IV*, 665; Silva Lopes, *Memórias...do bispado do Algarve*, 564.

[1] 'La entencion de todos sea en deffender la ecclesia de Dios por a Jhesu Christo dar sus animas e yr contra moros non por cosa de rapina mas por acrescemiento de la fe de Dios': thirteenth-century Rule of the Order of Santiago, cap. 34, in Lomax, *Orden de Santiago*, 225-6.

[2] Tejada y Ramiro, *Colección de cánones*, III, 411; Aguirre, *Collectio maxima conciliorum*, V, 208.

[3] In 1318: Tejada, III, 475.

[4] 'Unus ambassiatorum domini regis Castelle peciit nomine suo et suorum collegarum, quatenus in decreto concubinariorum addatur clausula "salvis remanentibus institutis et legibus regalibus"; alias protestatus est de non consenciendo': J. Haller, *Concilium Basiliense: Studien und Quellen zur Geschichte des Concils von Basel*, III (Basle, 1900), 293. Cf. Suárez Fernández, 117.

[5] Above, pp. 17, 37, 44.

of Catholicism as the State religion had been to declare that, 'in view of the great distances involved and the poverty of the churches of Spain', provincial synods should assemble not twice each year but once.[1] It is interesting because it is not the only feature that the Visigothic Church had in common with the thirteenth-century.[2] And it is opportune because it leads naturally to a final attempt to place in a wider historical context what has been said in this book about the conditions of the later period.

The belief is still held by some that ever since Reccared's conversion and the Third Toledo Council Spain has been a 'theocracy', by which is meant a 'clericocracy' with its secular rulers rulers in name only, so many Dalai Lamas, puppets manipulated by the priests.[3] But on a serious level this belief has been totally abandoned by historians of both the Visigothic and the Habsburg periods, none of whom could now subscribe to the judgement of a contemporary of Menéndez y Pelayo that the Visigothic State was 'a more completely priest-governed state than the world has perhaps ever seen, with the exception of Paraguay and the States of the Church'.[4] On the contrary, 'of the two parties to the Visigothic Councils, the Crown and the Church' – it can be asserted *tout court* – 'the Crown was dominant and the Church was subordinate'. The Visigothic Church was 'virtually a department of State', and its bishops 'supine supporters of the king'.[5] 'The Visigothic theocracy', Castro writes, 'is regarded by many as the logical antecedent of the Spain of Philip II, even though the major Spanish historians may not think so'.[6] And the many are right, though for quite the wrong reasons – unless by 'theocracy'

---

[1] Thompson, *Goths in Spain*, 36, 285–6.

[2] Two others of note were clerical concubinage and misappropriation of the *tercias*, particularly by the bishops. 'So many enactments were passed on these two subjects that offences would seem to have been widespread': *ibid*. 45 ff., 299 ff. For restrictions on foreign travel, *ibid*. 176–7; and above, Ch. 7.

[3] Thus Eduardo Romero, *Tiranía y teocracia en el siglo XX* (Mexico, 1958), esp. 18 ('el gobierno de los godos no fué otra cosa que una monarquía teocrático-militar' in the sense that, at the Visigothic Councils, 'los monarcas, prosternados ante los obispos y con el rostro en tierra, les suplicaban su apoyo y les pedían consejo'), 23, 42.

[4] Thomas Hodgkin, 'Visigothic Spain', *EHR*, II (1887), 209–34, at p. 222.

[5] Thompson, 281, 316; J. N. Hillgarth, 'Coins and Chronicles: Propaganda in sixth-century Spain, and the Byzantine Background', *Historia*, XV (1966), 483–508, at p. 500.

[6] *The Structure of Spanish History*, 68.

they mean 'that domination of the Church by the Crown' which 'was probably more complete in Spain in the sixteenth century than in any other part of Europe, including Protestant countries with an Erastian system'.[1] When benefices were granted by the monarch to such men of God as his barber's brother[2] the Church was clearly as little in control of its own destinies as it had been nine centuries earlier.

In order to accommodate the authorised version concerning the thirteenth century, therefore, it is necessary to assume that the Church first staged a rapid recovery consistent with its achieving the summit of 'power and prestige' in San Fernando's century,[3] and then, presumably, suffered a rather more rapid decline. The foregoing pages have argued that there had been no such rise and fall; that the Spanish Church was on the same plane in the thirteenth century as in the seventh or sixteenth. Felipe II's control of the Church dated from the reign of San Fernando, not from that of Fernando el Católico when Alexander VI had merely given his blessing to a *fait accompli* and ratified the king's possession of the *tercias*.[4] Hence the king's righteous indignation in 1485, for example, when Innocent VIII insisted that Spain contribute to the defence of Christendom against the Turks, and the time-honoured arguments in his protest which reminded the pontiff that what motivated the proposed final push to Granada was not desire for booty but devotion to Christ and to the cause of increasing the Catholic Faith (*que sea acrescentada*). To which end many past popes had granted the kings ecclesiastical revenue without diminution – including Nicholas IV at a time when the Holy Land had been in dire need, 'non habiendo por menos justa e nescesaria esta guerra de Granada que la dicha Tierra Santa'.[5] And he might have looked even further back – to 1247 and Innocent IV's grant to Fernando III.

Fernando III and his successors were able to help themselves to Church revenue when papal grants were not forthcoming, because

[1] J. Lynch, 'Philip II and the Papacy', *TRHS*, 5th ser., II (1961), 23–42, at p. 24.
[2] I. Cloulas, 'La Monarchie Catholique et les revenus épiscopaux', *Mélanges de la Casa de Velázquez*, IV (1968), 107–42, at p. 138.
[3] Thus Sobrequés (above, p. 102).
[4] Cf. W. E. Shiels, *The Rise and Fall of the Patronato Real* (Chicago, 1961), 82 ff.
[5] Publ. Goñi Gaztambide, *HS*, IV, 72. For the fifteenth-century background and the Church's contribution to the conquest of Granada, see *idem, Historia de la Bula de la Cruzada*, 404 ff.; M. A. Ladero Quesada, *Castilla y la conquista del reino de Granada* (Valladolid, 1967), 208–13.

the Church's leaders were as helpless and hopeless in the thirteenth century as they had been in the seventh. In 1219 Honorius III called them dumb dogs, the very same epithet as had occurred to Honorius I when he had chastised their predecessors in the 630s;[1] and by implication they defended their craven performance, as San Braulio had done on the earlier occasion, as politic not cowardly.[2] But in the 630s they had at least had the councils in which to make their voices heard, if they dared. In San Fernando's century the dumb dogs were effectively muzzled, and when they attempted to break out and hunt in a pack – notably in the late 1250s and at the end of Alfonso X's reign – they were soon cowed, so that their last state was worse than their first. In 1434 the bishop of Burgos could buttress his claim to consideration by reference to the Toledo Councils of the sixth and seventh centuries which had provided a hundred chapters of the *Decretum*; but he could not offer any such conciliar material from a later age.[3] It was from that source too that Vincentius Hispanus illustrated his point about the effectiveness of the pragmatic Spaniards of the 1230s who had gained their own empire and *elected their own bishops*, his authority, *via* Gratian, being a canon of the Twelfth Toledo Council of 681 which had described the appointment of bishops as a function of *regalis potestas*.[4] 'The entire dependence of the clergy on the court, which was traditional since the time of Valens and a fundamental characteristic of Teutonic society' and contributed to the failure of Arianism in Spain,[5] was carried over when Arianism gave way to Catholicism as the State religion and was a striking feature of public life in the thirteenth century – by which time the kings, largely with the help of the ecclesiastics, had ridded themselves of that other Teutonic bequest – elective kingship.[6]

---

[1] Above, Ch. 1; Thompson, 185.

[2] 'Dispensative potiusquam negligenter aut formidolose': *PL.* 80, 668C.

[3] *Ciudad de Dios*, xxxv, 527.

[4] 'Sed soli Yspani virtute sua obtinuerunt imperium et episcopos elegerunt' (above, p. 104). Gaines Post, *Studies*, 489, n. 197, gives the canonist's source as *Decretum*, dist. lxiii, c. 26. It is, in fact, c. 25 (Friedberg, *Corpus*, I, 242). Text in *Concilios visigóticos e hispano-romanos*, ed. J. Vives (Barcelona–Madrid, 1963), 393–4.

[5] C. A. A. Scott, *Ulfilas, Apostle of the Goths* (Cambridge, 1885), 220. Cf. c. 35 of the Council of Agde (506) on the bishops' solemn obligation to attend the metropolitan synod 'postpositis omnibus, excepta gravi infirmitate corporis, aut praeceptione regia': Mansi, VIII, 330–1.

[6] Cf. Sánchez-Albornoz, *Bol. de la Acad. Argentina de Letras*, XIV, 84, 91–4.

It was highly appropriate, therefore, that Felipe II should have pressed for the canonisation of Hermengild who had incurred martyrdom in 585, while attempting to be the first Catholic king of Spain four years before Reccared made the break. In February 1586 Sixtus V authorised the celebration of his feast in Spain.[1] An even more fitting symbol, though, would have been Reccared himself – or Fernando III. For it was, after all, due in large part to Fernando III that Felipe II could be described in 1566 as 'the greatest prelate in ecclesiastical rents that there is in the world, after the pope'.[2] Fernando had laid the foundations of the *Patronato Real*.[3] 'Dignior autem est qui decimas recipit quam qui decimas tribuit', in the words of the medieval pope who best understood the subject of sovereignty.[4] Fernando's canonisation, however, had to await the next century. And thereby hangs a tale.

In November 1598, a month after the death of Felipe II, Juan de Mariana felt it safe to proceed with the publication of his treatise on tyrannicide, the *De Rege et Regis Institutione* – 'le livre le plus remarquable et le plus hardi que possède la littérature politique de l'Espagne'.[5] Prudently, though, he made some excisions, and one of the passages left out was a reasoned reply of a historical nature to certain *allegaciones* made by a fully-fledged regalist to the effect that the kings of Spain long before had possessed all the ecclesiastical *diezmos* with the permission of the popes, and that the churches were beholden for their income to a gracious monarch who at that time – the late sixteenth century – was prepared to content himself merely with the *tercias*. This claim contained a total reversal of the actual historical process of the previous centuries, and Mariana's refutation of it was based on the evidence which he had already published in the

---

[1] Lucas Castellinus, *Tractatus de certitudine gloriae canonizatorum* (Rome, 1628), 438. Cf. *Acta Sanctorum: Aprilis: tom. II*, 138; and, for the 'official view' of Hermengild at this time, the account given by the royal chronicler, Ambrosio de Morales: *Corónica General de España*, lib. XI, cap. lxvii [ed. Madrid, 1791, V, 545–54].

[2] '...por ser Administrador de tres muy grandes Maestradgos, y de las tercias de los diezmos': Martín de Azpilcueta, *Tractado de las rentas de los beneficios eclesiásticos* (Valladolid, 1566), fo. 28v. For the *Maestradgos* – the Masterships of the three Military Orders – see L. P. Wright, 'The Military Orders in sixteenth- and seventeenth-century Spanish Society', *Past and Present*, XLIII (1969), 34–70.

[3] Cf. Mansilla, 88.

[4] *Regestum domni Innocentii tertii pape super negotio Romani imperii*, no. 18, ed. W. Holtzmann (Bonn, 1947), I, 29.

[5] G. Cirot, *Mariana historien* (Bordeaux, 1905), 35 ff.

History. Listing the instances of papal grants known to him, he was able to prove that, contrary to what had been alleged, it was the *tercias* and not the full *diezmos* that had been granted by a succession of spineless (*flacos*) popes, and, further, that these grants had been for limited periods only. Moreover, he suggested that the pope was forbidden by Canon Law to alienate the property of the churches without consulting the bishops concerned.[1]

Since, according to one estimate, more than half of the Spanish Church's income was appropriated by the Crown,[2] it is not difficult to understand why Mariana delayed publication and then toned down his observations on this point quite considerably. The morality of tyrannicide might be discussed openly, but too much was involved for Felipe II to countenance this sort of analysis of his financial affairs. It is not, however, true to say that all reference to this thorny subject was removed from the *De Rege*. For, in the belief that the first papal grant of this nature had been that of Gregory X to Alfonso X in 1275, Mariana made his point by implication, by casting Alfonso's immediate predecessor, Fernando III, in the role of the paradigmatically pious monarch who declined to tax the Church. At the siege of Seville, he claimed, Fernando had rejected the advice of those who had urged him to relieve their pressing need at the expense of the ecclesiastics. It was not the priests' money that he wanted – the king was reported to have said – but their prayers.[3]

The story seems to have been of quite recent invention. It does not occur either in the *Primera Crónica General* or in the *Crónica del Sancto Rey,* which had been compiled in 1526.[4] Mariana had not alluded to it in his *History*, published only seven years before. Possibly its pedigree goes no further back than the mid-sixteenth century and

---

1 *Ibid.* 414–16, for the text of the draft.
2 Don Sancho Busto, acting bishop of Toledo, in 1574: Lynch, 27.
3 *De Rege*, lib. I, cap. x (Toledo, 1599), 122–3, 119: 'Ferdinandus Castellae Rex cognomento Sanctus, Hispali obsessa in magna atque adeo suprema inopia suadentibus quibusdam, uti templorum donis eam inopiam levaret, ne nciepto abscedere cogeretur cum gravi dedecore nominis Christiani praecise facturum negavit, maius se praesidium ponere dictitans in precibus sacerdotum, quam in omnibus eorum copiis et auro.' Cf. above, Ch. 6.
4 *Crónica del Sancto Rey Don Fernando tercero deste nombre que ganó à Sevilla y à Cordoba y à Jaen y à toda el Andaluzia, cuyo cuerpo esta en la Sancta Yglesia de Sevilla* (Seville, 1526). The substance of the work is drawn from the *Primera Crónica General*. See Sánchez Alonso, *Historia de la historiografía*, I, 430.

the work of the Dominican, Domingo de Valtanàs Mexía, to whom, together with Mariana, reference was made in the 1620s when evidence was submitted to Rome in support of the cause of canonisation, and this instance of Fernando's piety was thrown into the scales to add weight to the various miracles ascribed to him.[1] So it appears that it was Mariana, of all people, who in his ignorance of the 1247 grant, and in the *De Rege*, of all books, first gave the legend currency and was responsible for its eventual acceptance as true history. And this suspicion is confirmed by the lack of attention given to it when the canonisation campaign was first mounted. In 1627 two books were published which might have been expected to have made much of the tale: Espinosa's *Historia de Sevilla*, and Pineda's *Memorial* of the king's 'excellent sanctity and heroic virtues' which, in the words of Menéndez y Pelayo, 'sirvió de pieza principal en el proceso de canonización'. Yet neither mentioned it. 'The fat rents' with which Fernando had endowed the churches, and his generosity to them in the *repartimiento* of Seville,were duly recorded, but not the king's worthy aphorism.[2] To the extent that it argued economic hardship it would, indeed, have been out of place in the *Memorial*, since Pineda was convinced by Lucas of Túy that 'todo el tiempo del Rey Santo' had been one of 'salud i abundancia', proof, he thought, of the Almighty's pleasure in the monarch, in contrast to 'the sword, the famine and the pestilence' which was the lot of the besieged Moors.[3] By 1673, though, two years after Fernando's canonisation, it was well

[1] *Interrogatorio de testigos para el processo de la causa que pende ante el Illmo Sr D. Diego de Guzmán, Patriarca arçobispo de Sevilla, cerca de la excelente vidà, heroicas virtudes y milagrosas obras del Señor Rey don Fernando el III que ganó à Sevilla y à toda la Frontera, llamado El Santo* (Seville?, n.d.), fo. 11, *item* 54. For Valtanàs, whom Carlos V consulted 'para negocios graves', see Ximena, *Catálogo de Jaén*, 459.

[2] Pablo de Espinosa de los Monteros, *Primera parte de la historia, antiguedades y grandezas de la muy noble y muy leal Ciudad de Sevilla* (Seville, 1627), 147r–8r; Joan de Pineda, *Memorial de la excelente santidad y heroycas virtudes del Señor Rey don Fernando, tercero deste nombre, primero de Castilla i de León* (Seville, 1627), 94–7, 119. Cf. Menéndez y Pelayo, *loc. cit.* 49. Nor did Pedro de Ribadeneyra (d. 1611), an expert on the subject of sanctity, allude to the incident, although chs. 37–8 of his *Libro Primero de las virtudes del principe*, entitled 'El recato que deven usar los principes en aprovecharse de los bienes de la Yglesia' [in *Obras* (Madrid, 1605), 469–74] provided him with an ideal opportunity for doing so.

[3] Pineda, 158–60. It should be noted that the information about the besieged Moors being reduced to eating roots and excrement ('i aun desto avian poco') came not from Lucas, as Pineda thought, but from his fifteenth-century vernacular continuator. See *Crónica de España por Lucas, obispo de Túy*, ed. J. Puyol (Madrid, 1926), 434.

established, and Núñez de Castro was able to provide a blow-by-blow account of the imagined conversation of 1248.[1] Ten years later, the Bollandist Papebroch noted it as a tradition which he had not been able to verify.[2] Then, in the mid-eighteenth century, Burriel included it in the *Memorias de San Fernando*, which he dedicated to Fernando VI at just about the time when that monarch was negotiating the Concordat of 1753 and securing the *Patronato Universal*.[3] Like Mariana, Burriel regarded 'nuestro divino rey San Fernando' as the embodiment of those royal virtues which later kings had not invariably displayed in their dealings with the Church. He believed that historical research would show that Rome's supreme authority had always been acknowledged there 'desde las primeras luces evangélicas hasta el día de hoy'.[4]

Burriel's stamp of approval settled the matter, so that in the present century it could be maintained that San Fernando never encroached on the *diezmos* or other *bienes privativos* of the clergy, even when the pope had given him permission to do so. Thus Padre Retana in 1941, disposing of an offensive suggestion to the contrary made by a 'certain obscure author'.[5]

Presumably the object the P. Retana's scorn was a historian rather than a hagiographer.[6] At all events, his utter certainty on this point –

[1] A. Núñez de Castro, *Vida de San Fernando el tercero, rey de Castilla y León* (Madrid, 1673), 110r–11v, citing Pineda, 24, though Pineda does not mention the exchange.

[2] D. Papebroch, *Acta vitae S. Ferdinandi III* (Antwerp, 1684), 180 = *Acta Sanctorum: Maii: tom. VII*, 346.

[3] Burriel, *Memorias*, 119–21; Shiels, 229 ff. I do not mean to suggest that Burriel was the author of the *Memorias*, which seem to have been written by another some fifty years earlier. Cf. Menéndez y Pelayo, *loc. cit.* 50; L. Redonet y López Doriga in *Centenario de la Conquista de Sevilla...conmemorada por El Instituto de España, el 24 de enero de 1948* (Madrid, 1948), 21.

[4] Burriel to Castro, 30 Dec. 1754: publ. Valladares, *Semanario Erudito*, II, 44–6.

[5] L. F. de Retana, *Albores del Imperio: San Fernando III y su época* (Madrid, 1941), 192–3: 'Me he detenido en este asunto, por cierto inútilmente, pues a nadie tengo que convencer; y no lo hiciera, a no ser por haber leído en cierto oscuro autor, frases ofensivas e irreverentes para la memoria del ilustre gobernante, haciendo hincapié en lo que su pequeño espíritu cree ser lo característico, por ser lo único visible para él en este gigante.' P. Retana seems not to understand the relationship between the *tercias* and the *diezmos*. Nor is he impressed by Gregory IX's criticism of Fernando's intervention in the diocese of Calahorra (above, p. 140). The king's relations with the Church 'fueron siempre de hijo amante y de poderoso y ferviente protector' who enriched it 'con grandes donadíos': *ibid.* 172–3.

[6] Possibly he had Cedillo in mind: *Contribuciones*, 298–9 (above, p. 111, n. 6).

and his failure to analyse Gregory IX's letter, to which he referred, from the point of view of *libertas ecclesiastica*[1] – are symptomatic of that 'rigidez de los viejos moldes eruditos' which, almost twenty years after Vicens lamented it,[2] still bedevils this subject. In 1941, however, half a century after Menéndez y Pelayo's exuberant speech, the issue was perhaps too uncomfortably contemporary to be susceptible of 'irreverent' analysis. Since 1892, self-assurance had evaporated: even in *L'École française de Rome* Serrano could see signs of 'anti-Spain'.[3] The national *complejo de inferioridad* had established itself. As early as 1902 another biographer of Fernando III had deplored all the elements of disorder swarming about that country. In the year of Alfonso XIII's coronation he had entreated the Almighty to send another San Fernando to the rescue.[4] It was to the canonised monarch and his age that the disaffected looked back longingly, as the antithesis now rather than as the prefiguration of their present condition. So too, in 1937 – after first Alfonso and then the Republic had failed to bring stability – it was to the bishops of the thirteenth century and of the seventh that, albeit unwittingly, the Spanish hierarchy referred in their Encyclical Letter to their brethren throughout the world. They had declared for the Nationalists, they explained, lest, by tolerating injustice, they should incur the title of 'dumb dogs'.[5] Appropriate though it may have been, it was not a happy precedent.

---

[1] Retana, 193, n. 53, quoting *Reg. Greg. IX*, 255 (Dec. 1228), as an example of papal authorisation of an ecclesiastical subsidy to the king. But Gregory's letter to the Castilian bishops also mentions – which Retana does not – that the pope had been much concerned 'a clamore tam querulo et clamosa querimonia' in their letter to him. He congratulated them as *athletas imperterritos* in the defence of *ecclesiastica libertas*. The *oportuna subsidia* and *congruum remedium* were to be assigned to Fernando 'sine prejudicio libertatis ecclesiastice'. Possibly they had reported the king's attempt on the *tercias*. See above, p. 111. John of Abbeville was in Spain at the time.

[2] *Aproximación a la historia de España*, 8.

[3] Above, p. xi.

[4] 'Quiera el cielo depararnos un monarca como San Fernando que logre sacarnos de tanto abatimiento': Santiago Rodríguez, *Vida del Santo Rey don Fernando III de España* (Barcelona, 1902), 124.

[5] 'No podíamos inhibirnos sin dejar abandonados los intereses de nuestro Señor Jesucristo y sin incurrir el tremendo apelativo de *canes muti*, con que el Profeta censura a quienes, debiendo hablar, callan ante la injusticia': Cardenal Isidro Gomá y Tomás, *Pastorales de la Guerra de España* (Madrid, 1955), 154.

BIBLIOGRAPHY

Material from the following archives and libraries has been used:

AD Astorga	AC Palencia
AC Ávila	AE Palencia
ACA Barcelona	AC Pamplona
AC Barcelona	AGN Pamplona
AD Barcelona	AM Pamplona
Arquivo Distrital, Braga	AC Salamanca
AC Burgo de Osma	AC Santiago de Compostela
BC Burgo de Osma	AC Segovia
AC Burgos	AC Seo de Urgel
AC Calahorra	AC Sigüenza
AC Ciudad Rodrigo	AHA Tarragona
AC Cuenca	BP Tarragona
AC Gerona	AC Toledo
AE Gerona	BC Toledo
AC Huesca	AC Tortosa
AC León	AC Tudela
AM León	AE Tudela
AC Lérida	AC Túy
AC Lugo	AC Valencia
AHN Madrid	ASV Vatican City
RAH Madrid	AC Vich
AC Mondoñedo	AC Zamora
AC Orense	AA Zaragoza
AC Oviedo	AC Zaragoza

The bibliography is divided into: 1, Manuscripts;[1] 2, Published catalogues and registers;[2] 3, Narrative sources and published documents; 4, Secondary material.

I. MANUSCRIPTS

Barcelona, Archivo de la Catedral:
Constitutiones Synodales et Provinciales
Liber I Antiquitatum
Libro de la Cadena

---

[1] Cartularies, etc. are not normally listed.
[2] The distribution of published material between sections 2, 3 and 4 is not meant to be exclusive. Only works cited in the text are mentioned.

335

Bibliography

Barcelona, Archivo de la Corona de Aragón:
  Registros de la Cancillería, vols 6, 8, 11–14, 16, 20, 22, 24, 37–9, 41–2, 49–50, 55,
    63, 77, 252, 321
Burgo de Osma, Biblioteca del Cabildo:
  Cód. 17 (Rodericus Palentinus, *Liber Septenarius de Visitatione Prelati*)
Cambridge, Trinity College:
  MS. B.15.21 (John of Abbeville, *Liber Omeliarum*)
Gerona, Archivo de la Catedral:
  Cartulario Carlomagno
  Causa del Any 1240
  Llibre Vert
Gerona, Archivo Episcopal:
  Liber Notularum (1294–1300)
Lérida, Archivo de la Catedral:
  Constitutiones Ecclesie Ilerdensis
  Regestre de presentasions de prebendes
London, British Museum
  Add. 20787 (*Primera Partida*)
  Egerton 442 (Papeles tocantes á asuntos eclesiásticos)
  Lansdowne 397 (Richard of Pophis Formulary)
Madrid, Archivo Histórico Nacional:
  Cód. 267B (Lugo, *Tumbo Nuevo*)
  Cód. 987B, 996B (Toledo, *Libros Becerros*)
  Cód. 1042B (Lugo, *Libro de Aniversarios*)
  Cód. 1443B (Ávila Cartulary)
Madrid, Biblioteca Nacional, Sección de Manuscritos:
  1529 (J. B. Pérez, *Archiepiscoporum Toletanorum Vitae*)
  5928 (F. A. Villaamil y Saavedra, *Noticias de la Santa Iglesia de Mondoñedo*)
  7112 (A. Sánchez Cavañas, *Historia Civitatense*)
  8997 (J. B. Pérez, *Liber de Rebus Sancte Ecclesie Toletane*)
  9552, 13018, 13022–3, 13028, 13035, 13039, 13041–2, 13069, 13074, 13089,
    13094–5, 13116 (Burriel MSS.)
  11263bis (R. Guise, *Extracto de Algunas Memorias Relativas a Concilios Generales de
    España*)
  13071–2 (Ascensio de Morales, *Compulsa de Instrumentos Pertenecientes a los Abusos
    de la Corte Romana, Recogidos en Virtud de Real Orden en los Archivos de la
    Ciudad de Cuenca, 1750*)
  13076 (A. Santos Calderón de la Barca, *Memorias para la Historia de la Iglesia de
    Coria, 1752*)
  Vit. 15–5
Madrid, Real Academia de la Historia:
  9–24–5/4558–4564 (Papeles de Villanueva, vols 61–7)
  C2/9.5422 (Ascensio de Morales, *Catedrales de España*: 'Privilegios y Escrituras
    que se hallan en el Archivo y Tumbo…de Astorga y su Obispado')
  C7/9.5427 (Morales, *Catedrales*…: 'Privilegios…de Plasencia')

C19/9.5439 (Morales, *Catedrales*...: 'Documentos...de Cuenca')

Santiago de Compostela, Archivo de la Catedral:
Constitutiones sinodales y capitulares antiguas
Libro I de Constituciones; Libro II de Constituciones
Tumbillo de Tablas, de Privilegios y Constituciones
Tumbo B

Seo de Urgel, Archivo de la Catedral:
Dotium sive dotaliarum ecclesie Urgellensis liber secundus
Cód. 2119 (*Constitutiones Synodales Ilerdenses et Tarraconenses*)
Registro episcopal fragmentario

Tarragona, Archivo Histórico Archidiocesano:
Index dels Indices..., (1679)
Cartoral AB
Libro de la Corretja
Thesaurus Sanctae Metropolitanae Ecclesiae Tarraconensis...a Mariano Mari (1783)

Tarragona, Biblioteca Pública:
MS. 176 (*Resumen cronológico de algunas documentos del Archivo de la Colegiata de S. Pedro de Ager*)

Toledo, Biblioteca del Cabildo:
Cód. 23–16
Cód. 39–12
Cód. 42–21

Tortosa, Biblioteca del Cabildo:
Cód. 187 (*Constituciones Synodales Ecclesie Tarraconensis*)

Vatican, Archivo Segreto Vaticano:
Reg. Avinionensia, 91
Arm. XXXI.72 (Marinus de Eboli Formulary)
Collectorie 397 (*Regestum causarum per Alexandrum papam IV Ottaviano S. Marie in Vialata diacono cardinali, commissarum, necnon acta quedam earumdem causarum, 1257–1263*)

Vatican, Biblioteca Apostolica Vaticana:
Cod. lat. 3975, 3976 (Marinus de Eboli Formulary)

Vich, Museo Episcopal:
Cód. 147 (*Confessionale, Constitutiones Sinodales Vicenses*)
Cód. 220 (*Constitutiones Synodales Vicenses et Provinciales Tarraconenses*)

Zamora, Archivo de la Catedral:
Liber Constitutionum

Zaragoza, Archivo Arzobispal:
Cartulario Pequeño

2. PUBLISHED CATALOGUES AND REGISTERS

A. *Papal Registers*

Les Registres d'Alexandre IV (1254–61), ed. C. Bourel de la Roncière, etc. (Paris, 1902–59).

337

Bibliography

Les Registres de Boniface VIII (1294–1303), ed. G. Digard, M. Faucon, A. Thomas, and R. Fawtier (Paris, 1907–39).

Les Registres de Clément IV (1265–68), ed. E. Jordan (Paris, 1893–1945).

Regestum Clementis papae V (1305–14), ed. monks O.S.B. (Rome, 1885–1957).

Les Registres de Grégoire IX (1227–41), ed. L. Auvray (Paris, 1890–1955).

Les Registres de Grégoire X (1271–76), ed. J. Guiraud (Paris, 1892–1906).

Regesta Honorii papae III (1216–27), ed. P. Pressutti (Rome, 1888–95).

Les Registres d'Honorius IV (1285–87), ed. M. Prou (Paris, 1888).

Les Registres d'Innocent IV (1243–54), ed. E. Berger (Paris, 1881–1921).

Le Registre de Jean XXI (1276–77), ed. L. Cadier (Paris, 1898).

Les Registres de Martin IV (1281–85), ed. par les membres de l'Ecole française de Rome (Paris, 1901).

Les Registres de Nicolas III (1277–80), ed. J. Gay (Paris, 1898–1938).

Les Registres de Nicolas IV (1288–92), ed. E. Langlois (Paris, 1886–1905).

Les Registres d'Urbain IV (1261–64), ed. J. Guiraud (Paris, 1892–1958).

B. *Other Catalogues and Registers*

Arco, R. del. 'El archivo de la Catedral de Jaca', *BRAH*, LXV (1914), pp. 47–98.

'Los archivos de Barbastro', *Universidad*, VII (1930), pp. 27 ff., 233 ff., 269 ff.

As Gavetas da Torre do Tombo, I– (Lisbon, Centro de Estudos Históricos Ultramarinos, 1960–).

Battelli, Giulio. *Schedario Baumgarten* [descrizione diplomatica di Bolle e Brevi originali da Innocenzo III a Pio IX, riproduzione anastatica con introduzione e indici a cura di G.B], 2 vols (Vatican City, 1965–6).

Batzer, E. *Zur Kenntnis der Formularsammlung der Richard von Pofi* (Heidelberg, 1910).

Bayerri Bertomeu, E. *Los códices medievales de la Catedral de Tortosa* (Barcelona, 1962).

Bujanda, F. *Inventario de los documentos del archivo de la insigne Iglesia Colegial de Logroño* (Logroño, 1947).

Castro, J. R. *Catálogo del Archivo General de Navarra: sección de comptos: documentos* I (años 842–1331) (Pamplona, 1952).

Durán Gudiol, A. 'La documentación pontificia del Archivo Catedral de Huesca hasta el año 1417', *AA*, VII (1959), pp. 339–93.

Eubel, C. *Hierarchia catholica Medii Aevi*, I (Munich, 1923).

Fransen, G. 'Manuscrits canoniques (1140–1234) conservés en Espagne', *Rev. d'Hist. Ecclésiastique*, XLVIII (1953), pp. 224–34.

Fuentes, F. *Catálogo de los archivos eclesiásticos de Tudela* (Tudela, 1944).

Gams, P. B. *Series episcoporum ecclesiae catholicae* (Ratisbon, 1873).

García Larragueta, S. *Catálogo de los pergaminos de la Catedral de Oviedo* (Oviedo, 1957).

García Villada, Z. *Catálogo de los códices y documentos de la Catedral de León* (Madrid, 1919).

Goñi Gaztambide, J. *Catálogo del Archivo Catedral de Pamplona*, I (Pamplona, 1965).

'Regesta de las bulas de los archivos navarros', *AA*, X (1962), pp. 253–354.

Bibliography

González Hurtebise, E. 'Recull de documents inédits del Rey En Jaume I', I. *CHCA* (1909), pp. 1183–1253.

Jesus da Costa, A. 'Documentos da Colegiada de Guimarães', *RPH*, III (1947), pp. 561–89.

Linehan, P. A. 'La documentación pontificia de Honorio III (1216–1227): unas adiciones a la Regesta de D. Demetrio Mansilla', *AA*, XVI (1968), pp. 385–408.

Llorens y Raga, P. L. 'Catálogo de los pergaminos de la santa Catedral de Segorbe', *RABM*, LXXII (1964–5), pp. 31–65.

López Polo, A. *Catálogo del archivo del Capitulo General Eclesiástico* (Teruel, 1965).

Loye, J. de. *Les archives de la Chambre Apostolique au XIVe siècle* (Paris, 1899).

Mansilla, D. 'La documentación española del Archivo Castel S. Angelo (395–1418)', *AA*, VI (1958), pp. 285–448.

'La diócesis de Burgos vista a través de la documentación del archivo capitular en los siglos XIII y XIV', *AA*, IX (1961), pp. 417–73.

Mañueco Villalobos, M. *Documentos de la Iglesia Colegial de S. María la Mayor (hoy Metropolitana) de Valladolid*, anotados por J. Zurita Nieto, 2 vols (Valladolid, 1920).

Marcos Rodríguez, F. *Catálogo de los documentos del Archivo Catedralicio de Salamanca* (Salamanca, 1962).

Martínez Ferrando, J. E. *Catálogo de la documentación relativa al antiguo reino de Valencia, contenida en los Registros de la Cancillería Real, del Archivo de la Corona de Aragón*, 2 vols (Madrid, 1934).

Matilla Tascón, A. *Guía-inventario de los archivos de Zamora y su Provincia* (Madrid, 1964).

Milian Boix, M. 'El fondo "Instrumenta Miscellanea" del Archivo Vaticano: documentos referentes a España (853–1782)', *AA*, XV (1967), pp. 489–1014.

Millás Vallicrosa, J. M. *Las traducciones orientales en los manuscritos de la Biblioteca Catedral de Toledo* (Madrid, 1942).

Miquel Rosell, F. J. *Regesta de letras pontificias del Archivo de la Corona de Aragón* (Madrid, 1948).

Olmos Canalda, E. *Códices de la Catedral de Valencia* (Valencia, 1943).

Inventario de los pergaminos del Archivo Catedral de Valencia (Valencia, 1961).

Pérez Martínez, L. 'Regesta de las bulas del Archivo Capitular de Mallorca', *AA*, XI (1963), pp. 161–88.

Potthast, A. *Regesta Pontificum Romanorum inde ab anno 1198 ad annum 1304*, 2 vols (Berlin, 1874–5).

Quintana Prieto, A. 'Registro de documentos pontificios de Astorga', *AA*, XI (1963), pp. 189–228.

Rocha Madahil, A. G. da. 'O Cartulario seiscentista da Mitra de Braga: "Rerum Memorabilium"', *Câmara Municipal do Porto: Boletim Cultural*, XXXI (1968), 92–234.

Rojo Orcajo, T. 'Catálogo descriptivo de los códices que se conservan en la S. I. Catedral de Burgo de Osma', *BRAH*, XCIV (1929), pp. 655–792.

San Martín Payo, J. 'Catálogo del Archivo de la Catedral de Palencia', *Publicaciones*

Bibliography

de la Institución Tello Téllez de Meneses, XI (1954), pp. 141–94; XIII (1955), 129–70; XVI (1956), 253–320; XVII (1958), 99–142; XXI (1961), 181–236.

Schillmann, F. *Die Formularsammlung des Marinus von Eboli* [Bibliothek des preussischen hist. Instituts in Rom, Bd 16] (Rome, 1929).

Stegmüller, F. *Repertorium Biblicum Medii Aevi*, III (Madrid, 1951).

Uhagón, F. R. de. 'Índice de los documentos de la Orden Militar de Calatrava', *BRAH*, XXXV (1899), pp. 1–167.

Zarco Cuevas, J. *Catálogo de los manuscritos castellanos en la Real Biblioteca de El Escorial*, III (San Lorenzo de El Escorial, 1929).

3. NARRATIVE SOURCES AND PUBLISHED DOCUMENTS

Abate, G. 'Lettere "secretae" d'Innocenzo IV e altri documenti in una raccolta inedita del secolo XIII', *Miscellanea Francescana*, LV (1955), pp. 317–73.

Acta Sanctorum...by the Bollandists, XI (t. II Aprilis), XX (t. VII Maii), ed. Paris–Rome (1866).

Aegidii Aureaevallensis: Gesta episcoporum Leodiensium, ed. I. Heller, *MGH*, Scriptores, XXV (Hanover, 1880).

Aguirre, J. Sáenz de. *Collectio maxima conciliorum omnium Hispaniae et novi orbis*... ed. altera, V (Rome, 1755).

Alamo, J. del. *Colección diplomática de San Salvador de Oña, 882–1284*, 2 vols (Madrid, 1950).

Albert's von Beham: Conceptbuch, ed. C. Höfler [Bibliothek d. lit. Vereins in Stuttgart, Bd 16] (Stuttgart, 1847).

Alberti Milioli...Liber de temporibus et aetatibus et chronica imperatorum, ed. O. Holder-Egger, *MGH*, Scriptores, XXXI (Hanover, 1903).

Albrici monachi Trium Fontium Chronica, ed. P. Scheffer-Boichorst, *MGH*, Scriptores, XXIII (Hanover, 1874).

Alfonso X. *Primera Crónica General de España*, ed. R. Menéndez Pidal, 2 vols (Madrid, 1955).

Las Siete Partidas...cotejados con varios códices antiguos, ed. Real Academia de la Historia, 3 vols (Madrid, 1807).

Setenario, ed. K. H. Vanderford (Buenos Aires, 1945).

Alfonso de Cartagena. 'Discurso pronunciado por...en el Concilio de Basilea acerca del derecho de precedencia del rey de Castilla sobre el rey de Inglaterra', *Ciudad de Dios*, XXXV (1894), pp. 122–9, 211–17, 523–42.

Alonso Alonso, M. (ed.) *Comentario al 'De Substantia Orbis' de Averroes por Álvaro de Toledo* (Madrid, 1941).

Alvarus Pelagius. *De Planctu Ecclesiae* (Venice, 1560).

Speculum Regum, ed. M. Pinto de Meneses (Lisbon, 1955).

Anales Toledanos, II and III, ed. Flórez, *España Sagrada*, XXIII (Madrid, 1767), pp. 401–23.

Annales Monastici, II–IV, ed. H. R. Luard, Rolls Ser. (London, 1865–9).

Annalium Laubiensium Continuatio, ed. G. H. Pertz, *MGH*, Scriptores, IV (Hanover, 1841).

Bibliography

Anónimo de Madrid y Copenhague, El, trans. A. Huici Miranda [Anales del Instituto de Valencia, II] (Valencia, 1917).

Artigas, M. (ed.) 'Un nuevo poema por la cuaderna via', *Boletín de la Biblioteca Menéndez y Pelayo,* I (1919), pp. 31–7, 87–95, 153–61, 210–16, 328–38; II (1920), pp. 41–8, 91–8, 154–63, 233–54.

Augustinus, A. *Opera omnia,* 8 vols (Lucca, 1765–74).

Balduini Ninovensis: Chronicon, ed. O. Holder-Egger, *MGH,* Scriptores, XXV (Hanover, 1880).

Baluze, S. *Miscellanea,* ed. J. Mansi, I (Lucca, 1761).

Bartholomei de Cotton: Historia Anglicana, ed. H. R. Luard, Rolls Ser. (London, 1859).

Berceo, Gonzalo de. *Veintetres milagros,* ed. C. Carroll Marden (Madrid, 1929).

Bujanda, F. 'Documentos para la historia de la diócesis de Calahorra: tres sínodos del siglo XIII', *Berceo,* I (1946), pp. 121–35.

Cancioneiro de Ajuda, ed. Carolina Michaëlis de Vasconcellos, 2 vols (Halle, 1904).

Cancioneiro da Biblioteca Nacional (antiguo Colocci–Brancuti), ed. Elza Paxeco Machado and José Pedro Machado, II (Lisbon, 1950); VI (1958).

Canivez, J. M. *Statuta Capitulorum Generalium Ordinis Cisterciensis ab anno 1116 ad annum 1786* (Louvain, 1933–41).

Carmen Apologeticum. See Grauert, section 4.

Carrión, L. 'Miscelánea', *AIA,* V (1916), pp. 127–31.

Castro, Américo, and Federico de Onís. (eds.) *Fueros leoneses* (Madrid, 1916).
'Une charte leonaise intéressante pour l'histoire des moeurs', *B. Hisp.,* XXV (1923), pp. 193–7.

Censual do Cabido da Sé do Porto (Porto, 1924).

Chartularium Studii Bononiensis: documenti per la storia dell' Università... pubblicati per opera della Commissione per la Storia dell' Università di Bologna, 13 vols (Bologna, 1909–40).

Chartularium Universitatis Portugalensis, I, ed. A. Moreira de Sá (Lisbon, 1966).

Charvin, G. *Statuts, chapitres généraux et visites de l'Ordre de Cluny,* I– (Paris, 1965–).

Chronica o Comentaris del gloriosissim e invictissim Rey En Jacme Primer, ed. M. Aguiló y Fuster (Barcelona, 1873).

Chronica Roberti de Torigneio [Chronicles of the Reigns of Stephen, Henry I and Richard I, IV], ed. R. Howlett, Rolls Ser. (London, 1889).

Chronicle of James of Aragon, trans. J. Forster, 2 vols (London, 1883).

Chronicón de Cardeña, ed. Flórez, *España Sagrada,* XXIII (Madrid, 1767), pp. 370–80.

Chronicon de Lanercost, ed. J. Stevenson (Edinburgh, 1839).

'Chronique latine inédite des Rois de Castille (1236)', ed. G. Cirot, *B. Hisp.,* XIV (1912), pp. 30–46, 109–18, 244–74, 353–74; XV (1913), pp. 18–37, 170–87, 268–83, 411–27.

Close Rolls: 1237–64, 7 vols (London, 1911–35); 1298–1302 (London, 1906).

Colección de documentos históricos, I, ed. Real Academia Gallega (La Coruña, 1915).

Collectionis Bullarum Sacrosanctae Basilicae Vaticanae tomus primus (Rome, 1747).

Cortes...de León y de Castilla, publ. por la Real Academia de la Historia, I (Madrid, 1861).

Bibliography

Crónica del Rey Don Alfonso X, ed. C. Rosell, *BAE,* LXVI (Madrid, 1875).

Crónica de San Juan de la Peña, publ. por la Excma Diputación Provincial de Zaragoza (Zaragoza, 1876).

David, C. W. (ed.) *De Expugnatione Lyxbonensi* (New York, 1936).

Delaville le Roulx, J. *Cartulaire général de l'Ordre des Hospitaliers de S. Jean de Jerusalem, 1100–1310,* 4 vols (Paris, 1894–1906).

Desclot, *Chronicle,* trans. F. L. Critchlow, 2 vols (Princeton, 1928–34).

Diego García, *Planeta,* ed. M. Alonso (Madrid, 1943).

Documentos para a história da Cidade de Lisboa: Cabido da Sé; Sumarios de Lousada; Apontamentos das Brandoẽs; Livro dos bens proprios dos Reis e Rainhas, publ. Câmara Municipal (Lisbon, 1954).

Douais, C. *Acta Capitulorum Provincialium Ordinis Fratrum Praedicatorum* (Toulouse, 1894).

'St Raymond de Peñafort et les hérétiques', *Le Moyen Âge,* III (1899), pp. 305–25.

Elze, R. (ed.) *Die Ordines für die Weihe und Krönung des Kaisers und der Kaiserin* [Fontes Germanici Antiqui] (Hanover, 1960).

Erdmann, C. *Papsturkunden in Portugal* (Berlin, 1927).

Fabre, P., and L. Duchesne. (eds.) *Le Liber Censuum de l'Église romaine,* 2 vols (Paris, 1905–52).

Férotin, M. *Recueil des chartes de l'abbaye de Silos* (Paris, 1897).

Finke, H. *Ungedruckte Dominikanerbriefe des XIII Jahrhunderts* (Paderborn, 1891).

Aus den Tagen Bonifaz VIII (Münster-in-W., 1902).

Acta Aragonensia, 3 vols (Berlin, 1908–22).

'Nachträge und Ergänzungen zu den Acta Aragonensia', *SpGG,* IV (1933), pp. 355–536.

Foulché-Delbosc, R. 'Une régle des Dominicains: texte castillan du XIVe siècle', *Rev. Hispanique,* VIII (1901), pp. 504–10.

Friedberg, E. *Corpus Iuris Canonici,* 2 vols (Leipzig, 1879–81).

García Larragueta, S. *El Gran Priorado de Navarra de la Orden de San Juan de Jerusalén,* 2 vols (Pamplona, 1957).

Gesta abbatum monasterii S. Albani, I, ed. H. T. Riley, Rolls Ser. (London, 1867).

Gil de Zamora. *De Preconiis Hispanie,* ed. M. de Castro y Castro (Madrid, 1955).

'Biografías de San Fernando y de Alfonso el Sabio', publ. F. Fita, *BRAH,* V (1884), pp. 308–28.

Giraldus Cambrensis. *De Principis Instructione,* ed. G. F. Warren, Rolls Ser. [Opera, VIII] (London, 1891).

González, Julio. *Alfonso IX,* 2 vols (Madrid, 1944).

Repartimiento de Sevilla, 2 vols (Madrid, 1951).

El reino de Castilla en la época de Alfonso VIII, 3 vols (Madrid, 1960).

González Palencia, A. *Los mozárabes de Toledo en los siglos XII y XIII,* 4 vols (Madrid, 1926–30).

Gonzalo de la Hinojosa. *Continuación de la Crónica de España del arzobispo D. Rodrigo Jiménez de Rada,* ed. Marqués de la Fuensanta del Valle, *CODOIN,* CV–CVI (Madrid, 1893).

Bibliography

Guillaume Anelier de Toulouse. *Histoire de la Guerre de Navarre en 1276 et 1277,* publ. F. Michel (Paris, 1856).

Hahn, S. F. *Collectio monumentorum,* I (Brunswick, 1724).

Höfler, C. (ed.) *Analecten zur Geschichte Deutschlands und Italiens* [Abhandlungen d. III Cl. d. k. Ak. d. Wiss., IV Bd, III Abthl] (Munich, 1846), pp. 18–28.

Jofré de Loaisa. 'Chronique des rois de Castille', ed. A. Morel-Fatio, *BEC,* LIX (1898), pp. 325–78.

Juan Manuel. *Libro de los Estados; Libro Infinido,* ed. P. de Gayangos, *BAE,* LI (Madrid, 1860).

Junyent, E. *Diplomatari de Sant Bernat Calvó, abat de Santas Creus, bisbe de Vich* (Reus, 1956).

Kaltenbrunner, F. *Actenstücke zur Geschichte des deutschen Reiches* [*Mittheilungen aus dem Vaticanischen Archive,* I] (Vienna, 1889).

Kehr, P. *Papsturkunden in Spanien: I. Katalonien* (Berlin, 1926).

Knust, H. *Juan Manuel: El Libro de los Enxiemplos del Conde Lucanor et de Patronio* (Leipzig, 1900).

Lea, H. C. (ed.) *A Formulary of the Papal Penitentiary in the Thirteenth Century* (Philadelphia, 1892).

Leyenda de San Isidro por Juan Diácono, ed. F. Fita, *BRAH,* IX (1886), pp. 97–157.

López Agurleta, J. *Bullarium Equestri Ordinis S. Iacobi de Spatha* (Madrid, 1719).

Lucas of Túy. *Chronicon Mundi,* ed. Schottus, *Hispania Illustrata,* IV (Frankfurt, 1603).

  De altera vita fideique controversiis adversus Albigensium errores libri tres, ed. J. Mariana (Ingolstadt, 1612).

Manning, W. F. (ed.) *The Life of St Dominic in Old French Verse* (Cambridge, Mass., 1944).

Mansi, J. D. *Sacrorum Conciliorum nova et amplissima collectio,* 56 vols (Florence etc., 1759–1927).

Mansilla, D. *La documentación pontificia hasta Inocencio III (965–1216)* (Rome, 1955). *La documentación pontificia de Honorio III (1216–1227)* (Rome, 1965).

Marsilio of Padua. *Defensor Pacis,* ed. R. Scholz [Fontes Iuris Germanici Antiqui] (Hanover, 1932).

Martène, E., and U. Durand. *Thesaurus novus anecdotorum,* 5 vols (Paris, 1717).

Martínez, E. *Colección diplomática del real convento de S. Domingo de Caleruega* (Vergara, 1931).

Matthew Paris. *Chronica Majora,* ed. H. R. Luard, 7 vols, Rolls Ser. (London, 1872–83).

Menéndez Pidal, R. *Documentos lingüísticos de España,* I (Madrid, 1919).

Miedes, Miguel Pérez. *Constitutiones sive Ordinationes Insignis Metropolitanae Ecclesiae Valentinae* (Valencia, 1546).

Monte Pereira, G. (ed.) *Documentos históricos da ciudade de Évora,* I (Evora, 1885).

Nicholas of Curbio. *Vita Innocentii IV* [Archivio della R. Soc. di St Patria, XXI] (Rome, 1890).

Paoli, Cesare, and Enea Piccolomini. (eds.) *Lettere volgari del secolo XIII scritte da Senesi* [Scelta di Curiosità, CXVI (Bologna, 1871)].

Bibliography

Pavo de Figura Seculi, ed. Th. v. Karajan [Denkschriften der kaiserlichen Ak. der Wiss: phil-hist. Cl., II] (Vienna, 1851), pp. 111–17.

Petri de Vineis...Epistolarum libri sex, ed. J. R. Iselius (Basle, 1740).

Poema de Fernán González, ed. C. Carroll Marden (Baltimore, 1904).

*Portugaliae Monumenta Historica...*jussu Academiae Scientiarum Olisponensis edita: *Leges et Consuetudines*, I (Lisbon, 1856).

Powicke, F. M., and C. R. Cheney. *Councils and Synods, with other Documents relating to the English Church*, II, 2 vols (Oxford, 1964).

Ptolemy of Lucca. *Breves Annales*; *Historia Ecclesiastica*, ed. Muratori, *RIS*, XI (Milan, 1727).

Raymond of Peñafort. *Summa de Poenitentia et Matrimonio* (Rome, 1603).

Raynaldi, O. *Annales Ecclesiastici*, ed. Mansi, III (Lucca, 1748).

Reichert, B. M. (ed.) *Acta Capitulorum Generalium Ordinis Praedicatorum*, I [Mon. Ord. Frat. Praed. Hist., I] (Rome, 1898).

Litterae encyclicae... [Mon. Ord. Frat. Praed. Hist., v] (Rome, 1900).

Relatio de Concilio Lugdunensi, ed. L. Weiland, *MGH*, Constitutiones, II (Hanover, 1896).

Ripoll, T. *Bullarium Ordinis Fratrum Praedicatorum*, 8 vols (Rome, 1729–40).

Ríus Serra, J. *Cartulario de San Cugat del Vallés*, 3 vols (Barcelona, 1945–7).

Rationes decimarum Hispaniae (1279–80), 2 vols (Barcelona, 1946–7).

San Raimundo de Penyafort: Diplomatário (Barcelona, 1954).

Robert, U. 'État des monastères espagnols de l'Ordre de Cluny aux XIII–XV siècles, d'après les actes des visites et des chapitres généraux', *BRAH*, XX (1892), pp. 321–430.

Rodericus Toletanus (Rodrigo Jiménez de Rada). *De Rebus Hispaniae*, ed. F. de Lorenzana [Patrum Toletanorum quotquot extant Opera, III] (Madrid, 1793).

Rodrigo y el Rey Fernando, ed. R. Menéndez Pidal, *Reliquias de la poesía épica española* (Madrid, 1951), pp. 257–89.

Rubió i Lluch, A. *Documents per la història de la Cultura catalana mig-eval*, 2 vols (Barcelona, 1908–21).

Rymer, T. *Foedera*, I, i (London, 1816).

Salimbene de Adam. *Cronica*, ed. O. Holder-Egger, *MGH*, Scriptores, XXXII (Hanover–Leipzig, 1905–13).

Sancho IV. *Castigos e documentos para bien vivir, ordenados por...*, ed. A. Rey [Indiana Univ. Publications: Humanities Ser., no. 24] (Bloomington, 1952).

Sicardi episcopi Cremonensis Chronica, ed. O. Holder-Egger, *MGH*, Scriptores, XXXI (Hanover, 1903).

Tangl, M. *Die päpstlichen Kanzleiordnungen v. 1200–1500* (Innsbruck, 1894).

Tejada y Ramiro, J. *Colección de cánones y de todos los concilios de la Iglesia de España y de América*, III, VI (Madrid, 1849, 1862).

Tobella, A. M., and Anscari Mundó. 'Documents del primer segle de la Congregació Claustral (1212–1317)', *Analecta Montserratensia*, X (1964) [= Miscellanea Albareda, II], pp. 399–454.

Torres Fontes, J. *Colección de documentos para la historia del reino de Murcia*: I. *Docu-*

Bibliography

mentos de Alfonso X el Sabio (Murcia, 1963); II. *Documentos del siglo XIII* (Murcia, 1969).

Valladares de Sotomayor, A. (ed.) *Semanario Erudito*, II (Madrid, 1787), XVI–XVII (1789).

Valls i Taberner, 'Diplomatari de San Ramón de Penyafort', *AST*, V (1929), pp. 249–304.

Villanuño, M. de. *Summa Conciliorum Hispaniae ad usque saeculum proxime praeteritum* (Madrid, 1784–5).

Vincke, J. *Documenta selecta mutuas civitatis Arago-Cathalaunicae et ecclesiae relationes illustrantia* (Barcelona, 1936).

Virgil of Córdoba. *Philosophia*, ed. G. Heine [Bibliotheca Anecdotorum seu Veterum Monumentorum Ecclesiasticorum Collectio Novissima, I (Leipzig, 1848), pp. 211–44].

Vita Sancti Raymundi, ed. F. Balme and C. Paban, *Raymundiana* [Mon. Ord. Frat. Praed. Hist., VI, i] (Rome, 1900).

Wadding, L. *Annales Minorum* (Rome, etc., 1731–1933).

Winkelmann, E. *Acta imperii inedita seculi XIII*, I (Innsbruck, 1880).

4. SECONDARY MATERIAL

Abadal, R. d'. *L'Abat Oliba* (Barcelona, 1962).

'La domination carolingienne en Catalogne', *Revue Historique*, CCXXV (1961), pp. 319–40.

'À propos de la "Domination" de la maison comtale de Barcelona sur le Midi français', *Annales du Midi*, LXXVI (1964), pp. 315–45.

Affo, I. *Memorie degli scrittori e letterati Parmigiani*, I (Parma, 1789).

Ajo González de Rapariegos y Sáinz de Zúñiga, C. Ma. *Historia de las universidades hispánicas*, I (Ávila–Madrid, 1957–8).

Alcalde, L. 'El Liber Anniversariorum del antiguo convento de Santa Catalina de Barcelona', *Homenatge a Antoni Rubió i Lluch*, II (Barcelona, 1936), pp. 519–39.

Almeida, F. de. *História da Igreja em Portugal*, I (Coimbra, 1910).

Ibid. [nova edição por Damião Peres, I (Porto, 1967)].

Alonso Alonso, M. 'Bibliotecas medievales de los arzobispos de Toledo', *Razón y Fe*, CXXIII (1941), pp. 295–309.

Altisent, A. 'Una societat mercantil a Catalunya a darreries del segle XII', *BRABL*, XXXII (1967–8), pp. 45–65.

Álvarez Martínez, U. *Historia general, civil y eclesiástica de la Provincia de Zamora* (re-ed., Madrid, 1965).

Amat. *Vida del Illmo Sr D. Felix Amat, arzobispo de Palmyra...*: la publican los testamentarios del Illmo Sr Amat (Madrid, 1835).

Arco, R. del. *El arzobispo don Antonio Agustín: nuevos datos para su biografía* (Tarragona, 1910).

'Vidal de Canellas, obispo de Huesca', *BRABL*, VIII (1915–16), pp. 463–80, 508–21, 545–50.

Bibliography

'El obispo D. Jaime Sarroca, consejero del rey D. Jaime el Conqueridor', *BRABL*, IX (1917), pp. 65–91, 140–67.

'La "Historia eclesiástica de la ciudad de Zaragoza" del Maestro Diego de Espés', *BRAH*, LXXII (1918), pp. 503–22.

'Vidal de Canellas: nuevas noticias', *BRABL*, X (1921), pp. 83–113.

Argáiz, G. de. *La Soledad laureada por San Benito y sus hijos en las iglesias de España, y teatro monástico de la provincia Cartaginense*, II (Madrid, 1675).

Arias, Gino. *Studi e documenti di storia del diritto* (Florence, 1902).

Ariz, Luys de. *Historia de las grandezas de la ciudad de Ávila*, I (Alcalá de Henares, 1607).

Arruego, Juan de. *Catedra episcopal de Zaragoza en el templo de San Salvador...* (Zaragoza, 1653).

Artonne, A. 'Le livre synodal de Lodève', *BEC*, CVIII (1949–50), pp. 36–74.

Auvray, L. 'Une acte de la législation du Cardinal Jean Halgrin en Espagne', *Mélanges d'archéologie et d'histoire*, XVI (1896), pp. 105–9.

Aynsa y de Yriate, F. de. *Fundación, excelencias y cosas memorables de la antiquísima ciudad de Huesca* (Huesca, 1619).

Azcona, T. de. *La elección y reforma del episcopado español en tiempo de los Reyes Católicos* (Madrid, 1960).

Baer, Yitzhak. *A History of the Jews in Christian Spain*, I: trans. L. Schoffman (Philadelphia, 1961).

Baethgen, F. 'Quellen und Untersuchungen zur Geschichte der Päpstlichen hof – und finanzverwaltung unter Bonifaz VIII', *QFIA*, XX (1928–9), pp. 114–237.

Baier, H. *Päpstliche Provisionen für niedere Pfründen bis zum Jahre 1304* [Vorreformationsgeschichtliche Forschungen, Bd 7] (Münster-i.-W., 1911).

Ballesteros y Beretta, A. *Sevilla en el siglo XIII* (Madrid, 1913).

Historia de España y su influencia en la Historia Universal, III (Barcelona, 1923).

Alfonso X el Sabio (Barcelona, 1963).

'Alfonso X de Castilla y la corona de Alemania', *RABM*, XXXIV (1916), pp. 1–23, 187–219.

'Itinerario de Alfonso X, rey de Castilla', *BRAH*, CIV (1934), pp. 49–88, 455–516; CV (1934), pp. 123–80; CVI (1935), pp. 83–150; CVII (1935), pp. 21–76, 381–418; CVIII (1936), pp. 15–42; CIX (1936), pp. 377–460.

'Don Remondo de Losana, obispo de Segovia', *Correo Erudito*, I (1940–1), pp. 313–18.

'La toma de Salé en tiempos de Alfonso X el Sabio', *Al-Andalus*, VIII (1943), pp. 89–128.

'Burgos y la rebelión del Infante Don Sancho', *BRAH*, CXIX (1946), 93–194.

Ballesteros Gaibrois, M. *Don Rodrigo Jiménez de Rada* (Barcelona, 1936).

'Don Rodrigo Ximénez de Rada, coordinador de España', *Príncipe de Viana*, II (1941), pp. 66–73.

Barraclough, G. *Papal Provisions* (Oxford, 1935).

'The Making of a Bishop in the Middle Ages: the Part of the Pope in Law and Fact', *Catholic Historical Review*, XIX (1933–4), pp. 275–319.

Public Notaries and the Papal Curia (London, 1934).

Bibliography

'The Constitution "Execrabilis" of Alexander IV', *EHR*, XLIX (1934), pp. 193–218.

'Bernard of Compostella', *EHR*, XLIX (1934), pp. 487–94.

Bayerri Bertomeu, E. *Historia de Tortosa y su comarca*, VII (Tortosa, 1957).

Bayley, C. C. *The Formation of the German College of Electors in the mid-thirteenth Century* (Toronto, 1949).

'The Diplomatic Preliminaries of the Double Election of 1257 in Germany', *EHR*, LXII (1947), pp. 457–83.

Beer, R. *Die Handschriften des Klosters Santa Maria de Ripoll* [Sitzungsberichte der phil-hist Kl. der kaiserlichen Ak. der Wiss., Bd 158] (Vienna, 1908).

Beltrán de Heredia, V. *Cartulario de la Universidad de Salamanca* (1218–1600), I (Salamanca, 1970).

'La formación intelectual del clero en España', *RET*, VI (1946), pp. 313–57.

Benavides, A. *Memorias de Don Fernando IV de Castilla*, 2 vols (Madrid, 1860).

Benito Ruano, E. *La banca toscana y la Orden de Santiago durante el siglo XIII* (Valladolid, 1961).

'Balduino II de Constantinopla y la Orden de Santiago: un proyecto de defensa del Imperio Latino de Oriente', *Hispania*, XII (1952), pp. 3–36.

'La Iglesia española ante la caída del Imperio Latino de Constantinopla', *HS*, XI (1958), pp. 5–20.

'Deudas y pagos del Maestre de Santiago, Don Pelay Pérez Correa', *Hispania*, XXII (1962), pp. 23–37.

Berganza, F. de. *Antigüedades de España propugnadas en las noticias de sus reyes en la Corónica del Real Monasterio de S. Pedro de Cardeña*, II (Madrid, 1721).

Berlière, U. 'Les chapitres généraux de l'Ordre de S. Benoît', *RB*, XIX (1902), pp. 38–75, 268–78, 374–411.

Bishko, C. J. 'The Cluniac Priories of Galicia and Portugal: their Acquisition and Administration, 1075–c. 1230', *SM*, VII (1965), pp. 305–56.

Blanch, Josep. *Arxiepiscopologi de la Santa Església Metropolitana i Primada de Tarragona*, transcripció i prologació de Joaquim Icart, I (Tarragona, 1951).

Blanco Díez, A. 'Los arcedianos y abades del Cabildo Catedral de Burgos', *BRAH*, CXXX (1952), pp. 267–98.

Boase, T. S. R. *Boniface VIII* (London, 1933).

Bonilla y San Martín, A. *Historia de la filosofía española*, I (Madrid, 1908).

Bourquelot, F. *Études sur les foires de Champagne...aux XIIe, XIIIe et XIVe siècles* [Mémoires présentés par divers savants à l'Académie des Inscriptions et Belles Lettres, 2e série, Antiquités de la France, V], 2 vols (Paris, 1865).

Brentano, Robert. *Two Churches: England and Italy in the thirteenth Century* (Princeton, 1968).

Brooke, C. N. L. 'Gregorian Reform in Action: Clerical Marriage in England, 1050–1200', *Cambridge Historical Journal*, XII (1956), pp. 1–21.

Bujanda, F. *Episcopologio calagurritano* (Logrono, 1944).

Burns, R. I. *The Crusader Kingdom of Valencia: Reconstruction on a thirteenth-century Frontier*, 2 vols (Cambridge, Mass. 1967).

Bibliography

'Journey from Islam: Incipient Cultural Transition in the Conquered Kingdom of Valencia', *Speculum*, XXXV (1960), pp. 337–56.

Burriel, A. M. *Memorias para la vida del Santo Rey Don Fernando III*, dadas a la luz con apéndices y otras ilustraciones por D. Miguel de Manuel Rodríguez (Madrid, 1800). (But cf. above, p. 333.)

Caamaño, C. 'El Fuero romanceado de Palencia', *AHDE*, XI (1934), pp. 503–22.

Calvo, A. *San Pedro de Eslonza* (León, 1957).

Cañizares, B. 'Los grandes pleitos de la iglesia de Lugo: la iglesia de Lugo y la iglesia de León', *BCM Lugo*, II (1946), pp. 137–52.

Cantera, F. 'La Judería de Calahorra', *Sefarad*, XVI (1956), pp. 73–112.

Capdevila, S. *La Seu de Tarragona* (Barcelona, 1935).

'Un concili provincial de Tarragona desconegut', *AST*, II (1926), pp. 495–521.

'Els Franciscans i l'arquebisbe de Tarragona Benet de Rocaberti', *Franciscalia* (Barcelona, 1928), pp. 39–45.

'Col.lecció diplomàtica de l'església de Tarragona en el pontificat d'En Benet de Rocaberti (1251–68)', *BAT*, LII (1952), pp. 182–5.

Capmany y de Montpalau, A. de. *Memorias históricas sobre la marina, comercio y artes de la antigua ciudad de Barcelona*, II (Madrid, 1779).

Cappelletti, G. *Le chiese d'Italia*, 21 vols (Venice, 1844–70).

Carlé, María del Carmen. 'El precio de la vida en Castilla del Rey Sabio al Emplazado', *CHE*, XV (1951), pp. 132–56.

'Mercaderes en Castilla, 1252–1512', *CHE*, XXI–II (1954), pp. 146–328.

Castejón y Fonseca, D. *Primacía de la iglesia de Toledo* (Madrid, 1645).

Castell Maiques, V. 'Hispano de Massas: un obispo desconocido de Olorón, Francia (h. 1237–1244)', *AA*, XIV (1966), pp. 11–64.

Castillo, Hernando de. *Primera Parte de la historia general de Sancto Domingo y de su Orden de Predicadores* (Madrid, 1584).

Castro, Américo. *The Structure of Spanish History*, trans. E. L. King (Princeton, 1954).

'Unos aranceles de aduanas del siglo XIII', *Rev. Filología Española*, VIII (1921), pp. 1–29.

Cedillo, Conde de. *See* López de Ayala.

Cerchiari, E. *Capellani papae et apostolicae sedis auditores causarum sacri palatii apostolici*, II (Rome, 1920).

Chabas, R. 'Çeid abu Çeid', *El Archivo*, V (1891), pp. 143–66, 283–304, 362–76; VI (1892), pp. 407–9.

Chaytor, H. J. *A History of Aragon and Catalonia* (London, 1933).

Cheney, C. R. *English Synodalia of the thirteenth Century* (Oxford, 1941).

'The Earliest English Diocesan Statutes', *EHR*, LXXV (1960), pp. 1–29.

See also sec. 3, Powicke.

Chiaudano, M. 'I Rothschild del Duecento: la gran tavola di Orlando Bonsignori', *Bullettino Senese di St. Patria*, n.s., VI (1935), pp. 103–42.

Chiffletius, J. J. *Vindiciae Hispaniae* (Antwerp, 1645).

Cocheril, M. *Études sur le monachisme en Espagne et au Portugal* (Lisbon, 1966).

'L'Ordre de Cîteaux au Portugal: le problème historique', *SM*, I (1959), pp. 51–96.

Bibliography

'L'implantation des abbayes cisterciennes dans la péninsule ibérique', *AEM*, I (1964), pp. 217–87.

C(ollantes) de T(erán), F(rancisco). 'Noticias y documentos para la historia de la Catedral de Sevilla', *Archivo Hispalense*, IV (1888), pp. 39–42.

Colmeiro, M. *Historia de la economía política en España*, ed. G. Anes Álvarez (Madrid, 1965).

Colmenares, D. de. *Historia de la insigne ciudad de Segovia y compendio de las historias de Castilla* (Segovia, 1637).

Cuervo, J. *Historiadores del convento de San Esteban de Salamanca*, 3 vols (Salamanca, 1914–16).

Cunha, Rodrigo da. *Catálogo e história dos bispos do Porto* (Porto, 1623).

História ecclesiástica dos arcebispos de Braga, II (Braga, 1635).

História ecclesiástica da igreja de Lisboa, I (Lisboa, 1642).

Daumet, G. *Mémoire sur les relations de la France et de la Castille de 1255 à 1320* (Paris, 1913).

'Les testaments d'Alphonse X le Savant', *BEC*, LXVII (1906), pp. 70–99.

David, P. *Études historiques sur la Galice et le Portugal du VIe au XIIe siècle* (Lisbon–Paris, 1947).

Davis, G. 'The Development of a National Theme in Medieval Castilian Literature', *Hispanic Review*, III (1935), pp. 149–61.

Deeley, A. 'Papal Provisions and the Royal Rights of Patronage in the early fourteenth century', *EHR*, XLIII (1928), pp. 497–527.

Defer, E. *Histoire de l'abbaye de St-Martin-ès-Aires* (Troyes, 1875).

Defourneaux, M. *Les Français en Espagne aux XIe et XIIe siècles* (Paris, 1949).

Denifle, H. 'Assignationen und Austausch der Bücher im Kloster zu Barcelona nach der Mitte des 13 Jahrhunderts', *ALKG*, II (1886), pp. 202–3, 241–8.

Devic, C., and J. Vaissete. *Histoire générale de Languedoc*, VIII (Toulouse, 1879).

Deyermond, A. D. *Epic Poetry and the Clergy: Studies on the 'Mocedades de Rodrigo'* (London, 1969).

'La decadencia de la epopeya española: "Las Mocedades de Rodrigo"', *AEM*, I (1964), pp. 607–17.

Diago, F. de. *Historia de la Provincia de Aragón de la Orden de Predicadores* (Barcelona, 1599).

Anales del reyno de Valencia, I (Valencia, 1613).

Digard, G. *Philippe le Bel et le Saint-Siège de 1285 à 1304*, I (Paris, 1936).

Dondaine, A. 'Le Manuel de l'Inquisiteur (1230–1330)', *AFP*, XVI (1946), pp. 85–194.

Dorado, B. *Compendio histórico de la ciudad de Salamanca* (Salamanca, 1776).

Dufourcq, C.-E. *L'Espagne catalane et le Maghrib aux XIIIe et XIVe siècles* (Paris, 1966).

'La question de Ceuta au XIIIe siècle', *Hespéris*, XLII (1955), pp. 67–127.

'Un projet castillan du XIIIe siècle: la Croisade d'Afrique', *Revue d'histoire et de civilisation du Maghreb*, I (1966), pp. 27–51.

Durán Gudiol, A. 'El derecho capitular de la Catedral de Huesca desde el siglo XII al XIV', *REDC*, VII (1952), pp. 447–515.

349

Bibliography

'Un viaje por la diócesis de Huesca en el año 1338', *Argensola*, VII (1956), pp. 367–72.

'García de Gudal, obispo de Huesca y Jaca (1201–36)', *HS*, XII (1959), pp. 291–331.

Duro Peña, E. 'Los códices de la Catedral de Orense', *HS*, XIV (1961), pp. 185–212.

'Las dignidades de la Catedral de Orense', *AEM*, I (1964), pp. 289–332.

Ehrle, F. 'Zur Geschichte des Schatzes der Bibliothek und des Archivs der Päpste im vierzehnten Jahrhundert', *ALKG*, I (1885), pp. 1–48, 228–364.

Elliott, J. H. 'Revolution and Continuity in Early Modern Europe', *Past and Present*, XLII (1969), pp. 35–56.

Engels, O. 'Die weltliche Herrschaft des Bischofs von Ausona–Vich (889–1315)', *SpGG*, XXIV (1968), pp. 1–40.

Escagüés Javierre, I. 'Catálogo de los libros existentes en dos bibliotecas del siglo XIII', *Rev. Bibliografía Nacional*, VI (1945), pp. 195–209.

Escalona, R. *Historia del Real Monasterio de Sahagún* (Madrid, 1782).

E(scudero) de la P(eña), J. M. 'Variedades', *RABM*, II (1872), pp. 58–60.

España Sagrada. See Flórez, E.

Espejo, C., and J. Paz. *Las antiguas ferias de Medina del Campo* (Valladolid, 1908).

Esperança, M. de. *História seráfica da Ordem dos Frades Menores de S. Francisco na Provincia de Portugal*, I (Lisbon, 1656).

Estella Zalaya, E. *El fundador de la Catedral de Toledo: estudio histórico del pontificado de D. Rodrigo Ximénez de Rada* (Toledo, 1926).

Eubel, C. 'Der Registerband des Cardinalgrosspönitentiars Bentevenga', *Archiv für kath. Kirchenrecht*, LXIV (1890), pp. 3–69.

'Die Bischöfe, Cardinäle und Päpste aus dem Minoritenorden', *RQ*, IV (1890), pp. 185–258.

Eydoux, H.-P. 'L'abbatiale de Moreruela et l'architecture des églises cisterciennes en Espagne', *Cîteaux in de Nederlanden*, V (1954), pp. 173–207.

Fabre, P. 'La perception du Cens Apostolique dans l'Italie Centrale en 1291', *Mélanges d'archéologie et d'histoire*, X (1890), pp. 369–83.

Fanta, A. 'Ein Bericht über die Ansprüche des Königs Alfonsos auf den deutschen Thron', *MIöG*, VI (1885), pp. 94–104.

Feio, A. 'Um ignorado concílio provincial Bracarense (1261)', *RPH*, I (1941), pp. 141–3.

Felíu, Ll. 'Diplomatari de Sant Ramon de Penyafort: nous documents', *AST*, VIII (1932), pp. 101–16.

Feret, P. *La faculté de théologie de Paris*, I (Paris, 1894).

Fernández, A. *Historia y anales de la ciudad y obispado de Plasencia* (Madrid, 1627).

Fernández, L. 'La Abadía de S. María de Benevivere durante la Edad Media', *Miscelánea Comillas*, XXXVII (1962), pp. 9–254.

Fernández Catón, J. M. 'El cardenal leonés: Pelayo Albanense (1206–1230)', *Archivos Leoneses*, VII (1953), pp. 97–113.

Fernández de Madrid, A. *Silva Palentina*, I, anotada por M. Vielva Ramos (Palencia, 1932).

Fernández del Pulgar, P. *Historia secular y eclesiástica de Palencia*, 3 vols (Madrid, 1679–80).

Bibliography

Ferreira, J. A. *Fastos episcopaes da Igreja Primacial de Braga*, I–II (Famalicão, 1928–31).

Ferrer Flórez, M. 'Mallorca y la teocracía pontificia', *AST*, XXIII (1950), pp. 15–30.

Finistres y de Monsalvo, J. *Historia del Real Monasterio de Poblet*, II (Cervera, 1753: 2nd ed. Barcelona, 1948).

Finke, H. *Konzilienstudien zur Geschichte des XIII Jahrhunderts* (Münster-i.-W., 1891). *See also* Gaibrois de Ballesteros, *and* Jaffé.

Fita, F. *Actas inéditas de siete concilios españoles celebrados desde el año 1282 hasta el de 1314* (Madrid, 1882).

'La Catedral de Murcia en 1291', *BRAH*, III (1883), pp. 268–75.

'Testamento del rey Don Alfonso VIII (8 diciembre 1204)', *BRAH*, VIII (1886), pp. 229–48.

'Madrid desde el año 1228 hasta el de 1234', *BRAH*, VIII (1886), pp. 399–424.

'Concilio de Alcalá de Henares (15 enero 1257)', *BRAH*, X (1887), pp. 151–9.

'Once bulas de Bonifacio VIII inéditas, y biográficas de San Pedro Pascual, obispo de Jaén y mártir', *BRAH*, XX (1892), pp. 32–61.

'Inscripciones toledanas inéditas del siglo XIII', *BRAH*, XX (1892), pp. 449–62.

'Concilios españoles inéditos: provincial de Braga en 1261 y nacional de Sevilla en 1478', *BRAH*, XXII (1893), pp. 209–56.

'El Concilio de Lérida en 1193 y S. María la Real de Nájera: bulas inéditas de Celestino III, Inocencio III y Honorio III', *BRAH*, XXVI (1895), pp. 332–83.

'Fundación y primer periodo del monasterio de S. Clara de Barcelona. Bulas inéditas', *BRAH*, XXVII (1895), pp. 273–314, 436–89.

'Doce bulas inéditas', *BRAH*, XXIX (1896), pp. 94–117.

'Patrologia latina', *BRAH*, XXXIX (1901), pp. 524–30.

'Don Pedro de Albalat, arzobispo de Tarragona, y Don Ferrer Pallarés, obispo de Valencia. Cuestiones cronológicas', *BRAH*, XL (1902), pp. 335–52.

'Concilios tarraconenses en 1248, 1249 y 1250', *BRAH*, XL (1902), pp. 444–58.

'Santiago de Galicia: nuevas impugnaciones y nueva defensa', *Razón y Fe*, II (1902), pp. 35–45, 178–95; III (1902), pp. 49–61.

'Concilio nacional de Burgos (18 febrero 1117)', *BRAH*, XLVIII (1906), pp. 387–407.

See also López Ferreiro.

Fleckenstein, J. 'Heinrich IV. und der deutsche Episkopat', in *Adel und Kirche* (*Festschrift für Gerd Tellenbach*) (Freiburg–Basle–Vienna, 1968), pp. 221–36.

Fliche, A. *La réforme grégorienne*, I (Paris, 1924).

Flórez, E., and M. Risco, *et al*. *España Sagrada*, 51 vols (Madrid, 1747–1879).

Folz, R. *L'idée d'empire en Occident du Ve au XIVe siècle* (Paris, 1953).

Font y Ríus, J. M. 'La reconquista y repoblación de Levante y Murcia', in *La Reconquista española y la repoblación del país* (Zaragoza, 1951), pp. 85–126.

'Les villes dans l'Espagne du Moyen Âge', *Recueils de la Société Jean Bodin*, VI (1954), 263–95.

Foreville, R. 'L'iconographie du XIIe Concile Oecuménique: Latran IV (1215)', *Mélanges offerts à René Crozet* (Poitiers, 1966), pp. 1121–30.

Fournier, P. 'Le cardinal Guillaume de Peyre de Godin', *BEC*, LXXXVI (1925), pp. 100–21.

Bibliography

Frizon, P. *Gallia Purpurata* (Paris, 1638).

Gaibrois de Ballesteros, M. *Historia del reinado de Sancho IV de Castilla*, 3 vols (Madrid, 1922–8).

'Tarifa y la política de Sancho IV de Castilla', *BRAH*, LXXIV (1919), pp. 418–36, 521–9; LXXV (1919), pp. 349–55; LXXVI (1920), pp. 53–77, 123–60, 420–48; LXXVII (1920), pp. 192–215.

(with H. Finke) 'Roma después de la muerte de Bonifacio VIII', *BRAH*, LXXXIV (1924), pp. 351–6, 435–8.

'Fray Munio de Zamora' in *Finke Festschrift* [Vorreformationsgeschichtliche Forschungen] (Münster-i.-W., 1925), pp. 127–46.

Gaiffier, B. de. 'Sainte Ide de Boulogne et l'Espagne, à propos de reliques matériales', *Analecta Bollandiana*, LXXXVI (1968), pp. 67–81.

Gallardo Fernández, F. *Origen, progresos y estado de las rentas de la Corona de España, su gobierno y administración*, III (Madrid, 1805).

Gams, P. B. *Die Kirchengeschichte von Spanien*, III, i (Regensberg, 1876).

García y García, A. *Laurentius Hispanus* (Rome–Madrid, 1956).

'Nuevas decretales de Gregorio IX en la Biblioteca del Cabildo de Córdoba', *REDC*, XV (1960), pp. 147–52.

'Los manuscritos del Decreto de Graciano en las bibliotecas y archivos de España', *Studia Gratiana*, VIII (1962), pp. 159–94.

'Valor y proyección histórica de la obra jurídica de S. Raimundo de Peñafort', *REDC*, XVIII (1963), pp. 233–51.

'La canonística ibérica medieval posterior al Decreto de Graciano', in *Repertorio de Historia de las Ciencias Eclesiásticas*, I: siglos III–XVI (Salamanca, 1967), pp. 397–434.

García Gómez, E. 'El conde mozárabe Sisnando Davídiz y la política de Alfonso VI con los taifas', *Al-Andalus*, XII (1947), 27–33.

García Rámila, I. 'Ordenamientos de Posturas, y otros capitulos generales otorgados a la ciudad de Burgos por el rey Alfonso X', *Hispania*, V (1945), pp. 179–235, 385–439, 605–50.

Garganta, J. M. de. 'Un obituario del convento de S. Domingo de Gerona', *AIEG*, VI (1951), pp. 137–78.

Geanakoplos, D. J. *The Emperor Michael Palaeologus and the West, 1258–1282* (Cambridge, Mass., 1959).

Ghedira, A. 'Un traité inédit d'Ibn al-Abbār', *Al-Andalus*, XXII (1957), pp. 31–54.

Gil Farrés, O. *Historia de la moneda española* (Madrid, 1959).

Giménez y Martínez de Carvajal, J. 'El Decreto y las Decretales, fuentes de la Primera Partida de Alfonso el Sabio', *AA*, II (1954), pp. 239–348.

'San Raimundo de Peñafort y las Partidas de Alfonso X el Sabio', *AA*, III (1955), 201–338.

Giménez Soler, A. *Don Juan Manual* (Zaragoza, 1932).

Girona Llagostera, D. 'Mullerament del Infant En Pere de Catalunya ab Madona Constança de Sicilia', I. *CHCA* (1909), pp. 232–99.

Giudice, G. del. *Don Arrigo Infante di Castiglia* (Naples, 1875).

Giunta, F. 'Federico II e Ferdinando III di Castiglia' in *Studies in Italian Medieval*

Bibliography

History pres. to Miss E. M. Jamison, eds. Philip Grierson and John Ward Perkins [Papers of the British School at Rome, xxiv (n.s., xi)] (London, 1956), pp. 137–41.

Glorieux, P. *La littérature quodlibetique, 1260–1320* [*Bibliothèque Thomiste*, v (1925)].

Répertoire des maîtres en théologie de Paris au XIIIe siècle, i (Paris, 1933).

Göller, E. *Die Einnahmen der Apostolischen Kammer unter Johann XXII* (Paderborn, 1910).

'Zur Geschichte des zweiten Lyoner Konzils und des Liber Sextus', *RQ*, xx (1906), pp. 81–7.

Golubovich, G. *Biblioteca bio-bibliografica della Terra Santa e dell' Oriente Francescano*, 5 vols (Florence, 1906–23).

Gómez Bravo, J. *Catálogo de los obispos de Córdoba*, i (Córdoba, 1778).

Goñi Gaztambide, J. *Historia de la Bula de la Cruzada en España* (Vitoria, 1958).

'La Santa Sede y la Reconquista del reino de Granada', *HS*, iv (1951), pp. 43–80.

'Bula de Juan XXII sobre reforma del episcopado castellano', *HS*, viii (1955), pp. 409–13.

'Los obispos de Pamplona del siglo XIII', *Príncipe de Viana*, xviii (1957), pp. 41–237.

'El fiscalismo pontificio en España en tiempo de Juan XXII', *AA*, xiv (1966), 65–99.

Gonzaga de Azevedo, L. *História de Portugal*, iv (Lisbon, 1942).

González, Julio. 'El deán de Santiago, Don Fernando Alfonso, y su hijo Don Juan', *Correo Erudito*, iii (1942), pp. 194–204.

'Repoblación de la "Extremadura" leonesa', *Hispania*, iii (1943), pp. 195–273.

'La clerecía de Salamanca durante le Edad Media', *Hispania*, iii (1943), pp. 409–30.

'Reconquista y repoblación de Castilla, León, Extremadura y Andalucía (siglos XI al XIII)', in *La Reconquista española y la repoblación del país* (Zaragoza, 1951), pp. 163–206.

González Davila, G. *Historia de las antigüedades de Salamanca* (Salamanca, 1606).

Teatro eclesiástico de las iglesias metropolitanas y catedrales de los reinos de las dos Castilla, i–iii (Madrid, 1645–50).

González Texada, J. *Historia de Santo Domingo de la Calzada* (Madrid, 1702).

Gorosterratzu, J. *Don Rodrigo Jiménez de Rada, gran estadista, escritor y prelado* (Pamplona, 1925).

Gottlob, A. *Aus der Camera Apostolica des 15. Jahrhunderts* (Innsbruck, 1889).

Grauert, H. *Magister Heinrich der Poet in Wurzburg und die römische Kurie* [Abhandlungen der königlich bayerischen Ak. der Wiss., phil-hist. Kl., Bd 27] (Munich, 1912).

Gutiérrez, B. *Historia del estado presente y antiguo de la mui noble y mui leal ciudad de Xerex de la Frontera*, ii (Jerez, 1887).

Guzmán y Gallo, J. P. 'La princesa Cristina de Norvega y el Infante Don Felipe', *BRAH*, lxxiv (1919), pp. 39–65.

Haller, J. 'Die Verteilung der "Servitia Minuta" und die Obligation der Praelaten im 13. und 14. Jahrhundert', *QFIA*, i (1898), pp. 281–95.

Haskins, C. H. *Studies in the History of Medieval Science* (Cambridge, Mass., 1927).

Bibliography

Hauréau, B. *Notices et extraits de quelques manuscrits latins de la Bibliothèque Nationale,* I–IV (Paris, 1890–3).

Heckel, R. von. 'Das Aufkommen der ständigen Prokuratoren an der päpstlichen Kurie im 13. Jahrhundert', *Studi e Testi,* xxxvIII [Miscellanea F. Ehrle, II] (1924), pp. 290–321.

Hefele, J. (trans. H. Leclercq). *Histoire des conciles d'après les documents originaux,* v, I–vI, I (Paris, 1912–14).

Heller, E. 'Der kuriale Geschäftsgang in den Briefen des Thomas von Capua', *Archiv für Urkundenforschung,* xIII (1933–5), pp. 197–318.

Herculano, A. *História de Portugal desde o começo da monarquia até o fim do reinado de D. Afonso III,* 8 vols, 9th ed, (Lisbon, n.d.)

Herde, P. *Beiträge zum päpstlichen Kanzlei und Urkundenwesen im 13. Jahrhundert* (Kallmünz, 1961).

'Ein Formelbuch Gerhards von Parma mit Urkunden des Auditor Litterarum Contradictarum aus dem Jahre 1277', *Archiv für Diplomatik,* xIII (1967), pp. 225–312.

Hergueta, N. 'Apuntes para la biografía de D. Martín García, o González, secretario de D. Sancho el Bravo y obispo de Calahorra y Astorga', *RABM,* IX (1903), pp. 328–38.

'Noticias históricas de D. Jerónimo Aznar, obispo de Calahorra, y de su notable documento geográfico de siglo XIII', *RABM,* xVII (1907), pp. 411–32; xVIII (1908), pp. 37–59; xIX (1908), pp. 402–16; xx (1909), pp. 98–116.

Herlihy, D. *Pisa in the Early Renaissance* (New Haven, 1958).

Medieval and Renaissance Pistoia (New Haven, 1967).

Hernández Parrales, A. 'El Infante Don Felipe primer arzobispo electo de Sevilla', *Archivo Hispalense,* xxxI (1959), pp. 195–204.

Herriot, J. H. 'A thirteenth-century Manuscript of the Primera Partida', *Speculum,* xIII (1938), pp. 278–94.

'The Validity of the Printed Editions of the Primera Partida', *Romance Philology,* v (1951–2), pp. 165–74.

Highfield, J. R. L. 'The English Hierarchy in the Reign of Edward III', *TRHS,* 5th ser., vI (1956), pp. 115–38.

Higounet, Ch. 'Mouvements de population dans le Midi de la France du XIe au XVe siècle', *Annales-Économies-Sociétés-Civilisations,* vIII (1953), pp. 1–24.

Hirsch, B. 'Zur "Noticia Seculi" und zum "Pavo"', *MIöG,* xxxvIII (1918–20), pp. 571–610; xL (1924–5), pp. 317–35.

Histoire littéraire de la France …par des membres de l'Institut, xVIII (Paris, 1835)

Hoberg, H. *Taxae pro communibus servitiis ex libris obligationum ab anno 1295 usque ad annum 1455 confectis* [*Studi e Testi,* cxLIV (1949)].

Hoyos, M. Ma de los. 'Convento de San Pablo de Burgos', *BIFG,* xLIII (1964), pp. 182–90.

Huesca, Ramón de. *Teatro histórico de las iglesias del reyno de Aragón,* vI, vIII (Pamplona, 1796, 1802).

Hüffer, H. J. 'Die leonesischen Hegemoniebestrebungen und Kaisertitel', *SpGG,* III (1931), pp. 337–84.

Bibliography

Huidobro y Serna, L. 'Burgos en la conquista de Sevilla', *BIFG*, xxxi (1952), pp. 51–5, 99–108.

Huillard-Bréholles, J. L. A. *Historia diplomatica Friderici Secundi* (Paris, 1852–61).

Incarnatione, Thomas ab. *Historia ecclesiae Lusitanae*, iv (Coimbra, 1763).

Irurita Lusarreta, M. A. *El Municipio de Pamplona en la Edad Media* (Pamplona, 1959).

Jaffé, E., and H. Finke. 'La dispensa de matrimonio falsificada para el rey Sancho IV y María de Molina', *AHDE*, iii (1927), pp. 298–318.

Janauschek, L. *Originum Cisterciensium*... *tomus* i (Vienna, 1877).

Jimeno, E. 'La población de Soria y su término en 1270', *BRAH*, cxlii (1958), pp. 207–74, 365–494.

Jordan, E. *De mercatoribus camere apostolicae saec. XIII* (Rennes, 1909).

Junyent, E. 'Un importante legado de libros en el siglo XIII', *HS* ii (1949), pp. 425–9.

'El necrologio del monasterio de San Juan de las Abadesas', *AST*, xxiii (1950), pp. 131–91.

'Lista de las parroquias del obispado de Vich según la visita pastoral del obispo Galcerán Sacosta (1330–39)', in *Miscelánea filológica dedicada a Mons. A. Griera*, i (Barcelona, 1955), pp. 369–89.

Kaepelli, T. 'Dominicana Barcinonensia', *AFP*, xxxvii (1967), pp. 47–118.

Kay, Richard, 'A Critique of the Conciliar Collections', *Catholic Historical Review*, lii (1966–7), pp. 155–85.

Kirsch, J. P. *Die Finanzverwaltung des Kardinalkollegiums im XIII. und XIV. Jahrhundert* (Münster-i.-W., 1895).

Kleffens, E. N. van. *Hispanic Law until the End of the Middle Ages* (Edinburgh, 1968).

Klüpfel, L. *Die äussere Politik Alfonsos III von Aragonien* [Abhandlungen z. mittleren u. neueren Gesch., Heft 35] (Berlin, 1911–12).

Kuttner, S. *Repertorium der Kanonistik (1140–1243)* (Vatican City, 1937).

'The Barcelona Edition of St Raymond's first Treatise on Canon Law', *Seminar*, viii (1952), pp. 52–67.

'Zur Entstehungsgeschichte der "Summa de Casibus Poenitentiae" des hl. Raymund von Penyafort', *ZSSR*, LXX, iii (*kan. Abt.*, xxxix, 1953), pp. 419–34.

(with A. García y García) 'A New Eyewitness Account of the Fourth Lateran Council', *Traditio*, xx (1964), pp. 115–78.

'Wo war Vincentius Hispanus Bischof?', *Traditio*, xxii (1966), pp. 471–4.

Lacarra, J. M. 'La restauración eclesiástica en las tierras conquistadas por Alfonso el Batallador (1118–34)', *RPH*, iv (1949), pp. 263–86.

'Les villes-frontières dans l'Espagne des XIe et XIIe siècles', *Le Moyen Âge*, lxix (1963), pp. 205–22.

Lafuente, V. de. *Historia eclesiástica de España,* iv, 2nd ed. (Madrid, 1873).

'Archivos de Tarazona, Veruela, Alfaro, Tudela, Calatayud y Borja', *BRAH*, xxiv (1894), pp. 209–15.

Lambert, E. *L'art gothique en Espagne aux XIIe et XIIIe siècles* (Paris, 1931).

Laurent, M. H. *Le bienheureux Innocent V – Pierre de Tarentaise – et son temps* [*Studi e Testi*, cxxixx (1947)]

Bibliography

Lea, H. C. *An Historical Sketch of Sacerdotal Celibacy in the Christian Church* (Boston, 1884).

A History of the Inquisition in the Middle Ages, II (London, 1888)

Lecoy de la Marche, A. *La chaire française au moyen Âge* (Paris, 1886).

Lecuona, M. de 'Los sucesos calceatenses de 1224–1234', *Scriptorium Victoriense*, I (1954), pp. 134–46.

Lewis, A. R. 'The Closing of the Mediaeval Frontier, 1250–1350', *Speculum*, XXXIII (1958), pp. 475–83.

Linehan, P. A. 'Documento español sobre la Quinta Cruzada', *HS*, XX (1967), pp. 177–82.

'Pedro de Albalat, arzobispo de Tarragona, y su "Summa Septem Sacramentorum", *HS*, XXII (1969), pp. 9–30.

'The *Gravamina* of the Castilian Church in 1262–3', *EHR*, LXXXV (1970), pp. 730–54.

'Councils and Synods in thirteenth-century Castile and Aragon', in *Studies in Church History*, VII, ed. G. J. Cuming (Cambridge, 1971), pp. 101–11.

'La carrera del obispo Abril de Urgel: la Iglesia española en el siglo XIII', *AEM*, forthcoming.

'*Ecclesie non Mittentes*: the thirteenth-century Background', in *Studia Albornotiana*, II, forthcoming.

Livermore, H. *A History of Portugal* (Cambridge, 1947).

Lladonosa Pujol, J. 'Proyección urbana de Lérida durante el reino de Alfonso el Casto', VII. *CHCA* (1962), II, 195–205.

Llorente, J. A. *Historia de la Inquisición en España*, I (Barcelona, 1870).

Lognon, A. *La formation de l'unité française* (Paris, 1922).

Lomax, D. W. *La Orden de Santiago (1170–1275)* (Madrid, 1965).

'The Order of Santiago and the Kings of León', *Hispania*, XVIII (1958), pp. 3–37.

'El arzobispo Don Rodrigo Jiménez de Rada y la Orden de Santiago', *Hispania*, XIX (1959), pp. 323–65.

'The Authorship of the *Chronique Latine des Rois de Castile*,' *BHS*, XL (1963), pp. 205–11.

'Don Ramón, Bishop of Palencia (1148–84)' in *Homenaje a Jaime Vicens Vives*, I (Barcelona, 1965), pp. 279–91.

Loperráez, J. *Descripción historica del obispado de Osma*, 3 vols (Madrid, 1788).

López, A. *La provincia franciscana de España de los Frailes Menores* (Santiago de Compostela, 1915).

Estudios crítico-históricos de Galicia (Santiago de Compostela, 1916).

Memoria histórica de los obispos de Marruecos desde el siglo XIII (Madrid, 1920).

'Confessores de la familia real de Castilla', *AIA*, XXXI (1929), pp. 5–75.

'Fr. Valasco, nuncio apostólico en los reinos de España y Portugal, y obispo de Idanha o Guarda', *Biblos*, XVIII (1942), pp. 249–58.

López, J. *Tercera parte de la historia general de Sancto Domingo y de su Orden de Predicadores* (Valladolid, 1613).

López-Arévalo, J. R. *Un cabildo catedral de la Vieja Castilla: Ávila: su estructura jurídica, siglos XIII–XX* (Madrid, 1966).

Bibliography

López de Ayala Álvarez de Toledo y del Hierro, J. (Conde de Cedillo). *Contribuciones é impuestos en León y Castilla durante la Edad Media* (Madrid, 1896).

López Ferreiro, A. *Historia de la santa iglesia de Santiago de Compostela,* v (Santiago de Compostela, 1902).

(and F. Fita) *Monumentos antiguos de la iglesia compostelana* (Madrid, 1882).

López de Meneses, A. 'Documentos acerca de la Peste Negra en los dominios de la Corona de Aragón', *Estudios de Edad Media de la Corona de Aragón,* vi (1956), pp. 291–447.

Luchaire, A. 'Un document retrouvé', *Journal des Savants,* iii (1905), pp. 557–68.

Lunt, W. E. *Financial Relations of the Papacy with England to 1327* (Cambridge, Mass., 1939).

Luquet, G. H. 'Hermann l'Allemand', *Revue de l'histoire de religions,* xliv (1901), pp. 407–22.

Macedo, A. de. *Lusitania Infulata et Purpurata* (Paris, 1663).

Maisonneuve, H. *Études sur les origines de l'Inquisition,* 2nd ed., (Paris, 1960).

Manning, W. F. 'An Old Spanish Life of St Dominic: Sources and Date', in *Mediaeval Studies in Honor of J. D. M. Ford* (Cambridge, Mass., 1948), pp. 139–58.

Manrique, A. *Cisterciensium... Annalium...* tomus iv (Lyons, 1659).

Mansilla, D. *Iglesia castellano-leonesa y Curia Romana en los tiempos del Rey San Fernando* (Madrid, 1945).

'Episcopologio de Burgos en el siglo XIII', *HS,* iv (1951), pp. 313–34.

'El cardenal hispano Pelayo Gaitán', *AA,* i (1953), pp. 11–66.

'El cardenal Petrus Hispanus, obispo de Burgos, 1300–1303', *HS,* ix (1956), pp. 244–80.

'Creación de los obispados de Cádiz y Algerciras', *HS,* x (1957), pp. 243–71.

'Formación de la provincia bracarense después de la invasion árabe', *HS,* xiv (1961), pp. 1–21.

Maravall, J. A. *El concepto de España en la Edad Media,* 2nd ed. (Madrid, 1964).

'La idea de Reconquista en España durante la Edad Media', in *Estudios sobre Historia de España,* ed. M. Fernández Álvarez [El Legado de la Historia, 4] (Madrid, 1965), pp. 177–212.

Marca, P. de. *De primatibus,* in *Dissertationes tres...* Stephanus Baluzius collegit (Paris, 1669).

Marca hispanica sive limes hispanicus (Paris, 1688).

Marcos Pous, A. 'Los dos matrimonios de Sancho IV de Castilla', *CTEER,* viii (1956), pp. 7–108.

Mariana, J. de. *De Rebus Hispaniae,* i (Mainz, 1605).

Martorell, F. 'Fragmentos inéditos de la " Ordinatio Ecclesiae Valentinae "', *CTEER,* i (1912), pp. 81–127.

Matute y Gavira, J. (and J. Hazañas y la Rúa). 'Memorias de los obispos de Marruecos y demás auxiliares de Sevilla', *Archivo Hispalense,* i (1886), pp. 121–8, 197–212, 225–40, 273–89.

Maubach, J. *Die Kardinäle und ihre Politik um die Mitte des 13. Jahrhunderts* (Bonn, 1902).

357

Bibliography

Meireles, A. da Assunção. *Memórias do mosterio de Pombeiro*, publ. A. Baião (Lisbon, 1942).

Menéndez y Pelayo, M. *Historia de los heterodoxos españoles*, ed. Biblioteca de Autores Cristianos, 2 vols (Madrid, 1956).

'El siglo XIII y San Fernando', in *Estudios y discursos de crítica histórica y literaria*, VII [Ed. Nacional...*Obras Completas*, XII (Santander, 1942)], pp. 47–61.

Menéndez Pidal, R. *Crónicas generales de España* (Madrid, 1918).

El Imperio Hispánico y los Cinco Reinos (Madrid, 1950).

'Sicilia y España ante de las Visperas Sicilianas', *Bollettino Centro di studi Filologici e linguistici Siciliani*, III (1955), pp. 5–14.

See also section 3, *Rodrigo y el Rey Fernando*.

Mercati, A. *Saggi di storia e letteratura*, I (Rome, 1951).

'Frammento di un registro di Nicolo IV', *Bullettino dell' Istituto Italiano e Archivo Muratoriano*, XLVI (1931), pp. 109–28.

Merêa, P. 'Domingos Domingues, canonista português do século XIII', *Boletim da Faculdade de Direito: Universidade de Coimbra*, XLIII (1967), pp. 163–9.

Michaud Quantin, P. 'Deux formulaires pour la confession du milieu du XIIIe siècle', *RTAM*, XXXI (1964), pp. 43–62.

Millares Carlo, A. 'La cancillería real en León y Castilla hasta fines del reinado de Fernando III', *AHDE*, III (1926), pp. 227–306.

Minguella y Arnedo, T. *Historia de la diócesis de Sigüenza y de sus obispos*, 3 vols (Madrid, 1901–13).

Miret y Sans, J. *Investigación histórica sobre el vizcondado de Castellbó* (Barcelona, 1900).
Itinerari de Jaime I 'el Conqueridor' (Barcelona, 1908).

Moncada, J. L. *Episcopologio de la iglesia de Vich*, ed. J. Collell, I–II (Vich, 1891–4).

Mondéjar, Marqués de. *Memorias históricas del rei Don Alfonso el Sabio* (Madrid, 1777).

Morel-Fatio, A. 'Textes castillans inédits du XIIIe siècle', *Romania*, XVI (1887), pp. 364–82.

Morera Llauradó, E. *Tarragona cristiana*, II (Tarragona, 1899).

Moret, J. de. *Annales del reyno de Navarra*, III (Pamplona, 1704).

Mortier, D. A. *Histoire des Maîtres Généraux de l'Ordre des Frères Prêcheurs* (Paris, 1903–9).

Müller, J. 'Die Legationen unter Papst Gregor X., 1271–6', *RQ*, XXXVII (1929), pp. 57–135.

Mundó, A. 'La renúncia del bisbe de Vic, Guillem de Tavertet (1233) segons la correspondència de Bages i els Registres Vaticans', *VII.CHCA*, III (1964), pp. 77–95.

See also Tobella.

Muñoz de la Cueba, J. *Noticias históricas de la santa iglesia catedral de Orense* (Madrid, 1727).

Muñoz Torrado, A. *La iglesia de Sevilla en el siglo XIII* (Seville, 1914).

Muñoz Vázquez, M. 'Notas sobre el repartimiento de tierras', *Boletín de la Real Acad. de Córdoba*, XXV (1954), pp. 251–70.

'Documentos inéditos para la historia del Alcázar de Córdoba de los reyes cristianos', *Boletin de la R. Acad. de Córdoba*, XXVI (1955), pp. 69–88.

Bibliography

Nebot, M. 'Don Poncio de Jardí, tercer obispo de Mallorca (1283–1303)', *BSAL*, XIII (1910–11), pp. 345–9, 360–4, 376–80; XIV (1912–13), 12–16, 25–9, 108–12, 125–8.

'El segundo obispo de Mallorca, Don Pedro de Muredine (1266–82)', *BSAL*, XIII (1910–11), pp. 134–6, 149–53, 161–6, 183–8, 195–7, 218–20, 238–40, 252–4, 267–9, 295–7, 316–18, 333–6.

Nogales-Delicado y Rendón, D. de. *Historia de la muy noble y muy leal ciudad de Ciudad Rodrigo* (Ciudad Rodrigo, 1882).

Núñez de Castro, A. *Historia eclesiástica y seglar de la muy noble y muy leal ciudad de Guadalaxara* (Madrid, 1653).

Ochoa Martínez de Soria, J. M. 'El Centro de Estudios Medievales del Seminario de Vitoria en los archivos de las catedrales gallegas', *Scriptorium Victoriense,* VII (1960), pp. 345–68.

Ochoa Sanz, J. *Vincentius Hispanus: canonista bolonés del siglo XIII* (Madrid, 1960).
'Problemas biográficas de Vincentius Hispanus' [Congrès de Droit Canonique Médiéval – Louvain–Bruxelles, 22–6 juillet 1958 (*Bibl. de la Rev. d'Hist. Eccl.,* XXXIII (1959)], pp. 162–75.

Olagüe, I. *La decadencia española,* 4 vols (Madrid, 1950–1).

Olmos Canalda, E. *Los prelados valentinos* (Valencia, 1949).

Omont, H. 'Catalogue de la bibliothèque de Bernard II, archévêque de St-Jacques-de-Compostelle', *BEC,* LIV (1893), pp. 327–33.

Ortega y Cotes, I. J. *Bullarium Ordinis Militiae de Calatrava* (Madrid, 1761).

Ortiz de Zúñiga, D. *Anales eclesiásticos y seculares de la muy noble y muy leal ciudad de Sevilla* (Madrid, 1677).

Pano, M. 'Nuevos documentos para la historia de Aragón', *BRAH,* XXIX (1896), pp. 421–3.

Paz, J. *See* Espejo, C.

Pelzer, A. 'Un traducteur inconnu, Pierre Gallego', *Studi e Testi,* XXXVII (1924) [*Miscellanea F. Ehrle,* I], pp. 407–56.

Pereyra da Sylva Leal, M. *Catálogo dos bispos da Idanha e Guarda* [Collecçam dos documentos e memórias da Academia Real da Historia Portugueza (Lisbon, 1722)].

Pérez Alhama, J. 'Concatedrales en España', *REDC,* XV (1960), pp. 373–443.

Pérez de Urbel, J. *Los monjes españoles en la Edad Media,* 2 vols (Madrid, 1933–4).
Sancho el Mayor de Navarra (Madrid, 1950).

Peters, E. M. '*Rex inutilis*: Sancho II of Portugal and thirteenth-century Deposition Theory', *Studia Gratiana,* XIV [Collectanea Stephan Kuttner, IV (1967)], pp. 255–305.

Pontich, M. *Synodales gerundenses* (Gerona, 1691).

Poole, R. L. *Lectures on the History of the Papal Chancery* (Cambridge, 1915).

Portela Pazos, S. *Decanologio de la iglesia catedral de Santiago de Compostela* (Santiago de Compostela, 1944).

Post, Gaines. *Studies in Medieval Legal Thought* (Princeton, 1964).

Procter, E. S. *Alfonso X of Castile* (Oxford, 1951).
'The Castilian Chancery during the Reign of Alfonso X, 1252–84', in *Oxford*

Bibliography

Essays in Medieval History pres. to H. E. Salter, ed. F. M. Powicke (Oxford, 1934), pp. 104–21.

Puig y Puig ,S. *Episcopologio de la sede barcinonense* (Barcelona, 1929).

Puyol, J. 'El presunto cronista Fernán Sánchez de Valladolid', *BRAH*, LXVII (1920), pp. 507–33.

Quétif, J. (and J. Échard) *Scriptores Ordinis Praedicatorum*, 2 vols (Paris, 1719–21).

Quintana Prieto, A. 'La sucesión en la sede de Mondoñedo en 1248', *AA*, XIII (1965), pp. 11–34.

Rades de Andrada, F. *Historia de las tres ordenes de caballería* (Madrid, 1572).

Rau, V. 'A Family of Italian Merchants in Portugal in the XVth Century: the Lomellini', in *Studi in onore di Armando Sapori* (Milan, 1957), pp. 715–26.

Renouard, Y. 'Comment les papes d'Avignon expédiaient leur courrier', *Revue Historique*, CLXXX (1937), pp. 1–29.

'1212–1216: comment les traits durables de l'Europe occidentale moderne se sont définis au début du XIIe siècle', *Annales de l'Université de Paris*, XXVIII (1958), pp. 5–21.

'Un sujet de recherches: l'exportation de chevaux de la péninsule ibérique en France et en Angleterre au Moyen-Âge', in *Homenaje a Jaime Vicens Vives*, I (Barcelona, 1965), pp. 571–7.

Reuter, A. E. *Königtum und Episkopat in Portugal im 13. Jahrhundert* [Abhand. z. mittleren u. neueren Gesch., Heft 69] (Berlin, 1928).

Rico, F. 'Aristoteles Hispanus: en torno a Gil de Zamora, Petrarca y Juan de Mena', *Italia Medioevale e Umanistica*, X (1967), pp. 143–64.

Ríos, J. A. de los. *Historia crítica de la literatura española*, II (Madrid, 1862).

Risco, M. *Historia de la ciudad y corte de León y de sus reyes*, I (Madrid, 1792). *See also* Flórez, E.

Ríu y Cabanas, R. 'El monasterio de Santa Fe de Toledo', *BRAH*, XVI (1890), pp. 51–7.

Ríus Serra, J. 'El bisbat de Vich en el segle XIII', *AST*, I (1925), pp. 397–411.

Rivera Recio, J. F. *La iglesia de Toledo en el siglo XII (1086–1208)*, I (Rome, 1966). 'Personajes hispanos asistentes en 1215 al IV Concilio de Letrán, *HS*, IV (1951), pp. 335–55.

Rodríguez Amaya, E. 'Inventario general de los archivos de la S. I. Catedral y ciudad de Badajoz, formado por D. Ascensio Morales en 1753–4', *Rev. de Estudios Extremeños*, CIII (1952), pp. 389–492.

Rodríguez López, P. *Episcopologio asturicense*, II (Astorga, 1907).

Rosa Pereira, I. da. 'Sínodos da diocese de Lisboa: notas históricas', *Lumen*, XXV (May 1961), pp. 385–98.

Ruffi, A. de. *Histoire de la ville de Marseille* (Marseille, 1696).

Ruiz Jusué, T. 'Las cartas de hermandad en España', *AHDE*, XV (1944), pp. 387–463.

Ruiz de Larrinaga, J. 'Las clarisas de Santa Catalina de Zaragoza', *AIA*, IX (1949), pp. 351–77.

Runciman, Steven. *A History of the Crusades*, 3 vols (Cambridge, 1954).

Säbekow, G. *Die päpstlichen Legationen nach Spanien und Portugal bis zum Ausgang des XII Jahrhunderts* (Berlin, 1931).

Bibliography

Sáez, E. *et al. Los Fueros de Sepúlveda* (Segovia, 1953).

Sagarra, F. de. 'Noticias y documentos inéditos referentes al Infante Don Alfonso, primogénito de Don Jaime I y de Dona Leonor de Castilla', *BRABL*, IX (1917–20), pp. 285–301.

'Antics segells dels arquebisbes de Tarragona', *AST*, V (1929), pp. 191–205.

Sanabre, J. *El archivo diocesano de Barcelona* (Barcelona, 1947).

Sánchez-Albornoz, C. *España y el Islam* (Buenos Aires, 1943).

España: un enigma histórico, 2 vols (Buenos Aires, 1956).

Estudios sobre las instituciones medievales españolas (Mexico, 1965).

'Un ceremonial inédito de coronación de los reyes de Castilla', *Logos*, II, iii (1943), pp. 75–97.

'La sucesión al trono en los reinos de León y Castilla', *Boletín de la Acad. Argentina de Letras,* XIV (1945), pp. 35–124.

Sánchez Alonso, B. *Historia de la historiografía española,* I (Madrid, 1947).

Sánchez Belda, L. 'La cancillería castellana durante el reinado de Sancho IV, 1284–95', *AHDE*, XXI–II (1951–2), pp. 171–223.

Sánchez Candeira, A. *El 'Regnum-Imperium' leonés hasta 1037* (Madrid, 1951).

Sanchis Sivera, J. *La diócesis valentina* (Valencia, 1922).

'El obispo de Valencia, Arnaldo de Peralta', *BRAH*, LXXXII (1923), pp. 40–64, 104–21.

'Para la historia del derecho eclesiástico valentino', *AST*, IX (1933), pp. 137–47; X (1934), pp. 123–49.

Sancho de Sopranis, H. 'La incorporación de Cádiz a la Corona de Castilla bajo Alfonso X', *Hispania*, IX (1949), pp. 355–86.

Sandoval, P. de. *Antigüedad de la ciudad, y la iglesia caredral de Túy* (Braga, 1610).

Catálogo de los obispos que ha tenido la santa iglesia de Pamplona (Pamplona, 1614).

Sangorrin, D. *El libro de la Cadena del Concejo de Jaca,* (Zaragoza, 1921).

Sanjurjo y Pardo, R. *Los obispos de Mondoñedo* (Lugo, 1854).

San Martín Payo, J. *La antigua Universidad de Palencia* (Madrid, 1942).

Santa María, N. de. *Chronica da Ordem dos conegos regrantes do patriarcha S. Agostinho,* II (Lisbon, 1668).

Sapori, A. *Studi di storia economica medievale,* 2nd ed. (Florence, 1946).

Le marchand italien an Moyen Âge (Paris, 1952).

Sarrailh, J. *L'Espagne éclairée de la seconde moitié du XVIIIe siècle* (Paris, 1954).

Sayous, A.-E. 'Dans l'Italie, a l'intérieur des terres: Sienne de 1221 à 1229', *Annales d'Histoire économique et sociale,* III (1931), pp. 189–206.

'Les méthodes commerciales de Barcelona au XIIIe siècle, d'après des documents inédits des archives de sa cathédrale', *EUC*, XVI (1931), pp. 155–98.

Schäfer, K. H. *Die Ausgaben der Apostolischen Kammer unter Johann XXII. nebst den Jahresbilanzen von 1316–1375* (Paderborn, 1911).

Scheffer-Boichorst, P. 'Zur Geschichte Alfons X. von Castilien', *MIöG*, IX (1888), pp. 226–48.

Schramm, P. E. 'Die Krönung im Katalanisch-aragonesischen Königreich', *Homenatge a Antoni Rubió i Lluch,* III (Barcelona, 1936), pp. 577–98.

Bibliography

'Das kastilische König- und Kaisertum während der Reconquista', in *Festschrift für Gerhard Ritter* (Tübingen, 1950), pp. 87–139.

'Das kastilische Königtum in der Zeit Alfonsos des Weisen (1252–84)', in *Festschrift für E. E. Stengel* (Münster-Cologne, 1952), pp. 385–413.

Schulten, A. *Tartessos* [Univ. Hamburg Abhandlungen aus dem Gebiete des Auslandskunde, XIII (1922)].

Serrano, L. *Cartulario del Infantado de Covarrubias* (Valladolid, 1907).

Don Mauricio, obispo, de Burgos y fundador de su catedral (Madrid, 1922).

Cartulario de San Pedro de Arlanza (Burgos, 1925.)

El obispado de Burgos, y Castilla primitiva desde el siglo V al XIII, III (Madrid, 1936).

'El mayordomo mayor de Dona Berenguela', *BRAH*, CIV (1934), pp. 101–98.

'El canciller de Fernando III de Castilla', *Hispania*, I, fasc. v (1941), pp. 3–40.

'Nuevos datos sobre Fernando III de Castilla', *Hispania*, III (1943), pp. 569–79.

Serrano y Sanz, M. 'Memoria librorum quos dompnus Sancius Jordani dimisit in ecclesia S. Maria de Unicastro', *Erudición Ibero-Ultramarina*, III (1932), pp. 117–19.

Sierra Corella, A. 'El cabildo de párrocos de Toledo', *RABM*, XLIX (1928), pp. 97–114.

Silva Lopes, J. B. da. *Memórias para a história ecclesiástica do bispado do Algarve* (Lisbon, 1848).

Smalley, Beryl. *The Study of the Bible in the Middle Ages*, 2nd ed. (Oxford, 1952).

'Robert Bacon and the Early Dominican School at Oxford', *TRHS*, 4th ser., XXX (1948), pp. 1–19.

Smith, R. S. *The Spanish Guild Merchant: A History of the Consulado, 1250–1700* (Durham, N. Carolina, 1940).

Sobrequés Vidal, S. *La época del patriciado urbano* [in *Historia social y económica de Espana y América*, II, ed. J. Vicens Vives (Barcelona, 1957)].

Solano de Figuerora y Altamirano, J. *Historia eclesiástica de la ciudad y obispado de Badajoz*, I, iii (re-ed. Badajoz, 1931).

Soldevila, F. *Pere el Gran*, II–I, i (Barcelona, 1950, 1962).

Sousa Costa, A. D. de. *Mestre Silvestre e Mestre Vicente, juristas da contenda entre D. Afonso II e suas irmãs* (Braga, 1963).

'Cultura medieval portuguesa. Português, o Cardeal Gil?', *Itinerarium*, I (1955), pp. 296–306.

Southern, R. W. *St Anselm and his Biographer* (Cambridge, 1963).

Suárez Fernández, L. *Castilla, el Cisma y la crisis conciliar (1378–1440)* (Madrid, 1960).

'Evolución histórica de las hermandades castellanas', *CHE*, XVI (1951), pp. 5–78.

Tate, R. B. 'The *Anacephaleosis* of Alfonso García de Santa María, bishop of Burgos, 1453–56', in *Hispanic Studies in Honour of I. González Llubera* (Oxford, 1959), pp. 387–401.

Teetaert, A. 'La doctrine pénitentielle de St Raymond de Penyafort', *AST*, IV (1928), pp. 121–82.

Thompson, E. A. *The Goths in Spain* (Oxford, 1969).

'The Barbarian Kingdoms in Gaul and Spain', *Nottingham Mediaeval Studies*, VII (1963), pp. 3–33.

Bibliography

Thorkelin, G. J. *Diplomatarium Arna-Magnaeanum*, I (Copenhagen, 1786).

Tihon, C. 'Les expectatives "in forma pauperum", particulièrement au XIVe siècle', *Bulletin de l'Institut Hist. Belge de Rome*, v (1925), pp. 51–118.

Tobella, A. M. 'Dues actes capitulars dels anys 1227 i 1229', *Catalonia Monastica*, I (1927), pp. 131–45.

and A. Mundo. 'Cronologia dels capítols de la Congregació Claustral Tarraconense i Cesaraugustana (1219–1661)', *Analecta Montserratensia*, x (1964) [= Miscellanea Albareda, II], pp. 221–398.

Torre, A. de la. 'Relaciones de España con Federico II e el Imperio', *Atti del Convegno Internazionale di Studi Federiciani*... 10–18 dicembre 1950 (Palermo, 1952), pp. 161–7.

Torres Fontes, J. *Repartimiento de Murcia, 1272–3* (Madrid, 1961).

'El obispado de Cartagena en el siglo XIII', *Hispania*, XIII (1953), pp. 339–401, 515–80.

'Jaime I y Alfonso X: dos criterios de repoblación', *VII.CHCA*, II (1964), pp. 329–40.

Trabut-Cussac, J.-P. 'Don Enrique de Castille en Angleterre, 1256–9', *Mélanges de la Casa de Velázquez*, II (1966), pp. 51–8.

Tramontana, S. 'La Spagna catalana nel Mediterraneo e in Sicilia', *Nuova Rivista Storica*, L (1966), pp. 545–79.

Treharne, R. F. 'An Unauthorised Use of the Great Seal Under the Provisional Government in 1259', *EHR*, XL (1925), pp. 403–11.

Tubino, F. M. 'Códice de la coronación: manuscrito en pergamino del siglo XIV', *Museo Español de Antigüedades* v, (1875), pp. 43–68.

Ubieto Arteta, A. 'Puntualizaciones sobre reconquista valenciana', *Ligarzas*, I (1968), pp. 161–78.

Ughelli, F. *Italia Sacra*, I (Venice, 1717).

Usher, A. P. *The Early History of Deposit Banking in Mediterranean Europe* (Cambridge, Mass., 1943).

Valdeavellano, L. G. de. *Historia de España*, I, 4th ed. (Madrid, 1968).

'El mercado: apuntes para su estudio en León y Castilla durante la Edad Media', *AHDE*, VIII (1931), pp. 201–405.

Valls i Taberner, F. *San Ramón de Penyafort* [*Obras selectas*, I, ii] (Madrid–Barcelona, 1953).

'Relacions familiars i polítiques entre Jaume el Conqueridor i Alfóns el Savi', *B.Hisp.*, XXI (1919), pp. 9–52.

'Notes sobre la legislació eclesiàstica provincial que integra la compilació canònica Tarraconense del Patriarca d'Alexandria', *AST*, XI (1935), pp. 251–72.

Vázquez de Parga, L. *La División de Wamba* (Madrid, 1943).

Ventura Subirats, J. 'El catarismo en Cataluña', *BRABL*, XXVIII (1959–60), pp. 75–168.

Verlinden, C. 'La Grande Peste de 1348 en Espagne', *Rev. Belge de philologie et d'histoire*, XVII, i (1938), pp. 103–46.

'Le influenze italiane nella colonizzazione iberica (uomini e metodi)', *Nuova Rivista Storica*, XXXVI (1952), pp. 254–70.

Bibliography

Vicens Vives, J. *Manual de historia económica de España*, 5th ed. (Barcelona, 1967).
  Aproximación a la historia de España, 3rd ed. (Barcelona, 1962).
Villagrasa, F. de. *Antigüedad de la iglesia catedral de Segorbe* (Valencia, 1664).
Villanueva, J. *Viage literario a las iglesias de España*, 22 vols (Madrid, 1803–52).
Vincke, J. *Staat und Kirche in Katalonien und Aragon während des Mittelalters* (Münster-i.-W., 1931).
  'Els comtes-reis de Barcelona i els "servitia" papals vers el 1300', *AST*, VII (1931), pp. 339–50.
  'Die Anfänge der päpstlichen Provisionen in Spanien', *RQ*, XLVIII (1953), pp. 195–210.
  'Los familiares de la Corona aragonesa alrededor del año 1300', *AEM*, I (1964), pp. 333–51.
Waley, D. *The Papal State in the Thirteenth Century* (London, 1961).
Wieruszowski, H. 'Conjuraciones y alianzas políticas del rey Pedro de Aragón contra Carlos de Anjou antes de las Visperas Sicilianas', *BRAH*, CVII (1935), pp. 547–602.
Wilhelm, F. 'Die Schriften des Jordanus v. Osnabrück', *MIöG*, XIX (1898), pp. 615–75.
Wolff, R. L. 'Mortgage and Redemption of an Emperor's Son: Castile and the Latin Empire of Constantinople', *Speculum,* XXIX (1954), pp. 45–84.
Ximena, M. de. *Catálogo de los obispos de las iglesias catedrales de la diócesi de Jaén* (Madrid, 1654).
Zaccagnini, G. 'Ancora dei banchieri e mercanti pistoiesi a Bologna e altrove nei secoli XIII e XIV', *Bullettino Storico Pistoiese,* XXXVI (1934), pp. 149–58.
Zanelli, A. 'Il giuramento di fedeltà di Buoso da Dovara ad Alfonso X di Castiglia (1271)', *Archivo Storico Italiano,* 5th ser., X (1892), pp. 122–6.
Zimmermann, H. *Die päpstliche Legation in der ersten Hälfte des 13. Jahrhunderts* (Paderborn, 1913).
Zunzunegui Aramburu, J. 'Para la historia de la diócesis de Segorbe-Albarracín en la primera mitad de siglo XIV', *AA*, XVI (1968), pp. 11–24.
Zurita, J. *Anales de la Corona de Aragón*, I (Zaragoza, 1610).

DOCUMENTS IN THE ARCHIVO NACIONAL, MADRID (SECCION DE CLERO)
Material from the *carpetas* listed below has been cited in the text

carpetas	
79–93	Baleares: Palma. Santo Domingo, O. P.
161	Barcelona. Valdaura, O. Cist.
181–5	Burgos. San Pablo, O. P.
230–2	Gumiel de Izán, O. Cist.
353–4	Ríoseco, O. Cist.
425	Castellón. Benifazá, O. Cist.
541–5	Coruña. Sobrado, O. Cist.
594	Huesca. Nra Sra de los Angeles, O. P.

Bibliography

carpetas

642–53	Montearagón, O. S. A.
772	San Victorián, O. S. B.
968	León. Eslonza, O. S. B.
1031	Logroño. Nájera, O. S. B.
1331B	Lugo. Catedral
1398	Navarra. Fitero, O. Cist.
1407–8	Leyre, O. Cist.
1421	La Oliva, O. Cist.
1422	: Pamplona. San Pedro de Rivas, O. S. A.
1488	Orense. Montederramo, O. Cist.
1526	Osera, O. Cist.
1646	Oviedo. Documentos sin procedencia
1702	Palencia. Carrión, O. S. B.
1724	San Pablo, O. P.
1762	Pontevedra. Armentera, O. Cist.
1874	Santo Domingo, O. P.
1893–4	Salamanca. San Esteban, O. P.
1917	Santander. Liébana, O. S. B.
1977	Segovia. Los Huertos, O. Praem.
2129–355	Tarragona. Poblet, O. Cist.
3019–22	Toledo. Catedral
3224	Valencia. San Vicente Roqueta, O. Cist.
3430	Valladolid. Palazuelos, O. Cist.
3592	Zaragoza: Calatayud. Iglesia de S. María
3667	Piedra, O. Cist.
3755–6	Rueda, O. Cist.
3767–9	Veruela, O. Cist.

sellos 5, 49, 65, 72, 90: Tarragona. Poblet, O. Cist.

INDEX

Proper names of both Catalans and Castilians are listed in their Castilian form. In cases of uncertainty of origin the Latin form is used.

The following abbreviations have been employed: abp: archbishop; archd: archdeacon; bp: bishop; card: cardinal; dioc: diocese; prov: province.

Index

Index

Index

Conti, Raynald dei, card-deacon of S. Eustacius, 301; *see also* Alexander IV, pope

converts: *see* Jews; Moors

Corbeil, Treaty of (1258), 153

Córdoba, church of, 180n, (affiliation with church of Burgos) 116n, (constitutions of) 258n, 270; capture of, 105, 107, 111; diocesan visitation, 264; episcopal elections at in 1290s, 258; Virgil of, 104; bps of: *see* Fernando I; Fernando II; Gil Domínguez; Gutierre; Juan Fernández (bp-elect); Lope Pérez; Pedro Yáñez

Coria, church of, 114, 172; diocese of, 17; bps of: *see* Alfonso; Fernando; Pedro; Sancho

Corias, abbey of Santa María y San Juan (Asturias), 305n

Cortes (of Castile), (1252) 121–2; (1258) 166, 168; (1259) 154, 169; (1271–2) 107n; (1277) 122; (1329) 185

Coserans, bp of: *see* Navarrus

cost of living (in Castile, 1314), 248

councils: in 11th and 12th centuries, 34; scarcity of in 1220s and 1230s, 16–17, 35–8; John of Abbeville's legislation regarding, 33–4; excessive legislation of, 89, 310; political significance of, 118–19, 164–5; in 1292, 241–2, 307; of Tarragona, 54–82 *passim*, 94–7, 119, 307, 326, (venue of) 81–2, 96; forbidden in Castile, 219n; plans for in Castile–Leon, 166–74, 221; ordered by Clement V, 246; at Alcalá de Henares (1257), 166–7; at Santiago (1259–60), 172; at Ponferrada (pre-1267), 176n; at Peñafiel (1302), 174; forbidden in Portugal, 220n

court, royal: and bishops, 13, 15, 187, 221, 238–41; *see also* chancery; Curia

Covarrubias, abbey of (Burgos), 16, 296n

Crecencius, abp of Athens, 309n

Crete: *see* Angelo, patriarch of Grado

Crusade: 87; Spanish (papal view of) 207–9, (in Africa) 202; Fifth, 8, 10, 19, 291; *see also* Holy Land

Cubellas, 199

Cuenca, cathedral-church of, 27, 32, 114, 151n, (archive of) 158, ('one year rule' at) 271; diocese of, 12–13, (*tercias* of) 121n; episcopal elections at (1280, 1290), 256n; bps of: *see* Bernardo; García; Gonzalo; Gonzalo García Gudiel; Gonzalo Palomeque; Mateo Riñal; Pascal; Pedro Lorenzo

Cum quidem (constitution of 1244–5 Tarragona Council), 181n

Curia (papal), 50, 129; award of benefices to habitués of, 94, 149, 284ff; borrowing at, 131–51 *passim*; costliness of, 307–10; effects of episcopal stay at, 138–50; exclusion from, 150–1; at Lyons, 129–30; Spaniards at, 251ff; Spanish attitude to, 251–4

Curia (royal): churchmen banished from (1295), 243–4; etymology of the word, 187; *see also* court, royal

currency, reform of, 122; exchange rates, 134, 211–12; that of Portugal *vilis*, 130

'custom', 17, 176n

D. presbiter, candidate for Salamanca canonry, 274

Dante: on Card John Gaetan Orsini, 217; on Card Octavian Ubaldini, 300

Daroca, 309

De archiepiscopo Toletano (constitution of 1240 Tarragona Council), 95n

debts, episcopal at Curia, 128–51

decima: grant to Alfonso X, 213–14, 331; grant to Alfonso XI, 245–50

Desclot, Bernat, 152–3

Desiderius, O.F.M., collector, 195–6

Diago Rois, O.F.M., 320

Diego, bp of Cartagena, 324n

Diego Garcés, *subcollector*, 248

Diego García: on Castilian Church, 12; on clerical attire, 30

Diego García, son of García Martínez, 204n

dineros prietos, 122

Dinis, king of Portugal, 216n, 220n, 259n

distance; sense of between Rome and Spain, 103, 185, 306–7

Domingo, bp of Baeza, 116n, 234, 316n

Domingo, bp of Plasencia, 10n

Domingo, bp of Salamanca, 308

Domingo Domínguez, cleric of Soria, 275n

Domingo González, Master, *clericus chori* of León, 307n

Domingo Martínez, bp of Ciudad Rodrigo, 256

Domingo Martínez, cleric of Soria, 275n

Domingo Pascal, abp-elect of Toledo, 143, 254

Domingo Pérez, abbot of Castrojériz (Burgos), 283, 287

Domingo Pérez, archd of Cuenca, 284

Domingo de Sola, bp of Huesca, 66n, 206, 318n

Domingo Suárez, bp of Ávila, 115n, 316

Domingo Ximénez, canon of Plasencia, 141n

Domingos Domingues, canonist, 283n

Domingo Peres, *magister scolarum* of Braga, 299

Dominic, St, 146, 314

Index

Index

374

Index

Index

Index

Index

Lisbon, 23, 103, 183; church of, 305n; dean of, 18n; siege of (1147), 5; bps of: *see* Aires Vasques; João Martins; Johannes Hispanus; Matheus; Soeiro

Logroño, 66, 98n

Lombardy, 43; Alfonso X and, 212; military operations in, 192

London, citizens of and Infante Sancho of Castile, 110n; orfrey of, 134n

Lope, bp of Sigüenza, 320

Lope, Master, treasurer of Toledo, 283

Lope, Zamora proctor, 288n

Lope Fernández de Aín, bp of Morocco, 202–3; Spanish estate of, 130n

Lope Pérez, bp of Córdoba, 116n, 285n, 316n

Lope Rodríguez, Master, cleric of Toledo, 301

Lorenzo de Portugal, O.F.M., bp of Ceuta, 203

Louis IX, king of France, 153, 209

Lucas, bp of Túy, 333; makes Aristotle a Spaniard, 126; on church of León, 148, 162, 268; on IV Lateran, 6; on Castile in the 1230s, 105, 125

Lucca, merchants of: *see* Bactoli Company, Orlandi Company, Riccardi Company

Lugo, 22, 48, 109; chapter of, 269, 313; deanery of, 260n; distance from León, 26; diocese of, 50; bps of: *see* Alfonso; Arias; Juan Martínez; Miguel

Lyons, 67n, 69n, 149; Council of (1245), 50, 145, 237, 269, 310n, (can. 14 of) 159n, (Spanish bishops at) 102, 142, 159–62, 193–4, (taxes authorised by) 194–9; Council of (1274), 84, 217; (Jaime I of Aragon at) 210, (Spanish bishops at) 212, (taxes authorised by) 130

Madrid, 162; Augustinian nuns of, 225n; Cortes at (1329), 185; meeting of bps at, (1258), 171

Magaz (prov. León), 249

Mallorca, church of, 52, 69, 95, (and Gregory IX) 324n; climate of, 326n; Dominicans of, 318; siege of, 25n; synods of, 98; bps of: *see* Pedro de Morella; Raimundo de Torrelles

Manfred of Hohenstaufen, 206

Manfred de' Roberti, Master, *collector,* 197; bp-elect of Verona, 208n

Mansilla, Demetrio, 2; on Mondoñedo election (1248), 109; on papal provisions, 294; on Spaniards and the papal Curia, 253

Margaritus, archd of Palermo, *rector de Reddis,* 94n

María Martínez, prioress of S. María de Zamora, 224–7

María de Molina, queen of Castile, 104, 132, 223

Mariana, J. de; on Fernando III, 331–2; on Alfonso X, 122

Marie de Brienne, empress of Constantinople 181

Marinus of Eboli, Formulary of, 157

Marseilles, 123, 203

Marsilio of Padua, 86

Marsupinus Meliorati, agent at Avignon of Chiarenti Company, 136n

Martène, E., 28

Martin IV, pope, 45n, 152, 210, 214, 221, 230

Martín, bp of Jaén, 234

Martín, O.P., bp of Segovia, 316n, 319n

Martín, bp of Sigüenza, 260n; dean of Burgos, 256, 300n

Martín, abp of Toledo, 2

Martín, abbot of *Elisontia,* 128n

Martín, Lugo proctor, 300

Martín, Master, canon of Orense, 237

Martín, O.F.M., *subcollector,* 196

Martín Arias, bp of Zamora, 12, 160, 292

Martín Fernández, bp of León, 115, 145, 150n, 151, 167, 168, 245n, 284; and the friars, 319

Martín Fernández, bp of Salamanca, 160, 193, 271n

Martín Gómez, Master, abbot of Cervatos (Burgos), 263

Martín González, bp of Calahorra and Astorga, 115n, 232, 244; married, 235n

Martín González de Contreras, dean of Burgos, 116n, 163

Martín González, archd of Cuenca, 283–4

Martín Peláez, practor of bp Suero Pérez of Zamora, 301–2

Martín Pérez, cantor of Ávila, 283

Martín Pérez, dean of Plasencia, 273

Martín Pérez, archd of Tarragona, 64n

Martín Rodríguez, bp of Zamora and León, 22n, 320n, (Zamora constitutions of) 47, 63n; and papal provisions, 292–3

Martín Vicéntez, cleric of Zamora, 301

Martín Yáñez, canon of León, 266

Martinho, abp of Braga, 184n, 206, 261, 267; prior of Guimarães, 296

Martinho, bp of Porto: at IV Lateran, 6; at Palencia, 148

Martinho Peres de Portucarrario, 259n

Martinus Lucensis, proctor, 300n

Martos, 179

Martorell, 25

379

Index

Index

Nuño Velázquez, *magister scolarum* of Astorga, career of, 284–5

Ocaña, 24
Octaviani Company (of Florence), 131–2
Olim excommunicasse (constitution of 1246 Tarragona council), 81n, 95n
Oliva, bp of Vich, 3
Oliva, abbey of S. María, O. Cist. (Navarre), 281n
Oliverio, 248
Olmedo (Ávila), archdeaconry of, 261
Olmutz: *see* Bruno, bp
Oña, abbey of San Salvador (Burgos), 27, 120n, (*census* of) 211
'one year rule', 270–1
Ordinatio Valentina, 38n, 67n, 282n
Ordonho Álvares, abp of Braga, 259n; card-bp of Tusculum, 224, 229n, 295
Orense, church of, 19, 47, 313; bps of: *see* Juan Díaz; Laurentius Hispanus; Pedro Yáñez
oriundi, 273–5
Orlandi Company (of Lucca), 130n
Orobona, nun of Zamora, 227
Orsini, John Gaetan, card-deacon of S. Nicholas in Carcere Tulliano: and Spain, 217–18, 299n; *see also* Nicholas III, pope
Orsini, Matthew Rosso, card-deacon of S. Maria in Porticu, 299
Orsini, Napoleon, card-deacon of S. Adrian, 253
Orvieto: Spaniards at, 136n, 230
Osera, abbey of S. María, O. Cist. (Orense), 199
Osma, 248; church of, 25, 180n, (benefices at) 261; bps of: *see* Agustín; Gil; Juan; Melendo
Osnabrück: *see* Jordan; Benno, bp
Oviedo, 22; archd of, 184; church of, 116, 123, 151n, 278n, 298, (chapter of) 304n, 305n (claim of church of Braga to jurisdiction over) 242; diocese of, 7, 19; episcopal election at (1275), 256n; bps of: *see* Álvaro (bp-elect); Fernando Álvarez, O.F.M. (bp-elect); Ferrán Alfonso; Ferrán Martínez (bp-elect); Fredulus; Miguel; Pedro; Rodrigo Díaz

P., Master, cleric of John of Abbeville, 27
P. Aurie, dean of Salamanca, 292
P. B. Cist., Roman proctor, 281
P. de Olivaria, Aragonese agent at papal Curia, 308n
P. Yáñez, treasurer of León, 144n

Palazuelo, O. Cist. (Palencia), 281
Palencia, 22, 168, 191n, (famine at, in late 1250s) 178; (population of, in 14th century) 245n; archdeacon of, 267; church of, 115n, 123, 146–50, 177, 180n, 261n, 295, 305n, (illiteracy of chapter of) 237, ('one year rule' at) 270, (proctor of) 282, (and Sancho IV) 243n, 245; clergy of, 31, 186; *concejo* of, 230n; deanery of, 231; Order of Preachers at, 22n, 317, (General Chapter of) 229n; university at, 31, 146, 171; bp of (in 1314) 248–9; *see also*: Alfonso; Álvaro; Fernando; Juan Alfonso; Juan de Saavedra; Munio of Zamora; Rodrigo; Tello
Palenciola: *see* Palenzuela
Palenzuela (Burgos), 148n; archd of, 261
Palermo: *see* Margaritus; Petrus, nepos... Margariti
Palma de Mallorca, 98n
Pamplona, 258n, (fair at) 132; church of, 61, (literacy of chapter of) 237, (sacking of cathedral of) 216, (claim of church of Toledo to) 67; clergy of, 84–5; diocese of, 97, 99, 191; Franciscan convent at, 198n; synods of, 38, 67, 97n, 93, (in 1216?) 16; bps of (proctor of), 282; *see also* Miguel; Pedro Ramírez; Pedro Ximénez de Gazolaz; Sparago
Paolo di Sulmona, 180, 203, 304
papacy: and kings of Castile, 103–12; Spanish attitude to, 304–5; treasurer of, attacked, 183–4; treasury of, and Spanish documents, 188
Papebroch, D: on Fernando III, 333
Paris, 163; debt settlements at, 131–3; Portuguese negotiations at (1245), 109; Spanish delegation at, 204; University of, 20, 66n, 139, 236n; bp of: *see* Eudes de Sully
Pascal II, pope, 17n
Pascal, bp of Cuenca, 261, 262, 265, 309n
Pascal, bp of Jaén, 113, 234, 261; represented at episcopal gathering (1267), 176n
Pascal Cornelio, Master, 283, 285
Pascal Garcés, treasurer of Toledo, 141n
Pascal Pérez, cleric of Zamora, 255, 301–3
Pavia, 212
Pecoraria, James, card-bp of Palestrina, 190, 276
Pedagaes (Braga), 186
Pedraza (prov. Segovia), 16
Pedro II, king of Aragon, 5, 59, 68, 102, 210
Pedro III, king of Aragon, 136n, 152–3, 155, 210; as Infante, 206n; and *decima*, 215–16
Pedro IV, king of Aragon, 325n

Index

Index

Pelayo, Master, canon of Zamora, physician to Infante Alfonso of Castile, 296n
Pelayo Pérez Correa, Master of Order of Santiago, 142
Pelayo Rodríguez, canon of Zamora, 300n
Peñafiel, Council of (1302), 174, 244n
penance, 29; contemporary attitudes to, 77, 319
penitentiary, papal, 186
Perales, 184n
Perpignan, 211
Pers de Ffriac, merchant of Cádiz, 143n
Perugia, 88n, 148n, 208n, 258, 279n, 280, 281, 286n
Peter, card-deacon of S. Maria in Aquiro, 189
Peter Aigueblanche, bp of Hereford, 202n
Peter Lombard, MS of, 116n
Peter the Venerable, abbot of Cluny, 1
Petrus, nepos ... Margariti (archd of Palermo), 94n
Petrus Berengarii, Roman proctor, 282, 307n
Petrus Cinchii de Turre, Roman merchant, 129
Petrus Gaietanus, Toledo and Segovia pensioner, 149n, 286–7
Petrus Hispanus, bp of Burgos, card-bp of Sabina: and Dominicans of Burgos, 317n; and election of Pope Clement V, 253
Petrus Hispanus, canon of Mondoñedo, 254
Petrus Johannis de Lavania, Senator, 149n
Petrus de Piperno, *collector*, 198, 199
Petrus de Regio, *familiaris pape*, 225n
Petrus Teobaldiscus de Urbe, nuncio, 220
Petrus Tusci, papal scribe, 189
Petrus de Viccovario, Master, *collector*, 198
Petrus de Ysidolio, merchant of St Jean d'Angely, 131
Peyre de Godin, Guillaume de, card-bp of Sabina, 101
Philip the Fair, king of France, 158n, 210
Philip of Swabia, 155
Philip, bp of Camerino: in Aragon, 1246, 195n
Philip de Ceccano, Master, nuncio, 191
Philip, abp of Ravenna: Salimbene's anecdote concerning, 236n
Piacenza, merchants of, 130
Piedra, abbey of Ntra Sra, O. Cist (Tarazona), 281n
Piedrahita del Barco, 272
Piero della Vigna, 162n
Pierre de Montebruno, abp of Narbonne, 216
Pierre de Poitiers, 77n

Pietro, bp of Rieti, nuncio, 139, 218–20
Pietro de Assisi, Roman proctor, 281, 307n
Piperno, Peter de, card-deacon of S. Mariae Novae: on Abp Gonzalo III of Toledo, 306
Pirenne thesis: and Spanish history, 1
Pirunti, John, 300
Pirunti, Jordan, card-deacon of SS Cosmas and Damian, 300, 302, 303n, 308n
Pisa, merchants of, 130; capture of prelates by fleet of, 160
Pistoia, merchants of, 130n, 131–3, 141; *see also* Ammanati; Chiarenti
Planeta: see Diego García
Plasencia: Card. Gil Torres' constitutions for church of, 270, 273; diocese of, 17; bps of: *see* Adán Pérez; Domingo
pluralism, 66n, 97; John of Abbeville and, 31–2
Poblet, abbey of S. María, O. Cist. (Tarragona), 67, 84, 281, 192n, 282; abbot of, 57, (and prior) 132
Poema de Fernán González: eulogy of Spain in, 105
Pombeiro, abbot of, 53
Ponce, bp of Tortosa, 59, 61n, 63n, 65, 92
Ponce de Vilamur, bp of Urgel, 61n, 64, 78n; election of, 56–7; suspended from office, 87–9; Roman debts of, 129–30
Ponferrada: episcopal assembly at, 176n
Pontius de Broet, nuncio, 220
population: of Castile, 106
Porto, church of, 6, 23, 27, 50; citizens of, 205n; bps of: *see* Julião; Martinho; Pedro; Pedro Salvador; Vicente
Portugal, 5, 18; Augustinians of, 39n; Church taxed, in 130; churchmen exiled from, 148; Nicholas III and, 219n
Primera Partida, 52, 68, 147, 324; on bps at papal Curia, 138; silent on subject of councils, 120; on monastic chapters, 39; on need for solidarity of bishops and chapters, 255; on 'Rome', 251; on royal rights in episcopal elections, 108
proctors, 94, **280–90**; of Sancho IV, 103–4
prostitutes: at Barcelona, 80
Provins, 145, 150
provisions (papal): and Spain, 292ff
Ptolemy of Lucca: on Pope John XXI, 236n, 325n

Quinqueyuga (dioc. Toledo), 177
quinta (papal tax, 1241), 191–2

R. Gonzálvez, agent of bp of Zamora at Provins, 145

Index

Index

Index

Sande (Túy), 259n
Santander, 167; abbacy of, 170n, 235n
Santiago, 23; legendary dean of, 265; universal title of bps of, 183; *see also* Compostela
Santiago, Order of, 55n, 106, 110, 130, 152n, 191n, 200n, 326n; Master of, 27; *see also* Pelayo Pérez Correa
Santillana (Santander), abbacy of, 170n
Saracens: *see* Moors
Sardinia, 153
Saturnia (Italy), 259n
Savelli, Centius, card-bp of Porto, 189n
Savelli, James, card-deacon of S. Maria in Cosmedin: and Spanish clerics, 299n; *see also* Honorius IV, pope
Saxutius, Florentine merchant, 141
Schramm, P. E.: on imperial pretensions of Fernando III, 124n
Segorbe, church of, 89, 193, 282n; diocese of, 170; bps of, at IV Lateran, 4; *see also* Aparicio; Pedro Garcés
Segovia, 156, 203; collapse of royal palace at (1258), 116n, 163; church of, 151n, 256n, 309n, (constitutions of) 271–2, 273, (reduced rents of) 178; diocese of, 2–3, 8, 9, (*tercias* of) 110; bps of: *see* Bernardo; Fernando Sarracín; Fernando Velázquez; Giraldo; Gonzalo; Martín; Remondo; Rodrigo Tello
Senobaldus Fassol, Florentine debt-collector in Spain, 131n
Sepulchre, Order of, 79n
Sepúlveda, 2–3, 16; abbot of San Tomé, 3n; archd of, 271–2; *fuero* of, 3
Serrano, Dom Luciano, x, 334
servitia (papal), 307n
Setenario (of Alfonso X), 106–7
Seville, 117, 180, 203n; capture of, 105, 107, 121, 124–5, 156; *repartimiento* of, 113, 123–4, 177, 203n, 266, (and churchmen) 113–16; Alfonso X on wealth of, 106; church of, 110, 231, 298; Cistercians at, 68; tale of Fernando III at siege of, 331–2
Shem Tob Falaquera, 207n
Sicilian Vespers, 152, 210
Siena, merchants of, 130, 131n, 132n, *see also* Bonsignori; bp of Lugo at, 141n; Alfonso X and, 156
Sigüenza, 24–5, 163, 248, 249; chapter of, 267; church of, 180, 231, 239, 280n, 320–1; bps of: *see* Andrés; Lope; Martín; Pedro; Rodrigo; Simon de Carrión
Sijena (Lérida), church of, 202
Silves, church of, 326n; bps of: *see* Alvarus

Pelagius; Bartolomé; García; Roberto
Silvestre Godinho, abp of Braga, 50; will of, 280n
Simon de Carrión, bp of Sigüenza, 184n, 265n
Sinibaldus de Labro, Toledo pensioner, archd of Bologna, 133n, 135n, 141, 288n
simony, 29
Sinitius, Master, *collector*, 206–7
Sisnando, Count, 179n
'six-month rule', 270n
Sixtus IV, pope: on *tercias*, 112n
Sixtus V, pope, 330
Sobrado (Orense), 144; abbey of SS Justo and Pastor, 281n
Sodoruel (Huesca), archdeaconry of, 287n
Soeiro, bp of Lisbon, 6n, 209n, 239
Soeiro, Master, dean of Lisbon, 283
Sojo (prov. Alava), 27
Soria, 164, 203; natives of at Jaén, 234–5; proposed for cathedral status, 234
Soros, church of, 57
Sotosalvos, abbey of S. María, O. Cist. (Segovia), 272
Spain: *see* Hispania
Spaniards: *see* hispani
Sparago, bp of Pamplona, abp of Tarragona, 9, 16, 19n, 25, 35–6, 38n, 41–2, 56, 57, 69n, 72n; death of, 59
spitting, clerical, 76n
Stefanía, nun of Zamora, 227
Stephanus, armiger of Card. Guillermo of XII Apostles, 279n
Stephanus 'dictus Surdus', 145
Suero Pérez, bp of Zamora, 115, 117, 183, 220n, 261, 285n, 289n, 301; and Dominicans, 225–9
Summa de Poenitentia: *see* Raymond of Peñafort, St
Summa Septem Sacramentorum, 71–7; provenance, 71–2; sources, 72–4, 76–8; content, 74–6, 98
synods, 73, 75; excess of, 89, 310; used as pretext for holiday, 74n, 81n; timing of, 81; *see under individual churches*

Talamanca, 126
Talavera, *apoteca de*, 126; clergy of, 165, 239
tapestries, Greek, 134n
Tarazona, 18; cathedral archive destroyed, 24n; Council (1229), 34; church of, 184n, (provisions at) 304; episcopal proctor, 289; bps of: *see* García Frontón; Pedro
Tarifa, siege of, 243
Tarragona, 24, 64, 199, (John of Abbeville at) 40, 94; church of, 32, 47, 63, 65, 200.

386

Index

(archiepiscopal election, 1268) 304, (cathedral archive of) 55, 95n, (*cameraria* of) 89–90, 94n, 195, 280n, (cantor of) 27, (chapter of) 304n, (*sede vacante* in 1230s) 60n; fair at, 82; province of, 25, 28, 37–8, 39, 51, 95, 140, (councils of) 36, 38n, 51, 56, *see also* councils, (synod of) 71, 89; abps of: *see* Agustín, Antonio; Benito de Rocaberti; Bernardo de Olivella; Guillermo; Guillermo de Mongrí (abp-elect); Pedro de Albalat; Pedro Clasquerin; Rodrigo Tello; Sparago

Tarshish, 182

Tartars: councils summoned on account of, 94n, 96n, 201, 242n

Tello, abp of Braga, 53, 310

Tello, bp of Palencia, 11, 15, 16, 31, 147–8, 177

Tello, archd of Palencia, 204n

Temple, Masters of, 7

Teobaldo I, king of Navarre, 65n, 67, 119, 161, 192, 280n

Teobaldo II, king of Navarre, 93n

tercias, 145, 158, 243; grants of, to Fernando III, 111–12, 119n, to Abp Rodrigo of Toledo, 125, to Abp Sancho I of Toledo, 169–70, 179–80; of Osma, 167; of Palencia, 146, 149; of Seville, 124; of the Portuguese Church, 220n; Alfonso X and, 121, 123; Fernando IV and, 249–50; Clement IV on, 207–8; Nicholas III on, 219; and Alexander VI, 328; *see also* tithes

Teruel, 184n

Theobald, brother of Petrus Johannis de Lavania, Senator, 149n

theologians, 86, 95; lack of among Spanish bishops, 236, 313

Thomas, *cubicularius pape*, nuncio, 190

Thomas de Cantilupe, bp of Hereford, 309

Tibur, el Consyl de, 98n

Tiburcio, bp of Coimbra, 148, 280n

Tielmes, 184n

Timothy, canon of Pécs, bp of Zagreb: and Urgel archdeaconry, 299n

tithes: payment of, 29, 66n, 123, 174; *de oleo*, 124n; *see also tercias*

Tocqueville, A. de, 175

Todi, bp of: *see* Petrus Gaietanus

Tojal, 23

Toledo, 19; archd of, 116n; archdiocese of, 8, 214, (clergy of) 165–6, 168, 169, (state of in 1314) 248, (*tercias* of) 110; archiepiscopal election (1264), 260n; cathedral of, 24, 27, 32, 125; (archive of) 173; church of, 130, 149n, 180, 234n, 296, 298, (chapter of) 10n, 180, 196, 310, (claim of to church of Pamplona) 67; Cortes at (1259), 154, 169; province of, 7, 28, 124; Visigothic Councils at, 327, 329–30; abps of: *see* Bernardo; Domingo Pascal (abp-elect); Fernán Rodríguez de Cabañas (abp-elect); Gonzalo (II) García Gudiel; Gonzalo (III) Palomeque; Juan de Medina; Martín; Rodrigo Ximénez de Rada; Sancho I; Sancho II

Toledo, John of, card-priest of S. Lawrence in Lucina, 281, 301n; chaplain of, 283

Tonnerre (Yonne), archdeaconry of, 110n

Tormes, River: in flood (1256), 226n

Toro, 22n; clergy of, 303

Torres, Gil, card-deacon of SS Cosmas and Damian, 27, 46, 51–2, 60n, 67, 80n, 84, 85n, 142, 144, 148, 149n, 178n, 195n, 197n, 217, **276–95**; origins of, 277–8; and sees of Tarragona and Toledo, 276; reputation of, 278; correspondence of with Grosseteste, 278; on clerical concubinage, 279; Innocent IV on, 276, 279; and Card. Pelayo Gaitán, 279; and Spaniards at papal Curia, 280–5; and petitioners for benefices, 290; and church of Zamora, 292–4; and church of Salamanca, 275; constitutions of, 260, 268–75

Tortosa, church of, 69; diocese of, 63; episcopal election at (1254–5), 90–2; synod at (1274), 65n; bps of: *see* Arnaldo de Jardino; Bernardo de Olivella; Ponce

Tours, Council of (1163), 24n, 32, 67n; province of, 241

Toulouse, 66

Tractatus de Sacramentis: *see* Ramón Despont, bp of Valencia

translations from Arabic, 236

Tremp (Urgel), 78; archdeaconry of, 299n

Triacastela, archdeaconry of (Lugo), 284n, 299n

tribute: Spanish attitude to payment of, 104, chap. 9, *passim*

Troyes, 128, 129

truculence: as episcopal attribute, 12, 14, 90

Tuacius Bernaldi, Florentine debt-collector in Spain, 131n

Tudela, 207, 211, 216n; *census* of, 199; prior of, 18; proctor of, 282, 289–90

Tudela del Duero (prov. Valladolid), 248

Tura Bartholomei, member of Bonsignori Company, 141

Túy, archd of, 205n, 306–7; church of (and Innocent IV), 257–8; diocese of, 215n; bps of: *see* Fernando Arias; Lucas

Index

Ubaldini, Octavian, card-deacon of S. Maria in Via Lata, 205n, 278n; and Spanish clerics, 300
Úbeda, archd of, 235n
Uclés, convent of, 27
unanimity: as requisite for capitular action, 304–5
Urach, Conrad of, card-bp of Porto, 189n
Urban IV, pope, 62, 94, 103, 157, 158, 162, 171, 183, 185, 260n; Castilian appeals to, 177–81
Urgel, 26, 196, 209; chapter of, 191, 211; church of, 32, 177n, (census of) 198–9, (sacrist of) 56–7; diocese of, 38n, 192, (episcopal visitation of) 99n; bps of: see Abril; Guillermo de Moncada; Pedro; Pedro de Puigvert; Ponce de Vilamur
Urraca (sister of King Sancho III of Navarre), 3
Urraca (daughter of King Alfonso VI of Castile and León), 3
Ursino, Jordan de, card-deacon of S. Eustacius; and Sancho IV, 232

Valdemora (León), archdeaconry of, 307n
Valence, bp of: see Jean
Valencia, 99, 209; chapter of, 81n, 298; church of, 55, 61n, 63, 89, (poverty of) 208, (state of in later 13th century) 311–14; clergy of, 74; diocese of, 96–7, 99; siege of, 60, 118; synods of, 81n, 81n, 97, 98n; bps of: see Andrés de Albalat; Arnaldo de Peralta; Berenguer de Castelbisbal; Ferrer; Jazpert de Botonach; Ramón Despont
Valeria, 13
Valladolid, 203n, 248; abbot of, 19; cantor of, 116n; chapter of, 132, (census of) 211–12; Cortes at (1258), 166, 168, (1295), 243–4; Council at (1228), 22, 28, 32, 51, (1292), 241–2; prior of, 225; rebel bishops at (1282), 220–1
Valtanas Mexía, Domingo de, 332
Valverde, abbey of (Lugo), 39n
Vasconia: illiteracy in, 237
Velasco Fernandes, canon of Lisbon, 299
Velasco Pérez, bp-elect of Ciudad Rodrigo, 306n
Velascus, O.F.M., bp of Guarda, collector, 199
Vellido Adolfo, 231
Venerabilem: Vincentius Hispanus on, 104
Venetians, 181
Vercelli, bp of: see Aymo
Verdun, church of, 278, 294
Verona, bp of: see Manfred de' Roberti

Veruela, abbey of S. María, O. Cist. (Tarazona), 79n, 81n, 84, 318
vestiarium, 33, 65, 85, 90
Vicens Vives, J., ix–x
Vicente, bp of Guarda, 27, 104, 105, 154, 183n, 197, 329–30
Vicente, bp of Porto: expenditure of, 258
Vicente, bp of Zaragoza, 66n, 69
Vicente Rodrigues, native of Guarda, 296
Vicentius Hispanus: see Vicente, bp of Guarda
vicesima: grant of Aragonese Church to Jaime I, 119n
Vich, 26; chapter of, 57, 189, 298; church of, 28, 32, 47, 50, 62, 68; clergy of, 85; episcopal visitation of diocese, 99n; John of Abbeville at, 41; bps of: see Bernardo Calvó, St; Bernardo Mur; Guillermo; Oliva
Vidal de Canellas, bp of Huesca, 59n, 61n, 62, 66, 194, 195
Vienna: Dominican General Chapter at (1282), 137n
Vienne, General Council at, 246
Villabuena, abbey of, O. Cist. (Astorga), 22
Villafranca de Vallecarceris, 284n
Villafranca del Vierzo: monastic general chapter at (1228–9), 28n
Villamayor de los Montes (Burgos), 281
Villamor (de Cadoz?), Zamora, 285n
Villanueva, J., 46, 54–5, 74
Villarreal (Toledo), 248
Violante, queen of Castile, 320
Virgil of Córdoba: see Córdoba
Visigothic Church, control of, 139, 327–8
visitations, archiepiscopal, 61–3; episcopal, 99, 238–9, 264; Rodrigo of Palencia on, 238
visits ad limina, 92; absolution from obligation, 149n, 263
Viterbo: Abp Gonzalo II of Toledo at, 134; canon of Oviedo at, 133
Vivián, bp of Calahorra, 288
vota Sancti Jacobi, 266

weather, Spanish, 162–3
Willelmus, frater, 23n
William of Parma, vice-chancellor of Roman Church, 146, 150, 287
wine: Spanish debts to Italians in, 132
wool: Spanish debts to Italians in, 132

abu-Yacub, 125
Yspania: see Hispania

388

Index